Logistics in Greek Sanctuaries

Monumenta Graeca et Romana

NEW DIRECTIONS IN
MEDITERRANEAN ARCHAEOLOGY

Editor-in-Chief

Troels Myrup Kristensen (*Aarhus University, Denmark*)

Editor-in-Chief Emeritus

John M. Fossey† FRSC (*Musée des beaux-arts de Montréal, Canada*)

Editorial Board

Anna Collar (*University of Southampton, UK*)
Søren Handberg (*University of Oslo, Norway*)
Kathleen M. Lynch (*University of Cincinnati, USA*)

Editorial Advisory Board

Andreas Konecny (*Universität Graz, Austria*)
Duane Roller (*Ohio State University, USA*)
Massimo Osanna (*Ministry of Culture, Italy*)
Peter Stewart (*University of Oxford, UK*)
Lea Stirling (*University of Manitoba, Canada*)

VOLUME 30

The titles published in this series are listed at *brill.com/mgr*

Logistics in Greek Sanctuaries

Exploring the Human Experience of Visiting the Gods

Edited by

Judith M. Barringer
Gunnel Ekroth
David Scahill

BRILL

LEIDEN | BOSTON

This is an open access title distributed under the terms of the CC BY-NC 4.0 license, which permits any non-commercial use, distribution, and reproduction in any medium, provided the original author(s) and source are credited. Further information and the complete license text can be found at https://creativecommons.org/licenses/by-nc/4.0/

The terms of the CC license apply only to the original material. The use of material from other sources (indicated by a reference) such as diagrams, illustrations, photos and text samples may require further permission from the respective copyright holder.

Published as open access with the aid of grants from the Royal Swedish Academy of Letters, History and Antiquities and Riksbankens Jubileumsfond for the Advancement of the Humanities and Social Sciences, Sweden.

Cover illustrations: (*front*) Woman cooking, watched by a girl. Greek (Boiotia, Tanagra), Late Archaic Period, about 500–475 BC, terracotta, 10.7 × 11.3 × 8 cm. Museum of Fine Arts, Boston, Acc. no.: 01.7788; (*back*) Weight from Olympia with Zeus' name and eagle, bronze. Berlin, Staatliche Museen, Antikensammlung, Ol. 12177 (Photo: Staatliche Museen zu Berlin, Antikensammlung / Mirko Vonderstein).

Library of Congress Cataloging-in-Publication Data

Names: Barringer, Judith M., 1959– editor | Ekroth, Gunnel editor | Scahill, David editor
Title: Logistics in Greek sanctuaries : exploring the human experience of visiting the gods / edited by Judith M. Barringer, Gunnel Ekroth, David Scahill.
Other titles: Monumenta Graeca et Romana.
Description: Leiden ; Boston : Brill, 2025 | Series: Monumenta Graeca et Romana, 3050–5186 ; volume 30. New directions in Mediterranean archaeology | Includes bibliographical references and index.
Identifiers: LCCN 2025010729 (print) | LCCN 2025010730 (ebook) | ISBN 9789004720893 hardback | ISBN 9789004720909 ebook
Subjects: LCSH: Temples—Greece | Religion and sociology—Greece—History—To 1500 | Architecture and society—Greece—History—To 1500 | Architecture—Human factors—Greece—History—To 1500
Classification: LCC NA275 .L64 2025 (print) | LCC NA275 (ebook) | DDC 726/.120809385—dc23/eng/20250429
LC record available at https://lccn.loc.gov/2025010729
LC ebook record available at https://lccn.loc.gov/2025010730

Typeface for the Latin, Greek, and Cyrillic scripts: "Brill". See and download: brill.com/brill-typeface.

ISSN 3050-5186
ISBN 978-90-04-72089-3 (hardback)
ISBN 978-90-04-72090-9 (e-book)

Copyright 2025 by Judith M. Barringer, Gunnel Ekroth and David Scahill. Published by Koninklijke Brill BV, Plantijnstraat 2, 2321 JC Leiden, The Netherlands.
Koninklijke Brill BV incorporates the imprints Brill, Brill Nijhoff, Brill Schöningh, Brill Fink, Brill mentis, Brill Wageningen Academic, Vandenhoeck & Ruprecht, Böhlau and V&R unipress.
Koninklijke Brill BV reserves the right to protect this publication against unauthorized use.
For more information: info@brill.com.

This book is printed on acid-free paper and produced in a sustainable manner.

Contents

MGR Editorial Preface to Introduce the Subseries *Monumenta Graeca et Romana, New Directions in Mediterranean Archaeology* (*MGR-NDMA*)   VII
Figures   VIII
Abbreviations   X

Introduction   1
   Judith M. Barringer, Gunnel Ekroth, and David Scahill

1   Managing the Ebb and Flow of Competing Claims on Sacred Space   10
   Laura Gawlinski

2   Locked in/Locked out: How Was Access to Greek Sanctuaries and Temples Controlled in Practice?   22
   Jenny Wallensten

3   Policing Sanctuaries in Ancient Greece   35
   Jan-Mathieu Carbon and Edward Harris

4   Tegean Regulations for the *Panegyris* in Alea Athena's Sanctuary: An Arkadian *Festwiese* (c.400–380 BCE)   52
   Christophe Chandezon

5   Utilitarian Uses of Water at Greek Sanctuaries   68
   Patrik Klingborg

6   Sanitation in Greek Sanctuaries   81
   Monika Trümper

7   Hotels, Tents, and Sacred Houses: Spaces for Human Accommodation in Greek Sanctuaries   103
   Gunnel Ekroth

8   The Architectural Evidence for Dining in Greek Sanctuaries   115
   David Scahill

9   The Divine *Symposion*: Logistics and Significance of Drinking Wine in Greek Sanctuaries   138
   Floris van den Eijnde

10   What's for Dinner? The 'Menu' in Greek Sanctuaries   158
   Michael MacKinnon

11 Food in Sanctuaries: Markets and Consumption   176
    Annalisa Lo Monaco

12 The Question of Temple Merchants: Buying and Selling in Greek Sanctuaries   193
    Véronique Chankowski

13 '… A Piglet to Clean the Sanctuary': Recurring Costs and the Logistics of Greek Sanctuaries   203
    Jeremy McInerney

14 Handworkers and Repair in Greek Sanctuaries   215
    Judith M. Barringer

15 Handling of Hides in Greek Sanctuaries: Practical, Spatial, and Conceptual Considerations   236
    Petra Pakkanen

Index of Inscriptions   251
Index Locorum   255
General Index   258

MGR Editorial Preface to Introduce the Subseries *Monumenta Graeca et Romana, New Directions in Mediterranean Archaeology* (*MGR-NDMA*)

Monumenta Graeca et Romana (*MGR*) has since the publication of its first volume in 1963 served as an important publication venue for scholarship on the material and visual culture of the Greek and Roman worlds. However, much has changed in classical archaeology over the course of the past 70 years, and as the new editorial board for the series, it is our express objective for *MGR* to reflect these new developments in the field.

As part of this renewed mission for *MGR*, we welcome new submissions. We also introduce both a new format and a new subseries. The new subseries, *Monumenta Graeca et Romana, New Directions in Mediterranean Archaeology* (*MGR-NDMA*), will be devoted to theoretically informed and agenda-setting studies that push the methodological and disciplinary scope of the fields of Mediterranean and classical archaeology (both terms here understood in the broadest possible sense) in new directions. These may take the form of both monographs and coherently structured edited volumes and can be organised in thematic, geographical or chronological terms, as long as they seek to provide new directions for future practitioners of the disciplines. Comparative work across traditional boundaries in existing scholarship is especially welcome. To broaden the remit of MGR, we are also introducing a survey-volume format that offers cohesive surveys of specific types of objects, monuments, or regions. The survey format is flexible, but authors should aim to be as inclusive as possible in their coverage and approaches, designing each volume to be a useful starting point for scholars and students who are making their way into a new area of research or material.

The present volume is the first in the *Monumenta Graeca et Romana, New Directions in Mediterranean Archaeology* subseries. It makes an important and innovative contribution to the study of Greek sanctuaries by expanding our field of vision beyond the narrow focus on ritual and on to the nitty-gritty details of their daily operation, thereby opening a new window onto Greek religion and its material culture.

Troels Myrup Kristensen
MGR Editor-in-Chief

Anna Collar, Søren Handberg, Kathleen Lynch
MGR Editorial Board

Figures

1.1 Athens, Agora, limestone supports for the *perischoinisma* set into the Panathenaic Way near the entrance to the Athenian Agora, looking west   19
4.1 Tegea, Archaeological Museum, inscribed stele *IG* v.2 3   53
4.2 Variations in the course of the Sarandapotamos River   55
4.3 Tegea, temple of Alea, plan   56
6.1 Pergamon, Asklepieion, reconstructed plan of southwest corner with latrines   84
6.2 Kos, Asklepieion, plan of the latrine   84
6.3 Olympia, distribution of bathing facilities and latrines   86
6.4 Olympia, Kladeos Baths with combined guesthouses   87
6.5 Epidauros, sanctuary of Asklepios, distribution of baths and latrines   89
6.6 Epidauros, sanctuary of Asklepios, stoa of Kotys and northeast baths   90
6.7 Olympia, pool, evidence and reconstructed plan   95
6.8 Olympia, pool, reconstruction   95
6.9 Agrigento, pool south of the Olympieion, view from northeast   96
6.10 Syracuse, altar of Hieron II, plan   97
8.1 Athens, Kerameikos, Pompeion, restored plan   116
8.2 Perachora, Dining Building, restored plan   117
8.3 Argive Heraion, West Building, restored plan   118
8.4 Troizen, Peristyle Courtyard Dining Building, *Left*: reconstruction of the 'Long Hall' with beds after Welter 1941, pl. 16; *Right*: restored plan after Welter 1941, pl. 12   119
8.5 Corinth, Asklepieion, a) section looking south after Roebuck 1951, Plan D; b) dining rooms after Roebuck 1951, 52, fig. 13; c) photo after Roebuck 1951, pl. 14: 4   119
8.6 Epidauros, Banquet Building ('Gymnasion'), *Left*: west rooms with restored couches after Leypold 2008, pl. 47b; *Center*: restored plan after Pakkanen 2019, fig. 1; *Right*: east hall with stone supports for beds after Frickenhaus 1917, fig. 10   120
8.7 Athens, Akropolis, South Slope, Asklepieion, plan   121
8.8a Brauron, sanctuary of Artemis, Π-shaped stoa, isometric view of a room   122
8.8b Brauron, sanctuary of Artemis, state plan   123
8.9 Labraunda, Andron B, restored plan *klinai* (J. Blid)   125
8.10 Aigeira, Buildings D and E, plan by Alexandra Tanner   126
8.11 Athenian Akropolis, Propylaia, Pinakotheke (Northwest hall), plan restored with *klinai*   127
8.12 Lissos, Asklepieion, Building A, restored section looking east by C. Kanellopoulos   128
8.13 Aigeira, Guesthouse, aerial view (above), restored plan of Phase 1 by G. Ladstetter (below)   129
8.14 Athens, Agora, South Stoa I, reconstruction of dining room by Piet De Jong   130
8.15a Corinth, South Stoa, plan of the late fourth century BCE by author   131
8.15b Corinth, South Stoa, reconstruction of rooms with benches by author   132
9.1 Athens, Agora H 487, krater-*skyphos* from the sanctuary of Zeus on Mt. Hymettos, Attika   144
9.2 Athens, Agora, South Stoa I, reconstruction of dining room by Piet de Jong   147
9.3 Naxos, Yria, sanctuary of Dionysos, gateway and banquet buildings   149
9.4 Naxos, Yria, sanctuary of Dionysos, gateway and banquet buildings during the eighth, seventh and sixth centuries, respectively   150
9.5 Aigina, sanctuary of Aphaia   151
9.6 Athens, Akropolis, South Slope, sanctuary of Asklepios   152

9.7	Corinth, sanctuary of Demeter and Kore, lower terrace, *c*.400 BCE. Plan by D. Peck, American School of Classical Studies at Athens, Corinth Excavations 153	
10.1	Location of Sites with zooarchaeological remains 161	
10.2	NISP (= Number of Identified Specimens) Frequency values for cattle, sheep/goat and pig among sites 162	
10.3	Ratios of sheep:goat for sites 163	
10.4	Nemea, plan with locations of zooarchaeological deposits examined 167	
10.5	NISP (= Number of Identified Specimens) frequency values for 'supplemental' taxa (equids, dogs, and wild animals) among sanctuary assemblages 168	
10.6	NISP (= Number of Identified Specimens) frequency values for pigs among sites 168	
10.7	Logarithm difference values (and distribution curves) for sheep measurements among contexts at Nemea 169	
10.8	Logarithm difference values (and distribution curves) for cattle measurements among contexts at Nemea 169	
10.9	Logarithm difference values (and distribution curves) for pig measurements among contexts at Corinth 170	
10.10	Logarithm difference values (and distribution curves) for cattle measurements among sites (Note: with addition of site of Argilos, northern Greece, Classical timeframe) 172	
11.1	Olympia, Archaeological Museum, vessel for the sale of fruit, *karpometron*, terracotta 180	
11.2	Berlin, Antikensammlung, Ol. 12177, bronze weight from Olympia with Zeus' name and eagle 181	
11.3	New York, The Metropolitan Museum of Art 06.1021.241, South Italian red-figure fishplate, perhaps from Cumae, attributed to the Helgoland Painter, *c*.360–325 BCE, terracotta 183	
11.4	Olympia, Archaeological Museum, inscribed pointed amphora, terracotta 188	
14.1	Olympia, plan of the Roman period 216	
14.2	Athens, Agora, House of Simon, plan 222	
14.3	Athens, Agora, House of Simon, view to west 223	
14.4	Athens, Agora, combined state plan and restored plan of the houses (at left) of Mikion and Menon House (5th–3rd c. BC) and (at right) the Triangular Shrine (5th c. BC) 224	
14.5	Olynthos, plan of House A viii 7 and House A viii 9 225	
14.6a	Troy, phase plan of the sanctuary prepared by Elizabeth Riorden, Hellenistic period 226	
14.6b	Troy, drawing of bronzeworking pits in front of the North Building by Maureen Basedow 227	
14.7	Olympia, workshop, plan 229	
14.8a	Athens, Cape Zoster, plan by D. Giraud, late sixth or early fifth century BCE 230	
14.8b	Athens, Cape Zoster, plan by D. Giraud, fourth century BCE 231	
14.9	Kroton, sanctuary of Hera Lakina, plan, late Classical/early Hellenistic 232	
15.1	Simplified structure of animal skin and leather layers. Above, A: skin structure of porcine animals; B: skin structure of most animals. Below: layers of leather processed from dermis of most animals 238	

Abbreviations

The abbreviations used in this text are those of the *American Journal of Archaeology* https://www.ajaonline.org/submissions/abbreviations and the *Oxford Classical Dictionary*, 4th edition https://oxfordre-com.ezproxy.is.ed.ac.uk/classics/page/ocdabbreviations. Additional abbreviations are as follows:

AGRW	*Associations in the Greco-Roman World* (https://philipharland.com/greco-roman-associations/)
AIO	*Attic Inscriptions Online* (https://www.atticinscriptions.com/)
BÉ	*Bulletin Épigraphique*
CGRN	*Collection of Greek Ritual Norms* (http://cgrn.ulg.ac.be/)
CID	Rougemont, G. 1977. *Corpus des inscriptions de Delphes*. Paris
CIRB	Gavrilov, A., N. Pavlichenko, D. Keyer, and A. Karlin, eds. 2004. *Corpus Inscriptionum Regni Bosporiani*. St. Petersburg
I.Amyzon	Robert, J., and L. Robert. 1983. *Fouilles d'Amyzon en Carie 1. Exploration, histoire, monnaies et inscriptions*. Paris
I.Chalcedon	Merkelbach, R., F. Dörner, and S. Şahin, eds. 1980. *Die Inschriften von Kalchedon*. Bonn
I.Ilion	Frisch, P. 1975. *Die Inschriften von Ilion*. Bonn
I.Knidos	Blümel, W., ed. 1992. *Die Inschriften von Knidos*. Bonn
IK.Priene	Blümel, W., and R. Merkelbach, eds. 2014. *Die Inschriften von Priene* 1. Bonn
I.Lampsakos	Frisch, P. ed. 1978. *Die Inschriften von Lampsakos*. Bonn
I.Lindos	Blinkenberg, C. 1941. *Lindos. Fouilles et recherches 2. Fouilles de l'acropole. Inscriptions*. Berlin
IMT NördlTroas	Barth, M., and J. Stauber, eds. 1996. *Inschriften Mysia & Troas*. Munich. Version of 25.8.1993 (Ibycus). Packard Humanities Institute CD #7, 1996. Troas, Nördliche Troas, nos. 1–90
IMT Skam/NebTäler	Barth, M., and J. Stauber, eds. *Inschriften Mysia & Troas*. Munich. Version of 25.8.1993 (Ibycus). Packard Humanities Institute CD #7, 1996
I.Smyrna	Petzl, G., ed. 1982–1987. *Die Inschriften von Smyrna*. Bonn
I.Stratonikeia	Çetin Sahin, M. 1981. *Die Inschriften von Stratonikeia*. Bonn
I.Thasos 3	Hamon, P. 2019. *Corpus des inscriptions de Thasos 3. Documents publics du quatrième siècle et de l'époque hellénistique*. Paris
LSAM	Sokolowski, F. 1955. *Lois sacrées de l'Asie Mineure*. Paris
LSCG	Sokolowski, F. 1969. *Lois sacrées des cités grecques*. Paris
LSS	Sokolowksi, F. 1962. *Lois sacrées des cités grecques. Supplément*. Paris
NGSL²	Lupu, E. 2009. *Greek Sacred Law*, 2nd ed. Leiden
OR	Osborne, R., and P.J. Rhodes. 2017. *Greek Historical Inscriptions, 478–404 BC*. Oxford
RO	Rhodes, P.J., and R. Osborne. 2004. *Greek Historical Inscriptions, 404–323 BC*. Oxford

Introduction

That was the time, too, when one could hear crowds of wretched sophists around Poseidon's temple [at Isthmia] shouting and reviling one another, and their disciples, as they were called, fighting with one another, many writers reading aloud their stupid works, many poets reciting their poems while others applauded them, many jugglers showing their tricks, many fortune-tellers interpreting fortunes, lawyers innumerable perverting judgment, and peddlers not a few peddling whatever they happened to have.

DIO CHRYSOSTOM, *Discourses* 8.9–10, trans. COHOON

⋯

But some unpleasant and hard things happen in life. And do they not happen in Olympia? Do you not swelter? Are you not cramped and crowded? Do you not bathe with discomfort? Are you not drenched whenever it rains? Do you not have your fill of tumult and shouting and other annoyances? But I fancy that you hear and endure all this by balancing it off against the memorable character of the spectacle.

EPIKTETOS, *Discourses* 1.6.26–28, trans. OLDFATHER

⋰

Sanctuaries were the assembly point for large numbers of people in the ancient Greek world, including worshippers, athletes, tourists, merchants, dignitaries, and philosophers among many others. Local sanctuaries served the regional population, while Panhellenic sanctuaries, such as those of Apollo at Delphi and Zeus at Olympia, catered to the entire Mediterranean.[1] Unlike the sanctuary at Delphi, which stood within the town, Olympia, like many other large sanctuaries, was located many kilometers from the city, Elis, that governed it.[2] We know that the Panhellenic Olympic games and their accompanying religious festival attracted some 45,000 visitors to the sanctuary at Olympia in the fourth century BCE.[3] The games lasted five days,[4] and we must imagine that many, if not all, visitors remained at Olympia for the duration of the events. How did this enormous number of visitors cope with their practical needs over nearly a week, and how did sanctuary administrators manage the crowds and maintain order?

Although scholars have studied ancient Greek sanctuaries for more than a century and a half, such questions are rarely addressed. Instead, work has tended to focus on religious activity,[5] deities,[6] and sacrifice.[7] Treatments of material remains of religious activity in the form of votive dedications, e.g., terracottas, reliefs, pottery, and metal objects, often focus on identifying and discussing design and function.[8] Using both material evidence (e.g., architecture, altars, animal bones, vase painting, sculpture) and written sources (ancient literature and inscriptions), studies concentrate on sacrificial practice and the relationship between human worshippers and divinities. Numerous studies are devoted to inscriptions, e.g., dedications, contracts, alliances, regulations, and ritual norms,[9] as well as topography and land use.[10]

Greek temples and large-scale marble sculpture remain some of the most prestigious items in the study of Classical antiquity, just as sacrificial rituals and worship constituted the core activities in sanctuaries, and consequently

---

1   E.g., Polinskaya 2013; Scott 2014; Pilz 2020; Barringer 2021; Beck and Kindt 2023.
2   E.g., Chaniotis 1988; de Polignac 1995. On the town surrounding Delphi, see Luce 2016; 2021. On Elis and Olympia, see, e.g., Roy 2013; 2015.
3   See Barringer 2021, 10, 44–45.
4   From the fifth century BCE on; see Barringer 2021, 10, 46, 104.
5   The bibliography on this subject is vast. See, e.g., *ThesCRA*; Mikalson 2005; Ogden 2008; Kearns 2010 for overviews of various topics. For an offering of other themes, including regional studies, specific practices, and various approaches to sanctuaries, see, e.g., Marinatos and Hägg 1993; Rietmüller 2005; Flower 2009; Parker 2011; Larson 2016; Mazarakis Ainian 2017; Freitag and Haake 2019; Collar and Kristensen 2020; Pirenne-Delforge 2020; Eidinow, Geertz, and North 2022; Woolf, Bultrighini, and Norman 2024.
6   E.g., Riethmüller 2005; Parker 2017; Lalonde 2019; Galoppin et al. 2022; Pirenne-Delforge and Pironti 2023.
7   The scholarship on Greek sacrifice is extensive. For overviews, see Hermary et al. 2004; Ekroth 2014; Carbon and Ekroth 2024. On the iconographical evidence, see van Straten 1995, and for the zooarchaeological remains, Ekroth and Wallensten 2013.
8   Lombardi 2009; Papalexandrou and Sowder Koch 2023. For votive reliefs, see van Straten 1995.
9   See the extensive database Collection of Greek Ritual Norms (*CGRN*: http://cgrn.ulg.ac.be/); Grzesik 2021.
10 Chaniotis 1988; Sinn 1993; de Polignac 1995; Sporn 2002; Chandezon 2003; Cole 2004; Horster 2004; Papazarkadas 2011; Sporn 2019; Pilz 2020; Angliker and Bellia 2021; Williamson 2021; Gerlach, Lindström, and Sporn 2022.

attracted—and still do attract—the greatest attention from scholars.[11] Scholars have examined architecture and monuments (which can also be votives), such as temples, treasuries, altars, *stoai*, *hestiatoria* (dining spaces), and gymnasia,[12] as well as individual monuments (their meaning, placement, cost, technical details), and the appearance of sanctuaries and votive gifts. Catalogues amply document materials, e.g., bronze, ceramics, stone, inscriptions, recovered from sanctuaries, as well as the excavated areas and monuments within.[13]

Yet beyond supplying a compendium of material, these catalogues offer a treasure trove of information and rich discussion of material and religious matters, which provide the basis to investigate many of the questions addressed in this volume. And monuments such as temples and treasuries did not exist in a vacuum but appeared in an elaborate context of other buildings and activities, including—but not limited to—sacrifices to please, appease, and honor the gods. While temples, altars, and statues catered to divinities and marked sanctuaries as spaces belonging to deities and their worship, sanctuaries usually included structures, areas, and infrastructure necessary for human visitors.[14] As modern viewers, we tend to disconnect these practical matters from practiced religion and beliefs.

The previous lack of interest in more mundane aspects of Greek sanctuaries is partly a result of the empirical material that has dominated the field. The practical and logistical needs of human visitors in sanctuaries are rarely apparent in the evidence most commonly used: ancient architecture and art, and ancient written evidence, although the citations at the beginning of this Introduction indicate that ancient visitors certainly were keenly aware of them.

A gradual realization that material culture, including everyday objects, is essential for a comprehensive understanding of Classical antiquity, including religion, has opened up the field to new insights and approaches. This development can be seen as linked to the growing awareness of the importance of everyday material culture for the exploration of Greek antiquity at large, related to the so-called 'material turn' that emerged in archaeology and social anthropology in the second half of the last century.[15] This theoretical development raised the awareness of the possibilities to access the less high-minded aspects of the Greek sanctuary experience.

Considering the current state of the material evidence and the increased interest in bottom-up perspectives of everyday life and personal experiences, the time is ripe to address the human experience of visiting the gods. Where did all the visitors, as well as the sanctuary personnel, stay? How did they obtain food and water for themselves, their animals, their slaves, and what sanitation facilities were available to them? Did the sanctuary address these needs, and if so, how? By what means did sanctuaries manage the behavior of crowds and the waste that they produced? Who maintained the physical aspects of the sanctuary, and where did they live? What were the sources of sanctuary revenue, and how were these managed? What provisions and votives were available for sale, and how were such markets governed? This collection addresses precisely these—and other—questions. We refer to these matters as 'logistics,' a term originally used to describe preparations for military operations. Here, we apply it to the coordination and implementation of a number of activities for the effective or successful delivery of services.

Of paramount importance in this context are advances in the study of the less spectacular forms of material evidence, such as undecorated pottery, kitchenware, terracotta figurines, and roof tiles, as well as architecture beyond temples and monumental altars.[16] The consistent collection and analysis of animal bones from Greek sanctuaries has, in the last decades, provided fundamentally different perspectives on one of the major activities in Greek sanctuaries—animal sacrifice and the cooking and consumption of meat by the human visitors.[17] These categories of ancient evidence provide completely new avenues for investigating sanctuaries from the point of view of the human visitor. While these categories of evidence, e.g., wells, latrines, cooking ware, leftover meals and food residue are documented in archaeological studies (where they often receive short shrift), their integration into the workings and everyday realia for visitors and sanctuary personnel has not been explored.

At a moment of 'crisis' in the field of Classical Studies when scholars and the public are questioning the bases and rationale for what we do, the volume is timely in offering a new perspective on how we might think about and

---

11 Pedley 2005; Partida and Schmidt-Dounas 2019; Smith 2021.
12 Leypold 2008; Mania and Trümper 2018; Partida and Schmidt-Dounas 2019.
13 E.g., the series *Corinth*; *Ephesos*; *Études Thasiennes*; *FdD*; *Kerameikos*; *Milet*; *OlForsch*; *OlBer*; *Olynthos*; *Samos*.
14 See, e.g., Sinn 1996; Kyrieleis 2011.
15 See, e.g., the series *Material Religion in Antiquity*.
16 E.g., Tomlinson 1980; Hemans 1989; Heiden 1995; Leypold 2008; Serino 2021.
17 For overviews, see Wallensten and Ekroth 2013; Carbon and Ekroth 2024.

understand the ancient past.[18] Every child—and every adult—wants to know (and children dare to ask): "where did they go to the bathroom?" We want to know how ancient people lived, not only what they created. Rather than concentrating on the religious significance of major structures and monuments at sanctuaries, the chapters in this volume investigate how sanctuaries functioned at the pragmatic level. A closer examination of this area expands the traditional focus on Greek cult places and reveals facets of ancient Greek culture beyond those usually explored.

1 Bringing Logistics to the Forefront

The essays presented here chiefly derive from a conference on "Logistics in Greek Sanctuaries," which was held in Athens in September 2018 and co-organized by the three editors of this volume; these studies are supplemented by additional commissioned contributions from leading scholars in the field designed to fill in some gaps. The works were written by an international group of senior scholars and those earlier in their career, who have expertise in the issues addressed and who offer new, challenging ideas concerning logistics involved in the running and use of Greek sanctuaries. The authors also represent a range of disciplines and specialties, including archaeology, zooarchaeology, history, law, epigraphy, religion, and anthropology.

The first four papers concern how large crowds were managed at major sanctuaries. Human presence as well as natural events, such as earthquakes and floods, took a toll on sanctuary facilities. Sanctuaries received the most visitors and therefore the most managerial attention during major festivals and ritual events, but the use and control of space at those times differed from sanctuary administration on a day-to-day basis. Who had access to sanctuary space, under what circumstances, and how was visitors' conduct monitored even if no sanctuary personnel were present? **Laura Gawlinski** explores such questions in her investigation of sanctuary 'time management': whether regular activities were administered differently from less-frequent festival events, and what happened when the routine and the exceptional came into conflict, e.g., when the right to asylum or a private act of veneration clashed with a festival. Although there is much less direct testimony about the regulation of space for non-festival activities, incidental evidence, such as the use of informers, regulation of access to paraphernalia, such as offering boxes,[19] and the deployment of temporary markers to organize space, affords us a more nuanced understanding.

Travelling to a sanctuary or participation in festive procession towards one has been of interest in recent scholarship. The journey is often intentionally arduous, time-consuming, sometimes dangerous and/or costly, and in the case of Christian pilgrims, intended both to test the traveler's resolve and as an act of abasement before the deity.[20] The moment of arrival and entry, however, remain largely uninvestigated. Whether one was free to enter at will and how one's movements were regulated within the sanctuary are the subjects of **Jenny Wallensten**'s essay. The author 'walks' step by step with the sanctuary visitor from the entrance towards the focus of his or her journey: the temple with its cella and cult statue within. Given the great variety of sanctuary character and the state of our sources, this contribution offers a diachronic overview. Wallensten also surveys the sanctuary personnel and argues that 'manufactured' staff, such as sculpted portraits of priestesses, assisted their human counterparts.

Sanctuary personnel were charged with maintaining order and upholding legal and religious norms in sanctuaries. **Edward Harris** and **Jan-Mathieu Carbon** take a wide view to consider several aspects of this topic: the exclusion of those disqualified from entering a sacred precinct, maintaining order inside sanctuaries; the regulation of offerings made in sanctuaries; and the accountability of religious officials. In many instances, the enforcement of regulations explicitly required the intervention of specific officials, while published sanctions in the form of inscribed laws or signs might have served as deterrents in smaller sanctuaries. Both methods of 'enforcement' were essential to advertising the expected norms of behavior.

Christoph Chandezon takes up the same topic but focuses on a single example: an often referenced, but highly complex, inscription of the beginning of the

---

18 E.g., Hanson and Heath 2001; Zuckerberg 2018; https://newcriterion.com/issues/2019/3/decline-fall-classics-edition (last accessed 28.03.2024); https://www.nytimes.com/2021/04/25/us/howard-classics-department.html (last accessed 28.03.2024); https://theweek.com/articles/965573/cancel-classics (last accessed 28.03.2024); https://www.goacta.org/2021/10/is-classics-empire-in-terminal-decline/ (last accessed 28.03.2024); https://vtcynic.com/news/an-academic-persecution-the-death-of-classics-at-uvm/ (last accessed 28.03.2024); https://www.nytimes.com/2021/02/02/magazine/classics-greece-rome-whiteness.html (last accessed 28.03.2024); https://www.currentaffairs.org/2021/06/calm-down-the-classics-arent-going-anywhere (last accessed 28.02.2024); https://www.theatlantic.com/ideas/archive/2021/06/princeton-classics-major-latin-greek/619110/ (last accessed 28.03.2024).

19 Kaminski 1991.
20 E.g., Dillon 1997; Rutherford 2013; Collar 2020.

fourth century BCE (*IG* v.2 3). The document organizes the provision of a plot of land belonging to the city of Tegea in Arkadia for the festival of the goddess Alea at Tegea and regulates the stay of pilgrims and their animals. Chandezon provides a detailed line-by-line discussion and commentary of the text and its terminology and contents (the first time in English). The subsequent review of the archaeological study of the temple and its environs concludes by employing Ulrich Sinn's idea of *Festwiesen* to analyze the use of space.

The indispensable question of water and sanitation, and how sanctuaries provided for these needs are the focus of the following contributions. Water was an essential resource at sanctuaries, not just for human consumption but also for watering animals, cleaning, toilet facilities, and bathing. In contrast to previous studies that focus on water infrastructure in terms of its religious significance, e.g., for rituals of purification, cleaning of cult images, and healing, **Patrik Klingborg** discusses the utilitarian needs for water at Greek sanctuaries. Klingborg's study of the archaeological and written evidence for drinking, food preparation, washing, cleaning, and gardening, along with estimates of quantities needed for various purposes demonstrates that these necessities are likely to have required considerably larger volumes of water than religiously significant activities.

One of the most fundamental issues concerning large gatherings of human beings—then and now—is sanitation, a topic that has received little scholarly attention in discussions of Greek sanctuaries. **Monika Trümper** considers the archaeological evidence for sanitation provisions in extra-urban Greek sanctuaries of the eastern Mediterranean. Although evidence is scattered and sometimes ephemeral, comparisons with modern religious festivals in India help to illuminate the ancient evidence and enable us to understand the concepts and tools of sanitation in sanctuaries and whether and how two major human bodily needs—urination and defecation—as well as washing and bathing, were met. Clearly identifiable purpose-built structures were first introduced in the fourth century BCE, but became more common only in the late Hellenistic, and particularly the Roman Imperial, periods. The current state of research suggests that bathing facilities were far more common than latrines, although, of course, users of these sanctuaries surely urinated and defecated much more frequently than they bathed.

Many Greek sanctuaries attracted visitors far beyond their local setting, sometimes for stays of several days; one can think of island sanctuaries on Delos or Samothrace and other mainland sanctuaries, such as Delphi, attracting distant visitors. Accommodation was necessary for visitors and worshippers, but also for the priestly personnel and refugees seeking the protection of the god. **Gunnel Ekroth** discusses what kind of accommodation was available—hotels, tents, or houses—and who provided such lodging for the visitors: the sanctuary or private individuals. How did these installations relate to the sanctuary proper, and to what extent was the management of accommodation a concern for the sanctuary administration? To what degree did humans, whether religious personnel or regular visitors, actually stay inside the *temenos* of the god, that is, on sacred space? Because the evidence—material remains and written sources—is not plentiful, modern parallels are recruited to tease out a fuller picture of the ancient situation, not least to illustrate the infrastructure needed to manage large crowds coming to sacred places and spending the night.

Similarly, **David Scahill** investigates the ancient archaeological evidence for built spaces used for dining in sanctuaries. This chapter starts by examining the criteria for dining infrastructure in sanctuaries and moves on to examine a select group of buildings—among them *hestiatoria*, and banquet buildings with courtyards—along with associated evidence of furniture (i.e., *klinai*, benches, and tables) to explore what the distinctions of building type mean with regard to who might be dining, as well as when and how. Different building types and furniture arrangements raise questions concerning the dining experiences of worshippers. What provisions were necessary for dining? Where were buildings located in sanctuaries with respect to temples and altars? The different building types and variety of furniture layouts for dining in sanctuaries suggest that specific arrangements for worshippers were calculated in the design process, but this also raises questions regarding flexibility over the lifetime of a building's use.

Food and drink comprised an essential part of the sanctuary experience, and several essays explore where this took place, who participated, what was eaten, and where food was obtained. The communal consumption of wine in sanctuaries is an undertheorized aspect of Greek religion. Reviewing epigraphic, literary, and archaeological evidence, **Floris van den Eijnde** offers inroads into this complex topic. While the banquet is generally treated as a natural corollary of animal sacrifice—often understood as defining civic inclusivity—the question as to the social meaning of wine consumption in Greek sanctuaries is commonly overlooked by historians, although archaeologists dealing with sacred contexts have long recognized that drinking was an essential component of ritual proceedings at cult sites throughout the Greek world. Among other things, van den Eijnde considers how wine was used during various ritualized stages of banqueting in Greek sanctuaries, if drinking in sanctuaries was limited to specific social groups, and how the consumption of wine in sacred settings compares to that in the domestic *symposion*.

Worship of the gods centered on animal sacrifice and rituals, which concluded with the communal consumption of meat distributed to the participants. There is extensive literature on the theoretical and practical aspects of animal sacrifice itself, but far less on the practical activities that resulted from it. How and where was this food cooked and consumed? Analysis of zooarchaeological data from 'dining deposits' recovered in ancient Greek sanctuary sites (chiefly of the Archaic through Hellenistic periods) reveals details about practical aspects in provisioning meat and other animal resources to participants and diners.[21] Rather than focusing on remains of altar offerings designed for the gods, as is usually the case for zooarchaeological studies of sanctuaries, **Michael MacKinnon**'s contribution zeroes in on consumption debris from the sanctuaries' human celebrants (although as the author admits, distinctions between categories of debris are not always neat). This essay first considers general trends among various sanctuary sites on the Greek mainland (including data from non-sanctuary sites to compare availability of animal species), then focuses on three case studies to explore which animals (as well as breeds or varieties) appear in deposits; the origin of animal victims; whether seasonal trends are detectable; demographic patterns; which skeletal elements are represented; and how parts were obtained, processed, butchered, cooked, and prepared. This study touches on a wide range of issues, including how the tabulated results compare with sacrificial regulations/instructions specified in epigraphic documents.

For longer stays, visitors had to obtain various commodities, and many sanctuaries also seem to have had organized markets with their own standardized weights and measures.[22] Two essays discuss the wares, animals, and food and drink available for purchase in sanctuaries, as well as sales regulations. Thanks to the refinement of the analysis of faunal remains and organic residues in containers, it is now possible to investigate issues relating to the life and subsistence of the believers at the sanctuaries on feast days, including what was eaten and in what quantities, and the roles of dried food (e.g., figs, cheese, dried fish) brought by visitors and freshly prepared food.

Annalisa Lo Monaco discusses the nature, supply, and demand in these markets: what food was offered for sale, how transactions were regulated, what prices were set, the origin of food, and how goods were handled. Literary and epigraphic documentation, together with archaeological evidence, illuminate our knowledge about the consumption of vegetables, fish, meat, and liquids.

Famous sanctuaries brought an influx of consumers to Greek cities. In addition to regular religious events, some sanctuaries also hosted fairs at certain times of the religious year. They provided a service but also helped to create a demand for the various needs of the pilgrims: drink and food, as well as animals for sacrifices and artefacts to offer to the gods. **Véronique Chankowski**'s careful examination of the Samos decree regarding the *kapeloi* in the Heraion (*IG* XII.6 169), considered together with other epigraphic testimony from the Aegean islands and Asia Minor, shed light on the commercial activities that took place in the *temenos* and its environs. These activities had to follow specific regulations because of the sacred status of the place, which usually required specific behavior, but cities and sanctuaries also accepted certain adjustments to foster commercial developments according to the attractiveness of the god concerned.

Principal festivals were not the only times when sanctuaries were used: sanctuaries had visitors on a daily basis, and this was especially true for major sanctuaries. Food and water had to be available to these visitors, and religious personnel were needed to oversee daily religious affairs, such as oracular consultations or ministrations at altars. Workers and other craftsmen were required to maintain altars and buildings and to produce votive objects. All of this cost money, and some sanctuaries were indeed large financial operations, generating revenue from leasing land, making loans, and 'industry.' The final three chapters investigate sanctuary finances, evidence for sanctuary staff, and revenues generated from animal by-products.

When large sanctuaries upscaled their operations and sources of income grew, the range of expenses also increased. Epigraphic records allow us to measure the impact of this upscaling and to understand the logistical challenges facing such sanctuaries. **Jeremy McInerney**'s examination of two Delian inscriptions, *IG* XI.2 154 and *ID* 98, reveals that this increased complexity of Delos' operations conceals important features of the Delian accounts. Elites who served as ambassadors for Delos received extraordinarily high levels of compensation for their service, and as an economic agent, Delos profited the wealthy. Yet the general populace also shared in the sanctuary's wealth through a constant stream of small, unskilled jobs that brought low levels of financial reward, thus the

---

21 See, for examples, the contexts addressed in Ekroth and Wallensten 2013.
22 E.g., Hitzl 1996.

sanctuary of Delos reflected the economic inequalities that characterized the Hellenistic Greek world. Although the piecemeal activities and record-keeping of a major sanctuary like Delos seem odd, they are indicative of the economic operation of sanctuaries.

Evidence of workers in Greek sanctuaries includes inscribed accounts; tools; debris from marble, metal, and ceramic working; kilns; and smelting pits. We know about itinerant workers and workers from various locations laboring on special projects, and we are informed, either through written accounts or from archaeology, about repairs that went on in sanctuaries, especially temple repair after major natural disasters. What is much harder to detect is the presence of a permanent staff of workers in sanctuaries, day-to-day tendance of sanctuaries, and accommodation for these laborers; in large part, this 'absence' is due to past scholarly disinterest in such issues. Using both archaeological and epigraphical evidence, **Judith Barringer** examines what we know or can surmise about sanctuaries' 'skeleton staff,' their identities and duties, and their dwellings—or where we might seek them.

The final paper of the volume addresses the sanctuary as a producer of goods distributed and used outside the sacred area. An example of this is leather: sacrificial ritual provided raw material for leather-making and supported the temple economy as a source of revenue. Moreover, leather originating from sacrificial ritual (ἱερόθυτα) was perceived as special, better-quality leather and therefore, guaranteed its commercial, as well as symbolic, worth. Although skins from sacrifices figure frequently in epigraphical material relating to sacrifice, scholars have rarely addressed the role of skins and leather production in sanctuaries. **Petra Pakkanen** takes up this theme and demonstrates that (especially) major sanctuaries where public, large-scale sacrifices took place provided this by-product for leather production rather systematically and that skins were handled within sanctuaries for further trade in a regulated manner. Classical/Hellenistic Halaesa (Alesa) in Sicily and the sanctuary of Herakles by the Ilissos River in Classical Athens provide examples to explore the connection between tanning establishments and sanctuaries, while the latter part of this essay describes the main stages of ancient Greek leather-making procedures.

2   Looking to the Future

The studies presented here are by no means the last word on logistics in Greek sanctuaries. Many topics are unaddressed, and many questions remain. It is not always evident that our extant sources will be able to answer them, but by posing these questions, we aim to widen the approach to investigating Greek sanctuaries. As only a few examples, we might pose the following: what perils did travelers to sanctuaries face, and what was the risk of physical harm or even of being killed by traveling to and visiting a sanctuary?[23] During the stephanitic games at Olympia, Delphi, Isthmia, and Nemea, periods of *ekecheiria* (sacred truce) were enacted an an effort to provide safe travel. This was not always successful: arrests, attacks, and seizure by pirates who ransomed their captives are all attested as occurring during the *ekecheiria*.[24] What about travel to sanctuaries at other times when this was not in effect?[25]

Given the inherent and/or possible dangers of large gathering places of people, what nefarious elements might be associated with sanctuary visits, and how were they mitigated? Did people travel alone or in groups? Ancient evidence indicates that some sanctuary officials, such as *theoroi* and *spondophoroi*, traveled this way, and one reason was to mitigate danger; in some cases, they were provided with escorts.[26] Did families, including children (and possibly nursemaids?), travel together, and were they moving as mixed or single-sex groups? Traveling by cart, rather than on foot, may have increased the possibility of escaping danger (although it could also act as a magnet; the animal drawing the cart was certainly worth something), but how costly was travel by cart? And the perils of sea travel were many,[27] but were they more than travel by land?

Did one organize one's own journey or were there travel 'agents'? Did pilgrims travel in organized groups as is possible today? And how did people find their way to sanctuaries sometimes very far distant from their homes? Were there maps, guides, or (marked) landmarks, or was such information learned by exchanges at sanctuaries themselves? Is there evidence of fixed rest stops, tourist attractions, and entertainment between destinations? Having arrived at the sanctuary, was there an official reception,

---

23 Lucian (*Dial. Mort.* 27.2) writes of a certain Ismenodoros, who, while traveling with only two servants to protect him and carrying four cups and five bowls of solid gold in his baggage, was murdered by robbers along a deserted road over Mt. Kithaeron to Eleusis.

24 Rutherford 2013, 186.

25 Casson (1974) is still fundamental on travel and its perils, whether by sea (pirates) or land (highwaymen). He writes that roads leading to and from big festival sites were well maintained and "broad enough to take wheeled traffic," while other 'roads' might be essentially goat paths (69).

26 Rutherford 2013, 176, 185–187.

27 Rutherford 2013, 186–187.

information, or organization office, e.g., to allocate sleeping spaces?

Regulating human behavior in the sanctuary is a topic dealt with in several papers in this volume, but a number of themes would benefit from future research. What was the extent of the sanctuary authorities' power over visitors, including those from other cities? What means did they have to enforce their rules (i.e., sanctuary police)? Markets for buying and selling various goods are well-known at several sanctuaries and also explored in this tome, but the particular goods on offer deserve further attention. What was the source of the animals and produce? Isotopic analysis may be able to clarify whether the animals sacrificed and consumed were brought by the worshippers or procured locally. Another commodity for sale were human beings. Did markets for buying and selling slaves exist in every sanctuary? A wealth of written evidence for manumissions of slaves exists at Delphi. To what extent did this occur in other sanctuaries? We might also consider to what extent prostitutes (*hetairai*), thieves, and/or tricksters operated in sanctuaries. Was prostitution a regular part of sanctuary visits, and was there any official resistance to it or administration of it? Were special facilities available to *hetairai* for cleaning and beautification to attract more revenue? The visit to sanctuaries for such non-ritual purposes and to what extent these activities affected sanctuary logistics need further study.

Apart from accommodation and possibilities to purchase food, one would like to know more about other provisions and services available to middle- and long-distance travelers to sanctuaries. Possible services might encompass the following: laundry; workers to repair travelers' necessities, e.g., wagons; money changing/methods of payment (itinerant bankers seem to have circulated);[28] craftsmen, e.g., sculptors, potters, and coroplasts, offering services (e.g., mending a pot) or their wares for sale; votive offerings, souvenirs, e.g., objects—secular or religious to take home; scribes to write dedications; medical help;[29] and burial of the dead.

Beyond these pragmatic concerns, the intellectual activity, e.g., epinician poetry authored by Pindar or Bacchylides, at sanctuaries merits further study. Was it marketed in some way? Who made arrangements for rhetoricians to speak? Did figures, such as Plato, visit sanctuaries for religious purposes or for self-promotion or both? What is known about guides in sanctuaries: who were they, and how were they engaged (and by whom other than Pausanias)? What fees did they charge, and were they regulated in some way? Were there different kinds of guides, i.e. those who gave specialized tours or those writing publications?

While we know that Plato shared a tent when he visited Olympia,[30] did VIPs, such as donors or philanthropists (e.g., Herodes Atticus, who funded the Nymphaion at Olympia), embassies, or visitors from differing political systems (e.g., the tyrannies of Sicily) enjoy special treatment beyond earmarked dining facilities, such as the Leonidaion at Olympia?

Few topics are more pressing in the modern world than the impact of human beings on the environment, and thus, we might consider the concentration of sometimes tens of thousands of human beings in a relatively small space over a period of days. What was the impact on the sanctuary environment?[31] And what about safety concerns? Where were fires permitted in the environs of the sanctuary for cooking and heat? Was there a fire service of some kind to start fires and to extinguish them? Where and how was garbage and trash disposal handled? Ancient writers attest to the gathering of waste for sale, e.g., as fertilizer; how was this managed?

The economic importance of sanctuaries has received intense scrutiny in recent years.[32] Among the many ways that funds could be raised for infrastructure, what role did philanthropy play? What exceptional treatment beyond special dining facilities did VIP visitors receive? What was the experience like for embassies and visitors from differing political systems or status categories?

These many questions are but a sampling of the logistics topics that merit further investigation. Whether one can answer such questions depends on the available evidence and its chronological limits. And, of course, these subjects require exploration from a diachronic perspective, including changes and developments that occurred in the Roman and early Christian periods. We hope that the essays presented here will encourage and prompt others to take up the search and continue the investigation into the logistics of Greek sanctuaries.

---

28 Aurigny 2020, 96 on *FD* III 2, 139; *Syll.*³ 729. She also mentions an inscription of the third or fourth century CE on the Athenian treasury at Delphi indicating that the building was transformed into a money-changing location (97).

29 Cf. Horster (2020, 123), who also cites *I.Ilion* 3 (= *IMT Skam/NebTäler* 191) of the third century BCE, an honorific decree for a patron from Paros, who, among other things, provided a physician for the Panathenaia.

30 Infra p. 107.

31 Studies indicate that the impact of modern festival goers on the environment is massive. For the interesting results from the excavations at Roskilde, Denmark, see Albris, Beck, and Sørensen 2009. For the ancient situation, see also Dillon 1997a.

32 E.g., Chandezon 2000; Dignas 2002; Collar and Kristensen 2020; Lo Monaco 2020.

Finally, it is our pleasure to acknowledge and thank the many people and institutions that made the conference and this book possible. Generous funding from the Riksbankens Jubileumsfond for the Advancement of the Humanities and Social Sciences made this conference possible, and the Swedish Institute at Athens, its director, Jenny Wallensten, and staff offered gracious hospitality and support during the conference. The Akropolis Museum and the Italian Archaeological School at Athens provided comfortable and convenient venues, and questions and discussion from the highly engaged audience enriched the experience. We offer warm thanks to them all. A great highlight of the conference was the lively summation and response offered by Nancy Bookidis and Vinciane Pirenne-Delforge, and we are grateful to these two generous scholars, whose contributions stimulated our thought processes and discussion. The editors of this Brill series, Anna Collar, Søren Handberg, Kathleen Lynch, and Troels Myrup Kristensen, along with Giulia Moriconi, the Associate Editor of Classical Studies at Brill, deserve acknowledgment and our thanks for their encouragement and patience in this endeavor. We are especially grateful to Gera van Bedaf, the Production Editor at Brill, for her hard work on this manuscript, particularly on the layout. Our greatest debt is to the conference speakers and contributors of this volume, whose enthusiastic acceptance of the conference invitation, thought-provoking papers, and spirited participation buoyed us along. We thank them for their patience, good humor, and hard work.

Judith M. Barringer, Gunnel Ekroth, and David Scahill
7 July 2025

Works Cited

Albris, S.L., A.S. Beck, and L. Sørensen 2009. "'Smattens' arkæologi. Arkæologer på Roskilde Festival." *Siden Saxo* 2: 4–13.

Angliker, E., and A. Bellia, eds. 2021. *Soundscape and Landscape at Panhellenic Greek Sanctuaries*. Pisa.

Aurigny, H. 2020. "Gathering in the Panhellenic Sanctuary at Delphi: an Archaeological Approach." In *Pilgrimage and Economy in the Ancient Mediterranean*, edited by A. Collar and T.M. Kristensen, 93–115. Leiden.

Barringer, J.M. 2021. *Olympia: A Cultural History*. Princeton.

Beck. H., and J. Kindt, eds. 2023. *The Local Horizon of Ancient Greek Religion*. Cambridge.

Carbon, J.-M., and G. Ekroth, eds. 2024. *From snout to tail. Exploring the Greek sacrificial animal from the literary, epigraphical, iconographical, archaeological and zooarchaeological evidence*. Stockholm.

Casson, L. 1974. *Travel in the Ancient World*. Baltimore.

Chandezon, C. 2000. "Foires et panégyries dans le monde grec classique et hellénistique." *RÉG* 113: 70–100.

Chandezon, C. 2003. *L'élevage en Grèce (fin V^e–fin Ier s. a.C.). L'apport des sources épigraphiques*. Bordeaux.

Chaniotis, A. 1988. "Habgierige Götter, habgierige Städte. Heiligtumsbesitz und Gebietsanspruch in den kretischen Staatsverträgen." *Ktema* 13: 21–39.

Cole, S.G. 2004. *Landscapes, Gender, and Ritual Space: The Ancient Greek Experience*. Berkeley.

Collar, A. 2020. "Movement, Labour and Devotion: A Virtual Walk to the Sanctuary at Mount Kasios." In *Pilgrimage and Economy in the Ancient Mediterranean*, edited by A. Collar and T.M. Kristensen, 33–61. Leiden.

Collar, A., and T.M. Kristensen, eds. 2020. *Pilgrimage and Economy in the Ancient Mediterranean*. Leiden.

Dignas, B. 2002. *Economy of the Sacred in Hellenistic and Roman Asia Minor*. Oxford.

Dillon, M. 1997a. "The Ecology of the Greek Sanctuary." *ZPE* 118: 113–127.

Dillon, M. 1997b. *Pilgrims and Pilgrimage in Ancient Greece*. London.

Eidinow, E., A. Geertz, and J. North. 2023. *Cognitive Approaches to Ancient Religious Experience*. Cambridge.

Ekroth, G. 2014. "Animal sacrifice in antiquity." In *The Oxford Handbook of Ancient Animals*, edited by G.L. Campbell, 324–354. Oxford.

Ekroth, G., and J. Wallensten, eds. 2013. *Bones, behaviour and belief. The zooarchaeological material as a source for ritual practice in ancient Greece and beyond*. Stockholm.

Flower, M. 2009. "Spartan 'Religion' and Greek 'Religion.'" In *Sparta: Comparative Approaches*, edited by S. Hodkinson, 193–229. Swansea.

Freitag, K., and M. Haake, eds. 2019. *Griechische Heiligtümer als Handlungsorte. Zur Multifunktionalität supralokaler Heiligtümer von der frühen Archaik bis in die römische Kaiserzeit*. Stuttgart.

Galoppin, T. et al., eds. 2022. *Naming and Mapping the Gods in the Ancient Mediterranean 1: Spaces, Mobilities, Imaginaries*. Berlin.

Gerlach, I., G. Lindström, and K. Sporn, eds. 2022. *Kulttopographie und Kommunikationsformen im sakralen Kontext. Ergebnisse der Clustertagungen (2012–2018)*. Berlin.

Grzesik, D. 2021. *Honorific Culture at Delphi in the Hellenistic and Roman Periods*. Leiden.

Hanson, V.D., and J. Heath. 2001. *Who Killed Homer?* New York.

Heiden, J. 1995. *Die Tondächer von Olympia, OlForsch* 24. Berlin.

Hemans, F.P. 1989. "The Archaic Roof Tiles at Isthmia: A Re-examination." *Hesperia* 58: 251–266.

Hermary, A. *et al.* 2004. 'Les sacrifices dans le monde grec', *ThesCRA* I, 59–134.

Hitzl, K. 1996. *Die Gewichte griechischer Zeit aus Olympia, OlForsch25*. Berlin.

Horster, M. 2004. *Landbesitz griechischer Heiligtümer in archaischer und klassischer Zeit*. Berlin.

Horster, M. 2020. "Hellenistic Festivals: Aspects of the Economic Impact on Cities and Sanctuaries." In *Pilgrimage and Economy in the Ancient Mediterranean*, edited by A. Collar and T.M. Kristensen, 116–139. Leiden.

Kaminski, G. 1991. "Thesauros." *JdI* 106: 63–181.

Kearns, E. 2010. *Ancient Greek Religion*. Malden, MA.

Kyrieleis, H. 2011. *Olympia: Archäologie eines Heiligtums*. Mainz.

Lalonde, G. 2019. *Athena Itonia: Geography and Meaning of an Ancient Greek War Goddess*. Leiden.

Larson, J. 2016. *Understanding Greek Religion: A Cognitive Approach*. London.

Leypold, C. 2008. *Bankettgebäude in griechischen Heiligtümern*. Wiesbaden.

Lo Monaco, A., ed. 2020. *Spending on the Gods: Economy, Financial Resources and Management in the Sanctuaries in Greece*. Athens.

Lombardi, P. 2009. "Ἀναθέτω ἐν τὸ ἱερόν. Esempi di regolamentazione della dedica votive nel mondo greco." In *Dediche sacre nel mondo greco-romano. Diffusione, funzione, tipologie*, edited by J. Bodel and M. Kajava, 95–126. Rome.

Luce, J.-M. 2015–2016. "La ville de Delphes." *BCH* 139–140: 726–766.

Luce, J.-M. 2021. "Programme 'Ville de Delphes'." https://hal.science/hal-03614002, last accessed 23.3.2024.

Mania, U., and M. Trümper, eds. 2018. *Development of Gymnasia and Graeco-Roman Cityscapes*. Berlin.

Marinatos, N., and R. Hägg. 1993. *Greek Sanctuaries: New Approaches*. London.

Mazarakis Ainian, A. 2017. *Les sanctuaires archaïques des Cyclades*. Rennes.

Mikalson, J. 2005. *Ancient Greek Religion*. Malden, MA.

Ogden, D., ed. 2008. *A Companion to Greek Religion*. Malden, MA.

Papalexandrou, N., and A. Sowder Koch, eds. 2023. *Hephaistus on the Athenian Acropolis: Current Approaches to the Study of Artifacts Made of Bronze and Other Metals*. Boston.

Papazarkadas, N. 2011. *Sacred and Public Land in Ancient Athens*. Oxford.

Parker, R.C.T. 2011. *On Greek Religion*. Ithaca.

Parker, R.C.T. 2017. *Greek Gods Abroad: Names, Natures, and Transformations*. Berkeley.

Partida, E., and B. Schmidt-Dounas, eds. 2019. *Listening to the Stones: Essays on Architecture and Function in Ancient Greek Sanctuaries in Honour of Richard Alan Tomlinson*. Oxford.

Pedley, J. 2005. *Sanctuaries and the Sacred in the Ancient Greek World*. Cambridge.

Pilz, O. 2020. *Kulte und Heiligtümer in Elis und Triphylien. Untersuchungen zur Sakraltopographie der westlichen Peloponnes*. Tübingen.

Pirenne-Delforge, V. 2020. *Le polythéisme grec à l'épreuve d'Hérodote*. Paris.

Pirenne-Delforge, V., and G. Pironti. 2023. *The Hera of Zeus: Intimate Enemy, Ultimate Spouse*. Cambridge.

de Polignac, F. 1995. *Cults, Territory, and the Origins of the City-State*, trans. by J. Lloyd. Chicago.

Polinskaya, I. 2013. *A Local History of Greek Polytheism: Gods, People, and the Land of Aigina, 800–400 BCE*. Leiden.

Riethmüller, J.W. 2005. *Asklepios. Heiligtümer und Kulte*. Heidelberg.

Roy, J. 2013. "Olympia, Identity and Integration: Elis, Eleia, and Hellas." In *Greek Federal States and Their Sanctuaries: Identity and Integration*, edited by P. Funke and M. Haake, 107–121. Stuttgart.

Roy, J. 2015. "The Distribution of Cult in the Landscape of Eleia." In *Human Development in Sacred Landscapes: Between Ritual Tradition, Creativity and Emotionality*, edited by L. Käppel and V. Pothou, 173–188. Göttingen.

Rutherford, I. 2013. *State Pilgrims and Sacred Observers in Ancient Greece: A Study of Theōriā and Theōroi*. Cambridge.

Scott, M. 2014. *Delphi: A History of the Center of the Ancient World*. Princeton.

Serino, M. 2021. "Some remarks on Greek ritual meals. Preliminary results of the study on cooking and plain pottery from the sanctuary of Apollo at Soros (Thessaly)." *Mare Internum* 13: 19–44.

Sinn, U. 1993. "Greek sanctuaries as places of refuge." In *Greek Sanctuaries: New Approaches*, edited by N. Marinatos and R. Hägg, 88–109. London.

Sinn, U. 1996. *Olympia: Kult, Sport und Feste in der Antike*. Munich.

Smith, T.J. 2021. *Religion in the Art of Archaic and Classical Greece*. Philadelphia.

Sporn, K. 2002. *Heiligtümer und Kulte Kretas in klassischer und hellenistischer Zeit*. Heidelberg.

Sporn, K. 2019. "Natural Features in Greek Cult Places: The Case of Athens." *Natur—Mythos—Religion im antiken Griechenland*, edited by T.S. Scheer, 29–48. Stuttgart.

Tomlinson, R.A. 1980. "Two Notes on Possible *Hestiatoria*." *BSA* 75: 221–228.

van Straten, F.T. 1995. *Hierà kalá: Images of animal sacrifice in Archaic and Classical Greece*. Leiden.

Williamson, C.G. 2021. *Urban Rituals in Sacred Landscapes in Hellenistic Asia Minor*. Leiden.

Woolf, G., I. Bultrighini, and C. Norman, eds. 2024. *Sanctuaries and Experience: Knowledge, Practice and Space in the Ancient World*. Stuttgart.

Zuckerberg, D. 2018. *Not All Dead White Men: Classics and Misogyny in the Digital Age*. Cambridge, MA.

CHAPTER 1

Managing the Ebb and Flow of Competing Claims on Sacred Space

Laura Gawlinski

In his book *Greek Religion*, Walter Burkert identifies two guiding elements for the organization of ancient Greek religious practice: "As the sanctuary articulates space, so the festival articulates time."[1] These two elements were, in practice, quite interdependent. Sacred space was not static, but reacted to changing needs, not just throughout a longer, historical trajectory over time, but also in the short-term, throughout the year. Most sanctuaries contained a permanent built infrastructure, even if some of that infrastructure might only be used on an irregular basis when hosting occasional festivals.[2] But temporary alterations or additions offered momentary adaptability to changing circumstances. Human resources also varied; an influx of personnel and their official rules and regulations arrived alongside crowds of worshipers, but in less visited times, a sanctuary could deploy different arrangements to compensate for diminished oversight. We need to conceptualize the sanctuary as a living, changing entity and look beyond its static architectural plan. Sacred space has a lifecycle—an ebb and flow—to which space, policies, and personnel respond.

Most of our information about the customs, regulations, and authority figures governing sanctuary life comes from sources that are concerned with festivals or other momentous occasions, such as annual state-funded sacrifices, because those are the matters and moments that require the most logistical work.[3] Sanctuaries received the maximum number of visitors, and therefore the most managerial attention, during major festivals and ritual events, but how space was used and controlled at those times differed from how it was managed day-to-day. We should expect a functional contrast between these major days in the calendar and the times that were much less busy. This paper first offers a general picture of the traffic fluctuations in a sacred space and then explores two questions related to 'time management:' 1) were regular activities administered differently from less frequent festival events, and if so, in what way?; and 2) what happened when the routine and the exceptional came into conflict with one another, as, for example, when the right to asylum or a private act of veneration clashed with a festival? Although there is not much explicit testimony about the regulation of space for non-festival activities, we can begin to gain a more nuanced understanding of the sanctuary lifecycle by reading between the lines of the evidence we do have.

Because the goal is to uncover the kinds of circumstances that affected the sanctuary cycle in general, this examination will not be limited to a particular time frame or region; a variety of evidence can be used as a tool for rethinking the expectations about how sanctuaries fit into the complex lives of their communities of users. Inscriptions that record regulations for sanctuary activities and resources are particularly valuable, as these also provide insight into the range of people who frequented sanctuaries, from the visiting worshipers to the priests and other officials who were responsible for their management. What also arises from this investigation is a heightened distinction between public and private, not just between active and idle, which is especially notable as scholarship turns to considering individual and personal religion in addition and in relation to that of the *polis*.

1 The Rhythm of Sacred Time

What determined the schedule of a sanctuary and constituted this ebb and flow would have differed from site to site. A sanctuary that was centrally located or urban, such as the Akropolis in Athens, was characterized by an event schedule, level of attention, and number of visitors that would be quite different from those of a site that was less eminent or more rural, such as the cave shrine to Pan on Mount Parnes near Phyle. Some sites were visited rarely, some were closed part of the time, and still others met specialized needs that determined their availability.[4] For

---

1 Burkert 1985, 9. See also Blömer (2021, 165) on the 'convergence' of festival time with festival space.
2 Dignas 2007, 164.
3 Barringer (2021, 44–62) addresses the number of visitors at Olympia during festivals and the personnel and logistics required.

4 Hewitt (1909) and Corbett (1970) outline the evidence; the latter focuses specifically on the temple building. Mylonopoulos (2011) examines interior statue barriers and their implications for temple accessibility. Kobusch (2020b) considers the variable form and use of the temple *pronaos* (the front portico) and demonstrates that it was sometimes a publicly accessible, multifunctional space. See also Wallensten in this volume.

example, most healing sanctuaries seem to have accepted visitors at practically any time, since most of the medical issues they treated were not themselves beholden to a convenient schedule.[5] Despite this overwhelming variety and the fact that our evidence does not allow us to plausibly reconstruct the full agenda for any one single space, it is at least possible to become more aware of the effects of the ebb and flow.

A first step towards understanding sanctuary timetables comes from the so-called sacrificial calendars, which provide lists of offerings organized by month, and sometimes day, usually alongside the costs that the issuing body would provide for each item or payment. These calendars typically feature the annual ritual expenditures and events of the community that published them, but some events were more occasional than others and organized on a different cycle. Many sacrifices, for example, were scheduled at regular intervals that were not annual. A fragment of the large sacrificial calendar of 403/2–400/399 BCE from Athens, originally displayed in the Stoa Basileios, preserves the heading τάδε τὸ ἕτερον ἔτος θυέται, "make these sacrifices during the other year," that is, every other year.[6] An inscription of c.500–475 BCE on an altar from Thalami in Messenia requires a sacrifice in the fifth year,[7] a quadrennial schedule, as does Face A of the 'sacred law' of c.500–450 BCE from Selinous.[8] A number of complementary 'calendars' were in effect at the same time. In addition to the *polis*-calendar of Athens in the Stoa Basileios, there were also deme calendars, such as that of c.440–430 BCE from Thorikos, now on display in the Epigraphical Museum in Athens.[9] Such schedules reached even beyond the *polis* when Panhellenic sanctuaries and events were involved. The Olympic games were only every four years, and other stephanitic games were biennial. The Panathenaia was yearly, but intensified and enlarged only every fourth, when it was opened to outsiders. There were limitations on the consultation of the oracle at Delphi; not only were appointments available only one day a month, but also only for nine months of the year. Consideration of the timing of major events matters because these would be the times that sanctuaries had the greatest number of visitors.

Some of this intensive sanctuary activity was ruled by the seasons.[10] The Eleusinian first-fruits decree of the 430s BCE organized the grain offerings brought into Eleusis.[11] The decree does not specify a date for the commencement of the collection and suggests that this gathering would be dealt with over a period of time, not at one moment, but the timing must have coincided with the harvest at least in a general way. Other seasonal activities affecting the number of people traveling to sanctuaries included warfare and sailing. For example, a contract of the late second century BCE for the sale of the priesthood of Aphrodite Pandamos and Pontia on Kos prescribes that the men stationed on warships sacrifice after they have returned from their sailing duties (τοὶ στρατευόμενοι ἐν ταῖς μακραῖς ναυσὶν ἐ[πεί]| κα καταλύωντι τὸν πλοῦν θυόντω).[12] Similarly, initiations at the sanctuary of the Great Gods on Samothrace took place throughout the sailing season; Roman-period lists of initiates record dates in April through early November, with June being the most common.[13] There are no known rules against initiation at other times, but it is clear from the lists that there were high and low seasons. Since Samothrace is an island, and its mystery festival was particularly popular with sailors, the uptick in visitors was influenced by the best weather for sailing. Finally, there is even some evidence that construction and building maintenance in sanctuaries would have been influenced by seasonal labor and equipment availability.[14]

In addition to the activities governed by a regularized calendar or the flow of the seasons, a number of substantive events took place at times that were pre-arranged but not precisely fixed. For example, some regulations attest to a configuration that limited sacrifice to specific days. Two contracts of the first century BCE for priesthoods on Kos refer to days that were *hosion* or proper in a religious sense. One instructs the priestess of Artemis to open the sanctuary at dawn "on each of the days on which it is proper [*hosion*] to open the sanctuaries" (ἑκάσ|[τα]ς

---

5   Dignas (2007) focuses on the 'daily life' of healing sanctuaries.
6   *CGRN* 45, A, frag. 3, l. 30. See Lambert 2002 for this calendar; the text cited here is also his face A, frag. 3. Translations throughout are my own.
7   *IG* V.1 1312=*CGRN* 11, ll. 2–3.
8   *CGRN* 13, A, ll. 1–2.
9   *IG* I³ 256bis=*CGRN* 32.
10 For a thought-provoking attempt to uncover the timing of a festival based on the growing cycle, see Bookidis et al. 1999, 29–30. The discovery of the remains of a whole grape at the sanctuary of Demeter and Kore at Corinth suggests an autumn date for some ritual activities. For the 'archaeology of seasonality,' see now the contributions in Lichtenberger and Raja 2021.
11 Clinton 2005–2008, 28a=*IG* I³ 78a.
12 *IG* XII.4 319=*CGRN* 220, ll. 5–6.
13 Dimitrova 2008, 245–247. I thank Yannis Nakas for sharing information about the Greek sailing season with me. The evidence from Samothrace also fits the observations by Feuser 2021 on the sea-based activities of the Mediterranean basin.
14 Carusi 2021. Barringer (2021, 59) notes the existence of facilities at Olympia for on-site maintenance.

ἀμέρας αἷς ὅσιόν ἐστιν ἀνοίγειν τὰ ἱερά).[15] In a contract for a priest of Nike, worshipers who are not offering a marriage sacrifice, but still wish to offer an animal, should do so "on the days on which it is proper [*hosion*] to sacrifice" (θυέτω δὲ κ[αὶ] | [τῶ]ν ἄλλων ὁ χρῄζων ἱερεῖον ὃ νομίζετα[ι ἐν] | [αἷ]ς ἀμέραις ὅσιόν ἐστιν θύεν).[16] Unfortunately, it is unclear to us from these texts how the priests or the visitors would have known or marked which days were *hosion*.[17] Other uses of sacred space, such as oathtaking, could happen as needed. Some oath ceremonies were related to activities of the sanctuaries where the oaths were administered, such as the one taken by the *athlothetai* (games officials) for Herakles at Marathon (*IG* I³ 3, ll. 6–10, *c*.490–480 BCE), but a sacred location could add efficacy to any oath.[18] Similarly, sanctuaries could serve as a meeting place for *polis* or federation officials or, more irregularly, for interstate arbitrations.

At the opposite end of the spectrum from busy, regulated days of communal worship were the personally motivated visits by individuals or families who desired to make private sacrifice or set up dedications. The timing might coincide with a festival, but issues such as financial difficulties, illness, and natural disasters would have driven people to visit sanctuaries on an irregular, *ad hoc* basis.[19] An upcoming marriage, for example, might necessitate attendance at sanctuaries. A regulation of the beginning of third century BCE concerning a family cult and sanctuary on Kos allows its indigent male members to celebrate even the wedding itself in the sanctuary, but only in a particular month, and the group set the activities for the various days.[20] The contract for a priest of Nike on Kos referenced above also permits marriages within a sanctuary,[21] but if there were further details, we no longer have access to them (Face A is illegible, and the weddings are first mentioned on Face B). It was more common for premarital rituals to take place in a sanctuary, such as the preliminary, first-fruits offering to Aphrodite Ourania at Athens. This was given in the form of 1 dr deposited into a *thesauros* (offering-box), which was inscribed with these details about the process.[22] The *thesauros* seems to have been available most of the time, and the locking mechanism of the stone box would have made it safe to deposit the coins even when no priestess was present.[23]

Offerings could be made in response to a message from a god, which might arrive at any time. In the *Dyskolos* by Menander, the mother of Sostratos arranges a sacrifice at a nearby cave of Pan after she has a dream that Pan chained up her son and made him dig up a field; Getas, who is enslaved to the family and thus carries out the arrangements, explains to the audience that this ritual act will change the outcome seen in the dream (ll. 406–418). Although Menander's comedy is fiction, its plot does seem to reflect lived experience, as votive offerings frequently record that they were the result of a divine message. Gil Renberg has collected 1,300 dedicatory inscriptions from Greece, Rome, and Egypt that declare to the reader that they were set up by order of a god, so this practice was far from unusual.[24] The earliest Greek example is a votive relief of the second half of the fourth century BCE, which was found in the area of the Athenian Agora. It depicts the dedicator, the cobbler Dionysios, at work in his shop; the recipient was the hero Kallistephanos. The hexameter inscription below the image includes the impetus for the dedication: Dionysios "saw a divine vision in his sleep" (ὄψιν ἰδὼν θείαν ἐν ὕπνω[ι]).[25]

From this very broad sketch of the complicated lifecycle of a sacred space, we learn that activities and guests were at their most numerous on the set sacrificial and festival days, and that seasons and the environment mattered. Work (agriculture, war, manufacturing, etc.) affected visitation, and people had personal needs that did not fit neatly into any predetermined schedule. Someone who had a dream from a god or needed to fulfill a vow might have been able to wait until an appropriate or convenient time to deposit a votive, but some circumstances, such as sudden illness, required more immediate action. Religious

---

15   *CGRN* 188, ll. 8–13.
16   *IG* XII.4 330=*CGRN* 163, ll. 2–4.
17   For more on the term *hosios*, see Peels 2016, esp. 36–55.
18   Torrance 2014, 132–142.
19   The corollary to individual worshipers choosing to visit sanctuaries for personal reasons is that they could also be kept out of sanctuaries based on personal circumstances. Purity regulations were concerned with how recently a visitor had attended a funeral, killed someone in battle, had intercourse, menstruated, or given birth to a child. For these purity notices, see Parker 2018. See also Carbon and Harris in this volume.
20   *IG* XII.4 348=*CGRN* 96, ll. 86–113.
21   *IG* XII.4 330=*CGRN* 163, ll. 1–2.
22   *SEG* 41.182 of the early fourth century BCE. For the security features and locking mechanisms of this *thesauros*, now on display in the Akropolis Museum, see Kazamiakes 1990–1991.
23   For coin rituals and *thesauroi*, see Pafford (2013), who notes "Cult fees are expressed in a different way than other sacred laws or sacrificial calendars in that *they involve activity that will be impromptu and worshiper driven*" (57, emphasis mine). A regulation concerning the healing sanctuary of Amphiaraos at Oropos (*CGRN* 75, *c*.386–374 BCE) is explicit that fees and fines are to be deposited in the presence of a sanctuary official (ll. 12–13, 23–24).
24   Renberg 2003.
25   *SEG* 55.307, E, l. 5; Lawton 2017, 2017, 89–91 no. 89, and 17–19 for a summary of the use of votives, especially the fact that they depict private worship.

life was embedded in the culture, intertwined with other institutions, and affected by an individual's life events. So-called 'everyday life' in a Greek sanctuary is difficult to uncover because there was perhaps no such thing as a typical day.

2 Sanctuary Life outside the Calendar

How were sanctuaries managed outside of the major sacrificial and festival days? Although regulations rarely provide an explicit reference to "all days" or "every day," the nature of some texts seems to imply just that. The inscriptions that instructed worshipers about purity requirements or unusual sacrificial specifications must have been in effect all the time. For example, the Hellenistic copy of a sign of c.450 BCE posted at a shrine on Thasos informed visitors that a goat, otherwise a common sacrificial animal, was not a part of this particular Hera cult: "For Hera At-the-Harbor, a goat is unacceptable" ("Ἥρηι Ἐπιλιμενίηι | αἶγα ὦ θέμις).[26] Such notices would have been especially useful in the absence of a priest or other official.

An inscribed regulation of c.386–374 BCE concerning the healing sanctuary of Amphiaraos at Oropos offers further insight about arrangements for intermittent visits. It opens with an explicit statement that the priest does not have to be present all the time, but just seasonally from the end of winter to the time for plowing (autumn), a time span when people were most likely to travel. But even during that period, he may be absent quite frequently, as long as the total number of days away is not more than ten per month (τὸν ἱερέα τοῦ Ἀμφιαράου φοιτᾶν εἰς τὸ ἱερό|ν, ἐπειδὰν χειμὼν παρέλθηι μέχρι ἀρότου ὥρης, μὴ πλέον δια-λείποντα ἢ τρεῖς ἡμέρας καὶ | μένειν ἐν τοῖ ἱεροῖ μὴ ἔλαττον ἢ δέκα ἡμέρα|ς τοῦ μηνὸς ἐκ⟨ά⟩[[σ]]στου).[27] The sanctuary visitors were also served by a *neokoros*, a temple warden, under the authority of the priest (ll. 6–8); because the *neokoros* oversaw the payments made by the visitors who requested incubation and recorded information about them (ll. 20–24, 39–43), those in need could access healing even when the priest was not there. The priest, however, was responsible for praying over the sacrifices on the altar (ll. 25–26), and what is especially valuable about this text is that it articulates to the worshipers how they are to handle this potential issue. When the priest was not present, those sacrificing could just perform the prayers themselves (ὅταν δὲ μὴ παρεῖ, τὸν θύοντα καὶ τεῖ θυσίει α|ὐτὸν ἑαυτοῖ κατεύχεσθαι ἕκαστον, ll. 27–28).

Consideration for the priest's absence from the Amphiaraon may reflect the fact that it was a healing sanctuary, which was especially prone to irregular patterns of visitation. However, similar practices are attested in two inscriptions from Chios, in which the goal is to ensure the perquisites are distributed to the priest whether he is present or not.[28] A regulation or sale from the end of the fifth century BCE for the priesthood of Zeus Pelinaios on Chios spells out what a visitor is to do if the priest is absent: he can make the sacrifice himself, but only after shouting three times (βωσάτω [ἐ]ς | τρὶς ὁ θέλων γεγω|νεῖν καὶ αὐτὸς π[ο]|είτω τὰ ἱερά).[29] In a slightly later contract for a *genos*-priesthood of Herakles, also from Chios, the sacrificer is similarly asked to voice his intentions first.[30] But in this case, the worshiper will turn to a preselected alternate if the priest is not there: "The sacrificer must call out to the priest, but if the priest is not present, one of the allotted ones must serve as acting priest" (ἐπαγγειλ[άτω] | δὲ ὁ θύων τῶι ἱερεῖ, ἐὰν δ[ὲ ὁ] | ἱερεὸς μὴ παρῆι προιερη[τευ]|έτω τις ὢν αἱ λόγχαι εἰσ[ίν], ll. 9–12).

The text of the sale of the priesthood of Zeus Pelinaios concludes with a punishment clause levying a fine of five staters for anyone who breaks the rules therein (ll. 13–16). Certainly, when the priest was present, infractions could be caught by him, but the text does not indicate how a misstep would be noticed or the fine exacted if he was not. This clause invites consideration of an important issue: who might have been responsible for policing or enforcing regulations on a slow day in a sanctuary?[31] One option was to rely on other members of the community by involving them in the process as informers, a quasi-legal procedure called *phasis*.[32] Numerous sources refer to someone who is not in an official position of authority 'catching' a wrongdoer, and in some cases, regulations even define an incentive for the informer in the form of a portion of the fine levied. An example from Delos pertains to offenders who bring animals onto sanctuary land for grazing (banned) instead of for sacrificing (permitted). In this inscription, several officials (the *hieropoioi*, the *boule*,

---

26   *CGRN* 23. Peels (2016, 168–179) considers when these kinds of rules were made explicit.
27   RO no. 27; *CGRN* 75, ll. 2–6.

28   In *CGRN* 36, ll. 11–13, the sacrificer to Zeus Pelinaios may not give any of the portions of the animal to anyone else if he sacrifices alone; in *CGRN* 50, ll. 12–14, the priest of Herakles will also still receive his portion, even if the sacrifice was overseen by an alternate instead.
29   *CGRN* 36, ll. 8–11.
30   *CGRN* 50, c.400–350 BCE.
31   See Chandezon and Carbon and Harris in this volume. See also Gawlinski 2014, 73–76.
32   MacDowell 1991.

and the rest of the *archontes*) are granted the right to fine the offender directly, but the text also empowers anyone else who wishes to report the infraction to the magistrates and receive half the fine, whatever that might end up being (ἐξεῖναι δὲ καὶ εἰσαν|γέλλ[ει]ν εἰς τὰ[ς ἀρ]χὰς τῶι βουλομένωι | καὶ λαμ[βά]νειν τὸ ἥμισυ, ll. 9–11).[33]

Lene Rubinstein has collected 80 texts from the sixth through second centuries BCE that feature provisions for fine sharing. She identifies a general pattern for the use of this relatively infrequent incentive:

> Common to most offenses of these types is that *they would be difficult to police effectively* [emphasis mine], that they were 'victimless' crimes in that they did not cause harm to any particular individual, and that each of them might come across as rather inconspicuous when considered on its own, yet had the potential to cause major damage if committed repeatedly. Moreover, the reporting in most of these cases was likely to have been based on a direct encounter between perpetrator and denunciator.[34]

Many of the infractions to which fine sharing applied concern sanctuary resources. Wood in sacred groves, pastureland, or water pipes would not be watched closely by officials day-to-day, and even on busy festival days would have been difficult to "police effectively." In the lengthy regulation of 91 BCE or 23 CE about the Andanian mystery festival in Messenia, there is only one transgression whose recorded fine could be shared with an informer: cutting wood from the sanctuary grove. If a visitor caught someone using sanctuary resources in this way, he was obligated to report it to the Sacred Men (μηδεὶς κοπτέτω ἐκ τοῦ ἱεροῦ τόπου· | ἂν δέ τις ἅλωι…ὁ δὲ ἐπιτυχὼν ἀγέτω | αὐτοὺς ἐπὶ τοὺς ἱεροὺς καὶ λαμβανέτω τὸ ἥμισυ),[35] officials responsible for the festival specifically, but it is reasonable to expect that this ban, and perhaps even its incentive, would be in place at other times, too. Not only is this the only infraction in the document with a fine-sharing clause, but it is also the only one that involves a permanent physical feature of the sanctuary.[36] Authorities do not appear to have used this fine-sharing system regularly, but it was one option available for managing sanctuary space when it was considered necessary to rely on informers.

3   Conflicts and Priorities

As recounted by Livy (31.14.6–11), two Akarnanian men visiting Athens in 201 BCE found themselves inside the sanctuary of the goddesses at Eleusis, although uninitiated. This was an accident that occurred simply because they had happened to follow the crowd (*imprudentes religionis cum cetera turba ingressi sunt*, 31.14.7), but when they were discovered, they were executed. This result is an unusually extreme example of what might befall a visitor whose presence at a site came into conflict with that site's rules, but there must have been at least occasional tensions caused by the diverse purposes for which a sanctuary could be used. Clashes between major public events and private activities provide an opportunity to investigate the logistics for managing competing claims over space and resources. These moments can also serve as an indirect testament to some of the everyday activities that would not have been recorded otherwise.

Several regulations that set the order of sacrificial rituals distinguish between the treatment of public and private sacrifices and thus offer incidental information about this divide. The solution for managing sacrifices from multiple sources was a hierarchy in which the public sacrifices always took precedence. For example, at the procession during the festival for Artemis at Amarynthos (Euboia), the animals are to be arranged with the public ones and the best-in-show first, then the 'choice' (*krita*) animals, and then finally the private ones, if anyone wishes to join the procession (πρῶτομ μὲν τὰ δ|ημόσια καὶ τὸ καλλιστεῖον, ἔπειτα τὰ κριτά, ἔπειτα | τῶν ἰδιωτῶν, ἐάν τις βόληται συμπομπεύειν).[37] Similarly, the woman who purchases the

---

33   SEG 48.1037, B, ll. 2–11 of *c*.180–166 BCE (for discussion *NGSL*² 22–25). Other pertinent examples include the regulations of the Labyadai at Delphi (fifth–fourth centuries BCE), in which there is even a fine for the officials (the *tagoi*) if they do not ensure that the informer is paid (RO no. 1, C, ll. 10–16). At Arkesine on Amorgos, a lease of the sacred land calls for the informer to get half the fine in cases where someone brings in forbidden flocks or sells off items that are in dispute (mid-fourth century BCE; RO no. 59, ll. 36, 50). Instead of offering an incentive to report those who use the sanctuary for grazing or dumping, a fourth-century BCE regulation from Chios indicates that those who see but do not report face a fine themselves (*LSCG* no. 116, ll. 17–20, 27–30). See also Carbon and Harris in this volume.

34   Rubinstein 2016, 429.

35   *IG* V.1 1390=*CGRN* 222, ll. 78–80. For a text and commentary of this regulation, see Gawlinski 2012.

36   The other transgressions that result in fines pertain to festival activities: refusing to take oaths (ll. 6–7), stealing from other worshipers (ll. 76–77), mismanaging accounts (ll. 51–52, 60–62), cheating in the temporary marketplace (ll. 101–102), restricting access to water (ll. 105–106), breaking the contract about setting up the bath (ll. 110–111), and committing general malfeasance (ll. 160–163). The fine for disrupting the asylum process went to the owner of the enslaved suppliant (ll. 81–82).

37   *IG* XII.9 189=*CGRN* 91, ll. 36–38 of *c*.340 BCE.

priesthood of Dionysos at Miletos would receive the right to make the raw meat offering on behalf of the city before anyone else could (μὴ ἐξεῖναι ὠμοφάγιον ἐμβαλεῖν μηθενὶ πρότερον | [ἢ ἡ ἱέ]ρεια ὑπὲρ τῆς πόλεως ἐμβάληι).[38] Private groups also had to wait to set up their own *thiasoi* until the public one was prepared (μὴ ἐξεῖναι δὲ μηδὲ | [συν]αγαγεῖν τὸν θίασον μηθενὶ πρότερον τοῦ δημοσίου, ll. 3–4). At Erythrai, sacrifices for Asklepios and Apollo by private individuals seem to be allowed, but the sacrifices on behalf of the public occur first. In addition, this text temporally spaces some offerings even further apart by prohibiting any special preliminary sacrifices by individuals during the festival:

ὅταν δὲ ἡ πόλις τὴν θυσίην | τῶι Ἀσκληπιῶι ποιῆι, τὰ τῆς πόλεως | προτεθύσθαι ὑπὲρ πάντων, ἰδιώτης δὲ | μηδεὶς προθυέτω ἐν τῆι ἑορτῆι· ἀνὰ δὲ | τὸν ἄλλογ χρόνον προθυέτω κατὰ τὰ | προγεγραμμένα.[39]

When the city makes the sacrifice to Asklepios, the offerings of the city should be made first, on behalf of everyone, and let no private individual offer a preliminary sacrifice during the festival. But during the rest of the time, they may offer a sacrifice according to what has been written.

This acceptable private ritual is regulated when it comes into conflict with an occasional, special event.

The placement of votives dedicated by individuals could also be regulated, and the objects might be moved around or even discarded.[40] An inscription of the mid-second century BCE from Athens specifies that the priest has the right to relocate the dedications so that they do not block the statue (*LSCG* no. 43 = *IG* II² 995). It also seems to reassert the priest's right to give the permission to leave a dedication in the first place (though the text requires substantial restoration at this point): "In the future, no one can dedicate anything in the sanctuary without the priest, just as it was originally" (καὶ εἰς τὸ [λοιπὸν μη]θένα ἀν]ατιθέναι μηθὲν ἐν τῶι [ἱ]ερ[ῶι ἄνευ τοῦ ἱε]ρέως κα]θάπερ ἐξ ἀρχῆς ὑπῆρχεν, ll. 10–12).[41] Enough problems must have been caused by unsupervised personal devotion so that increased oversight, codified in a written text, was sought to resolve them.

Supplication and asylum-seeking were much more fraught for a sanctuary; the tensions were not just between private and public, but also between different types of uses for the space. Sanctuaries were the main locations where suppliants could make a petition or seek refuge, though some were used more frequently for this than others. Our sources suggest that the Theseion in Athens, for example, was especially known as an asylum for enslaved persons. Among the oldest references is a joke in Aristophanes about a trireme sailing off to "sit" at the Theseion, i.e., act as a suppliant (*Eq.* 1311–1312); later sources such as Plutarch (*Thes.* 36.4), along with scholia, imply that it was a popular destination for enslaved suppliants who were attempting to flee from those who owned them, but possibly only with the hope to be resold.[42] None of the sources are clear about that process, nor do they offer information about how the suppliants affected other activities in the sanctuary. Evidence from other sanctuaries, however, shows that the process could be regulated or limited. Angelos Chaniotis and others argue that sanctuaries intentionally developed methods to manage the number of suppliants without breaking the religious requirements of asylum.[43] For example, the regulation of markets at the sanctuary of Hera at Samos forbids shopkeepers from doing business with any suppliants, and, in the case of enslaved asylum-seekers, the shopkeepers could neither hire them nor give them food (οὐχ ὑπ[οδέξον|ται δὲ ἐν τοῖς κα]πηλείοις τοὺς καθίζοντας οἰκέτας εἰς τὸ ἱερὸν ο[ὐδὲ παρ|έξουσιν οὔτε ἔργα ο]ὔτε σῖτα οὐδ' ὑποδέξονται παρ' αὐτῶν οὐδὲν [τρόπωι | οὐδὲ παρευρέσ]ει οὐδεμιᾶι).[44] These rules were intended to make the situation so uncomfortable and difficult that suppliants would choose to leave.

Other regulations display a particular concern for the festival calendar and mitigate the effects of supplication when other activities needed to take priority. In the defense speech of Andokides from around 400 BCE, Andokides recounts that he previously had been charged with depositing a suppliant branch on the altar of the Eleusinion during the Mysteries—an act forbidden during the festival time (ll. 110–116). The asylum of enslaved

---

38 *CGRN* 138, ll. 2–3, 275/4 BCE.
39 *CGRN* 76, ll. 25–30, 380–360 BCE.
40 Mylonopoulos, 2013, 123 (with n. 9); van Straten 2000, 213–214.
41 Any interpretation of the priest's role must contend with the fragmentary text. Here I have provided the lines with the restorations of Sokolowski (*LSCG* no. 43), but compare the text of *IG* II² 995: καὶ εἰς τὸ [λοιπὸν μη]θένα μετ]ατιθέναι μηθὲν ἐν τῶι [ἱ]ερ[ῶι ἀλλ' ἐὰν | πάντα κα]θάπερ ἐξ ἀρχῆς ὑπῆρχεν. An inscription from Loryma (*LSAM* no. 74, third century BCE) also appears to give the priest control over whether offerings can be brought into a temple, but it is even more heavily restored.
42 Christensen 1984; Gottesman 2014, 160–179. For the sources, see also Wycherley 1957, 113–114. It is often assumed that this reselling would involve some sort of trial as at Andania (see below), but this is not made explicit in any of the sources.
43 Chaniotis 1996; Peels 2016, 120–124. See also Sinn 1993.
44 *IG* XII.6 169=*NGSL*² no. 18, ll. 20–23.

persons was regulated in multiple ways during the Andanian Mysteries:[45]

> ᵛ φύγιμον εἶμεν τοῖς δούλοις· ᵛ τοῖς δούλοις φύγιμον ἔστω τὸ ἱερόν, καθὼς ἄν οἱ ἱεροὶ | ἀποδείξωντι τὸν τόπον, καὶ μηθεὶς ὑποδεχέσθω τοὺς δραπέτας μηδὲ σιτοδοτείτω μηδὲ ἔργα παρεχέτω· ὁ δὲ ποιῶν παρὰ τὰ γεγραμ|μένα ὑπόδικος ἔστω τῶι κυρίωι τᾶς τοῦ σώματος ἀξίας διπλασίας καὶ ἐπιτιμίου δραχμᾶν πεντακοσιᾶν, ὁ δὲ ἱερεὺς ἐπικρινέ|τω περὶ τῶν δραπετικῶν, ὅσοι κα ἦνται ἐκ τᾶς ἁμετέρας πόλεος, καὶ ὅσους κα κατακρίνει, παραδότω τοῖς κυρίοις· ἂν δὲ μὴ παραδιδῶι ἐξέσ|τω τῶι κυρίωι ἀποτρέχειν ἔχοντι.

That There Be a Place of Refuge for the Enslaved. The sanctuary must be a refuge for the enslaved, as the Sacred Men appoint the place, and no one is to harbor the fugitives or give them provisions or offer them work. Anyone acting contrary to what is written is to be liable to the master for twice the value of the enslaved person and a fine of 500 dr. The priest must decide about the fugitives, whichever ones are sitting (in supplication) from our city, and whichever ones he condemns he must hand over to their masters. But if he does not hand over, the master is allowed to go away in possession of him.

As was the case at the Heraion on Samos, no one is allowed to feed the suppliants or support them through employment. The priest carries out trials to decide whether they must go back to their original owner or get sold to someone new. But what is especially valuable about this passage for understanding logistics is the reference to marking space: as the Sacred Men prepare for the influx of visitors for the event, they reserve a *topos* (area) for refuge. This act preserves the right to asylum even during the festival but establishes a separation from other activities and other visitors.[46] It also implies that there was no restricted, specialized space at other times. Since supplication within a sanctuary usually takes place at an altar or statue, it is possible that the *topos* would have included one or more; the Mysteries were held in the Karnasian Grove, which was home to the worship of multiple deities.[47] The necessity of a prohibition against harboring, feeding, or employing the enslaved suggests that they did not have to stay within the *topos* at all times, and it is possible that the purpose of the *topos* was the initial request for asylum and the later trial. It is significant that the priest, not the Sacred Men, carry out the trials (ll. 82–83). The duties of the Sacred Men are focused on the festival, but the priest would be the one responsible for the sanctuary year round.

The Andanian Mystery regulations contain at least two other references to spaces defined during the time of the festival. The same phrasing for the refuge is repeated for the location of the temporary market "where everything can be sold" (οἱ ἱεροὶ τόπον ἀποδειξάντω, ἐν ᾧ πραθήσεται πάντα, l. 99).[48] There also seems to be an area for visitors' tents, which are regulated by size, material, and contents (ll. 34–39).[49] Although it is not specified how that space as a whole is allocated or arranged, a subdivision exists within it: in a *topos* that the Sacred Men mark, only the Sacred Men can have tents, and no one who is uninitiated may enter. This forbidden space is outlined, perhaps by garlands (*peristemma*), and further delineated by means of *hydranai*, containers for purificatory water (μηδέ, ἐν ὧι ἂν τόπωι περιστεμ|ματώσωντι οἱ ἱεροί, μηθένα τῶν μὴ ὄντων ἱερῶν ἔχειν σκανάν· μηδὲ παρερπέτω μηθεὶς ἀμύητος εἰς τὸν τόπον, ὅν κα περιστεμμα|τώσωντι· χωραξάντω δὲ καὶ ὕδρανας, ll. 35–37).[50]

This text offers a rare glimpse into the adjustments that could be put in place in a sanctuary not just to handle an increased number of visitors, but also to accommodate

---

45 *IG* V.1 1390=*CGRN* 222, ll. 80–84, 91 BCE or 23 CE.
46 Naiden (2006, 149–150) interprets this passage as increasing space for refuge, but I find that less likely since the other references to space-making (see below) concern reserving a limited space for festival activities.
47 In addition to the textual references to altars and statues, these objects also are common images in vase paintings featuring supplication in sanctuaries; see sources collected in Pedrina 2017. On the use of altars to ensure accessibility, see Naiden 2006, 36–41. It is possible that statues within temples were also used for supplication; Plutarch places the supplication of Kylon and his followers in a temple (*Sol.* 12), but Herodotos (5.71) just refers to a statue, *agalma*, and Thucydides (1.126) locates the act at an altar. For the Andanian deities and sanctuary features associated with them, see Gawlinski 2012, 17–22, 41–49. The site is not excavated, so the specifics of the organization of the sanctuary cannot be confirmed.
48 When Dikaiopolis in Aristophanes' *Acharnians* arranges his own market, he first points to its boundaries (ὅροι μὲν ἀγορᾶς εἰσιν οἵδε τῆς ἐμῆς, 719). See Chankowski in this volume.
49 See Ekroth in this volume. On tents at Olympia with further bibliography, see Barringer 2021, 58.
50 Compare the process in *CGRN* 167 (*IG* XII.4 328, first century BCE), a priest sale contract from Kos, which mentions an area (*topos*) that had to be set aside for tents for the *kanephoroi* and offerings (A, ll. 20–24). The space is defined with respect to permanent buildings, being on the right side of the *stadion*, extending to the *nakoreion* and *oikia*: τὸν δὲ τόπον τὸν εἰσπορευόμενον ἐν | δεξιᾷ ἐκ τοῦ σταδίου μέχρι τῶν νακορείων καὶ τᾶ[ς] | οἰκίας. On the use of water basins (and their associated rituals) both around and within sanctuaries to delineate space, see Kobusch 2020a, 77–81.

special situations like initiation. This flexible transformation of space must have been more common than material remains indicate; in addition to camping, supplication, commerce, and initiation, activities such as choral dancing, public singing, or agonistic events required room. Some sanctuaries, of course, maintained permanent built space for occasional activities such as these, but many others did not, especially not in every chronological phase. Some areas would not have been formally demarcated, and any signage or boundary markers (*horoi*) made from anything other than stone would not be identifiable archaeologically. Temporary campsites and markets can leave behind postholes that indicate their general location, but their boundaries were impermanent by nature and are now difficult to verify. For example, at the sanctuary of Demeter and Kore at Corinth, a series of postholes have been interpreted as the remains of market stalls based on their patterns.[51] At the Heraion at Samos, holes in the ground near the altar have been tied to ritual dining, a fairly common activity.[52] In the sanctuary of Athena at Sounion, a group of reused architectural elements in stone, cut with holes, may have been supports for a semipermanent structure. How these five column capitals and four rectangular blocks were arranged is now unclear, and possible structures include an awning for visitors, bleachers (*ikria*), or an enclosure.[53]

None of these archaeological remains can be associated with written sources that explain their use, so we must turn elsewhere, outside sanctuary contexts, to consider further how temporary boundaries might have worked. The source material illustrating the practices of the Athenian democracy includes both written and physical evidence for temporary enclosures, which were used for courts and activities that required voting.[54] Although many of these sources are late and preserve only a garbled version of earlier sources, the abundance of information at least forms a general picture.

Spaces in and around the Agora were modified for exceptional trials or meetings. Pollux describes a case in which the Archon Basileus, the Archon charged with religious matters, oversaw a special trial related to matters at the Eleusinian Mysteries (8.123–124, second century CE). The court was open only to those who had made it to the highest grade of initiation (*epoptai*), and others had to be kept out: "The court was encircled by a rope. When the *basileus* gave the command, the *thesmothetai* filled the court. The rope barrier (*perischoinisma*) was set fifty feet away, and the assistants were posted so that no one uninitiated approached" (τὸ δὲ δικαστήριον περισχοινίζετο, τοῦ μὲν βασιλέως παραγγείλαντος, τῶν δὲ θεσμοθετῶν πληρούντων τὸ δικαστήριον. τὸ δὲ περισχοίνισμα ἀπὸ πεντήκοντα ποδῶν ἐγίγνετο. καὶ οἱ ὑπηρέται ὑφειστήκεισαν ὅπως μηδεὶς ἀνεπόπτευτος προσίηι).[55] A speech in the Demosthenic corpus records a similar situation concerning the Areopagos using the Stoa Basileios for trials: "The council of the Areopagos, when sitting in session in the Stoa Basileios, has it roped off; by itself, it is much at peace, and everyone stays out of the way" (τὸ τὴν ἐξ Ἀρείου πάγου βουλήν, ὅταν ἐν τῇ βασιλείῳ στοᾷ καθεζομένη περισχοινίσηται, κατὰ πολλὴν ἡσυχίαν ἐφ' ἑαυτῆς εἶναι, καὶ ἅπαντας ἐκποδὼν ἀποχωρεῖν, 25.23). Although this speech can no longer be ascribed to Demosthenes and is probably Hellenistic in date, for my purposes, this text remains useful for the concepts of temporary barriers and guards and the ancient reader's familiarity with them.[56]

A number of sources indicate that the vote taken for the ostracism of Athenian politicians required that a temporary location be organized, but they lay out the details using a variety of terms. For example, Philochoros writing in the fourth–third centuries BCE says that the Agora was "fenced with boards," ἐφράσσετο σανίσιν ἡ ἀγορά (frag. 30) to prepare for ostracism, and according to Plutarch (*Arist.* 7.4), voters brought their sherds to a spot in the Agora that was "fenced around in a circle with barriers" (εἰς ἕνα τόπον τῆς ἀγορᾶς περιφραγμένον ἐν κύκλῳ δρυφάκτοις). But it is the *perischoinisma*, a "roping off," that comes closest to the archaeological evidence. Pollux (8.20) says that they roped

---

51 Bookidis and Stroud 1997, 201.
52 Kron 1988, 144. Holes in the steps of the 'Heraion' at Olympia may have held posts used for tethering animals; the possible interpretations are intriguing. See Barringer 2021, 59–60.
53 Barletta 2017, 46–51. Theodoropoulou-Polychroniadis (2015, 111) notes that it is not impossible that the two blocks with circular cuttings that she examines at the site could have been used for stands for offerings, citing parallels. The *perischoinisma* posts in the Athenian Agora (discussed below) are similar, but the holes are square; all but two of the Sounion blocks have round holes. I suspect there are more posts like this that have yet to be recognized in sanctuaries. Frejman's (2020) survey of Labraunda, Sunuri, and Nemea highlights the need to look for impermanent and semipermanent structures in what he terms extra-*temenal* areas.
54 For the sources, see Wycherley 1957, 163–165; Boegehold 1995, 194–201. Raubitschek (1956) also discusses some of the relevant sources for barriers and boundaries. I thank J. Sickinger and K. Daly for suggesting that I examine these civic barriers as a model for the ones in use in sanctuaries.
55 Pollux 8.141 also mentions roping-off for cases concerning the Mysteries.
56 Harris 2018, 193–196; Trevett 2019, 422. Harris (2018, 204, n. 41) points out that there is no evidence that the Areopagos council ever met elsewhere and that the Stoa Basileios is too small to hold them. He sees this detail as part of the evidence of inauthenticity and the argument for a date in the Hellenistic period.

off an area, *perischoinizo*, to create a temporary space for the vote: "having roped off a certain part of the Agora, any Athenian who wished had to carry to this demarcated spot a sherd inscribed with the name of the man intended for ostracism" (περισχοινίσαντας δέ τι τῆς ἀγορᾶς μέρος ἔδει φέρειν εἰς τὸν περιορισθέντα τόπον Ἀθηναίων τὸν βουλόμενον ὄστρακον ἐγγεγραμμένον τοὔνομα τοῦ μέλλοντος ἐξοστρακίζεσθαι). The site of this vote has now been identified in the Athenian Agora.[57] It features a series of limestone posts set in a square shape along the Panathenaic Way, which allowed ropes to be put up on wooden posts to cordon off the area, and then taken back down when the vote concluded (Fig. 1.1).

Drawing on these and other similar sources, we can identify the range of terms that illustrate the actions and materials involved in the construction of temporary boundaries. *Schoinos*, rope, appears as an important root in both verbs (the action of roping off) and nouns (an enclosure of rope).[58] Another terminological group is based around *phrasso*, fencing; one reference specifies that the fence be made of *sanides*, wooden boards, while another is comprised of another kind of barrier, *dryphaktoi*, which can refer to low parapets and railings, usually made of wood.[59] There is one lone reference to a *pegma*, another fence word.[60] To these can be added, from the celebration of the Mysteries of Andania, a word with *stemma*, ribbons, as its root.[61] This brief list offers an introduction to the range of temporary barriers with which the ancient Greeks were familiar. Some were more permanent than others. The materials from which they were made do not tend to survive in the archaeological record; some created identifiable postholes, and others did not.[62] But these terms and their contexts can open our imaginations to the ways that space allocation, crowd control, and privacy could have been managed flexibly in sanctuaries.

4 Conclusions: Whose Logistics?

Most of our information about what happened in sanctuaries on 'off days' is incidental or indirect. One reason for this must be the nature of the documents—the inscribed sources that provide the rules for rituals and sanctuary management do not normally concern these kinds of matters. It is somewhat surprising that there are not more records about conflicts between individuals arising over sanctuary use. One might hazard an argument from silence and conclude that clashes did not happen very often, and that part of knowing and following the *patrios nomos* (ancestral custom) meant that most of these matters worked out the way they were supposed to without incident. On the other hand, complaints about conflicts might be absent because the ones who would have made a complaint were powerless in the situation: the texts indicate that civic sacrifices and the official duties of priests always took precedence over private veneration. If someone arrived at a sanctuary on a festival day and was denied the opportunity to make an offering, the refusal would not have been documented from the point of view of the worshiper in a way that would be preserved in the historical record. Considering time management, then, not only influences the understanding of the physical experience of malleable sanctuary space, but also invites broader questions related to religious authority and the distinctions between public and private.

Most sanctuary regulations were published to map out the responsibilities of priests and other officials. This volume focuses on the experiences of the human visitors to a sanctuary, and those sanctuary administrators are human visitors, too. It is not just an abstract notion, such as 'the *polis*' or the 'council' that oversees sanctuary maintenance; some middle-manager of religion must figure out how to put the logistics into practice. How do his duties—making sure no one steals wood, keeping visitors informed about unusual stipulations, etc.—affect his experience of the sacred? This essay has tried to get at some of these tensions to invite further thinking about how those real-world issues may have been worked out in practice, from regulating sacrifice to setting up temporary adjustments to sacred space.

---

57 Saraga 2013, 134–137; Camp 2015, 473–475.
58 περισχοινίζω ([Dem.] 25.23; Pollux 8.20, 123, 141; Harp., gloss on [Dem.] 25.23, first or second century CE), περισχοίνισμα (Alkiphron *Epist.* 2.3.11, second century CE; [Plut.] *X orat.* 847a; Pollux 8.124), περισχοινισμός, ἀπεσχοινίζω (Harp., gloss on [Dem.] 25.23).
59 φράσσω σανίσιν (Philoch. frag. 30), περιπεφραγμένον ἐν κύκλῳ δρυφάκτοις (Plut. *Arist.* 7.4). For *dryphaktoi* in courts, see Boegehold 1995, 195–201; in temples, see Mylonopoulos 2011.
60 πῆγμα = something fastened together, fence, scaffolding (Timaios Sophistes, *Lexicon Platonicum*, fourth century CE).
61 περιστεμματόω, ll. 35–36 (see above on the area for tents).
62 Lanni 1997, 184–185, on the barriers for crowds at courts, including *dryphaktoi*, and the slim archaeological evidence for them.

FIGURE 1.1 Athens, Agora, limestone supports for the *perischoinisma* set into the Panathenaic Way near the entrance to the Athenian Agora, looking west
COURTESY: AMERICAN SCHOOL OF CLASSICAL STUDIES AT ATHENS: AGORA EXCAVATIONS

Works Cited

Barringer, J.M. 2021. *Olympia: A Cultural History*. Princeton.

Barletta, B.A. 2017. *The Sanctuary of Athena at Sounion*. Princeton.

Blömer, M. 2021. "The Sanctuary of Jupiter Dolichenus at Doliche and the Seasonality of Sacrifice." In *The Archaeology of Seasonality*, edited by A. Lichtenberger and R. Raja, 165–178. Turnhout.

Boegehold, A.L. 1995. *The Lawcourts at Athens: Sites, Buildings, Equipment, Procedure, and Testimonia. Agora 28*. Princeton.

Bookidis, N., J. Hansen, L. Snyder, and P. Goldberg. 1999. "Dining in the Sanctuary of Demeter and Kore at Corinth." *Hesperia* 68: 1–54.

Bookidis, N., and R.S. Stroud. 1997. *Corinth 18.3: The Sanctuary of Demeter and Kore: Topography and Architecture*. Princeton.

Burkert, W. 1985. *Greek Religion*, trans. by J. Raffan. Cambridge, MA.

Camp, J. 2015. "Excavations in the Athenian Agora, 2008–2012." *Hesperia* 84: 467–513.

Carusi, C. 2021. "The Seasonality of Building Works in the Athenian Epigraphic Evidence." In *The Archaeology of Seasonality*, edited by A. Lichtenberger and R. Raja, 73–84. Turnhout.

Chaniotis, A. 1996. "Conflicting Authorities: Asylia between Secular and Divine Law in the Classical and Hellenistic Poleis." *Kernos* 9: 65–86.

Christensen, K. 1984. "The Theseion: A Slave Refuge at Athens." *AJAH* 9: 23–32.

Clinton, K. 2005–2008. *Eleusis: The Inscriptions on Stone: Documents of the Sanctuary of the Two Goddesses and Public Documents of the Deme*. Athens.

Corbett, P.E. 1970. "Greek Temples and Greek Worshippers: The Literary and Archaeological Evidence." *BICS* 17: 149–158.

Dignas, B. 2007. "A Day in the Life of a Greek Sanctuary." In *A Companion to Greek Religion*, edited by D. Ogden, 161–171. Malden, MA.

Dimitrova, N.M. 2008. *Theoroi and Initiates in Samothrace*. Princeton.

Feuser, S. 2021. "Seasonality and the Sea." In *The Archaeology of Seasonality*, edited by A. Lichtenberger and R. Raja, 59–72. Turnhout.

Frejman, A. 2020. *With Gods as Neighbours: Extra-Temenal Activity at Greek Rural Sanctuaries, 700–200 BCE*. Ph.D. diss., Uppsala University.

Gawlinski, L. 2012. *The Sacred Law of Andania: A New Text with Commentary*. Berlin.

Gawlinski, L. 2014. "Securing the Sacred: The Accessibility and Control of Attic Sanctuaries," In *Cities Called Athens: Studies Honoring John McK. Camp II*, edited by K.F. Daly and L.A. Riccardi, 61–87. Lewisburg, PA.

Gottesman, A. 2014. *Politics and the Street in Democratic Athens*. Cambridge.

Harris, E. 2018. *Demosthenes, Speeches 23–26*. Austin.

Hewitt, J.W. 1909. "The Major Restrictions on Access to Greek Temples." *TAPA* 40: 83–91.

Kazamiakes, K.N. 1990–1991. "Θησαυρός Ἀφροδίτης Οὐρανίας· ἡ κατασκευή." *Horos* 8–9: 29–44.

Kobusch, P. 2020a. "Fountains and Basins in Greek Sanctuaries: On the Relationship Between Ritual Performance and Architecture." In *The Power of Urban Water. Studies in Premodern Urbanism*, edited by N. Chiarenza, A. Haug, and U. Müller, 69–84. Berlin.

Kobusch, P. 2020b. "The Usage of the Pronaos of Hellenistic Temples." In *Hellenistic Architecture and Human Action. A Case of Reciprocal Influence*, edited by A. Haug and A. Müller, 81–99. Leiden.

Kron, U. 1988. "Kultmahle im Heraion von Samos archaischer Zeit. Versuch einer Rekonstruktion." In *Early Greek Cult Practice*, edited by R. Hägg, N. Marinatos, and G.C. Nordquist, 135–148. Stockholm.

Lambert, S.D. 2002. "The Sacrificial Calendar of Athens." *BSA* 97: 353–399.

Lanni, A.M. 1997. "Spectator Sport or Serious Politics? οἱ περιεστηκότες and the Athenian Lawcourts." *JHS* 117: 183–189.

Lawton, C.L. 2017. *Votive Reliefs. Agora 38*. Princeton.

MacDowell, D.M. 1991. "The Athenian Procedure of *Phasis*." In *Symposion 1990: Vorträge zur griechischen und hellenistischen Rechtsgeschichte*, edited by M. Gagarin, 187–198. Cologne.

Mylonopoulos, J. 2011. "Divine Images Behind Bars: The Semantics of Barriers in Greek Temples." In *Current Approaches to Religion in Ancient Greece. Papers Presented at a Symposium at the Swedish Institute at Athens, 17–19 April 2008*, edited by M. Haysom and J. Wallensten, 269–291. Stockholm.

Mylonopoulos, J. 2013. "Commemorating Pious Service: Images in Honour of Male and Female Priestly Officers in Asia Minor and the Eastern Aegean in Hellenistic and Roman Times." In *Cities and Priests: Cult Personnel in Asia Minor and the Aegean Islands from the Hellenistic to Imperial Period*, edited by M. Horster and A. Klöckner, 121–153. Berlin.

Naiden, F.S. 2006. *Ancient Supplication*. Oxford.

Pafford, I. 2013. "Priestly Portion and Cult Fees—The Finances of Greek Sanctuaries." In *Cities and Priests: Cult Personnel in Asia Minor and the Aegean Islands from the Hellenistic to Imperial Period*, edited by M. Horster and A. Klöckner, 49–64. Berlin.

Parker, R.C.T. 2018. "*Miasma*: Old and New Problems." In *Purity and Purification in the Ancient Greek World: Texts, Rituals, and Norms*, edited by J.-M. Carbon and S. Peels-Matthey, 23–33. Liège.

Pedrina, M. 2017. *La supplication sur les vases grecs. Mythes et images*. Pisa.

Peels, S. 2016. *Hosios: A Semantic Study of Greek Piety*. Leiden.

Raubitschek, A. 1956. "The Gates in the Agora." *AJA* 60: 279–282.

Renberg, G. 2003. *'Commanded by the Gods': An Epigraphical Study of Dreams and Visions in Greek and Roman Religious Life*. Ph.D. diss., Duke University.

Rubinstein, L. 2016. "Reward and Deterrence in Classical and Hellenistic Enactments." In *Symposion 2015. Conferências sobre a História do Direito grego e helenístico/Vorträge zur griechischen und hellenistischen Rechtsgeschichte*, edited by G. Thür and D. Leão, 419–449. Vienna.

Sinn, U. 1993. "Greek Sanctuaries as Places of Refuge." In *Greek Sanctuaries: New Approaches*, edited by N. Marinatos and R. Hägg, 88–109. London.

Saraga, N. 2013. "Νέα στοιχεία από τη σωστική ανασκαφική έρευνα της Α΄ Εφορείας στην Αρχαία Αγοράτης Αθηνάς." In *Αρχαιολογικές συμβολές 2. Αττική—Α΄ και Γ΄ Εφορείες Προϊστορικών & Κλασικών Αρχαιοτήτων*, edited by M. Dogka-Toli and S. Oikonomou, 129–147. Athens.

Theodoropoulou-Polychroniadis, Z. 2015. *Sounion Revisited: The Sanctuaries of Poseidon and Athena at Sounion in Attica*. Oxford.

Torrance, I.C. 2014. "Ways to Give Oaths Extra Sanctity." In *Oaths and Swearing in Ancient Greece*, edited by A.H. Sommerstein and I.C. Torrance, 132–155. Berlin.

Trevett, J. 2019. "Authenticity, Composition, Publication." In *The Oxford Handbook of Demosthenes*, edited by G. Martin, 419–430. Oxford.

van Straten, F. 2000. "Votives and Votaries in Greek Sanctuaries." In *Oxford Readings in Greek Religion*, edited by R. Buxton, 191–223. Oxford.

Wycherley, R.E. 1957. *Literary and Epigraphical Testimonia. Agora 3*. Princeton.

CHAPTER 2

Locked in/Locked out: How Was Access to Greek Sanctuaries and Temples Controlled in Practice?

Jenny Wallensten

1 Introduction

Going to a sanctuary could entail a trip next door or several days of traveling. It could be in the context of a private visit or of a state delegation; a brief daily visit could be intended, as well as a planned longer stay, perhaps in preparation for sacred games or for medical treatment. Such 'sacred traveling,' on one's own or walking in a communal festive procession to a sanctuary, has lately received a lot of scholarly attention.[1] But what happened once the worshiper entered sacred ground? The entrance into, and the movements performed once inside, the sanctuary have not been as frequently discussed:[2] those are the topics that I wish to examine here. Was one free to enter a sanctuary at will? Could one enter a temple easily, and if one's movements were monitored, how was this done? Given the great variety of sanctuary character and the state of our sources, this paper will necessarily be of a diachronic character and limited to buildings within the sanctuary with a focus on the temple itself.

2 Standing before the *Temenos*

Going into a sanctuary first meant entering its *temenos*, the territorial designation of sanctuary ground: land cut off from the surroundings and dedicated to the cult of one or several gods.[3] Because of the divine ownership of the *temenos*, human visitors could only go inside on certain conditions. Sometimes these were presented to the visitor *in spe* in the shape of inscribed regulations just outside or inside the *temenos* or in connection with specific buildings or altars within.[4] Thus, we know that some individuals should not enter a certain sanctuary due to their origin or sex,[5] for example, but also due to their previous actions or behavior. Murderers should not go into sacred space without having gone through purification rituals, and sexual acts, as well as dietary choices, could bar someone from a visit for a certain period of time.[6] The reason for such instructions was that a person who entered where he or she should not or who failed to observe the rules would cause ritual to fail and bring pollution to the sanctuary, thereby provoking the need for purification rituals. These could be expensive and time-consuming and would disrupt the normal day-to-day working of the sanctuary in question.[7] Such violations would, of course, also strongly displease the gods.

---

1 Amongst others, Elsner and Rutherford 2005 (including an introductory discussion of the use of the terms pilgrims and pilgrimage in Graeco-Roman antiquity, 1–38, cf. Rutherford 2013, 12–14); Dillon 1997, 2012; Rutherford 2013; Kristensen and Friese 2017; Friese, Handberg, and Kristensen 2019; Collar and Kristensen 2020.
2 Albeit less, there certainly is excellent work on this too, e.g., Gawlinski 2015.
3 For the *temenos* concept, see, e.g., Bergquist 1967; Ekroth 2024.
4 By the entrance, see for example *CGRN* 90, ll. 14–18, Ialysos, 350–300 BCE; *CGRN* 121, Priene, 200–130 BCE; probably *SEG* 32.1167, ll. 9–11, cf. Lucian, *De sacrificiis*, 13. Pausanias (8.37.2) saw a tablet with a text about the mysteries in the stoa "by the Mistress," and Cole suggests that what he saw was the text of *CGRN* 126, which regulated dress for entering the sanctuary, initiands, and sacrifices (Cole 2004, 42, n. 54). Much important work has been done recently to clarify the meaning and categories of so-called sacred or ritual norms or sacred laws, as they were—and sometimes still are—called: see, e.g., Parker 2004; Georgoudi 2010; Carbon and Pirenne-Delforge 2012; 2017; Harris 2015.
5 Special rules for foreigners: *CGRN* 4, Olympia 524–500 BCE; *CGRN* 156, ll. 24–26 Mykonos, 230–200 BCE. Women excluded from entering or sacrificing: *CGRN* 27, Thasos, 450–425 BCE; *CGRN* 33, Elateia, end of the fifth century BCE; *CGRN* 62–63, Lindos. Dorians not allowed: Hdt. 5.72.3; *IG* XII.5 225=*LSCG* no. 110. For a further discussion of these and other examples, see Cole 2004.
6 Sex and food: *CGRN* 203, Delos, after 166 BCE. Sex, food, and birth: *CGRN* 217, Delos, late second century BCE. Sex and death: *CGRN* 71, Metropolis, fourth century BCE. Sex, death, and birth, *CGRN* 144, Ptolemais, first century BCE. Murderers: Dem. 20.158; Parker 1983, 104–105 (Antiphon), 125, 185. A ritual norm from the cult of the Egyptian gods in Megalopolis, *c*.200 BCE, gives purity regulations for those wishing to sacrifice and to enter the *hieron* after childbirth, abortion, menstruation, bloodshed, after having eaten goat or sheep and other meats, or after sexual pleasure: *CGRN* 155.
7 Failed ritual: Antiph. 5.82; Cole 2004, 36; Naiden 2013, 147–148; Harris 2015, 13; 2018; 423; 2019, 144–145 with further references.

Apart from local details relating to specific cults, the general rule that a sanctuary was to remain pure would certainly have been well known to Greeks of all ages. Because of this, one would expect that a human visitor who approached a sanctuary, with or without the wish to enter, would consciously and clearly know when he or she arrived at a *temenos* in order to be able to prepare for the right behavior. However, this was not always the case. Visible walls and elaborate entrance buildings were probably more the exception than the rule. Although strong *temenos* walls with gates guarded some of the most famous sacred places of the Greek world, notably the Akropolis of Athens and Demeter's sanctuary at Eleusis, Laura Gawlinksi has recently shown that these Attic fortifications should perhaps firstly be understood in historical and geographical context and in connection with their function as military strongholds.[8] Gunnel Ekroth has collected a *temenos* dossier that demonstrates that hundreds of years could pass before major sanctuaries, such as that at Olympia, were walled. At Isthmia, sections of the Archaic *temenos* wall were taken down after a fire in the temple in 470 BCE.[9] It seems not to have been reconstructed and instead, only *horoi* stones indicated the limit of the sanctuary. This was deemed sufficient, although there certainly were riches inside, and also, of course, owner gods who demanded that their *temene* were kept pure.[10] Ekroth shows that the building of walls was context-dependent and never an obligatory feature of sacred space. Horos stones or lustral basins at regular intervals were an option to demarcate sacred space, as were trees and other plants, but again, these features were not necessary. Examples from literature indicate that one literally could stumble upon a sanctuary: Antigone is asked by her father in the beginning of the *Oedipus Colonus* whether the place where they are is "of the gods" or if it is permissible to tread there. Although they have not entered through any formal or built structure, Antigone answers that the place is surely sacred to the gods, and her interpretation rests only on the character of the physical environment: laurel, olive, and vine grow densely and the nightingales sing.[11] When Sokrates and Phaidros walk along the Ilissos River, they pass an altar to Boreas that Phaidros had never noticed, and when they finally stop in a lovely spot by a spring, Sokrates says that it "seems" to be sacred to the nymphs and Acheloos judging only by scattered dedications.[12] Any discussion of access to sacred places must thus look far beyond 'textbook' sanctuaries featuring *peribolos* walls with designated entrances, monumental altars and temples, and include *temene* that may be no more than a cave, an altar hidden by shrubbery, or cuttings in bedrock, such as the small cult space of Ge Karpophoros on the Athenian Akropolis in the shadow of the Parthenon.[13] Could access to such sacred areas really be controlled at all?

3   Walking into the Sanctuary

In Herodas' famous fourth mime, we meet women about to sacrifice in a sanctuary, perhaps to be identified with that of Asklepios in Kos.[14] They seem to stroll around the *temenos*, admiring the votive sculpture, not prevented by fences or any such installations, nor stopped by a guard. They proceed towards the temple, where they are admitted when the doors have been opened, possibly on their request.[15] Once inside the *temenos*, however, a visitor may have been subjected to a second round of restrictions or demands for additional sacrifices in order to proceed. Worshippers who had entered Apollo's sanctuary at Delphi had to offer a honey cake before approaching the altar and could not enter the interior of the temple of Apollo before the sacrifice of a sheep.[16] Moreover, a worshipper to a sanctuary could find that access to certain areas within were off-limits, although 'general' entrance was allowed. Such limitations were often connected to gender. In the central sacred area of Olympia, the Altis, only a female priestess could enter the inner part of the temple of Eileithyia, where the deity Sosipolis was worshipped, for example, whereas only men were allowed to sacrifice at the highest point of the great ash altar of Zeus.[17]

---

8   Gawlinski 2015, 62, 63–68 *et passim*.
9   Gebhard and Hemans 1992, 23, 42, 47–48; Gebhard 1993, 164–165; Ekroth 2024.
10 Ekroth 2024, 71–73. Wall used as statue base, see Scott 2010, 209 with references in n. 134. Paus. 2.25.6, 5.25.2–4, 5.25.7.
11 Soph. *OC* 9–20. For sensory identification, see also Brulé 2012, 39–40.
12 Pl. *Phdr.* 230b–c; Brulé 2012, 35–39.
13 Wallensten 2014.
14 Herod. 4; Zanker 2009, 98–131.
15 Herod. 4.45; Zanker 2009, 110, l. 12, 114, ll. 39–56.
16 Eur. *Ion* 226–232. The chorus of slave women in Euripides' *Ion* cannot, for example, enter for these reasons.
17 Paus. 6.20.3 (Sosipolis), 5.13.10 (ash altar). For the discussions around the shape and extent of the Altis, see now Barringer 2021, 34–44. The Spartan king Kleomenes, having entered the Akropolis, was stopped from entering the *adyton* of Athena because of being Dorian (Hdt. 5.72.3). He had thus already been able to enter the sacred area of the Akropolis without being cited for his ethnicity.

4 Temple Access and Use

Until quite recently, most scholars would have argued that sanctuary visitors, even when allowed to enter a sanctuary, rarely actually entered the temple or temples housed within the *temenos*.[18] According to this point of view, the temple was primarily the house of the god and a safe house for his or her riches, and so there would have been no need for people other than priests and sanctuary staff to enter. Allowing entry to others would put the sacred property at risk—potentially significant quantities of valuable votives and ritual utensils—as well as compromising the safety of the cult statue. This object could be of considerable monetary value quite aside from its worth as a sacred image. Even if it would have been difficult to steal a life-size marble or chryselephantine image, parts of it certainly could be removed.[19] In addition, the statue could become the victim of sexual assault, as was the case with the Aphrodite of Knidos, or manhandled, as happened to the Artemis of Arkadian Kaphyai, which was hanged by a group of children.[20] Since the altar, where the pivotal act of blood sacrifice took place, most often stood outside the temple, this, not the temple interior, would have been the main place of congregation.[21]

However, the view that temples were the domain of a select few has come under increasing scrutiny. P.E. Corbett opened the discussion in 1970 with an article that collected archaeological and textual indications of a much freer access to the interior of Greek temples than previously thought, and many of his suggestions have been corroborated further by recent archaeological findings. It is now clear that worshippers had greater access to temple buildings than previously thought for the simple reason that temples played a much more important role in performed ritual than earlier scholarship recognized. New scholarly perspectives underline that temple architecture should not only be understood in aesthetic terms or as passive monuments, but also as interactive arenas of ritual use. When we regard the architecture as designed to allow frequent passage in and out of the sacred space, our vision of pilgrims' movements through the space suddenly becomes manifest.[22]

In fact, we can find tangible remains indicative of humans entering the temple already at its entrance. Katja Sporn suggests that ramps leading to the stylobate, a feature often observed in Peloponnesian temples of the Doric order,[23] probably were constructed in order to ease access to the entrance of the temple for a large group of people walking at a measured pace, that is, in procession.[24] Simultaneously, ramps would have eased the transportation of cult utensils and larger dedications, such as statues, including the cult image, in and out of the temple.[25] Furthermore, it has recently been suggested that ramps provided access for disabled worshippers.[26] Ramps and their counterpart in western Greece, i.e., stairs, invited worshippers to go towards the temple doors and not necessarily stay by the altar. Rather, all areas surrounding the cella not only seem to have been frequented, but also actively used. *Perirrhanteria* placed by the temple entrance demonstrate that visitors were expected to enter—after cleansing.[27] Furthermore, the peristyle could, in fact, be considered as part of the temple interior, and worshippers certainly made use of this space.[28] Literary sources speak of hymns performed in the peristyle,[29] and the screen walls connecting the columns of the colonnade

---

18 See, e.g., Sporn 2015, 349–350 with further references.
19 Diod. Sic. 10.28.1–2 on Syracusans entering the temple of Zeus and trying to remove his robe "in the making of which a large amount of gold had been used." Famously, the statue of Athena in the Parthenon could be stripped of her gold sheets (Thuc. 2.13.5), as was done by Lachares in 296 BCE (Paus. 1.25.7) although Lapatin (2001, 88–89; 2005, 274) believes the ancient traditions about the "stripping" to be problematic. The existence of the terms *hierosylia*, *hierosylos*, temple-robbery, and temple-robber, also testifies to the possibility of theft from the gods' belongings: *LSJ*, s.v. Ἱεροσυλία, Ἱεροσύλησις, Ἱερόσυλος; Pritchett 1991, 160–161; Dignas 2007, 174. This was such an abominable crime that it entailed the death penalty, according to Xen. *Ap.* 25.
20 Pseudo-Lucian, *Erotes* 15–16; Paus. 8.23.6.
21 Corbett 1970, 149; Hollinshead 1999, 189; Larson 2007, 8; Mikalson 2010, 19; Marconi (2016, 79) regards Temple C at Selinous as the god's dwelling and backdrop for rituals performed by the altar in the open. Cf. Burkert (1985, 92) for the idea of the temple as magnificent background to the rites under the sky by the altar. He, however, also underlines that the worshiper entered the temple to pray.
22 Corbett 1970; Williamson 2018, 311.
23 I am grateful to David Scahill for reminding me that Apollo's temple at Delphi also had a ramp, built under Peloponnesian influence by Corinthian architects.
24 Sporn 2015, 355–360,
25 I thank David Scahill for pointing this out. The cult image of Athena Polias was, for example, removed from her temple during the Plynteria festival: Parker 2005, 478. Admittedly, this most likely was a relatively small statue.
26 Sneed 2020.
27 Kerschner 1996, 107–116; Pimpl 1997; Sporn 2015, 361. Of course, as a reviewer points out, it is possible that the *perirrhanteria* were meant for sanctuary personnel. The existence of *perirrhanteria* by the temple entrance by itself cannot be taken as proof that ordinary worshippers may have entered but is certainly evidence of human entrance into the cella. See further Klingborg, von Ehrenheim, and Frejman 2023, 19–23 and *passim*.
28 As suggested by Sporn 2015, 359–230; Miles 2016, 209–210.
29 Paus. 3.26.10, 6.20.3.

on Archaic Temple F in Selinous may have been designed to conceal ritual action inside the *peristasis*.³⁰

There is also evidence for use of the pronaos or opisthodomos areas.³¹ Wreaths given to victors in the Olympic games were on display in the pronaos of the temple of Zeus in Olympia at least at the time of Pausanias' visit, and Herodotos is said to have read his works in its corresponding opisthodomos.³² Dio Chrysostom saw the chest of Kypselos displayed in the opisthodomos of the temple of Hera at Olympia.³³ The north porch of the Erechtheion famously included an altar of Zeus Hypatos, where, according to the testimony of Pausanias, cakes (but not wine) were offered, while the interior housed several other altars.³⁴

5 Through the Temple Doors

Dowel holes on columns, antae, and pavements in many temples indicate the installation of metal or wooden grilles in the intercolumniations of the pronaos and opisthodomos to restrict (certain) visitors from entering and protect the contents within: the temple of Aphaia on Aigina and the Parthenon are but two examples.³⁵ Not all temples were thus equipped, but the ones that were could, of course, be opened when needed.³⁶ Thus, even before entering a closed cella, worshippers might marvel at dedications fixed to the walls in the peristyle—objects and inscriptions that indicated the interests of the god—and prepare for a visit in the cella itself,³⁷ although visibility would probably have been somewhat restricted in this area. Daylight was limited behind the columns, which furthermore would have made objects visible from certain angles only, but this obstruction may have engaged the visitor even more: he or she would have needed to come close to a dedicated object to read its dedicatory text and would have walked among the gifts rather than looking at them only from the outside. Thus, the dim light may have enhanced the objects' allure, just as in the even more tenebrious cella.³⁸ In all probability, most worshippers expected to be able to enter and come face to face with the cult statue, i.e., with the god or goddess.³⁹ But before entering the cella, a clear physical boundary may have been present, in sharp contrast to the sanctuary entrance.⁴⁰ In order to walk over the threshold, visitors would, in most cases, have had to pass through temple doors, usually wooden, bronze or bronze-clad, and possibly but rarely, stone.⁴¹ Particularly luxurious doors may have had decoration of ivory and precious metals. For example, we know of chryselephantine doors on the early Classical temple of Athena in Syracuse and the temple of Asklepios in Epidauros, and perhaps the Parthenon itself, as a recent article proposed.⁴² Through echoes of the material used for the chryselephantine cult statue, the ornate materials of the latter two sets of temple doors prepared the viewer

---

30 Marconi (2016, 81), who notes that Apollo Temple BII in Metapontion also had a closed colonnade, which served to protect votive gifts.

31 Williamson 2018, 316, on the attraction of places of entry.

32 Wreaths and other dedications: Paus. 5.12.5; Lucian, *Her.* 62.1.

33 Dio Chrys. *Or.* 11.163.15; Pausanias (5.17.5) seems to have seen it inside the temple of Hera. For further references, see Hollinshead 1999, 213. For the history of the chest, see Barringer 2021, 98–102.

34 Paus. 1.26.5. "Inside the entrance." Pausanias saw altars to Poseidon and Erechtheus, Butes, and Hephaistos.

35 Korres 1996, 46; Hollinshead 1999, 203; Barletta 2005, 84 (wooden grilles); Linders 2007, 778; Gawlinski 2015, 70, who also points out that treasuries, too, could be fitted with metal grilles, thus hindering theft while still displaying the riches inside. See also Miles 2016, 218. For the occurrence of temple-robbery, see nn. 20, 85.

36 In the first Kallias decree, certain officials are charged with opening, closing, and sealing the doors of the opisthodomos; see Linders 2007, 777. The opisthodomos has been suggested to be either the west chamber behind the Parthenon cella (Hollinshead 1999, 211–213; van Rookhuijzen 2020, 12–19, 32) or the backroom of the partly destroyed old temple of Athena Polias and later the west room (Linders 2007, *passim*).

37 Miles 2016, 209; Williamson 2018, 321.

38 Mattern 2006, 173; Miles 2016, 207; Williamson 2018, 321. Infra n. 65 for the possible effect of light in the cella due to the use of thin marble roof tiles.

39 Williamson 2018, 321–323. Ancient literary and epigraphical sources usually make no distinction between the statue of a god and the god. In the famous episode in *Il.* 6.303, the priestess Theano enters the temple and puts her gift, a beautiful textile, "on the knees of Athena," i.e, in the lap of the seated cult statue. Likewise, having entered Asklepios' sanctuary in Herodas' fourth mime, ll. 19–20, Kynno asks Kokkale to place her votive tablet to the right of Hygieia: again, no difference is made between the statue of a god and the god. In the inventories from the sanctuary of Artemis Brauronia on the Athenian Akropolis, a chiton is described as "around the statue," that is, the garment was draped on the statue (*IG* II² 1514, col. III, ll. 22–23; Linders 1972, 11–12 with n. 42), while in the inventories of the Athenian Asklepieion, objects can be "on the hand of the god," e.g., *IG* II² 1534, l. 102.

40 As Williamson notes, the door did not constitute a "boundary between the pure and the polluted" (2018, 309), but its elaborate design would certainly have differentiated the space within from that without.

41 Williamson 2018. Williamson points out (with reference to Ath. 15.672b–c) that the temple of Hera at Samos, which at some time did not have any doors, is the exception that proves the rule (309, n. 2). Few temple doors survive; see Gerding 2014 for comparanda from funerary contexts.

42 Pope and Schultz 2014; Prignitz 2014, 23, 50–51; Williamson 2018, 318.

standing outside of the cella for entry into it and the vision of the divine within. The actual passage through the doors enhanced this effect. Christina Williamson analyzes how the senses could be affected through a sudden change in lighting and the encounter with other sensorial stimuli while passing through temple doors and draws attention to how cognition is impacted by going from one space to another through a doorway. Once over the threshold, the temple visitor had a "changed mindset and raised awareness," prepared to meet the divine.[43]

Although temple doors usually opened inwards as if welcoming the person entering, visitors alone probably could not have opened the doors if they were found closed. In most instances, a priest or priestess controlled the keys and locking and unlocking of the door.[44] An emblematic illustration of this is, of course, found in the *Iliad* when the Trojan women ask the priestess Theano to open the temple of Athena, that they may pray to her to take pity on Troy.[45] Epigraphic sources evidence this convention, such as a document from Chalkedon that indicates that the priest of Asklepios should open the temple every day, or a Koan inscription stating that the priestess of Artemis Pergaia was to see that the sanctuary was open at dawn "on all the days on which it is religiously sanctioned to open the sanctuaries."[46]

Very few temple locks or keys have survived the millennia. However, we know of their existence because of their important role in iconography. Safeguarding the key to the temple and opening the temple in the morning and closing it in the evening,[47] were important enough tasks for priests and priestesses that the key became the symbol of the latter.[48] A large key of the so-called Homeric type (a bar, twice bent either straight at 90° or slightly curved), is the visual attribute of the priestess. This iconography was established by the late sixth or early fifth century BCE, but images of male keyholders do exist, and the office of the *kleidouchos* could refer to both male and female.[49] The title also appears in the epigraphic dossier of the Asklepieion in Athens, where it may have denoted responsibility for sacred property in need of locks and keys, i.e., a temple guardian charged with supervision of daily worship.[50]

6 Entering the Cella

The lesser importance of the inner rooms of a temple as arenas for the performance of ritual has been taken to explain why the interiors of Greek temples supposedly were given less attention than their elaborate exterior decoration.[51] This idea cannot be corroborated: as we know from written and archaeological evidence, temple interiors offered a variety of visual stimuli for visitors, including painted walls; furnishings, such as benches, beds, and tables, pillows and rugs; as well as all sorts of dedications attached to the walls, stacked on shelves, and standing on the temple stylobate.[52] There seems to have been an almost 'homely' milieu for the main inhabitant: the statue.[53]

The temple was indeed the house of the god, and the interior of the cella was the setting for its image, the cult statue, which constituted the central focus of the room. Testimony for hymn singing inside the temple should come as no surprise then. Like tangible dedications, which, preferably, were placed close to or even on the deity,[54] a sung gift would naturally be performed in front of the deity. The ephebes and the priest τῶν παίδων sung a hymn at the opening of the temple of Dionysos in Teos

---

43 Williamson 2018, 320–321.
44 The doors were also extremely heavy, but if kept well-maintained, one individual could probably open them by him or herself. I thank J. Barringer and D. Scahill for discussing the matter.
45 Hom. *Il.* 6.297–301.
46 *I.Chalcedon* 12 ll. 23–24 (=*LSAM* no. 5) of the first century BCE-first century CE; *CGRN* 188 of the first century BCE.
47 It should be noted that the opening and closing of temple or sanctuary may not have been done daily. Inscribed ritual norms occasionally mention a duty to open sanctuaries "on days on which it is religiously sanctioned" (*hosion*) to do so: *CGRN* 188, ll. 8–10; cf. *CGRN* 163 with commentary on ll. 3–4.
48 Temple keys are thought to have been large enough to hang from a person's shoulder. Smaller keys found in sanctuaries are usually interpreted as dedications: Schaus 2014, 177. For the iconography of keys and key-bearers, see, e.g., Mantis 1990; Karatas 2019; Wallensten 2021, 173–174.
49 Williamson 2018, 319; Wallensten 2021, 173–174. On Delos, for example, families dedicated statues of their sons who had held the title, although it is somewhat unclear what exactly this office entailed: see, e.g., *ID* 1830, 1875, 1876.
50 Aleshire 1989, 89–90. Cf. the Heros Klaikophoros, attested in Epidauros, *IG* IV².1 297 and Troizen, *IG* IV 768; Pfaff 2018, 369, 424.
51 Sporn 2015, 350.
52 Wall paintings at Kalapodi: Niemeier 2008, 305; Niemeier, Niemeier, and Brysbaert 2012, 83–84, pls. XIII and XIV; Vlachopoulos 2020, 422–423. Wall paintings at Isthmia: Broneer 1971, 33–34, pls. A–C; Niemeier, Niemeier, and Brysbaert 2012, 81–82, pl. XII; Hurwit 2014, 69, 71, pl. 2.1; Vlachopoulos 2020, 424. Furniture could be both dedications and utilitarian objects, e.g., Andrianou 2006a, esp. 233–234, 251; 2006b, 566–568, 573–579; Miles 2016, 214–215.
53 Andrianou 2006b, 573, 581.
54 Supra n. 40.

on certain days.⁵⁵ Evidence for singing also comes from Pausanias, who tells of women and girls—apparently not priestesses, but worshippers—singing in the temple of Eileithyia in Olympia.⁵⁶ And perhaps, as some scholars have recently suggested, another ephemeral offering to the gods, the procession or parts thereof, continued to the inside of the temple and ascended interior staircases, which were common mainly in western Greece. This access to the attic may have offered another arena for ritual enactment.⁵⁷

In addition to rethinking accessibility to temple interiors, scholars also now question the usual scholarly presumption that altars, the focal point of ritual action, chiefly stood only outside of temples. Pausanias mentions well-known examples from major temples like that of Apollo in Delphi and Zeus in Olympia, the Erechtheion, as well as less well-known examples such as that of Artemis Soteira in Troizen.⁵⁸ Archaeological evidence for interior altars has been found in Antikyra, Aulis, and Ikarion.⁵⁹ Within temples, sacrifices may have been mainly of cakes and similar foodstuffs, and only incense was burnt, but not always: mention can also be made of the strange ritual in Hermione where sacrifice (Pausanias uses the word *thysia*) of four young cows, was performed inside, behind closed doors in the temple of Demeter Chthonia.⁶⁰ An inscription from Kos mentions a hearth inside the temple of Hera.⁶¹ Moreover, we also find remains of cult tables in temples in Aulis, on Cape Zoster, in the late Archaic temple of Aphaia on Aigina, and in the fourth-century BCE temple of Amphiaraos at Oropos,⁶² while textual evidence mentions *klinai* (couches) and *thronoi* (chairs), perhaps also indicative of rituals, such as *theoxenia*, inside temples.⁶³

7   Closer to the Gods

The interior space of Greek temples could be elaborately decorated, with rich ornaments and furnishings, attention to lighting arrangements, and often intricately fashioned coffered ceilings in the peristyle.⁶⁴ This rich display was not only visible or known solely to the gods but also clearly indicates consideration and use of temple interiors as components of visitor experience. As mentioned above, the interior served as backdrop for the cult statue, i.e., the god who dwelled in the building. Since there cannot be any doubt that cult statues were mostly meant to be seen,⁶⁵ it is surprising that the idea of general inaccessibility of the cella to the public has persevered.⁶⁶ Since the primary goal of sanctuary visits must have been interaction with the divine, a climactic experience surely was to stand before the manifestation of the god, i.e., his or her cult statue. Prayers to the deity were certainly more efficacious if made 'in person,' and certainly physical contact with the god or goddess, such as the placing of gifts or sacrificial parts on the god's hands or knees would ensure the correct recipient. In one of Cicero's speeches against Verres, we hear of a statue of Herakles, whose mouth and chin were worn from worshippers touching and kissing them.⁶⁷ Current research, in fact, traces an apparent evolution of temple spaces gradually adapting for viewing and visitors' experiences of the divine.⁶⁸

---

55 *LSAM* no. 28, ll. 7–10. The hymns were probably performed on the birthday of the god. For the priest of "the children or boys," see Robert and Robert 1954, 225; *MAMA* 5, no. 205.
56 Paus. 3.26.10, 6.20.3.
57 Miles 1998–1999, 18, 22–25; Marconi 2016, 82–83; Miles 2016, 212. Certainly, maintenance of the roof and attic was also a reason for these stairs.
58 For rituals, including burning, inside temples, see now Ekroth 2021. Delphi: Paus. 4.17.4, 10.24.4 (altars of Poseidon and Apollo). Olympia: Paus. 5.14.4. Troizen: 2.31.2.
59 Hollinshead 1999, 204.
60 Paus. 2.35.8.
61 *LSCG* no. 151B.
62 Frank (2014, 38, 51, 53, 56, 98–99, 105, 144, 184) lists further example of offering tables inside temples in Alipheira, Perivolia, Phigaleia, and Pheneos. Cuttings in the floor indicate the existence of offering tables in Epidauros, Kelonai, and Messene (Temple of Artemis Oupisias/Orthia/Phosphoros); see Frank 2014, 68, 74, 96. See also Gill 1991, 39–40, 47, 48–50; Hollinshead 1999, 204.
63 Andrianou 2006a, 233–234; 2006b, 571; Hölscher 2007, 30; Jameson 2014, 165–168; Paus. 10.32.12 (Temple of Asklepios near Tithorea).
64 The marble tiles of the Classical temple of Zeus in Olympia and the Archaic temple of Demeter in Sangri, Naxos may have been so thin as to admit sunlight. Olympia, where the lighting may have created a glow around the statue: Hennemeyer 2012, 123; 2015, 26–27; Barringer 2021, 132; Sangri: Ohnesorg 1993, 68, 118–119.
65 Pausanias (e.g., 2.35.11, 6.20.3) specifically points out when a statue is secret or hidden for all except the priestly personnel, presumably because one normally could see it.
66 Corbett 1970, 149; Bruit Zaidman and Schmitt Pantel 1992, 58; Larson 2007, 8. Of course, a temple may not have been open to the public every day, as Bruit Zaidman and Schmitt Pantel point out. In Herodas' fourth mime, ll. 41–56, it appears that visitors could ask for the temple to be opened in some cases: Kynno asks the slavegirl to find the *neokoros*, whereupon the temple is opened.
67 Cic. *Verr.* 2.4.94.
68 Miles 2016, 206. Cf. Hennemeyer 2015, 29.

The ability to get close to the cult statue so as to kiss its cheek or place an offering at its knees precludes impenetrable physical boundaries inside the cella. However, it is clear that close access to the statue was not always granted. Worshippers could only address and watch the chryselephantine Aphrodite at Sikyon from the temple doorstep,[69] and in certain cases, a wish to protect, or at least separate, the cult statue from visitors is apparent in the architecture of the sacred building. Some temples, such as that of Athena at Sounion, restricted access to the cult statue by some sort of barrier, and a parapet was built in front of the statue of Zeus in his temple at Olympia.[70] These impediments may not always have thwarted a disrespectful visitor intent on breaching that boundary and approaching the deity. Hennemeyer suggests that far from stopping people from coming closer to the statue, the parapet in the Zeus temple, which featured doors, instead articulated and emphasized the nucleus of the cella, i.e., the statue and the space directly in front of it.[71] Rather than fully separating gods and men, barriers before cult images could signify, and give material expression to, the religious borders between god and human, indicating where each had his or her place.[72]

A smaller, closed-off space behind the cella and usually accessible only from it, may yet have constituted a physical limit inside some temples. This space is often referred to as the *adyton*, literally a place that is not to be entered, but is often translated as the innermost sanctuary.[73] In spite of the forbidding name, the *adyton* could be entered, but only by certain people on certain occasions for very specific reasons. The *adyton* used to be interpreted as a space for rituals of so-called chthonian cults, but is now usually regarded as designed for secure storage,[74] and as such, the domain only of temple personnel, who inventoried, counted, and arranged valuable objects. Oracular temples are an exception; in these venues, *adyta* were needed for ritual use,[75] as is the case for some of the temples in Selinous, where an inner room together with other architectural features may have been a way of articulating a focal object, most likely the cult statue.[76]

8 Surveying the *Temenos*

Summing up this overview, it appears as if physical boundaries restricting entry to sacred space were, in fact, not very prominent, and not always deemed necessary despite the need to keep the sanctuary pure by excluding some people. Moreover, temples within the *temenos* were not limited to serving as luxurious storage or housing only for the statue but also attracted visitors and involved participants beyond the sanctuary staff, who congregated in temple interiors, where they engaged in specific rituals. Contrary to scholars' expectations, sacred space and its temples were rather easily accessed. But would this not require more control to avoid pollution, theft, and other improper behavior? As mentioned above, traces of barriers placed in front of the cult statue have been identified, and literary sources speak of curtains used to hide or reveal cult statues.[77] We should probably assume that the surviving evidence does not provide the whole picture. It is likely that material barriers that once restricted or channeled movement inside sacred space were of perishable material; we can imagine wooden fences and ropes, as well as textiles, providing both temporary and permanent obstructions.[78]

However, I think it probable that much supervision was performed not by structures, but by something as perishable as wood or textile: humans. From certain sanctuaries, we know of officials specifically charged with keeping order during large festivals, such as the *gynaikonomos* of the Andanian Mysteries, who was charged with ensuring decorum as regards dress and the *hieroi*. The *gynaikonomos* was further supported by a troupe of 20 *rhabdophoroi*, whose duties included detecting and scourging those who

---

69 Paus. 2.10.4.
70 Hollinshead 1999, 204; Mylonopoulos 2011; Barletta 2017, 103.
71 Hennemeyer 2015, 30–31. A shallow pool may have separated the visitor from the statue once the visitor was behind the parapet.
72 Mylonopoulos 2011; Williamson (2018, 313) uses the pertinent term "filter."
73 *LSJ*, s.v. ἄδυτος. For a survey of the use of the term, see Hollinshead 1999, 190–194. The inner space occasionally could also be called the opisthodomos (Hollinshead 1999, 198).
74 Hollinshead 1999, 207.
75 Hollinshead 1999, 192–193.
76 Hollinshead 1999, 206–207.
77 A fourth-century BCE inscription from Samos mentions a curtain in front of the goddess, and Pausanias describes exquisite veils used in front of the statue of Zeus at Olympia and that of Artemis in Ephesos: *SEG* 47.1314; *IG* XII.6 261; Paus. 5.12.4; Williamson 2018, 323. The women in Herodas' mime (4.55–56) refer to open temple doors and a *pastos*, probably a curtain, drawn aside. It is, however, unclear if curtains and other textiles were used for security reasons, ritual demands, or visual effect. This issue should probably be considered on a case-by-case basis.
78 For fencing off areas of sanctuaries, see Gawlinski and Ekroth in this volume. However, anyone who has been to a music festival or stood in line at an airport may question the efficacy of roping off an area.

disobeyed or conducted themselves indecently. *Hieropoioi* were elected to assure proper conduct at the procession for the festival of Hephaistos in fifth-century BCE Athens. Likewise, two men were charged with keeping an eye on general good order during a procession in honor of Athena in second-century BCE Ilion.[79] To such officials, we could probably add slaves, often present in large numbers, who could be assigned to monitor visitors' correct conduct.

One could argue moreover that a well-organized procession, i.e., a controlled pattern of movement, given a rhythm by singing or accompanying musicians, is itself a way to maintain order during a festival. Thus, the construction of a ramp leading up to a temple, suitable for only a few people walking adjacent to, or just behind one another, would impose a somewhat controlled entrance to the peristyle or temple. But even allowing for (long-vanished) wooden structures restricting the path of a big crowd on sanctuary ground, extra personnel during festivals, a choreography for moving crowds, or even religious staff positioned at the edge of a *temenos* or on the stairs of a temple, how could the staff know if someone was pure enough to enter? To detect the sex of the visitor may be easy enough (if the context is not a comedy by Aristophanes), and ethnicity may perhaps be revealed by accent or dress, but what about diet or sex? In a famous passage, the priestess of Athena on the Athenian Akropolis tries to stop the Spartan king Kleomenes from entering the *hieron*, claiming that it is not allowed for him as a Dorian to enter.[80] Apparently, she was sitting close to the doors, monitoring visitors, and recognized him. But what if the rules stipulated that someone was unclean from a death in the family and not for being a Dorian? If the visitor was from a small local community, the priestess would perhaps have been aware if someone had died and who his or her relatives were, and fellow community members could perhaps inform on transgressors. But what about sanctuaries that attracted an international crowd? In those circumstances, there may have been less, or even no, such social control. To a considerable degree, control of movement into and within sanctuaries must surely have been impossible. However, most Greek visitors to a sanctuary were aware of social and religious norms and would have approached knowing that specific demands put restrictions on their behavior and that their fellow humans also knew these rules and could denounce improper behavior.

Moreover, sanctuary visitors must have been prepared for or hoped for the possibility of actually meeting the god in the *temenos*, inside or outside the temple, since the god, even if not constantly present, lived there.[81] Even if entering a *temenos* unexpectedly, as Sokrates did on the banks of the Ilissos, most Greeks likely would have adjusted their behavior once they had identified the character of the place. And whereas a human being could fail to see a ritual impurity or a breach of decorum, the god would not. Asklepios inflicted what has been termed punishing miracles on those who mocked his power or on disbelievers who entered his *temenos*.[82] Having unlawfully entered a Thesmophorion, Miltiades died from gangrene in a wound that he suffered when escaping from that sanctuary.[83] Apollo saved his sanctuary at Delphi from Xerxes' Persian army in 480 BCE and from the attacking Galatians in 279 BCE; on the first occasion, he even told the Delphians explicitly that he was able to protect what belonged to him.[84] The gods looked out for their property and their rules, and stories promoted this divine interest and what happened when the protocol was violated. Diodoros touches upon this when speaking of a sanctuary of Hemithea: "… the sacred precinct is filled with votive offerings, nor are these protected by guards or by a strong wall, but by the habitual reverence [or superstition, *deisidaimonia*] of the people." No external security arrangement was needed since humans had internalized correct behavior.[85] The gods held their sanctuaries under a watchful eye, and we could therefore add the gods themselves as a category of overseers who potentially monitored visitors to their sacred space.

However, Diodoros' anecdote about the sanctuary of Hemithea does not tell the whole story. Sometimes the gods apparently were not ready to engage in combat for their temples, priests, or belongings, and sometimes accepted rules were disregarded. Sacred sites *were* sacked, and the existence of the term *hierosylia*, sacrilege or temple-robbery, testifies strongly to the lack of religious respect of certain individuals, both Greek and foreigner.[86]

---

79 *CGRN* 222, ll. 25–28, 42–45 (Andania); *CGRN* 43, ll. 24–28 (Athens); *CGRN* 186, ll. 27–29; see also *CGRN* 97, esp. ll. 2–4 (Mylasa). For the policing of sanctuaries, see also Harris and Carbon in this volume.
80 Hdt. 5.72.3.
81 This is perhaps especially the case for healing sanctuaries, where the cure was often thought to be distributed by the god him- or herself while sleeping in the sanctuary.
82 Von Ehrenheim 2019, 104–106.
83 Hdt. 6.134–136.
84 Persians: Hdt. 8.36–37. Galatians: Paus. 10.23.2–3.
85 Diod. Sic. 5.63.3.
86 See, e.g., Trampedach 2005; Nevin 2017; and supra n. 20 for further references. For gods taking revenge after a sacrilege in their sanctuaries, see for example Hdt. 6.134–136 (Militades, a man, enters a Thesmophorion of Demeter); Apollod. *Epit*. E. 6.6 (Athena and Poseidon kill Ajax after the desecration of Athena's statue and the rape of Cassandra in her temple); Paus. 3.23.3–5

Furthermore, some sanctuaries must occasionally have been understaffed in relation to the big crowds attracted by important festivals.[87] Epigraphic sources reveal efforts to regulate priests' absences from the sanctuary. A famous inscription tells that the priest of Amphiaraos does not have to be present daily, but "from when winter has passed until the season of ploughing, not leaving an interval between visits of more than three days and staying in the sanctuary not less than ten days each month."[88] At the same sanctuary, a *neokoros* possessed many responsibilities in regard of the sanctuary and its visitors. But the overburdened *neokoros* was, of course, needed in many places simultaneously. While overseeing the patients' deposition of the treatment fee,[89] he may have had to leave the votives on their own in the temple. While recording the names and origin of the incubants, he could not make sure that no one carried meat out of the sanctuary.[90] It is not surprising that the ladies in Herodas' mime, could not find the *neokoros* immediately when they wish to enter the temple of Asklepios.[91]

9 Extra Staff

However, perhaps there was tangible extra help to be had in the form of portrait statues honoring priests and priestesses, which were set up in sanctuaries? Inscriptions attest to this practice for priestesses from the early fourth century BCE onwards.[92] Connelly has suggested that as symbols evoking traditions, history, and religious customs to the worshippers/beholders, these statues became part of the ritual of visitation itself. At the same time, their portraits, presented as praying or holding sacral implements, materialized the rites they had performed and so kept the prayers to the gods alive.[93] I would like to add another aspect to this. Scholars have noted that statues of priestesses tended to be placed near entrances of sanctuaries and temples, i.e., placed near the building or space where they served the gods, thus clearly drawing attention to the office of the person commemorated.[94] At fourth-to-third-century BCE Priene, for example, statues of the priestesses Nikeso and Timonassa stood on one side of the entrance to the sanctuary of Demeter and Kore.[95] The statue of Syeris, a *diakonos* of the priestess Lysimache stood by the temple of Athena at the Athenian Akropolis, likely near the eastern façade of the Erechtheion, and the statue of the priestess Philtera was likewise placed near Athena's temple.[96] Pausanias saw the statue of Syeris and encountered many more statues of priestesses in such locations: in front of the temples of Demeter Chthonia in Hermione, of Hera in Argos, and near the entrance to the sanctuary of the Eumenides in Achaian Keryeneia, to name but a few.[97] A visitor would thus have entered sacred ground under watchful eyes of sculptured temple servants, mirroring the duties of the living priestesses, and, I would argue, thereby reinforcing the presence of the latter. A gathering of similar looking statues, clustered

---

(Apollo takes vengeance on Menophanes and Mithradates after the sack of Delos) and discussion of this passage and its implications in Padilla Peralta 2020.

87 I am grateful to Gunnel Ekroth for bringing the matter of slaves to my attention. Slaves could certainly have been used for this task, but even if sanctuary slaves were an important oversight force, it is hard to see how they could have monitored the enormous crowds attending major festivals. Between 45,000 and 50,000 visitors are thought to have visited Olympia during the games in the fourth century BCE; see Barringer 2021, 10.

88 *CGRN* 75, ll. 2–6, trans. by Carbon, Peels, and Pirenne-Delforge. I know of no instance that specifically states that the priest must be permanently present in his or her sanctuary. Some priests had to live in the sanctuary, although most such cases are fictional or mythical; see Ekroth and Gawlinski in this volume.

89 *CGRN* 75, ll. 20–24.

90 *CGRN* 75, ll. 31–32, 39–43.

91 Herod. 4.45.

92 Connelly 2007, 118.

93 Connelly (1991, 93–94) suggests that the image of a praying worshipper is the prayer, which remains active in the sanctuary; 1989, 211–212; 2007, 119, 163.

94 Mylonopoulos 2013, 141–142.

95 Nikeso: *IK.Priene* 192, third century BCE; Timonassa: *IK.Priene* 191, fourth–third century BCE; Eule 2001, 105–107, KI 66, 69, KS 43, plan 8; Connelly 2007, 137.

96 Syeris, fourth century BCE: *IG* II² 3464; Keesling 2012. The base of a statue of Lysimache, *IG* II² 3453, fourth century BCE, also survives, but not *in situ*. However, it is likely that it would have stood near that of her *diakonos*, whose portrait was put up later with an accompanying epigram, the wording of which focuses on the temple of Athena/the Erechtheion. The portrait of Syeris, a "minor cult employee" could only make sense in close connection with that of the priestess she served: Keesling 2012, 497. For their placement, see Kron 1996, 144; Keesling 2012, 498. The location of Syeris' and Lysimache's statues thus calls to mind the priestess trying to hinder Kleomenes from entering (Hdt 5.72.3). The portrait of Lysimache, an under life-size bronze statue, datable to the first half of the fourth century BCE is mentioned by Pliny, *NH* 34.19. For the interesting suggestion of a custom of honoring the first priestess to serve in a new temple, see Keesling 2012, 495. See also the statue of the priestess of Athena Philtera: *IG* II² 3474, second century BCE. The epigram of Philtera mentions the placement *kata naon*, but is it the statue, the living priestess, or both that is meant? See also Barringer (2021, 219), who discusses the *in situ* honorific statue bases for priestesses of Hera (and perhaps Demeter Chamyne) in the pronaos of the Heraion at Olympia.

97 Paus. 2.17.3, 2.35.8, 7.25.7.

in the same locations, accrued over time to create a collective of priestesses. This group represented the office, and its watchful presence, permanently standing silently, contributing to the supervision over visitors as they came and went.

Dan-el Padilla Peralta has recently discussed norm-compliance in relation to the dedicatory landscape of Hellenistic Delos, arguing that people responded to the religious monuments, which acted as a dynamic agent,[98] prompting "prosocial behaviour."[99] Thus, a person surrounded by the notion that the cult statue was in fact the god—a fundamental mindset in the ancient world[100]—and that the sanctuary was filled with this god's belongings, would be inclined to behave in compliance with religious norms in the vicinity of the divine presence, and offerings and altars to the deity. Padilla Peralta writes in the context of creating generosity and trust between merchants of different origins in the commercial crucible of Delos, but the reasoning resonates well with my proposal that the statues of priests and priestesses placed by temple and sanctuary entrances provided an active guardianship of sacred ground. For a visitor entering a sanctuary, the statues of the servants of the god should have imposed a sense of respect and pious behavior.[101]

In a society where the cult statue could equal the god, it is not farfetched to believe that the statues of the servants of the gods also embodied prestige, charisma, and authority enough to encourage correct conduct, perhaps especially at the moment when the worshipper walked by the metal or stone crowd of priestly staff and saw next to them the living, breathing priestess with whom the statues shared dress and attribute.

10 Conclusions

To enter a sanctuary was to enter a space owned by the gods. Inside the *temenos*, one could wander among the gods' possessions, including riches and valuable objects and enter temples and other buildings, and one was expected to adhere to rules other than those of secular, human-owned space. This survey has shown that physical boundaries played a smaller role in controlling access to holy ground that one might expect, and that access to the inside of temple buildings and to the cult statue was common and probably often an expected highlight of a sanctuary visit. Sanctuary staff, sometimes with order and decorum as their main task, as the *gynaikonomos* and the *rhabdophoroi* of the Andanian Mysteries, or the *hieropoioi* of a festival of Hephaistos in Athens certainly kept an eye on the visitors. But to a large extent, control of movement and correct behavior relied on the visitor him- or herself, through respect for the rules of the sanctuary, and more likely than not, fear of being caught and shamed by the surrounding community of fellow men and women. Furthermore, I argue that by their permanent, watchful presence, portrait statues of priestly personnel assisted the living staff: it is noticeable that statues of priestesses often were placed at the entrance of a sanctuary or temple.

That this system of trust did not always work is clear from the historical record that tells of men walking into women-only sanctuaries, theft of divine property, and full-scale sacks of sanctuary ground. But that it usually operated as well as it did may be due to yet another important factor: fear of divine retribution. When disrespected, the Greek gods could hold a terrible grudge, as Miltiades found out.[102]

---

98 Padilla Peralta 2020, 341. I thank Judy Barringer for drawing my attention to this article.
99 Padilla Peralta 2020, 343.
100 Supra n. 40.
101 This may be corroborated by studies in behavioral psychology at Newcastle University, examining why people are generous even to strangers and cooperate when there is no immediate reciprocal gain. Previous studies had indicated that one explanation lies in the will to keep up a pro-social reputation, without which one may be shunned. Corroborating models that illustrate this behavior, laboratory experiments show that people tend to cooperate more when they know that someone else observes them. The Newcastle team wished to investigate "whether subtle cues of being watched can increase contributions to a public good in a real-world setting where people have the option of contributing or not, using their own money." The research team proceeded to place images of human eyes at eye level next to an 'honesty box' in which consumers of coffee and tea were supposed to pay for their drinks. The researchers could conclude that when people felt watched, even by eyes on a poster, they were more prone to pay, in comparison to when the illustration of eyes was replaced by an image of flowers. The gaze of the eyes, although only an image, triggered the feeling of being watched, since the human perceptual system responds to stimuli involving faces and eyes. The coffee drinkers, eager to keep up their social reputation, therefore behaved as if someone could check whether they actually paid; see Bateson, Nettle, and Roberts 2006, 412–414 (also discussed by Padilla Peralta 2020, 346). This is interesting not only for statues placed outside the temple, but also has implications for portrait *pinakes* placed inside temples, such as that of

Kleidike in Kyzikos (Mylonopoulos 2013, 142). Her watchful eyes would have overseen cella visitors wandering among its riches.
102 Hdt. 6.134–136; Paus. 3.23.3–5.

Acknowledgments

My warmest thanks go to Gunnel Ekroth, Judy Barringer, and David Scahill for their thorough editing and inspiring comments. Any remaining mistakes are, of course, my own.

Works Cited

Aleshire, S.B. 1989. *The Athenian Asklepieion: The People, their Dedications and the Inventories*. Amsterdam.

Andrianou, D. 2006a. "Chairs, Beds and Tables: Evidence for Furnished Interiors in Hellenistic Greece." *Hesperia* 75: 219–266.

Andrianou, D. 2006b. "Late Classical and Hellenistic Furniture and Furnishings in the Epigraphical Record." *Hesperia* 75: 561–584.

Barringer, J.M. 2021. *Olympia: A Cultural History*. Princeton.

Barletta, B. 2005. "Architecture and Architects of the Classical Parthenon." In *The Parthenon: From Antiquity to the Present*, edited by J. Neils, 67–99. Cambridge.

Barletta, B. 2017. *The Sanctuary of Athena at Sounion*. Princeton.

Bateson, M., D. Nettle, and G. Roberts. 2022. "Cues of Being Watched Enhance Cooperation in a Real-World Setting." *Biology Letters* Sept. 22, 2(3): 412–414.

Bergquist, B. 1967. *The Archaic Greek Temenos: A Study of Structure and Function*. Lund.

Broneer, O.T. 1971. *Isthmia 1: The Temple of Poseidon*. Princeton.

Brulé, P. 2012. *Comment percevoir le sanctuaire grec?* Paris.

Bruit Zaidman, L., and P. Schmitt Pantel. 1992. *Religion in the Ancient Greek City*, trans. P. Cartledge. Cambridge.

Burkert, W. 1985. *Greek Religion*, trans. J. Raffan. Oxford.

Carbon, J.-M., and V. Pirenne-Delforge. 2012. "Beyond Greek 'Sacred Laws.'" *Kernos* 25: 163–182.

Carbon, J.-M., and V. Pirenne-Delforge. 2017. "Codifying 'Sacred Laws' in Ancient Greece." In *Writing Laws in Antiquity/ L'écriture du droit dans l'antiquité*, edited by D. Jaillard and C. Nihan, 141–157. Wiesbaden.

Cole, S.G. 2004. *Landscapes, Gender, and Ritual Space: The Ancient Greek Experience*. Berkeley.

Collar, A., and T.M. Kristensen, eds. 2020. *Pilgrimage and Economy in the Ancient Mediterranean*. Leiden.

Connelly, J.B. 1991. "Continuity and Change: The Cypriote Votive Tradition and the Hellenistic Koine." In *Cypriote Terracottas*, edited by F. Vandenabeele and R. Laffineur, 93–99. Brussels.

Connelly, J.B. 2007. *Portrait of a Priestess*. Princeton.

Corbett, P.E. 1970. "Greek Temples and Greek Worshippers: The Literary and Archaeological Evidence." *BICS* 17: 149–158.

Dignas, B. 2007. "A Day in the Life of a Greek Sanctuary." In *A Companion to Greek Religion*, edited by D. Ogden, 163–177. Malden, MA.

Dillon, M. 1997. *Pilgrims and Pilgrimage in Ancient Greece*. New York.

Ekroth, G. 2021. "Behind Closed Doors: Greek Sacrificial Rituals Performed inside Buildings in the Early Iron Age and the Archaic Period." In *Autour du foyer. Pratiques rituelles et modes de commensalité dans la Méditerranée de l'Âge du fer, de l'Égée à la péninsule Ibérique*, edited by M. Bastide and J. Lamaze, 13–39. Berlin.

Ekroth, G. 2024. "A Room of One's Own?" In *Stuff of the Gods: The Material Aspects of Religion in Ancient Greece*, edited by M. Haysom, M. Mili, and J. Wallensten, 69–82. Stockholm.

Elsner, J., and I. Rutherford. 2005. *Pilgrimage in Graeco-Roman and Early Christian Antiquity*. Oxford.

Eule, J.C. 2001. *Hellenistische Bürgerinnen aus Kleinasien. Weibliche Gewandstatuen in ihrem antiken Kontext*. Istanbul.

Frank, S.J. 2014. *Bucolic Architecture: Hellenistic Pastoral Temples in the Peloponnese*. Ph.D. diss., University of Minnesota.

Friese, W., S. Handberg, and T.M. Kristensen, eds. 2019. *Ascending and Descending the Acropolis: Movement in Athenian Religion*. Aarhus.

Gawlinski, L. 2015. "Securing the Sacred: The Accessibility and Control of Attic Sanctuaries." In *Cities Called Athens: Studies Honoring John McK. Camp II*, edited by K.F. Daly and L.A. Riccardi, 61–87. Lanham, MD.

Gebhard, E.R. 1993. "The Evolution of a Pan-Hellenic Sanctuary: From Archaeology towards History at Isthmia." In *Greek Sanctuaries: New Approaches*, edited by N. Marinatos and R. Hägg, 154–177. London.

Gebhard, E.R., and F.P. Hemans. 1992. "University of Chicago Excavations at Isthmia, 1989: I." *Hesperia* 61: 1–7.

Georgoudi, S., 2010. "Comment régler les theia pragmata. Pour une étude de ce que l'on appelle 'lois sacrées.'" *Mètis* n.s. 8: 39–54.

Gerding, H. 2014. "The Stone Doors of the Erechtheion." *ΛΑΒΡΥΣ: Studies Presented to Pontus Hellström*, 251–269. Uppsala.

Gill, D. 1991. *Greek Cult Tables*. New York.

Harris, E.M. 2015. "The Family, the Community and Murder: The Role of Pollution in Athenian Homicide Law." In *Public and Private in Ancient Mediterranean Law and Religion*, edited by C. Ando and J. Rüpke, 11–35. Berlin.

Harris, E.M. 2018. "Pollution and Purification in Athenian Law and in Attic Tragedy: Parallels or Divergences?" In *Συναγωνίσεσθαι. Studies in Honour of Guido Avezzù*, edited by S. Bigliazzi, F. Lupi, and G. Ugolini, 419–454. Verona.

Harris, E.M. 2019. "Pollution for Homicide after 400 BCE: More Evidence for the Persistence of a Belief." In *Dike. Essays on Greek Law in Honor of Alberto Maffi*, edited by L. Gagliardi and L. Pepe, 143–149. Milan.

Hennemeyer, A. 2012. "Der Zeus-Tempel von Olympia." In *Mythos Olympia. Kult und Spiele*, edited by W.-D. Heilmeyer et al., 121–125. Munich.

Hennemeyer, A. 2015. "The Temple Architecture and its Modifications during the Fifth Century BCE." In *New Approaches to the Temple of Zeus at Olympia*, edited by A. Patay-Horváth, 16–38. Newcastle-upon-Tyne.

Hollinshead, M.B. 1999. "'Adyton,' 'Opisthodomos,' and the Inner Room of the Greek Temple." *Hesperia* 68: 189–218.

Hölscher, F. 2007. "Götterstatuen bei Lectisternien und Theoxenien?" In *Römische Bilderwelten. Von der Wirklichkeit zum Bild und zurück*, edited by F. Hölscher and T. Hölscher, 27–42. Heidelberg.

Hurwit, J.M. 2014. "The Lost Art: Early Greek Wall and Panel Painting, 760–480 B.C." In *The Cambridge History of Painting in the Classical World*, edited by J.J. Pollitt, 66–93. Cambridge.

Jameson, M.H. 2014. "Theoxenia." In *Cults and Rites in Ancient Greece. Essays on Religion and Society*, edited by A. Stallsmith, 145–176. Cambridge.

Karatas, A.M.S. 2019. "Key-bearers of Greek Temples: The Temple Key as a Symbol of Priestly Authority." *Mythos* 13: 1–48.

Keesling, C.M. 2012. "Syeris, Diakonos of the Priestess Lysimache on the Athenian Acropolis (*IG* II^2 3464)." *Hesperia* 81: 467–505.

Kerschner, M. 1996. "Perirrhanterien und Becken." In *Alt-Ägina 2: 4. Die Sphinxsäule: Votivträger, Altäre, Steingeräte*, edited by K. Hoffelner, 59–132. Mainz.

Klingborg, P., H. von Ehrenheim, and A. Frejman 2023. "Ritual Usage of Water in Greek Sanctuaries." *Klio* 105: 1–50.

Korres, M. 1996. "Restoring the Architecture: Pronaos, West Wall." In *The Parthenon. Architecture and Conservation*, edited by M. Korres, G.A. Panetsos, and T. Seki, 45–47. Athens.

Kristensen, T.M., and W. Friese, eds. 2017. *Excavating Pilgrimage: Archaeological Approaches to Sacred Travel and Movement in the Ancient World*. Leiden.

Kron, U. 1996. "Priesthoods, Dedications and Euergetism: What Part Did Religion Play in the Political and Social Status of Greek Women?" In *Religion and Power in the Ancient Greek World*, edited by P. Hellström and B. Alroth, 139–182. Uppsala.

Lapatin, K. 2001. *Chryselephantine Statuary in the Ancient Mediterranean World*. Oxford.

Larson, J. 2007. *Ancient Greek Cults: A Guide*. New York.

Linders, T. 1972. *Studies in the Treasure Records of Artemis Brauronia Found in Athens*. Stockholm.

Linders, T. 2007. "The Location of the Opisthodomos: Evidence from the Temple of Athena Parthenos Inventories." *AJA* 111: 777–782.

Mantis, A.G. 1990. Προβλήματα της εικονογραφίας των ιερειών και των ιερέων στην αρχαία Ελληνική τέχνη. Athens.

Marconi, C. 2016. "The Greek West: Temples and their Decoration." In *A Companion to Greek Architecture*, edited by M.M. Miles, 75–91. Hoboken, NJ.

Mattern, T. 2006. "Architektur und Ritual. Architektur als funktionaler Rahmen antiker Kultpraxis." In *Archäologie und Ritual. Auf der Suche nach der rituellen Handlung in den antiken Kulturen Ägyptens und Griechenlands*, edited by J. Mylonopolos and H. Roeder, 167–183. Wien.

Mikalson, J.D. 2010. *Ancient Greek Religion*, 2nd ed. Chichester.

Miles, M.M. 1998–1999. "Interior Staircases in Western Greek Temples." *MAAR* 43–44: 1–26.

Miles, M.M. 2016. "The Interiors of Greek Temples." In *A Companion to Greek Architecture*, edited by M.M. Miles, 206–222. Hoboken, NJ.

Mylonopoulos, J. 2011. "Divine images behind bars. The semantics of barriers in Greek temples." In *Current Approaches to Religion in Ancient Greece*, edited by M. Haysom and J. Wallensten, 269–291. Stockholm.

Mylonopoulos, J. 2013. "Commemorating Pious Service: Images in Honour of Male and Female Priestly Officers in Asia Minor and the Eastern Aegean in Hellenistic and Roman Times." In *Cities and Priests. Cult Personnel in Asia Minor and the Aegean Islands from the Hellenistic to the Imperial Period*, edited by M. Horster and A. Klöckner, 121–153. Berlin.

Naiden, F.S. 2013. *Smoke Signals for the Gods: Ancient Greek Sacrifice from the Archaic through Roman Periods*. Oxford.

Nevin, S. 2017. *Military Leaders and Sacred Space in Classical Greek Warfare: Temples, Sanctuaries and Conflict in Antiquity*. London.

Niemeier, W.-D. 2008. "Καλαπόδι." In Εύβοια και Στερεά Ελλάδα, edited by A.G. Vlachopoulos, 302–305. Athens.

Niemeier, W.-D., B. Niemeier, and A. Brysbaert. 2012. "The Olpe Chigi and New Evidence for Early Archaic Greek Wall-Painting from the Oracle Sanctuary of Apollo at Abai (Kalapodi)." In *L'Olpe Chigi. Storia di un agalma*, edited by E. Mugione, 79–86. Salerno.

Ohnesorg, A. 1993. *Inselionische Marmordächer*. Berlin.

Padilla Peralta, D. 2020. "Gods of Trust: Ancient Delos and the Modern Economics of Religion." In *Pilgrimage and Economy in the Ancient Mediterranean*, edited by A. Collar and T.M. Kristensen, 329–356. Leiden.

Parker, R.C.T. 1983. *Miasma: Pollution and Purification in Early Greek Religion*. Oxford.

Parker, R.C.T. 2004. "What Are Greek Sacred Laws?" In *The Law and the Courts in Ancient Greece*, edited by E. Harris and L. Rubinstein, 57–70. London.

Parker, R.C.T. 2005. *Polytheism and Society at Athens*. Oxford.

Pfaff, C.A. 2018. "Late Antique Symbols and Numerals on Altars in the Asklepieion at Epidauros." *Hesperia* 87: 387–428.

Pimpl, H. 1997. *Perirrhanteria und Louteria. Entwicklung und Verwendung großer Marmor- und Kalksteinbecken auf figürlichem und säulenartigem Untersatz in Griechenland*. Berlin.

Prignitz, S. 2014. *Bauurkunden und Bauprogramm von Epidauros (400–350). Asklepiostempel, Tholos, Kultbild, Brunnenhaus*. Munich.

Pritchett, W.K. 1991. *The Greek State at War 5*. Berkeley.

Pope, S., and P. Schultz. 2014. "The Chryselephantine Doors of the Parthenon." *AJA* 118: 19–31.

Robert, J., and L. Robert. 1954. *La Carie. Histoire et géographie historique avec le recueil des inscriptions antiques*. Paris.

Rutherford, I. 2013. *State Pilgrims and Sacred Observers in Ancient Greece. A Study of Theoria and Theoroi*. Cambridge.

Schaus, G.P. 2014. *Stymphalos: The Acropolis Sanctuary*. Toronto.

Scott, M. 2010. *Delphi and Olympia: The Spatial Politics of Panhellenism in the Archaic and Classical Periods*. Cambridge.

Sneed, D. 2020. "The Architecture of Access: Ramps at Ancient Greek Healing Sanctuaries." *Antiquity* 94: 1015–1029.

Sporn, K. 2015. "Rituale im griechischen Tempel. Überlegungen zur Funktion von Tempelrampen." In *Ein Minoer im Exil. Festschrift für Wolf-Dietrich Niemeier*, edited by D. Panagiotopoulos, I. Kaiser, and O. Kouka, 349–374. Bonn.

Trampedach, K. 2005. "Hierosylia. Gewalt in Heiligtümern." In *Die andere Seite der griechischen Klassik. Gewalt im 5. und 4. Jahrhundert v. Chr.*, edited by S. Moraw and G. Fischer, 143–165. Stuttgart.

van Rookhuijzen, J. 2020. "The Parthenon Treasury on the Acropolis of Athens." *AJA* 124: 3–35.

Vlachopoulos, A.G. 2020. "Wall Paintings." In *A Companion to the Archaeology of Early Greece and the Mediterranean* I, edited by I. Lemos and A. Kotsonas, 407–432. Chichester.

von Ehrenheim, H. 2019. "Causal explanation of disease in the iamata of Epidauros." *Kernos* 32: 101–118.

Wallensten, J. 2014. "Karpophoroi Deities and the Attic Cult of Ge. Notes on *IG* II^2 4758." *OpAthRom* 7: 193–203.

Wallensten, J. 2021. "The Key to Hermione? Notes on an Inscribed Monument." *OpAthRom* 14: 169–180.

Williamson, C.G. 2018. "Filters of Light. Greek Temple Doors as Portals of Epiphany." In *Sacred Thresholds: The Door to the Sanctuary in Late Antiquity*, edited by E.M. van Opstall, 309–340. Leiden.

Zanker, G. 2009. *Herodas: Mimiambs*. Oxford.

CHAPTER 3

Policing Sanctuaries in Ancient Greece

Jan-Mathieu Carbon and Edward Harris

Logistics typically designate the administration, organization, and/or coordination of complex operations, a process that involves a variety of interrelated factors: facilities, people, things, etc. The word is heuristically apt for understanding the detailed and complex processes that went on in Greek sanctuaries, involving actions—rituals such as dedication, purification, and sacrifice—by the cult personnel and worshippers within specific parameters. None of these logistical aspects—divine, human, material, etc.—can truly be separated from the others, an interconnection that is obvious when considering the written evidence. In the present case, we consider how written regulations reflect a concern with the oversight and control of these logistics. We designate here the administration and the enforcement of such rules relating to Greek sanctuaries and their human participants as 'policing.' Though much of the written evidence—literary and epigraphical—focuses on ritual activities, we attempt to bring out the impact of policing on human agents, such as the cult personnel and worshippers.

Specifically, we examine four logistical aspects of policing sanctuaries: first, the exclusion of worshippers and particularly those disqualified from entering a sacred precinct; second, maintaining order inside sanctuaries (crowd-control and other factors); third, the regulation of sacrificial offerings and dedications made by priests and worshippers in sanctuaries; and fourth, the accountability of religious officials. Rules could be oral and/or written. In many cases, the enforcement of regulations explicitly required the intervention of specific officials belonging to the sanctuary or specially appointed officers responsible for a festival, e.g., the staff-bearers (*rhabdouchoi*) or other officials for direct policing, as well as higher officials for adjudicating more serious cases. 'Keepers' or officials who permanently resided in sanctuaries, such as *neokoroi*, played a prominent role in supervising the day to day logistics of many sanctuaries and, where the rules were not written down, would often be responsible for orally communicating them to visiting worshippers and enforcing them.[1] In smaller and less frequented sanctuaries, published sanctions may have served primarily as deterrents: the precise mechanisms of their enforcement often remain unclear to us given the concision of the rules. Still, in sanctuaries large or small, the publication of laws or signs was viewed as an essential step in making rules visible to worshippers and advertising the expected norms of behavior in these sacred sites.[2] That visibility was a key desideratum for the publication of signs in particular is frequently underlined by the inscribing of such smaller sacred norms on boundary stones, stelai, or plaques near entrances to sanctuaries, or on the door-frame or lintel of a shrine itself. In other words, the visitors to Greek sanctuaries entered a tightly regulated and controlled environment, where, as we will see, the threat of physical, monetary and/or divine punishment loomed.

To set the stage, we may consider two infamous incidents involving the policing of major sanctuaries, Olympia and Samothrace. In 420 BCE, the Spartans were accused of violating the truce for the Olympic games because the people of Elis charged that they had attacked the fort at Phyrkos and invaded Lepreon with hoplites, though they had accepted the truce for the festival.[3] The Eleans, who were in charge of the sanctuary, imposed a fine of 2000 minas, 2 minas for each hoplite as the law (*nomos*) ordered.[4] The Spartans sent envoys to protest that the hoplites had been sent to Lepreon before the truce was announced at Sparta. The Eleans replied that the truce was already in effect throughout Elis and should have been respected. The Spartans countered that if the Eleans thought that the truce had been violated, they should not

---

1 Cf. Ricl 2011, esp. p. 21: "*neokoroi* were an essential part of the logistics of Greek cults." For some relevant examples, see the sections below on *Exclusion from Sanctuaries* and *Maintaining Order in Sanctuaries*.
2 On shorter sacred norms—sometimes abbreviated decrees, other times laws or regulations with a less clear source of authority—that were published as 'signs' in sanctuaries, see Harris 2015, 58–60 and the accompanying appendices by Carbon and Harris.
3 Thuc. 5.49.1–5. Cf. Xen. *Hell.* 3.2.21; Paus. 5.2.2.
4 This exact law is not otherwise attested but must have been part of the body of laws at Elean Olympia. The payment of fines to Zeus Olympios is envisaged in several other inscribed laws from Olympia, e.g., Minon 2007, no. 13 (*c.*475 BCE), cf. esp. ll. 1–5, which refer to an earlier precedent: [τ]ὰ ζίκαια · κα' τὸ γράφος · τἀρχαῖον.

have announced it later in Sparta.[5] The Eleans rejected this argument but offered to cancel the fine and pay the percentage due to the god on their behalf if the Spartans returned Lepreon to them. When the Spartans rejected this solution, the Eleans made another proposal: if the Spartans did not wish to return Lepreon but wished to have access to the sanctuary, they should stand before the altar of Olympian Zeus and swear that they would pay the fine after the festival. The Spartans also refused this proposal and were banned from the sanctuary.[6]

When the 90th Olympic games were celebrated in 420 BCE, the Eleans took elaborate precautions to prevent the Spartans from sacrificing (Thuc. 5.50.3). They placed an armed guard of younger men, who were joined by a thousand troops from Argos, another thousand soldiers from Mantinea, and cavalry from Athens. Lichas, the son of Arkesilas, a Spartan, entered a chariot in the race under the name of the Boiotians because of the ban on the Spartans.[7] After his chariot won, and Lichas went onto the racetrack and crowned his charioteer to show that the chariot belonged to him, the staff-bearers (*rhabdouchoi*) beat him.[8] Even though it was feared that something terrible would happen, the Spartans kept their peace.

Several centuries later in 172 BCE, king Perseus of Macedon sent Evander of Crete and three Macedonians to murder King Eumenes II of Pergamon.[9] When Eumenes was approaching Delphi from Cirrha, the conspirators rolled down two boulders, which struck his head and his shoulder. The conspirators fled and were not caught, but Eumenes was able to recover from his injuries. Several years later in 168 BCE, the Roman Lucius Atilius addressed the people of Samothrace. He reminded them that the island was sacred and then asked how a murderer could pollute the island with the blood of Eumenes, citing the proclamation (*praefatio sacrorum*) that all those with unclean hands were banned from taking part in sacred rites. Atilius was referring to Evander, who was visiting the island after his attempt on Eumenes' life. The people of Samothrace therefore sent Theondas, who held the office of *basileus*, to Perseus to announce that Evander was being charged with murder at the court in which those who entered the sacred boundaries of the sanctuary (*terminos sacros templi*) with unclean hands were tried.[10] If Evander were confident of his innocence, he should entrust his case to the court. Perseus took Evander aside and advised him not to submit to trial because his case was weak. In reality, Perseus was worried that his own role in the affair would be exposed and suggested that Evander should take his own life. When Evander began to plan his escape, Perseus gave orders to have him killed. This put Evander out of the way, but Perseus incurred pollution (*labem*) by having Evander killed in a sanctuary (Livy acutely comments that Perseus had actually incurred blood pollution at two of the most sacred shrines, Delphi and Samothrace). To avoid blame, Perseus had Theondas announce that Evander had committed suicide. In and of itself, pollution as a barrier to entering a sanctuary was not remarkable, and the case is as politically charged as the exclusion of the Spartans from Olympia. Nevertheless, it precisely demonstrates that officials were charged not only with making the rules of sanctuaries clear to worshippers (here, the proclamation), but also with pursuing those who did not follow these rules and enacting punishment (here, the lawsuit).

---

5   The truce was probably thought to last for a whole 'sacred month' (*hieromenia*), regardless of when it had been announced outside of Elis: see Minon 2007, no. 7, l. 2 (['Ολ]υμπικô μενὸς, c.500–475 BCE), with commentary. Following from the dispute reported by Thucydides, there has been some debate as to whether the Olympic *ekecheiria* offered a generalized form of amnesty and *asylia* for all communities (Siewert 1981, 244) or only a temporary protection for the *theoroi* and the participants in the festival (Rougemont 1973). For local dating according to the widely disseminated Olympic truce, see *CGRN* 13 (Selinous, c.500–450 BCE).

6   Thuc. 5.50.1. For another case of exclusion from the Olympic games, see Paus. 5.21.13.

7   Thuc. 5.50.3–4; cf. Xen. *Hell.* 3.2.21.

8   On *rhabdouchoi* at Olympia, as well as in other festival and athletic venues, see Harris 2019c, 112–113.

9   Livy 42.15–16. For an analysis of the implications of this incident see Harris 2019b, 146–147; with a different emphasis, see also Salvo 2018, 164–168.

10 Livy 45.5–6. Public courts (*dikasteria*) were in session outside the period of the sacred truce (*ekecheiria*) of the major festivals, which normally marked a suspension of public and judicial activities. A regulation from Thasos (Salviat 1958, *LSS* no. 69, *I.Thasos* 3 9, *SEG* 17.415) of c.325–300 BCE lists the festival days during which it is not possible to accuse or bring anyone to trial (αἷς ἡμέραις οὐκ ἔξεστιν ἐνδεικνύε[ιν ο]ὐδὲ ἀπάγειν· κτλ.; all of the occasions mentioned thereafter are major festivals of the community). A fragmentary decree or law from Lampsakos (*I.Lampsakos* 9, *LSAM* no. 8, *CGRN* 185, ll. 24–28) of the second–first century BCE specifies that no seizures of property from debtors or trials are to be held during the days in which the Asklepieia were held (cf. Dem. 21.11 discussed below). However, it is also probable that *ad hoc* trials were held in the context of festivals, as seems to be suggested by the authority of the Sacred Men (*hieroi*) to act as judges in specific cases at Andania (*LSCG* no. 65, *CGRN* 222, ll. 36–37, 78–80). As we discuss further below, there are instances where religious officials were granted the power to act as the equivalent of the judiciary within certain limits.

These two vivid incidents illustrate the importance placed on policing sanctuaries to enforce sacred norms and their direct impact on worshippers. The norms in question could be orally and/or textually transmitted: in our two examples, the Olympic sacred truce disseminated to other cities and the proclamation made at Samothrace were fundamentally oral laws; however, we can assume that sacred truces were also recorded: for example, rules were published at Athens about the truce for the Eleusinian Mysteries.[11] Most importantly, the legal frameworks present in both sanctuaries clearly employed a variety of written rules about behavior, stipulating the means of enforcement, as well as the sanctions (such as fines) or other concrete measures to be taken.[12] In the first case, the Eleans excluded the Spartans from the shrine at Olympia for violating the sacred truce and had officials of the festival (*rhabdouchoi*) beat a Spartan who violated the ban.[13] In the second, the authorities at the sanctuary on Samothrace were about to try Evander who was polluted due to attempted homicide and who entered the temple precinct in violation of the sacred norm about murderers.

1 Exclusion from Sanctuaries

Individuals or groups could be excluded from sanctuaries for different reasons.[14] Some types of sanctuaries, for example certain *abata*, were apparently not to be frequented at all.[15] In other cases, the word *abaton* could apply to a more welcoming, usually open sacred precinct or *temenos*.[16] Yet although this was not always clearly stated, many sanctuaries were probably off-limits to those who had no demonstrable business there. In fact, some rules make this explicit: only those intending to offer a sacrifice or participate in some kind of ritual could legitimately enter.[17] Such rules also clearly served to protect the integrity of the sanctuary, particularly its possessions. The precise details of their enforcement are not always very clear, however.

To indicate which area lay within the territory of the sanctuary and which lay outside, the community might place boundary-stones (*horoi*) around the sacred space or precinct (*temenos*). In other cases, the community might encircle the sanctuary with an enclosure wall (*peribolos*) with a monumental gate to control access. The most famous are the walls surrounding the Athenian Akropolis with the impressive Propylaia. The authorities at Delphi enclosed the sixth-century Apollo sanctuary with a polygonal masonry wall.[18] The area of the sanctuary was later extended by constructing a new wall to the south. These walls further helped to protect the rich dedications in and around the temple of Apollo and in the many treasuries (which, when they were not in use, would have been kept under lock and key), while carefully demarcating the precinct from the surrounding city and its potential sources of pollution (people, animals, etc.).

Enclosure walls were especially important to help keep the uninitiated out of sanctuaries at which mysteries were celebrated. As early as the sixth century, the sanctuary of Demeter and Kore at Eleusis was surrounded by a wall, which was expanded in the fifth and again in the fourth

---

11 *LSS* no. 3, B, *AIO-AIUK* 4.2 no. 1, *c*.460 BCE.
12 For orality in sacred norms, cf., e.g., Hitch 2011. On sanctions, see Naiden 2008.
13 For rules concerning foreigners (ξένοι) at Olympia, see Minon 2007, no. 3 (*CGRN* 4, *c*.525–500 BCE); 4 (*CGRN* 5, *c*.525–500 BCE); 8 (Siewert and Taeuber 2013, 29–31, no. 4, specifically concerning citizens of Epidamnos, Libyans and Cretans, *c*.500 BCE). Conversely, another interesting case known to us is that of Timokrates, son of Malex, who was apparently condemned for detaining a foreign *thearos* in chains (Minon 2007, no. 19, *c*.475–450 BCE); much of Timokrates' property seems to have been sold as a result.
14 See already Hewitt 1909, with an early attempt at classifying restrictions of access to sanctuaries.
15 Most signs typically mention that a sanctuary is an *abaton* with few other specifications, cf., e.g., the boundary stone *IG* II² 4964 (400–350 BCE, which only adds the deity, Zeus Kataibates, and the further qualifier ἱερόν). An analogous boundary stone from Chios specified: "Sacred/sanctuary: no entry" (ἱρόν· οὐκ ἔσοδος, *LSCG* no. 121). Another similar rule on a limestone plaque was found at Kallion in Aitolia (*LSS* no. 128, fifth century BCE); this imposed a fine of 4 staters on anyone accessing the sanctuary. Such rules seem to have restricted entry altogether, though it is also possible that certain exceptions, e.g., the role of a priest or priestess, were not spelled out in these brief texts. See also the collection of evidence drawn from Pausanias in Corbett 1970, 150–151 with n. 11.
16 Cf. for example the use of this word to refer to the well-frequented sanctuary at Epidauros, where incubation took place (*IG* IV².1 121–123, *passim*).
17 Especially clear in this regard is a relatively recently published sign from a privately consecrated sanctuary of Asklepios at Pythion in Thessaly (*BÉ* 2017 no. 299, *SEG* 68.288, fourth century BCE); a later text (third century BCE) was appended to this and clarified that a fine of 5 dr was imposed on anyone who crossed the *temenos* without intending to sacrifice. See also, e.g., *SEG* 26.1225 from Halikarnassos: A, ll. 1–2, boundary stone of Apollo, fourth century BCE; B, ll. 3–10, regulation concerning access to the *akra*, prohibited "for one who has no business (there)," third or second century BCE. The latter seems to correspond also to rules restricting access to fortresses, such as the recently published example from Zarax in Lakonia (Lanérès 2022).
18 For the enclosure walls at Delphi, see Bommelaer and Laroche 2015, 116–120.

century BCE.[19] The City Eleusinion in Athens was also surrounded by an enclosure wall as early as the Archaic period.[20] This wall was extended in the Classical period when the area of the sanctuary was expanded. An impressive gateway also controlled access.

For the most part, walled sanctuaries or temples that had doors were designed to prevent access by worshippers, except at specific times.[21] It was an act of sacrilege to enter a shrine by jumping over the enclosure wall when the gate was locked. The Parians told the following story about the time when Miltiades was besieging Paros: a captive slave called Timo who was *hypozakoros* (assistant to the attendant) of the Chthoniai Theai told Miltiades to enter the sanctuary of Demeter Thesmophoros for a purpose that is not certain—perhaps to remove one of the sacred, indeed immoveable (*akineta*), objects from the part of the sanctuary called the *megaron*, as Herodotos tentatively suggests.[22] Miltiades climbed over the enclosure wall (*herkos*) of the sanctuary of Demeter Thesmophoros because he could not open the door (which was probably locked) and was seized by panic and fled. Leaping back down from the wall, he twisted his thigh or his knee. Later the wound became gangrenous, and Miltiades died, which was apparently reckoned by the Parians to be a just punishment for his intrusion into the sacred space at a time when the sanctuary was closed off to commit his intended crime (whatever it was); Timo herself was accused of having "revealed to Miltiades sacred things that could not be spoken to a male" (though she was later acquitted by a Pythian oracle). At any rate, the story certainly suggests that the wall was high enough to deter intruders and for Miltiades to suffer a serious injury when leaping from it.

As in Miltiades' case—a foreign man who trespassed on a Thesmophorion—exclusions from sanctuaries could concern specific categories of people. Most importantly, individuals could be banned from sanctuaries because they were temporarily or permanently unclean.[23] As a famous late regulation for the cult of Athena at Lindos states: from certain crimes (*paranoma*), most individuals were never to be considered pure.[24] In this category, we especially find those who had committed murder. Such individuals were permanently debarred from the Eleusinian Mysteries.[25] A recently published inscription from Thyateira dated to the second century BCE contains rules about who can enter a sanctuary and forbids those who have willingly killed someone friendly (that is, not an enemy in war) from ever entering. However, the inscription allows someone who has killed involuntarily to enter after having performed the prescribed purification.[26]

Other categories of people could be debarred from sanctuaries. As mentioned previously, uninitiated individuals were banned from entering sanctuaries where mysteries were celebrated. A pair of signs in Greek and Latin found at the shrine of the Great Gods at Samothrace dated to the first century BCE and CE forbids those who are uninitiated from going into the shrine.[27] At Athens, the penalty for violating this rule was harsh. Livy states that two young men from Akarnania entered the temple of Demeter following the crowd, unaware that they were committing a sacrilege.[28] When they asked foolish questions, which

---

19 On enclosure walls at Eleusis, see Mylonas 1961, *passim*. On *peribolos* walls in general, see Hellmann 2006, 175–186.

20 Miles 1998, 25–32. Only the foundations or lower courses of this wall are preserved, but their thickness (0.9–1.15 m) suggests a probably substantial impediment to access.

21 See notably Corbett 1970, 150–151, discussing some of the literary evidence. Cf. Wallensten in this volume.

22 Hdt. 6.133–136.

23 Numerous examples of inscribed regulations defining sacred norms of these kinds are known. Cf., for instance, a regrettably fragmentary, but seemingly originally quite detailed regulation concerning conduct in the sanctuary and purity is CGRN 65, Tegea, of the fourth century BCE. The subject of *hagneia* and temporary impurity is rich and deserves a fuller treatment than is possible here; see the fundamental work of Parker 1983, esp. 332–356.

24 *I.Lindos* 487, LSS no. 91 (second or third century CE). An exception was made for certain sacred officials, priests, singers (*molpoi, hymnodoi*), musicians, and other servants of the temple, who were to be viewed as 'always pure,' having performed the necessary purification after involuntary offenses (*akousia*). For a new edition of this text, see I. Petrovic and A. Petrovic 2018. For the *paranoma*, the authors (245, n. 65) think particularly of incest or illicit intercourse, noting a possible parallel with the rules of the *oikos* of Dionysios, LSAM no. 20, CGRN 191, ll. 25–32 (Philadelphia in Lydia, c.125–75 BCE). However, crimes such as (voluntary) homicide were perhaps also covered by the blanket statement of the law from Lindos.

25 Isok. 4.157.

26 Malay and Petzl 2017, 1, cf. esp. ll. 10–11, 11–12. For the distinction between deliberate homicide and involuntary homicide, see Dem. 21.43, 37.59 (the involuntary killer had to remain in exile, until pardoned by the relatives of the victim; the return was accompanied by a purificatory ritual), with the commentary of Harris 2013, 182–189. On the text from Thyateira, see further Parker 2018 and Harris 2019b, 147; see also Parker 1983, 370–374 and CGRN 13 (Selinous, c.500–450 BCE) on purification from homicide. An unfortunately fragmentary law from Lato (LSS no. 112, CGRN 166, Lato, second century BCE) provided an apparently much more specific series of scenarios concerning voluntary or involuntary harm and homicide, probably within the city as a whole, rather than a specific sanctuary, and notably involving fire in a few cases. However, the terms ἄκων and ἀκόντως are both restored in the text; nevertheless, this document gives us some hint of the level of detail we might have expected from purity regulations in Greek cities and sanctuaries.

27 LSS nos. 75, 75a.

28 Livy 31.14.7–8.

revealed their ignorance of the rites, they were arrested and put to death, presumably by the Athenian authorities. At the Mysteries of Andania, the Sacred Men had the power to exclude the uninitiated from the place they marked off.[29]

A few sanctuaries did ban foreigners completely,[30] though this was not a universal norm, since specific rules concerning the presence or sacrifices of foreigners were often published.[31] Sanctuaries or cults that excluded foreigners were typically reserved for an exclusive group, such as a city or smaller community. The sanctuary of the Archegetes on Delos is one clear case: the inscriptions on the two lintels of the temple explicitly forbade any strangers to enter.[32] It is not clear how these rules were enforced, but presumably group cohesion was at play: non-Delians were probably expected to be singled out by those who belonged to the closed circle of the Delians. Those contravening the rule could then have been appropriately punished. Smaller groups, such as civic subgroups and associations, kept and sometimes published lists of their members.[33] A detailed example of a regulation concerning the scrutiny of members is that of the phratry of the Demotionidai in Athens and its cult of Zeus Phratrios.[34] In the aforementioned cases, it seems that foreigners or non-members were simply expected to stand out or be noticed, much like the unfortunate Akarnanian pair at Eleusis.

More intriguing and equally difficult to enforce were rules concerning particular types of strangers. A well-known, albeit difficult, case comes from Paros, which may relate to a local sanctuary of [Demeter and] Kore (yet, however tempting that inference might be, it is entirely unclear whether this might be the same as the Thesmophorion visited by Miltiades).[35] Through its specific prohibition of Dorian *xenoi*, this inscription from Paros parallels the famous case of the Spartan king Kleomenes' visit to the temple of Athena on the Athenian Akropolis.[36] The officials of the sanctuaries clearly tried to prevent Kleomenes' intrusion on the Akropolis or, in another case, in sacrificing at the Argive Heraion.[37] Policing did occur, though what the consequences may have been for the Spartan king are less clear (probably a degree of impurity, the possibility of divine punishment, etc.). At the sanctuary of Leukothea in Chaironeia, Plutarch reports that the *neokoros* made the following proclamation with a whip in hand (*labōn mastiga*): "Neither a male nor female slave is to enter, neither an Aitolian man or woman."[38] Here, then, there was tangible threat of physical punishment, which would have resonated in visitors' ears and excluded specific groups from the sanctuary.

As we saw in the case of the Spartans at the Olympic games, the authorities of a sanctuary might also temporarily ban all the members of a community for some collective offense or disqualification. At Delphi, the members of any community that had not accepted the sacred truce were excluded from the sanctuary.[39] After their defeat in the Third Sacred War, the Amphictyony banned the Phokians from the shrine at Delphi as one of the punishments for their sacrilege.[40] The military occupation of a sanctuary by a foreign power is an offence that is often reported in the sources: anyone visiting or living in a sanctuary was expected to respect its sacrality and to conduct themselves appropriately.[41]

---

29 *LSCG* no. 65, *CGRN* 222, ll. 36–37.
30 On this subject, see Butz 1996; Wächter (1910, 118–123) already provided an extensive list of sources.
31 See, e.g., *LSCG* no. 101, *CGRN* 234, Decree B (Arkesine, fourth century BCE), apparently restricting any camping by foreigners, but not forbidding their presence in the sanctuary otherwise. The decree made clear that the keeper of the temple or sanctuary (*neokoros*) was the agent empowered to prevent this and that he would be fined if he failed in his duty. The inscription was set up to be visible in front of the doors of the sanctuary and thus served as a warning sign to visitors. On accommodation and camping in Greek sanctuaries, see also Ekroth and Scahill in this volume.
32 *ID* 68 a–b, *LSS* no. 49, end of fifth–beginning of fourth century BCE.
33 On rules for associations as well as lists of members, see now Arnaoutoglou 2021 and Carbon 2021 (among other essays in that collection). See also Gawlinski in this volume.
34 *IG* II² 1237, *LSCG* no. 19, RO no. 5, 396/5 BCE. See Joyce 2021 for a detailed discussion of this text and the role of the phratry as a decision-making body.
35 *LSGC* 110, *c*.450 BCE; cf. also Sammartano 2019. The text is inscribed on a column drum. Kore appears to be mentioned in the fragmentary text, but several of its aspects are uncertain; see also below.
36 Hdt. 5.72; cf. Parker 1998; on Kleomenes and rules against foreigners, see now esp. Pirenne-Delforge 2020, 187–204. Yet the stone from Paros has been variously restored: e.g., it could have concerned sacrificial participation rather than entry to the sanctuary in question.
37 Hdt. 6.81. For the enforcement of such customary rules against foreigners, see Harris 2015, 60.
38 Plut. *Quaest. Rom.* 16. For entry restricted on an 'ethnic basis,' see the brief treatment in Corbett 1970, 151. For slaves and whipping, see the case of the *hetaira* at Thyateira discussed below.
39 *IG* II² 1126, *LSCG* no. 78, ll. 47–48.
40 Diod. Sic. 16.60.1–3. For discussion and references to other sources, see Sánchez 2001: 203–213.
41 Cf. for example the occupation of Delion by the Athenians during the Peloponnesian War (Thuc. 4.97), which was said by the Boiotians to have "transgressed the *nomima* of the Hellenes" in treating a sacred place (and notably its water) as profane. This also appears to be, e.g., the general context of numerous edicts regarding the presence of Seleukid troops in, or in close

Whether policed through group cohesion or specific individuals empowered to act for the community, norms of exclusion were publicly enforced. There was a law at Athens banning women who had been seduced from attending publicly funded sacrifices. If such a woman did attend, anyone who wished was allowed to use physical violence but could not kill her.[42] The relatively new inscription from Thyateira is also interesting concerning the rights of a *hetaira* to visit the sanctuary: she could only do so after having purified herself with the blood of a piglet and while being observed by the *neopoiai* in service.[43] If she contravened the rules, she would be liable to a fine of 1 mina of silver, and if a slave, or perhaps *as* a slave (the text is a bit unclear), she would receive lashes, each of which would correspond to 3 obols. As the editors have well noted, this would be a particularly brutal punishment, necessitating a whipping of 200 lashes to make up the amount of 600 obols needed for the stated fine of 1 mina. The new regulation from Thyateira thus brings two essential aspects of policing to our attention: first, the role of sanctuary officials—here, the *neopoiai* who happened to be in office—in controlling the purity of women, and particularly women falling outside the expected norms of citizen marriage; and second, the severe sanctions imposed on offenders against these particular rules. While it is clear that the officials of the sanctuary played a role in witnessing purifications, collecting fines, or whipping offenders, it is hard to see how they could enforce other rules about temporary impurity which are stated in the inscription, such as the one about not entering the temple until three days after eating garlic or touching garlic (ll. 7–8)—unless, of course, these *neopoiai* had a highly developed sense of smell. The rule thus seems to lead us away from policing to the subject of conforming to normative expectations, to having a crime on one's conscience, and to the idea of divine punishment, other fascinating and crucial aspects of many sacred norms, which we cannot investigate further here.[44]

It was also forbidden to have sexual relations inside sacred precincts, and various rules to that effect are known.[45] Sex could be a factor in exclusion, though typically Greek sanctuaries were not fully male- or female-only. Instead, certain celebrations or festivals required the participation of one sex to the exclusion of the other.[46] Thus, men were normally banned from sanctuaries where women's rites, such as the Thesmophoria, were celebrated (recall the case of Miltiades mentioned above). Aristophanes in his *Thesmophoriazousai* gives a comic account of what happened to a man who violated such a ban, though death may have been a punishment in many cases.[47] At Methymna, probably during a Dionysiac *pannychis*, there was a law that prevented men from entering the temple and ordered the *gynaikonomos* to stand outside the doors to keep them out.[48]

---

proximity to, Karian sanctuaries: *I.Amyzon* 10–11; *I.Labraunda* 46 (all from *c*.203 BCE).

42 [Dem.] 59.85–86; Aischin. 1.183: "If any woman [who has been seduced] enters or adorns herself, (the law) orders whoever encounters her to tear her *himatia* and to rip off her jewelry and to beat her without killing or maiming her (τὸν ἐντυχόντα κελεύει καταρρηγνύναι τὰ ἱμάτια καὶ τὸν κόσμον ἀφαιρεῖσθαι καὶ τύπτειν, εἰργόμενον θανάτου καὶ τοῦ ἀνάπηρον ποιῆσαι) in order to humiliate her and to make her life unlivable." Τὰ ἱμάτια is normally translated as 'clothes' (cf. Hdt. 1.9; Pl. *Plt.* 279e), but the term can be very specific and refer to the mantle worn by a woman over her chiton. Does the law limit the punishment to the mantle and not include the chiton, which, if removed, would have left the woman naked? Or is it more general? Note that the term *himation* does not occur until the fifth century BCE. Canevaro 2013, 190–196 shows that the document at [Dem.] 59.87 is a forgery.

43 Malay and Petzl 2017, 1, ll. 15–20. Only one other inscription specifies the possibility for a *hetaira* to enter the sanctuary (*LSAM* no. 18, *CGRN* 211, Maionia in Lydia, 147/6 BCE) but it only alludes to the woman "having purified herself all around, as is customary" (probably with the blood of a piglet, as at Thyateira); no other details are listed, and sanctions are not specified on this sign.

44 On 'purity of the mind,' see I. Petrovic and A. Petrovic 2016. On having crimes weighing on one's conscience, often denoted with the terms *enthymios* or *enthymistos*, see Karila-Cohen 2010. For the divine punishment that could be perceived to have occurred after certain crimes, see also e.g. *I.Smyrna* 728, *LSAM* no. 84 (second–third century CE; exposure of a child: μὴ δὴ μήνειμα γένηται); more generally, see the so-called 'Confession stelai,' Petzl 1994 with several new examples in Petzl 2019. Other important cases are the regulations for the cult of Men at Sounion, *IG* II² 1365–1366, *LSCG* no. 55 (first century BCE–CE?), which state that anyone disrespecting or interfering with the cult would owe a debt to Men Tyrannos "for which it was not possible to atone;" 'purity of the mind' was also a desideratum in this cult (cf. *IG* II² 1366, ll. 11–12, 26).

45 See Parker 1983, 74–103 for pollution caused by sexual relations; cf. also Carbon 2018, with further references. For purity rules specifically concerning associations or other groups, see Carbon 2021.

46 For example, in a regulation from Elateia (*CGRN* 33, end of fifth century BCE), the clause γυναῖκα μὲ παρίμε[ν] may not exclude women from the Anakeion altogether, but rather from being present during dining and overnight camping (σκανεν̑), a subject mentioned in the preceding clause. Even in the sacred grove of Ares at Geronthrai, for instance, women were apparently only debarred from entry during the festival (Paus. 3.22.7: ἑορτὴν ... ἐν ᾗ ...); this probably implies that women could enter at other, unspecified times. On rules concerning the exclusion of women, see Cole 1992; Osborne 1993.

47 Ar. *Thesm.* 181–182, 625ff.

48 *LSCG* no. 127, ll. 7–10, *IG* XII.2 499, end of fourth century BCE. For a probably similar type of regulation concerning a women-only festival with only a male sacrificer being present and with an

There were also rules in place constraining the behavior of women during these kinds of festivals. For example, while the Thesmophoria were being held on Thasos, no woman was allowed to enter the neighboring sanctuary of Apollo Delios and Artemis, on whose door-frame (*parastas*) a series of decrees were inscribed to that effect.[49] The cult official (*hieropoios*) of Apollo was to make sure that the sanctuary remained locked during this period, and a woman who contravened this rule would have the offense weigh on her conscience. As a decree inscribed near the entrance to the Thesmophorion in the deme of Piraeus indicated, the *demarch* had to make sure that no rituals or assemblies of worshippers took place in the sanctuary outside of the expected festivals (Thesmophoria, etc.) and other occasions on which women traditionally and legitimately (*kata ta patria*) assembled; those breaking the rules were to be brought to court by the *demarch*.[50] In no case do we seem to find the *wholesale* and *permanent* exclusion of men or women as a category from a sanctuary.

Other specific types of exclusion were possible. We occasionally hear that priests and other officials who did not conform to the prescribed expectations concerning sacrificial prerogatives and votive offerings would be excluded from the sanctuary in which they had hitherto served.[51] Those who had committed a lesser offense might be excluded for a limited period of time. Rules could also concern the exclusions of animals. The famous regulation concerning what could be brought into the sanctuary of Alektrona at Ialysos is a case in point.[52] This decree of Ialysos published a law concerning what was forbidden to enter the sanctuary, and three copies of the text were inscribed and set up in prominent locations giving access to the sanctuary; introducing such things as a horse or donkey would necessitate purification of the sanctuary and the offering of a sacrifice afterward, or the one disobeying the rule would be liable to a charge of impiety. Smaller cattle could be brought in at lesser cost (1 obol per animal). Denunciations to the major civic officials (the *mastroi*) were encouraged by the law as a deterrent and as a means of policing the extra-urban sanctuary.

The aforementioned list of temporary exclusions from sanctuaries could be greatly expanded, notably with regard to purity regulations, but the enforcement of the rules in question is not always obvious.[53] The picture we have sketched here runs contrary to the image presented by many inclusive places of worship today (though of course several modern cults are quite restrictive too) or even by Pausanias' seemingly casual perusal of certain shrines in Greece. Visitors to any Greek sanctuary would have been well advised to arrive at an appropriate time and to become acquainted with the specific rules of the place. Otherwise, they might well find out on arrival that they were not welcome at all; or having entered unknowingly, they might be punished in different ways.

2   Maintaining Order in Sanctuaries

Inside the sanctuary, the logistics continued to be carefully defined and orchestrated for human participants. The task of maintaining order here was placed mainly in the hands of the priests and other officials of the sanctuary but might also be entrusted to officials of the *polis*. Combining a variety of concerns regarding conduct by worshippers on the Akropolis is a famous decree of Athens dated to the early fifth century BCE, the so-called 'Hekatompedon inscription.'[54] In order to safeguard the site, one of the treasurers is to remain on the Akropolis within the precinct on the required days; if he cannot, the *prytanis* is to stay there (ll. A16–18).[55] No one is to throw dung inside the Kekropeion or along the *hekatompedon*; if anyone does, the treasurers are to fine him up to 3 obols (ll. B10–13).[56] There appears to be a rule against baking in any oven—no doubt reflecting a widespread concern about possible damage from fire—and a fine of (100?) dr to be imposed by the treasurers, who are themselves fined

---

assembly of women involved, see *LSAM* no. 61, *CGRN* 97 (Mylasa, *c*.350–300 BCE). There, it appears that a post-sacrificial dinner may have included male participants, but the regulation also enacted sanctions against certain types of misbehavior (cf. ll. 10–16). For the role of a male attendant, sacrificer, or *mageiros*, in women-only festivals, see also, e.g., *NGSL*² no. 20, A, *CGRN* 38 (Chios, *c*.400 BCE), ll. 2–4; *LSAM* no. 6 (Chios, first–second century CE), ll. 1–3.

49   *I.Thasos* 3 4, *SEG* 56.1017, *c*.375–350 BCE.
50   *LSCG* no. 36, *CGRN* 78 (cf. also the *AIO* version), mid-fourth century BCE.
51   Cf. *CGRN* 42, ll. 6–7, Iasos, *c*.425–375 BCE.
52   *LSCG* no. 136, *CGRN* 90, *c*.350–300 BCE.
53   See, e.g., Horster 2019 on purity and *eukosmia*.
54   *IG* I³ 4, *AIO* 1692; cf. Butz 2010, 161–167.
55   An analogous situation is implied by the collection of rules and decrees regarding the Nikephorion, the sanctuary of Athena Nikephoros, issued by a *hieronomos* called Dionysios probably in post-Attalid Pergamon (*LSAM* no. 12, *CGRN* 212): at ll. 22–28, a *neokoros* is mentioned as one of the supervisors of the money-box in the sanctuary (on this subject, see below), while the *akra* itself was permanently guarded by a gatekeeper (πυλωρός), who received sacrificial prerogatives.
56   On sanitation in Greek sanctuaries, see notably Trümper in this volume.

if they allow such a thing to happen (ll. B14–17). This regulation is not only indicative of the wide range of concerns communities had regarding the behavior of worshippers, but also of the concrete steps that were taken to police important sanctuaries, particularly requiring sacred and civic officials to perform these tasks and empowering them to impose penalties, as well as penalizing these officials for failing to uphold their responsibilities.

An inscription found at Oropos and dated to 386–374 BCE contains detailed provisions about the policing duties of the priest of Amphiaraos.[57] During the time of highest frequentation, the priest is required to be present in the sanctuary from the end of winter until the ploughing season not fewer than ten days a month and not to be absent more than three days (ll. 2–6). The priest is to compel the *neokoros* to supervise the sanctuary and its visitors according to the law (ll. 6–8). The office of *neokoros*, whose wide-ranging duties often included permanent residence in sanctuaries and policing them, is attested at several sanctuaries throughout the Greek world.[58] At Oropos, the priest has the power to impose fines up to 5 dr for offenses and to seize the property (*enechyra lambaneto*) of those who do not pay (ll. 9–12).[59] If the offender pays, he should place the fine in the collection-box (*thesauros*) in the presence of the priest (ll. 12–13).[60] If someone commits an offense against a private individual in the sanctuary, the priest is to decide in cases up to 3 dr (ll. 13–16). If the amount is larger, the case is to be adjudicated in the place assigned by the laws, which should be the courts of the city (ll. 16–17).[61] The summons is to be made on the same day (as the trial) unless the defendant asks for a delay to the next day (ll. 18–20). The regulation at Oropos thus informs us about how the periodically present priest and the probably ever-present *neokoros* worked in tandem to maintain order in the sanctuary and control the behavior of worshippers, while more serious offenses would be relegated to the authority of the city.

In places like Oropos, crowd-control could become a significant issue. Major and well frequented sanctuaries required the physical presence of officials responsible for the supervision of the numerous worshippers.[62] A decree (*psephisma*) from Korope dated to around 100 BCE concerns rules for keeping order at the local oracle.[63] The generals and *nomophylakes* appointed *rhabdouchoi* (recall the 'police officers' at Olympia) to punish the disorderly (ll. 23–26).[64] Similarly, in the regulation of the deme of Paiania concerning festivals of Demeter, it is specified that the *hieropoioi* would carry *rhabdoi* (ῥαβδοχε̑ν) for maintaining order during festivals and could also order other people (hὸς ἂν κελεύοσιν) to act with them in this capacity, essentially as 'deputies.'[65] Once again, physical punishment was used not only as a deterrent, but also as an effective means of enforcement.

One of the most extensive set of regulations for maintaining order at a festival in a sanctuary are those for the Mysteries of Andania.[66] The regulation is a logistical compendium, of which we can only offer an overview here. For example, the law contains detailed rules about what women can wear during the Mysteries. If any woman violates these rules, the *gynaikonomos*, an official of the city of Messene, has the right to damage (or tear off?) the offending garment or accoutrement, which then becomes the property of the god (ll. 15–26; compare the treatment of the woman who had been seduced in Athens, discussed

---

57 *LSCG* no. 69, *CGRN* 75.
58 In these respects—the duties of the priest and the *neokoros* regarding the maintenance of order—the rules at Oropos are probably the most detailed preserved. To a certain degree, they anticipate later finds, such as the detailed regulation from Marmarini, which assigns purificatory duties to the *neokoros* alongside the priestess of the goddess, the female cult officials called φοιβατρίαι, and other participants in the cult (*CGRN* 225, A, 6–8, B, 2–6, 33–34, *c*.225–150 BCE). Most tellingly, the last of these clauses appears to imply that the *neokoros* was always expected to be present in the sanctuary, while, by contrast, the attendance of the φοιβατρίαι was not guaranteed (καθαίρειν δὲ τὸν νεωκόρον ταῦτα καὶ τῶν φοιβατριῶν ἥτις ἂμ παρῆι). On *neokoroi* in general, see the very useful discussion by Ricl 2011. As we discuss throughout this paper, *neopoiai* and other officials often have similar duties.
59 For the correct interpretation of the phrase *enechyra lambaneto*, see Harris 2008.
60 For the collection box, see *LSCG* no. 69, *CGRN* 75 ad loc., as well as Naiden 2020.
61 For similar rules about imposing fines, see *IG* I³ 82, ll. 24–28; Woodhead 1997, no. 56, l. 32.
62 Guards or guardians of sanctuaries are known in a variety of guises across the Greek world. At Epidauros, for example, we hear of guards (*phrouroi*) who were tasked with protecting the sanctuary and were compensated with some sacrificial portions (*IG* IV².1 40 and 41, *LSCG* no. 60, *CGRN* 34, end of fifth century BCE); guardians of the temple (*nauphylakes*) are found in later sources at the site (*IG* IV².1 393, 401–402, late second–early third century CE). The precise contours of *naophylakia* or *hierophylakia* are not well known.
63 *LSCG* no. 83, *Syll.*³ 1157.
64 Note that the rule does not make a distinction between free persons and slaves: both could apparently be subject to corporal punishment in such cases.
65 *CGRN* 25 (cf. also the *AIO* version), A, ll. 9–11, *c*.450–425 BCE.
66 *LSCG* no. 65, *CGRN* 222, probably dating to 23 CE. For a more detailed edition and commentary, see Gawlinski 2012. On the legal procedure, see Harter-Uibopuu 2002. For ll. 25–26, cf. the commentary of Gawlinski (2012, 132–133) on the difficulties in understanding the word λυμαίνεσθαι. The word has clear connotations of pollution, violence, and dishonor.

above). The Sacred Men (*hieroi*)—*ad hoc* officials probably selected by lot in Messene—are to enforce rules about the construction of tents (size, material, contents),[67] as well as to forbid the uninitiated from entering the area cordoned off, to publish signs about purity for those entering it, and to provide basins for initiates to perform the requisite lustrations (ll. 34–37). Controlling the worshippers with physical violence or the threat of this and other punishments once again played a part. All those participating must keep *euphemia*, 'ritual silence' or 'seemly speech,' during the ceremony and obey orders. The Sacred Men can scourge anyone who disobeys (ll. 39–41). To assist the Sacred Men there were 20 *rhabdophoroi* under their command (ll. 41–45). The Sacred Men also punished the crime of theft and other offenses (ll. 75–78). If anyone caught someone cutting wood in the sanctuary, he was to bring the offender to the Sacred Men, who would flog slaves and collect a fine from free men, half of which went to the informant (ll. 78–80). The Sacred Men were to mark out a place for selling, but the *agoranomos*, a city official, was to enforce rules about unadulterated goods and weights and measures.[68] If he caught offenders, he was to whip slaves and to fine free men 20 dr but do so in the presence of the Sacred Men (ll. 99–103). There are similar provisions concerning water for the *agoranomos* to enforce (ll. 103–6).[69]

Several other rules concern proper behavior during festivals, which always require a group of cult officials to maintain order and ensure that the rules are observed.[70] In Athens, a board of *hieropoioi* was charged with the performance of the procession during the Hephaisteia;[71] anyone breaking the expected order and decorum (*kosmos*) of the occasion could be liable to a fine of up to 50 dr under the authority of the *hieropoioi*, who were responsible for reporting the guilty party (perhaps to the *praktores*, for exaction of the fine; ll. 24–26); if heavier fines were considered, these would need to be brought before a court (the *dikasterion* of the archon, ll. 27–28).[72] Groups, such as associations, are also known to have published rules that were concerned notably with maintaining order or due decorum in their sanctuaries, specifically during celebrations.[73]

In addition to the aforementioned laws, Athenians also had a procedure called *probole* against injustices committed in sanctuaries during festivals.[74] This procedure was first created for offenses at the Dionysia and was later extended to cover transgressions at the Eleusinian Mysteries.[75] A meeting of the Assembly was held after the festival (in the case of the Dionysia, around 20 Elaphebolion) at which anyone who wished could bring a charge against an offender. For instance, at the Dionysia of 346, Meidias punched Demosthenes in the middle of the theater after attempting to destroy the costumes for his chorus, and Demosthenes initiated a vote against him in the Assembly.[76] The charge could also be brought by foreigners. When Evander of Thespiai seized Menippos from Karia during the Eleusinian Mysteries, Menippos brought a *probole* in the Assembly because it was illegal to seize debtors during the festival.[77] In such cases, the Assembly would either pass a vote of censure (*katacheirotonia*) or not.[78] This censure was only an expression of disapproval and did not impose a fine or other punishment. The person who proposed the vote could then bring

---

67 On accommodation and camping in Greek sanctuaries, see again Ekroth and Scahill in this volume.

68 On *agoranomoi*, see Migeotte 2005 and the essays in Capdetrey and Hasenohr 2012. For markets during festivals, see also Lo Monaco and Chankowski in this volume.

69 For utilitarian uses of water in Greek sanctuaries, see Klingborg in this volume.

70 Cf., e.g., an allusion to a punishment inflicted by the *demarchs* against anyone behaving out of order during the contest of the Artemisia at Eretria, *LSCG* no. 92, *CGRN* 91 (*c.*340 BCE), ll. 24–26; this is to be made "according to the law," but the precise details remain murky to us.

71 *CGRN* 43, *AIO* 1304, 421/0 BCE. On this text, see also Makres 2014, suggesting that it deals with the Theseia (critiqued in *AIO*, *CGRN*, and by Harris 2022, 70, n. 31).

72 Compare also the requirement that the *hieropoioi* of Athena punish anyone who was disobedient with regard to the suitable conduct of the procession of the Lesser Panathenaia "with the fines specified in the laws" (*IG* II³ 447, *CGRN* 92, RO no. 81, *AIO*, *c.*335–330 BCE; cf. Shear 2021, 83–115). Numerous regulations from the island of Kos grant priestly personnel or occasionally other individuals the right to impose fines "exactly as if in fulfilment of a legal verdict" (ἁ πρᾶξις ἔστω ... καθάπερ ἐγ δίκας): cf. *i.a.* *IG* XII.4 72, *CGRN* 148, ll. 75–78, *IG* XII.4 319, ll. 1–2; and cf. the examples in n. 95 infra.

73 On the subject of order in associations, see now the discussion of Arnaoutoglou 2021. Cf. also the rules on correct behavior published by the Labyadai at Delphi (*CGRN* 82, D, ll. 19–29, *c.*400–350 BCE): those persons disregarding the rules of the group would be fined, but those contesting the fine could swear an oath in order to be acquitted (if truly transgressors, they would thus incur a religious punishment instead); absentees from the group assembly were also liable to a small fine (1 obol); a disturbance at the assembly would lead to a similar fine.

74 On this procedure, see Harris 2019a; cf. Harris in Canevaro 2013, 211–223, showing that the documents at Dem. 21.8 and 10 are forgeries.

75 Dem. 21.175–176.

76 Incidents: Dem. 21.13–21; vote: Dem. 21.1–2.

77 Incident: Dem. 21.175; *probole*: Dem. 21.11.

78 Aischin. 3.52.

a private action or a public action against the offender.⁷⁹ For instance, after the vote in the Assembly, Menippos brought a private action (*ex idiou pragmatos*) for damages against Evander, and the court awarded him a judgment cancelling the payment to Evander and charging him for the time Menippos was forced to remain in Athens.⁸⁰ On the other hand, after the Assembly voted to condemn Meidias, Demosthenes waited two years and brought a public action (*graphe hybreos*) for outrage against Meidias in 346 BCE, which may have resulted in a fine paid to the state.⁸¹

Where these forms of policing were not possible for various reasons, we often find rewards for those who denounce transgressors. For example, we may consider the late Archaic sign at the *stadion* of Delphi, which forbade carrying wine out of the racecourse (*dromos*), where it was presumably both offered to the gods and drunk.⁸² This racecourse lay to the west of the main *temenos*, as a sort of appendage to it, and controlling behavior here may accordingly have required a special rule. The regulation apparently specifies where a particular kind of ritual drinking was to take place, though it is not clear if it testifies, e.g., to a need to control drunken crowds and the possible unrest that they would create.⁸³ The inscribed rule specified both a religious sanction—propitiation and a sacrifice—and a fine; for the latter, half of the fine of 5 dr was awarded to the one who had denounced the guilty party. In some cases, as mentioned above and discussed further below, the authorities could not effectively police sacred norms and had to leave enforcement to the individual's conscience, use curses, or find still other means of circumscribing the participation of worshippers in the cult.

3 Regulating Human Actions in Sanctuaries: Sacrifice and Dedications

Visitors who entered sanctuaries would be expected to make an offering of some kind and/or offer a sacrifice, even if they were casual passersby or sightseers.⁸⁴ The priest and other cult officials were principally responsible for controlling the rituals performed in sanctuaries, such as dedication and sacrifice, and the products of these rituals (objects, meat, etc.).⁸⁵ Priests were typically in charge of one of the most important gestures in the ritual, placing the *hiera*, the sacred portions on the altar for burning or on a cult-table. This obligation, for example, is repeatedly stated in the priestly contracts from the island of Kos.⁸⁶ Priestesses or priests could occasionally appoint a deputy (a *hyphiereus* or *hyphiereia*, someone to *proierateuein*, or the like) to act in this capacity.⁸⁷

What would happen if a visitor came to a sanctuary but failed to find the person responsible for sacrificing? In some smaller or originally private sanctuaries, such as the cult of Men founded by Xanthos at Sounion, there might be no replacement for this fundamental role of the priest or leader of the cult.⁸⁸ The regulation from Sounion specifies that no one is to make a sacrifice without the founder of the cult (Xanthos) or his appointed successor being present. In most other sanctuaries, worshippers might only perform the sacrificial rites and place the *hiera* in specific circumstances, such as when the priest was absent.

The regulation from the Amphiareion at Oropos discussed above indicates that a priest was not always expected to be present at every sacrifice. This regulation makes it explicitly clear that the priest, when present,

---

79   Note that after he brought his *probole* against Meidias, Demosthenes (21.28) states that he had a choice between bringing a private action or a public action. For analysis of this key passage, see Harris 2019c.
80   Dem. 21.176.
81   Dem. 21.28.
82   *CGRN* 12, *c*.530–500 BCE.
83   Rules against the presence of drunken individuals are occasionally found in other contexts, such as the Greek gymnasion, cf. esp. *NGSL*² no. 14 (Beroia, *c*.200–170 BCE), B, ll. 26–28: "Those who ought not to share the gymnasion: The following shall not strip off (to exercise) in the gymnasion: a slave, a freedman and their sons, an *apalaistros*, a prostitute, anyone of those who have business at the marketplace, a drunk, and an insane person." But a certain level of inebriation was presumably tolerated during lodging and banquets in sanctuaries: we do not otherwise tend to find behavioral rules specifically about wine-drinking in connection with Greek sanctuaries. For perspectives on wine-drinking in sanctuaries, see van den Eijnde in this volume.

84   For a particularly clear expression of this expectation, see the example cited supra n. 18 for further references. For gods taking revenge after a sacrilege in their sanctuaries, see for example Hdt. 6.134–136 (Militades, a man, enters a Thesmophorion of Demeter); Apollod. *Epit.* E. 6.6 (Athena and Poseidon kill Ajax after the desecration of Athena's statue and the rape of Cassandra in her temple); Paus. 3.23.3–5 (Apollo takes vengeance on Menophanes and Mithradates after the sack of Delos) and discussion of this passage and its implications in Padilla Peralta 2020.
85   On the sources of priestly authority and the subject of ritual expertise, see esp. Stravrianopoulou 2009. On the consumption of sacrificial meat in sanctuaries, see notably MacKinnon in this volume; for the treatment of hides derived from sacrificial animals, cf. Pakkanen in this volume.
86   Cf., e.g., *CGRN* 147 (*c*.250–200 BCE), ll. 10–11, 117–118, 124–126; 164 (*c*.200–150 BCE), ll. 8–9; 208 (*c*.150–101 BCE), ll. 18–19.
87   See, e.g., the sale of the priesthood of Dionysos Thyllophoros on Kos, *IG* XII.4 304 (*c*.200–150 BCE), ll. 39–40.
88   *IG* II² 1366, *LSCG* no. 55, ll. 12–15, first century BCE or CE?

was in charge of placing the *hiera* on the altar and making the prayer, all the more so when public sacrifices were concerned.[89] When the priest was absent, however, the worshippers could take matters into their own hands and proceed with the sacrifice. Still, things needed to be done correctly, and certain expectations were imposed upon worshippers. At the Amphiareion, some form of oversight of the sacrifice might still have taken place in the absence of the priest, perhaps on the part of the *neokoros* or other officials of this kind since the skin of the sacrificial animal was deemed sacred according to the regulation and thus belonged to the sanctuary.

Some sanctuaries were more remote or less regularly frequented than Oropos. A pair of celebrated examples about what might be expected to take place in such cases comes from Chios. One of the regulations, for the cult of (Zeus) Pelinaios (on the principal mountain of the island), specifies that if the priest seemed to be absent, the worshipper was expected to call out three times: only then could he or she perform the sacrifices themselves; the worshipper was also prevented from providing anything else to any third party (who might implicitly be attempting to usurp the priest's authority).[90] In this regulation, the priest's prerogatives and the right of the worshipper to act on his/her own behalf should the priest be absent were enforced: a fine of 5 staters was levied on those failing to follow this procedure. However, it is not clear how, in the absence of any authority figure, the fine could be exacted, unless the rule implicitly relied on informants. Most probably, the rather heavy fine of 5 staters must have acted principally as a deterrent. In the other case from Chios regarding the privileges of the priest of Herakles, a cult that was connected with a *genos*, a private worshipper was also to call out for the priest.[91] Should he be absent, a deputy priest would be selected by lot, presumably from among the members of the *genos*. No fine was specified in this case, perhaps because a replacement for the priest was expected to be found, and the circle of worshippers was relatively small (restricted mostly or perhaps exclusively to members of the *genos* in question?). In both of these instances from Chios, as in many other regulations concerning priests and priestesses, including contracts of sale of these offices, the aim was to give priests their due (normally called by the term *geras*): a specific set of portions from the sacrifice and occasionally other prerogatives.

In some cases, sacrifices are known to have been declared illegal or literally "unsacrificed."[92] When the Spartan king Agesilaos attempted to sacrifice at Aulis before setting off on his campaign to Asia Minor in 396 BCE, much as Agamemnon was thought to have done before him, the Boiotarchs sent cavalry to forbid him from sacrificing and to prevent him from obtaining the results of the rituals, which were essentially completed: the horsemen literally threw Agesilaos' offerings from the altar (καὶ οἷς ἐνέτυχον ἱεροῖς τεθυμένοις διέρριψαν ἀπὸ τοῦ βωμοῦ).[93] These actions can, of course, be attributed to political tension between Boiotia and Sparta, but they might also point to underlying rules about how—if at all—foreigners could sacrifice at Aulis (supra p. 39 on exclusion of foreigners). Epigraphical evidence about sacrifices being rejected by political authorities is also found. On Kos, where sacrificial perquisites were so consistently and precisely defined in priestly contracts issued by the *polis*, we occasionally also find a clause that for those who did not offer the portions (*gere*) that had been prescribed for the cult personnel, the entire ritual would be declared invalid: literally "the sacred portions are to be unsacrificed" (τὰ ἱερὰ ἄθυτα ἔστω).[94] Worshippers therefore needed to pay a close eye to this aspect of logistics or their ritual efforts would end up being invalidated.

Priests or priestesses who themselves broke these rules, taking more than their due, would tend to be punished even more heavily than worshippers who omitted one of their customary *gere*.[95] For example, another priestly contract from Chios, though more fragmentary, appears to state that any worshipper removing one of the prerogatives would owe a fine of 10 dr; by contrast, if the

---

89 See again *CGRN* 75, *c*.386–374 BCE, ll. 25–32.
90 *CGRN* 36, end of fifth century BCE. On absent priests, see also Gawlinski and Wallensten in this volume.
91 *CGRN* 50, *c*.400–350 BCE.

92 The subject of a sacrifice being rejected by a divinity, for different reasons, is another matter; on this, see recently Naiden 2013, 131–182. There also could be elaborate rules for removing an illicit sacrifice (e.g., of a forbidden animal species) and purifying the altar, cf. *CGRN* 99, A, ll. 26–32 (Kyrene, *c*.325–300 BCE).
93 Xen. *Hell.* 3.4.3–4.
94 Cf. *IG* XII.4 304, ll. 38–39 and 326, ll. 66–67, two versions (*c*.200–150 and 100–50 BCE, respectively) of the sale of the priesthood of Dionysos Thyllophoros. See also the restorations at *IG* XII.4 297 and 337, l. 14, fragmentary Hellenistic *diagraphai* for priesthoods of unknown gods.
95 The subject is less often treated in the evidence, however. For worshippers fined for removing one or more of the priestly *gere*, see also the clauses found in the priestly contracts from Kos, e.g., *CGRN* 142 (*c*.100–50 BCE), ll. 20–23 (50 dr, which the priest could exact "exactly as if in fulfilment of a legal verdict"—see supra n. 72) and *CGRN* 208, l. 20 (when a group of people failed to sacrifice, they had to pay 30 dr for each portion (of the γέρη) that was not given to the priest; a similar clause concerning the legal validity of the fine applied). See also *CGRN* 249 (Miletos, *c*.15–100 CE), C, ll. 10–12 (12 dr).

priestess who had purchased the office took more than her due, she would owe double that, a fine of 10 staters (i.e., 20 dr).[96] Even more drastic punishments are attested: as mentioned above, the priest of Zeus Megistos at Iasos who failed to conform to the law about his dues would be debarred from the sanctuary.[97]

Turning away from sacrifice, we move to dedications. Could worshippers simply add a votive object to a sanctuary as they pleased? A substantial number of inscriptions are concerned not only with the complex question of the placement of dedications in sanctuaries, but also with the protection of these objects as sacred property. A now fragmentary but originally probably quite comprehensive law concerning the portico (*pastas*) of Attalos II is contained in a decree of the Delphic Amphictyony: not only did this forbid worshippers from setting up dedications in this area, but also camping/dining and probably the lighting of fires; a fine sacred to Apollo was imposed on those contravening the rule.[98] Other regulations concerning dedications tended to be passed as the need for them arose. An interesting decree from Hellenistic Laodikeia-by-the-Sea (Beirut) reflects the concerns of a group of priests about the increasing number of dedications in their privately owned sanctuary of Isis and Sarapis: the city was asked to confirm that the tax it imposed on dedications concerned the objects themselves, not their placement on private land; thus, the priests retained their authority over the private sanctuary.[99] Other rules were also concerned with decluttering and combatting the enthusiasms of worshippers. A decree of Rhodes restricted any dedications in the walkways (*peripatoi*) or the lower part of the *temenos* of Asklepios, which had no doubt become overcrowded; urban officials called *astynomoi* were empowered to relocate dedications that contravened this rule.[100] A decree of Miletos concerning one of the stoas of the sanctuary of Apollo Delphinios—conspicuously inscribed on the architrave of this building—restricted the placement of tablets (*pinakes*) or other votives by worshippers to the lower part of walls, and prevented them from being affixed to the woodwork or the columns of the building.[101] A fine of 10 staters sacred to the god Apollo was imposed on any infractions; how the fine was administered or who was responsible for its exaction is not explicitly stated, but through its placement, the regulation clearly addressed a broad audience.

As the texts from Laodikeia-by-the-Sea and Rhodes make clear, the authority of the cult personnel was crucial in supervising dedicatory practices and protecting dedications. While some dedications, namely silver money that was deposited in the sanctuary, would be directly given to the priest of Zeus Megistos at Iasos, any other kinds remained the property of the sanctuary and were administered by a separate board of officials, the *neopoiai*.[102] Treasurers were, of course, responsible for maintaining detailed accounts of dedications in sanctuaries, such as those on the Athenian Akropolis and Delos; periodically, votives could be recycled or metal objects melted down.[103]

Closer to the subject of policing, the decree concerning the Thesmophorion in the Piraeus mentioned above makes it clear that the priestess' supervision was necessary for those wishing to install sacred objects of any kind in the sanctuary (*hiera enidreuontai*) except during certain festivals or other customary occasions (when the priestess of Demeter would, in any case, be expected to be present); offenders would be prosecuted by the *demarch*, as outlined earlier.[104] A regulation from the Rhodian fort at Loryma in southwest Asia Minor sought to protect the dedications in a local sanctuary and may have mentioned the role of the priest as the cult official responsible for introducing new dedications or removing old ones.[105] As far as dedications were concerned, priests or other officials were therefore closely involved in administering these logistical aspects of the rituals enacted by worshippers and the resulting property of the sanctuary.

---

96 *CGRN* 37, *c*.425–375 BCE, ll. 14–16. A similar fine for a priestess taking more than her due appears to be specified in a contemporaneous Chian text, *CGRN* 38, B, ll. 9–11, but the conclusion of this passage is difficult to understand and could be restored differently, perhaps as a specific fine (see the commentary in *CGRN* ad loc.).
97 *CGRN* 42, *c*.425–375 BCE.
98 *LSS* no. 43, *c*.218 BCE.
99 Cf. the detailed discussion of Sosin 2005, also collecting other evidence from across the Greek world about the placement of dedications.
100 *LSS* no. 107, third century BCE.
101 *LSS* no. 123, third century BCE.
102 *CGRN* 42, *c*.425–375 BCE.
103 Cf., e.g., Wagner 1997; see also Aleshire 1991, esp. 94 on the role of priests. For a specific order to melt down dedications in the sanctuary of the Heros Iatros in Athens, see *LSCG* no. 41 (221/0 BCE); compare *LSCG* no. 80 (Oropos, third century BCE), discussed below.
104 *LSCG* no. 36, *CGRN* 78 (cf. also the version in *AIO*), mid-fourth century BCE. The role of a priest in controlling dedications also appears in another regulation from Athens (*LSCG* no. 43, second century BCE), though is heavily dependent on restorations.
105 *LSAM* no. 74, third century BCE. The responsibility of the priest is again dependent on a restoration in the final lines of the text.

4 Accountability of Religious Officials in Sanctuaries

In the *Politics*, Aristotle considers priests and those in charge of sanctuaries as civic officials: like all officials of the state, religious officials were subject to the law and accountable to the Council and Assembly.[106] At Athens, all priests of public cults had to submit their accounts after their term of office.[107] From a legal point of view, priests and other religious officials were just as accountable to the *polis* as other public officials. Their religious function did not give them a privileged position vis-à-vis the Assembly and the courts. Apollodoros mentions the case of a priest being convicted in an Athenian court for not carrying out his religious duties in the prescribed manner.[108] In the lengthy decree concerning Eleusinian first-offerings, the *hieropoioi* of Eleusis were to be fined for failure of their duty if they did not receive the offerings of crops within five days after the donation had been announced.[109]

Examples from outside of Athens amply parallel these observations. The accountability of religious officials in terms of their normally expected duty—especially in terms of logistical supervision—is repeatedly made clear. The aforementioned law of Korope, dated to around 100 BCE, fines officials who do not carry out their duties supervising the oracle.[110] A law of Eretria dated to the fourth or third century BCE contains rules about the festival of the Asklepieia and imposes a penalty of 5 dr on each of the *hieropoioi* who do not follow these prescriptions.[111] In a regulation from Chalketor dated to the second century BCE, instructions are given to a board of officials (perhaps *neopoiai*) to distribute meat to the participants; if they do not follow the rules, they are to pay the expenses for the festival.[112]

Allowances could be made for absences in certain cases, a subject already introduced above with the examples from Chios and Oropos. In the case of major duties, such as the oversight of a festival or celebration, a suitable replacement had to be found, and the officials were held accountable for this. For example, in an inscription dated to the third century BCE from Samos, the *epimenioi* appointed by the *chiliasteroi* are to supervise the sacrifice and gathering of worshippers; if they are absent, they are to appoint someone to perform their task. If, however, someone elected does not carry out his duty, he is to pay a fine of 200 dr imposed by the *nomophylakes* and other *epimenioi*.[113]

The religious duties expected could also be more specific or *ad hoc*, but the officials were still held to their task. A decree of the Boiotian Federation about melting down dedications imposes a fine on any elected official, either *hierarchai*, *syllogeus* or Treasurers who violate the rules.[114] A decree from Halasarna dated to around 200 BCE instructs various officials to draw up a new list of those qualified to participate in religious rites.[115] If any of these officials does not obey, he is to owe 500 dr to Apollo.

Failure to impose the required punishment on offenders was itself threatened with punishment. In an official act at Olympia concerning the protection of the γροφεύς Patrias, the accused was to be banished.[116] A series of officials successively appear as responsible for proclaiming and enacting the sanctions—the *basileis* and their head, the *hellanodikai*, the *damiourgoi*; failures in their duty would be punished with heavy fines payable to Zeus Olympios.[117] Another inscription from Thasos of the

---

106 Arist. *Pol.* 1322b, 17–25. For the accountability of officials in the Greek city-states, see Fröhlich 2004.
107 Aischin. 3.18.
108 [Dem.] 59.116. Mikalson 2016, 201 believes that priests were only accountable in financial matters, but the evidence of Apollodoros and the inscriptions examined here shows that they also could be punished for not carrying out their religious duties. Though it probably belongs in special circumstances (perhaps a military catastrophe or more probably an earthquake), a late third–early second century BCE text from Iasos explicitly states that private individuals had the right to accuse priests and other relevant magistrates before the *prostatai* in order that the administration of sanctuaries be correctly performed according to ancestral tradition and the laws: cf. Fabiani 2019, ll. 3–8.
109 Clinton 2005–2008, no. 28, *CGRN* 31, OR no. 141 (cf. also the version in *AIO*), ll. 18–21, *c*.435 BCE?
110 *LSCG* no. 83, ll. 28–30 [*rhabdophoroi*], 61–63 [*exetastai*].
111 *LSCG* no. 93, ll. 29–31. The examples of fines imposed on officials for failures in their duties could, of course, be multiplied: for example, a regulation about the Eleusinian Mysteries dated to the first century BCE instructs the *mystagogoi* about the procession from Athens to Eleusis—if one of the *mystagogoi* fails to follow the rules, he is subject to the fines indicated (*LSS* no. 15, ll. 40–43); in an inscription from Ephesos dated to the third century CE, the *prytanis* who omits certain details of the prescribed rituals is to pay a fine of ten staters (*LSS* no. 121, ll. 25–30).
112 *LSAM* no. 79, *CGRN* 183, ll. 8–10.
113 *LSCG* no. 122, ll. 1–5 and 6–8 respectively.
114 *LSCG* no. 70, ll. 48–52.
115 *LSCG* no. 173, ll. 110–114.
116 Minon 2007, no. 20, *c*.475–450 BCE.
117 Once again, the parallels are many: for example, a regulation from Lebena of the second century BCE requires the *iarorgos* to exact a fine; if he does not, he must pay the fine himself (*LSCG* no. 144, A, ll. 5–6). A law of Tegea dated to the fourth century BCE requires that a *hieromnemon* who does not fine offenders must pay 1 dr and is cursed (*LSCG* no. 67, ll. 4–5; for discussion of this text, see Chandezon 2003, 33–40 and especially now Chandezon in this volume). Compare also an inscription from Euboia, which starts with a fragmentary rule about a sacred grove and imposes a penalty of 500 dr on the *demarch* who does not receive an oath or distrain offenders (*LSCG* no. 91, ll. 2–6).

fourth century BCE orders the *agoranomos* and the priest of Asklepios to ensure that a piece of public land (*chorion*) next to the garden of Herakles is kept clean by the lessee. If they do not, they are to owe a fine of a *hemiektos* sacred to Asklepios per day (ll. 6–10). The *apologoi* are to try the case; if these officials fail to do so, i.e., if they neglect their duty and do not try the case, they themselves are to owe the fine (l. 10).[118] Rules concerning accommodation and cleanliness in a sanctuary also conform to this pattern. A law of Arkesine forbids any foreigner to camp in the Heraion and stipulates a fine of 10 dr a day on the *neokoros* who does not drive them out.[119] An inscription from Epidauros about keeping the sanctuary clean instructs the *hieromnamones* to judge those violating the rules. If they do not, they are to each owe a fine of 100 dr.[120]

These numerous examples underscore the accountability of religious officials and the punishments that could be imposed on them for failing in their prescribed duty, notably with regard to policing. The law about the Mysteries at Andania prescribes several penalties for religious officials who do not carry out their tasks or violate rules.[121] The Sacred Men and the Sacred Women had to swear an oath to carry out the Andanian Mysteries justly and honestly (ll. 1–6). If any of these officials did not swear the oath, the secretary was to impose a fine of 1,000 dr (ll. 6–8). If any of the *rhabdophoroi* did not follow the rules about their duties, he was to be judged by the Sacred Men and excluded from the Mysteries (ll. 43–45). The Five elected by the people were to handle funds acquired during the Mysteries (ll. 45–46) assisted by the *argyroskopos*, whose duty was probably to check for counterfeits (ll. 47–48).[122] After the Mysteries, the Five had to report to the *synedroi* and deliver their accounts to the *epimeletes* (ll. 48–51). If they did not pay the funds to the Treasurer, they were subject to prosecution and had to pay double the amount missing and an additional 1,000 dr (ll. 51–52; cf. ll. 55–59). To protect the funds, an entrenchment clause that outlawed proposals to divert the money to other purposes was inserted, and this addition included penalties for the proposer and the Treasurer (ll. 60–63).[123]

In other words, while sanctuaries were sacred ground, this did not place priests and other religious officials beyond the long arm of the law. Officials were responsible for policing sanctuaries, and they themselves would be held accountable for failing to punish transgressors. From worshippers visiting sanctuaries to the officials responsible for policing their visit, the ancient Greek sanctuary was a carefully regulated environment.

5 Conclusions

Three main conclusions arise from the four principal parts of this essay. First, as in the rest of the *polis*, Greek sanctuaries empowered specific officials to enforce important regulations designed for logistical purposes: excluding banned individuals or groups, maintaining order (especially during festivals), and generally securing the good will of the gods. This related to long-standing traditions or norms of behavior preserved orally or in writing. Policing sanctuaries was normally a matter of civic regulation; private sanctuaries had their own structures, but ones that were either closely modelled or dependent on the institutions of the *polis*.[124] Distinctive circumstances could grant the role of policing to private individuals, as when sanctuaries allowed individuals to take charge of sacrifices, but such occasions tended to be limited or exceptional (aside from, e.g., incentives offered for denunciations, which were a common practice in most contexts in the ancient Greek world). The law about seduced women at Athens is one such remarkable case. Other outliers were sanctuaries that were less visited or which belonged to sub-civic groups, associations, or private individuals. Moreover, some matters that would be hard to detect or regulate were left to the conscience of the offender or were the subject of curses, a strategy also employed by the *polis* to enforce norms.[125]

Second, logistical aspects, such as maintaining order in sanctuaries, were often in the hands of *polis* officials and institutions, just as they were in other parts of the *polis*.[126] The decree about the Sacred Orgas provides a good illustration: the rules were to be enforced by the

---

118 *LSCG* no. 115.
119 *LSCG* no. 101, *CGRN* 234, B, third century BCE. On accommodation, see again Ekroth and Scahill in this volume.
120 *LSS* no. 24, ll. 4–7. On cleanliness and good order or appearance (*eukosmia*) in the sanctuary, see further Horster 2019, notably discussing Euripides' *Ion*. On sanitation specifically, see also Trümper in this volume.
121 *LSCG* no. 65, *CGRN* 222; cf. Gawlinski 2012.
122 Deshours (2006, 85), followed by Gawlinski (2012, 158), believes that this official assessed the value of different coinages, but the suffix *-skopos* indicates that this official inspected coins and did not exchange them. He thus was similar to the *dokimastes* at Athens. For this official and his task, see Feyel 2009, 86–111.

123 On entrenchment clauses, see Harris 2006, 22–25 with the literature cited there.
124 See Harris 2021, 28–31. For the rules of a phratry imitating the rules of the polis, see again Joyce 2021.
125 Rubinstein 2007.
126 Cf. Harris 2013, 21–59.

Areopagos, the general for the countryside, the *peripolarchoi*, the *demarchs*, the Council of five hundred, and any Athenian who wished to do so. At Athens, the Council played a major role in administering religious festivals. For instance, according to Andokides, there was a law inscribed on stone in the city Eleusinion that anyone who placed a suppliant bough on the altar during the Mysteries would pay a fine of 1,000 dr.[127] As Andokides' account shows, accusations were brought before the Council, which imposed the fine. Many of the examples collected in the preceding section (4) demonstrate that this conclusion also applied outside of Athens. In a recently published inscription from Epidauros of the fourth century BCE, a theft of material from the sanctuary was reported to the building commissioners (*epistatai tou ergou*), the *hiaromnamones* (magistrates of the state responsible for the administration of the sanctuary), and the priests, but tried in the civic court of the Three Hundred.[128] Even in rare cases when priests took the initiative to publish regulations about order in sanctuaries, as did the priest of Apollo Erithaseos in Athens, they clearly did so by relying on official enactments of the *polis*.[129]

Third, the rule that all officials are accountable—a key tenet of the rule of law—extended to priests and other religious officials. Perrin-Saminadayar puts it very well: "les prêtres athéniens étaient considérés exactement comme les autres détenteurs d'une *archè* dans la cité, c'est-à-dire qu'ils n'étaient ni mis sur un piédestal, ni tenus à l'écart."[130] Sanctuaries are thus not to be viewed as outside the *polis*, but as part of the *polis* when it comes to enforcing norms.[131] They were especially carefully and precisely regulated spaces. The officials who were tasked with policing sanctuaries were responsible for fulfilling this expectation, just as the worshippers they supervised needed to adhere to precise codes of conduct.

---

127 Andok. 1.116; cf. 110.
128 Kritzas and Prignitz 2020.
129 *IG* II² 1362, *LSCG* no. 37, *AIO* (cf. also *Axon* 3.1 (2019) 93–108); punishments in the case of a slave involved 50 lashes and reporting the name of the offender to his master according to a public decree (κατὰ τὸ ψήφισ[μ]α τῆς βουλῆς καὶ τοῦ δήμου τοῦ Ἀθηναίων, ll. 12–13); in the case of a free man, the priest had to collaborate with the *demarch* in order to exact the stated fine of 50 dr and to report the name of the offender, again according to an official decree of Athens. The case of the *hieronomos* Dionysios at Pergamon (*LSAM* no. 12, *CGRN* 212, after 133 BCE; supra n. 55) is an analogous example: he collected a series of purity regulations followed by two official decrees of the state.
130 Perrin-Saminadayar 2012, 148.
131 See further Harris 2021.

Acknowledgments

We were not originally participants in the conference from which this volume has resulted, but we both attended and profitably engaged in its proceedings. We are very grateful to the editors for their invitation to contribute this paper, as well as for their helpful suggestions and revisions. A version of the essay was given at the Athens Greek Religion Seminar of the Swedish Institute on 12 December 2022. We warmly thank Jenny Wallensten and the other participants for their comments.

Works Cited

Aleshire, S.B. 1991. *Asklepios at Athens: Epigraphic and Prosopographic Essays on the Athenian Healing Cults*. Amsterdam.

Arnaoutoglou, I. 2021. "Greek thorybos, Roman eustatheia: The Normative Universe of Athenian Cult Associations." In *Private Associations in the Ancient Greek World: Regulations and the Creation of Group Identity*, edited by V. Gabrielsen and M.C.D. Paganini, 144–162. Cambridge.

Bommelaer, J.-F., and Laroche, D. 2015. *Guide de Delphes: le site*. Athens.

Butz, P.A. 1996. "Prohibitionary inscriptions, ξένοι, and the influence of the early Greek polis." In *The role of religion in the early Greek polis*, edited by R. Hägg, 75–95. Stockholm.

Butz, P.A. 2010. *The Art of the Hekatompedon Inscription and the Birth of the Stoikhedon Style*. Leiden.

Canevaro, M. 2013. (with E.M. Harris) *The Documents in the Attic Orators: Laws and Decrees in the Public Speeches of the Demosthenic Corpus*. Oxford.

Capdetrey, L., and C. Hasenohr. 2012. *Agoranomes et édiles, institutions des marchés antiques*. Bordeaux.

Carbon, J.-M. 2018. "Introduction: Probing the 'Incubation Chamber.'" In *Purity and Purification in the Ancient Greek World: Texts, Rituals and Norms*, edited by J.-M. Carbon and S. Peels-Matthey, 11–20. Liège.

Carbon, J.-M. 2021. "The Place of Purity: Groups and Associations, Authority and Sanctuaries." In *Private Associations in the Ancient Greek World: Regulations and the Creation of Group Identity*, edited by V. Gabrielsen and M.C.D. Paganini, 86–116. Cambridge.

Chandezon, C. 2003. *L'élevage en Grèce (fin V^e–fin Ier s. a.C.), l'apport des sources épigraphiques*. Bordeaux.

Clinton, K. 2005–2008. *Eleusis: The Inscriptions on Stone: Documents of the Sanctuary of the Two Goddesses and Public Documents of the Deme*. Athens.

Cole, S.G. 1992. "Γυναιξὶ οὐ θέμις: Gender Difference in the Greek Leges Sacrae." *Helios* 19: 104–122.

Corbett, P.E. 1970. "Greek Temples and Greek Worshippers: The Literary and Archaeological Evidence." *BICS* 17: 149–158.

Deshours, N. 2006. *Les mystères d'Andania. Étude d'épigraphie et d'histoire religieuse*. Bordeaux.

Fabiani, R. 2019. "*Kathoti kai proteron*: un contributo all'interpretazione di I.Iasos 219." In *Forme del sacro. Scritti in memoria di Doro Levi*, edited by F. Berti, 111–128. Athens.

Feyel, C. 2009. *Δοκιμασία, la place et le rôle de l'examen préliminaire dans les institutions des cités grecques*. Nancy.

Fröhlich, P. 2004. *Les cités grecques et le contrôle des magistrats (IVe–Ier siècle avant J.-C.)*. Paris.

Gawlinski, L. 2012. *The Sacred Law of Andania: A New Text with Commentary*. Berlin.

Harris, E.M. 2006. *Democracy and the Rule of Law in Classical Athens: Essays on Law, Society and Politics*. Cambridge.

Harris, E.M. 2008. "Two Notes on Legal Inscriptions." *ZPE* 167: 81–84.

Harris, E.M. 2013. *The Rule of Law in Action in Democratic Athens*. Oxford.

Harris, E.M. 2015. "Toward a Typology of Greek Regulations about Religious Matters: A Legal Approach." *Kernos* 28: 53–83 (with online appendices by J.-M. Carbon and E.M. Harris).

Harris, E.M. 2019a. "Hybris nelle corti giudiziarie ateniesi: Il profilo legale dell'accusa nella Contro Midia di Demostene." *Rivista di diritto ellenico* 9: 143–170.

Harris, E.M. 2019b. "Pollution for Homicide after 400 BCE: More Evidence for the Persistence of a Belief." In *Dike: Studies in Greek Law in Honour of Alberto Maffi*, edited by L. Gagliardi and L. Pepe, 143–150. Milan.

Harris, E.M. 2019c. "Violence and the State in Xenophon: A Study of Three Passages." In *Xenophon on Violence*, edited by A. Kapellos, 103–123. Berlin.

Harris, E.M. 2021. "Religion and the Rule of Law in the Greek Polis". In *Rhetoric and Religion in Ancient Greek and Rome*, edited by S. Papaioannou, A. Serafim, and K. Demetriou, 17–36. Berlin.

Harris, E.M. 2022. "Notes on the New Law of Epicrates from the Athenian Agora." *ZPE* 222: 65–81.

Harter-Uibopuu, K. 2002. "Strafklauseln und gerichtliche Kontrolle in der Mysterieninschrift von Andania (*IG* v,1 1390)." *Dike* 5: 135–159.

Hellmann, M.-C. 2006. *L'architecture grecque 2*. Paris.

Hewitt, J.W. 1909. "The Major Restrictions on Access to Greek Temples." *TAPA* 40: 83–91.

Hitch, S. 2011. "Embedded Speech in the Attic Leges Sacrae." In *Sacred Words: Orality, Literacy and Religion*, edited by A.P.M.H. Lardinois, J.H. Blok, and M.G.M. van der Poel, 113–141. Leiden.

Horster, M. 2019. "Apollo's Servants—Cleaning the Sanctuary and Keeping Things in Order." In *Natur-Mythos-Religion im antiken Griechenland*, edited by T.J. Scheer, 201–217. Stuttgart.

Joyce, C. 2021. "A New Solution to the 'Demotionidai Inscription' (*IG* II^2.1237=Rhodes, Osborne, n. 5)." *Rivista di diritto ellenico* 9: 121–160.

Karila-Cohen. K. 2010. "L'étude du sentiment religieux à partir du lexique: l'exemple d'ἐνθύμιος et ἐνθυμιστός." In *Paysage et religion en Grèce antique, Mélanges offerts à Madeleine Jost*, edited by P. Carlier and C. Lerouge-Cohen, 109–121. Paris.

Kritzas, C., and S. Prignitz. 2020. "The 'Stele of the Punishments': A New inscription from Epidauros." *AE* 159: 1–61.

Lanérès, N. 2022. "'Entrée interdite.' Une inscription de Zarax (Laconie)." *RÉG* 135: 271–278.

Makres, A. 2014. "*IG* I^3 82 Revisited." In Ἀθηναίων ἐπίσκοπος: *Studies in Honour of Harold B. Mattingly*, edited by A.P. Matthaiou and R. Pitt, 185–202. Athens.

Malay, H., and G. Petzl. 2017. *New Religious Texts from Lydia*. Vienna.

Migeotte, L. 2005. "Les pouvoirs des agoranomes dans les cités grecques." In *Symposion 2001: Vorträge zur griechischen und hellenistischen Rechtsgeschichte*, edited by R.W. Wallace and M. Gagarin, 287–301. Vienna.

Mikalson, J.D. 2016. *New Aspects of Religion in Ancient Athens: Honors, Authorities, Esthetics, and Society*. Leiden.

Miles, M.M. 1998. *The City Eleusinion. Agora 31*. Athens.

Minon, S. 2007. *Les inscriptions éléennes dialectales (vi^e–iie siècle avant J.-C.)*. Geneva.

Mylonas, G.E. 1961. *Eleusis and the Eleusinian Mysteries*. Princeton.

Naiden, F.S. 2008. "Sanctions in Sacred Laws." In *Symposion 2007: Vorträge zur griechischen und hellenistischen Rechtsgeschichte*, edited by E.M. Harris and G. Thür, 125–138. Vienna.

Naiden, F.S. 2013. *Smoke Signals for the Gods: Ancient Greek Sacrifice from the Archaic through Roman Periods*. Oxford.

Naiden, F.S. 2020. "The Monetisation of Sacrifice." In *Pilgrimage and Economy in the Ancient Mediterranean*, edited by A. Collar and T.M. Kirstensen, 163–186. Leiden.

Osborne, R. 1993. "Women and Sacrifice in Classical Greece." *CQ* 43: 392–405.

Parker, R.C.T. 1983. *Miasma: Pollution and Purification in Early Greek Religion*. Oxford.

Parker, R.C.T. 1998. *Cleomenes on the Acropolis: An Inaugural Lecture Delivered Before the University of Oxford on 12 May 1997*. Oxford.

Parker, R.C.T. 2018. "The New Purity Law from Thyateira." *ZPE* 205: 178–183.

Perrin-Saminadayar, É. 2012. "Prêtres et prêtresses d'Athènes et de Délos à travers les décrets honorifiques athéniens (167–88 a.C.)." In *Civic Priests: Cult Personnel from the Hellenistic Period to Late Antiquity*, edited by M. Horster and A. Klöckner, 135–159. Berlin.

Petrovic, I., and A. Petrovic. 2016. *Inner Purity and Pollution in Greek Religion 1: Early Greek Religion*. Oxford.

Petrovic, I., and A. Petrovic. 2018. "Purity of Body and Soul in the Cult of Athena Lindia: On the Eastern Background of Greek Abstentions." In *Purity and Purification in the Ancient Greek World: Texts, Rituals, and Norms*, edited by J.-M. Carbon and S. Peels-Matthey, 225–258. Liège.

Petzl, G. 1994. *Die Beichtinschriften Westkleinasiens*. Bonn.

Petzl, G. 2019. "Die Beichtinschriften Westkleinasiens: Supplement." *EA* 52: 1–105.

Pirenne-Delforge, V. 2020. *Le polythéisme grec à l'épreuve d'Hérodote*. Paris.

Ricl, M. 2011. "Neokoroi in the Greek World." *Belgrade Historical Review* 2: 7–26.

Rougemont, G. 1973. "La hiéroménie des Pythia et les 'trêves sacrées' d'Éleusis, de Delphes et d'Olympie." *BCH* 97: 75–106.

Rubinstein, L. 2007. "'ARAI' in Greek Laws in the Classical and Hellenistic Periods: Deterrence or Concession to Tradition?" In *Symposion 2005: Vorträge zur griechischen und hellenistischen Rechtsgeschichte*, edited by E. Cantarella, 269–286. Vienna.

Salviat, F. 1958. "Une nouvelle loi thasienne. Institutions judiciaires et fêtes religieuses à la fin du IVe siècle av. J.-C." *BCH* 82: 193–267.

Salvo, I. 2018. "Blood Pollution and Macedonian Rulers: Narratives between Character and Belief." In *Purity and Purification in the Ancient Greek World: Texts, Rituals, and Norms*, edited by J.-M. Carbon and S. Peels-Matthey, 157–169. Liège.

Sammartano, R. 2019. "Esclusioni etniche nei regolamenti cultuali greci: la norma di Paros (*IG* XII.5 225)." *Axon* 3: 389–410.

Sánchez, P. 2001. *L'amphictionie des Pyles et de Delphes. Recherches sur son role historique, des originies au 2e siècle de notre ère*. Stuttgart.

Siewert, P. 1981. "Eine Bronze-Urkunde mit elischen Urteilen über Böoter, Thessaler, Athen und Thespiai." *OlBer* 10: 228–248.

Siewert, P., and H. Taeuber, eds. 2013. *Neue Inschriften von Olympia*. Vienna.

Shear, J. 2021. *Serving Athena: The Festival of the Panathenaia and the Construction of Athenian Identities*. Cambridge.

Sosin, J. 2005. "Unwelcome Dedications: Public Law and Private Religion in Hellenistic Laodicea by the Sea." *CQ* 55: 130–139.

Stavrianopoulou, E. 2009. "Norms of public behaviour towards Greek priests: Some insights from the leges sacrae." In *La norme en matière religieuse*, edited by P. Brulé, 213–229. Liège.

Wächter, T. 1910. *Reinheitsvorschriften im griechischen Kult*. Giessen.

Wagner, C. 1997. *Dedication Practices on the Athenian Acropolis, 8th to 4th centuries B.C.* D.Phil. diss., Oxford University.

Woodhead, A.G. 1997. *Inscriptions: The Decrees. Agora 16*. Princeton.

CHAPTER 4

Tegean Regulations for the *Panegyris* in Alea Athena's Sanctuary: An Arkadian *Festwiese* (c.400–380 BCE)

Christophe Chandezon

One of the most famous Arkadian inscriptions, that which carries the number *IG* V.2 3 in the *Inscriptiones Graecae*, has resisted analysis since its discovery in December 1888 in spite of numerous publications dedicated to it.[1] The stone comes from a prestigious sanctuary, that of Alea Athena. Victor Bérard and Gustave Fougères discovered the stone near the hamlet of Piali, some tens of meters north of the ruins of the temple of the goddess.[2] It is now displayed in the Archaeological Museum of Tegea (Fig. 4.1).

The engraving is *stoichedon*-style with 39 letters per line, and clauses are separated by interpuncts. The text is easy to read until at least clause VIII. The stone is broken at the bottom and the end of the text is lost, which may have led to the disappearance of important rulings. That which remains is dominated by problems raised by the presence of animals and grazing rights,[3] which distorts its scope. The Arkadian dialect in which the inscription is written is often difficult.[4] Several words or expressions in the inscription are not usual Greek and only vaguely understood. The text was not issued by the sanctuary of Alea Athena, but by the city of Tegea, which places a plot of public land at the disposal of the sanctuary for the festival of the goddess. It lays down the rules and provides for cases where the authorities of the sanctuary, including the priest, may contravene them.[5]

The inscription has been dated 400–380 BCE on the basis of letter forms.[6] The old temple of Alea,[7] built at the end of the seventh or beginning of the sixth century, was destroyed by fire in 395/4 BCE.[8] The law could date either before or after this disaster, and the clause forbidding fire (VI) can be understood as either a normal regulation or as a lesson learned from the fire (see below).[9] The law undoubtedly predates the construction of the new temple of Skopas, which was not begun until the third quarter of the fourth century BCE and lasted several decades.[10]

Greek text according to Thür and Taeuber 1994, 11–20 (= *IPArk* 2):

(I) Τὸν ἱερὲν πέντε καὶ εἴκοσι οἶς νέμεν καὶ ζεῦγο-
ς καὶ αἶγα· εἰ δ' ἂν καταλλάσσε, ἰνφορβισμὸν ἔναι τ-
ὸν ἱερομνάμονα ἰνφορβίεν· εἰ δ' ἂν λευτὸν μὲ ἰνφ-
4 ορβίε, hεκοτὸν δαρχμὰς ὀφλὲν ἰν δᾶμον καὶ κάταρ-
ϝον ἔναι ⋮ (II) Τὸν ἱεροθύταν νέμεν ἰν Ἀλέαι ὅ,τι ἂν ἀ-
σκεθὲς ἔ, τὰ δ' ἀνασκεθέα ἰνφορβίεν, μὲ δ' ἐσπεράσα-
ι πὰρ ἂν λέγε ἱεροθυτές· εἰ δ' ἂν ἐσπεράσε, δυόδεκ-
8 ο δαρχμὰς ὀφλὲν ἰν δᾶμον. ⋮ (III) Τὰς τριπαναγόρσιος τ-
ὰς ὑστέρας τρὶς ἁμέρας νέμεν ὅτι hὰν βόλετοι ὂς
μὲ ἰν τοῖ περιχόροι· εἰ δ' ἂν ἰν τοῖ περιχόροι, ἰνφορβίεν ⋮ (IV) Ἰν Ἀλέαι μὲ νέμεν μέτε ξένον μέτε ϝαστὸν
12 εἰ μὲ ἐπὶ θοίναν hίκοντα, τοῖ δὲ ξένοι καταγομέν-
οι ἐξεῖναι ἀμέραν καὶ νύκτα νέμεν ἐπιζύγιον· εἰ δ'
ἂν πὰρ τάνυ νέμε, τὸ μὲν μέζον πρόβατον δαρχμὰν ὀ-
φλὲν, τὸ δὲ μεῖον ἰνφορβίεν ⋮ (V) Τὰ hιερὰ πρόβατα μὲ
16 νέμεν ἰν Ἀλέαι πλὸς ἀμέραυ καὶ νυκτός, εἰκ ἂν διε-
λαυνόμενα τύχε· εἰ δ' ἂν νέμε, δαρχμὰν ὀφλὲν τὸ πρόβατον ϝέκαστον τὸ μέζον, τὸν δὲ μείονον προβάτο-
ν ὀδελὸν ϝέκαστον, τᾶν συῶν δαρχμὰν ϝεκάσταυ, ε[ἰ]
20 μὲ παρhεταξάμενος τὸς πεντέκοντα ἒ τὸς τριακα-
σίος. ⋮ (VI) Εἰκ ἐπὶ δόμα πῦρ ἐποίσε, δυόδεκο δαρχμὰς
ὀφλέν, τὸ μὲν ἔμισυ τᾶι θεοῖ, τὸ δ' ἔμισυ τοῖς hιερ[ο]-
μνάμοσι ⋮ (VII) Εἰκ ἂν παραμαξεύε θύσθεν τὰς
κελε[ύθ]-

---

1 Jost 1985, 382.
2 Bérard 1889, 280. This article forms the *editio princeps* of the text.
3 Guarducci 1952: "legge dei Tegeati intorno ai pascoli;" Thür and Taeuber 1994, 11–20: "Weidegesetz;" Hermary et al. 2004, 96: "règlement relatif au pacage;" Sourvinou-Inwood et al. 2005, 42: "règlement concernant principalement le droit de pacage sur certaines terres;" Dubois 2010, 19, "inscription sur le pacage des animaux."
4 Dubois 1986.
5 Jost 1985, 382.
6 Guarducci 1952, 52–54.
7 Jost 1985, 145–146, 151–154, 369–384; Østby 2014c.

8 Paus. 8.45.4. But the sanctuary operated from the Geometric period on: Østby 2014d.
9 Thür and Taeuber 1994, 12. Dubois (1986, 29) sees an allusion to the fire in this clause.
10 Paus. 8.45.5. In overview, Østby (2014a) particularly favors 348–342, a rather late date for the construction.

FIGURE 4.1 Tegea, Archaeological Museum, inscribed stele *IG* v.2 3
PHOTO: © HELLENIC MINISTRY OF CULTURE AND SPORTS/EPHORATE OF ANTIQUITIES OF ARKADIA, N. 3028/2002

24 ὀ τᾶς κακειμέναυ κατ' Ἀλέαν, τρῖς ὀδελὸς ὀφλὲ[ν ἀν]-
τὶ ϝεκάσται, τὸ μὲν hέμισυ τᾶι θεοῖ, τὸ δ' ἔμισ[υ τοῖ]-
ς hιερομνάμοσι ⋮ (VIII) Τᾶι παναγόρσι τὸς hιερ[ομνάμ]-
ονας ἀρτύεν τὰ ἰν ταῖς ἰνπολαῖς πάντα τά [δ' ἄλλα(?) τ]-
28 ὸς δαμιοργὸς ⋮ (IX) Τὸν κόπρον τὸν ἀπυδόσμ[ιον ἐξάγε]-
[ν] τᾶι hεβδόμαι τὸ Λεσχανασίο μενός· [εἰ δὲ μέ, δαρχ]-
[μὰ]ν ὀφλέν ⋮ (X) Τὸν Παναγόρσιον μένα τὸν
 . . . . 9 . . . .

. . . ἀζεν τοῖς ξένοις, εἰκ ἂν ἰόντα I#⁷ . . . . 9 . . . .
32 . . 5 . . εἰ δ' ἀπιόντα ει#⁷ . . . . 21 . . . .
. . 6 . . . ν δάμοι ἐφαγ . . . . 23 . . . .
. . . 8 . . . . αι τὸς ι . . . . 25 . . . .
. . . . 9 . . . . νον . . . . 27 . . . .

English translation:[11]

(I) The priest may pasture 25 sheep, a yoke of cattle, and a goat. If he exceeds this number, the animals will be seized (*inphorbismon enai*). The *hieromnamon* must seize them. If, having seen the offense, he does not seize them, he shall owe 100 drachmas to the People and be accursed. (II) The *hierothytes* may pasture any animal without blemish in Alea, but any animal with blemish will be seized. The *hierothytes* is not allowed to exceed the number of animals that he has declared; if he exceeds this number, he shall owe 12 drachmas to the People. (III) For the three days following the *Tripanagorsis* (or: For the last three days of the *Tripanagorsis*), anyone may pasture any animal he wants, but not in the *perichoros*; any animal being pastured in the *perichoros* will be seized. (IV) No foreigner or citizen is to pasture in Alea unless he has come for a banquet, but a stranger remaining in the halting-place may pasture one yoke for a day and a night. If he pastures any more than this, he is to pay a fine of 1 drachma per large animal, and a smaller animal will be seized. (V) The sacred animals are not to be pastured in Alea more than a day and a night if they happen to be driven through; if they are pastured for more, then the fine is to be 1 drachma for each larger animal, 1 obol for each smaller animal, and 1 drachma per pig unless they received special permission from the Fifty or the Three Hundred. (VI) If someone brings fire next to the building (*doma*), he shall owe 12 drachmas; half of it is for the goddess and half for the *hieromnamones*. (VII) If someone drives outside of the road through Alea, he shall owe 3 obols for each (?); half of it is for the goddess and half for the *hieromnamones*. (VIII) During the *Panagorsis*, the *hieromnamones* must regulate trader-related questions and the *damiorgos* has to regulate other questions (IX) Dung that can be sold has to be removed on the 7th of the month of Leschanasios; if not, 1 drachma is owed. (X) During the month of Panagorisios … to strangers … going away … People …

1 The Inscription in Its Setting

We are now able to place this inscription in its environmental context: the topography of the sanctuary is much better known since the Norwegian excavations directed by Erik Østby and carried out around the temple in 1990–1996 and 2004, the results of which were published in two volumes in 2014.[12] They deliver numerous facts that, in particular, reveal the surroundings of the temple.[13]

The sanctuary of Alea was located just south of the ancient city of Tegea.[14] The heart of the Tegean city-state was a basin surrounded by mountains, with Mount Parthenon to the east and the massif of Mount Mainalos to the west. The basin itself is at a fairly high elevation (about 670 m) and its karstic nature causes water drainage problems. The area included game, and bones of fallow deer, roe deer, and hare were found during excavations.[15] Around the sanctuary were fields of grain, grasslands, and a wide variety of trees, mainly birch (*Betula*), ash (*Fraxinus*), oak (*Quercus*), and pine (*Pinus*). Because of the climatic conditions, olive trees were not very abundant, but there were still some, probably on well-exposed soils. The area near the sanctuary offered an open landscape dominated by crops and grassland.[16]

Around 400 BCE, Tegea was a proper city with a wall, agora, and theater.[17] The temple of Alea was a little outside the walled area.[18] A river flowed nearby; its current name is the Sarantapotamos, but in ancient times it was referred to as the Upper Alpheios.[19] The Norwegian excavations showed that its course (riverbed) changed at the end of the Classical period; previously, it flowed around the temple area on its southern, western, and northern sides, after which the riverbed shifted to the eastern side of the sanctuary (Fig. 4.2).[20]

The Upper Alpheios was an important element of the local landscape, especially because it regularly flooded, leaving behind layers of sand and silt. This was obviously a source of regular destruction of buildings, but also, in other ways, presented advantages.[21] Knut Ødegård wrote,

---

11 For the translation of the Greek text into English, I thank Jim Roy, who kindly corrected it; this English translation is to my knowledge the first (partial translation in Osborne 1987, 49), although French (Dubois 1986, 2: 33–34) and German translations exist (Thür and Taeuber 1994, 13–15).

12 Østby 2014c; Østby 2014d. Results of this work in Tegea: Jost 2018, 123–127.
13 Zooarchaeology: Vila 2000; Vila 2014. Palynology: Bjune, Krzywinski, and Overland 2014.
14 Nielsen 2004, 297–533.
15 Vila 2014, 554–555.
16 Bjune, Krzywinski, and Overland 2014, 445.
17 Østby 2014d, 50–51.
18 Østby 2014d, 12.
19 Baladié 1980, 50.
20 Ødegård and Klempe 2014, 28, 35; Østby 2014d, 17.
21 Ødegård and Klempe 2014.

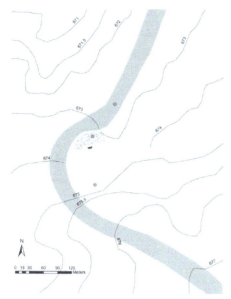
The riparian environment of the sanctuary in the Geometric period (8th century B.C.)

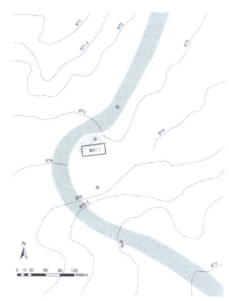
The environment of the Archaic temple, surrounded by a dry surface of silt and sand, since the late 7th century B.C.

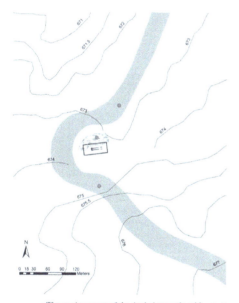
The environment of the Archaic temple with a wet backswamp area, after the end of the 6th century B.C.

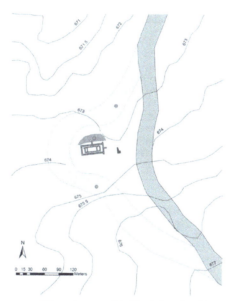
The environment of the Classical temple, with the deposit of waste marble chips mixed with soil from the temple construction, and a new course of the river. After ca. 300 B.C.

FIGURE 4.2 Variations in the course of the Sarandapotamos River
AFTER ØDEGÅRD AND KLEMPE 2014, 29, FIGS. 1–4 BY PERMISSION OF HARALD KLEMPE

"Because of the abundance of water, the area around the shrine must also have been an important area for livestock, with good grazing possibilities, even in dry summers."[22] The presence of water around the sanctuary is reflected by the remains of pond turtles and amphibians in the zooarchaeological material.[23] Just north of the temple were two statue bases from the Classical period,[24] as well as a fountain built during the fourth century BCE and linked to the legend of Auge and Herakles,[25] while the altar, also from the fourth century BCE, stood east of the temple.[26]

---

22   Ødegård and Klempe 2014, 33.
23   Vila 2000, 198; Vila 2014, 550.
24   Østby 2014d, 20–23.
25   Paus. 8.47.4. Østby 2014d, 16–18.
26   Paus. 8.47.3. Østby 2014d, 18–20. Nearby, there was also a *stadion* made of simple earthwork (χῶμα γῆς): Paus. 8.47.4. Østby 2014d, 20.

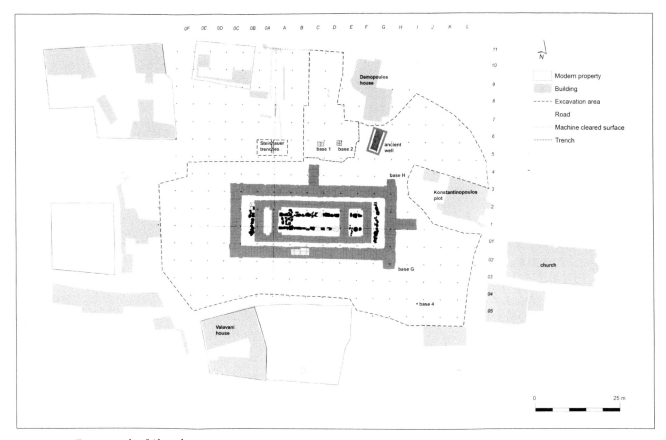

FIGURE 4.3 Tegea, temple of Alea, plan
AFTER ØSTBY 2014B, 11, PL. 1 BY PERMISSION OF ERIK ØSTBY

Otherwise, the area immediately north of the temple did not yield any other permanent installations.[27] As early as the seventh century BCE, this space was connected to the sanctuary, and on several occasions an east-west wall was built parallel to the temple, which may have marked the northern limit of the *hieron*. This wall, regularly destroyed by floods, was rebuilt each time at the same location. The occupation levels in the area only reveal light structures, which can be identified by postholes. Around 550 BCE, this land just north of the Archaic temple saw the building of a new wall, made of mudbricks, which was destroyed around 500 BCE. The ground was then levelled several times and strengthened by the laying of stones. The last time this happened coincided with the time of the fourth century BCE temple; the ground to the north of the temple was then covered with debris and left free of any permanent structure until the Imperial period. The whole area therefore formed a large open field, available for gatherings (Fig. 4.3).[28]

Another new development comes from the discovery of a 22-line lacunose inscription engraved on a bronze plaque, which was first published in 2015 and has aroused curiosity ever since.[29] Its appearance on the art market in London and Munich in 2010 has concealed its exact origin, but the dialect in which this religious calendar is inscribed and the toponyms it cites show that it comes from Arkadia. The proposed dates place it between 500 and 450 BCE.[30] The document poses complex problems, particularly relating to the understanding of the calendar of festivals, and the possible existence of a collective political structure in Arkadia from the beginning of the fifth century BCE, of which Mount Lykaion would have been the center. Both inscriptions, the Tegean and the new one, show points of convergence: in particular, both mention a festival called *tripanegyris*, which suggests a kind of systematic organization of the religious life in Arkadia during the Classical period.

27 Østby 2014d, 16.
28 Tarditi 2014, 85–86.
29 Heinrichs 2015. See especially Carbon and Clackson 2016, while waiting for the studies announced by several specialists on Arkadia (*BÉ* 2017, 229, 230; Dubois 2018). The text was integrated by J.-M. Carbon into the database *CGRN* 223.
30 Dubois 2018, XIII, citing the opinion of Sophie Minon, who places the text rather towards 475–450 BCE.

2 Two Preliminary Considerations on the Tegean Text

Two recurrent points need to be explained before the clause-by-clause analysis of *IG* v.2 3. It is impossible to clarify them completely, but probable solutions can be suggested. The first is topographical: it concerns the place called Alea (*in Aleai / kat'Alean*), which is mentioned four times in the Tegean inscription (ll. 5, 11, 16, 24).[31] A similar expression appears in the newly discovered Arkadian text mentioned above. It concerns (l. 4) a sacrifice to be made ἰν Ἀλέαν τὸν Μαραθιδᾶν. We will begin with this. The Marathidai have been interpreted as a kind of *genos* related to the place called Maratha near Gortys.[32] We must therefore rule out a link with the small Arkadian city of Alea,[33] and instead see it as a reference to the goddess Alea, honored in Tegea and also in Mantinea.[34] The sacrifice mentioned in the new inscription was performed in a sanctuary of the goddess Alea, perhaps in Maratha, and thus the comparison with our text is misleading. In the Tegean inscription, the link between this space and the name of the goddess is obvious, but the expression *in Aleai* cannot refer to the goddess because one does not see how one could have grazed animals (or not) *in Aleai* or have taken a road that crosses Alea.[35] Alea is therefore a spatial reference. It cannot be the sanctuary itself, because it would be unheard of for it to be used as a pasture or to be crossed by a vehicle. One also cannot interpret *in Aleai* in terms of rules applying to the city of Alea, and one cannot see how the sanctuary or the city of Tegea could grant grazing rights to the territory of another city. It is also not credible that this text would emanate from the city of Alea but be displayed in the sanctuary of Tegea, because the sanctuary authorities are those of Tegea.[36]

According to almost all commentators, Alea is a plot of land close to the sanctuary and used for festivals. Did it belong to the sanctuary or to the city? The authority exerted there was that of the magistrates of the city, such as the *hieromnamones* and the *damiourgoi*, under the control of the councils of the city, the Fifty and the Three Hundred. The priest and the *hierothytes* appear only as users of Alea with restricted rights. In all likelihood, the expression *in Aleai* refers to an otherwise unoccupied space used at the time of the festival. It must be compared to the one that was excavated in the 1990s, although this latter one, just north of the temple, was probably partly inside the *temenos*.[37]

The second point concerns the penalty for domesticated animals grazing "on Alea" outside the permitted instances. The text calls it *inphorbismos* (l. 2), and the verb designating the application of this sanction is *inphorbien* (ll. 3, 3–4, 6, 10–11, 15).[38] These words have two possible origins: either they are related to the verb *phorbein*, to graze, and to *phorbê*, grazing, or refer to the muzzle or halter (*phorbeia*) that is put around the head of animals, and which, by extension, also designates the leather strap that musicians use to secure their instruments firmly at their mouths.[39] Hence, there are two groups of possible meanings for *inphorbismos* and *inphorbien*: either placing the offending animals in a pasture reserved for them, or putting a controlling device, such as a muzzle, on them.

Scholars propose four possible interpretations:[40]

1) the use of a muzzle, preventing the animal from continuing to graze;[41]
2) payment of a grazing fee for use of a pasture available to visitors;[42]
3) a temporary seizure of the offending animal, which would then be kept in an area where it could no longer damage the trees of the sacred grove or roam;

---

31 Bérard 1889, 289–290 (district of Tegea, near the sanctuary).

32 Minon in *BÉ* 2017, 230; Dubois 2018, XIV; proposal taken up by the *CGRN* 223. The place called Maratha is mentioned by Paus. 8.28.1.

33 Nielsen 2004, 508–509.

34 Jost 1985, 373–375.

35 An inscription from Mantinea (first half of the fifth century BCE) gives a list of characters punished for violating the asylum of the Mantinean sanctuary of the goddess (*IG* v.2 262, l. 1: [Ϝο]φλέασι οἴδε ἰν Ἀλέαν).

36 The Council of the Three Hundred, ll. 20–21, also appears in the Tegean text on public works, *IG* v.2 6, l. 8. These councils are at the center of debates about the Arkadian Confederacy, and some have seen them as federal councils: Nielsen 2002, 125.

37 The different walls of the seventh and sixth century (the latter made of mudbrick) each may have served as a *peribolos* to separate this area of the *hieron* from the outer ground. In this case, the destruction of the mudbrick wall around 500 BCE would be the sign of northward expansion of the *temenos*: Ødegård 2014, 94; Tarditi 2014, 60–61, 64, 69–70, 75–76.

38 The only use of the noun ἰνφορβισμός (l. 2) in the expression ἰνφορβισμὸν ἔναι, expresses the action of ἰνφορβίεν.

39 Bélis 1986.

40 Guarducci 1937; Guarducci 1952, 54–59; Jost 1985, 383; Dubois 1986, 21–22; Thür and Taeuber 1994, 15–16, n. 2.

41 Danielsson 1890, 35–36.

42 This is the solution chosen by Dubois 1986, 2: 22. In the Greek cities, the most common name for the grazing tax was ἐννόμιον; see, for example, in Athens (*Syll.*³ 914, ll. 7, 33–34 of 326/5 BCE) or at Delos (*ID* 353, A, l. 28 of 219 BCE). The same tax was sometimes referred to as ἐμφόρβιον, cf. Hesychios *s.v.*, and was used in the plural at Kolophon at the end of the fourth century BCE: Maier 1959–1961, 1, no. 70, frag. f. l. 83.

this seizure would entail the payment of a fine for the return of the animal;[43]

4) a final seizure of the animal.[44]

The fourth solution seems the most likely: the confiscation of animals roaming on land to which they have no right of access is normal in such inscriptions. In Eretria, a law dating from about the same period as the Tegean text states: "if anyone grazes an animal or lets it in, the animal will be confiscated." In other circumstances, the sanction is only a fine, as in Korope in Thessaly: there, the amount is fixed, whereas in Ialysos on the island of Rhodes, the fine is calculated per head of livestock.[45] The Tegean text makes clear when fines are stipulated (clause V). Scholars have argued that it is difficult to interpret *inphorbismos* in clause IV as confiscation. A stranger hosted in Tegea (*xenos katagomenos*) who lets his animals graze on Alea for more than one day and one night must pay a fine of one drachma per head of large livestock, while sheep or goats are subject to the penalty of *inphorbismos*. In fourth-century Greece, a sheep was worth at least 10 drachmas (in Attika).[46] However, the penalty should not be heavier for the offence of a sheep than for a mule. But we must consider that the city of Tegea did not want to penalize a foreign visitor who came with a draught or riding animal and left Tegea with the animal after spending a night there.

3   The Text, Step by Step

[I] The priest may pasture 25 sheep, a yoke of cattle, and a goat. If he exceeds this number, the animals will be seized. The *hieromnamon* must seize them. If, having seen the offense, he does not seize them, he shall owe 100 drachmas to the People and be accursed.

Clauses I through V deal with the possibility of grazing animals. The presence of cattle near the sanctuary of Alea is not surprising. The wet character of this ground corresponds to a category of pasture, the *leimônes*, well defined in the eyes of the Greeks. Moreover, the presence of a watercourse and spring should have made this sector attractive to herders.[47]

Pausanias explains that Alea had a male priest, who was a child,[48] while high Imperial inscriptions speak of a priestess.[49] It would thus seem that in the time of Pausanias, an ancient situation dating back to the Classical period when the priest was male had been restored, but our text does not allow us to judge the age of the priest.[50] The modest herd given to the priest is indicative of those of ordinary families: it included 25 sheep, a couple of draft animals, probably two oxen or two mules that could be used for transport or ploughing, and a single goat, probably raised for its milk.[51] Pigs are not mentioned, although they were important animals in the Arkadian economy and appear in clause V, which concerns sacred livestock.[52] The composition of this herd presents a somewhat different picture to that provided by the zooarchaeological data from the Norwegian excavations. Goats and sheep were, by far, the most numerous, followed by pigs and cattle. However, it is true that the data of the Norwegian excavations comes from sacrificial activity, and dates from the eighth century BCE.[53]

The priest of Alea thus enjoyed a privilege granted by the city on this land near the temple and could use it at any time. The city wanted to avoid abuses, and the *hieromnamon* was to verify compliance with this clause. The heavy penalty to which he is subject if he does not do his duty may indicate concern about collusion with the priest. This mention of a priest's livestock has no parallel in the ancient record. The priest was supposed to be an ordinary Tegean citizen, living from agriculture and breeding. Of course, this does not mean that he was not richer than an owner of 25 sheep, two large animals, and one goat, which is only a limitation set by the city for a privilege. Clause I

---

43   Hypothesis retained by Guarducci 1952, 57–59, in her second article on this text. In this case, ἰνφορβισμός would be linked to φορβειά.

44   Guarducci (1937) opted for this solution in her first article, with the idea of an integration of these animals with the sacred cattle of the goddess.

45   Eretria: *LSCG* no. 91, ll. 11–12: ἐὰν δὲ βόσκων ἢ εἰρελῶν, / στερέσθω τοῦ βοσκήματος ("if someone graze animals or let them go inside, they will be confiscated;" beginning of the fourth century BCE). Korope: *LSCG* no. 84, ll. 82–87 (end of the second century BCE; the amount of 50 dr is completely returned, but the mention of a fine in cash is certain; moreover, if the shepherd is a slave, he will have to pay a fine per head of cattle in addition to the lashes). Text of Ialysos: *LSCG* no. 136 (*CGRN* 90), ll. 30–33: εἰ δέ κα / πρόβατα ἐσβάληι, ἀποτεισάτω ὑ/πὲρ ἑκάστου προβάτου ὀβολὸν / ὁ ἐσβαλών ("If someone brings in small cattle, then he must pay one obol for every animal;" end of fourth century BCE).

46   Van Straten 1987, 166; Jacquemin 1991, 97–98; Hermary et al. 2004, 101–103.

47   Østby 2014d, 17–18; Luce 2014, 49 for the Byzantine era.

48   Paus. 8.47.3.

49   *IG* V.2 81 where a certain Kleopatra is said to be ἱερασα/μένα Ἀλέᾳ / Ἀθάνᾳ καὶ / Δάματρι.

50   Jost 1985, 381–382.

51   Guarducci (1952, 59) explains the restriction to one goat by the damage that these animals can do.

52   Roy 1999, 329–333, 349–356.

53   Vila 2000, 197–202; Vila 2014, 552–555.

does not specify that this grazing right was to be applied "on Alea," and one cannot exclude the possibility that it concerns all the public pastures of Tegea.

[II] The *hierothytes* may pasture any animal without blemish in Alea, but any animal with blemish will be seized. The *hierothytes* is not allowed to exceed the number of animals that he has declared; if he exceeds this number, he shall owe 12 drachmas to the People.

The second clause of the text concerns the animals for sacrifice, not the private cattle of the *hierothytes*.[54] As elsewhere, this sanctuary staff member is in charge of the animals for public sacrifices. There is no limit to the number of animals he can graze *in Aleai*, but there is a religious condition: all must have been approved for sacrifice and be without stain (*askethea*), which designates animals that are both whole and without physical deformities, and thus suitable for sacrifice.[55] The *hierothytes* must declare (*legen*, l. 7) the number of animals meeting this condition, and it is likely that these animals were marked after a *dokimasia*, as was customary in sanctuaries.[56] Animals that are *anaskethea* (with blemish) will be confiscated. The excess *askethea* animals will not be confiscated because they are consecrated, but the *hierothytes* will have to pay a fine to the people of Tegea (ἰν δᾶμον, l. 8). The area known as Alea belonged to the city for it would be difficult to understand an interdiction decided by the sanctuary for a sacrificial animal on a parcel belonging to this sanctuary. This clause implies that the sacrificial animals had to be kept for at least a few days on a parcel of land near to the sanctuary before being slaughtered for the goddess. In the inscription of Andania, the animals for the sacrifice are presented to the sanctuary ten days before the sacrifice.[57] A regulation from Ios in the Cyclades contains similar provisions for sacrificial animals: declaration of their number and marking of future victims.[58]

[III] For the three days following the *Tripanagorsis*, anyone may pasture any animal he wants, but not in the *perichoros*; any animal being pastured in the *perichoros* will be seized.

This clause presents serious difficulties. What is the *perichoros*? The concept is that of an enclosed space or a space enclosing something.[59] This space is distinct from the land known as Alea (which is not mentioned in this passage). It could be the *temenos* of Alea Athena itself, delimited by a *peribolos*.[60] In this case, the idea would be that a pilgrim can keep his animals in the vicinity of the sanctuary for the three days following the *Tripanagorsis* under the condition that the *temenos* is not used as pasture: it is normal to exclude animals from the sanctuaries. If *perichoros* designates a space enclosing something, i.e., the sanctuary in this case, it means that clause III forbids pasturing in the immediate vicinity of the *temenos* and recommends pasturing animals only in the area referred to in the inscription as "in Aleai."

The *Tripanagorsis* is undoubtedly the major festival of the goddess, which later texts refer to as the Aleaia when they speak about the organization of contests.[61] Further on, the text uses the simple word *Panagorsis* (l. 26), which may be explained in two different ways.[62] The *Tripanagorsis* was either a trieteric festival—and the intercalated celebration would then be the *Panagorsis*—or a festival lasting three days. It may have taken place in the month of Panagorsios mentioned later in the inscription (l. 30). The recently published Arkadian inscription mentions a festival with an almost identical name, the *Tripanagoris* (τᾶι τριπαναγόρι, l. 3).[63] Here again, there are ambiguous elements: the inscription mentions another name for the festival, the *Trianbris*, in a short form, (τᾶι τριανβρί, e.g., l. 2) or long form (τᾶι παναγόρι τᾶι τριανβρ[ί], l. 3), which indicates a three-day festival.[64] Thus, the word *Tripanagoris* seems simply an all-embracing way of

---

54 Jost 1985, 383.
55 Sourvinou-Inwood et al. (2005, 42) commenting on the meaning of ἀσκηθής, tends to understand it as a synonym of ὁλόκληρος.
56 Feyel 2006.
57 *CGRN* 222, ll. 70–71; Deshours 2006, 35 (ll. 70–71), 87; Gawlinski 2012, 174.
58 *LSCG* no. 105 (third century BCE).

---

59 Dem. 19.266 uses περίχωρος to talk about the allies of Olynthos (περιχώρους … συμμάχους). See Dubois 1986, 26.
60 Guarducci 1937, 170.
61 Paus. 8.47.4 said that it was the name of the competitions when talking about the *stadion* near to the sanctuary: καὶ ἄγουσιν ἀγῶνας ἐνταῦθα, Ἀλεαῖα ὀνομάζοντες ἀπὸ τῆς Ἀθηνᾶς ("they celebrate games, one festival called Aleaea after Athena," trans. Jones). Inscriptions: *IG* V.2 22, ll. 8–9, ἐν τῶι ἀγῶνι τῶν Ἀλ[ε/αίω]ν ("during the competitions of the Aleaia") for the proclamation of honors in a decree of Tegea (late Hellenistic period); *IG* V.2 142, ll. 6, 12, 22, 32, 37, repeated mention of Ἀλέαια in an agonistic listing of an athlete from Tegea.
62 Jost 1985, 384; Dubois 1986, 25.
63 The expression ἰν Κορυνιτίοι has been interpreted by Carbon and Clackson (2016, 126) as meaning "to Gortys." Minon proposes a connection with Paus. 8.11.4, which mentions a place called Κορυνήτης between Tegea and Mantineia, cited and approved by Dubois (2018, xv in *BÉ* 2017, 229). This explanation was taken up by J.-M. Carbon in *CGRN* 223, and its meaning analyzed by Jost 2021, 177–179.
64 On the meaning of this word and its etymology, see Carbon and Clackson 2016, 146–148.

naming this same festival from which one can conclude either that it lasted three days or was trieteric.⁶⁵ This brings us back to the same problem as that with the Tegean inscription. It appears, however, that without doubt, *tripanagor(s)sis* was an Arkadian way of designating a festival.

The wording τᾶς τριπαναγόρσιος τ/ὰς ὑστέρας τρῖς μέρας is problematic. It could refer to the last three days of the Tripanagorsis or the three days following it. The text allows visitors to graze as many head of livestock as they wish. This can concern animals for private sacrifices (a solution valid only for the first possibility), as well as animals to be sold or bought, and in the case of *Tripanagorsis* also offers the possibility of organizing a fair. At Tithorea in Phokis in the second century CE, Pausanias describes a festival of Isis, which involves a fair, and he writes that it takes place on the third and last day of the festival. Relevant to this discussion is the fact that livestock were sold there.⁶⁶ This explanation would make sense, especially because clause VIII also speaks of the commercial exchanges that take place during the *panegyris*.

[IV] No foreigner or citizen is to pasture in Alea unless he has come for a banquet, but a stranger remaining in the halting-place may pasture one yoke for a day and a night. If he pastures any more than this, he is to pay a fine of 1 drachma per large animal, and a smaller animal will be seized.

The banquets (*thoinai*) attract foreigners and Tegean citizens; the citizens can use Alea as pasture only on such occasions.⁶⁷ This provision is reminiscent of other examples showing that people living near a shrine tended to use it for grazing animals, if not prevented from doing so. It was tempting because there was often water, greenery, trees, and shade.⁶⁸ Foreigners enjoyed more lenient regulations while they were lodged there, which is the probable meaning of *katagomai*.⁶⁹ The authorization granted to them was, however, limited to one day and one night and was reserved for the draft animals (*epizygion*) with which they had arrived and would leave. Sheep and goats were thus excluded from this provision: in this way, clause IV ruled out shepherds trying to use Alea as a stopover during a journey with their animals. Exceeding the authorized length of stay was punishable by a fine of one drachma for large animals, while small livestock would be seized.⁷⁰ This clause recalls the provisions made by Xenophon at Skillous, which provides parking for visitors' animals (see below). This was a problem for Greek sanctuaries: a law of Ialysos in Rhodes excluded equines, as well as shoes and other objects made of pigskin, from the sanctuary of the goddess Alektrona.⁷¹

[V] The sacred animals are not to be pastured in Alea more than a day and a night if they happen to be driven through; if they are pastured for more, then the fine is to be 1 drachma for each larger animal, 1 obol for each smaller animal, and 1 drachma per pig, unless they received special permission from the Fifty or the Three Hundred.

Sacred herds are a well-known phenomenon in Greek sanctuaries, for example at Delphi.⁷² They had a different status from that of the sacred animals present for the pleasure of the divinity and which, in the sanctuary, constituted living *anathêmata*. The *hiera probata* should be considered as a resource for the sanctuary in the same sense as sacred land leased to farmers or as monetary reserves lent against interest. These animals could serve as sacrificial victims, but that was not their primary purpose. At Delphi, for example, the sacred beasts of Apollo included mares, but we have no evidence of horse sacrifice in Delphic religion.⁷³

That Alea of Tegea owned sacred beasts is not surprising. Arkadia is known to have been "rich in livestock,"⁷⁴ and the sanctuary of the goddess was one of the most prosperous of this part of Greece. The movement of livestock from winter to summer pastures is a known practice in Greece, and in the case of Arkadia, the livestock were pigs. This

---

65   Carbon and Clackson 2016, 146–148, 153; Dubois 2018, XV–XVII.
66   Paus. 10.32.15 (formulating πανηγυρίζουσι πιπράσκοντες to say that the participants hold a fair). For fairs at Greek sanctuaries, see also the contributions by Lo Monaco and Chankowski in this volume.
67   Horster 2020, 127.
68   *NGSL*² 26–27.
69   The suggestion that καταγομένος refers to the idea of staying in the vicinity of a sanctuary was made to me during the symposium in Athens by V. Pirenne-Delforge and J.-M. Carbon. I thank them very much.
70   This clause has intrigued: Jost 1985, 383. We can compare it with the fines of the following clause: 1 dr for large livestock and pigs, 1 obol for small livestock (ll. 17–19). This is what we would have expected here if the purpose was not to prohibit absolutely the presence of small livestock of individuals staying one night *in Aleai*.
71   *Syll.*³ 338 (*CGRN* 90), ll. 21–25: μὴ ἐσί/τω ἵππος ὄνος ἡμίονος γῖνος / μηδὲ ἄλλο λόφουρον μηθὲν μη/δὲ ἐσαγέτω ἐς τὸ τέμενος μη/θεὶς τούτων ("A horse, a donkey, a mule, hinny, and any other animal with a long-haired tail must not enter, and no one should lead into the sanctuary any of these"). On the handling of hides at Greek sanctuaries, see Pakkanen in this volume.
72   McInerney 2010, 153–164.
73   On sacred herds at Delphi, see Rousset 2002, 192–205. Villing (2017, 74–100) discusses cases in which sacred birds could serve as sacrificial victims. On unproductive sacred animals, see Bodson 1978; *NGSL*² 29–30.
74   Roy 1999, 331–332.

clause has been cited as a record of long-distance transhumance in ancient Greece.[75] It could testify at least to shorter movements of livestock, from the plain to the surroundings mountains. The sacred livestock included cows (and possibly horses), sheep, goats, and pigs. It reflects the Arkadian herds, and the use of *probaton* indicates that the word then had a broad meaning.[76]

Some researchers think that this clause concerned animals belonging to any sanctuary, not only those of Alea Athena in Tegea, but this is unlikely.[77] Even for the sacred *probata* of the goddess, the text would be very restrictive. It is only valid for passing herds and limits the authorization to one day and one night. An extension of this time limit may only be granted by one of the civic councils of the Fifty and the Three Hundred. This confirms that the land known as Alea was managed by the city, and certainly belonged to it. The Fifty probably formed the permanent commission of the Three Hundred, each board serving for two months.[78] The double mention of these bodies indicates the possibility of taking a quick decision, without necessarily convening the Three Hundred in a plenary session. In case of infringement, high fines had to be paid. These fines should not be considered as grazing rights permitting a longer stay.[79]

[VI] **If someone brings fire next to the building (*doma*), he shall owe 12 drachmas; half of it is for the goddess and half for the *hieromnamones*.**

This is the first clause that no longer concerns animals. In fact, the Tegea text as a whole was not a law concerning pastures and livestock, but a text regulating the use of land, that of Alea, which the city placed at the disposal of the sanctuary under certain conditions. Clauses VI–X represent the whole text's focus on regulations organizing everything concerning the *panegyris*, even if the loss of the lower part of the stone may give a distorted idea of the true value of this document. Clause VI relating to fire[80] should not necessarily be read as an allusion to destruction of the Archaic temple by fire. Rather, the *doma* is an ordinary building placed near the shrine, located on the grounds where pilgrims are welcomed.[81] The Norwegian excavations showed that the immediate surroundings of the temple to the north remained free of any durable constructions,[82] but the excavations are far from having exhausted the entire surroundings of the fourth-century BCE temple. Nothing excludes the existence of permanent buildings. The amount of the fine is high, and the proceeds are intended to be shared between the sanctuary and the city. The *hieromnamones* are mentioned here in the plural, whereas only one *hieromnamon* is mentioned in clause I. This difference is explained by the fact that the *hieromnamones* formed a board.[83] As such, it had to collect half of the fines under clauses VI and VII, but the executive board could operate on a rotational basis, so that one member of the *hieromnamones* always remained 'on call.' It would then be normal that only one *hieromnamon* would be obliged to denounce the offence committed by the priest if he abused his right to graze.[84]

[VII] **If someone drives outside of the road through Alea, he shall owe 3 obols for each (?); half of it is for the goddess and half for the *hieromnamones*.**

This clause on cart (*hamaxa*) traffic through the Alea grounds is mysterious. Was its purpose to protect the land by excluding heavy vehicles? To avoid accidents? The surroundings of the *temenos* of the goddess were marshy, and it was necessary in the Archaic period to drain them to make them more passable.[85] This road (here *keleuthos*) could have connected the city to the sanctuary.[86] In the area around the temple, the wet soil was reinforced on several occasions to facilitate circulation.[87] The ground to the north of the temple was first consolidated with pebbles in the sixth century BCE, then again during the fourth-century building works.[88] It is unclear how the cart traffic fine was calculated. Some scholars believe that ἀν]/τὶ ϝεκάσταυ means "each time the vehicle leaves the road," but I do not see how it was possible to count the

---

75 Georgoudi 1974, 178–180. Contra: Roy 1999, 381, n. 218.
76 Benveniste 1969, 1, 37–45.
77 Guarducci 1937, 172; Guarducci 1952, 63; Georgoudi (1974, 179), which postulates that the land known as Alea belonged to the sanctuary and that a fee could not be charged for animals that also belonged to the sanctuary.
78 Nielsen 2004, 532.
79 Contra: Dubois 1986, 29.
80 *NGSL*² 25. In Arkesine of Amorgos, a regulation of the fifth century BCE forbids making fire in the Heraion and in a building linked to it under penalty of a 10-drachma fine: *LSCG* no. 100 (*CGRN* 234), A, ll. 2–4: πῦρ μηδένα καίεν / [ἐν] τῶι Ἡρ[αίωι πρὸ]ς τὸ καινὸ οἴκο τῆς γω[ν]/ίας καὶ τὸ νε[ὼ τὸ πρ]ὸς τὸ Λυκείο ("that no fire is lit in the Heraion at the corner between the new building and the temple, and towards the Lykeion").
81 Guarducci 1937, 52–54; Guarducci 1952, 53; Jost 1985, 382. For Dubois (1986, 29), it would be the wooden building temporarily used as a temple after the Archaic temple was burnt.
82 Tarditi 2014, 86.
83 They also appear in the plural in another text of Tegea: *IG* V.2 4 (*CGRN* 65), l. 7.
84 Guarducci 1952, 61.
85 Tarditi 2005; Tarditi 2014. This character of the terrain has been evoked to explain the presence of frogs and pond turtles in the zooarchaeological material: Vila 2000, 198.
86 Østby 2014d, 12.
87 Ødegård and Klempe 2014, 31.
88 Tarditi 2014, 60–61, 69–70.

violations and instead suggest that it refers to "each person in the cart."

[VIII] **During the *Panagorsis*, the *hieromnamones* must regulate trader-related questions, and the *damiorgos* has to regulate other questions.**

This clause indicates that the *panegyris* was an opportunity to trade. That shrines help to structure trade is normal,[89] and the text shows that an exchange economy was present in Arkadia.[90] This is the most ancient epigraphic attestation of markets during *panegyreis*, evoked subsequently in other inscriptions, such as those from the sanctuary of Apollo Aktios in Akarnania or concerning the Mysteries of Andania (Messenia).[91] A periodic market was to be regulated by both the *hieromnamones* and the city of Tegea if we accept the propositions suggested in the edition of the text edited by Thür and Taeuber.[92] The inscription does not make it possible to say if this market was simply intended to supply the pilgrims or if it was a true fair.[93] Such an intervention by the civic authorities is normal for a property belonging to the city, especially as it generally fell to the city to make arrangements for a market that was developing on the fringe of a *panegyris*.

(IX) **Dung that can be sold has to be removed on the 7th of the month of Leschanasios; if not, 1 drachma is owed.**

The presence of humans and animals around the sanctuary, and probably on the place called Alea, generated waste of all kinds (*kopros*). Some of it would be useful for agriculture and gardening, hence its commercial value, and its removal was to take place by a specific date.[94] We do not know when Leschanasios was in the Tegean calendar. If the removal of the refuse was intended to clean the place before the *panegyris*, we must place Leschanasios before it. Who should remove this manure? In the text of Thür and Taeuber, the verb remains without a subject.

This clause providing for the cleaning of the site echoes archaeological data: the ground to the north of the temple, free of any permanent structure until the Imperial period, was useful for the fourth-century BCE works. The recent Norwegian excavation found little material on its surface and deduced that it was regularly cleaned of refuse.[95]

(X) **During the month of Panagorisios ... to strangers ... going away ... People ...**

The last clause is too fragmented to be understandable. We can only read the name of the month Panagorsios, in which the great festival of the goddess took place, and the mention of foreigners (*xenoi*), which shows that this text still concerns the *panegyris*.

4 Blanks on Archaeological Maps with a Xenophontian Excursus towards a *Festwiese* Solution

Madeleine Jost wrote of the Tegean inscription that it provides "a quick but suggestive overview" (*un aperçu rapide mais suggestif*) of a Greek *panegyris*.[96] This underlines the real value of this text, which is a kind of agreement between the sanctuary and the city concerning a piece of land that the latter puts at the disposal of the former under certain conditions. It is sufficient to know the multiple uses of land of this kind: 'parking' for the pilgrims' animals and sacrificial animals, a possible location for a market during the festival, and grazing land. The Norwegian excavations may not have taken place on the ground referred to as *in Aleai*, because they were concerned with a space partly inside the *peribolos*, but the findings shed light on the environmental data that conditioned the possible uses of the land referred to as *in Aleai*: marshy soil, where a cart could become stuck so consolidation of the ground was necessary, a space with little tall vegetation and few buildings, but offering a natural meadow for some animals provided that they were not numerous or did not stay too long. It should be added without drawing any firm conclusions that the inscription was found a little to the north of the temple, i.e., within the later excavated area or close to it.

The results of the Norwegian excavations suggest another potential use that is not mentioned in the text. When a large building, such as the temple of Skopas, is to be constructed, space that extends beyond the footprint of the future building is needed for the construction site. Today's Parisians are in a good position to know this: after

---

89   Aurigny 2020, 94–97; Kowalzig 2020. See also Chankowski and Lo Monaco in this volume.
90   Roy 1999, 338–340.
91   Kristensen 2020, 213–214. Law of Andania: *IG* V.1 1390 (*CGRN* 222), ll. 98–103 (Deshours 2006, 91–92; Gawlinski 2012, 214–219).
92   There is a problem here in the placement of punctuation, which was noticed by Thür and Taeuber 1994, 17, n. 11. Their solution was to say that δαμιοργός (l. 28) is the subject of the second part of the sentence that constitutes clause VIII, and should therefore not be attached to clause IX, as was done. The second sigma that we think we read in ΔΑΜΙΟΡΓΟΣΣ would be an unnoticed interpunction.
93   Horster 2020, 133; Kristensen 2020, 213.
94   *NGSL*² 28. In Chios, a regulation of the fourth century BCE forbade the grazing of cattle in the sacred woods and the leaving of manure: *LSCG* no. 116. In Delphi, the amphictyonic regulation of 380 BCE forbade the removal of manure from the sacred ground: Rousset 2002, 188 (l. 21), 192.
95   Tarditi 2014, 86.
96   Jost 1985, 384.

the roof of Notre-Dame de Paris burnt down, the restoration site immediately invaded all the free land near the cathedral. Not only was the square of the metropolitan church requisitioned, but also the nearby park, where for a while there was even a question of cutting down hundred-year-old yew trees because construction huts had to be set up to store materials. The land just north of the temple of Alea was, in the fourth century BCE, filled with building waste: marbleworkers toiled nearby, and the stone residue from their labor was recycled to create stable ground.[97]

For these logistical problems, the sanctuary needed the help of the city, and such an arrangement was probably not unique. The Tegea inscription invites us to map our understanding of the sacred spaces of the Greeks. This text finds no parallel in epigraphic sources, but Xenophon writes something similar in his *Anabasis* (5.3.7–13), when he explains how he created a sanctuary to Artemis Ephesia around 380 BCE in Skillous near Olympia to fulfill a vow made in Ephesos. He used part of his spoils recovered from the expedition of the Ten Thousand.[98] Xenophon's text is roughly contemporary with the Tegean inscription and also speaks of a Peloponnesian sanctuary:

> Ξενοφῶν δὲ λαβὼν χωρίον ὠνεῖται τῇ θεῷ ὅπου ἀνεῖλεν ὁ θεός. Ἔτυχε δὲ διαρρέων διὰ τοῦ χωρίου ποταμὸς Σελινοῦς. Καὶ ἐν Ἐφέσῳ δὲ παρὰ τὸν τῆς Ἀρτέμιδος νεὼν Σελινοῦς ποταμὸς παραρρεῖ. Καὶ ἰχθύες τε ἐν ἀμφοτέροις ἔνεισι καὶ κόγχαι· ἐν δὲ τῷ ἐν Σκιλλοῦντι χωρίῳ καὶ θῆραι πάντων ὁπόσα ἐστὶν ἀγρευόμενα θηρία. Ἐποίησε δὲ καὶ βωμὸν καὶ ναὸν ἀπὸ τοῦ ἱεροῦ ἀργυρίου, καὶ τὸ λοιπὸν δὲ ἀεὶ δεκατεύων τὰ ἐκ τοῦ ἀγροῦ ὡραῖα θυσίαν ἐποίει τῇ θεῷ, καὶ πάντες οἱ πολῖται καὶ οἱ πρόσχωροι ἄνδρες καὶ γυναῖκες μετεῖχον τῆς ἑορτῆς. Παρεῖχε δὲ ἡ θεὸς τοῖς σκηνοῦσιν ἄλφιτα, ἄρτους, οἶνον, τραγήματα, καὶ τῶν θυομένων ἀπὸ τῆς ἱερᾶς νομῆς λάχος, καὶ τῶν θηρευομένων δέ. Καὶ γὰρ θήραν ἐποιοῦντο εἰς τὴν ἑορτὴν οἵ τε Ξενοφῶντος παῖδες καὶ οἱ τῶν ἄλλων πολιτῶν, οἱ δὲ βουλόμενοι καὶ ἄνδρες ξυνεθήρων· καὶ ἡλίσκετο τὰ μὲν ἐξ αὐτοῦ τοῦ ἱεροῦ χώρου, τὰ δὲ καὶ ἐκ τῆς Φολόης, σύες καὶ δορκάδες καὶ ἔλαφοι. Ἔστι δὲ ἡ χώρα ᾗ ἐκ Λακεδαίμονος εἰς Ὀλυμπίαν πορεύονται ὡς εἴκοσι στάδιοι ἀπὸ τοῦ ἐν Ὀλυμπίᾳ Διὸς ἱεροῦ. Ἔνι δ' ἐν τῷ ἱερῷ χώρῳ καὶ λειμὼν καὶ ὄρη δένδρων μεστά, ἱκανὰ σῦς καὶ αἶγας καὶ βοῦς τρέφειν καὶ ἵππους, ὥστε καὶ τὰ τῶν εἰς τὴν ἑορτὴν ἰόντων ὑποζύγια εὐωχεῖσθαι. Περὶ δὲ αὐτὸν τὸν ναὸν ἄλσος ἡμέρων δένδρων ἐφυτεύθη ὅσα ἐστὶ τρωκτὰ ὡραῖα. Ὁ δὲ ναὸς ὡς μικρὸς μεγάλῳ τῷ ἐν Ἐφέσῳ εἴκασται, καὶ τὸ ξόανον ἔοικεν ὡς κυπαρίττινον χρυσῷ ὄντι τῷ ἐν Ἐφέσῳ. Καὶ στήλη ἕστηκε παρὰ τὸν ναὸν γράμματα ἔχουσα· ΙΕΡΟΣ Ο ΧΩΡΟΣ ΤΗΣ ΑΡΤΕΜΙΔΟΣ. ΤΟΝ ΕΧΟΝΤΑ ΚΑΙ ΚΑΡΠΟΥΜΕΝΟΝ ΤΗΝ ΜΕΝ ΔΕΚΑΤΗΝ ΚΑΤΑΘΥΕΙΝ ΕΚΑΣΤΟΥ ΕΤΟΥΣ, ΕΚ ΔΕ ΤΟΥ ΠΕΡΙΤΤΟΥ ΤΟΝ ΝΑΟΝ ΕΠΙΣΚΕΥΑΖΕΙΝ. ΑΝ ΔΕ ΤΙΣ ΜΗ ΠΟΙΗΙ ΤΑΥΤΑ ΤΗΙ ΘΕΩΙ ΜΕΛΗΣΕΙ.

Upon receiving it [his part of the spoils] Xenophon bought a plot of ground (*chorion*) for the goddess in a place which Apollo's oracle appointed. As it chanced, there flowed through the plot a river named Selinus; and at Ephesus likewise a Selinus river flows past the temple of Artemis. In both streams, moreover, there are fish and mussels, while in the plot at Skillous there is hunting of all manner of beasts of the chase. Here Xenophon built an altar (*bômos*) and a temple (*naos*) with the sacred money, and from that time forth he would every year take the tithe of the products of the land in their season and offer sacrifice to the goddess, all the citizens and the men and women of the neighborhood taking part in the festival (*heortê*). And the goddess would provide for the banqueters barley meal and loaves of bread, wine, and sweetmeats, and a portion of the sacrificial victims from the sacred herd (*hiera nomê*), as well as of the victims taken in the chase. For Xenophon's sons and the sons of the other citizens used to have a hunting expedition at the time of the festival, and any grown men who so wished would join them; and they captured their game partly from the sacred precinct (*hieros chôros*) itself and partly from Mount Pholöe—boars and gazelles and stags.

The place (*chôra*) is situated on the road which leads from Lakedaimon to Olympia and is about twenty stadia from the sanctuary (*hieron*) of Zeus at Olympia. Within the sacred precinct (*hiéros chôros*), there is meadowland (*leimôn*) and tree-covered hills, suitable for the rearing of swine, goats, cattle, and horses, so that even the draught animals which bring people to the festival (*heortê*) have their feast also. Immediately surrounding the temple (*naos*) is a grove (*alsos*) of cultivated trees, producing all sorts of dessert fruits in their season. The temple (*naos*) itself is like the one at Ephesos, although small as compared with great, and the image (*xoanon*) of the goddess, although of cypress wood as compared

---

[97] Ødegård 2014, 89–90; Tarditi 2014, 64.
[98] Xen. *An.* 5.3.7, describes his situation with a complex expression: κατοικοῦντος ἤδη αὐτοῦ ἐν Σκιλλοῦντι ὑπὸ τῶν Λακεδαιμονίων οἰκισθέντος παρὰ τὴν Ὀλυμπίαν ("and while he was living at Scillus near Olympia," trans. Todd). This could conceal an attempt to create a colony with Xenophon as *oikistes*.

with gold, is like the Ephesian image. Beside the temple stands a tablet (*stêlê*) with this inscription: "The place is sacred to Artemis. He who holds it and enjoys its fruits must offer the tithe every year in sacrifice, and from the remainder must keep the temple in repair. If anyone leaves these things undone, the goddess will look to it."[99]

This description has been linked to the Persian *paradeisoi* experienced by Xenophon in the Orient.[100] But is this sufficient? Are Xenophon's models necessarily oriental? In the center of the sacred space thus created is an altar (*bômos*) and a temple (*naos*) with a cult statue (*xoanon*). Around the area is a sacred wood, comprised of cultivated species whose fruits would be consumed during the festival. The *alsos* of Artemis is an orchard.[101] There is also that which Xenophon describes in the form of the *hieros chôros*, crossed by the river Selinus.[102] It was formerly an agricultural domain, a *chôrion*, which provided a meadow (*leimôn*) and hills (*orê dendrôn mesta*) for the goddess' herds (the *hiera nomê*, which included sheep, goats, oxen, and horses) and could accommodate the pilgrims' livestock. One could also hunt there. The text implies that cereals were cultivated on the nearby lands and that a tithe (*dekatê*) of the crops was taken for Artemis. Together, these spaces generated income to fund the life of the sanctuary.[103] There are other sanctuaries known to be embedded in an agricultural estate that provided them with income, such as that of Zeus Temenites in Arkesine on Amorgos.[104] The whole therefore formed a much larger space than the one evoked by the inscription of Tegea, but whose elements served to address the same issues. There are also logistical problems related to the accommodation of people and animals. It was necessary to ensure that visitors had a place to pitch their tents of canvas, wood, reeds, anything that could be found near the pilgrims' gathering place: it is natural that Xenophon uses the participle τοῖς σκηνοῦσιν, "for those who are in tents." The tents accommodated visitors for the night and welcomed vendors of drinks, food, and even merchants who came for the fair.[105] The management of their installation is an essential element of the regulations of Greek sanctuaries, and the law of Andania of the end of the first century BCE devotes five lines to this prosaic question.[106] There is also the issue of animals, and particularly of the carts of the visitors to the sanctuary. Not only do visitors need a place to stay, but the animals also need to be part of the festivities. The inscriptions complete the picture, addressing the matters of manure left by the animals and their need for water: in Skillous, the Selinus river helped to solve the problems, but elsewhere it was feared that the animals would gather around the sacred fountains.[107] In fact, the omnipresence of animals posed problems for the management of public and sacred spaces. Cities, as well as sanctuaries,[108] had these concerns, among other practical matters, as demonstrated by the Tegea inscription.

Our view of the opposition between sacred and profane lands is indeed simplistic, and even anachronistic,[109] relying on an artificially clear divisions of space (and matters) that do not fit with the Greek experience of what is sacred. In reality, the logistics of an ancient *panegyris* led to a spatial expansion far beyond the *temenos* because the *temenos* space was not always sufficient, and many of the rules that applied to it did not permit the fulfillment of

---

99 Trans. Todd.
100 Pomeroy 1994, 247–248; L'Allier 1998.
101 This sacred wood is perhaps not a unique case: an inscription of c.350 BCE from Kos situates an altar in the middle of an olive grove, associated with a sanctuary of the Charites: *CGRN* 86, C (*IG* XII.4 275), ll. 8, 13, with mention of a stone (λίθος) ἐν ταῖς ἐλαίαις, on which certain rites were performed.
102 The name suggests a plant, the σέλινον, celery (*Apium graveolens*). Its wild form, the marsh-celery, in Greek ἐλειοσέλινον, grows in wet areas, "by irrigation-ditches and in marshes" (παρὰ τοὺς ὀχετοὺς καὶ ἐν τοῖς ἕλεσι, Theophr. *Hist. pl.* 7.6.2). The horses of the Achaian army grazed this plant at the edge of Skamander (Hom. *Il.* 2.776, using σέλινον). It is not surprising that some Mediterranean rivers have taken their name from it (e.g., the name of the Greek city of Selinous in Sicily). About this species, see Amigues 2004, 169–170.
103 Papazarkadas 2011.
104 For the sanctuary of Zeus Temenites: Pernin 2014, 270–275, no. 131, ll. 35–37. The word τέμενος applies here only to the space of the sanctuary itself, and the divine owner is called Zeus Temenites. The surrounding land is cultivated and rented, but never designated by the word τέμενος.
105 Cf. the fair of Isis at Tithorea in mid-Imperial era Phokis, Paus. 10.32.15: ταύτῃ μὲν δὴ τῇ ἡμέρᾳ τοσαῦτα περὶ τὸ ἱερὸν δρῶσι, τῇ δὲ ἐπιούσῃ σκηνὰς οἱ καπηλεύοντες ποιοῦνται καλάμου τε καὶ ἄλλης ὕλης αὐτοσχεδίου· τῇ τελευταίᾳ δὲ τῶν τριῶν πανηγυρίζουσι πιπράσκοντες καὶ ἀνδράποδα καὶ κτήνη τὰ πάντα, ἔτι δὲ ἐσθῆτας καὶ ἄργυρον καὶ χρυσόν. ("So on this day they perform these acts about the sanctuary, and on the next day the small traders make themselves booths of reeds or other improvised material. On the last of the three days, they hold a fair, selling slaves, cattle of all kinds, clothes, silver, and gold," trans. Jones).
106 *IG* V.1 1390 (*CGRN* 222), ll. 34–37. Deshours 2006, 92; Gawlinski 2012, 143–148; Horster 2020, 129–131. For accommodation at Greek sanctuaries, see also Ekroth this volume.
107 One should also think about the means of tethering the animals and perhaps also about the need to guard against thieves of cattle, donkeys, mules, horses, who would find good opportunities for plunder there.
108 *NGSL*² 27–28.
109 Whatever the conceptual problems posed by these categories: Scullion 2005.

all needs. These problems arose even in sanctuaries such as Delphi, with its awkward terrain that forced many pilgrims to camp on the plain.[110] In this respect, the sanctuary of Alea Athena had an advantage over that of Apollo Pythios: the former, surrounded by free space, was on flat land in a suburb of the city.

We must therefore try to propose new interpretations on the question of spatial organization of Greek sanctuaries and festivals. In the 1990s, the German archaeologist Ulrich Sinn, who was attached to the excavations of Olympia, resumed the study of the spaces of this sanctuary. He noted that it was impossible to fit all the activities taking place at the time of the Olympic games into the sacred precinct. Where did the athletes and pilgrims camp? How were their basic needs met and the waste generated by their presence managed? Where were the large banquets held? Where did the fairs of the *panegyris* take place?[111] How did the sanctuary deal with the suppliants who took refuge in the sanctuary, sometimes for long periods of time?[112] What types of accommodation were available to the vendors of votives and all the shopkeepers who gravitated towards a Greek sanctuary? Finally, we must not forget that some sanctuaries could serve as a temporary place of refuge for the surrounding populations in times of war.[113] Ulrich Sinn concluded:

> To be able to measure precisely the need for space that a sanctuary required, one must keep in mind that the religious festivals of the Greeks were not limited to sacrifices at the altar, tributes paid to the statue of worship, and the reception of ex-voto. The religious festivals integrated elements fundamental to the processions and the sacred gathering for the dances and ritual banquets. We must also take into account the fact that the religious festivals lasted several days. For the pilgrims, accommodation was to be provided in the shrines, as well as the necessary facilities for daily life and hygiene.[114]

These questions could be solved in an ephemeral way: simple huts with materials gathered on site, tents erected here and there.[115] Moreover, participation in a festival was often referred to in ancient Greek by the expression "pitching a tent" (*skanopagesthai*).[116] Furthermore, Sinn notes the presence, around the *temenos* itself, of an unbuilt space that could be used for multiple purposes. Sinn opposes the idea of *inner* and *outer precincts* by making them two equally sacred spaces, but spaces where the demands of sacredness did not have the same intensity.[117] He even suggests that a reflection of this organization can be found in a passage of *The Suppliants*, where Aischylos evokes the suppliant, who, after having laid down his branches, passes through a flattened land without buildings (λευρόν ἄλσος, l. 508), which touches the sanctuary and whose ground you can walk on (βέβηλον ἄλσος, l. 509), and wonders to what extent it is protected by the god.[118] It is this kind of terrain that Sinn proposes to call the *Festwiese* (*festival meadow*) of the sanctuary, taking the name that in Bavaria is sometimes given to the land surrounding Catholic sanctuaries, land that is used occasionally at the time of a festival, and which is otherwise pasture.[119] The Sinn model allows us to think about what this terrain as described *in Aleai* was like, i.e., the *Festwiese* of the goddess. The activities that took place on the sidelines of the festival were concentrated there, while at other non-festival times, this pastoral region in Arkadia was used as pastureland.

The value of the Tegean case is that it is possible, thanks to the excavations, to see what this area of the *panegyris* was like, and to answer the challenge posed by Troels Myrup Kristensen: to collate textual and archaeological data to arrive at an image of the experience of *panegyris* for a pilgrim, and to understand to what the 'blanks,' the empty spaces, on maps of sanctuaries—with their numerous

---

110   Aurigny 2020, 97–103.
111   Fairs: De Ligt and De Neeve 1988.
112   See Gawlinski this volume.
113   Sinn 1988, 154–157 (Aigina); Sinn 1992, 180–183 (Sounion); Sinn 1993 (Olympia; supplicants; refuge in the vicinity of the sanctuary; context of this practice in Müller 1975). I sincerely thank Gunnel Ekroth for pointing me in the direction of the work of Ulrich Sinn.
114   Sinn 1992, 181 (quotation translated from the German).
115   Barringer 2021, 58–59.
116   See, e.g., the sacred regulation of Kos, *LSCG* no. 168 (first century BCE).
117   The sacredness of the *outer precinct* is contested by Scullion 2005, 115, who notes that the actual ritual activities must take place in the *temenos*.
118   Aisch. *Supp*. ll. 508–509. Sinn 1992, 183, draws attention to this text. The word ἄλσος does not designate here a sacred wood, but a plain: Bowen 2013, 251–252. It can be synonymous with 'sanctuary' even when there are no trees (Strabo 9.2.33=C412, about the sanctuary of Poseidon at Onchestos in Boiotia: οἱ δὲ ποιηταὶ κοσμοῦσιν, ἄλση καλοῦντες τὰ ἱερὰ πάντα, κἂν ᾖ ψιλά; "But the poets embellish things, calling all sacred precincts 'sacred groves,' even if they are bare of trees," trans. Jones). See Sinn 2005 et al., 12–13. See also Scullion 2005, 115, contrary to Sinn's idea that this land would also be consecrated.
119   Sinn 1992, 183; Sinn et al. 2005, 5, 10 (pages by Sinn) about the sanctuaries of Aphaia on Aigina, Hera in Perachora, Hera on Samos, etc. Sinn sometimes speaks about a *Festplatz* (plural, *Festplätze*): Sinn 1988, 154; Sinn 1993, 96–97.

post holes indicative of temporary constructions—might correspond.[120] At Tegea, the area north of the temple seems to have remained undeveloped for a long time, except for the mud-brick wall of the mid-sixth century BCE, which could have served as a *peribolos* in place of an earlier stone wall of the late seventh century BCE. The mud-brick wall was demolished at the end of the sixth century BCE, and the whole area was covered by a pebble surface, which could indicate an expansion of the sanctuary to the north.[121] Its ground then preserved the traces of trampling and occupation: bones, charcoal, and fragments of pottery littered it. It had to be strengthened with clay, probably because of floods. We can also suppose that the pilgrims could settle here for their meals. This is obviously the same site that was used for the construction of the temple of Skopas.

Acknowledgment

I would like to thank Madeleine Jost who kindly proofread this article and made some precious remarks.

Works Cited

Amigues, S. 2004. "Les plantes du ramassage dans l'alimentation gréco-romaine." *Pallas* 64: 169–182.

Aurigny, H. 2020. "Gathering in the Panhellenic Sanctuary at Delphi: An Archaeological Approach." In *Pilgrimage and Economy in the Ancient Mediterranean*, edited by A. Collar and T.M. Kristensen, 93–115. Leiden.

Baladié, R. 1980. *Le Péloponnèse de Strabon. Étude de géographie historique*. Paris.

Barringer, J.M. 2021. *Olympia: A Cultural History*. Princeton.

Bélis, A. 1986. "La phorbéia." *BCH* 110: 205–218.

Benveniste, É. 1969. *Le vocabulaire des institutions indo-européennes*. Paris.

Bérard, V. 1889. "Inscription archaïque de Tégée." *BCH* 13: 281–293.

Bjune, A.E., K. Krzywinski, and A. Overland. 2014. "Palynological Investigations in the Sanctuary of Athena Alea." In *Tegea 2, Investigations in the Sanctuary of Athena Alea 1990–94 and 2004*, edited by E. Østby, 443–449. Athens.

Bodson, L. 1978. *IEPA ZΩIA. Contribution à l'étude de la place de l'animal dans la religion grecque ancienne*. Brussels.

Bowen, A.J. 2013. *Aeschylus,* Suppliant Women, *Edited with an Introduction, Translation & Commentary*. Oxford.

Carbon, J.-M., and J.P.T. Clackson. 2016. "Arms and the Boy: On the New Festival Calendar from Arkadia." *Kernos* 29: 119–158.

Danielsson, O.A. 1890. "Epigraphica II: de titulo tegeatico." *UppsÅrsskr* 28–63.

De Ligt, L., and P.W. De Neeve. 1988. "Ancient Periodic Markets: Festivals and Fairs." *Athenaeum* 66: 391–416.

Deshours, N. 2006. *Les mystères d'Andania. Étude d'épigraphie et d'histoire religieuse. Scripta antiqua* 16. Bordeaux.

Dubois, L. 1986. *Recherches sur le dialecte arcadien*. Louvain-la-Neuve.

Dubois, L. 2010. "En relisant les inscriptions arcadiennes." In *Paysage et religion en Grèce antique. Mélanges offerts à Madeleine Jost, Travaux de la Maison René-Ginouvès* 10, edited by P. Carlier and C. Lerouge-Cohen, 17–25. Paris.

Dubois, L. 2018. "Une nouvelle inscription arcadienne." *RÉG* 131: XIII–XVII.

Feyel, C. 2006. "La dokimasia des animaux sacrifiés." *RPhil* 80: 33–55.

Gawlinski, L. 2012. *The Sacred Law of Andania: A New Text with Commentary*. Berlin.

Georgoudi, S. 1974. "Quelques problèmes de la transhumance en Grèce antique." *RÉG* 87: 155–185.

Guarducci, M. 1937. "Miscellanea I: i pascoli del santuario di Alea a Tegea." *RivFil* 65: 169–172.

Guarducci, M. 1952. "La legge dei Tegeati intorno ai pascoli di Alea." *RivFil* 80: 49–68.

Heinrichs, J. 2015. "Military Integration in Late Archaic Arkadia: New Evidence from a Bronze Pinax (ca. 500 BC) of the Lykaion." In *The Many Faces of War in the Ancient World*, edited by W. Heckel, S. Müller, and G. Wrightson, 1–89. Cambridge.

Hermary, A., M. Leguilloux, V. Chankowski, and A. Petropoulou. 2004. "Les sacrifices dans le monde grec." In *ThesCRA* 1, 59–134. Los Angeles.

Horster, M. 2020. "Hellenistic Festivals: Aspects of the Economic Impact on Cities and Sanctuaries." In *Pilgrimage and Economy in the Ancient Mediterranean*, edited by A. Collar, and T.M. Kristensen, 116–139. Leiden.

Jacquemin A. 1991. "Remarques sur le budget sacrificiel d'une cité: Délos indépendante." In *L'espace sacrificiel dans les civilisations méditerranéennes de l'Antiquité*, edited by R. Étienne and M.-T. Le Dinahet, 93–98. Paris.

Jost, M. 1985. *Sanctuaires et cultes d'Arcadie*. Paris.

Jost, M. 2018. "Sanctuaires d'Arcadie trente ans après: bilan des recherches." *BCH* 142: 97–144.

Jost, M. 2021. "Héros épiques en Arcadie." *RÉG* 134: 177–185.

Kowalzig, B. 2020. "Festivals, Fairs and Foreigners: Towards an Economics of Religion in the Mediterranean." In *Pilgrimage*

---

120 Kristensen 2020, 204, 214–217. The question of the festival experience (The Experience of Festivals) occupies the end of Parker 2011 (171–223).

121 Tarditi 2005, 199–201; Tarditi 2014, 75–76, 85–86.

and *Economy in the Ancient Mediterranean*, edited by A. Collar and T.M. Kristensen, 287–328. Leiden.

Kristensen, T.M. 2020. "Space, Exchange and the Embedded Economies of Greek Sanctuaries." In *Pilgrimage and Economy in the Ancient Mediterranean*, edited by A. Collar and T.M. Kristensen, 204–227. Leiden.

L'Allier, L. 1998. "Le domaine de Scillonte: Xénophon et l'exemple perse." *Phoenix* 52: 1–14.

Luce, J.-M. 2014. "Le secteur nord à partir de l'époque paléochrétienne." In *Tegea 2. Investigations in the Sanctuary of Athena Alea 1990–94*, edited by E. Østby, 37–54. Athens.

Maier, F.G. 1959–1961. *Griechische Mauerbauinschriften. Vestigia* 1–2. Heidelberg.

McInerney, J. 2010. *The Cattle of the Sun: Cows and Culture in the World of the Ancient Greeks*. Princeton.

Müller, H. 1975. "Φυγῆς ἕνεκεν." *Chiron* 5: 129–156.

Nielsen, T.H. 2002. *Arkadia and its Poleis in the Archaic and Classical Periods, Hypomnemata* 140. Göttingen.

Nielsen, T.H. 2004. "Arkadia." In *An Inventory of Archaic and Classical* Poleis, edited by M.H. Hansen and T.H. Nielsen, 505–539. Oxford.

Ødegård, K. 2014. "Excavation in Squares C9–C10 and D9–D10 in 1993." In *Tegea 2. Investigations in the Sanctuary of Athena Alea 1990–94 and 2004*, edited by E. Østby, 87–95. Athens.

Ødegård, K., and H. Klempe. 2014. "The Sanctuary of Athena Alea and its Setting." In *Tegea 2. Investigations in the Sanctuary of Athena Alea 1990–94 and 2004*, edited by E. Østby, 26–36. Athens.

Osborne, R. 1987. *Classical Landscape with Figures. The Ancient Greek City and its Countryside*. London.

Østby, E. 2014a. "The Classical Temple of Athena Alea at Tegea." In *Tegea 2. Investigations in the Sanctuary of Athena Alea 1990–94 and 2004*, edited by E. Østby, 317–351. Athens.

Østby, E. 2014b. "The Norwegian Excavation Project in the Sanctuary of Athena Alea at Tegea: An Introduction." In *Tegea 1. Investigations in the Sanctuary of Athena Alea 1990–94*, edited by E. Østby, 1–10. Athens.

Østby, E. 2014c. "The Sanctuary of Alea at Tegea in the Pre-Classical Period." In *Tegea 1. Investigations in the Sanctuary of Athena Alea 1990–94*, edited by E. Østby, 11–56. Athens.

Østby, E. 2014d. "The Sanctuary of Athena Alea at Tegea: The Topographical Evidence." In *Tegea 2. Investigations in the Sanctuary of Athena Alea 1990–94 and 2004*, edited by E. Østby, 11–26. Athens.

Papazarkadas, N. 2011. *Sacred and Public Land in Ancient Athens*. Oxford.

Parker, R.C.T. 2011. *On Greek Religion*. Ithaca.

Pernin, I. 2014. *Les baux ruraux en Grèce ancienne. Corpus épigraphique et étude. Travaux de la Maison de l'Orient* 66, Lyon.

Pomeroy, S.B. 1994. *Xenophon.* Oeconomicus *A Social and Historical Commentary*. Oxford.

Rousset, D. 2002. *Le territoire de Delphes et la terre d'Apollon, BÉFAR* 310. Athens.

Roy, J. 1999. "The Economies of Arkadia." In *Defining Ancient Arkadia*, edited by T.H. Nielsen and J. Roy, 320–381. Copenhagen.

Scullion, S. 2005. "'Pilgrimage' and Greek Religion: Sacred and Secular in the Pagan *Polis*." In *Pilgrimage in Graeco-Roman & Early Christian Antiquity*, edited by J. Elsner and I. Rutherford, 111–130. Oxford.

Sinn, U. 1988. "Der Kult der Aphaia auf Aegina." In *Early Greek Cult Practice*, edited by R. Hägg, N. Marinatos, and G.C. Nordquist, 149–159. Stockholm.

Sinn, U. 1992. "Das befestigte Heiligtum der Athena und des Poseidon an der 'Heiligen Landspitze Attikas.'" *AntW* 23: 175–190.

Sinn, U. 1993. "Greek Sanctuaries as Places of Refuge." In *Greek Sanctuaries. New Approaches*, edited by N. Marinatos and R. Hägg, 88–109. London.

Sinn, U., A. Seiffert, F. Hölscher, and C. Leypold. 2005. "Kultorte. Griechenland." In *ThesCRA* 4, 1–127. Los Angeles.

Sourvinou-Inwood, C., S. Georgoudi, V. Pirenne-Delforge, and J.B. Connelly. 2005. "Personnel de culte: monde grec." In *ThesCRA* 5, 1–65. Los Angeles.

Tarditi, C. 2005. "The Sanctuary of Athena Alea at Tegea: Recent Excavations in the Northern Area. Results and Problems." In *Ancient Arcadia. Papers from the third international seminar on ancient Arcadia held at the Norwegian Institute at Athens, 7–10 May 2002*, edited by E. Østby, 197–208. Athens.

Tarditi, C. 2014. "The Excavation in the Northern Sector: Classical and Pre-Classical Layers." In *Tegea 2. Investigations in the Sanctuary of Athena Alea 1990–94 and 2004*, edited by E. Østby, 55–86. Athens.

Thür, G., and H. Taeuber. 1994. *Prozessrechtliche Inschriften der griechischen Poleis. Arkadien*. Vienna.

van Straten, F.T. 1987. "Greek Sacrificial Representations: Livestock Prices and Religious Mentality." In *Gifts to the Gods, Boreas* 15, edited by T. Linders and G. Nordquist, 159–170. Uppsala.

Vila, E. 2000. "Bone remains from sacrificial places: the temples of Athena Alea at Tegea and of Asea on Agios Elias (The Peloponnese, Greece)." In *Archaeozoology of the Near East,4 B*, edited by M. Mashkour, A.M. Choyke, H. Buitenhuis, and F. Poplin, 197–205. Groningen.

Vila, E. 2014. "Étude archéozoologique des vestiges osseux de la fouille dans le temple." In *Tegea 1. Investigations in the Sanctuary of Athena Alea 1990–94*, edited by E. Østby, 547–562. Athens.

Villing, A. 2017. "Don't Kill the Goose that Lays the Golden Egg? Some Thoughts on Bird Sacrifices in Ancient Greece." In *Animal Sacrifice in the Ancient Greek World*, edited by S. Hitch and I. Rutherford, 63–101. Cambridge.

CHAPTER 5

Utilitarian Uses of Water at Greek Sanctuaries

Patrik Klingborg

In the well-known dossier of regulations for the Mysteries at Andania, it is stated that during the *panegyris*, the *agoranomos* is responsible for ensuring that "the water runs just as it is allotted and no one hinders those using it."[1] What the water was used for is not mentioned, but there can be little doubt that water had numerous functions within the context of Greek cults and sanctuaries, including basic needs, such as drinking, cooking, and washing. Nonetheless, modern scholarship has largely ignored utilitarian and practical uses of water at Greek sanctuaries. Instead, water supply infrastructure and sources have regularly been interpreted in terms of the religious significance of water: in particular, rituals of purification, cleaning of cult images, and healing.[2] The aim of this study is to move away from the focus on water in Greek sanctuaries as used for activities where it played a central religious function and instead explore other, 'utilitarian', forms of water use at these sites. Admittedly, there is no clear line between 'utilitarian' and 'non-utilitarian' activities, and these modern terms may not accurately represent activities in the ancient world. Is the use of water religiously significant when preparing a stew based on sacrificial meat or simply a necessity? Probably, it can be either depending on the type of ritual, context, and point of view. Unavoidably this paper will sometimes approach the grey area between 'utilitarian and 'non-utilitarian' uses.

In order to investigate pragmatic uses of water in Greek sanctuaries, this essay begins by focusing on four types of activities in, and in connection to, sanctuaries: drinking, food preparation, washing and cleaning, and gardening in a wide sense. Production and manufacturing in connection to sanctuaries, which is receiving increasing interest in scholarship, was also important and used a great deal of water. But such activities are best explored further in their own right before we can assess how they affected the water supply and usage in sanctuaries. Consequently, they will not be treated here.[3] Similarly, bathing is avoided, as it is discussed in the article by Monika Trümper in this volume. Many other miscellaneous activities that required water are not covered here, e.g., using water both when compacting the racing track in stadia and in order to bind the dust.[4] Construction works, often taking long periods of time, also required water in various stages.

Following the discussion of the various utilitarian uses of water, the essay will briefly address how the availability of water affected activities in sanctuaries. How much water was available, how was it acquired, and when? This is important as the access to water largely limits possible activities at a site.

1 Drinking

Both humans and animals need to consume liquids to survive, and this need is especially acute in warm and dry areas, such as the Mediterranean. If drinking only water, a human requires 2.5–3 liters per day to stay alive.[5] In the context of Greek sanctuaries, it is unknown whether the primary beverage for humans was water, wine, or something else. Cults are known where wine was not allowed.[6] Presumably no one generalization is valid for all sanctuaries. Similarly, figures for the minimum volume of water an individual consumed in practice per day in antiquity,

---

1 *IG* V.1 1390=*CGRN* 222, ll. 103–105, including translation; Gawlinski 2012. Infra n. 68.
2 E.g., Cole (1988), who does not mention any non-ritual aspects in an article on the use of water in Greek sanctuaries. See also Burkert 1985, 76; Parker 1996, 226–227; Bremmer 2006, 27; Pedley 2006, 77; Dignas 2007, 166. Water for healing is better explored, see e.g., Ginouvès 1962.
3 Industrial activity in connection to sanctuaries is well known, e.g., from the Rachi settlement near Isthmia published in preliminary reports, most recently Anderson-Stojanović 1996. For a general overview of metal working related to sanctuaries, see Risberg 1997. For specific sites, see, e.g., Isthmia (Rostoker and Gebhard 1980), Olympia (Heilmeyer, Zimmer, and Schneider 1987), and Tegea (Nordqvist 1997). For tanning in connection with sanctuaries, see Pakkanen in this volume. For a considerably more comprehensive study on activities outside of the *temenos*, including production, see Frejman 2020.
4 Miller 2001, 18, 37. The painting on an Attic *skyphos* of 460–450 BCE (*BAPD* 7205; Bloesch et al. 1982, no. 39) has been interpreted as depicting a man watering a sporting ground.
5 Reed and Reed 2013, table 9.1.
6 Cook and Plommer (1966, 32, 162, 164) state that wine was forbidden at the sanctuary of Hemithea at Kastabos, but their evidence is not conclusive. Wächter (1910, 113–114) mentions bans against "Weingenusses" to prevent worshippers from being drunk during ceremonies.

i.e., including limited hygiene and cooking, vary widely in modern scholarship, mostly from 5–15 liters.[7] But despite the importance of drinking, direct evidence for the consumption of water in sanctuaries is largely lacking. This is especially notable in sacred laws. In a rare case, an inscription dating to about 400 BCE from a sanctuary of the nymphs on the coastal road to Sounion records that anyone was allowed to take a drink from the sanctuary's spring at a cost of 1 obol, a price that also included the right to continue doing so for a full year. For those who needed more water, it was possible to pay 1 obol for drawing a full amphora one time.[8] Presumably the absence of further evidence of drinking water in sanctuaries is due to the unspectacular nature of the activity. But the lack of rules preventing worshippers from using 'the wrong' water sources for drinking or other activities also suggests that there was no strong divide between water sources supplying water for activities where the water played a special role and activities where it did not.[9]

Indirect evidence is more common, for example, in inscriptions recording what was consumed within the framework of cults. A series of inscriptions from Delos records that for the festival of Posideia, 3 *metretai* and 6 *choeis* of sweet wine, 12 jars of Knidian wine, and 35 jars of Koan wine were bought, a grand total of about 1,500 liters.[10] Philippe Bruneau suggested that this was enough for 1,000 persons and that the wine was mixed with at least another 1,500 liters of water. More extensive diluting of 1:3 as mentioned by Hesiod (*Op.* 596) would require 4,500 liters of water.[11] Consequently, in this case, regardless of the degree to which the wine was mixed, a lot of water was needed for drinking during the festival. Similar patterns should be expected at other major festivals. The available space in the stadia at Olympia and Nemea has been calculated to have been up to 40,000 people, giving a notion of the massive crowds attending the games.[12] If correct, this figure indicates that the minimum volume of water used per day in order to survive was close to 100,000 liters while a considerably more substantial figure of over 150,000 liters is more likely.

There were also a great number of animals in and around Greek sanctuaries, including sacrificial animals (both for sale and for immediate slaughter), sacred herds, profane flocks, beasts of burden and transportation, as well as animals used in ongoing building activities.[13] Irrespective of the animals' use, all would need drinking water, although it is uncertain whether animals to be sacrificed shortly were regarded as especially important to water in order to keep them fresh or whether they could be left thirsty since they were to die soon anyway. Oxen drinking water in connection with sacrifices are known from at least two Attic red-figure stamnoi, one from 490–480 BCE and another c.450–425 BCE.[14] In terms of volume, a single horse or ox needs between 15 and 30 liters of water per day in a warm and dry climate, and a donkey about 20 liters.[15] Goats, sheep and pigs need up to 20 liters per day.[16] This is considerably more than what a human requires. Considering the large number of animals that often must have been found in and around sanctuaries, especially major sanctuaries, they would have represented a considerable drain on resources, particularly during major festivals.

Figures recording the number of animals to be sacrificed give us an idea of how much water they would need if they were kept at the sanctuary for any time before being killed. In most cases, the volumes would be manageable as long as a water source was available in close vicinity; sacrificial calendars suggest frequent, but small-scale sacrifices of one or a small number as the norm.[17] Moreover, handling only a small number of animals reduced the need to collect them at the site beforehand, minimizing the need to water them. Larger sacrifices naturally would require greater organization, suggesting longer periods of time during which the animals would be gathered at the same spot, and consequently a larger need for water in many cases. A large hecatomb, such as the 109 oxen recorded

---

7   Connelly and Wilson 2002, 288–289; Mantellini 2015, 419; Klingborg and Finné 2018, 119–120.
8   Bousquet 1967, 92–95=*LSCG* no. 178; Koerner 1974, 173. The naming of the water source suggests that it is a spring or fountain rather than a well, cistern, or something similar.
9   There are exceptions, however, such as the water used only for ritual hand washing at Delion (Thuc. 4.97.3).
10 *ID* 440; *ID* 445=*CGRN* 199. See Bruneau 1970, 263, n. 1; Linders 1994.
11 Lynch 2007, 243; O'Connor 2015, 104–105. For other mixings, see Ath. 10.423–427; Plut. *Mor.* 657.
12 Birge, Kraynak, and Miller 1992, 178; Senff 2017, 197. Some estimates are even higher; Nielsen (2007, 55) estimates 45,000 spectators at Olympia in the mid-fourth century BCE.
13 For animals used for transport, see, e.g., the building nominated as a stable at the sanctuary of Artemis at Brauron (Themelis 2002, 106–107).
14 Van Straten 1995, 209, no. V90 (*BAPD* 213476), 217–218, no. V135 (Paris, Musée du Louvre C 10.754); Ekroth 2005, 16.
15 Engels 1978, 127 (horses); Dixon and Southern 1992, 206 (horses); Bachrach 1993, 720 (oxen); Roth 1999, 65 (donkeys). For a comparison, see also Roth 1999, 62–67. Donkeys can survive on considerably less water for short periods.
16 Reed and Reed 2013, table 9.2.
17 E.g., *IG* I³ 256bis=*CGRN* 32 (sacrificial calendar of the deme of Thorikos), *IG* II² 4971=*CGRN* 53 (sacrificial calendar of the deme of Erchia in Attika), *IG* II² 1358=*CGRN* 56 (sacrificial calendar of the Marathonian Tetrapolis).

at Delos around 375 BCE, would require 1635–3270 liters of water every day the animals were kept alive before the sacrifice; presumably they were delivered to the island as late as possible.[18] Similar volumes would be needed for the Great Panathenaia, which is usually assumed to have included a full hecatomb of 100 cattle.[19] In an extreme case, Xenophon recounts that at the Pythian festival in 370 BCE organized by Jason, tyrant of Pherai, 1,000 cattle and over 10,000 sheep, goats, and pigs were collected.[20] This represents somewhere between 35,000 and 280,000 liters of water per day with volumes at just under 100,000 liters per day as a realistic estimate. While the scale in this case is unprecedented, and may, in fact, never have taken place, it indicates the large volume of water required by the victims. Regardless of the actual number, it is likely that most of the animals for major occasions were kept away from the sanctuary until shortly before the sacrifice. This is also suggested by an inscription from Delphi recording a spring or fountain called the Kerameia outside of the sanctuary where only sacred beasts were allowed to drink.[21]

Building activity would also require the presence of large numbers of animals in and around sanctuaries. Notably, in contrast to sacrificial victims these animals would be needed over extended periods of time as construction projects could last for years or decades. They would therefore require an extensive and permanent water supply. However, only rarely do we have any figures suggesting how many animals were needed for specific building projects in sanctuaries. From Epidauros, the acquisition of 43 carts gives an idea of the number of animals used for transportation for one construction project.[22] More exact information is known from secular projects. For example, in 330/29 BCE, Eudemos of Plataia contributed 2,000 oxen, requiring 30,000–60,000 liters of water per day, for the construction of the Panathenaic *stadion* in Athens and its seating.[23] If this is any indication of how many animals were used when constructing monumental structures in sanctuaries, then it is likely that these created the single largest water demand during such periods, even if the majority of them were not kept in the vicinity of the site itself.

Finally, watering animals in and around sanctuaries could be problematic. Secular animals were not allowed to drink from the Kerameia spring at Delphi as noted above, testifying to a distinction between those animals that belonged to the god and those that did not. In a sacred law dating to the second or beginning of the first century BCE from an unknown sanctuary at Eresos, a final line reads "Do not give water to drink to flocks or pasture animals in the *temenos*."[24] The fact that the line appears after an empty row at the end of the inscription suggests that it was a later addition as, or when, the practice of watering animals within the sacred area became an issue. At Megalopolis, a water basin was found abutting the outside of the propylon, perhaps intended to allow animals to quench their thirst.[25] But while water sources have been found just outside of the *temenos* at some other sanctuaries as well, such as that of Artemis at Lousoi and Demeter at Priene, it is considerably rarer than perhaps expected.[26] Notably, grazing is treated far more commonly than drinking in sacred laws, suggesting that using water resources was not viewed as damaging to a similar degree.[27]

2   Cooking

Preparation of food was another activity requiring water. Animal sacrifices were of primary importance in Greek religion as a way to communicate with the gods, ask for help, or give thanks. During the most common form of sacrifice, *thysia*, some bones and fat would be consumed by fire while the meat was divided between the participants of the ritual. Usually the meat was then consumed, either during a communal meal at the sanctuary or at home.[28] In many cases, the meat was also supplemented by that from other animals that had not been sacrificed.[29] The centrality of animal sacrifices and, following this, consumption of meat, are of major importance for the necessity

---

18   *IG* II² 1635, l. 36.
19   Pritchett and Pippin 1956, 256. See also *IG* II³ 447=*CGRN* 92, which records that 4,100 dr were set aside for cows for the Little Panathenaia, interpreted as enough for a full hecatomb.
20   Xen. *Hell*. 6.4.29; Jameson 1988, 95.
21   *CID* IV 108, ll. 25–27.
22   Burford 1969, 74, 184–187.
23   *IG* II³ 352. Note that this is phrased as 1,000 yokes of oxen, i.e., 2,000 animals. *AIO* no. 65 suggests that this relates to 1,000 days of work, not 2,000 actual animals.
24   *IG* XII.Supp. 126=*CGRN* 181, ll. 21–22. Cf. Chandezon, this volume.
25   Lauter-Bufe 2009, 33–34.
26   Kobusch 2020, 75. Note that it is often difficult to establish the relationship between the location of the water source and the *temenos*. Kobusch proposes that it is better to simply discuss water sources as located in the entrance area.
27   E.g., *LSCG* no. 84, ll. 8–14; *LSCG* no. 91, ll. 9–12; *LSCG* no. 116, ll. 2–6. For more examples, see Dillon 1997; Rostad 2006.
28   Ekroth 2007, 250. In some cases, the meat was sold. On the handling of the meat, including sales, see Lo Monaco in this volume.
29   Ekroth 2007, 268–269.

of water in Greek sanctuaries because, in contrast to the common idea that the meat was grilled, Gunnel Ekroth has convincingly shown that "[m]ost meat eaten in sanctuaries seems to have been boiled."[30] How much "most meat" was, as well as whether only water was used to cook it, or if other liquids such as wine were extensively used, is unknown.[31] Certainly the ratio between liquid and meat shifted from sacrifice to sacrifice depending on the number of people who were to take part in the meal (i.e., how much food was needed), other ingredients used, the wish to create a rich meal, as well as numerous other potential factors. At a bare minimum, the liquid would have to cover the meat and other ingredients. Moreover, the weight, and therefore amount of meat, of the victim also varied, both over time and between individuals.[32] Overall, however, cattle, pigs, and sheep/goats were considerably smaller in antiquity than today, perhaps only reaching a third of their modern size.[33] Following Michael Jameson, a cow may have provided 100 kg of meat, a pig 50 kg, and a sheep or goat 20–30 kg.[34] If we assume that a generous amount of water was used in relation to the meat, such as a 1:3 ratio, then preparing the meat from a cow would require 30 liters of water, and the food could feed 400 people if allowing for portions of 250 gr of meat each. The number of individuals is important because they would consume 1200 liters altogether if each drank 3 liters of water per day. Consequently, the need for drinking water thus exceeded that for cooking by a factor of 40.

The quantity of drinking water needed for animals also quickly exceeded that required for cooking, especially in the case of smaller victims. But since many such animals may not have spent any significant period of time in the sanctuary before being sacrificed, their impact on the water consumption was probably dictated by the cooking.

The number of people attending sacrifices and festivals is another way to approach how much water would be required for cooking. Turning again to the festival of Posideia on Delos, scholars calculate that the sacrificial meat (from an ox, as well as one or more goats, sheep, and pigs) was enough to feed 1,000 individuals.[35] If these meals were boiled with water, then a considerable volume must have been used regardless of the ratio of water to kilogram of meat.

One important consequence of thinking in terms of the water needed for preparing meat is that although major events obviously demanded a great deal of water, smaller sacrifices would require water on a regular basis, creating a semi-regular low-intensity demand. At Marathon, for example, six cattle, as well as 29–37 other victims, were sacrificed per year.[36] Additionally, it seems safe to assume that many additional animals would be sacrificed by private individuals throughout the seasons.

Finally, boiling sacrificial meat was not the only type of food preparation requiring water. Bread was an important staple food in ancient Greece and in at least one case, the Eileithyia festival on Delos, an ἀρτοκόπος, baker, is attested.[37] While one rarely connects baking with water consumption, the activity requires a significant volume as liquid makes up between 25–75% of the weight of bread.[38]

3 Washing and Cleaning

Washing and cleaning formed another group of activities usually employing water. As with cooking, such activities range from religious to purely utilitarian. Epigraphic evidence indicates that various forms of ritual cleaning were the most commonly documented washing or cleaning activity.[39] There is also, however, evidence for activities that should not be classified as religiously significant.

Epigraphic sources indicate that statues should be washed.[40] An inscription from third-century BCE Kalaureia stipulates that the *epimeletes*, an official often in charge of some practical matter, in the sanctuary of Poseidon must clean the image (εἰκών) of the woman Agasikratis in the temple, as well as the images, presumably of her relatives, in an exedra.[41] Since these images

---

30 Ekroth 2007; Ekroth 2010; Ekroth 2017, 21.
31 It is possible that some of the 1,500 liters of wine recorded for the festival of Posideia on Delos (*ID* 440) was used in boiling sacrificial meat. Linders (1994, 76) suggests that some of the wine may have been used to make a hot barley soup.
32 There is considerable variation, as well as disagreement between scholars, in determining the size of ancient animals; see Jameson 1988, 95; Naiden 2013.
33 Naiden 2013, 252–253, 259.
34 Jameson 1988, 95.

35 *ID* 440; *ID* 445=*CGRN* 199; Bruneau 1970, 262–263; Vial 1984, 17–20; Linders 1994, 73.
36 Jameson 1988, 94.
37 *ID* 440A, l. 70.
38 Revel 1979, 40–41; Foxhall and Forbes 1982, 64, 79 (25–40%); Roth 1999, 47 (65–75%).
39 *IG* XII.4 332=*CGRN* 85; *IG* XII.4 274–278=*CGRN* 86; Dignas 2002=*CGRN* 98; *LSS* no. 115=*CGRN* 99; *IG* XII.4 72=*CGRN* 148, etc.
40 E.g., *IG* XII.4 348=*CGRN* 96; *IG* IV 840=*CGRN* 106; and *IG* II³ 879=*CGRN* 136.
41 *IG* IV 840=*CGRN* 106, ll. 10–14. Agasikratis had consecrated 300 dr, the interest of which was to be used for sacrifices to Poseidon.

were not of gods, deified rulers, or heroes but of a mortal woman and her family, the washing in this case should probably not be considered as religiously significant in the same way as, e.g., ritual purification. A more ambiguous example comes from a decree concerning the cult of Aphrodite Pandemos in Athens, which directs the *astynomoi*, one category of city magistrates, to anoint the altars, put pitch on the doors (of the temple?), and clean (λούω) the ἕδη, presumably sitting statues of gods, whenever the procession for Aphrodite Pandemos took place.[42] Do these three activities differ in nature regarding religious significance? Is pitching the doors comparable to cleaning the image of the deity being worshipped during the procession?[43] Similarly, in the dossier of a familial cult of Diomedon at Kos from *c*.325 BCE, it is specified that the portraits of Diomedon's ancestors should be washed.[44] It is difficult to tell whether this should be considered a religiously significant or utilitarian activity in relation to the cult.

Not only statues needed cleaning. A late fourth-century BCE inscription from Kyrene states that if someone sacrifices an animal of a species not customary at a specific altar, then the individual must remove the grease from the altar and wash it.[45] It is not stated whether the washing agent is water, but it seems likely. The inscription is also interesting because it is likely that ash and blood were sometimes cleaned away from altars, and we know of other types of maintenance, such as refurbishing the stucco or lime.[46] Depictions on red-figure, and to some extent black-figure, vases, primarily from Attika, also show altars clean or splattered with blood, but it is difficult to ascertain how this should be interpreted. Is blood painted on an altar a decorative addition or a reflection of a real situation?[47] Similarly, do altars without blood stains in vase paintings, both before and after sacrifices, indicate that some altars were kept clean?[48] And if altars were cleaned, was this a religiously significant act or not?

Answers to these questions seem impossible to ascertain based on current evidence.

Images and altars were not the only things that required cleaning or washing, either sporadically or on regular basis. Based on a passage in Euripides' *Ion*, Matthew Dillon has argued that birds not only would build nests in temples and other buildings, but also presumably spread droppings over them, as the case is today.[49] A first-century CE inscription from Aphrodisias records that the pigeons there were to remain free.[50] We also know that large amounts of bird droppings could be a problem, and the excrement was even collected and sold, e.g., at Delos, presumably as fertilizer.[51] An article on modern water collection from roofs, an activity known from Greek sanctuaries, highlights the issue of droppings from birds, squirrels, rats, and opossums.[52] Presumably, such animal waste in Greek sanctuaries was removed on a regular basis, and water may very well have been used in the cleaning process.

Further evidence for the cleaning of buildings from sanctuaries comes from the sacred law of the Mysteries of the Goddess of Marmarini: "on the thirteenth [day], let the sacred places around/of the goddess be washed, the temple and the peristyle and the door panels and the propylon."[53] Again, this activity may be interpreted as religiously significant and symbolic or not. But there is also evidence suggesting utilitarian cleaning in the same inscription in the last two lines, which were perhaps added at a later point than the preceding regulations: "if anyone urinates or bleeds within the peristyle [in the Sanctuary], let him purify with the purification previously described."[54] Presumably, the stipulation was added after said infringement took place at some point. The instructions for the purification are unfortunately not preserved, but probably the ritual purification was complemented by a thorough utilitarian washing. Similarly, a fragment by the stoic Chrysippos states that "One [must] refrain from urinating against an altar or the shrine of a god."[55] As in the case with the sacred law from Marmarini, it is difficult to imagine that Chrysippos would say this unless

---

42 *IG* II³ 879=*CGRN* 136.
43 Pitching may, however, have had ritual relevance considering that the Athenians smeared black pitch on their doors during the Anthesteria to keep away ghosts (Burkert 1985, 238).
44 *IG* XII.4 348=*CGRN* 96, ll. 18–21.
45 Washing the altar, see *LSS* no. 115=*CGRN* 99, ll. 26–29.
46 Ekroth 2005, 25. The primary motivation for adding new stucco or lime seems to have been damage from the fire on the altar.
47 For the iconographic evidence for blood on altars, see Ekroth 2005, esp. 19–26. Ekroth attributes the difference in the frequency of blood stains of altars on black- and red-figure vases to the techniques of rendering altars. Blood on the altars is also mentioned in the literary sources, e.g., Bacchyl. 11.110–111; Ar. *Pax* 1020; Lycoph. *Alex.* 1193.
48 Ekroth 2005, 24.

49 Dillon 1997, 125; Eur. *Ion* 154–183.
50 *LSAM* no. 86=*CGRN* 233. See *NGSL*² no. 29.
51 Bruneau 1970, 420.
52 De Kwaadsteniet et al. 2013, 6. For water collection on roofs in Greek sanctuaries, see, e.g., the temple of Apollo at Corinth (Robinson 1976, 218–220) and the temple of Aphaia on Aigina (Furtwängler 1906, 86–87).
53 Decourt and Tziafalias 2015, A, ll. 4–6 (=*CGRN* 225), trans. Parker and Scullion 2016.
54 Decourt and Tziafalias 2015, B, ll. 80–82, trans. Parker and Scullion 2016.
55 Quoted by Plut. *Mor. De Stoic. Repugn.* 1045a.

it occurred, and again, as in the case of the previously discussed inscription, urinating on altars of shrines would require not only ritual purification, but also physical cleaning.[56]

There is also plenty of indirect evidence for the use of water for cleaning in Greek sanctuaries. In particular, the preparation and consumption of food and drink must have involved a great number of pots, drinking vessels, and other items, and after the meal, these items would either be disposed of or washed for reuse. Direct disposal is known from deposits found in sanctuaries,[57] but such finds can hardly represent more than a fraction of the total number of meals prepared and consumed within the context of sanctuaries even if many of the items employed may have been organic or even edible (e.g., using bread loaves instead of plates or plates made of wood), leaving no traces. Consequently, a lot of material used for the preparation and consumption of food must have been washed in or near the sanctuary, presumably using water, although the evidence for washing, cooking, and serving implements in sanctuaries is scant and often indirect. It is possible that some of the installations interpreted as baths in the *hestiatoria* (dining halls) at the sanctuary of Demeter and Kore in Corinth were intended for washing dishes, such as a plastered square area measuring 85 × 85 cm situated next to a low table in the kitchen of Building L–M:28.[58] The textual material is somewhat more informative. In Menander's *Dyskolos*, a slave complains that he must do all the work during a sacrifice saying that "I've made the charcoal glow for you. I [take (?)], fetch, wash, cut offal up, all in one breath. I make cakes, shift the [pots, by Pan (?)]. Here, and [get] blinded by the smoke."[59] It is unclear what the slave in the passage washed, but it does not sound as if the character refers to a religiously significant act.

Banning washing in a sanctuary's water sources may often have been necessary. Pausanias mentions that the spring in the sanctuary of Poseidon in Tainaros had once been a marvel as those who gazed into it could see harbors and ships. But in his days this effect had been destroyed by women washing dirty clothes in it.[60] Rules that forbid the washing in specific water sources are also recorded in a number of inscriptions.[61] A fifth-century BCE inscription from Delos forbids the washing, dipping, or dumping of anything in the Minoe spring,[62] and a similar regulation applied the same restrictions to the Inopos reservoir from c.400 BCE.[63] Considering the spring's and reservoir's locations close to some of the major sanctuaries on the island, it is tempting to suggest that cooking and dining implements may have been one cause of problems leading to the institution of the regulations. Similar bans on washing or otherwise polluting fountains are known both in connection to, and outside of, sanctuaries at Keos, Kos, and Pergamon.[64] A third-century BCE inscription found at a fountain near the Athena sanctuary at Priene is especially interesting in this context.[65] The first five lines are badly damaged but end with "to wash," where the word (πλύσιμα) probably indicates that this refers to washing in the everyday sense of dishes, clothes, and other objects. The next line is undamaged and explicitly bans ritual cleaning, καθαρμός, threatening a fine of 50 dr for offenders. Much later, Pausanias (1.34.4) mentions a similar ban at Oropos in Attika on using water for certain religiously significant purposes: "The Oropians have near the temple a spring, which they call the Spring of Amphiaraus; they neither sacrifice into it nor are wont to use it for purifications (καθάρσιος) or for lustral water (χέρνιψ)."[66]

It is also likely that animals were cleaned before being sacrificed considering the importance of the victims being pure and perfect or *kalliston*, as beautiful as possible. It is difficult to see how an animal covered in dust and waste, as animals penned up in large groups tend to be, could be considered as such.

There is also plenty of evidence for the washing of humans, often within a clearly religiously significant framework. Besides archaeological remains of baths in or near many sanctuaries, inscriptions sometimes detail

---

56 For further examples, see *SEG* 43.568: Andros c.350–300 BCE, prohibited defecation, possibly in a sanctuary to Demeter. Likewise, *CIRB* 939, Nymphaion, fifth century BCE, forbad defecation in a sanctuary. *LSS* no. 24, Epidauros, prohibited littering in the sanctuary's stoa, and *LSS* no. 53 banned the dumping of excrement or dung (κόπρος) in the sanctuary of Leto on Delos.
57 See, e.g., the sanctuary of Poseidon at Kalaureia (Wells et al. 2005, 155; Wells et al. 2008, 48) and the sanctuary of Poseidon at Isthmia (Gebhard and Reese 2005, 140).
58 Bookidis and Stroud 1997, 182–179.
59 Men. *Dys.* ll. 546–549, trans. Arnott.
60 Paus. 3.25.8.
61 Evidence for washing dishes is rare in general. Lewis (2002, 76–77, fig. 2.22) has interpreted at least one Attic vase painting in a kylix tondo as depicting a woman washing dishes (*BAPD* 202271). The fourth-century BCE comedian Antiphanes (frag. 152.2, see Ath. 4.170e) mentions dishwashing.
62 *LSS* no. 50, late fifth or early fourth century BCE.
63 *SEG* 56.950; Fincker and Moretti 2007, 187, 228.
64 Keos, early third century BCE, *IG* XII.5 569; Kos, c.300 BCE, *IG* XII.4, 285=*CGRN* 140; Pergamon, early second century BCE, *OGIS* 483. See also Hes. *Op.* 757–759. For humans washing in the Klepsydra in Athens, see Ar. *Lys.* 913, presumably playing on the unlawfulness of the action.
65 Kah 2012.
66 Trans. Jones.

practical aspects, such as the running of baths, especially in the context of healing sanctuaries.[67] One such example is recorded in the sacred law from Andania, probably from 92/1 BCE, which indicates the need to provide temperate water for the bathers.[68] Another inscription, from Epidauros, also deals with water channels for a bath.[69]

4 Plants and Vegetation

While Greek sanctuaries tend to be dry and desolate places today, textual sources often portray them as lush with trees, orchards, and sacred groves (ἄλση).[70] Archaeological evidence suggests that this is not merely an idealized image, but reflects the *de facto* situation at many sites, for example, the garden of the Hephaisteion in Athens and the less securely identified grove at Nemea.[71] Additionally, many inscriptions mention prohibitions against removing wood or letting animals graze within sanctuaries, further corroborating the impression of substantial greenery.[72] Despite evidence for the protection of vegetation in sanctuaries, there is little information on watering at these sites. This contrasts with advice in written sources concerning other contexts where watering was an important part of taking care of plants.[73] There is no reason to believe that the same care was not shown in sanctuaries.

Turning to sanctuaries, Plato states that spring water should be transported using water pipes in order to beautify *alse* and *temene*.[74] At least in the case of the *alse*, it seems reasonable to suggest that the water benefited the place not only by its own presence, but also by invigorating the vegetation in the groves. More specifically, a decree of 418/7 BCE from Athens on the administration of the property of Kodros, Neleus, and Basile states that the lessee of the sanctuary must plant no less than 200 olive-shoots, as well as control the ditches and the water of Zeus, i.e., rain.[75] These ditches were presumably used to collect rain, which could contribute to the watering of the trees, as olives require large volumes of water during the first years after planting.[76] It is also important that the quantity of water provided not fluctuate too much, meaning that we should expect stable water usage for this purpose throughout the year.[77]

In a similar case, a certain Diognetos, son of Archesilas of Melite, leased the sanctuary of Egretes in Athens in 306/5 BCE, and the agreement specifies that he is to take care of the trees in the sanctuary.[78] Whether this included watering is unclear, but the lease further requires that any tree that died be replaced, and, as in the case above, newly planted sprouts would need to be watered. In the case of the famous garden around the temple of Hephaistos in Athens, established in the early third century BCE, Dorothy Burr Thompson suggested that the underground water conduit leading to a basin in the southwest corner of the precinct could have been used to water the plants.[79]

5 Accessing Water at Greek Sanctuaries

Access to water was necessary for the activities discussed above, and in Greek sanctuaries, such access would be limited primarily by two factors: the resources available and the effort needed to distribute the water. Additionally, not all water sources were equal in terms of quality, although

---

67 See Trümper this volume.
68 *IG* V.1 1390=*CGRN* 222. The date of the inscription is disputed with some scholars preferring 23 CE (see Gawlinski 2012, 3–11). For water management and baths, see also *IG* VII 4255 (335–322 BCE) concerning the rainwater in the sanctuary of Amphiaraos at Oropos.
69 *IG* IV².1 116.
70 The greenery in sanctuaries is commonly mentioned in the textual evidence, including trees (Paus. 1.21.7, 2.1.7, 2.13.3) and gardens (*IG* I³ 977a). For iconographical evidence of vegetation in sanctuaries in the form of closely pruned trees, see vase paintings, such as *BAPD* 9559 (an Attic bell-krater), 14955 (an Attic *lekythos*), and 30321 (an Attic bell-krater), and Hurwit 1991 for the representation of vegetation in Greek art. Palm trees are often shown with altars, presumably signifying that the altar is dedicated to Apollo or Artemis (see Sourvinou-Inwood 1985). For *alse*, see, e.g., Hom. *Od*. 6.291; Hes. *Sc*. 99; Hdt. 5.119; Pl. *Leg*. 761c. See also Birge 1982; Bonnechere 2007; Brulé 2012, 31–66, 123–136.
71 Temple of Hephaistos in Athens (Thompson 1937); sanctuary of Zeus at Nemea (Birge, Kraynak, and Miller 1992, 85–96). For other examples, see the sanctuary of Apollo Hylates near Kourion (Soren 1987); sanctuary of Asklepios at Corinth (Roebuck 1951, 14, 41). See also Carroll-Spillecke 1992; Carroll 2003; Bowe 2011.
72 E.g., grazing in *LSCG* nos. 91, 104, 116. See also Dillon 1997.
73 Theophr. *Caus. pl*. 3.8.3–4; Philo, *On Sobriety* 36; Plut. *Mor. De Alex. fort*. 340d. For an iconographic example, see a mid-fourth century BCE Attic hydria (*BAPD* 42036) in the National Archaeological Museum in Athens (inv. 1424), which shows Eros watering plants using an amphora. On irrigation in general, see Oleson 2000.
74 Pl. *Leg*. 6.761c. The passage is, however, difficult to interpret from the point of the water supply due to the terminology used (μεταλλεῖαι νάματα, often translated as hewn tunnels, and ὑδρεῖαι, often rendered as water pipes).
75 *IG* I³ 84. See also Koerner 1974, 163; Dillon 1997, 117.
76 Foxhall 2007, 101–102.
77 Foxhall 2007, 101–102. Theophr. *Caus. pl*. 3.8.4.
78 *IG* II² 2499.
79 Thompson 1937, 398.

both ancient and modern authors disagree on basic factors, such as which water was potable, not to mention which was the preferred or healthiest.[80]

In terms of available water sources, it is notable that output varies greatly, both between and within types. The most bountiful source a sanctuary could have access to would be a water course, although these were usually seasonal, offering plentiful water during the winter and little or nothing during the summer. In the case of the Aliakmon in northern Greece, the winter flow is ten times larger than that during the summer.[81] Similar seasonal patterns are attested in antiquity.[82] While flowing, however, the volumes are far beyond what any sanctuary could ever need. The Alpheios, for example, provides 4,685,000 m^3/day on average in modern times.[83] The seasonal variance is less pronounced for springs and fountains, but the annual output varies widely from one source to another.[84] The Peirene fountain in Corinth usually produces between 168 m^3 and 288 m^3 per day, but can reach as much as 480 m^3 during rainy years.[85] The Klepsydra in Athens, on the other hand, only produces 2.4 m^3 per day during the summer.[86] In contrast to water courses and springs/fountains, the output of wells depends largely on how much water humans can draw during a day, which in turn is determined by the size of the vessel used and available manpower.[87] More than 1–1.5 m^3 per day seems unlikely without mechanized tools. Cisterns for rainwater, finally, rarely make more than 0.5 m^3 available per day during wet years and considerably less during dry years.[88]

Two important consequences arise from these differences in output. The first is that the volume of available water varies radically between types of water sources. Having access to a water course enables a far wider range of activities than cisterns or wells. The second is that we cannot automatically assume that a certain type of water source will produce enough water for the activities in a sanctuary. A small spring, such as the Klepsydra for example (summer output 2.4 m^3/day), could not have produced enough water for larger than average sacrifices and festivals; if the hecatomb of the Great Panathenaia included the full set of 100 cattle, then boiling the meat alone would require at least that volume of water before factoring in any other needs.[89] Similarly, just the water used to dilute wine (leaving aside any other needs) at the Posideia on Delos required up to 4,500 liters.[90]

The effort required to distribute the water would also be a limiting factor.[91] In one published case, a hydria full of water was found to weigh 16 kg.[92] While small volumes of water for personal use are reasonably easy to carry, larger volumes require intense and organized labor. Hence, activities requiring large volumes of water would ideally be situated near a source. In some cases, this allows us to speculate about where activities took place in sanctuaries. For instance, during the late Archaic period at the sanctuary of Poseidon at Isthmia, an abnormally large well, known as the Large Circular Pit, was dug about 25 m outside of the later Roman *temenos* wall. The well was then filled in shortly after the middle of the fifth century BCE.[93] At some point thereafter, probably not much later, an advanced and unusually large system of interconnected cisterns provided water to the same spot,[94] which operated until *c*.300 BCE. For which purpose(s) the water was required is unknown, although dining has been suggested.[95] Whether correct or not, the large investment in securing water at this location indicates the great importance of having water specifically *here* at this spot. This suggestion is strengthened by the fact that the cistern water could have been channeled to almost any location on the site so clearly the location of the water source was

---

80 Hodge 2000. Most scholars today, however, tend to hold that spring water was viewed as the healthiest in antiquity (Tölle-Kastenbein 1990, 21; Crouch 1993; Mithen 2012, 93–94). For diverging views, see, see Klingborg 2017, 83–86.
81 Styllas 2018, 36.
82 E.g., Arist. *Mete.* 349b; Klingborg 2017, 78.
83 Skoulikidis 2018, 100. Note that this does not take seasonal variation into consideration.
84 Springs and fountains are considered together here as most springs (*pegai*) were augmented in one or more ways by the Greeks to become what they considered fountains (*krenai*), e.g., by opening further tunnels to increase the water flow, adding staircases to facilitate access, or building roofs to protect the water source or constructed basins for extra storage. For the terminology, see Wycherley 1937; Tölle-Kastenbein 1985.
85 Hill 1964, 17; Robinson 2011, 5. There are, however, much more productive springs than this, such as the Jardo spring near Split, which has an output of almost 5,200,000 m^3 per day in the winter (Marasović, Perojević, and Margeta 2014, 166), as much as the average daily volume over a year for the Alpheios (Skoulikidis 2018, 100).
86 Parsons 1943, 223.
87 There is also a seasonality to the water level in wells; see Broneer 1973, 23 for an example.
88 Klingborg and Finné 2018.

89 Pritchett and Pippin 1956, 256.
90 Supra n. 68.
91 The physical effort of carrying water has been stressed by Brinker 1990, 15; Crouch 1993, 152; Thomas 2000, 3.
92 Rotroff and Lamberton 2005, 8.
93 Broneer 1962; Broneer 1973, 22–24. The extent of the Archaic and Classical *temenos* is uncertain (Broneer 1973, 9). The well is even further away from the earlier Roman *temenos* wall.
94 This cistern system is known as the "West Water Works." See Broneer 1973, 27–29, pls. 1–4; Klingborg 2017, nos. 261–263.
95 Ekroth 2007, 261.

an intentional choice. The same notion is also supported by studies at Olympia where Alfred Mallwitz has argued that the placement of the many wells near the Stadion was not accidental or connected to the local soil conditions. Rather, he links the location of the wells to the needs of the participants and spectators of the games in this specific area.[96] Thus, looking at where water sources, large and small, are found in sanctuaries, can help us better understand the activities and needs at these sites.

The extant water supply infrastructure in sanctuaries differed radically from site to site. At Olympia, the Alpheios River offered a practically inexhaustible volume of water for the activities in connection to the sanctuary; the greatest issue in this case would be transporting the water to where it was needed.[97] Despite this, Lucian's *On the Death of Peregrinus* states that people died of thirst at the sanctuary before Herodes Atticus built his water supply for the site.[98] This seems difficult to reconcile with the access to water at the site and is probably an exaggeration. It may also reflect the effort needed to transport large volumes of water.

In stark contrast to the situation at Olympia, the use of even small volumes of water could become problematic in sanctuaries with limited resources. At the sanctuary of Poseidon at Kalaureia, only two small, interconnected cisterns are securely attested.[99] They would not be able to sustain more than about a dozen individuals, not to mention sacrificial animals, over an extended period of time. There is also good reason to believe that water was used for cleaning at the site, as discussed above.[100] The demand created by sporadic utilitarian uses at a sanctuary, largely dictated by festivals and sacrifices, is impossible to calculate in this case, but any large-scale activity would soon exhaust the supply, especially during the summer.

Despite such divergent situations, some generalizations can be made in regard to the water supply of sanctuaries. First, very few had access to a water course, especially a perennial one, so that few sanctuaries would have had a more or less unlimited supply available. Second, the presence of a spring or fountain was far less common than modern literature indicates. Franz Glaser's catalogue of ancient fountains in the area of modern Greece indicates that only 36 are found in sanctuaries, while another 12 may have had cultic significance.[101] Furthermore, of these 36 fountains, 15 are located in sanctuaries of Asklepios.[102] The presence of fountains in sanctuaries should therefore primarily be connected to Asklepios and the need, in many cases, to stay for periods of time at healing sites rather than to Greek religion and cult in general.

In comparison to rivers and springs/fountains, wells and cisterns are common, although considerably less so in sanctuaries than in domestic contexts.[103] Wells formed a central part of the water supply at Nemea, 46 have been found at the Heraion on Samos, and an Archaic well was located close to the later third or fourth century BCE propylon at Epidauros.[104] The most famous example is, however, Olympia where more than 240 wells have been excavated, although only a small number were used at the same time.[105] Very small sacred spaces could also have a well, such as that sacred to Pan, Men, and the Nymphs at the Kerameikos.[106] Cisterns are known to have supplied water to the Menelaion at Sparta, the sanctuary of Demeter and Kore at Corinth, and the sanctuary of Poseidon at Kalaureia, among others.[107] The primary advantage of relying on a well or cistern is that it could be located almost anywhere, allowing those using the water to place the source where it was needed. Accordingly, wells and cisterns can be used to some degree to infer where water was needed in sanctuaries, as we saw in the case of Isthmia. For example, one well (N17:2) at Nemea has been interpreted as used for ceramic production. Most of the others at this site are located between the *Oikoi* and *Xenon* (see p. 167, Fig. 10.4: square N17), possibly because of the need for water in areas of the sanctuary where individuals

---

96   Mallwitz 1988, 98.
97   The contribution of the many wells is, however, more questionable in relation to the large number of visitors during the games, and no permanent wells existed at Olympia until the fourth century BCE.
98   Luc. *De mort. Peregr.* 19. See also Epiktetos 1.6.26.
99   Klingborg 2017, nos. 264, 265. The extent of the *temenos* is, however, not established with certainty. A further, unexplored cistern opening is located outside of the sanctuary, and a few pieces of water pipes have been found in other areas of the site (Wide and Kjellberg 1895, 282; see also inv. no. 2693, a clay pipe, from the excavations at the site).
100   *IG* IV 840=*CGRN* 106, ll. 10–14.
101   Glaser 1983, 176.
102   Glaser 1983, 177.
103   For cisterns, see Klingborg 2017, 108. For a comparison to wells in domestic contexts, see for example the 230 wells found around the Athenian Agora (Camp 1977, 183).
104   Nemea: Kimmey 2017; Kimmey 2023. Samos: Fuchs 2023. Epidauros: Tomlinson 1983, 46. The context of the ten wells excavated at Lerna has been interpreted as domestic rather than cultic, although the material is not conclusive (Erickson 2018, 337).
105   Kyrieleis 2011, 114.
106   Stroszeck 2017, 46 (Kerameikos well B 19).
107   Menelaion: Klingborg 2017, no. 271. Sanctuary of Demeter and Kore: Klingborg 2017, nos. 250–253. Sanctuary of Poseidon at Kalaureia: Klingborg 2017, nos. 264–265.

stayed for periods of time.¹⁰⁸ The well at the propylon at Epidauros may have been intended both to provide water for ritual purification when entering the sanctuary and to water men and beasts arriving at the site. The cisterns in the sanctuary of Demeter and Kore, on the other hand, seem to have supplied water for the participants in the meals at the *hestiatoria*, as well as the preparation of these meals and cleaning thereafter.¹⁰⁹ Bathing has also been suggested.¹¹⁰ The location of the cisterns at Kalaureia indicates similar uses with the exception of bathing.

But most sanctuaries enjoyed access to more than one type of water source. This is indeed the case for all the sites mentioned above, with the possible exception of Kalaureia. Recent studies on the water supply in the Roman world have stressed the importance of such variety in terms of sustainability.¹¹¹ Having more than one type of water source at a site would allow activities there to benefit from the advantages of each type. At Olympia, the river would ensure that nobody had to die of thirst (in spite of Lucian's claim), while wells presumably provided water of a higher quality at the location where it was needed. In fact, the massive water supply may have contributed to the ability of the sanctuary to host such large games from an early stage. Similarly, the presence of wells, in addition to the aqueduct feeding the bath at Nemea, ensured that there was sufficient water for various activities.

One important observation is that the size of the water supply system in most sanctuaries was built to allow for consumption far beyond that required by religiously significant acts. There would be no need to construct a massive well in Archaic Isthmia to provide water for ritual purification, nor would 12 wells be required at Nemea.

6 Conclusions

We can draw a number of important conclusions based on the evidence presented above. Most conspicuously, little direct evidence exists for the most fundamental need for water, i.e., drinking; rather than indicating that water was not drunk, pure or mixed with wine, I argue that the lack of regulations suggests that there seldom was an inherent difference between water used for religiously significant and utilitarian needs. In most cases, water from any source could be used for any purpose, religiously significant or not, rendering rules in this regard unnecessary. My examination of the available evidence also suggests that the consumption of water, especially by animals, required large volumes—up to hundreds of thousands of liters per day during major events.

Water was also required to prepare sacrificial meat. While cooking was considerably less water intensive than drinking, it would have added to temporary peaks in the consumption pattern in a sanctuary, especially during large festivals. The preparation of meat may also have created a constant low intensity demand for water in sanctuaries with many private sacrifices throughout the year.

The material also indicates that water was used for cleaning things, and possibly animals, in sanctuaries, as well as watering plants and trees. It is not possible to say how much water was consumed by these activities, but it cannot have been inconsiderable, especially in view of the intensive need for watering vegetation during the summer months.

Overall, the evidence gives the impression that the volume of water needed was closely related to the number of individuals and animals present at a specific sanctuary at any given time with large peaks during festivals and large sacrifices. The strain on the water supply would also be directly related to resources available at individual sites, as even a small festival could present challenges if no reliable water source were available. We should therefore not compare the water consumption between different cults, but in the context of the cult itself. Furthermore, unless considerably more water was used for activities with ritual significance, e.g., ritual purification, cleaning of sacred images, than currently believed, it seems likely that the water supply in Greek sanctuaries would have been primarily adapted to serve utilitarian needs.

Further research on this topic is clearly needed, especially at largely excavated and well-known sanctuaries where use patterns can be traced more closely. How much water was needed at places such as Isthmia, Delphi, and Olympia? Only further studies can begin to answer that question.

Acknowledgments

This article was written within the framework of the project *Water at ancient Greek sanctuaries: medium of divine presence or commodity for mortal visitors?* (WaGS) funded by the Swedish Research Council (no. 2018–01414), with additional support from Enboms donationsfond and the Swedish Institute at Athens. I would like to thank Gunnel

---

108   Kimmey (2017, 297) suggest that the concentration of wells was the consequence of an underground water course but evidence for this is lacking to my knowledge.
109   Klingborg 2017, 110.
110   Bookidis and Stroud 1997, 404.
111   Locicero (2018, 389) has stressed sustainability made possible by access to several water sources in Roman Ostia.

Ekroth, Judy Barringer, and David Scahill for inviting me to participate in this volume, as well as their comments on my paper, and Axel Frejman for his comments on a draft version of the essay.

Works Cited

Anderson-Stojanović, V.R. 1996. "The University of Chicago Excavations in the Rachi Settlement at Isthmia, 1989." *Hesperia* 65: 57–98.

Bachrach, B.S. 1993. "Animals & Warfare in Early Medieval Europe." In *Armies and Politics in Early Medieval West*, edited by B.S. Bachrach, 708–751. Hampshire.

Birge, D.E. 1982. *Sacred Groves in the Ancient Greek World*. Ann Arbor.

Birge, D.E., L.H. Kraynak, and S.G. Miller. 1992. *Excavations at Nemea 1. Topographical and Architectural Studies: The Sacred Square, the Xenon, and the Bath*. Berkeley.

Bloesch, H., H.P. Isler, C. Isler-Kerényi, A. Lezzi-Hafter, and M. Sguaitamatti 1982. *Greek Vases from the Hirschmann Collection*. Zurich.

Bonnechere, P. 2007. "The Place of the Sacred Grove (Alsos) in the Mantic Rituals of Greece: The Example of the Alsos of Trophonios at Lebadeia (Boeotia)." In *Sacred Gardens and Landscapes: Ritual and Agency*, edited by M. Conan, 17–41. Washington D.C.

Bookidis, N., and R.S. Stroud. 1997. *Corinth 18:3: The Sanctuary of Demeter and Kore: Topography and Architecture*. Princeton.

Bousquet, J. 1967. "Deux inscriptions attiques." *BCH* 91: 90–95.

Bowe, P. 2011. "Civic and Other Public Planting in Ancient Greece." *Studies in the History of Gardens & Designed Landscapes* 31: 269–285.

Bremmer, J. 2006. *Greek Religion*. Oxford.

Brinker, W. 1990. *Wasserspeicherung in Zisternen. Ein Beitrag zur Frage der Wasserversorgung früher Städte*. Braunschweig.

Broneer, O. 1962. "Excavations at Isthmia 1959–1961." *Hesperia* 31: 1–25.

Broneer, O. 1973. *Isthmia 2: Topography and Architecture*. Princeton.

Brulé, P. 2012. *Comment percevoir le sanctuaire grec? Une analyse sensorielle du paysage sacré*. Paris.

Bruneau, P. 1970. *Recherches sur les cultes de Délos à l'époque hellénistique et à l'époque impériale*. Paris.

Burford, A. 1969. *The Greek Temple Builders at Epidauros*. Liverpool.

Burkert, W. 1985. *Greek Religion*, trans. J. Raffan. Cambridge. Mass.

Camp, J. 1977. *The Water Supply of Ancient Athens from 3000 to 86 B.C.* Ph.D. diss., Princeton University.

Carroll, M. 2003. *Earthly Paradises: Ancient Gardens in History and Archeology*. London.

Carroll-Spillecke, M. 1992. "The Gardens of Greece from Homeric to Roman Times." *Journal of Garden History* 12: 84–101.

Cole, S.G. 1988. "The Uses of Water in Greek Sanctuaries." In *Early Greek cult practice* edited by N. Hägg, N. Marinatos, and G. Nordquist, 161–165. Stockholm.

Connelly, J.B., and A.I. Wilson. 2002. "Hellenistic and Byzantine cisterns on Geronisos island. With a mortar analysis by C. Doherty." *RDAC*: 269–292.

Cook, J.M., and W.H. Plommer. 1966. *The Sanctuary of Hemithea at Kastabos*. Cambridge.

Crouch, D.P. 1993. *Water Management in Ancient Greek Cities*. New York.

De Kwaadsteniet, M., P.H. Dobrowsky, A. van Deventer, W. Khan, and T.E. Cloete. 2013. "Domestic Rainwater Harvesting: Microbial and Chemical Water Quality and Point-of-Use Treatment Systems." *Water, Air, & Soil Pollution* 224: 1–19.

Decourt, J.C., and A. Tziafalias. 2015. "Un règlement religieux de la région de Larissa: cultes grecs et 'orientaux.'" *Kernos* 28: 13–51.

Dignas, B. 2002. "Priestly Authority in the Cult of the Corybantes at Erythrae." *EA* 34: 29–40.

Dignas, B. 2007. "A Day in the Life of a Greek Sanctuary." In *A Companion to Greek Religion*, edited by D. Ogden, 163–177. Oxford.

Dillon, M.P.J. 1997. "The Ecology of the Greek Sanctuary." *ZPE* 118: 113–127.

Dixon, K.R., and P. Southern. 1992. *The Roman Cavalry: From the First to the Third Century AD*. London.

Ekroth, G. 2005. "Blood on the Altars? On the Treatment of Blood at Greek Sacrifices and the Iconographical Evidence." *AntK* 48: 9–29.

Ekroth, G. 2007. "Meat in Ancient Greece: Sacrificial, Sacred or Secular?" *Food & History* 5: 249–272.

Ekroth, G. 2010. "'En grillad, tack!' Varför homeriska hjältar inte kokade sin mat." In *Tankemönster. En festskrift till Eva Rystedt*, edited by F. Faegersten, J. Wallensten, and I. Östenberg, 53–60. Lund.

Ekroth, G. 2017. "Bare Bones: Zooarchaeology and Greek Sacrifice." In *Animal Sacrifice in the Ancient Greek World*, edited by S. Hitch and I. Rutherford, 15–47. Cambridge.

Engels, D.W. 1978. *Alexander the Great and the Logistics of the Macedonian Army*. Berkeley.

Erickson, B. 2018. *Lerna 8: The Historical Greek Village*. Princeton.

Fincker, M., and J.-C. Moretti 2007. "Le barrage du réservoir de l'Inopos à Délos." *BCH* 131: 87–228.

Foxhall, L., and H.A. Forbes 1982. "Σιτομετρεία: The Role of Grain as a Staple Food in Classical Antiquity." *Chiron* 12: 41–90.

Foxhall, L. 2007. *Olive Cultivation in Ancient Greece: Seeking the Ancient Economy*. Oxford.

Frejman, A. 2020. *With Gods as Neighbours: Extra-Temenal Activity at Greek Rural Sanctuaries, 700–200 BCE*. Ph.D. diss., Uppsala University.

Fuchs, J. 2023. "The Water Supply of the Heraion of Samos." In *Going Against the Flow. Wells, Cisterns and Water in Ancient Greece*, edited by P. Klingborg, 135–159. Stockholm.

Furtwängler, A. 1906. *Aegina. Das Heiligtum der Aphaia*. Munich.

Gawlinski, L. 2012. *The Sacred Law of Andania*. Berlin.

Gebhard, E.R., and R.S. Reese. 2005. "Sacrifices for Poseidon and Melikertes-Palaimon at Isthmia." In *Greek Sacrificial Ritual, Olympian and Chthonian*, edited by R. Hägg and B. Alroth, 125–154. Stockholm.

Ginouvès, R. 1962. *Balaneutiké. Recherches sur le bain dans l'antiquité grecque*. Paris.

Glaser, F. 1983. *Antike Brunnenbauten (KRHNAI) in Griechenland*. Vienna.

Heilmeyer, W., G. Zimmer, and G. Schneider. 1987. "Die Bronzegiesserei unter der Werkstatt des Phidias in Olympia." *AA*: 239–299.

Hill, B.H. 1964. *Corinth 1:6: The Springs: Peirene, Sacred Spring, Glauke*. Princeton.

Hodge, A.T. 2000. "Purity of Water." In *Handbook of Ancient Water Technology*, edited by Ö. Wikander, 95–99. Leiden.

Hurwit, J.M. 1991. "The Representation of Nature in Early Greek Art." In *New Perspectives in Early Greek Art*, edited by D. Buitron-Oliver, 33–62. Hanover.

Jameson, M.H. 1988. "Sacrifice and animal husbandry in Classical Greece." In *Pastoral economies in classical antiquity*, edited by C.R. Whittaker, 87–119. Cambridge.

Kah, D. 2012. "Eine neue Brunneninschrift aus Priene." *EA* 45: 55–70.

Kimmey, S. 2017. *The Nemean Wells: Sanctuary Context and Ritual Activity in the Northeast Peloponnese*. Ph.D. diss., University of Missouri, Columbia.

Kimmey, S. 2023. "The Nemean Wells: Water Management and Sanctuary Deposition." In *Going Against the Flow. Wells, Cisterns and Water in Ancient Greece*, edited by P. Klingborg, 113–134. Stockholm.

Klingborg, P. 2017. *Greek cisterns. Water and risk in ancient Greece, 600–50 BC*. Ph.D. diss., Uppsala University.

Klingborg, P., and M. Finné 2018. "Modelling the Freshwater Supply of Cisterns in Ancient Greece." *Water History* 10: 113–131.

Kobusch, P. 2020. "Fountains and Basins in Greek Sanctuaries." In *The Power of Urban Water: Studies in Premodern Urbanism*, edited by N. Chiarenza, A. Haug, and U. Müller, 69–84. Berlin.

Koerner, R. 1974. "Zu Recht und Verwaltung der griechischen Wasserversorgung nach den Inschriften." *Arch. Pap.* 22–23: 155–202.

Kyrieleis, H. 2011. *Olympia. Archäologie eines Heiligtums*. Darmstadt.

Lauter-Bufe, H. 2009. *Das Heiligtum des Zeus Soter in Megalopolis*. Mainz am Rhein.

Lewis, S. 2002. *The Athenian Woman: An Iconographic Handbook*. London.

Linders, T. 1994. "Sacred Menus in Delos." In *Ancient Greek Cultic Practice from the Epigraphic Evidence*, edited by R. Hägg, 71–79. Stockholm.

Locicero, M. 2018. *Liquid Footprints. Water, Urbanism, and Sustainability in Roman Ostia*. Ph.D. diss., Leiden University.

Lynch, K.M. 2007. "More Thoughts on the Space of the Symposium." *BSA* 15: 243–249.

Mallwitz, A. 1988. "Cult and Competition Locations at Olympia." In *The Archaeology of the Olympics: The Olympics and Other Festivals in Antiquity*, edited by W.J. Raschke, 79–109. Madison.

Mantellini, S. 2015. "The Implications of Water Storage for Human Settlement in Mediterranean Waterless Islands: The Example of Pantelleria." *Environmental Archaeology* 20: 406–424.

Marasović, K., S. Perojević, and J. Margeta. 2014. "Water supply system of Diocletian's palace in Split-Croatia." In *IWA Regional Symposium on Water, Wastewater and Environment: Traditions and Culture*, edited by I.K. Kalavroutsiotis and A.N. Angelakis, 163–173. Patras.

Miller, S.G. 2001. *Nemea 2. The Early Hellenistic Stadium*. Berkeley.

Mithen, S. 2012. *Thirst: Water and Power in the Ancient World*, with S. Mithen. Cambridge, MA.

Naiden, F.S. 2013. *Smoke Signals for the Gods: Ancient Greek Sacrifice from the Archaic through Roman Periods*. Oxford.

Nielsen, T.H. 2007. *Olympia and the Classical Hellenic City-State Culture*. Copenhagen.

Nordquist, G. 1997. "Evidence for Metalworking in Late Geometric Tegea." In *Trade and Production in Premonetary Greece. Production and the Craftsman*, edited by C. Gillis, C. Risberg, and B. Sjöberg, 197–205. Jonsered.

O'Connor, K. 2015. *The Never-Ending Feast: The Anthropology and Archaeology of Feasting*. London.

Oleson, J.P. 2000. "Purity of Water." In *Handbook of Ancient Water Technology*, edited by Ö. Wikander, 183–215. Leiden.

Parker, R.C.T. 1996. *Miasma: Pollution and Purification in Early Greek Religion*. Oxford.

Parker, R.C.T., and S. Scullion 2016. "The Mysteries of the Goddess of Marmarini." *Kernos* 29: 209–266.

Parsons, A.W. 1943. "Klepsydra and the Paved Court of the Pythion." *Hesperia* 12: 191–267.

Pedley, J. 2006. *Sanctuaries and the Sacred in the Ancient Greek World*. Cambridge.

Pritchett, W.K., and A. Pippin 1956. "The Attic Stelai: Part II." *Hesperia* 25: 178–328.

Reed, B., and B. Reed 2013. "How Much Water is Needed in Emergencies." In *Technical Notes on Drinking-Water, Sanitation and Hygiene in Emergencies. World Health Organization (WHO)*, edited by B. Reed, R. Shaw, and K. Chatteron, 9: 1–4. Leicestershire.

Revel, J. 1979. "A Capital City's Privileges: Food Supplies in Early Modern Rome." In *Food and Drink in History*, edited by R. Forster and O. Ranum, 37–49. Baltimore.

Risberg, C. 1997. "Evidence of Metal Working in Early Greek Sanctuaries." In *Trade and Production in Premonetary Greece. Production and the Craftsman*, edited by C. Gillis, C. Risberg, and B. Sjöberg, 185–196. Jonsered.

Robinson, B.A. 2011. *Histories of Peirene: A Corinthian Fountain in Three Millenia*. Princeton.

Robinson, H.S. 1976. "Excavations at Corinth: Temple Hill, 1968–1972." *Hesperia* 45: 203–239.

Roebuck, C. 1951. *Corinth 14: The Asklepieion and Lerna*. Princeton.

Rostad, A. 2006. *Human Transgression-Divine Retribution. A study of religious transgressions and Punishments in Greek cultic regulations and Lydian-Phrygian reconciliation inscriptions*. Ph.D. diss., University of Bergen.

Rostoker, W., and E.R. Gebhard 1980. "The Sanctuary of Poseidon at Isthmia: Techniques of Metal Manufacture." *Hesperia* 49: 347–363.

Roth, J.P. 1999. *The Logistics of the Roman Army at War (264 B.C.–A.D. 235)*. Oxford.

Rotroff, S.A., and R.D. Lamberton. 2005. *Women in the Athenian Agora*. Princeton.

Senff, R. 2017. "Olympia, Heiligtum und Wettkampfstätte mit wasserwirtschaftlichen Problemen." In *Cura Aquarum in Greece*, edited by K. Wellbrock, 193–213. Siegburg.

Skoulikidis, N. 2018. "The State and Origin of River Water Composition in Greece." In *The Rivers of Greece: Evolution, Current Status and Perspectives*, edited by N. Skoulikidis, E. Dimitriou, and I. Karaouzas, 97–127. Heidelberg.

Soren, D. 1987. *The Sanctuary of Apollo Hylates at Kourion, Cyprus*. Tucson.

Stroszeck, J. 2017. "Wells in Athens." In *Cura Aquarum in Greece*, edited by K. Wellbrock, 43–88. Siegburg.

Styllas, M. 2018. "Natural Processes Versus Human Impacts During the Last Century: A Case Study of the Aliakmon River Delta." In *The Rivers of Greece. Evolution, Current Status and Perspectives*, edited by N. Skoulikidis, E. Dimitriou, and I. Karaouzas, 31–49. Heidelberg.

Sourvinou-Inwood, C. 1985. "Altars with palm-trees, palm-trees and parthenoi." *BICS* 32: 125–146.

Themelis, P. 2002. "Contribution to the topography of the sanctuary at Brauron." In *Le orse di Brauron: Un rituale di iniziazione femminile nel santuario di Artemide*, edited by B. Gentili and F. Persusino, 103–116. Pisa.

Thomas, R.G. 2000 "Geological Background, Climate, Water Resources." In *Handbook of Ancient Water Technology*, edited by Ö. Wikander, 3–20. Leiden.

Thompson, D.B. 1937. "The Garden of Hephaistos." *Hesperia* 6: 396–425.

Tölle-Kastenbein, R. 1985. "Der Begriff Krene." *AA*: 451–470.

Tölle-Kastenbein, R. 1990. *Antike Wasserkultur*. Munich.

Tomlinson, R.A. 1983. *Epidauros*. London.

van Straten, F.T. 1995. *Hierà kalá: Images of Animal Sacrifice in Archaic and Classical Greece*. Leiden.

Vial, C. 1984. *Délos Indépendante (314–167 avant J.-C.). Étude d'une communauté civique et de ses institutions*. Athens.

Wächter, T. 1910. *Reinheitsvorschriften im griechischen Kult*. Gießen.

Wells, B., A. Penttinen, J. Hjohlman, and E. Savini 2005. "The Kalaureia Excavation Project: The 2003 Season with an Appendix by K. Göransson." *OpAth* 30: 127–215.

Wells, B., A. Penttinen, and J. Hjohlman. 2008. "The Kalaureia Excavation Project: The 2004 and 2005 Seasons with Contributions by K. Göransson, A. Karivieri, and M.D. Trifirò." *OpAth* 31–32: 31–129.

Wide, S., and L. Kjellberg. 1895. "Ausgrabungen auf Kalaureia." *AM* 20: 267–326.

Wycherley, R.E. 1937. "ΠΗΓΗ and ΚΡΗΝΗ." *CR* 51: 2–3.

CHAPTER 6

Sanitation in Greek Sanctuaries

Monika Trümper

μὴ χέσες
ἱεροῦ

Don't shit in the sanctuary

∴

This inscription was carved on a block in the fifth century BCE and displayed in the sanctuary of an unknown deity on the Akropolis of Nymphaion in Crimea.[1] It suggests that human bodily evacuation was a concern in this sanctuary, which had to be controlled and regulated. Defecation and urination are today a major problem at sacred sites, and particularly at large religious festivals where millions of people gather. Both are the primary concern of sanitation for reasons of public health, but also for social and environmental reasons. In its guidelines on sanitation and health, the World Health Organization defines sanitation as "access to and use of facilities and services for the safe disposal of human urine and feces. A safe sanitation system is a system designed and used to separate human excreta from human contact at all steps of the sanitation chain."[2] Central to health is also the provision of clean drinking water that is not contaminated by urine and feces. Sanitation is mutually bound with hygiene, which means conditions conducive to maintaining health and preventing disease, especially through cleanliness and practices, such as defecation in controlled spaces and hand washing.

Scholars have convincingly argued that ancient societies would not have met modern standards of sanitation and hygiene, first and foremost, because they did not know how diseases are transmitted and that human excreta are a major health hazard.[3] However, ancient societies implemented some modern sanitation tools, such as toilets and bathing facilities. Furthermore, the above-mentioned inscription and other written sources suggest that practices related to modern concepts of sanitation were discussed and regulated in sanctuaries and beyond. This raises the question of what significance concepts and tools of sanitation had in Greek sanctuaries and how logistics of sanitation shaped the human experience of visiting the gods. It is the aim of this paper to discuss this question.

The topic is vast and related to many different areas, including concepts of sacred versus profane; of pollution and purification; of dirt and cleanliness; or the nature, supply, use, and disposal of water. Since several contributions in this volume discuss these topics by investigating archaeological and written sources,[4] this paper focuses on examining archaeological evidence in order to answer the following question: whether and how two major human bodily needs, namely urination and defecation, as well as washing and bathing, were met in Greek sanctuaries. While ritual as well as profane washing and bathing have been studied in scholarly literature,[5] the problem of urination and defecation in sanctuaries has not yet been investigated.[6]

Since Greek sanctuaries differed widely in location, size, equipment, and function, requirements for meeting bodily needs must also have differed significantly. The following criteria must be considered:

– Length of stay of visitors (short- to long-term)
– Status (social status, sex) and purpose of users (pilgrims, personnel, athletes)
– Number of users and uses (regularly vs. irregularly)
– Contemporary standards and practices (private vs. public, rural vs. urban)

---

1 *CIRB* 939; Zuchtriegel 2006, 22; *NGSL*² 501; Ohlerich 2009, 98, 105, 374, no. 28.
2 *WHO Guidelines 2018*, XII, https://apps.who.int/iris/bitstream/handle/10665/274939/9789241514705-eng.pdf?ua=1 (last accessed 18 August 2023).
3 Of the vast literature on this topic, see Dupré Raventós and Remolà 2000; Jansen 2000; Lindenlauf 2004; Zuchtriegel 2006; Bradley and Stow 2012; Mitchell 2015; 2016; 2017.
4 See Klingborg and Pakkanen in this volume; cf. recently also Kobusch 2020.
5 Central still Ginouvès 1962, 231–427. For 'profane' bathing, see Trümper 2013; Trümper 2014a; Yegül 2015.
6 For ancient latrines in general: Zuchtriegel 2006; Antoniou 2010; Jansen, Koloski-Ostrow, and Moormann 2011; Antoniou and Angelarakis 2015; Hoss 2018.

Furthermore, it is crucial to identify the topography, spatial extension, and accessibility of sanctuaries with certainty in order to determine whether bodily needs could be met within the confines (*temenos*) of, or close to, sanctuaries. While the logistics of sanitation should be studied for all sanctuaries, the state of research and space do not allow for a comprehensive discussion here. Instead, the focus here is on sanctuaries with maximum requirements, i.e., well-defined extra-urban sanctuaries where large numbers of visitors often stayed for an extended period during important festivals, but which were also frequented on a regular basis year-round. Other sanctuaries are occasionally included when they provide important evidence. While the geographical focus is the eastern Mediterranean, western Greek sanctuaries are briefly mentioned. The chronological frame is necessarily broad, as will become clear, ranging from about 450 BCE to the Roman Imperial period.

Taking the state of research and preliminary remarks into account, I discuss urination and defecation, as well as bathing, separately. For both needs, I begin with some well-documented modern examples, which highlight central problems and solutions. I then briefly outline general standards in the Greek world before analyzing the archaeological evidence of Greek sanctuaries.

1 Urination and Defecation

India has numerous religious festivals. Within the frame of the "Clean India Campaign," recently initiated by the government, sanitation at these festivals became a major target, as two examples may illustrate. The city of Pandharpur with a population of 98,000 houses an important temple of the Hindu god Vithoba, which attracts 10,000–15,000 pilgrims every weekend throughout the year and 1.5 million pilgrims during the annual Ashadi Ekadasi festival. The large city of Allahabad, with a population of over one million, is the destination of a mass Hindu pilgrimage, the Kumbh Mela, at regular intervals. During the major festival in 2013, 120 million people visited the town over a two-month period, including 30 million on a peak day. The main ritual involves bathing in sacred rivers. Sanitation is a major problem at both the regularly and irregularly visited sites, particularly because open defecation pollutes ground water, rivers, and the environment, and the lack of personal hygiene promotes the spread of infectious diseases and raises the danger of epidemics. Local authorities of these two cities recently adopted different strategies to address these problems.

In Pandharpur, the world's largest public toilet-complex was built in 2016, following the governmental guideline that one toilet must be available for every 40 devotees. Eight permanent mega toilet-complexes were built in the city, each including 282 toilet and bath compartments, lockers, and changing rooms. These were complemented by 1,500 mobile toilet-complexes and toilets in the city's 18,000 households that are open to pilgrims during the annual festival. The city provided a team of 50 workers, who monitored behavior in the city and regularly cleaned the toilet complexes.[7]

For the large 2013 Kumbh Mela in Allahabad, a creative combination of temporary technological solutions appropriate to a range of literacy levels and cultural preferences was implemented. The main concern was to avoid contamination of ground water and the sacred rivers used for bathing. The options included specifically designated, fenced open-defecation fields, roadside urinals, pit latrines with and without water flushing, and bio digester toilets, in total 35,000 toilet seats located at least 15 m away from the rivers (one for every 8–10 pilgrims during average attendance). The human waste of these facilities was either digested by bacterial cultures or left in pits to decompose naturally and eventually be taken away by the rising fast-flowing rivers in rainy seasons.[8] About 9,000 workers were employed around the clock for maintaining, repairing, and cleaning the various facilities. Sex specificity and illiteracy of pilgrims, 80% of whom came from rural areas where open defecation is common, were taken into account in providing toilet signage and familiar types of facilities. However, personal hygiene behaviors were not addressed, and only a few facilities were furnished with sinks, spigots, soap, and towels for hand washing.[9]

Purpose-built toilets (or latrines) of the Graeco-Roman world have been extensively investigated in recent years. Studies have focused on key factors, such as the urban and architectural context, location, accessibility, size, plan, technical standard, and decoration.[10] Therefore, purpose-built latrines can be relatively securely identified in the archaeological record, and their development, distribution, and standards can be assessed in their larger traits.

---

7   https://www.ndtv.com/india-news/maharashtras-pandhar pur-gets-worlds-largest-toilet-facility-1428678 (last accessed 18 August 2023). Several online news reports about the mega toilet-complexes that were still accessible in September of 2018 have now disappeared. Cf. also Kahlid 2018.
8   Vortmann et al. 2015.
9   Vortmann et al. 2015, 5.
10 Neudecker 1994; Hobson 2009; Jansen, Koloski-Ostrow, and Moormann 2011; Koloski-Ostrow 2015; Hoss 2018; Bouet 2022.

Purpose-built latrines are installations or rooms that provide holes or channels along one wall or several walls; these were commonly covered with wooden or stone seats and connected with a cesspit or with a sewer in an adjoining street. Waterproof decoration was standard and ranged from simple stone or cement floors and hydraulic stucco to lavish variants with figured *opus tessellatum* mosaics and paintings, as well as marble revetment for floors and walls. Most often, water was required for flushing, but again options varied significantly, from flushing with buckets of used water to running fresh water. The number of seats (or intended users) per room ranged from 1 to 75.[11] Accessibility depended upon the architectural context, but also the location of entrances. While latrines in houses or complexes, such as *palaistrai* and baths, were commonly entered from inside the buildings, thus limiting access to the users of these buildings, these latrines sometimes provided independent entrances from the street. There were also entirely independent latrines with street entrances, which were not part of any specific building and open to the general public, who probably had to pay for the use.[12] The first purpose-built latrines have been dated to the fourth century BCE, but latrines only became really common from the late Hellenistic period (second century BCE) onwards and particularly in the Roman Imperial period. The distribution and availability of latrines in various contexts has been studied for some well-preserved cities, such as Delos, Priene, Pergamon, Pompeii, and Ostia.[13] These studies suggest that latrines never became standard in any context, even if numbers generally increased during the Roman Imperial period. Differences may go back to the availability of resources, such as water supply and drainage, but also to local sociocultural customs and preferences.

The debated sanitary and hygienic qualities of ancient latrines notwithstanding, they unquestionably concentrated the unpleasant activities and products of urination and defecation in clearly confined spaces, hidden from public view, and in this sense can clearly be identified as a significant cultural innovation. The commercial impact may have been ambiguous: solid excrement and urine were used and even sold for profit in antiquity, as fertilizer and for artisanal purposes; collection may have been facilitated by concentrating excrement in certain spots, but in high-end facilities with running water, excrement was washed away and thus 'wasted.'[14]

The central question is whether sanctuaries benefitted from the introduction and socio-cultural concept of purpose-built toilets. While the state of research prevents comprehensive assessment, the following list of relatively well-known examples is still astonishingly short. Focus is on the construction date of latrines because their period of use cannot usually be determined.

The extra-urban Asklepieion of Pergamon was provided with a complex of two latrines in the Hadrianic period, when the sanctuary experienced a major embellishment and remodeling process (Fig. 6.1).[15]

Located remotely in the southwest corner of the confined precinct, the latrines could be entered from the southern portico and a corridor that gave access to three rooms: a room with benches (2.38 × 4.90 m), which provided seats for about 15 waiting guests; a large latrine room with 43 seats (8.38 × 8.20 m), which was richly decorated with marble and provided with four columns and an *impluvium*; and a more modestly decorated small latrine room with 18 seats (4.45 × 4.45 m), which, however, had its own anteroom. Water was supplied from various higher lying areas and roofs but may not have been abundant year-round. Both latrines were drained via a channel from the northeastern side of the large latrine to a nearby river.[16] The remote location was probably chosen to keep the sanctuary free from unpleasant disturbances and smells. While it cannot be securely determined who used the different rooms, the duplication may have served different purposes: to simply increase capacities or to allow for a differentiation of users according to specific criteria, such as sex, age, social status, or needs (e.g., type of disease). If the rooms were designed for differentiated use by men and women, the latter would probably have used the more secluded and less lavishly decorated smaller room. The latrines were located next to an ornately decorated large room, which was identified as a room for banquets and cultural activities and performances.[17]

---

11 Neudecker 1994, 51.
12 Jansen, Koloski-Ostrow, and Moormann 2011, 154–155.
13 Neudecker 1994; Hobson 2009; Jansen, Koloski-Ostrow, and Moormann 2011; Trümper 2011; Koloski-Ostrow 2015, 3–32; Bouet 2022.
14 Wilson 2011, 155.
15 Neudecker 1994, 162, no. 81; Radt 1999, 236–237; Hoffmann 2011, 111–133.
16 Hoffmann 2011, Beil. 3c: the latrine channels were connected. Water must have entered in the northeast corner of the small latrine and was drained from the northeast corner of the large latrine; at the bottom of the channels, the height difference between these two points (northeast corner of the small latrine and northeast corner of the large latrine) was 1.29 m.
17 Radt 1999, 236; Hoffmann 2011, 238–239.

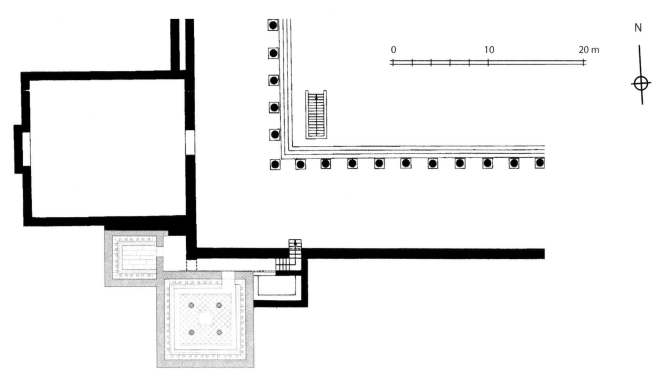

FIGURE 6.1 Pergamon, Asklepieion, reconstructed plan of southwest corner with latrines
IMAGE: K. BOLZ AND AUTHOR AFTER HOFFMANN 2011, 121 FIG. 77; BEIL. 9

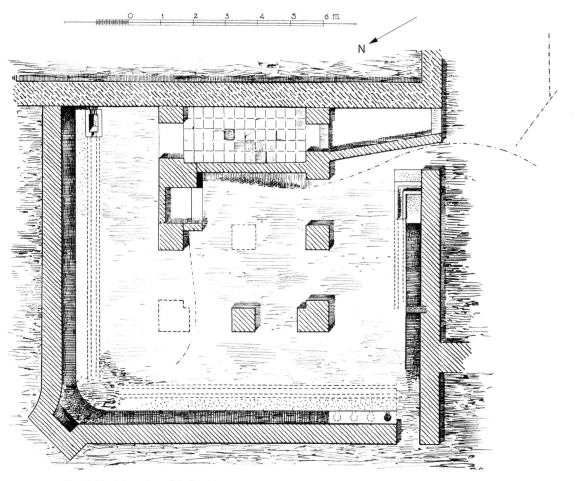

FIGURE 6.2 Kos, Asklepieion, plan of the latrine
AFTER SCHAZMANN 1932, PL. 34A

A latrine with more than 50 seats was added to the extra-urban Asklepieion of Kos in the Imperial period (Fig. 6.2). Well hidden behind the western portico of the lowest terrace, it was accessible from the courtyard and a secondary western entrance to this terrace.[18] The room (10 × 12 m) had marble seats along three sides and a central peristyle with six or more pillars and marble pavement in the porticoes. Running water was supplied by a nearby fountain house in the southeast, and the wastewater was drained through a kind of niche in the northwest corner. Construction is dated to the third century CE solely based on the wall technique, but the latrine may well have belonged to a large remodeling program that was initiated after a major earthquake in 142 CE and included some water works and the construction of one or even two baths to the north and northeast of the lowest terrace.[19] The latrine was apparently remodeled. The two small (service?) rooms in the east and the basin attached to the northern pillars were certainly inserted later into the peristyle courtyard, and the strangely placed entrance in the southwest corner seems to be later, too, if ancient at all.[20]

In the intraurban sanctuary of Artemis at Magnesia on the Maeander, a richly decorated latrine-complex was added to the sanctuary's northern portico in the third or fourth century CE. It included an anteroom (5.20 × 3.34 m) with a fountain-basin, and a large room (13.55 × 7.28 m) with channels on three sides and seats for 32 persons. Both rooms were finely adorned with polychrome marble slabs and had fountains with running water. Waste was drained through a pipe in the northeast corner, probably even to the Lethaios River, which was 150–200 m away.[21]

For other large extra-urban sanctuaries that were frequented in the Hellenistic and Imperial periods, among them those in Delphi, Eleusis, Epidauros, Isthmia, Olympia, and Samothrace, no separate latrine complexes are currently known. In these sanctuaries, toilet facilities were at best included either in baths or in confined complexes of different functions.

None of the four baths built between the fourth and first century BCE at Olympia had a latrine, but latrines were simply not common in baths of these periods.[22] Of the eight baths that were built outside the Altis from the late first century CE onwards, at least three were provided with a latrine (Fig. 6.3).

The Southwest Baths were built in the late first century CE, with a large multi-seater latrine for about 32 persons, which was accessible from a portico in front of the east façade and thus apparently also open to people who did not visit the baths. The latrine was flushed with used water from the bathing rooms and emptied to the east.[23] The Kladeos Baths, built around 100 CE or in the early second century CE, gained a modestly decorated four-seater latrine when the adjacent Roman guesthouses were remodeled in 220/230 CE (Fig. 6.4).

The latrine was supplied by wastewater from the bathing rooms and drained to the southwest. After the remodeling, the baths and the latrine were only accessible through the guesthouses and formed a conceptual and functional unit with the guesthouses.[24] The barely known South Baths were probably constructed in the late third century CE. They offered a latrine with space for about 20–24 persons next to the entrance, but within the confined space of the baths.[25] The other baths, especially the large East Baths, may also have included latrines, but none of these has been published so far.[26]

---

18 Schazmann 1932, 68–69; Neudecker 1994, 160, n. 48; Interdonato 2013, 67, 303 reconstructs only 16 seats. For the debated chronology of the sanctuary, see Ehrhardt 2014, who does not, however, mention the latrine.

19 Schazmann (1932, 68) suggests "spätrömische Zeit … kaum vor dem III. Jahrhundert n. Chr." Interdonato (2013) dates the latrine variously to the Antonine period (66–67, fig. 29) and the third century CE (303, catalog). Interdonato's dating of the Roman baths is similarly inconsistent (71, fig. 36; 303–308). A second, smaller bath building was found to the north of the lowest terrace, called terrace IV by Interdonato 2013, 71, fig. 36; 310–311, and dated to the second/third century CE on her plan of wall techniques (313, fig. 98).

20 This remodeling is clearly suggested by the plan and typology, but has not been discussed by any scholar.

21 Kadıoğlu 2005; Bingöl 2007, 90–94.

22 Infra n. 53.

23 Haseley 2012, 104, fig. 2; Sinn 2012, 106.

24 Schleif and Eilmann 1944, 57–69, esp. 66–67. On p. 95 the baths are dated to the Trajanic or Hadrianic period at the latest, but on p. 96 to around 100 CE. The mosaics have been dated to the Trajanic-Hadrianic or the late Hadrianic/early Antonine period; Kankeleit 1994, II 211, http://www.kankeleit.de/kladeosthermen .php (last accessed 18 August 2023); Sinn 2012, 107. Mallwitz (1972, 274–277) assigns them c.100 CE, while Yegül (2015, 252) does not provide a date.

25 Mallwitz 1972, 245–246: Diocletian period. Manderscheid 1988, 158; and Yegül 2015, 253: "no earlier than ca. A.D. 200." http:// www.kankeleit.de/suedthermen.php (last accessed 18 August 2023) mentions an earlier bath-complex, where some mosaic floors survive.

26 East Baths: Manderscheid 1988, 158; Kankeleit 1994, 2: 225–227; Yegül 2015, 254; http://www.kankeleit.de/oktogon.php (last accessed 18 August 2023). Kronion Baths: Sinn 1992, 77–79; Kankeleit 1994, 2: 214–219; http://www.kankeleit.de/kronion thermen.php (last accessed 18 August 2023). Leonidaion Baths: Sinn, Ladstätter, and Martin 1993, 158; Sinn, Ladstätter, and Martin 1994, 241–247; Sinn et al. 1995, 169–171; Kankeleit 1994, II 219–221; Senff 2018, 46; http://www.kankeleit.de/leonidaionther men.php (last accessed 18 August 2023). Two further unexcavated

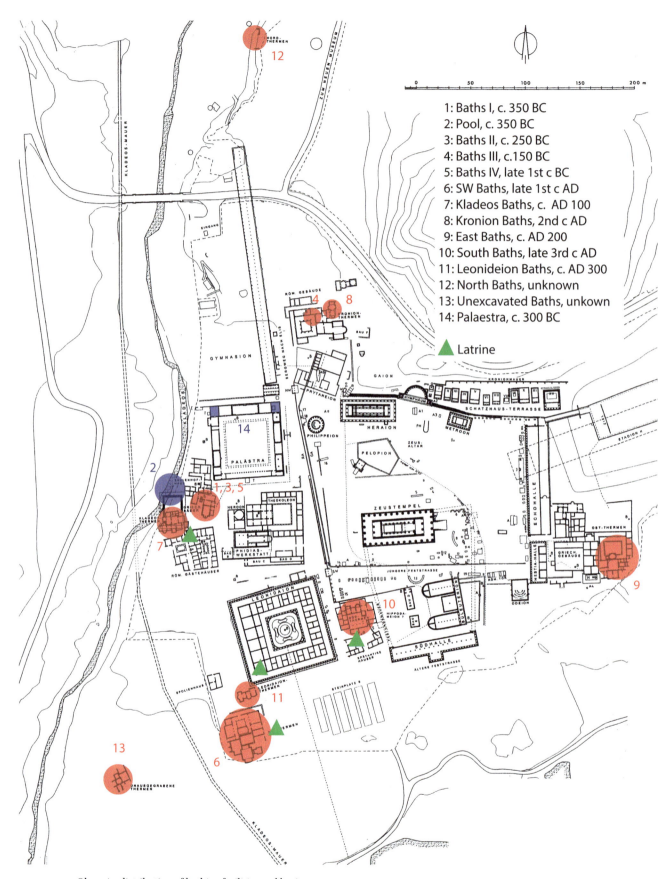

FIGURE 6.3 Olympia, distribution of bathing facilities and latrines
IMAGE: AUTHOR AFTER KYRIELEIS 2002, BEILAGE

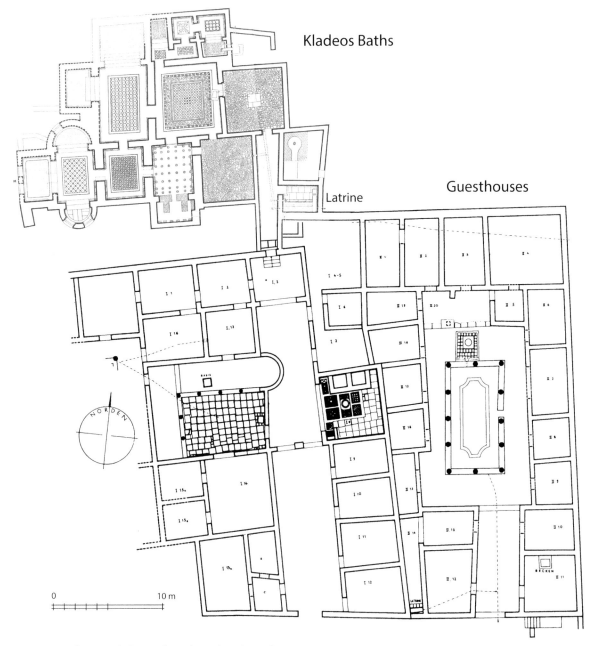

FIGURE 6.4 Olympia, Kladeos Baths with combined guesthouses
IMAGE: AUTHOR AFTER SCHLEIF AND EILMANN 1944, PL. 22 AND MALLWITZ 1972, 277 FIG. 230

The Leonidaion, built around 330/320 BCE, was later embellished with a latrine located in the southwest corner of the building and accessible from a secondary southern entrance to the building and an atrium to the north. It provided about 10–12 seats, was supplied by rainwater from the *impluvium* of the atrium and drained to the south. The date and function of the latrine are debated: the facility has been identified as part of the large remodeling program of the Leonidaion in the Flavian period or early Hadrianic period,[27] or as part of a new guesthouse-baths complex that was built after the earthquake of 280 CE.[28] Recent research has convincingly shown, however, that the first option is correct and that the latrine was central

baths are shown to the north and southwest of the sanctuary on the plan Kyrieleis 2002, Beilage.

27 Fuchs 2013, 294–295. For the date of this remodeling, see Mächler 2019; 2020, 301–302. Fuchs (2013, 295) argues that the latrine went out of use quickly and would have been replaced by a latrine built between the fourth and sixth column from the west of the southern portico. The plan Beil. 2 does not show any channels for supply and drainage, however.

28 Leonidaion Baths: Mallwitz 1972, 254; Sinn 1997, 215; Sinn 2012, 107.

to the concept of the remodeling process; it significantly helped to increase the convenience for users.[29]

A strong connection between baths and guesthouses has often been emphasized and claimed for most of Olympia's excavated baths,[30] and the construction of latrines may have been central to both building types. While the latrines were supplied with wastewater from the surrounding rooms, it is currently unknown where the sewage was ultimately drained, but possibly to one of the two rivers that border the sanctuary in the west and south. While the rivers may also have been an important source of fresh water for the sanctuary, contamination with sewage may have been avoided by obtaining water upriver, at points far away from drainage inlets;[31] alternatively, contamination may not have been recognized as a major problem in antiquity, because the health risks of feces were not known, as mentioned above.

Similar or even more dire pictures emerge for other sanctuaries, such as Epidauros. No latrine has been identified in any of the late Classical and Hellenistic buildings, among them a banquet building, a large guesthouse, a bath complex, and various stoa complexes (Fig. 6.5). In the little studied Roman Imperial period, the Northeast Baths were built next to the Stoa of Kotys complex, which was originally constructed in the third century BCE, probably as a guesthouse (Fig. 6.6).

This stoa complex was significantly repaired in the second century CE, most likely contemporaneously with the construction of the baths that were only accessible from the stoa-complex. Both buildings may have been financed by the Roman senator Antoninus, who, according to Pausanias and various inscribed finds, was responsible for numerous *euergetic* activities in Epidauros.[32] At the junction of the stoa complex and the baths, a latrine was built, with channels on three sides and about 32 seats and access from the stoa complex via an anteroom; its water management is unknown. René Ginouvès identifies two phases in the baths based on the building technique and assigns the latrine to the later phase, dated to the fourth/fifth century CE.[33] While the date of the second phase is debated by later scholars, nobody even mentions the latrine,[34] which is part of the row of rooms that connected the stoa complex and the baths; phase plans show that this room was built together with the baths and, at best, remodeled later.[35] Therefore, it seems very likely that the latrine belonged to the original concept of guesthouse-baths complex, similar to the situation at Olympia, and that it was maintained when the baths were remodeled.

It is likely that other buildings in Epidauros were provided with latrines, particularly the baths, but none have been securely identified to date.[36] Richard Neudecker argues that Roman baths were often, but not always, provided with latrines. The lavishly decorated 'Prachtlatrinen' that were built particularly from the second century CE onwards were mostly connected with baths, but belonged to the secondary outer areas of baths that were designed for various cultural activities.[37] The evidence from sanctuaries confirms this picture. Many sanctuary baths had no latrine, among them even richly decorated large examples, e.g., in Isthmia, Delphi, and Eleusis.[38] While small, modestly endowed latrines may have been overlooked in scholarship, this is hardly likely in the case of monumental 'Prachtlatrinen'. Only the three independent sanctuary latrines cited above qualify as 'Prachtlatrinen' in Neudecker's catalogue.[39] In contrast, the latrines of the guesthouse-baths-complexes clearly had a utilitarian function and appropriately mundane decoration and did not inspire extended pleasurable stays within the frame of cultural activities and for sophisticated care of the body.

The situation of purpose-built latrines is even worse for intraurban sanctuaries. For example, no evidence of latrines was found in the Asklepieia of Athens and Corinth, both clearly confined, larger sanctuaries that were still frequented in the Roman Imperial period.[40] In the Asklepieion of Messene, a small installation has been identified as a latrine without, however, discussion of the evidence. This installation is located to the south of

---

29 Mächler 2020, 303–304.
30 Mallwitz 1972, 246, 274; Sinn 1997; Haseley 2012, 107; Sinn 2012, 107.
31 Trümper 2017, 228–230.
32 Paus. 2.27.6; Trümper 2014a, 220–230 with earlier literature.
33 Ginouvès 1955, 141–152; the latrine appears only on the plan fig. 7.
34 Tomlinson 1983, 53; Philipp 1991, 88–89.
35 Ginouvès 1955, fig. 7; Tomlinson 1983, 52, fig. 8; Yegül 2015, 257, fig. 12.11. No reliable state plan of the stoa has been published, and published schematic plans differ significantly, cf. here figs. 6.5 and 6.6. For reconstructions of the original plan, see Roux 1961, 292, fig. 88; Coulton 1976, 239, fig. 65; and for a rough phase plan, see Tomlinson 1983, 42, fig. 5.
36 Roux (1961, 300) mentions a latrine in Building Φ, but does not specify its exact location and appearance. Cf. Trümper 2014a, 227, fig. 9: a possible candidate is a niche on the west side of room 8b, which could have been flushed with water from the pool in room 9.
37 Neudecker 1994, 83–91.
38 Yegül 1993, 2015. Frey and Gregory (2016, 460–461) tentatively identified a latrine to the north of the Roman Baths in Isthmia based on the general spatial configuration and the presence of water lines, but the evidence is very tenuous.
39 Neudecker 1994, 160–162; the latrine in Magnesia had not yet been excavated in 1994.
40 Riethmüller 2005; Melfi 2007, 289–311, 313–409.

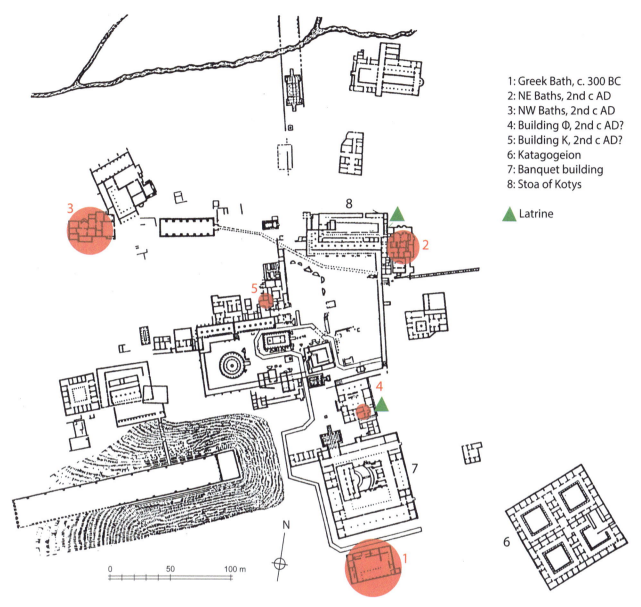

FIGURE 6.5 Epidauros, sanctuary of Asklepios, distribution of baths and latrines
IMAGE: AUTHOR AFTER RIETHMÜLLER 2005, 1: 292 FIG. 42

room X, on a lower level than this room, and to the west of an independent bath building. Its date and accessibility are nowhere mentioned, but apparently it could not be entered directly from the sanctuary; instead, it may conceptually have belonged to the bath building.[41] The latrine could have been supplied by the covered drainage channel that led from the southwest corner of the sanctuary's peristyle courtyard through room X. Comparable simple installations may have existed in or close to other intraurban sanctuaries, but await identification and comprehensive assessment.

Similarly, no latrines are currently known from the many western Greek sanctuaries for several reasons: their extension and *temene* are often not known, they were abandoned before purpose-built latrines became available or standard, and their development and use in the Hellenistic and Imperial period are far less studied than those in the Archaic and Classical periods.

Returning to large extra-urban sanctuaries in the eastern Mediterranean, several crucial questions arise: where did visitors with no access to any of the Imperial period buildings with latrines defecate, particularly during the Olympian games? More crucially even, how were human

---

41 The most detailed discussion is provided by Sioumpara 2011, 8–9, with stone plan on pl. 3. Cf. also Themelis 2003, 90; Müth 2007, 157; not mentioned in Riethmüller 2005, 2: 156–167; Melfi 2007, 256.

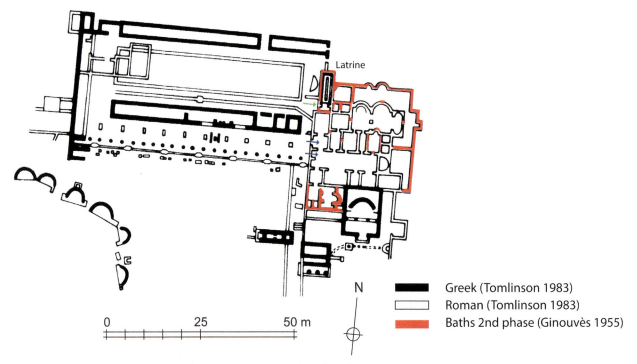

FIGURE 6.6 Epidauros, sanctuary of Asklepios, stoa of Kotys and northeast baths
IMAGE: AUTHOR AFTER GIONOUVÈS 1955, FIG. 7 AND TOMLINSON 1983, 42 FIG. 5

bodily needs met before the Imperial period, and where did the up to 40,000–50,000 visitors of the Olympic games in the Classical and Hellenistic periods relieve themselves? Since neither Olympia nor any other Greek sanctuary thus far has yielded any archaeological evidence that would answer these questions, one can only investigate written sources for information and discuss hypothetical solutions based on cross-cultural comparisons. While this is not the space to do this in due detail, the potential of both options is briefly explored.

The corpus of ancient written sources related to urination and defecation is overall small and heterogenous in genre and chronology, but provides important information, if only for a few towns, particularly Athens. Urination and defecation in public, especially in streets, was common. Waste in streets, including excrement of humans and animals, was considered a nuisance and hazard that obstructed streets and endangered adjacent buildings and pedestrians. Cities made laws that regulated the cleaning of streets and removal of waste, commonly delegating responsibility to houseowners and individuals who had dumped waste. Excrement (*kopros*) was also used as fertilizer or for crafts, such as tanning, and thus a source of profit. Private entrepreneurs (*koprologoi*) may have made waste a business, collecting it from houseowners (for a fee) and dumping it in appropriate locations outside the cities or selling it to farmers and craftsmen. City officials (usually the *astynomoi*) supervised the state of streets and public spaces, but were apparently not responsible for organizing municipal waste disposal.[42]

Similar to the control of waste management in urban public spaces, regulations existed in sanctuaries for social and environmental reasons or to ensure ritual purity. The inscription cited at the beginning of this essay indicates that defecation was a problem in the sanctuary of the Nymphs, but the spatial context of the inscription and the precise reason for its installation are unknown. Only a few of the hundreds of 'Greek sacred laws' or 'Greek ritual norms' explicitly mention human or animal waste, but most texts, even long ones, do not.[43] For example, the lengthiest and best preserved 'sacred law,' the *diagramma* of Andania, written in 91 BCE, is much concerned with water supply and bathing. The *agoranomos* of the city and the sacred men had to supervise and grant the proper regular function of water management and baths and punish

---

42 Owens 1983; Ault 1999; Zuchtriegel 2006, 20–38; Pakkanen in this volume.

43 The term 'sacred law' is much debated; Petrovic (2015, 341) mentions around 500 'sacred laws.' For a critical reassessment of written sources relating to Greek religion, see Carbon and Pirenne-Delforge 2012, who introduce the term 'Greek ritual norm.' Their online corpus of Greek ritual norms currently includes 250 entries; http://cgrn.ulg.ac.be/ (last accessed 18 August 2023), only one of which refers to urination/defecation (*CGRN* 225). For defecation in sanctuaries, cf. also *NGSL*² 501, n. 1.

unreliable contractors and offenders.⁴⁴ Urination and defecation or waste and its management are not mentioned at all.

By contrast, uncontrolled urination was a major concern in a sanctuary of an anonymous foreign goddess in Thessaly. While this sanctuary has not yet been found, its existence is known from a stele, which was probably set up between 225 and 150 BCE and is densely inscribed on both sides with regulations. The very last line of face B identifies urination in the inner precinct (peristyle) of the sanctuary as a source of pollution, which requires purification.⁴⁵

Similarly, a stele with a law or decree of 202 BCE was set up by the polis of Delos close to an altar of Dionysos. Its aim was to keep the recently cleaned area around the altar and the nearby sanctuary of Leto clean or pure, forbidding disposal of [*kopro*]*n*, ash, or any other trash in the sanctuaries. Offenders who were caught were reported to the *boule* (city council), with slaves receiving 50 lashes, and free offenders receiving a fine of 10 dr, half of which went to the informer. *Kopros* is not securely preserved in this inscription, but if correctly restored, may have referred to excrement of men and cattle. The stele was found 30 m to the north of Dionysos' altar and obviously kept in place, even when the area was densely built up and the terrain of Leto's sanctuary occupied by the Agora of the Italians in the last quarter of the second century BCE.⁴⁶

Even if urine is explicitly listed next to blood as a source of impurity in the inscription from Thessaly, this seems unique, and other factors requiring purification are mentioned much more frequently, among them blood, menstruation, sex, and certain foods.⁴⁷ Excrement may have been considered a nuisance more than a hazard for purity,⁴⁸ but even in this case its handling must have been regulated somehow. If not written in stone, regulations may have been communicated by signs, guards, or general behavior of personnel and pilgrims. Devotees may have been expected to avoid urination and defecation during short visits in intraurban sanctuaries, but a visit to the Olympian games certainly entailed bodily evacuations. Permanent personnel in sanctuaries had to relieve themselves in intra- and extra-urban sanctuaries alike.

Assuming that indiscriminate open defecation was undesirable in sanctuaries, such as Olympia, particularly during mass events, similar strategies to those adopted at modern festivals in India could have been implemented. Specific areas could have been designated for open defecation, keeping them at an appropriate distance from the drinking water wells, which were newly dug every four years. Human waste may have been left in pits and trenches, removed to fertilize fields, or discharged into nearby rivers (depending upon the water level in dry seasons and accessibility). Vessels may have been used in buildings, such as the baths, guesthouses, *Palaistra*, and stoas, which developed in Olympia from the fourth century BCE on; slaves could have taken care of emptying the vessels in appropriate designated places.⁴⁹ The *Festwiese* area in Olympia, where temporary tent towns may have been set up during the games, was conveniently located close to two rivers (Alpheios, Kladeos), which seem most appropriate for the efficient and fast removal of tons of human waste. If the rivers also served as a water supply, there would certainly have been need for regulations, entailing a clear spatial differentiation between upstream sampling points and downstream drainage points.⁵⁰

Similar designated areas could be hypothetically identified in other intraurban and particularly extra-urban sanctuaries, taking the topography, water supply (especially rivers), circulation patterns, and varying needs into account. For example, the Poseidon sanctuary of Isthmia was bordered by ravines in the west and north, the sanctuary of Epidauros by ravines in the north and south, and the sanctuary of Samothrace was crossed by two ravines. In contrast, no rivers were available close to the sanctuary of Nemea.⁵¹ These locations must have had consequences for the handling of human and other waste.

---

44   Gawlinski 2012, 86–89, 229–226.
45   *CGRN* 225, B, ll. 80–81: ἐὰν δέ τις ἐν τῶι περιστύλωι ἢ οὐρήσει ἢ αἷμα ποήσει, καθαιρέτω τὸν προγεγραμμένον καθαρμόν "If anyone either urinates or spills blood in the peristyle, let him perform the aforementioned purification." For translation and extensive comments: http://cgrn.ulg.ac.be/file/225/ (last accessed 18 August 2023).
46   *LSCG* no. 53; *SEG* 23.498; Moretti and Fincker 2008, 139.
47   See the 200 texts dealing with purification collected in *CGRN*, http://cgrn.ulg.ac.be/browse/theme/purification/ (last accessed 18 August 2023).
48   Literary sources that treat urinating at altars or sacred statues, for example Plut. *Mor.* 1045a, or Latin sources, such as Juv. 1.131 and Pers. 1.113 cannot be discussed here.

49   Neudecker 1994, 73 (1994, 73) assumes that temporary and portable latrines must have been available during the large Roman entertainment events.
50   Supra n. 31. The pace of flows and strength of currents of both rivers may have played an important role for the organization of water management in the sanctuary, but cannot be discussed in detail here.
51   The Nemea River was created only at the end of the fourth century CE. See Trümper 2018b, 266, n. 22.

2 Bathing

At the Indian festivals mentioned above, washing and bathing are obviously luxuries rather than necessities, if not ritually required and naturally provided. At Allahabad, bathing in natural bodies of water is part of the main ritual, but in 2013, the various toilet options did not provide facilities for hand washing on a regular basis. The mega toilet-complexes in Pandharpur include some bathing facilities, but no numbers are given. Since ritual immersion is not practiced there, pilgrims presumably do not bathe regularly during the festival, if at all.

Facilities installed specifically for bathing are well known from the Graeco-Roman world and share significant similarities with latrines: they usually can be securely identified based on their waterproof decoration, water supply and drainage, and furniture, such as bathtubs, basins, and benches. Purpose-built baths were constructed from the fifth century BCE onward as independent publicly accessible facilities ('public baths') and private facilities in houses and were later also included in buildings, such as *palaistrai*. The bathing facilities in public baths and houses commonly included a warm bathing form (hip-bathtub or immersion-bathtub, sweat bath, collective heated pool), while facilities for athletes (*palaistrai*, athletes' baths) offered installations for cold-water washings and plunge baths. All of these bathing facilities were included in clearly confined buildings, which allowed control of access and visibility. The only notable exceptions are open-air cold-water pools appropriate for plunging or swimming. Since accessibility is a key factor in assessing bathing facilities, the bathing facilities included in buildings and the independent open-air pools are discussed separately in the following text.

Bathing facilities never became standard in houses, but the number of publicly accessible bath complexes increased significantly in the Hellenistic period, and most cities had at least one of them in the Roman Imperial period. Since bodies can be cleansed in a simple and improvised manner with a bucket of water or at natural bodies of water, providing a specific facility for this activity is a remarkable cultural achievement. The underlying cultural and social concepts changed significantly, transforming bathing from a primarily quick cleansing activity in the fifth century BCE to an increasingly pleasurable, relaxing social activity in the Hellenistic and Roman Imperial periods.[52]

2.1 *Bathing Facilities in Confined Buildings*

Achievements in bathing culture had a significantly larger impact on sanctuaries than the introduction of latrines, certainly in the Classical and Hellenistic periods, but also later. Bathing facilities were differentiated in size, location, and bathing program, probably with a view to different users. This can be best illustrated in Olympia, which seems to have been leading in the bathing business throughout the entire period of the sanctuary's use (Fig. 6.3). Four baths were built from the fourth to first century BCE that all provided some warm water facilities. While the three to the west of the Altis—Baths I, II, and IV—replaced each other, the baths to the north, Baths III, may have overlapped in use with the Baths II and IV.[53] The baths were constantly modernized and improved, but remained astonishingly small, providing space for no more than 20–40 bathers at a time. Baths III may have been attached to a dining complex, but the three western examples were independent and had no direct link with buildings built contemporaneously or later, such as the Leonidaion, *Palaistra*, or Theokoleon. During the games, but possibly also during visits year-round every year, use of the baths was most likely restricted to those who could pay, or even more severely to certain social groups. The luxury of agreeable bathing facilities was provided by very few Classical and Hellenistic sanctuaries and was—quite expectedly—a prerogative of sub- and extra-urban sanctuaries.[54]

---

52 Trümper 2009; Trümper 2010; Lucore and Trümper 2013; Trümper 2014b; Trümper 2014c.

53 Construction of the western baths was traditionally dated to 450 BCE with remodeling around 400 BCE (Baths I, termed "Älteres Sitzbad" in German scholarship because it included hip-bathtubs); 300 BCE with remodeling in the third century BCE (Baths II, designated "Jüngeres Sitzbad" in German scholarship); and 100 BCE (Baths IV, referred to as "Hypocaust Bath" in German scholarship). See Schleif and Eilmann 1944, and thus still Wassenhoven 2012, 129–130; Lo Monaco 2013, 128–130; Yegül 2015, 254. But recent research challenges these dates: 1) The well of Baths I has been redated to the Hellenistic period instead of the first half of the fifth century BCE, see Kyrieleis and Herrmann 2013, 12–14, 46–49; 2) sima fragments from the Leonidaion found reused in the remodeling of Baths I downdate this phase to 300 BCE, see Heiden 1995, 140 roof 51; and 3) stratigraphic excavations and reassessment of the typological development of ancient baths suggest construction of Baths IV in the late first century BCE, see Sinn 2004, 124, 238. Therefore, the following construction dates are proposed here (cf. Trümper 2017, 230–239): Baths I: 350 BCE, remodeling 300 BCE; Baths II: 250 BCE with modernization in the early second century BCE; Baths IV: late first century BCE. The recently excavated northern Baths III ("Späthellenistisches Bad" in German scholarship) were dated to the second half of the second century BCE with remodeling in the first century BCE; see Sinn, Leypold, and Schauer 2003.

54 Trümper 2013, with list of sanctuary baths.

The *Palaistra* in Olympia, built before 280 BCE, offered two bathing rooms (*loutra*) that were located in the northeast and northwest corners and provided with the typical tubs for cold-water washings (Fig. 6.3).[55] Ulrich Mania recently argued that this *Palaistra* even had a predecessor, the Echo Stoa complex built 340–330 BCE, which included a typical *loutron* in the eastern courtyard.[56] In other sanctuaries, notably Nemea, and possibly also Epidauros, such *loutra* were found in independent bath complexes. The best-known example is the building in Nemea, located next to a guesthouse (*Xenon*) and built in the late fourth century BCE, where two tub rooms framed a small plunge pool (see p. 167, Fig. 10.4).[57] The much larger so-called Greek Bath in Epidauros was probably also built in the fourth century BCE next to a large guesthouse (*katagogion*) and a spacious banquet building; according to finds on site, this bath-complex may have provided a similar bathing program as the one in Nemea (Fig. 6.5).[58] It has been argued that the sanctuary in Nemea was mainly frequented during the games, which took place every two years in July and August, and that the bath and *Xenon* during this time were reserved for use by athletes. Such a temporary and restricted use is unlikely in the case of the bath at Epidauros, a famous healing sanctuary visited year-round, and at the *Palaistra* at Olympia, where competing athletes trained only for a few days during the penteteric games. It seems more likely that these facilities could also be used by other groups outside the festival periods even if they provided a much more mundane and inconvenient bathing standard than the aforementioned independent baths.

The trend to provide bathing facilities increased significantly in sanctuaries during the Roman Imperial period. At least eight public baths were built in Olympia from the first to third century CE (Fig. 6.3). As mentioned above, many of these were closely linked with guesthouse-dining-complexes, thus offering restricted, privileged groups a set of pleasurable, if not luxurious, amenities for dining, sleeping, and sanitation. More detailed studies of both baths and guesthouse-dining-complexes are required, however, in order to determine when they were built, how consistently they were conceived as functional sets in Olympia, and how they developed.[59]

Epidauros received at least two new public baths in the Imperial period, which were probably also correlated with guesthouses (Figs. 6.5–6.6).[60] The old Greek Bath was probably still used and renovated, continuously forming a functional unit with the remodeled banquet-odeion complex and the *katagogion*. In addition, small bath suites were integrated into buildings of debated function (Κ, Φ), which may have served as meeting places and habitations (of priests, cult personnel, or specific cultic groups or schools).[61] Other sanctuaries, such as Delphi, Eleusis, Isthmia, and Kos, were provided with at least one new public bath complex. But these baths and their surroundings have not been studied in detail. Therefore, their possible combination with guesthouses—an equally neglected building type—currently cannot be assessed.[62]

The location and context of baths are, however, central to answering the much-debated question of whether sanctuary baths were specifically constructed and used for ritual-religious and therapeutic-curative purposes. Recently, such a function has been challenged for several reasons. Only very few sanctuaries were provided with baths, particularly before the Imperial period, and therefore the baths could not have been central to cult and rituals of any deity. Bathing facilities were not even standard in sanctuaries of Asklepios. The location of baths in secondary areas outside the *temenos* proper and the combination with other buildings (guesthouses, dining complexes) suggest correlated use as agreeable amenities for secular purposes.[63]

---

55   For the design and construction date, possibly even at the end of the fourth century BCE, see Emme 2018, 146, 154, pl. 5; Mania 2018, 182.

56   Mania 2018.

57   Kraynak 1992; Miller 1992.

58   Trümper 2014a, 216–219; this building is commonly identified with the *balaneion* mentioned in several building accounts that Prignitz (2022, 391, 435) dates to 310–300 BCE.

59   Remains of multifunctional guesthouses/banquet buildings/dining pavilions have been identified next to the following baths at Olympia: Late Hellenistic Baths, Hypocaust Bath, Kladeos Baths, Kronion Baths, East Baths, South Baths, and Leonidaion Baths; the baths and adjacent structures were not always built at the same time, however. Haseley (2012, 107) correlated the Southwest Baths with the Leonidaion despite their considerable spatial distance.

60   Northeast Baths with Stoa of Kotys; Northwest Baths with a complex of debated function; see Trümper 2014a.

61   Trümper 2014a, 220–222.

62   Delphi: Bommelaer 1991, 196–198; Eleusis: Travlos, *Attika*, 154, fig. 187, where guesthouses are marked next to the bath-complex, cf. also Nielsen 2017, 35; Kos: Interdonato 2013, 303–313; Isthmia: Yegül 1993, 2015. Guesthouses/hostelries in sanctuaries have not yet been studied comprehensively, let alone for the Roman Imperial period; for Greek hostelries of the sixth to second century BCE, see Kraynak 1984; 1991; 1992. See also Ekroth in this volume.

63   Trümper 2013; 2014a; Yegül 2015. For a different interpretation, see Lo Monaco 2013.

2.2 Open-Air Pools

Some sanctuaries also provided large cold-water pools. Such pools were rare in the Mediterranean world before the early Imperial period when supplies of running water from aqueducts became widely available, and public baths began regularly to include cold-water pools of various sizes (*frigidaria, natationes*). These pools commonly required running water, particularly when they were uncovered in order to keep them clean and usable and avoid dangers of stagnant water; correspondingly, efficient drainage was crucial.[64]

Leaving aside pools included in baths of the Roman Imperial period, which were part of the bathing program, four sanctuaries provide evidence of independent large pools. In Olympia, a pool was built between the Altis and the Kladeos Rivers, probably in the first half of the fourth century BCE (Figs. 6.3, 6.7).[65] It was reconstructed as a rectangular open-air facility with a size of 24 × 16 m at the bottom and a maximum depth of 1.60 m, as well as with five steps and a paved walkway of about 2.50 m width on all four sides. The water supply cannot be securely determined, but water may have been provided from the north by the Kladeos River or via channels from a nearby spring. Water was drained to the south, probably back into the Kladeos River. In reconstructions of the sanctuary, the pool is commonly shown as freely accessible and fully visible (Fig. 6.8),[66] and the question of users has scarcely ever been addressed in scholarship.

The sanctuary of Poseidon in Isthmia was provided with an open-air pool around the mid-fourth century BCE, which measured 30 × 30 m and was about 1.20 m deep. No access steps have been found so far. At least in the east, it was flanked by a paved walkway of 2.10 m width and an adjacent wall. Water arrived from a ravine in the southwest and was drained into a great ravine in the north. While the spatial context of this pool cannot be fully reconstructed, an area to its east has recently been identified as a gymnasion, notably an area of 170–185 × 70 m, which possibly was surrounded by colonnades on all sides. However, this gymnasion, together with a public bath-complex, was only built in the second century CE.[67] Therefore, similar to the situation in Olympia, how the area around the Greek pool was designed and used is currently unknown.

While barely any bathing facilities have been identified in western Greek sanctuaries so far, those that have include two pools, one in Agrigento, and the other in Syracuse.[68] After the battle of Himera in 480 BC, the victorious tyrant Theron built a monumental temple for Zeus in Agrigento. The ambitious building program included the construction of a complex to the south of the temple. This complex was completed around 450 BCE and comprised a small *oikos* with a *theatron* (two large steps in front of the *oikos*), a large hall (35 × 11 m), a smaller building with three square rooms (each 5.40 × 4.20–4.80 m), three cisterns, and a large open-air pool of 10 × 11 m and 1.55–2.00 m depth (Fig. 6.9).

The hall and building with three square rooms have recently been identified as banquet buildings and have been reconstructed with a total of 80 *klinai*.[69] The pool and large hall were separated, but conceptually linked by a small open square where a large door led to the hall. A staircase descended from the square along the north wall of the pool, with five steps from west to east, providing easy access to the pool; a bench along the west wall at a height of 0.60–0.80 m above the floor provided comfortable seating if the pool was not entirely full. A sophisticated channel system from the east supplied the pool and was presumably part of an ambitious water management program, which, according to Diodoros Siculus, the engineer Phaiax had built for the entire city after 480 BCE at the request of Theron.[70] The pool could be fully drained via a drainage hole in the southeast corner at the bottom and was also provided with several overflow channels that partially supplied the cisterns of the complex.[71] The spatial and conceptual relationship between the Temple of Zeus and the southern complex cannot be securely determined. Furthermore, it is unknown how large the sanctuary of Zeus was and whether it was clearly confined within a *temenos* wall. Therefore, how access to, and visibility of, the pool could be controlled are not known.

The pool was found filled with debris, which suggested its abandonment around 300 BCE and included, among other items, ointment vessels in the shape of female heads

---

64 Trümper 2018b.
65 Trümper 2017; 2018b, 257–261.
66 References in Trümper 2017, 240.
67 Frey and Gregory 2016, see also https://www.youtube.com/watch?v=aRYMvXQihEg: (last accessed 18 August 2023); Trümper 2018b, 262–265.
68 Trümper 2019.
69 De Cesare and Portale 2017; De Cesare and Portale 2020, 114, fig. 10; De Cesare, Furcas, and Lionetti 2020, 161, fig. 4.
70 Diod. Sic. 11.25.4; De Cesare, Furcas, and Lionetti (2020) provide a detailed discussion of this channel system, which originated somewhere in the east and also included the Temple of Herakles (Temple A).
71 De Cesare, Furcas, and Lionetti 2020, 160: the original overflow outlet at 1.25 m above the floor was later replaced by a higher one, when presumably the pool would also have been used as a water reservoir.

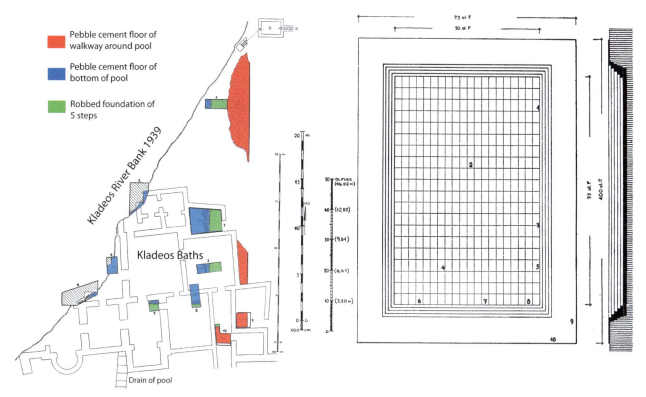

FIGURE 6.7   Olympia, pool, evidence and reconstructed plan
IMAGE: AUTHOR AFTER SCHLEIF AND EILMANN 1944, PL. 15

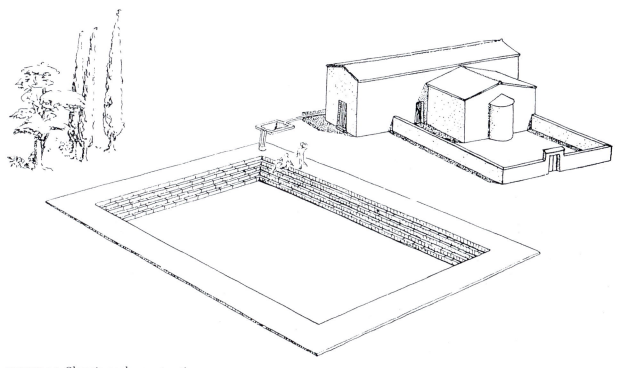

FIGURE 6.8   Olympia, pool, reconstruction
AFTER SCHLEIF 1943, PL. 9A

FIGURE 6.9 Agrigento, pool south of the Olympieion, view from northeast
IMAGE: AUTHOR

and fragments of local red-figured vases painted with images of women. Similar finds were made in one of the cisterns and in the area of the small *oikos*. Based on this material, Monica De Cesare and Chiara Portale argued that a female deity was venerated in the small oikos, "with a sphere of activities linked to female maturation."[72] According to this view, the pool would have been used for ritual purposes within the frame of this cult, which would have been practiced by women.[73] Cults of female deities that were particularly popular in Sicily and Southern Italy, such as Demeter and Kore or the nymphs, were commonly practiced in different settings, particularly when linked to the use of water. For example, remotely located grottoes with natural scenery and small water basins were used to venerate the nymphs in Lokri Epizefiri.[74] No sophisticated bathing facilities were identified in sanctuaries of Demeter and Kore.[75] Against this background, the large and potentially highly visible pool in the immediate vicinity of Agrigento's Olympieion clearly stands out. One wonders whether it could not (also) have been conceived for male visitors or personnel of Zeus' sanctuary, who may have dined or assembled in the adjacent rooms. While the pool has in general few parallels in Greek sanctuaries of

---

72 De Cesare and Portale (2020, 99), which emphasizes the importance of Helena for the sexual maturation of women and ritual baths linked to the respective rites of passage.

73 De Miro 1963; De Cesare 2012; Danile, De Cesare, and Portale 2013; De Cesare and Portale 2017; 2020; De Cesare, Furcas, and Lionetti 2020.

74 Costabile 1991; Hinz 1998, 208–209. Cf. also the Santuario rupestre below San Biagio in Agrigento, where grottoes and a fountain house were used for cultic activities from the fourth century BCE onward. See Hinz 1998, 74–79; Fino 2014.

75 The only securely identifiable bathing facilities are tiny rooms with waterproof decoration and drainage in the South and North Sanctuaries of Demeter and Kore at Morgantina, which may have been used for ritual ablutions. See Hinz 1998, 127–131.

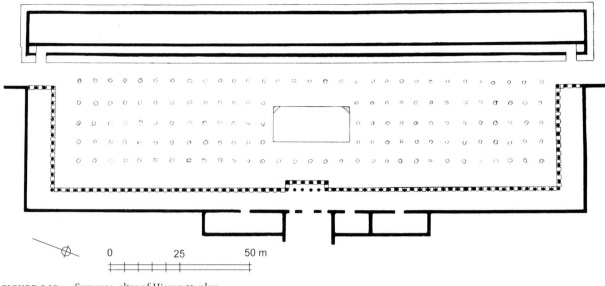

FIGURE 6.10   Syracuse, altar of Hieron II, plan
AFTER NEUTSCH 1954, 594 FIG. 71

the Classical and Hellenistic periods, it currently has none in sanctuaries dedicated solely to female rituals.

During his reign (275–215 BCE), Hieron II built a large altar, most likely for Zeus, in Syracuse. The altar (195.85 × 20.85 m) was bordered by a large square in the west (174 × 40.90 m) that was surrounded by Doric porticoes and accessible from an Ionic propylon in the west (Fig. 6.10).

The square itself included a centrally placed large open-air pool (27 × 12.75 m, 1.30–1.80 m deep), which was provided with stairs in two corners and a base in its center. The water management of the pool is unknown. Five parallel rows of cavities found in the open square were interpreted differently: first, as evidence of trees, which would have belonged to a *palaistra*-setting (the porticoes, courtyard with trees, and pool would have been used by athletes); and second, as evidence of stones with iron rings for fixing sacrificial animals. In the latter scenario, the pool would have been used for some cultic purposes, which are not defined any further.[76] Like the entire monumental altar-precinct, the pool is clearly an impressive feature. Accessibility to the precinct most likely could have been controlled, but the pool seems to have been freely accessible and visible within the confines of the complex.

All four pools presented above were ambitious building projects that belonged to monumentalizing building programs initiated by a tyrant and a king in Sicily and by the important Panhellenic sanctuaries in Olympia and Isthmia. Two pools were part of extra-urban sanctuaries and two of intraurban sanctuaries. The sanctuaries in Isthmia and Agrigento and the spatial context of their pools are not fully known, but the pool at Olympia was built roughly at the same time as other bathing facilities (Baths I, *loutron* in the Echo Stoa complex) and amenities for visitors (Leonidaion, Echo Stoa complex, South Stoa, Southeast complex, Fig. 6.3), thus forming part of a differentiated program. In contrast, the pool in Syracuse was the only bathing facility—indeed, water feature—in the altar precinct.

While it is by no means clear that these pools had similar functions and users, it is remarkable that three were built in, or close to, highly important sanctuaries of Zeus, and one in an equally significant sanctuary of Poseidon. Accessibility and visibility, central to determining possible functions and users, cannot be securely reconstructed for any of the pools. Three pools were built in contexts where athletic games and exercises certainly (Olympia, Isthmia) or possibly (Syracuse) took place. As smaller pools were included in some gymnasia or athletes' baths,[77] cold-water pools may have had an athletic connotation. But at least in the Imperial period, athletes participating in the Olympic games did not train in Olympia except during the five days of the games.[78] Therefore, as an athletes' only pool, the pool in Olympia would have been an enormous luxury. While the four pools discussed here would have allowed for some swim strokes or even athletic lap-swimming, with depths of 1.20–2.00 m, swimming was not part of the Olympic contests or any other athletic competitions in the Greek

---

76   For detailed discussion, see Trümper 2018a, 46–49.

77   Delphi, Nemea, and the palace of Pella. See Trümper 2017; 2018b.
78   Paus. 6.23.1; Philostr. *VA* 5.43: athletes trained in the gymnasion of Elis for 30 days before the games.

world, with the exception of a yearly festival in honor of Dionysos in Hermione, mentioned only by Pausanias in the second century CE without any indication of the age of this festival.[79] Thus, the pool in Olympia will hardly have been built for specific use during the Olympic games. Instead, the pool may have been *the* bathing facility that served for the sanitary (and recreational) needs of much larger crowds than the small bath complexes in Olympia, and most likely also outside the games. A plunge bath or some swimming strokes in cold water may have been particularly pleasant in the scorching summer months;[80] in colder seasons, cold bathing may have been impossible or at least significantly less comfortable than a warm shower bath, while sitting in a tub, but still more agreeable than a bath in one of the rivers or none at all.[81] Finally, it seems highly likely—but cannot be proven—that the pool was surrounded by something (fence, wall, trees) that would have allowed control of visibility and accessibility, for humans as well as animals—the number and status of users notwithstanding.

While similar arguments can be made for the pool in Isthmia, the function of the intraurban pools in Sicily is much harder to determine: washing and recreational pleasure bathing of privileged groups is conceivable, but ritual use—predominantly or at least occasionally—cannot be excluded.

Remarkably, the pools were less popular in the long run than other bathing facilities. The example in Agrigento was filled in with earth and debris around 300 BCE, suggesting that potential rituals performed here could not have been central to the cult. The pools in Olympia and Isthmia were abandoned in the Imperial period at the latest and replaced by modern bath complexes with warm water bathing facilities.[82] This spatial continuity may attest to conceptual continuity regarding the (profane) function and a broad variety of privileged paying users. The period of use of the Syracusan pool (and indeed of the entire altar precinct) is unknown. Maintenance of the pools may have been difficult and costly, but more importantly, bathing practices obviously changed, as clearly reflected in the Panhellenic sanctuaries.

3   Conclusions

Today, defecation and the disposal of human waste are the primary sanitary concerns in sacred places and during large religious festivals, while bathing plays a minor role, if any at all. In Greek sanctuaries, the present state of research suggests that purpose-built bathing facilities outdid purpose-built toilets by far, in terms of number, size, decoration, and possibly differentiation according to users. Purpose-built bathing facilities were introduced earlier in the Greek world than toilets, but even when both were available and standard designs had been developed for both, bathing facilities remained far more numerous than latrines from the late Hellenistic period on. Toilets were often even included in baths or combined with bathing facilities, but surprisingly not on a regular basis.

In reality, users of Greek sanctuaries must have urinated and defecated much more frequently than they bathed. Simply put, urination and defecation are always an unavoidable necessity, while bathing is not. To investigate further and possibly explain this intriguing gap between realistic need and currently known archaeological evidence and to advance the knowledge of sanitary infrastructure and logistics in Greek sanctuaries significantly, one should take the following steps:

1. The archaeological record of Greek sanctuaries should be systematically scrutinized for evidence of purpose-built latrines or other features, such as cesspits, ditches, and drains. This would most likely yield many more examples, at least for the Roman Imperial period. The latrines and other features should all be comprehensively assessed for their date, functioning, accessibility, and socio-cultural significance within the sanctuaries.

2. Even if bathing facilities of Greek sanctuaries are better known than latrines, many have not been sufficiently examined and published. Studying their context, design, construction date, and history is crucial for a differentiated assessment of sanitation in Greek sanctuaries. Furthermore, the combination

---

79 Paus. 2.35.1. For criteria to determine the possible function of pools (splashing and plunging vs. real swimming), see Trümper 2017, 239–240; 2018b.

80 The adverse climatic conditions were mentioned in literary sources, particularly for the games, which took place in July and August. Cf. infra n. 84 and Lo Monaco 2013, 139–140.

81 If the rivers were conveniently accessible at all and had sufficient water in the summer.

82 Kladeos Baths in Olympia; Roman Baths in Isthmia. Frey and Gregory (2016, 459–460) argue that use of the Greek pool ceased around 146 BCE when the Isthmian games were discontinued, but the pool would have been briefly revived in the mid-first century CE when the Isthmian games returned to Isthmia. The pool would, however, have been complemented by a modern Roman bathing facility identified further north (445, fig. 5), and only have been replaced by the lavishly decorated Roman Baths in the second century CE.

of bathing facilities with other buildings (e.g., guesthouses, dining-complexes, sports facilities) deserves closer analysis.

3. Water management is indispensable for sanitary facilities. While the significance of water in Greek sanctuaries is unanimously recognized, detailed comprehensive assessments of hydraulic systems in sanctuaries are absent.[83] Close analysis of the water management could elucidate the functioning of sanitary facilities in sanctuaries, and their rank in a hierarchy of various ritual and secular needs.

4. The increasingly popular methods of modeling and simulation could be applied to visualize and assess the use of Greek sanctuaries, particularly during mass events. For example, focusing on humans, one can calculate how many tents the *Festwiese* area in Olympia would have housed; how many tents would have been needed for 40,000–50,000 people;[84] how much toilet space would have been required and where this could have been located in relation to the sanctuary, tents, wells, and rivers; how much human waste would have been produced and must have been taken care of; how much food and water (for drinking, ritual needs, sanitation) must have been provided; and how water was managed, supplied, circulated, and drained. This should be done for different time periods, when the sanctuary saw major transformations, e.g., around 300 BC, the late first century CE, and the late second century CE, and for different seasons (during and outside games; summer vs. winter).

Modeling could also help to assess the possible social stratification of visitors more closely: the capacities of built bathing facilities, guesthouses, and latrines were limited, even in a sanctuary like Olympia, and suggest that there was a clear socially, financially, or otherwise motivated hierarchy in the use of these facilities.

Returning to the initial question regarding the concepts, tools, and logistics of sanitation in Greek sanctuaries and their impact on the visitors' experience: no clear and entirely satisfactory answer can be given at this point, let alone for Greek sanctuaries in general. Focusing on the best-known example with maximum requirements, Olympia, the bodily needs of some visitors could certainly be met with securely identifiable tools—latrines and bathing facilities—in the Roman Imperial period, and more modestly also earlier, between *c.*350 BCE and the first century CE. To what extent these permanent facilities were supplemented with temporary solutions, such as during festivals in modern India, must remain open for now.

Comparative archaeological analysis suggests that Olympia was at the forefront of sanitation, providing top-notch standards regarding permanent facilities throughout the sanctuary's period of use. But this picture is obviously flawed or at least incomplete for there were apparently not enough (permanent and temporary?) bathing facilities when the philosopher Epiktetos referred to the conditions during the Olympic games in the late first or early second century CE:

> But some unpleasant and hard things happen in life.—And do they not happen at Olympia? Do you not swelter? Are you not cramped and crowded? Do you not bathe with discomfort? Are you not drenched whenever it rains? Do you not have your fill of tumult and shouting and other annoyances? But I fancy that you hear and endure all this by balancing it off against the memorable character of the spectacle.[85]

Interestingly, Epiktetos does not specifically mention defecation and urination and bad smells, but these may have been discreetly subsumed under the "other annoyances."

Acknowledgments

I would like to thank the conference organizers, Judith Barringer, Gunnel Ekroth, and David Scahill, for inviting me to this very interesting and stimulating conference and for their generous hospitality. This paper was written in 2020; literature that appeared after this date could not be systematically included.

---

83 Von Ehrenheim, Klingborg, and Frejman 2019; Kobusch 2020; Klingborg in this volume.
84 For literary sources regarding tents, see Lo Monaco 2013, 137–139; Ekroth in this volume. See also Barringer 2021, 58, n. 87.
85 Epikt. *Diss.* 1.6.26–28. Trans. Oldfather.

Works Cited

Antoniou, G.P. 2010. "Ancient Greek Lavatories: Operation with Reused Water." In *Ancient Water Technologies*, edited by L.W. Mays, 67–86. Dordrecht.

Antoniou, G.P., and A. Angelarakis. 2015. "Latrines and Wastewater Sanitation Technologies in Ancient Greece." In *Sanitation, Latrines and Intestinal Parasites in Past Populations*, edited by P.D. Mitchell, 41–68. London.

Ault, B.A. 1999. "Koprones and Oil Presses at Haleis. Interactions of Town and Country and the Integration of Domestic and Regional Economies." *Hesperia* 68: 549–573.

Barringer, J.M. 2021. *Olympia: A Cultural History*. Princeton.

Bingöl, O. 2007. *Magnesia am Mäander*. Istanbul.

Bommelaer, J.-F. 1991. *Guide de Delphes. Le site*. Athens.

Bouet, A., ed. 2022. *Les latrines de Délos. Hygiène, salubrité et environnement d'une ville des Cyclades*. Bordeaux.

Bradley, M., and K. Stow, eds. 2012. *Rome, Pollution and Propriety: Dirt, Disease and Hygiene in the Eternal City from Antiquity to Modernity*. Cambridge.

Carbon, J.-M., and V. Pirenne-Delforge. 2012. "Beyond Greek 'Sacred Laws.'" *Kernos* 25: 163–182.

Costabile, F. 1991. *I ninfei di Locri Epizefiri. Architettura, culti erotici, sacralità delle acque*. Soveria Mannelli.

Coulton, J.J. 1976. *The Architectural Development of the Greek Stoa*. Oxford.

Danile, E., M. De Cesare, and E.C. Portale. 2013. "Agrigento: Nuove Indagini nell'area a sud del tempio di Zeus." *Mare Internum* 5: 133–144.

De Cesare, M. 2012. "Le nymphai e l'acqua in Sicilia: L'imagerie vascolare." In *Cultura e religione delle acque*, edited by A. Calderone, 141–168. Rome.

De Cesare, M., and E.C. Portale. 2017. "Le ricerche dell'università di Palermo nel santuario di Zeus Olympios ad Agrigento." In *Akragas: Current Issues in the Archaeology of a Sicilian Polis*, edited by N. Sojc, 81–94. Leiden.

De Cesare, M., and E.C. Portale 2020. "Il santuario di Zeus Olympios ad Agrigento. Al di là del tempio monumentale." In *The Akragas Dialogue. New Investigations on Sanctuaries in Sicily*, edited by M. De Cesare, E.C. Portale, and N. Sojc, 99–124. Berlin.

De Cesare, M., G.L. Furcas, and A.L. Lionetti 2020. "Considerazioni sull'approvvigionamento e smaltimento idrico dell'area centro-occidentale della Collina dei Templi di Agrigento in età classica." In *Le forme dell'acqua. Approvvigionamento, raccolta e smaltimento nella città antica*, edited by V. Caminneci, M.C. Parello, and M.S. Rizzo, 157–170. Bologna.

De Miro, E. 1963. "Agrigento. Scavi nell'area a sud del tempio di Giove." *MonAnt* 46: 82–198.

Dupré Raventós, X., and J.A. Remolà, eds. 2000. "Sordes urbis. La eliminación de residuos en la ciudad romana." *Actas de la reunión de Roma, 15–16 de noviembre de 1996*. Rome.

Ehrhardt, W. 2014. "Ergebnisse des DFG-Forschungsprojektes zum Asklepieion von Kos in den Jahren 2010–2013. Ein Resümee." *Kölner und Bonner Archaeologica* 4: 75–107.

Emme, B. 2018. "The Emergence and Significance of the Palaestra Type in Greek Architecture." In *Development of Gymnasia and Graeco-Roman Cityscapes*, edited by U. Mania and M. Trümper, 143–159. Berlin.

Frey, J.M., and T.E. Gregory. 2016. "Old Excavations, New Interpretations: The 2008–2013 Seasons of the Ohio State University, Excavations at Isthmia." *Hesperia* 85: 437–490.

Fuchs, W. 2013. "Untersuchungen zur Geschichte des Leonidaion in Olympia auf Grund des Ausgrabungsbefundes von 1954–1956." *OlBer* 13: 278–341.

Gawlinski, L. 2012. *The Sacred Law of Andania: A New Text with Commentary*. Berlin.

Ginouvès, R. 1955. "Sur un aspect de l'évolution des bains en Grèce vers le IVe siècle de notre ère." *BCH* 79: 135–152.

Ginouvès, R. 1962. *Balaneutikè. Recherches sur le bain dans l'antiquité grecque*. Paris.

Haseley, A. 2012. "Die Südwestthermen in Olympia." In *SPA Sanitas per aquam*, edited by R. Kreiner and W. Letzner, 103–108. Leuven.

Heiden, J. 1995. *Die Tondächer von Olympia, OF 24*. Berlin.

Hinz, V. 1998. *Der Kult von Demeter und Kore auf Sizilien und in der Magna Graecia*. Wiesbaden.

Hobson, B. 2009. *Pompeii, Latrines and Down Pipes: A General Discussion and Photographic Record of Toilet Facilities in Pompeii*. Oxford.

Hoffmann, A. 2011. *Das Asklepieion: Die Platzhallen und die zugehörigen Annexbauten in römischer Zeit, AvP* 11: 5. Berlin.

Hoss, S., ed. 2018. *Latrinae: Roman Toilets in the Northwestern Provinces of the Roman Empire*. Oxford.

Interdonato, E. 2013. *L'Asklepieion di Kos: archeologia del culto*. Rome.

Jansen, G.C.M. 2000. "Studying Roman Hygiene. The Battle between the Optimists and the Pessimists." In *Cura Aquarum in Sicilia. Proceedings of the Tenth International Congress on the History of Water Management and Hydraulic Engineering in the Mediterranean Region, Syracuse May 16–22, 1998*, edited by G.C.M. Jansen, 275–279. Leiden.

Jansen, G.C.M., A.O. Koloski-Ostrow, and E.M. Moormann, eds. 2011. *Roman Toilets: Their Archaeology and Cultural History*. Leuven.

Kadıoğlu, M. 2005. "Die Opus sectile Wandverkleidung der Latrine in Magnesia am Mäander." *IstMitt* 55: 309–336.

Kahlid, A. 2018. "Of Cholera, Colonialism and Pilgrimage Sites. Rethinking Popular Responses to State Sanitation,

c. 1867–1900." In *Society, Medicine and Politics in Colonial India*, edited by B. Pati and M. Harrison, 74–97. New York.

Kankeleit, A. 1994. *Kaiserzeitliche Mosaiken in Griechenland*. Bonn.

Kobusch, P. 2020. "Fountains and Basins in Greek Sanctuaries: On the Relationship between Ritual Performance and Architecture." In *The Power of Urban Water: Studies in Premodern Urbanism*, edited by N. Chiarenza, A. Haug, and U. Mueller, 69–84. Berlin.

Koloski-Ostrow, A.O. 2015. *The Archaeology of Sanitation in Roman Italy: Toilets, Sewers, and Water Systems*. Chapel Hill, NC.

Kraynak, L.H. 1984. *Hostelries of Ancient Greece*. Ph.D. diss., University of California, Berkeley.

Kraynak, L.H. 1991. "The Katagogion at Epidauros. A Revised Plan." *ArchNews* 16: 1–8.

Kraynak, L.H. 1992. "The *Xenon*." In *Excavations at Nemea 1. Topographical and Architectural Studies: The Sacred Square, the Xenon, and the Bath*, by D.E. Birge, L.H. Kraynak, and S.G. Miller, 99–187. Berkeley.

Kyrieleis, H. 2002. *Olympia 1875–2000: 125 Jahre deutsche Ausgrabungen*. Mainz.

Kyrieleis, H., and K. Herrmann. 2013. "Bericht über die Arbeiten in Olympia in den Jahren 2000 bis 2006." *OlBer* 13: 1–50.

Leypold, C. 2008. *Bankettgebäude in griechischen Heiligtümern*. Wiesbaden.

Lindenlauf, A. 2004. "Dirt, Cleanliness and Social Structure in Ancient Greece." In *Agency Uncovered. Archaeological Perspectives on Social Agency, Power, and Being Human*, edited by A. Gardner, 81–105. London.

Lo Monaco, A. 2013. "Fuori dall'Altis. Tende, bagni e propilei a Olimpia in età ellenistica." In *Roman Power and Greek Sanctuaries*, edited by M. Galli, 125–142. Athens.

Lucore, S., and M. Trümper. 2013. *Greek Baths and Bathing Culture: New Discoveries and Approaches*. Leuven.

Mächler, C. 2019. "Olympia, Griechenland. Das Leonideion. Die Arbeiten der Jahre 2016–2018." *E-Forschungsberichte des DAI* 1: 64–67.

Mächler, C. 2020. "Das Leonideion in Olympia. Umbaustrategien in panhellenischem Kontext." In *Umgebaut. Umbau-, Umnutzungs- und Umwertungsprozesse in der antiken Architektur*, edited by K. Piesker and U. Wulf-Rheidt, 298–312. Stuttgart.

Mallwitz, A. 1972. *Olympia und seine Bauten*. Munich.

Manderscheid, H. 1988. *Bibliographie zum römischen Badewesen unter besonderer Berücksichtigung der öffentlichen Thermen*. Munich.

Mania, U. 2018. "Gymnasial Buildings and Sanctuaries. A Contribution to the Formation of the Palaestra and an Interpretation of the So-Called 'Echo Stoa.'" In *Development of Gymnasia and Graeco-Roman Cityscapes*, edited by U. Mania and M. Trümper, 181–95. Berlin.

Melfi, M. 2007. *I santuari di Asclepio in Grecia*. Rome.

Miller, S.G. 1992. "The Bath." In *Excavations at Nemea 1. Topographical and Architectural Studies: The Sacred Square, the Xenon, and the Bath*, by D.E. Birge, L.H. Kraynak, and S.G. Miller, 188–262. Berkeley.

Mitchell, P.D., ed. 2015. *Sanitation, Latrines and Intestinal Parasites in Past Populations*. Farnham.

Mitchell, P.D. 2016. *Human Parasites in the Roman World: Health Consequences of Conquering an Empire*. https://doi.org/10.1017/S0031182015001651.

Mitchell, P.D. 2017. "Human Parasites in the Roman World: Health Consequences of Conquering an Empire." *Parasitology* 144: 48–58.

Moretti, J.-C., and M. Fincker. 2008. "Un autel de Dionysos à Délos." *BCH* 132: 115–152.

Müth, S. 2007. *Eigene Wege. Topographie und Stadtplan von Messene in spätklassisch-hellenistischer Zeit*. Rahden.

Neudecker, R. 1994. *Die Pracht der Latrine. Zum Wandel öffentlicher Bedürfnisanstalten in der kaiserzeitlichen Stadt*. Munich.

Neutsch, B. 1954. "Archäologische Grabungen und Funde im Bereich der Soprintendenzen von Sizilien (1949–1954)." *AA*: 466–706.

Nielsen, I. 2017. "Collective Mysteries and Greek Pilgrimage. The Cases of Eleusis, Thebes and Andania." In *Excavating Pilgrimage. Archaeological Approaches to Sacred Travel and Movement in the Ancient World*, edited by T.M. Kristensen and W. Friese, 28–48. London.

Ohlerich, I. 2009. *Kultorte und Heiligtümer auf dem Gebiet des Bosporanischen Reiches. Vom Beginn der Kolonisation bis zum Ende des 2. Jh. v. Chr.* Rostock.

Owens, E.J. 1983. "The Koprologoi at Athens in the Fifth and Fourth Centuries B.C." *CQ* 33: 44–50.

Petrovic, A. 2015. "Sacred Law" In *The Oxford Handbook of Ancient Greek Religion*, edited by E. Eidinow and J. Kindt, 339–352. Oxford.

Philipp, J.H. 1991. *The Asklepieion at Epidauros in Roman Times*. MA Thesis, Ohio State University.

Prignitz, S. 2022. *Bauurkunden und Bauprogramm von Epidauros II (350–300)*. Munich.

Radt, W. 1999. *Pergamon. Geschichte und Bauten einer antiken Metropole*. Darmstadt.

Riethmüller, J.W. 2005. *Asklepios. Heiligtümer und Kulte*. Heidelberg.

Roux, G. 1961. *L'architecture de l'Argolide aux IVe et IIIe siècles avant J.-C.* Paris.

Schazmann, P. 1932. *Asklepieion. Baubeschreibung und Baugeschichte*. Berlin.

Schleif, H. 1943. *Die neuen Ausgrabungen in Olympia und ihre bisherigen Ergebnisse für die antike Bauforschung*. Berlin.

Schleif, H., and R. Eilmann. 1944. "Die Badeanlage am Kladeos." *OlBer* 4: 32–104.

Senff, R. 2018. "Olympia, Griechenland. Die Arbeiten der Jahre 2016 und 2017." *E-Forschungsberichte des DAI* 1: 42–47.

Sinn, U. 1992. "Bericht über das Forschungsprojekt 'Olympia während der römischen Kaiserzeit,' 1. Die Arbeiten von 1987–1992." *Nikephoros* 5: 75–84.

Sinn, U. 1997. "Bericht über das Forschungsprojekt 'Olympia während der römischen Kaiserzeit und in der Spätantike,' 6. Die Arbeiten im Jahr 1996." *Nikephoros* 10: 215–216.

Sinn, U. 2004. *Das antike Olympia. Götter, Spiel und Kunst*. Munich.

Sinn, U. 2012. "Olympia und die Spiele in römischer Zeit." In *Mythos Olympia. Kult und Spiele*, edited by W.-D. Heilmeyer et al., 105–109. Munich.

Sinn, U., G. Ladstätter, and A. Martin. 1993. "Bericht über das Forschungsprojekt 'Olympia während der römischen Kaiserzeit,' 2. Die Arbeiten im Jahr 1993." *Nikephoros* 6: 153–158.

Sinn, U., G. Ladstätter, and A. Martin. 1994. "Bericht über das Forschungsprojekt 'Olympia während der römischen Kaiserzeit,' 3. Die Arbeiten im Jahr 1994." *Nikephoros* 7: 229–250.

Sinn, U., G. Ladstätter, A. Martin, and T. Völling. 1995. "Bericht über das Forschungsprojekt 'Olympia während der römischen Kaiserzeit und in der Spätantike,' 4. Die Arbeiten im Jahr 1995." *Nikephoros* 8: 161–182.

Sinn, U., C. Leypold, and C. Schauer. 2003. "Olympia. Eine Spitzenstellung nicht nur im Sport. Eine neuentdeckte Badeanlage der hellenistischen Zeit." *AW* 34: 617–623.

Sioumpara, E.P. 2011. *Der Asklepios-Tempel von Messene auf der Peloponnes*. Munich.

Themelis, P.G. 2003. *Das antike Messene*. Athens.

Tomlinson, R.A. 1983. *Epidauros*. Austin.

Trümper, M. 2009. "Complex Public Bath Buildings of the Hellenistic Period. A Case-Study in Regional Differences." In *Le bain collectif en Égypte*, edited by M.-F. Boussac, T. Fournet, and B. Redon, 139–179. Cairo.

Trümper, M. 2010. "Bathing Culture in Hellenistic Domestic Architecture." In *Städtisches Wohnen im östlichen Mittelmeer. 4. Jh. v. Chr.–1. Jh. n. Chr.*, edited by S. Ladstätter and V. Scheibelreiter, 529–572. Vienna.

Trümper, M. 2011. "Hellenistic Latrines." In *Roman Toilets: Their Archaeology and Cultural History*, edited by G.C.M. Jansen, A.O. Koloski-Ostrow, and E.M. Moormann, 33–42. Leuven.

Trümper, M. 2013. "Urban Context of Greek Public Baths." In *Greek Baths and Bathing Culture: New Discoveries and Approaches*, edited by S.K. Lucore and M. Trümper, 33–72. Leuven.

Trümper, M. 2014a. "Bathing in the Sanctuaries of Asklepios and Apollo Maleatas at Epidauros." In *Approaching the Ancient Artifact. Representation, Narrative, and Function*, edited by A. Avramidou and D. Demetriou, 211–232. Berlin.

Trümper, M. 2014b. "Baths and Bathing Culture, Greek." In *Encyclopedia of Global Archaeology*, edited by C. Smith et al., 784–799. New York.

Trümper, M. 2014c. "Privat versus Öffentlich in hellenistischen Bädern." In *Stadtkultur im Hellenismus*, edited by A. Matthaei and M. Zimmermann, 206–249. Göttingen.

Trümper, M. 2017. "Greek Swimming Pools: Case-Study Olympia." In *Cura Aquarum in Greece*, edited by K. Wellbrock, 215–250. Siegburg.

Trümper, M. 2018a. "Gymnasia in Eastern Sicily of the Hellenistic Period. A Reassessment." In *Development of Gymnasia and Graeco-Roman Cityscapes*, edited by U. Mania and M. Trümper, 43–73. Berlin.

Trümper, M. 2018b. "Swimming Pools and Water Management in the Eastern Mediterranean World of the 4th to 1st Century BC." In *Water Management in Ancient Civilizations*, edited by J. Berking, 255–296. Berlin.

Trümper, M. 2019. "Development of Bathing Culture in Hellenistic Sicily." In *Cityscapes of Hellenistic Sicily*, edited by M. Trümper, G. Adornato, and T. Lappi, 347–391. Rome.

von Ehrenheim, H., P. Klingborg, and A. Frejman. 2019. "Water at Ancient Greek Sanctuaries: Medium of Divine Presence or Commodity for Mortal Visitors?" *Journal of Archaeology and Ancient History* 26: 1–31.

Vortmann, M., S. Balsari, S.R. Holman, and P.G. Greenough. 2015. "Water, Sanitation, and Hygiene at the World's Largest Mass Gathering." *Current Infectious Diseases Report* 17: 1–7.

Wassenhoven, M. E. 2012. *The Bath in Greece in Classical Antiquity: The Peloponnese*. Oxford.

Wilson, A. 2011. "The Economy of Ordure." In *Roman Toilets: Their Archaeology and Cultural History*, edited by G.C.M. Jansen, A.O. Koloski-Ostrow, and E.M. Moormann, 147–156. Leuven.

World Health Organization https://apps.who.int/iris/bitstream/handle/10665/274939/9789241514705-eng.pdf?ua=1

Yegül, F. 1993. "Roman Baths at Isthmia in their Mediterranean Context." In *The Corinthia in the Roman Period: Including the Papers Given at a Symposium Held at the Ohio State University on 7–9 March 1991*, edited by T.E. Gregory, 95–113. Ann Arbor.

Yegül, F.K. 2015. "Roman Baths at Isthmia and Sanctuary Baths in Greece." In *Bridge of the Untiring Sea. The Corinthian Isthmus from Prehistory to Late Antiquity*, edited by T.E. Gregory and E. Gebhard, 247–269. Athens.

Zuchtriegel, G. 2006. "Wo kann man's wagen? Koprones, Latrinen und Ausgussstellen in griechischen Städten vor der Kaiserzeit. MA Thesis, Freie Universität. Berlin.

CHAPTER 7

Hotels, Tents, and Sacred Houses: Spaces for Human Accommodation in Greek Sanctuaries

Gunnel Ekroth

To visit the gods, for whatever purpose, often meant traveling and leaving one's home. The journey itself was necessary if the deities you wanted to contact were not located next door. Once at the site where the gods were thought to be present, you had to find a place to stay the night. But ordinary worshippers were not the only ones who would have stayed at sanctuaries. Religious personnel required housing for longer or shorter periods, and there were also refugees and even squatters.

To stay at a religious location involves logistics. What kind of accommodation could be found, and who would provide this for the visitors: the sanctuary or private initiatives? How do these installations relate to the sanctuary proper as to both space and function? Did humans actually stay inside the *temenos* of the god, that is, on sacred ground?

Just as for many other aspects of the logistics in Greek sanctuaries, the evidence for people staying there is not extensive, neither the material remains nor the written sources.[1] Modern parallels can therefore be useful to tease out a fuller picture of the ancient situation, and not least to illustrate the infrastructure needed to manage large crowds coming to sacred places and spending the night.[2]

That people do travel to sacred sites in very large numbers can be illustrated by some modern examples.[3] The small French city of Lourdes has 16,000 inhabitants but receives between 4 and 6 million visitors a year, who come to worship the Virgin and to be cured of illnesses.[4] In fact, Lourdes is the second most visited site in France and apparently, only Paris has more hotels per square kilometer.[5] In addition, there are private lodgings and apartments to rent, as well as camping grounds. The number of pilgrims arriving by camper vans is substantial. The pilgrimage of the French Roma population, which takes place in the end of August and is one of the largest religious events of this ethnic group, involves up to 1,200 camping cars and caravans, parked on fields outside the city.[6] In Saudia Arabia, the Tent city at Mina can house as many as 3 million Muslim pilgrims in more than 100,000 air-conditioned tents, covering an area of $c.20$ km².[7] Not everyone will stay in these tents though, and Mecca is full of hotels, booked year round, including international chains such as Hilton, Inter-Continental, and Mövenpick.[8] The housing situations at Mecca and Lourdes may seem to be exaggerated examples in comparison with ancient Greece. However, before access to cheap flights, the number of pilgrims at Mecca was much smaller—in the 1950s rarely more than 100,000, which is closer to the $c.40,000$ to 45,000 visitors that we assume may have come to ancient Olympia for the games.[9] So where and how did all these ancient visitors stay?

---

1 For previous work on accommodation in Greek sanctuaries, see Ziebarth 1935; Casson 1974, 197–218; Kraynak 1984; Kraynak 1992; Dillon 1997b, 206–211; Ault 2005, 150–155; Stewart 2009.
2 For the use of modern parallels, see also Trümper in this volume. For the logistics of lodging for travelers in Late Antiquity and the Middle Ages, see Constable 2003.
3 See Trümper in this volume for Indian religious festivals attracting huge crowds.
4 See https://sacredsites.com/europe/france/lourdes_facts.html (last accessed 25 April 2024).
5 https://www.reuters.com/article/us-pope-lourdes-history-idUKLB15892820080911 (last accessed 25 April 2024).
6 Peyron 2014, 209–218.
7 Saudi Arabia is currently launching an international competition to increase the capacity of the Mina tent city to 10 million pilgrims to as part of their Vison 2030 agenda, see https://uni.xyz/competitions/the-white-lands/info/about (last accessed 25 April 2024).
8 What is claimed to be the world's largest hotel once finished, the Abraj Kudai with 10,000 rooms and 70 restaurants and owned by Saudi Arabia's ministry of finance, is currently under construction at Mecca, see https://www.trendingbird.com/abraj-kudai-the-worlds-largest-hotel-in-makkah-saudi-arabia (last accessed 25 April 2024).
9 For the visitors to Mecca in the 1950s, see Bianchi 2004, 50–51, fig. 4.1. The figure for Olympia is calculated by how many spectators could watch the competitions in the *stadion* and the testimony of ancient written accounts, see Barringer 2021, 44–45, n. 26.

1 Hotels

Contrary to both Lourdes and Mecca, Greek sanctuaries were not overflowing with hotels.[10] Such installations are known from the written sources, designated as *katagogia*, *pandokeia*, or *xenones*.[11] In fact, most guesthouses mentioned in ancient texts and inscriptions are located at sanctuaries, and such facilities were probably more common than what our restricted evidence suggests.[12] On the other hand, our sources offer few details as to what these installations looked like and how they worked.[13] When going to a sanctuary, describing the available accommodation does not seem to have been at the top of the list for ancient authors. Pausanias, who probably visited more sanctuaries than most other Greeks, does not mention any hotels for people to stay in or give any indication of where he himself stayed during his journeys.[14]

The archaeological record for hotels at Greek sanctuaries is not extensive either and linked to methodological problems.[15] Excavations of cult places usually focus on the center of the sanctuary and the temple, and secular buildings situated further away tend to be neglected or not even sought. Ancient hotels are also difficult to distinguish both from dining halls and from the lodging for religious personnel or even private residences.[16] Keeping in mind the difficulties of finding and identifying hostels, such a facility was still apparently not a prerequisite for a sanctuary and of less importance than a stoa or a built installation for dining.

So why were hotels built? It is evident that it was not only a question of practicalities and comfort as important visitors also would stay in tents (see further below), and camping must have been the norm for most people coming to sanctuaries. A remote location of a sanctuary may have called for a hostel, while a position in or near a settlement provided options of staying with private individuals who rented rooms.[17] The particularities of the cult may have been another reason. Two of the possible guesthouses known from the archaeological record are located at Asklepieia, where people went to be cured and therefore would stay for a longer period, perhaps also accompanied by family and friends.[18] Oracle consultation may also have required an extended visit, and a *pandokeion* is known from Delphi.[19] Economy could have been an additional reason for the construction of a hotel, as the epigraphic record shows that some sanctuaries owned guesthouses that were leased to provide a source of income.[20]

In the few cases where we have more information, it is clear that the erection of a major hotel was due to particular circumstances. The late fourth-century BCE Leonidaion at Olympia was a private initiative, a dedication by Leonidas of Naxos to Zeus Olympios, which must have raised the status of the donor, as much as that of the sanctuary.[21] Leonidas may have been a *theoros*, *theorodokos*, or a *proxenos*, who built the hostel to house other *theoroi* coming

---

10   See Kraynak 1984; Dillon 1997b, 206–211; Sinn 2005, 51–52.
11   For the terminology, see Kraynak 1984, 9–21. See also Constable 2003, 144, for the development of the terminology in Late Antiquity.
12   McDonald 1951, 365–367; Kraynak 1984, 24. Sinn's discussion of *katagogion* in *ThesCRA* (4, 51–52) only includes two examples.
13   Most of the excavated structures identified as hostelries date to the second half of the fourth century BCE (Kraynak 1984, 24). The written evidence also suggests that hotels were more generally available during this period in sanctuaries, in cities and along the roadside.
14   Pausanias (5.15.1–4) mentions the Leonidaion at Olympia, but does not call it a hostel.
15   Lynn Kraynak's study of Greek hostelries from 1984 identifies ten or possibly eleven cases of which seven are located next to sanctuaries; that is, the presence of a sanctuary is the reason why the hotel was constructed. To these can be added seven instances of written mentions, see Kraynak 1984, A2, A11, A12, A19, A20, A24, and A95. For the *kapeleia* on Samos, which may have served as hostelries as well, see *NSGL*² no. 18, commentary on pp. 293–294; Habicht 1972, 220. On the archaeological evidence for Early Christian guesthouses for pilgrims, see Jensen 2020, 149–154.
16   For example, a building at Cape Zoster in Attika is classified as a possible hostelry by Kraynak (1984, 62–63) and as a dining building by Goldstein (1978, 133), but which may also have been the house of a priest in an earlier phase. For the interpretation of the Villa of Good Fortune at Olynthos as a high-class inn, see McDonald 1951. See also the contribution by Barringer in this volume. For the difficulties in identifying guesthouses for pilgrims at Early Christian sites, see Jensen 2020, 150.
17   Dillon 1997b, 208; Aurigny 2020, 102. For hostels at remote sanctuaries, such as the Lykaion and Aulis, see Kraynak 1984, 82–108.
18   Asklepieia with hotels: Epidauros (Kraynak 1984, 63–73) and Gortys (Kraynak 1984, 79–81). For longer stays at Asklepieia, see von Ehrenheim 2015, 199–200.
19   Kraynak 1984, no. A20; Rousset 2002, 207–208, no. 32. On spaces for lodging at Delphi, see also Aurigny 2020, 101–104.
20   On Delos, the sanctuary owned a *pandokeion* and a *xenon*, which they rented out. These structures were not necessarily located next to the sanctuary. See Kraynak 1984, 25; Chankowski 2008, 293. Even private cults could sublet their accommodations to raise funds, as was the case for the *xenones* in the sanctuary of Herakles Diomedonteios on Kos (325–300 BCE), *CGRN* 96, ll. 80–85 with commentary; Campanelli 2016, 157–158.
21   Boersma 1973; Kraynak 1984, 49–65; Leypold 2008, 104–110. Scott (2010, 239) sees its construction as particularly linked to the importance of the games as boosted by Philip and Alexander. The presence of other hotels at Olympia is suggested by a *xenon* mentioned in a bronze inscription from c.500 BCE; see Rutherford 2013, 31, 367–368, A5.

to the sanctuary. The building was in use well into the Roman period, when Pausanias reports that it acted as the lodging for the Roman governors of Greece.[22] The *Xenon* at Nemea, constructed in the late fourth century BCE after the site had been deserted for a century, can be connected to the re-organization of the sanctuary in relation to the political ambitions of Philip of Macedon, who may even have paid for the works.[23] The temple of Zeus was rebuilt, the altar extended, and a bath, as well as the hotel, were constructed (see p. 167, Fig. 10.4).[24] At Epidauros, the so-called *katagogion* was part of the major expansion of the sanctuary in the late fourth-early third century BCE, when the temples, the theater, and the Tholos were built (see p. 89, Fig. 6.5).[25] Attracting visitors and success in healing the sick were important issues for the sanctuary at Epidauros, which is evident from the prominent display of the *iamata* recording the experiences of those seeking the help of the god. The construction of the hostel may have been part of these efforts, as well. The most explicit literary description of a hotel is of the *katagogion* at the sanctuary of Hera at Plataiai, mentioned by Thucydides.[26] His description makes clear that this building was erected after the Thebans raised the city to the ground in 427, then used the stone and timber from Plataian houses to construct the hostel. Beds were made from brass and iron from the city and dedicated to Hera, so presumably they were placed in the *katagogion*. Possibly this hotel was aimed at attracting visitors to the Eleutheria festival after the city had been destroyed and providing housing for officials.[27]

The size and location of these structures are also noteworthy. The Leonidaion was the largest architectural complex at Olympia apart from the later gymnasion, and had as many as 50 rooms, lodging between 100 to 300 people.[28] It was situated next to the Altis, and oriented towards the main access routes to the sanctuary from the west and the south. The *katagogion* at Epidauros housed as many as 140–420 people, and this structure, as well as the *Xenon* at Nemea, were the largest buildings in these sanctuaries, both prominently situated overlooking the *temenos*.[29] The *katagogion* at Plataiai was also substantial. According to Thucydides, it faced the Heraion and measured "200 by 200 feet" with rooms in two stories around a courtyard.[30] Not only the size, but also the proximity to the religious center of the sanctuary, were apparently important for these constructions. The best hotels at Lourdes today are located just to the south of the large precinct of the Sanctuary of our Lady at Lourdes and the cave where the young Bernadette Soubirous saw the apparition of the Virgin Mary in 1858. At Mecca, the most prestigious hotels tower over the Great mosque and the Kaba, like the huge ZamZam Pullman Makkah, with 1,300 suites and deluxe rooms. Even lodging facilities and hostelries at Early Christian pilgrim sites were advertised as offering excellent views over the saint's shrine.[31]

Accommodation at such a location not only provides a roof over the visitors' heads, but also signals their status while being at the sacred site. Perhaps a similar attitude mind-set lay behind the more spectacular hotels at ancient Greek sanctuaries. The Leonidaion at Olympia not only occupied a prominent position in the sanctuary, but also was surrounded by an outer colonnade recalling a temple or a stoa, an unusual feature considering its function as a hotel. This embellishment caused Alfred Mallwitz to suggest that this architecture was perhaps meant to hint that those staying here saw themselves as no mere mortals.[32]

2 Tents

Contrary to Lourdes with its many hotels, and more similar to Mecca, Greek sanctuaries probably permitted pilgrims to stay in tents and not in buildings.[33] Our information about such accommodation is primarily known from the literary and epigraphical record.[34] The archaeological

---

22 Paus. 5.15.2; Specht 2001.
23 Miller 1979, 103; Kraynak 1984, 122–147; Miller 1988, 144–145; Kraynak 1992; Scott 2010, 247.
24 The *Xenon* may have been meant primarily for the competing athletes rather than for ordinary visitors. The explicit construction of such housing is known from later evidence, for example, at Isthmia, where athletes could stay for free in the *oikoi* during the festival. See Geagan 1989, 355–356.
25 For the date, see Kraynak 1991, 1; Riethmüller 2005, 1: 293–4; Melfi 2007, 45. The term is not attested in the Epidaurian inscriptions.
26 Thuc. 3.68.3; Kraynak 1984, 34–37.
27 Dillon 1997b, 208.
28 Heermann 1984; Kraynak 1984, 49–56; Ault 2005, 152; Leypold 2008, 107–110; Barringer 2021, 54–58, 233–234. The Leonidaion measures 80 × 80 m.

29 Epidauros: Kraynak 1991, 7; Riethmüller 2005, 1: 294. The incubants would sleep in the sanctuary, in the *abaton*, for one or more nights to encounter the god in a dream and presumably then be housed outside the sacred area if staying longer. Nemea: Kraynak 1984, 122–147; Kraynak 1992.
30 Thuc. 3.68.3; Kraynak 1984, 8.
31 Jensen 2020, 146.
32 Mallwitz 1972, 252.
33 Some ancient visitors, like the Roma visiting modern-day Lourdes (see above), may have slept on their wagons or carts after their arrival.
34 For the evidence of tents, see Goldstein 1978, 12–27, 58–59; Deshours 2006, 92, 132; Gawlinski 2012, 142–145. Tents could also be used for commerce, ritual purposes, and most of all, for

material is slight, for example, metal stakes from tents found under the courtyard of the *Palaistra* at Olympia and postholes at some other sites.³⁵ The tents would have been made of cloth, leather, or even reeds, and the supporting structure of wood.³⁶

To get a better grasp of the scattered ancient evidence for the use of tents when visiting sanctuaries, comparison with a modern festival's provisions for camping may be useful. The Roskilde music festival in Denmark now attracts more than 100,000 visitors annually, and the logistics of camping are laid out in detail on their web site.³⁷ Our ancient evidence is obviously less full, but reveals how sanctuaries took active means to regulate and organize the campers, which is understandable if their numbers counted tens of thousands. We should imagine popular sanctuaries as surrounded by camping grounds, like the festival of Artemis at Skillous, to which all citizens and inhabitants of the region would come and stay in tents.³⁸

Many sanctuaries had empty spaces nearby that served to house the dining that followed sacrifices, the famous *Festwiesen* identified by Ulrich Sinn, which could also have been used for tents.³⁹ Such areas have rarely been investigated in a consistent manner archaeologically, but a recent survey at the sanctuary of Zeus at Labraunda has identified a number of possible camping sites.⁴⁰ At Olympia, the area outside the Altis was to be used for dining and staying as is evident from Pindar and the scholia, while at a sanctuary of Zeus at Stratonikeia, camping was to take place in a specific location reserved for humans, presumably contrary to the areas for trade and keeping animals.⁴¹ Within the camping grounds, particular areas could be set aside for certain types of visitors. The extensive regulations of the Mysteries at Andania (late first century BCE) stipulate a specific area reserved for the Sacred Men's tents, and the uninitiated could not even enter this part of the camp.⁴² This restriction implies a particular sacred character ascribed to this area, especially as lustral basins and written instructions regulated the purity inside. On the other hand, it also suggests a kind of VIP area for the Sacred Men. It seems unlikely that prestigious visitors, such as Dionysios of Syracuse, who sent several lavish tents to Olympia in 388 BCE, would have camped with the *hoi polloi*.⁴³ Likewise, a late third-century regulation from Delphi prohibits anyone but the king himself from pitching a tent in the area of the stoa of Attalos, thus pointing to the exclusivity of this area.⁴⁴ At modern festival sites, such as Roskilde, there are also different camps depending on whether or not you bring your own tent or rent one on site, as well as how much you want to pay, but also depending on your resilience towards noise and garbage.⁴⁵

Securing a good spot for your tent was important. At Roskilde, festivalgoers traditionally arrive four days before the actual music festival begins. Those bringing their own tents queue up in front of the gates to the camping ground, and once the gates open, they run to the area where they prefer to pitch their tent. A mid-third-century decree from Delphi honors Mentor from Naupaktos with the right to place the first tent at the meeting of the Amphictyony.⁴⁶

---

banqueting; see Schmitt Pantel 1997, 312–313, suggesting that the verb *skanein* could be synonymous with "to banquet." A late fifth-century BCE sacrificial regulation concerning the Anakeion at Elateia urges worshippers to sacrifice and raise a tent, presumably stipulating that the meat was to be eaten on the spot; see *CGRN* 33 with commentary. See also *LSCG* no. 168 (early second century BCE); Goldstein 1978, 41–43.

35 Olympia: Wacker 1996, 91, n. 67; Kyrieleis 2003, 95; Barringer 2021, 58. See also Sinn's comment on the finding of a bronze tip from a tent among remnants of meals at Olympia in the discussion of Kron 1988, 148. For postholes, see Kron 1988, 142–144, who also addresses tents erected for banqueting rather than sleeping at the Samian Heraion, where no *hestiatoria* have been found. Some *skenai* mentioned in texts and inscriptions may refer to improvised huts constructed at particular festivals rather than to proper tents; see Burkert 1985, 107.

36 For huts (used in the market) made of reeds, see Paus. 10.35.15. The use of well-built *skenomata* to construct a stockade by the Arkadians when they were attacked at Olympia (Xen. *Hell.* 7.4.32) suggests more sturdy structures, but these may have been shops rather than tents to live in. For the temporality of such structures, especially round ones, see Cooper and Morris 1990, 71–72.

37 https://www.roskilde-festival.dk/en/camping (last accessed 25 April 2024).

38 Xen. *An.* 5.3.9. Polyainos, *Strat.* 6.45 describes how the Samians gathered in the sanctuary of Hera to celebrate her festival and erect tents (*eskenepoiounto*), see Goldstein 1978, 22–23. For tents surrounding the Altis at Olympia, see Taita 2014, 124–126.

39 Sinn 1988, 154–157; Sinn (1992, 180–183), who takes this space to be part of the *temenos*. The use of *Festwiesen* both for cooking and eating and for camping and sleeping needs further consideration. At the Roskilde festival, there is a separation between sleeping and cooking areas due to fire risks.

40 Frejman 2020, 71–78, and for criteria of identification, see 16–17 and 45–48. For the identification of camping grounds at the sanctuary of Sinuri, see Frejman 2020, 145–146, and at Nemea, Frejman 2020, 169–171. See also the contribution by Chandezon in this volume.

41 Pind. *Ol.* 10.46–47 with scholia; *I.Stratonikeia* 203, ll. 17–21.

42 *CGRN* 222, ll. 34–37; Gawlinski 2012, 145–148.

43 Diod. Sic. 14.109.

44 *CID* IV 85, l. 9; Goldstein 1978, 13–14; Aurigny 2020, 101. A tent could have been placed in the eastern area of the terrace, or awnings may have been installed between the columns or monuments by the help of ropes.

45 https://www.roskilde-festival.dk/en/camping (last accessed 24 April 2024).

46 *CID* IV 54, ll. 7–11: Goldstein 1978, 14.

Presumably, he first of all was able to choose where to put his tent. In Aristophanes' *The Peace*, a servant marks the space where the tent is to be erected at Isthmia by peeing in a circle on the ground.[47] The scholia to the passage are more matter-of-fact and clarify that people tried to secure a spot in advance and that this was the recommended way to proceed at crowded sanctuaries in order not to miss out on the best locations.[48]

We do not know to what extent visitors to ancient sanctuaries brought their own tents or if they could be rented on the spot. The second-century CE inscription from Stratonikeia mentioned earlier records that the priest of Zeus Panamaros provided tents for the citizens, *xenoi*, and slaves.[49] Polyainos' *Strategmata* from the second century CE tells of the Samians going to the sanctuary of Hera and erecting their tents, presumably their own, while the women in Aristophanes' *Thesmophoriazousai* probably also had their own tents.[50] You could also lodge in someone else's tent, as Plato apparently did when visiting Olympia, which may have meant eating and spending time with a group of strangers.[51] The Andania inscription regulates the size of the tents; Laura Gawlinski calculates them to have been $c.5$ m², which would be small, but useful, and could accommodate four people lying next to each other tightly with $c.50$ cm width per person.[52] The campers at Andania were not permitted to put curtains or hangings around the tents in the manner of modern tents equipped with porches, presumably to prevent people from occupying more space than absolutely necessary. This suggests that the visitors would bring their own tents, but also that the organizers wanted to maximize the use of camping ground space.[53]

On the other hand, a tent did not have to mean simple accommodation, and a private tent may have been a chance to outshine other visitors. Just as the tents at Roskilde range from the ultra-cheap mass-produced Chinese versions to the spacious cloth tents, so-called tenthouses with raised wooden floors and electricity, the ancient sources also mention large and luxurious tents.[54] Ion's tent described in Euripides' play is one example: $c.900$ m² and decorated with lavish textiles from the temple treasury.[55] This is a fictional case, and the tent may also have been used for ritual activities, which may have called for a more spectacular setting. As historical examples, we can cite the case of Alkibiades at Olympia, where the Ephesians provided him with a tent twice the size of the tent of the Athenian delegation, and Dionysios I of Syracuse sent tents made of colorful material and decorated with gold to Olympia, where they generated a lot of attention.[56]

Once again, the modern analogy of Roskilde offers a useful comparison. The tents at Roskilde are organized in plots separated by lanes between them. In the *Thesmophoriazousai*, the women search tents and passageways to find the intruder Mnesilochos, suggesting an organization of the camp in a similar manner.[57] The Andania inscription stipulates the marking of the area for the Sacred Men's tents with *stemmata*, wreaths, or fillets.[58] Ropes used in public spaces may also have been an option.[59] On the other hand, Lucian complains that Olympia is crowded with tents and huts and is stifling hot, suggesting that all camp grounds were not well-organized.[60] At Roskilde, the plots are marked by strips of paint on the grass, and each quadrant is identified by a letter and a number. Festivalgoers are urged to memorize their quadrant's designation and location in order to find their way back to their tent.[61] We have no ancient evidence for this practice, but one might assume that similar problems of getting lost cannot have been unheard of in the *Festwiese* at Olympia.

Too closely spaced and disorganized placement of tents would make fires a perpetual risk. The Greek regulations

---

47 Ar. *Pax* 879–880.
48 Or even end up without lodging, see Goldstein 1978, 14–16. What qualified as a good location may have been near important facilities, such as springs and baths, in the shade, or with a clear view of the processions and sacrificial activities; see Dio Chrys. *Or.* 9.22.
49 *I.Stratonikeia* 203, ll. 17–21; Dillon 1990, 83.
50 Polyainos, *Strat.* 6.45; Ar. *Thesm.* 624, 658. See also the discussion by Goldstein 1978, 23–26.
51 Ael. *VH* 4.9. Dillon (1990, 81) finds that this particular setting was a detail added by Aelian to create a better context for the ensuing dialogue.
52 Gawlinski 2012, 144.
53 The ban on *klinai* in the tents at Andania was perhaps also a way to squeeze in more sleepers (*CGRN* 222, l. 38; Gawlinski 2012, 148). A family may still have had several tents. Such tent groupings are common in Roskilde where they are often centered on a canopy, an installation recalling an ancient tetrastylon; see Albris, Beck, and Sørensen 2009, 8.
54 Roskilde: https://www.roskilde-festival.dk/en/camping (last accessed 2 April 2024).
      For glamping tents: https://www.bestproducts.com/fitness/equipment/g3197/glamping-luxury-tents/ (last accessed 24 April 2024).
55 Eur. *Ion* 1122–1166; Goldstein 1978, 9–13.
56 Alkibiades: [Andok.], *Against Alkibiades* 4.30; Goldstein 1978, 17. Dionysios: Diod. Sic. 14.109.
57 Ar. *Thesm.* 655–658. See Goldstein 1978, 23–26 for the discussion of where the play is set, on the Pnyx or in the City Eleusinion, and whether the tents were erected inside or outside the sanctuary.
58 *CGRN* 222, ll. 36–37.
59 For ropes, see Gawlinski 2012, 146; and Gawlinski in this volume.
60 Luc. *Her.* 8.
61 *Roskilde Festival Guide* 2019, 94.

forbidding lighting fires in sanctuaries may have concerned the campsites, as well.⁶² We may note that the Delphic inscription that prohibits camping in the area of the stoa of Attalos also bans the use of fire.⁶³ Campfires, torches, candles, camping stoves, and barbecues are strictly forbidden in the camping areas at Roskilde, and the fire access routes must be free of tents and garbage.⁶⁴ One is not allowed to cook in the camping plots due to risk of fire.⁶⁵

Our ancient sources do not elaborate on the negative sides of camp life apart from Lucian's complaint that it was crowded and hot. Even if a festival was well organized, camping must have affected the environment substantially. The many regulations protecting trees, bushes, and grass in Greek sanctuaries certainly address the negative impact of visitors and their animals and carts to the site, inside, as well as outside, the *temenos*.⁶⁶ To better understand the camping experience at a Greek sanctuary, we would have to excavate the areas used for these activities. This has actually been done at Roskilde, revealing the huge impact of the festivalgoers on the ground surface, which needs to be ameliorated with gravel on a regular basis.⁶⁷ Rich finds of beer caps and condoms reflect activities other than the music, the main event of the festival.⁶⁸ Moreover, the soil still smelled of beer and urine when excavated. The phosphate levels were similar to those of a pigpen, and their intensity suggests that systematic soil sampling would allow the mapping of the location and extent of the camps even several thousands of years later. Considering that ancient inscriptions prohibit people from urinating in sanctuaries, and Plutarch even states that you are not to urinate against the altar or the god's building, peeing in campsites is likely to have occurred in ancient Greece, as well.⁶⁹ This unappealing practice may, on the other hand, help us to locate ancient campsites, if we so desire.⁷⁰

Greek sanctuaries had personnel in charge of the logistics of the camping. At Andania, they were the Sacred Men.⁷¹ The Karneatai organized the Karneia festival for Apollo at Sparta, and Aristotle mentions officials managing public festivals, which may have included practicalities, such as housing, in addition to the purely cultic rituals.⁷² The number of such persons is difficult to assess; the Karneatai were only five, but all such officials must have been assisted by slaves.⁷³ In comparison, Roskilde in 2019 had *c.*130,000 festivalgoers, while the volunteers numbered more than 30,000. Presumably, there are greater demands on security and comfort today, but festival logistics in antiquity also must have needed substantial human resources.

3   Sacred Houses

Some of those staying at a sanctuary had to do so in their capacity as religious personnel. Where and for how long depended on the character of the cult, the requirements of the office, and the location of the sanctuary vis-à-vis other habitation and activities.⁷⁴ Some inscriptions regulate the time a priest had to be present in the sanctuary or make clear that if the priest does not appear even when the visitors call out, the latter may perform the sacrifices themselves.⁷⁵ If the sanctuary was located in a settled area, the priest or priestess may have lived at 'home,' and

---

62   Dillon 1997a, 124; Stewart 2009, 64, n. 128.
63   *CID* IV 85, l. 9.
64   *Roskilde Festival Guide* 2019, 86 and 94.
65   There are particular cooking areas, central squares in the neighborhood of the camping areas, where open fires are allowed and where visitors can prepare food. Tent fires have been a recurrent problem at Mecca, and after the major fire in 1997, 40,000 fireproof fiberglass tents were installed; see Imam and Alamoudi 2014, 1360; Bianchi 2004, 12, table 1.2; https://specialtyfabricsreview.com/2008/09/01/fireproof-tents-shelter-visitors-at-mecca/ (last accessed 25 April 2024).
66   For regulations protecting the greenery in sanctuaries, see Dillon 1997a, 115–120; Brulé 2012, *passim*. See also Chandezon in this volume.
67   Albris, Beck, and Sørensen 2009. I thank Axel Frejman for this reference.
68   The most common finds were the bracelets worn by the festivalgoers to indicate their right to access the site.

69   For urination in sanctuaries, see Plut. *Mor.: De stoic. repugn.* 22; *CGRN* 225, B, ll. 80–81; Decourt and Tziaphalias 2015, 20, B 81–82; Ar. *Plut.* 1183–1184, where the priest complains that people only visit the sanctuary to relieve themselves.
70   The areas where animals for transport or sacrifice were kept at ancient sanctuaries might also be located by mapping phosphate levels.
71   *CGRN* 222, ll. 1–11 and commentary; Gawlinski 2012, 102–105.
72   Hesychios, *s.v.* Karneatai; Nilsson 1957, 120–121; Arist. *Pol.* 1322b; [*Ath.Pol.*] 56.3. At Epidauros, officials called *phrouroi* (*IG* IV².1 40, 41) and *nauphylakes* (IG IV² 1 393, 401) oversaw the site; for discussion of their tasks, see Stewart 2009, 53–63. For other officials concerned with the practicalities of the management of sanctuaries, such as *epimeletai*, *neokoroi*, and *zakoroi*, see Georgoudi 2005, 51–60; Stewart 2009, 5–7.
73   The Sacred Men at Andania were overseen by the council of the Ten Men, while the finances of the Mysteries were managed by the Five Men, see Gawlinski 2012, 154–157, 234–239.
74   See also Barringer this volume.
75   *CGRN* 175, ll. 2–6 (Amphiareion, Oropos, 386–374 BCE); *CGRN* 36, ll. 7–11 (cult of Zeus Pelinaios, Chios, end of fifth century BCE).

the house of the religious official may even have been attached to the sanctuary.[76]

Securely identified priestly abodes are few, mainly due to the fact that they are difficult to distinguish from private houses, but also from structures in sanctuaries set apart for dining and storage or even from hostels. Buildings located near sanctuaries but lacking the trappings of regular Greek houses, for example installations for agricultural production, such as olive presses and grain mills, have been suggested as housing religious functionaries.[77] Multiple dining rooms can indicate that a building was not a private house, and some priestly houses could have been used as official dining spaces for participants of high status. In a sense, the official abode of the priest might resemble a modern ambassador's residence, which comprises a large official part for receptions and dinners, and a smaller part where the ambassador lives with his/her family. The idea behind this arrangement is that the ambassador hosts the guests in his/her home. Still, a particular building for the priest or priestess was not necessarily of major importance for Greek sanctuaries.

The epigraphical record from Greek sanctuaries often mentions houses, *oikiai* or *oikoi*.[78] At Eleusis, a late fourth-century BCE inscription lists the House of the Kerykes, as well as several other houses, some specified as sacred.[79] One of these sacred houses is described as the one where the priestess lives and this house is also to be purified, suggesting a location inside the sanctuary and that this building was not a regular residential one.[80] Both the House of the Kerykes and the sacred house of the priestess have been tentatively identified among the excavated remains based on the criteria outlined above,[81] but in most cases, such houses cannot be tied to any archaeological remains. The problem with the terms *oikos* and *oikia* is that they have a broad meaning and could be used for regular houses outside the *temenos* owned by the sanctuary and leased, but also for other buildings within the sanctuary, such as treasuries for storing votives, dining rooms, and even cult buildings.[82] The difficulties of identifying an *oikos* for religious personnel in the archaeological record can be illustrated by a small two-room complex with a porch located behind the temple in the sanctuary of Zeus at Labraunda in Turkey.[83] The inscription on the architrave identifies the building as the *oikoi* dedicated to Zeus by the ruler Idrieus, but although we know this structure was called *oikoi*, its function remains unclear, and suggestions have ranged from a residence or office for the priest to a dining hall, archive, or prytaneion.[84]

4   Other Types of Accommodation

Hotels, camping grounds and priestly houses are all official means for accommodating people visiting Greek sanctuaries. Sleeping in other buildings was also a possibility, although not always sanctioned.

Stoas are sometimes assumed to have been used for accommodation, but the question is to what extent ordinary visitors would be allowed to sleep in such buildings on a regular basis.[85] Cultic regulations sometimes explicitly ban staying in stoas except under certain contitions.[86] Incubants definitely would sleep here when seeking to be healed by the god through a dream, but such overnight stays could also cause problems. At Chalcedon,

---

76 For the archaeological, as well as written evidence, for priestly housing, see Deborah Stewart's excellent dissertation from 2009, esp. pp. 1–2 for different residential scenarios for cultic personnel. For the house of the priest of the Dionysiasts at Piraeus bordering the sanctuary, see Jaccottet 2003, 1: 163–170, 2: 25–27; Sosin 2005, 131, n. 10.

77 For a discussion of identifying criteria, see Stewart 2009, 372–379.

78 For the use and meaning of the terms, see Hellmann 1992, 291–294, 298–304; Stewart 2009, 70–72. An *oikia* might not have been more substantial than a tent, see Goldstein 1978, 44.

79 *Oikos* of the Kerykes: *IG* II² 1672; for other mentions of houses in this inscription, see ll. 17, 28, 47, 69, 70, 71, 74, 75, 77, 86, 91, 94, 119, 127, 293.

80 *IG* II² 1672, l. 127; Clinton 1974, 20.

81 Stewart (2009, 119–123) identifies the House of the Kerykes with the so-called Sacred house south of the sanctuary, and the house of the priestess with a building complex inside the *temenos* wall to the west of the fifth-century entrance to the north (Stewart 2009, 112–113).

82 Hellmann 1992, 299, 304: *ID* 97, l. 36. Designation of a house as sacred does not mean that it was used for a sacred purpose, but that it was owned by a sanctuary; for Delos, see Hennig 1983, 417; Chankowski 2008, 292. In the Delian accounts, several *hierai oikiai* and *hieroi oikoi* are rented out by the sanctuary, but none is linked to religious functionaries; see Kent 1948; Hellmann 1992, 189, 292, 298, 304.

83 Crampa 1972, 14–15; Hellström 2007, 119–125; Leypold 2008, 96–98. This is the earliest case of a building bearing an inscription marking it as an *oikos* (mid-fourth century BCE). The porch may have received a new roof c.100 CE. See Crampa 1972, 20, no. 21.

84 For the function, see Hellström 1989, 102–104.

85 This use of stoas seems often to be more of a generalized assumption by scholars than based on firm ancient evidence, see Pedley 2005, 75; *NGSL*² no. 26. For the South Stoa at Corinth interpreted as a hostelry with sleeping quarters, see Broneer 1954, 98–99. Perhaps visitors may also have slept in the colonnade around the Leonidaion in Olympia.

86 At the Letoon at Xanthos, only those who had offered sacrifice could stay in the stoas, see Le Roy 1986, 280, ll. 11–14, 295–296 (late second century BCE); *NGSL*² nos. 16, 26.

for example, the priest of Asklepios was responsible for keeping the stoas clean, while another inscription stipulates that bleeding or urinating in the stoas necessitated purification.[87] Asylum seekers seem to have slept in stoas, but their presence in sanctuaries was more *ad hoc*, and in some cases, the sanctuary tried to limit their stay.[88] Religious personnel could be housed in stoas, as well. An explicit example is an inscription laying out the creation of a new sanctuary to Apollo Helios Kisauloddenos at Smyrna, which included the building of a stoa with a tiled roof to lodge the sacred slaves and servants of the god.[89]

To what extent dining rooms, either in stoas or as separate structures, were used for sleeping, is a question that deserves more attention.[90] Would the banqueters in the *hestiatoria* simply roll over and fall asleep on their *klinai* at the end of the evening? The dining room couches, which are designed for reclining, are sometimes too short for people to stretch out fully, considering the fact that they were made to recline on.[91] The Π-shaped stoa at Brauron has been suggested to have housed the young girls, the *arktoi*, staying at the sanctuary, but they were children, and most scholars today see these rooms as regular dining facilities for adults.[92] A separation between eating and sleeping space is clear from the late Classical historian Dosiades, quoted by Athenaios, who reports that there were two houses for the *syssitia* on Crete, one called the *andreion*, where banquets took place, and the other, where the visitors slept, the *koimeterion*.[93] On the other hand, such an arrangement may not have been the norm and was therefore noteworthy.

5 Location of the Accommodation: Staying with the Gods?

This leads us to the last aspect to consider, the relation between the different modes of accommodation and sanctuary space. Were hotels, camping grounds, and houses designated for religious personnel located inside or outside the sanctuary? Would one be staying with the god or near the god? This question depends on how we define a sanctuary and most of all the *temenos*, the sacred area where the god's worship took place, and which was set apart and demarcated to keep it free from pollution.[94] What constitutes a *temenos* is a complex issue, which I am pursuing elsewhere, but a few comments should be made here.[95]

Ulrich Sinn has argued that Greek sanctuaries had a sacred center, the *hieron alsos*, but also a subsidiary area, what he calls the *bebelon alsos*.[96] Here lodging, dining rooms, baths, and other kinds of infrastructure were located, and this area would also have been part of sacred space. By contrast, Marietta Horster sees a distinction in time and activities, where the sacred area can become 'smaller' or at least partly less sacred, when used for festivals with fairs and markets.[97] In his recent study of 'extra-temenal' areas, Axel Frejman identifies an extra-temenal zone outside the actual *temenos*, which was functionally, administratively, and conceptually connected to the sanctuary by the activities carried out in this area, but not sacred to the same extent.[98]

---

87   Chalcedon: *LSAM* no. 5, ll. 24–26. Bleeding and urinating: *CGRN* 225, B, ll. 80–81. At Epidauros, the latrines attached to the early fifth-century BCE stoa serving as the *abaton* also may be related to the needs of the incubants staying overnight; see Lambrinoudakis 2002, 220.

88   On suppliants staying in sanctuaries on a regular basis requiring particular installations, see Sinn 1990, 67–69, 77, 83–97, 106–111; Sinn 1993, 95–97. The Andania inscription establishes a refuge for runaway slaves during the festival (*CGRN* 222, ll. 80–84; Gawlinski [2012, 187–194], who also discusses the practical implications of housing asylum seekers more generally). For hindering or expelling of asylum seekers, see Sinn 1990, 78–80, 97, 109–111; Sinn 1993, 91–93; and Chaniotis 1996. See also Gawlinski in this volume.

89   *I.Smyrna* 753, ll. 27–29 (second or third century CE). Pausanias (10.34.7–8) mentions stoas and dwellings built for the deity's servants at the sanctuary of Isis at Tithorea. See also Pausanias 10.32.12, who mentions housing (*oikeseis*) for asylum seekers and sacred slaves at the sanctuary of Athena at Elateia.

90   Cf. modern Japanese ryokans, where you both eat and sleep in the same room after a change of furniture. See also Scahill in this volume.

91   For couch dimensions, see Goldstein 1978, 300, 356. Attic vase paintings of *symposia* never show banqueters sleeping.

92   For the stoa at Brauron used as a sleeping space for the *arktoi*, see Papadimitriou 1963, 118–120; Bouras 1967, 75; Travlos, *Attika*, 55–56; for the interpretation as a dining space, see Leypold 2008, 51–52.

93   Ath. 4.143a–b.

94   The god could also own more land than the actual *temenos* (the sanctuary), and this additional terrain, often leased to generate income for the cult, could be located quite far away from the sanctuary proper; see Papazarkadas 2011 for the numerous Athenian examples. A sanctuary could also own land, which was neither used for cult nor agriculture, e.g., the *hiera ge* or *chora* at Delphi consisting of the plain of Kirrha below the sanctuary and the rocky peninsula that formed the western part of the Kirphis massif; see Rousset 2002, 183–192, fig. 5.

95   I am exploring this question in my project *The 'profanity' of Greek sanctuaries? Defining the* temenos *as a space for divine-human interaction 600 BC–200 AD*.

96   Sinn 1988, 154–157; Sinn 1990, 85–86; Sinn 1993, 95–97.

97   Horster 2010, 454.

98   Frejman 2020, 194–200.

The basic problem is that some human activities such as birth, death, and sex are incompatible with divine space and have to be located outside the *temenos*.⁹⁹ Many inscriptions regulating worshippers' visits to sanctuaries concern how to deal with the pollution arising from these actions before you enter, while others aim at controlling human impact once at the site, e.g., from fire, littering, and felling the god's trees.¹⁰⁰ Human presence in Greek sanctuaries was never uncomplicated or self-evident.¹⁰¹ Some regulations ban lodging in the *hieron* outright, such as a decree from the sanctuary of Dionysos at Knidos prohibiting male, as well as female, worshippers from staying there.¹⁰² In Arkesine on Amorgos, the *neokoros* was to prevent foreigners from entering and lodging in the Heraion.¹⁰³ A crisis may allow for more liberal access and use, such as in the *temenos* of Herakles Diomedonteios, where the buildings could be used as dwellings if there was a war.¹⁰⁴ Other inscriptions define who had the right to stay; for example, only those sacrificing could camp in the *temenos* of Zeus Labraundos at Patara or sleep in the stoas at the Letoon at Xanthos.¹⁰⁵ The question is whether or not sanctuaries would have taken the risk of housing the visitors inside the *temenos* unless this was absolutely necessary. Could they trust the visitors not to have sex in their hotel rooms, or risk the very pregnant to give birth or the very sick to die at the Asklepieia, if the hostels were located inside the *hieron*? Such aspects must be considered when we define the extent of *temene* and the location of different activities.

It seems that none of the hotels and camping grounds that we can identify are securely located inside *temene* unless we adopt a very wide and flexible definition of what constitutes the sacred area, and I am not sure that such a definition corresponds to the ancient *temenos* concept.¹⁰⁶ Certain visitors did sleep inside the *temenos*, like those incubating, but they may not have slept in the *abaton* for more than a few nights. Some cures also called for them to leave the sacred area to be fully healed, such as pregnant women giving birth.¹⁰⁷ Asylum seekers were provided with temporary lodging inside the *temenos* or else they would not have been sufficiently protected, but their presence could also cause problems.¹⁰⁸ The complications of staying in sanctuaries for long periods are evident from the Spartan king Pleistoanax, who lived for 19 years as an asylum seeker in the sanctuary of Zeus Lykaios.¹⁰⁹ He built a house, half of which was located inside the *hieron* and the rest outside, presumably to be able to enjoy both the benefits of divine protection and secular life.

If we look at the extant evidence, there are few archaeologically attested cases where priestly personnel lived inside the *temenos*.¹¹⁰ Judging from the written sources, it seems that when religious functionaries resided inside the sanctuary proper, they often seem to have been children, virgins, persons who had to remain chaste, or sacred slaves.¹¹¹ In short, these were individuals whose sexuality was restricted and therefore complied more easily with the purity regulations of *temene*. Religious personnel being housed inside the sacred area may also have been

---

99   Parker 1983, 32–104 and esp. 160–170.

100 For an overview, see Dillon 1997a and for the vegetation in particular, Brulé 2012.

101 For the negative human impact on sanctuaries even when visiting to worship the gods, see Ekroth 2024.

102 *I.Knidos* 160; *LSAM* no. 55 (350–300 BCE). See Feyel and Prost 1998, 458, ll. 6–7 (with commentary) for the ban on sleeping in the *hieron* of Apollo on Delos. Thucydides (4.97) mentions the misuse of the sanctuary of Apollo at Delion by the Athenian soldiers staying there. The contract for the lease of the sanctuary of the Athenian hero Egretes (*IG* II² 2499) stipulates that it had to be used as a *hieron*, perhaps to prevent people from staying in the buildings. For this particular sanctuary, see also McInerney in this volume.

103 *LSCG* no. 101 (350–300 BCE).

104 *CGRN* 96, C, ll. 82–86 concerning the *xenones* and the *oikia*.

105 Patara: *CGRN* 129. Xanthos: Le Roy 1986; *NGSL*² nos. 16, 26. In the Anakeion at Elateia, those sacrificing had to put up a tent, presumably for the post-sacrificial meal; see *CGRN* 33 with commentary.

106 Goldstein's conclusion (1978, 51) that there is no indication of tents outside the *hieron* is hard to accept. None of the dining halls that he discusses is located outside the sacred ground (1978, 297). Of the 37 dining buildings analysed by Leypold (2008), a third are located inside the temenos and five more possibly so, depending on how the limits of the sanctuary are defined.

107 The *iamata* from Epidauros make clear that incubating women seeking release from extended pregnancies leave the *hieron* before giving birth; see LiDonnici 1995, 84–87, A1, A2. On the heavily pregnant and severely sick being housed outside the *hieron* at Epidauros, see Paus. 2.27.1, 6.

108 For the handling of asylum seekers, see Sinn 1990, 78–80, 97, 109–111; 1993, 91–93; Chaniotis 1996; Stewart 2009, 12–23.

109 Thuc. 5.16.3.

110 Of the possible sacerdotal houses discussed by Stewart (2009), location inside the *temenos* is only suggested for the sacred house of the priestess at Eleusis and the Arrephoroi on the Athenian Akropolis.

111 The boy priest of Athena Kranaia at Elateia boarding with the goddess (Paus. 10.34.7–8); Corinthian boys and girls serving and residing in the sanctuary of Hera Akraia (Paus. 2.3.7); the Arrephoroi living on the Athenian Akropolis (Paus. 1.27.3; Stewart 2009, 223–249); Lokrian maidens at Troy living in the precinct of Athena, perhaps in one of the porticoes (Rose 2012, 170, n. 20); the god's slaves having dwellings inside the precinct of Asklepios at Tithorea (Paus. 10.32.12). The priestess of Herakles Charops at Thespiai had to be a virgin during her lifelong service (Paus. 9.27.6–7). On the chasteness of the priestesses at Dodona, see Stewart 2009, 196–204.

expected to be segregated from the community in order to remain pure in preparation for contact with the god.[112]

We also have to separate fictional and mythical cases in the literary sources from inscriptions stipulating the housing conditions at a particular site. Maron, the priest of Apollo, who lived with his wife and child in the god's grove, described in the *Odyssey*; Iphigeneia staying in the temple of Artemis at Tauris; Charikleia residing in Apollo's precinct at Delphi; and the examiners in Plato's *Laws* who resided in the sanctuary of Helios and Apollo while holding office do not necessarily reflect real life practice.[113] Living in the sanctuary may have been the result of particular circumstances, rather than the regular situation for religious functionaries, and was far from a prerequisite. Occasionally, such a residence could work as a means for constructing a special persona; Apollonios of Tyana, according to Philostratos, stayed in an Asklepieion already as a young boy and later was made a guest in Zeus' sanctuary at Olympia after having lectured from the temple and amazing everyone.[114]

6   Concluding Remarks

People going to Greek sanctuaries must have stayed somewhere during their visits but this was not an infrastructure that the sanctuaries prioritized for investment. Such structures were never a prerequisite of a sanctuary, and their construction often seems to have been due to particular requirements of the cult or local circumstances. Rather, efforts seem to have been directed toward managing the use of space around the sanctuary, in particular for camping, i.e., an activity that took place for a short duration, but involved large crowds. The management of these camping grounds, some of which must have housed tens of thousands of people, surely constituted a substantial logistical undertaking and also put serious strains on the local environment. Future exploration by survey and excavation of the surroundings of sanctuaries are desirable in order to fill out the picture provided by the written evidence so that we better understand the logistical challenges that faced those responsible for the upkeep of ancient Greek sanctuaries.[115] As a rule, all forms of accommodation seem to have been located outside the *temenos*. Even religious personnel rarely seem to have stayed inside sanctuaries, and most such cases concern mythical or fictional figures or particular cults. Although the god could be perceived as living in the sanctuary and even in his temple, humans generally would not, as mortal and immortal lifestyles were to a large extent incompatible. The space of the god would not serve as a hostel for men.[116]

Works Cited

Albris, S.L., A.S. Beck, and L. Sørensen 2009. "'Smattens' arkæologi. Arkæologer på Roskilde Festival." *Siden Saxo* 2: 4–13.

Ault, B.A. 2005. "Housing the Poor and the Homeless in Ancient Greece." In *Ancient Greek Houses and Households: Chronological, Regional, and Social Diversity*, edited by B.A. Ault and L.C. Nevett, 140–159. Philadelphia.

Aurigny, H., 2020. "Gathering in the Panhellenic Sanctuary at Delphi: An Archaeological Approach." In *Pilgrimage and Economy in the Ancient Mediterranean*, edited by A. Collar and T.M. Kristensen, 93–115. Leiden.

Barringer, J.M. 2021. *Olympia: A Cultural History*. Princeton.

Bianchi, R.R. 2004. *Guests of God: Pilgrimage and Politics in the Islamic World*. Oxford.

Boersma, J.S. 1973. "Leonidas of Naxos: architect and founder of the Leonidaion." In *Archeologie en historie. Opgedragen aan H. Brunsting bij zijn zeventigste verjaardag*, 169–178. Bussum.

Bouras, C. 1967. Ἡ ἀναστήλωσις τῆς στοᾶς τῆς Βραυρῶνος. Τὰ ἀρχιτεκτονικά τῆς προβλήματα. Athens.

Broneer, O. 1954. *Corinth 1:4: The South Stoa and its Roman Successors*. Princeton.

Brulé, P. 2012. *Comment percevoir le sanctuaire grec? Une analyse sensorielle du paysage sacré*. Paris.

Burkert, W. 1985. *Greek Religion*, trans. J. Raffan. Cambridge, MA.

Campanelli, S. 2016. "Family Cult Foundations in the Hellenistic Age: Family and Sacred Space in a Private Religious Context." In *Understanding Material Text Cultures: A Multidisciplinary View*, edited by M. Hilgert, 131–202. Berlin.

---

112 The priestess living in the sacred house at Eleusis may have done so, see Stewart 2009, 99, and also 38–41 on the marginalization of cultic personnel for purity reasons. The priest and priestess of the goddess Ma at Komana Pontika in the Pontos lived within the *temenos* (Strabo 12.8.9) and abstained from eating pork to preserve the sanctity of the precinct.

113 Hom. *Od.* 9.196–215; Eur. *IT* 65–66; Heliod. *Aeth.* 2.33.7; Pl. *Leg.* 945e, 946d. See also Diod. Sic. 5.44.1–5: the priests of Zeus Triphylios have their houses (*oikiai*) around the temple of the god on the fictional island of Panchaia.

114 Phil. *VA* 1.8, 1.16, 4.31.

115 Axel Frejman's doctoral thesis (2020) constitutes a most welcome contribution to this issue.

116 A church of St. George at Zorava, Syria, built in 515 CE on the site of a pagan temple, carries the following inscription above the door, which serves to illustrate who would stay where in a religious setting: "The *katagogion* of the *daimones* became the house (*oikos*) of God". For the text, see Kraynak 1984, 259, no. 106; *OGIS* 610.1; Trombley 2001, 363–364.

Casson, L. 1974. *Travel in the Ancient World.* London.

Chaniotis, A. 1996. "Conflicting Authorities. Asylia between Secular and Divine Law in the Classical and Hellenistic Poleis." *Kernos* 9: 65–86.

Chankowski, V. 2008. *Athènes et Délos à l'époque classique. Recherches sur l'administration du sanctuaire d'Apollon délien.* Athens.

Clinton, K. 1974. *The Sacred Officials of the Eleusinian Mysteries.* Philadelphia.

Constable, O.R. 2003. *Housing the Stranger in the Mediterranean World: Lodging, Trade, and Travel in Late Antiquity and the Middle Ages.* Cambridge.

Cooper, F., and S. Morris. 1990. "Dining in Round Buildings." In *Sympotica: A Symposium on the Symposion*, edited by O. Murray, 66–85. Oxford.

Crampa, J. 1972. *Labraunda. Swedish Excavations and Researches 3:2, The Greek Inscriptions.* Jonsered.

Decourt, J.C., and A. Tziaphalias. 2015. "Un règlement religieux de la région de Larissa: cultes grecs et 'orientaux.'" *Kernos* 28: 13–51.

Deshours, N. 2006. *Les mystères d'Andania. Étude d'épigraphie et d'histoire religieuse.* Bordeaux.

Dillon, M. 1990. "'The House of the Thebans' (FD iii.1 357–58) and Accommodation for Greek Pilgrims." *ZPE* 83: 64–88.

Dillon, M. 1997a. "The Ecology of the Greek Sanctuary." *ZPE* 118: 113–127.

Dillon, M. 1997b. *Pilgrims and Pilgrimage in Ancient Greece.* London.

von Ehrenheim, H. 2015. *Greek Incubation Rituals in Classical and Hellenistic Times.* Liège.

Ekroth, G. 2024. "A Room of One's Own? Exploring the *Temenos* Concept as Divine Property." In *Stuff of the Gods. The Material Aspects of Religion in Ancient Greece*, edited by M. Haysom, M. Mili, and J. Wallensten, 69–82. Stockholm.

Feyel, C., and F. Prost. 1998. "Un règlement délien." *BCH* 122: 455–468.

Frejman, A. 2020. *With Gods as Neighbours: Extra-Temenal Activity at Greek Rural Sanctuaries, 700–200 BCE.* Ph.D. diss., Uppsala University.

Gawlinski, L. 2012. *The Sacred Law of Andania: A New Text with Commentary.* Berlin.

Geagan, D.J. 1989. "The Isthmian Dossier of P. Licinius Priscus Juventianus." *Hesperia* 58: 349–360.

Georgoudi, S. 2005. "Personnel de culte: mode grec. III. Magistrats, fonctionnaires, agents au service des dieux." *ThesCRA* 5, 31–60.

Goldstein, M.S. 1978. *The Setting of the Ritual Meal in Greek Sanctuaries: 600–300 BC.* Ph.D. diss., University of California, Berkeley.

Habicht, C. 1972. "Hellenistische Inschriften aus dem Heraion von Samos." *AM* 87: 191–228.

Hennig, D. 1983. "Die 'heiligen Häuser' von Delos." *Chiron* 13: 411–495.

Heermann, V. 1984. "Banketträume im Leonidaion." *AM* 99: 243–250.

Hellmann, M.-C. 1992. *Recherches sur le vocabulaire de l'architecture grecque, d'après les inscriptions de Délos.* Paris.

Hellström, P. 1989. "Formal Banqueting at Labraunda." In *Architecture and Society in Hecatomnid Caria: Proceedings of the Uppsala Symposion 1987*, edited by T. Linders and P. Hellström, 99–104. Uppsala.

Hellström, P. 2007. *Labraunda. A Guide to the Karian Sanctuary of Zeus Labraundos.* Istanbul.

Horster, M. 2010. "Religious Landscape and Sacred Ground: Relationships between Space and Cult in Greek World." *RHR* 227: 435–458.

Imam, A., and M. Alamoudi 2014. "Mina: The City of Tents. Origination and Development." In *9° Congresso città e territorio virtuale, Roma, 2–4 ottobre 2013*, 1351–1365.

Jaccottet, A.-F. 2003. *Choisir Dionysos. Les associations dionysiaques ou la face cachée du dionysisme.* Lausanne.

Jensen, R.M. 2020. "Housing Pilgrims in Late Antiquity: Patrons, Buildings, and Services." In *Pilgrimage and Economy in the Ancient Mediterranean*, edited by A. Collar and T.M. Kristensen, 140–159. Leiden.

Kent, H.J. 1948. "The Temple Estates of Delos, Rheneia, and Mykonos." *Hesperia* 17: 243–338.

Kraynak, L.H. 1984. *Hostelries of Ancient Greece (Hotels, Inns).* Ph.D. diss., University of California, Berkeley.

Kraynak, L.H. 1991. "The *Katagogion* at Epidauros: A Revised Plan." *ArchNews* 16: 1–8.

Kraynak, L.H. 1992. "The *Xenon*." In *Nemea 1: Topographical and Architectural Studies: the Sacred Square, the Xenon, and the Bath*, by D. Birge, L.H. Kraynak, and S.G. Miller, 99–187. Berkeley.

Kron, U. 1988. "Kultmahle im Heraion von Samos archaischer Zeit. Versuch einer Rekonstruktion." In *Early Greek Cult Practice*, edited by R. Hägg, N. Marinatos, and G.C. Nordquist, 134–146. Stockholm.

Kyrieleis, H. 2003. "Die Untersuchungen zur Frühzeit Olympias im Bereich des Prytaneions, 1986/87 und 1990/91." In *OlBer* 12: 66–154.

Lambrinoudakis, V. 2002. "Conservation and Research: New Evidence on a Long-Living Cult. The Sanctuary of Apollo Maleatas and Asklepios at Epidauros." In *Excavating Classical Culture. Recent Archaeological Discoveries in Greece*, edited by M. Stamatopoulou and M. Yearolanou, 213–224. Oxford.

Le Roy, C. 1986. "Un règlement religieux au Létôon de Xanthos." *RA*: 279–300.

Leypold, C. 2008. *Bankettgebäude in griechischen Heiligtümern.* Wiesbaden.

LiDonnici, L.R. 1995. *The Epidaurian Miracle Inscriptions: Text, Translation, and Commentary*. Atlanta.

McDonald, W.A. 1951. "Villa *or* Pandokeion." In *Studies Presented to David Moore Robinson on His Seventieth Birthday*, edited by G. Mylonas, 365–373. St Louis.

Mallwitz, A. 1972. *Olympia und seine Bauten*. Munich.

Melfi, M. 2007. *I santuari di Asclepio in Grecia*. Rome.

Miller, S.G. 1979. "Excavations at Nemea, 1978." *Hesperia* 48: 73–103.

Miller, S.G. 1988. "Excavations at the Panhellenic Site of Nemea. Cults, Politics, and Games." In *The Archaeology of the Olympics: The Olympics and Other Festivals in Antiquity*, edited by W.J. Raschke, 141–151. Madison.

Nilsson, M.P. 1957. *Griechische Feste von religiöser Bedeutung mit Ausschluss der attischen*. Stuttgart.

Papadimitriou, J. 1963. "The Sanctuary of Artemis at Brauron." *Scientific American* 208.6: 110–120.

Papazarkadas, N. 2011. *Sacred and Public Land in Ancient Athens*. Oxford.

Parker, R.C.T. 1983. *Miasma: Pollution and Purification in Early Greek Religion*. Oxford.

Pedley, J. 2005. *Sanctuaries and the Sacred in the Ancient Greek World*. Cambridge.

Peyron, J. 2014. "Les pèlerinages des populations tsiganes en France." In *Politiques du pèlerinages: du XVIIe siècle à nos jours*, edited by L. Chantre, P. d'Hollander, and J. Grévy, 209–218. Rennes.

Riethmüller, J.W. 2005. *Asklepios. Heiligtümer und Kulte*. Heidelberg.

Rose, C.B. 2012. "Architecture and Ritual in Ilion, Athens, and Rome." In *The Construction of Sanctity*, edited by B. Wescoat and R. Ousterhout, 152–174. Cambridge.

Roskilde Festival Guide 2019. https://www.roskilde-festival.dk/media/2741/rf19-guide-uk.pdf

Rousset, D. 2002. *Le territoire de Delphes et la terre d'Apollon*. Paris.

Rutherford, I. 2013. *State Pilgrims and Sacred Observers in Ancient Greece: A Study of Theōriā and Theōroi*. Cambridge.

Schmitt Pantel, P. 1997. *La cité au banquet. Histoire des repas publics dans les cités grecques*. Rome.

Scott, M. 2010. *Delphi and Olympia: The Spatial Politics of Panhellenism in the Archaic and Classical Periods*. Cambridge.

Sinn, U. 1988. "Der Kult der Aphaia auf Aegina." In *Early Greek Cult Practice*, edited by R. Hägg, N. Marinatos, and G.C. Nordquist, 147–160. Stockholm.

Sinn, U. 1990. "Das Heraion von Perachora. Eine sakrale Schutzzone in der korinthischen Peraia." *AM* 105: 53–116.

Sinn, U. 1992. "Sunion: Das befestigte Heiligtum der Athena und des Poseidon an der 'Heiligen Landespitze Attikas.'" *AntW* 23: 175–190.

Sinn, U. 1993. "Greek Sanctuaries as Places of Refuge." In *Greek Sanctuaries. New Approaches*, edited by N. Marinatos and R. Hägg, 88–109. London.

Sinn, U. 2005. "Katagogion." *ThesCRA* 4, 51–52.

Sosin, J.D. 2005. "Unwelcome Dedications: Public Law and Private Religion in Hellenistic Laodicea by the Sea." *CQ* 55: 130–139.

Specht, S. 2001. "Ein Stück Rom in Griechenland: Der kaiserzeitliche Umbau des Leonidaion in Olympia." In *Griechenland in der Kaiserzeit. Neue Funde und Forschungen zu Skulptur, Architektur und Topographie*, edited by C. Reusser, 33–41. Bern.

Stewart, D.E.B. 2009. *οἱ περὶ τὸ ἱερόν. A Study of Sacerdotal Housing at Ancient Greek Sanctuaries*. Ph.D. diss., Bryn Mawr College.

Taita, J. 2014. "Quando Zeus deve far quadrare il bilancio: osservazione sul tesoro del santuario di Olimpia." In *Sport und Recht der Antike*, edited by K. Harter-Uibopuu and T. Kruse, 107–145. Vienna.

Trombley, F.R. 2001. *Hellenic Religion and Christianization c. 360–529*. Leiden.

Wacker, C. 1996. *Das Gymnasion in Olympia: Geschichte und Funktion*. Würzburg.

Ziebarth, H. 1935. "Gasthäuser im alten Griechenland." In *Εἴς μνήμεν Σπυριδώνος Λάμπρου*, edited by Γ. Χαριτάκης, 339–348.

CHAPTER 8

The Architectural Evidence for Dining in Greek Sanctuaries

David Scahill

A building has at least two lives—the one imagined by its maker and the life it lives afterward—and they are never the same.

KOOLHAAS 2012

∴

We think of buildings as being designed for a purpose. Ancient Greek buildings are no exception; however, just as with modern buildings to which Koolhaas refers, ancient buildings can exhibit aspects of design that indicate or suggest that function could be flexible, which might be necessary if a building has a long history of use in a sanctuary. Whether the architect anticipated flexibility of use over time or we only intuit this in retrospect is a question about which the evidence is largely silent. In this paper, I focus on a selection of well-studied examples of dining buildings and a few less known instances to explore questions regarding their logistical aspects.[1]

We might first ask, what are the architectural requirements for dining, feasting, drinking, and other accommodation in a sanctuary? A sheltered space is required if there is inclement weather or a need for privacy. If there is a desire for comfort, couches or benches and tables are necessary. There should be access to clean water. Cooking facilities should be nearby. One might expect access to facilities for relief of bodily functions, whether a latrine or otherwise. For more permanent built structures, the function of the space might be more prescribed, although the possibility for flexibility of function should not be overlooked.

Temporary structures, such as tents (*skenai*), would have sufficed in many cases for dining in sanctuaries, as we know from literature, inscriptions, and archaeological evidence.[2] Postholes beneath the Pompeion in the Kerameikos in Athens have been interpreted as holes for supports of shelter structures (*skenai*?) used for ritual meals associated with the Panathenaic procession.[3] The evidence of a burnt stratum associated with the postholes led Hoepfner to suggest that the temporary structures may have caught fire during a festival, which could have been a deciding factor for construction in the subsequent phase of a sturdier venue in the form of a stone building with dining rooms.[4] At a practical level, the choice of construction using more resilient material (stone) was sensible, and the erection of the Pompeion can be seen as a mere continuation of a more permanent structure to host the same activities in the same place. The monumental size of the building, then, was at least partly the result of having spaces (rooms, courtyard, etc.) to accommodate the activities that previously had occurred in the area (Fig. 8.1).

The Pompeion in Athens shows evolution of space toward a permanent building complex to handle the provisions of activities related to dining. As we shall see, several types of buildings in Greek sanctuaries served for dining. I discuss here eight categories: 1) *Hestiatorion*/Perachora type, 2) 'Sacred Houses,' 3) Dining rooms with a Courtyard, 4) Stoas, 5) *Andrones*, 6) *Naiskoi*, 7) the Pinakotheke in the Propylaia on the Athenian Akropolis, and 8) Other Building Types. Scholarly terminology for dining buildings is sometimes problematic due to modern versus ancient designations and inconsistencies of definition. In the following, I address problems concerning the nomenclature of building types as each case arises.

1 Hestiatorion/Perachora Type

Tomlinson assigned the name *hestiatorion* to a late-sixth-century BCE building in the sanctuary of Hera at Perachora

---

1 On dining buildings, see Leypold 2008 for a compendium and discussion of the evidence; Goldstein 1978; Bergquist 1990, 37–65. For previous discussion of the criteria regarding identification of dining buildings, see Scahill 2023. The present article goes further in exploring the logistics of these architectural spaces.
2 See Goldstein 1978, 8–59 on temporary structures for sacred meals. See Ekroth in this volume regarding tents.
3 Hoepfner 1976, 16–23, 126–129.
4 Hoepfner 1976, 22; Leypold 2008, 40–48.

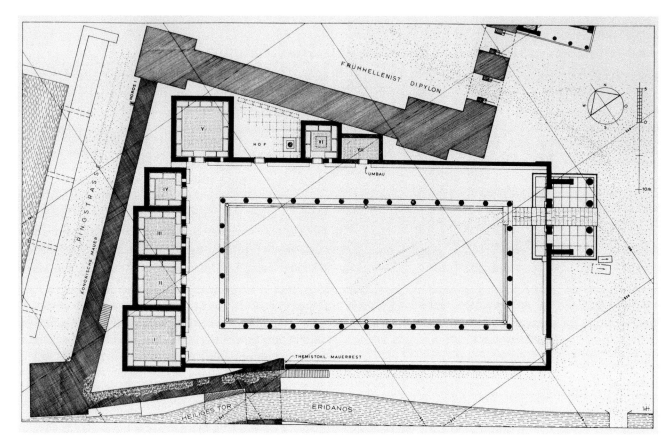

FIGURE 8.1 Athens, Kerameikos, Pompeion, restored plan
AFTER HOEPFNER 2002, FIG. 67

that has clear evidence of dining in rooms with *klinai*; this designation arose from the similarities of the Perachora building to a *hestiatorion* with *klinai* mentioned in the Delian accounts, although there is no ancient mention of a *hestiatorion* at Perachora (Fig. 8.2).[5] The Perachora dining building type, as we shall call it, is the most easily identifiable extant type of dining building, although by no means is it canonical. Two rooms are set side by side, with off-center doorways for the placement of stone *klinai* around the perimeter and sockets in the ground for wooden tables, all of which is fronted by a vestibule space.[6] Based on the *in situ* evidence of some of the stone *klinai* set on plaster flooring lining the perimeter of the room, each room can be reconstructed with 11 *klinai*.[7] The door is offset toward the western side of both rooms, i.e., the right side as one entered from the vestibule, to accommodate an arrangement of *klinai* for right-handed diners reclining on their left sides. Spatially, this dining building is located to the east of, and away from, the main sanctuary, together with a large double-apsidal cistern immediately to the north, which provided an abundant supply of fresh water.[8]

With only a few rooms, the Perachora dining building type could have accommodated the most important members of the cult, or to put it another way, a relatively small and elite group of worshippers.[9]

---

5 Tomlinson 1969a, 170 for discussion of a Delian inscription (*IG* XI 144, l. 65) that mentions wooden *klinai* for a room called a *hestiatorion*. The date of the building was initially thought to be *c*.300 BCE, but subsequently revised by Tomlinson (1990, 98) to the end of the sixth century BCE.

6 Tomlinson 1969; 1990. Three *klinai* and part of a fourth are preserved. The *klinai* are 1.80 m long × 0.35 m high × 0.89 m wide (Tomlinson 1969a, 168–169). Off-center doorways are one of the criteria for suggesting the placement of *klinai* around the perimeter of a room due to the way that *klinai* are positioned for reclining diners (on criteria, see Scahill 2023, 183).

7 Tomlinson 1969a, 168.

8 For the cistern, see Tomlinson 1969a, 157–163. See also Klingborg in this volume for a discussion of water for non-religious purposes in sanctuaries.

9 See Tomlinson 1990, 100. This building type spread widely by the end of the sixth century as witnessed at Megara Hyblaia in Sicily, where there is a similar building with three rooms (Gras, Tréziny, and Broise 2005, 419), which may reflect transmission of design through regional influence from the mother city of Megara. On

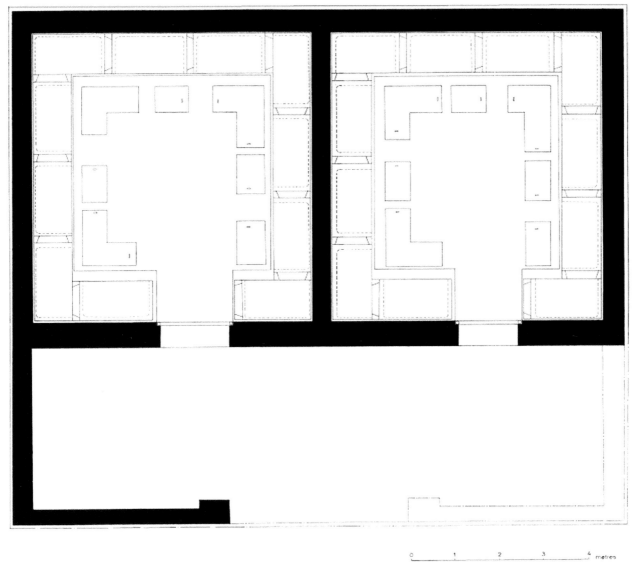

FIGURE 8.2 Perachora, Dining Building, restored plan
AFTER TOMLINSON 1969, 167, FIG. 5

The basic features that define this dining building type are:
1) rooms set next to each other with off-center doorways
2) plaster lining the perimeter of the room for *klinai* or benches
3) evidence for tables in front of the *klinai*
4) a vestibule space in front of the rooms

While the Perachora dining building type enabled scholars to identify a possible dining function for many of the more enigmatic buildings uncovered in sanctuaries, not every building where dining occurred exhibits all of these features.[10]

2 Sacred Houses

Sacred Houses (ἱεραὶ οἰκίαι) are mentioned in inscriptions, but efforts to identify specific buildings with this term are inconclusive.[11] Scholars sometimes label buildings

---

design transmission of architectural forms from mainland cities to Sicilian colonies, see Scahill 2017.

10   Miller (1978, 219–224) discusses criteria for rooms that may have contained *klinai*, including couch dimensions as a module for construction.
11   See especially Stewart 2009, 92–95 on ἱεραὶ οἰκίαι in Eleusinian accounts.

in sanctuaries with two or more rooms and no definite function as Sacred Houses or Priest Houses. Stewart has applied the term 'Sacerdotal Housing' as a catch-all phrase to encompass their possible functions.[12] Sacred Houses, such as those at the sanctuary of Aphaia at Aigina and at Marmaria at Delphi, share some architectural features with the Perachora type due to layout, and their proximity to, or placement in, sanctuaries although these structures lack definite signs of dining furniture.[13] As Stewart points out, these buildings may have been used for dining, but it does not seem to have been their primary function.[14]

3   Dining Rooms with a Courtyard

Dining rooms connected to a courtyard, such as those in the Pompeion in the Kerameikos in Athens discussed above, offer a more expansive building type with more opportunities for flexibility of use, including space that could be used for food preparation or other activities. The West Building in the Argive Heraion is one such example with three northern rooms fronting a courtyard, off-center doorways, and evidence of stone supports for wooden beds or wooden benches (Fig. 8.3).[15] The West Building sits on a lower terrace to the west of the Classical temple platform, separate from, but close to, the cult activity associated with the Archaic and Classical temple terraces above. The entrance to the building lies between the rooms on the north side, which slopes up to a higher elevation, providing convenient access to and from the two temple terraces. It is possible that the West Building was two-storied, although the evidence is inconclusive.[16] If it did have two storeys, the upper floor would have offered

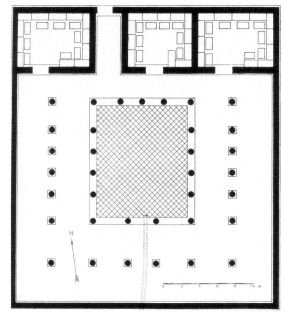

FIGURE 8.3   Argive Heraion, West Building, restored plan
AFTER FRICKENHAUS 1917, 129, FIG. 8

the possibility of more space to house overnight guests if they were allowed to stay in the sanctuary.[17]

In keeping with these larger spaces, the Square Peristyle Building with interior courtyard in the Asklepieion at Troizen has a long hall on the southwest side with stone supports for wooden benches or *klinai*, and rooms of varying sizes for dining around the other three sides of the building (Fig. 8.4).[18] The building is physically separated from, but near, the temple and altar area, with entrance through a doorway in its northwestern wall that divides the dining space from the temple precinct to the west. Rectangular hearths in the long hall and in some rooms would have provided warmth, light, and a place to cook meals (see discussion of hearths below).[19]

The expanded courtyard building type can also be seen at Corinth in the Asklepieion; however, here the building complex is more intricately designed on two levels (Fig. 8.5). Below the terrace of the Temple of Asklepios at Corinth, the east end of a large peristyle building with

---

12   Stewart 2009.
13   See Stewart 2009 on sacerdotal housing in Greek sanctuaries. See also Klebinder-Gauss 2019; Ekroth in this volume on Sacred Houses. For the possible dining building in the Marmaria at Delphi, see Bookidis 1983. A recent study of the Marmaria terrace by a team working under the auspices of the École française d'Athènes concurs with Bookidis' identification of L'edifice SD 44 as a dining building (Jacquemin, et al. 2021, 90–91).
14   Stewart 2009, 374.
15   See Leypold 2008, 28–33 with earlier bibliography. The date is controversial, and the building might belong to the fifth rather than the sixth century BCE (see Miller 1973).
16   Leypold 2008, 30 argues *ex silentio* that it is unlikely, but so much of the Argive Heraion evidence is gone that it is difficult to say for sure. The wall foundations of the building are substantial enough to support a second storey easily, and the topographical situation of the building would also work better if the roof were higher with respect to the adjacent temple terrace. Tilton (Waldstein et al., 1902, fig. 66) restored a hypothetical second storey. See Miller (1973, 14) on the evidence.

17   See Ekroth in this volume on overnight stays in sanctuaries. *Katagogia*/hostels provided a separate space for overnight guests. See Kraynak 1984, 63–73 (Epidauros), 79–81 (Gortys).
18   See Leypold 2008, 132–136. For the Asklepieion at Troizen, see Welter 1941, 32, pl. 12 (overall plan), pl. 14 (plan with *klinai*), pl. 16 (reconstruction of hall with *klinai*); Riethmüller 2005, 105–116.
19   Welter (1941, 69) refers to this building as an Inkubationshaus, with the understanding that the long hall was an *enkoimeterion/abaton*, while the smaller rooms were reserved for dining; however, incubation and dining in the same building is an unlikely combination.

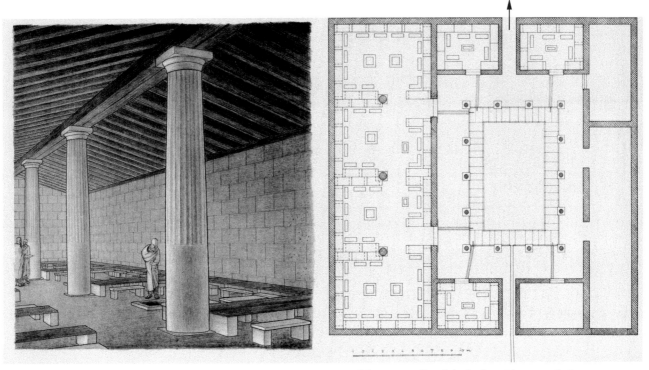

FIGURE 8.4 Troizen, Peristyle Courtyard Dining Building, *Left*: reconstruction of the 'Long Hall' with beds after Welter 1941, pl. 16; *Right*: restored plan after Welter 1941, pl. 12

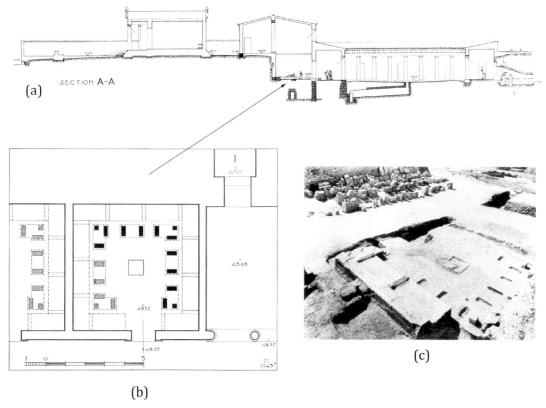

FIGURE 8.5 Corinth, Asklepieion, a) section looking south after Roebuck 1951, Plan D; b) dining rooms after Roebuck 1951, 52, fig. 13; c) photo after Roebuck 1951, pl. 14: 4

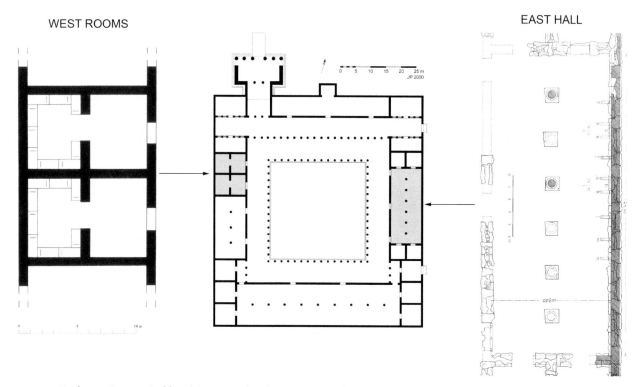

FIGURE 8.6 Epidauros, Banquet Building ('Gymnasion'), *Left*: west rooms with restored couches after Leypold 2008, pl. 47b; *Center*: restored plan after Pakkanen 2019, fig. 1; *Right*: east hall with stone supports for beds after Frickenhaus 1917, fig. 10

a courtyard has three rooms with stone *klinai* and sockets for tables, presumably made of wood.[20] The complex dates to the fourth century BCE, and the similarities of the *klinai* with those at Perachora suggest that the Perachora dining building, if it indeed dates from the late sixth century BCE as noted above, may have influenced the design of the dining rooms and furniture in the Asklepieion at Corinth.[21] The *enkoimeterion* for incubation is thought to have been just above the dining area on the temple terrace, meaning that dining activity was tucked below the temple platform away from this sacred activity.[22] This arrangement may have been implemented to separate the noisy banqueting proceedings from the sacred proceedings on the temple terrace. Hearths in the dining rooms are comparable to those at Troizen. The south side of the courtyard has access to a more than ample supply of water for dining and any other activities in the sanctuary via a spring/fountain house and storage reservoirs, suggesting that the reservoirs served more than the sanctuary.[23] In this case, the split-level design of temple platform and *enkoimeterion* on the upper level and dining on the lower level is especially well-organized to handle the traffic of participants in the sanctuary, still within a relatively compact spatial configuration.

An even more expansive spatial layout for dining exists in the sanctuary of Asklepios at Epidauros, where the 'Gymnasion,' now identified as a banquet building with rooms around a central courtyard, has stone supports with sockets for *klinai* and/or benches, similar to the West Building at the Argive Heraion and the Square Peristyle Building at Troizen, on the east side, and *klinai* have been reconstructed in the smaller rooms on the west side (Fig. 8.6).[24]

Buildings with courtyards offering more space for dining, either for one large group or multiple groups in various rooms, connotes a relaxed conviviality offset by the smaller rooms. At Troizen and Epidauros, the additional long halls invite more interaction and noise, while the smaller rooms, a more intimate and quiet setting, especially if doors were closed. At Epidauros, incubation in the *enkoimeterion/abaton* is thought to have occurred in the stoa beside the Tholos where a flight of stairs leads

---

20 Roebuck, 1951, 51–55; Leypold 2008, 79–84. On the Asklepieion at Corinth, see also Riethmüller 2005, 1:123–130, 2:54–61; Melfi 2007, 289–312, esp. 296–298 on the courtyard and dining rooms.

21 This parallel was noted by Roebuck 1951, 53. See also the section on *klinai* below.

22 Roebuck 1951, 42.

23 Roebuck 1951, 85, 96–106; Melfi 2007, 301–302.

24 Leypold 2008, 60–68. For the latest documentation and architectural study of this building, see Kiriaki 2012. On its identification, see also Tomlinson 1969, 111; Melfi 2007, 41, n. 142.

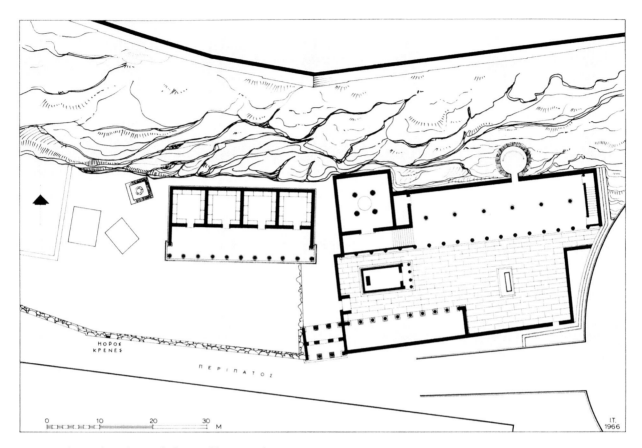

FIGURE 8.7 Athens, Akropolis, South Slope, Asklepieion, plan
AFTER RIETHMÜLLER 2005, 253, FIG. 36

to a basement level below a western extension, which also could have held stone and/or wooden benches.[25] The *abaton* stoa, the dining building with courtyard, and the so-called *katagogion*[26] or hostel further south provide accommodation on at least three different levels and three different points of proximity to the center of cult activity (see p. 89, Fig. 6.5). By closeness to the center of cult, I do not mean to imply 'more sacred.'[27] Rather, the distinction seems to reflect logistical measures of controlling traffic in the sanctuary. In the case of the *katagogion*, it is also

a way to keep profane aspects (sex, death, birth) outside the *temenos*.[28] We should probably exclude the possibility that incubation spaces were also used as dining spaces in Asklepios sanctuaries, but some overlap of activities would be architecturally possible even if it did not occur due to practicalities and rules in the sanctuary.

We might dub these dining buildings the 'expanded courtyard type,' a format that allows a more flexible use of space for people and other activities, including food preparation in addition to dining. The large dining spaces at Epidauros and Troizen, for example, would indicate planning for larger numbers of diners than, for instance, those who visited Perachora, irrespective of the number of actual visitors.

4   Stoas

Arguably, the most flexible ancient Greek building was a stoa with rooms. In addition to offering accommodation for commercial or civic functions in public spaces, stoas

---

25 Melfi 2007, 41–42. Modern restoration includes benches inside the lower level. For various identifications of the function of the Tholos, see Schultz et al. 2017, 23, n. 9. For the western extension of the *abaton* possibly dating to the Roman period, see Coulton 1976, 42, n. 4 for a summary of the dating controversy in which he notes that the moldings of the western section should also belong to the fourth century BCE, contemporary with the eastern section. Tomlinson (1983, 68) suggests a Hellenistic date for construction of the extension.

26 See Ekroth's discussion of this building in this volume. See also Kraynak 1991, 7; Riethmüller 2005, 294.

27 Stewart (2009, 376) makes this point using the phrase "degrees of sanctity." See also Ekroth on the issue of *temenos* boundaries in this volume.

28 I thank Gunnel Ekroth on this point.

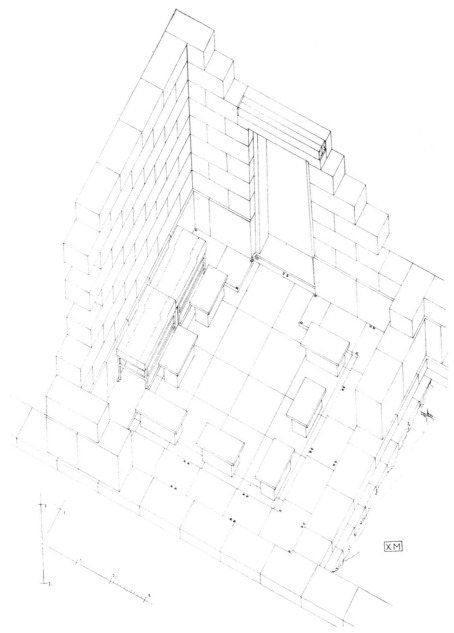

FIGURE 8.8A Brauron, sanctuary of Artemis, Π-shaped stoa, isometric view of a room
AFTER BOURAS 1967, 72, FIG. 54

within public and sacred spaces served as repositories for important equipment, war booty, or art (e.g., the Stoa Poikile in the Athenian Agora), or were places for congregation involving political or religious significance, including dining activity.[29]

Two stoas in close proximity and on different terraces grace the Asklepieion on the south slope of the Akropolis in Athens. The West Stoa (fifth century BCE) has been identified as a dining building, as it possesses four rooms of equal size with off-center doorways, each of which could accommodate 11 couches (Fig. 8.7).[30] The East Stoa (fourth century BCE) had a second storey, the exact configuration of which is unknown. If this building was the *enkoimeterion*, we do not know if patients slept in rooms, a hallway upstairs, or in the downstairs colonnade.[31] The West Stoa is separated by a propylon entranceway and *temenos* wall from the sacred precinct where the temple

---

29 Coulton 1976; Scahill 2012; 2016; 2023. See Kuhn 1985 on the religious function of stoas.

30 For the West Stoa, see Versakis 1908; Tomlinson 1969b, 112–117; Leypold 2008, 37–40. For the East Stoa, see Allen and Caskey 1911.

31 Allen and Caskey (1911, 43) assign a cult function to the square chamber at the west end of the East Stoa and place incubation in the upper floor this stoa.

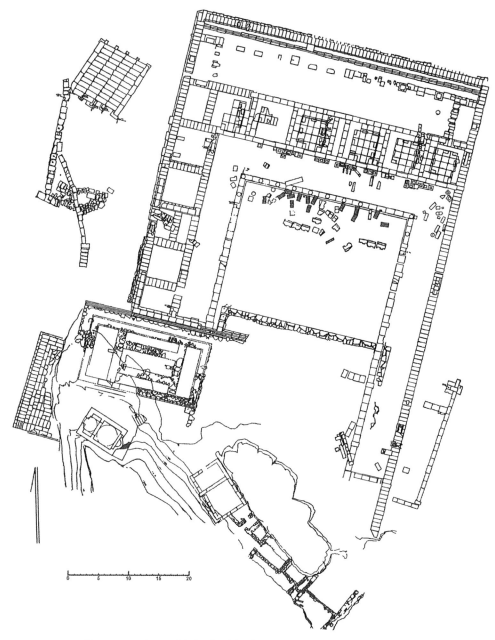

FIGURE 8.8B Brauron, sanctuary of Artemis, state plan
AFTER BOURAS 1967, FIG. 1

and *abaton* are located. This close proximity of secular and sacred activities may have occurred because the Asklepieion in Athens is a small, even cramped, sanctuary space compared to that at Epidauros for instance, for which reason the *temenos* boundary at Athens would mark a clear separation of activities. For the sanctuary's needs, the south slope of the Akropolis provided ample sources of fresh water nearby, including a Sacred Spring above the East Stoa and a spring with fountainhouse constructed to the west in the Archaic period.[32]

A more elaborate stoa for dining that borrows from the courtyard type discussed above is the Π-shaped stoa of the fifth century BCE in the sanctuary of Artemis at Brauron (Fig. 8.8a–b). The stoa had a northern wing accessed through entrances on the east and west sides. A series of rooms facing south sit behind the northern wing and extend partly down the west side of a courtyard. 13 Doric columns front the central rooms, forming the beginning of a peristyle. From the remains, we can restore 11 wooden *klinai* and seven stone tables per room, but not all the rooms have evidence to show they were used for dining.[33]

32 Crouch 1993, 265–268, 275–276, 278–280, 295.

33 Bouras 1967; Leypold 2008, 48–52.

The dining rooms and courtyard are accessed from the northern wing through a central corridor between the rooms, while the southern end of the courtyard is open toward the temple precinct at the south. Ekroth points out that the courtyard, which is secluded from the main part of the sanctuary, would interact visually with the space in front of the temple, but was "not directly part of the ritual actions" there.[34]

We have written evidence documenting buildings at Brauron in the fourth century BCE, an inscribed law concerning repairs to buildings in the sanctuary, but whether or not the text of the law mentions the Π-shaped Stoa is unclear.[35] A second inscription from Brauron, an inscribed catalogue of the late fifth century BCE, lists furniture and cooking items presumably in use at the site.[36] Especially noteworthy is the joining of cooking items with *klinai*, which suggests that cooking and dining were taking place in the same area. J.J. Coulton argued that the rooms with *klinai* in the stoa were for formal dining, but there is still debate over who used the building and how it was used.[37]

5   Andrones

The monumental *Andrones* at Labraunda, commissioned in the first half of the fourth century BCE by the ruling family, the Hekatomnids, of Karia, endowed dining with prestige and grandeur. *Andron* B (*Andron* built by Maussollos, r. 377/6–353/2 BCE) and *Andron* A, built slightly later, at Labraunda are temple-like buildings in appearance that served as extravagant banqueting rooms within the sanctuary (Fig. 8.9).[38] They are impressive in size. *Andron* B, measuring 11.78 m × 19.235 m, is the earliest preserved structure of the numerous Hekatomnid projects at Labraunda.[39] It is distyle in-antis with two columns on the front. Behind the porch, a large door leads into the cella, with large windows on either side of the door between the porch and the cella. The cella is deeper than it is wide with a boss along the wall that now indicates where a platform for *klinai* or benches was once located. A raised rectangular niche dominates the back of the cella. *Andron* A, also distyle in antis, is the better preserved of the two buildings with remains of the *klinai* platform around the edges of the cella.[40]

The *Andrones* were positioned in the sanctuary near the processional road leading to the terrace on which the temple of Zeus stood, a prime location for ritual dining associated with the cult of Zeus.[41] Both *Andrones* were used for banqueting and receptions of the Karian satrapy.[42] The layout of *klinai* versus benches around the rooms in the *Andrones* at Labraunda is not certain, but the *Andron* of Maussollos could have held c.18 *klinai*, according to Hellström and Blid.[43] They suggest the possibility that the reclining guests all faced toward the central niche at the back of the cella, in which a larger *kline* reserved for the satrap stood on a raised platform.[44] If all the guests were facing toward the back, those on the right side of the room would have to recline on their right elbow and dine with their left hand, which would be an awkward arrangement. Hellstrom and Blid, while pointing out that dining is not a static event and participants can shift around on their beds or even be in a sitting position, offer an alternative reconstruction with a continuous bench instead of *klinai*, an arrangement that would mitigate the problem.[45]

---

34   Ekroth 2003, 90.
35   *SEG* 46.133, 47.134, 52.104, 53.103.
36   *SEG* 37.34; Linders 1975, 75, n. 12; Andrianou (2006, 577) provides a partial list of the items.
37   Coulton 1976, 9, 43. See especially Ekroth 2003, 87–93 on the possible functions related to the stoa and 83–87, on other possible dining spaces at Brauron, including the cave and the 'Small Temple' in addition to the Π-shaped Stoa. For the stoa used as sleeping space, see Papadimitriou 1963, 118–120. The inscribed law mentions an upper level (ὑπερῷα) in the context of a discussion of the rooms (οἶκοι), and scholars have interpreted this as referring to the rooms of the Π-shaped Stoa (Mylonopoulos and Bubenheimer 1996, 7–23, esp. 17–18 on the upper storey). However, Bouras (1967, fig. 76b) reconstructs a one-storey building based on his assessment of the available architectural evidence. If this stoa possessed an upper storey, it would be the earliest attested example.

38   Leypold 2008, 92–96; Hellström and Blid 2019.
39   Hellström and Blid 2019, 11, 22 and fig. 21; for *Andron* B remains and proposed reconstruction, 17–116.
40   Hellström and Blid 2019. For *Andron* A remains and proposed reconstruction, 125–198.
41   Hellström and Blid 2019, 273.
42   Hellström and Blid 2019, 269–272.
43   Hellström and Blid (2019, 271, n. 819, fig. 471) discuss possible numbers of diners per *kline* and offer four possible alternatives for arrangement, including *klinai* and benches.
44   Hellström and Blid 2019, 270.
45   Hellström and Blid 2019, 269–272 on the possibility of left-handed diners in the *Andrones* at Labraunda.

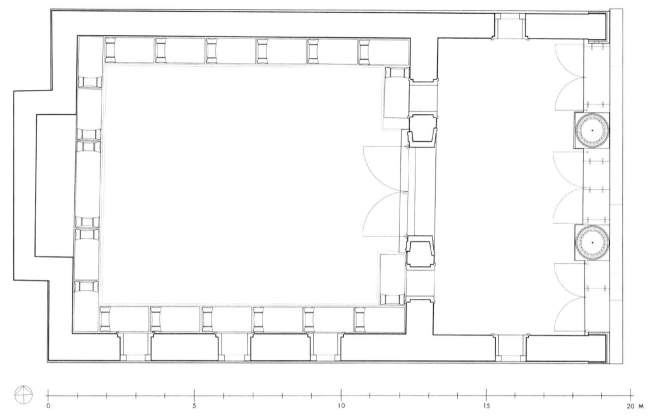

FIGURE 8.9 Labraunda, Andron B, restored plan *klinai* (J. Blid)
AFTER HELLSTRÖM AND BLID 2019, 117, FIG. 228

6 Naiskoi

Other monumental, temple-like buildings used for dining include three so-called *Naiskoi* of the Hellenistic period in front of the theater area at Aigeira, a city in the northwestern Peloponnesos.[46] Although these three buildings are reconstructed as tetrastyle prostyle buildings temple-like in appearance, each has a space for *klinai* or benches in the 'cella,' suggestive of dining.[47] This has led Alexandra Tanner to argue that the more neutral term 'building' rather than *naiskos* should be used, because their function as temples is questionable.[48]

The best preserved is Building D, which has a mosaic floor inside the 'cella,' with a raised border around the perimeter for the placement of *klinai* or benches (Fig. 8.10). Tanner reconstructs the dimensions of the building as 8.29 × 17.56 m, which is slightly smaller than *Andron* B at Labraunda, but still impressive.[49] Excavation has not yet clarified if the area in front of the theater was a sanctuary or civic space and both uses are possible.[50] Tanner notes that the arc-like placement of the three buildings in front of the theater is without direct parallel.[51]

By comparison with the *Andrones* at Labraunda, the Aigeira buildings are slightly smaller and the space in the 'cella' for dining significantly so, because the configuration of the space for dining is square rather than running the full length of the room. If all three of these *naiskoi*, hosting seven to ten people per *naiskos*, were in use at the same time, they offer the possibility of three extravagant rooms for intimate dining.

---

46 Tanner 2020; 2022; Gauss 2022.
47 Tanner 2020, 78.
48 Tanner 2020, 74. The interior of the Aphrodision on Delos presents a similar situation. The cella is divided into two rooms, and the front room has a marble floor mosaic with benches against the walls (Durvye 2009, 198–207, esp. 199–202). I thank Gunnel Ekroth for bringing this example to my attention.
49 Tanner 2020, 80.
50 Tanner 2020, 84.
51 Tanner 2020, 73.

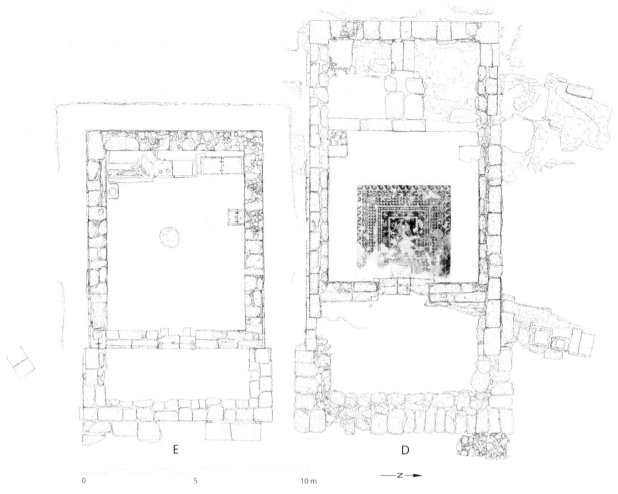

FIGURE 8.10   Aigeira, Buildings D and E, plan by Alexandra Tanner
COURTESY: ÖSTERREICHISCHES ARCHÄOLOGISCHES INSTITUT, ATHENS

7 The Pinakotheke in the Propylaia on the Athenian Akropolis

In the realm of possible dining buildings in sanctuaries that project monumentality and occupy a special place, the northwest wing, or 'Pinakotheke,' of the Propylaia on the Akropolis in Athens arguably surpasses them all (Fig. 8.11).[52] The Pinakotheke is so called because Pausanias says this building (*oikema*) housed famous paintings, but its function has been a matter of debate.[53] The northwest wing conspicuously has an off-center doorway, and John Travlos was the first to hypothesize that the reason for this was to place *klinai* around the perimeter of the room.[54] Pontus Hellström, went further in proposing that the unrealized eastern halls of the Propylaia were intended as banquet halls to be used in conjunction with the Panathenaic festival and that the entire Propylaia was designed to be a giant banqueting building.[55]

In addition to these design changes during construction of the Propylaia after the mid-fifth century BCE, a relatively small porticoed building with two rooms, the so-called Northwest Building on the Akropolis was begun northeast of the Propylaia's central structure, and its foundations look in all respects like those of a *hestiatorion* with two rooms and a porch/vestibule. According to Tanoulas, the foundations of the Northwest Building were laid, but then abandoned when Mnesikles began construction on

---

52   Leypold 2008, 33–37.
53   Paus. 1.22.6. Pausanias' statement that there were pictures (ἔχον γραφάς) in the northwest room has been taken to mean that it served as a picture gallery, but this does not preclude its use as a dining room, as well. Hellström has rightly pointed out that Pausanias' wording when describing the paintings is ambiguous; if they were wall paintings, rather than wooden panels as some have argued, these would be well-suited for a dining room (Hellström 1988, 118; Morris 1995, 313).
54   See Travlos, *Athens* 482, figs. 614, 618–619. See Hellström 1975; Dinsmoor, Jr. 1982; Hellström 1988.
55   Hellström 1988, 114, 120, fig. 21.

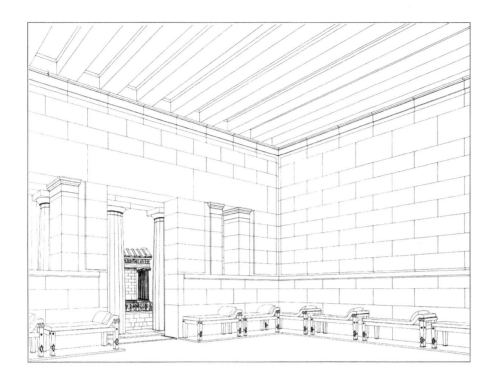

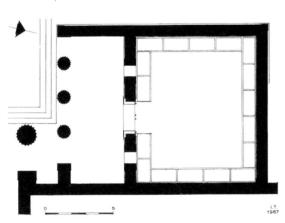

FIGURE 8.11   Athenian Akropolis, Propylaia, Pinakotheke (Northwest hall), plan restored with *klinai*
AFTER TRAVLOS, *ATHENS* 491, FIGS. 618–619

the Northeast wing of the Propylaia; the former structure was transformed into a courtyard when the Northeast wing was abandoned.[56] Therefore, the Propylaia area would have been earmarked to have a dining function from very early in the Periklean building project. The move to plan the Propylaia wings ultimately allowed the building to include dining on a grand scale positioned at the liminal space of entry to the Akropolis.[57]

8   Other Building Types

Architectural design of ancient buildings is not always a clear indicator of function—or not as clear as modern scholars would like. The sanctuary of Asklepios at Lissos on Crete, positioned on a semi-circular terraced hillside overlooking a harbor, contains a temple and several buildings, located near a spring water source.[58] No *abaton* or dining building has yet been identified in the sanctuary, but there

---

56   Tanoulas 1992a; 1992b.
57   See van den Eijnde in this volume on use of liminal space at the edges of sanctuaries for drinking parties.

58   Kanellopoulos 2019 brings new attention to this important site.

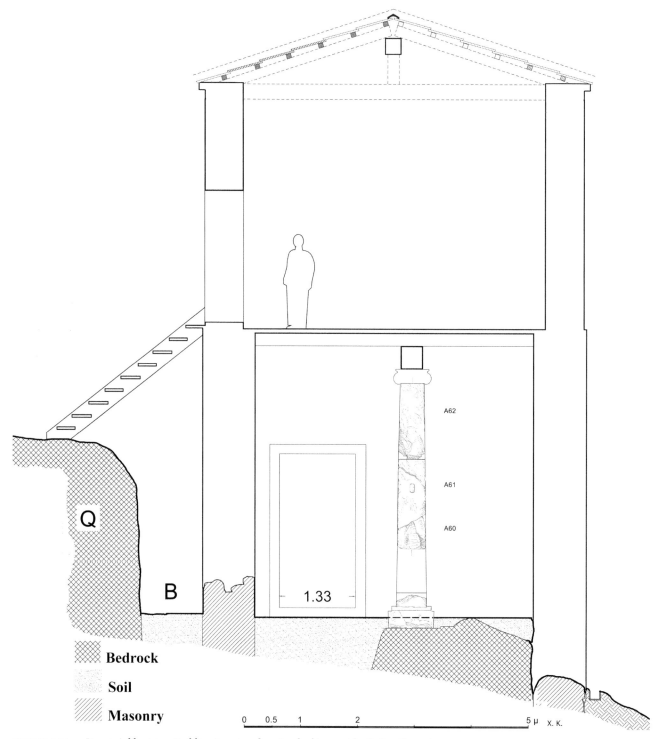

FIGURE 8.12   Lissos, Asklepieion, Building A, restored section looking east by C. Kanellopoulos

is at least one candidate for each of these two functions. Building A has an off-center doorway; this apparently was not for placement of dining couches, as one might expect, but because the door is on the short side, and the interior colonnade would impede the entrance were the door centered (Fig. 8.12).[59] That this door is the only access point to the building, on the lower level, would suggest a function related to privacy and exclusivity. The building is less than five meters in width, meaning the interior colonnade would only be necessary as support for an upper storey. The ample thickness of the preserved wall foundations also suggests a second level; benches or couches would fit along the walls downstairs and/or upstairs. Based on comparison to the two-storied buildings in

---

59   Kanellopoulos, personal communication, July 2023.

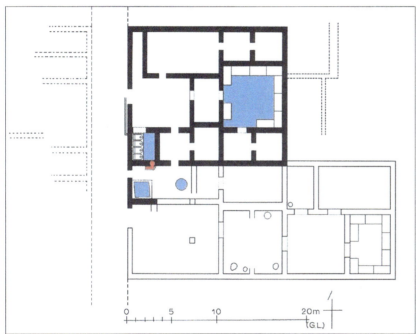

FIGURE 8.13
Aigeira, Guesthouse, aerial view (above), restored plan of Phase 1 by G. Ladstetter (below)
COURTESY: ÖSTERREICHISCHES ARCHÄOLOGISCHES INSTITUT, ATHENS

the west complex at the Asklepieion at Corinth (Fig. 8.5) and East Stoa in the Asklepieion at Athens (Fig. 8.7), at least one floor of Building A at Lissos is a candidate for incubation use. A water basin/bath downstairs against the wall on the north interior side would have provided for the guests. If not for incubation, then the downstairs room may have been designated for dining, and the upstairs for sleeping. Without more evidence, the use(s) of this building remains open to discussion. The design of Building A does not fit any of the building types already discussed, and the architect seems to have followed his own rules in accordance with the topography of the sanctuary.

The preceding examples suggest that dining may be located away from the center of cult activity and toward the edges of the sanctuary. Buildings that may have accommodated dining connected to cult activity, along with other activities, highlight flexibility of use.

9   Dining Outside the *Temenos*

The so-called 'Solon building' at Aigeira (Fig. 8.13), a complex begun in the fourth century BCE and located just below the akropolis on the northern lower terrace, has elements that indicate it probably served as a guesthouse

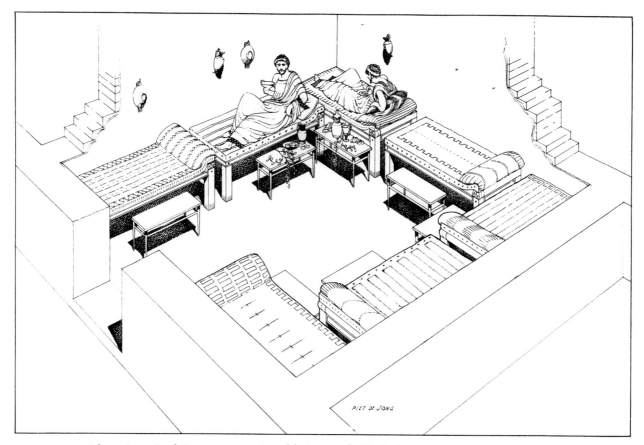

FIGURE 8.14   Athens, Agora, South Stoa I, reconstruction of dining room by Piet De Jong.
COURTESY: ARCHIVES OF THE AMERICAN SCHOOL OF CLASSICAL STUDIES AT ATHENS

with infrastructure for banqueting, overnight stays, and bathing.[60] The building is rectangular with many rooms and phases, a full accounting of which has not been made yet.[61] The main *andron* can accommodate 11 couches around the perimeter. Water supply was piped in from a nearby fountain connected to a naturally occurring spring at the edge of the plateau to the west. A terraced path leads up from this building complex to a gate in the akropolis fortification wall. The space on the higher plateau of the akropolis, on which a temple and altar were situated, appears to have been too small and crowded to accommodate a building for banqueting, and no possible dining structures have been detected there. Therefore, it is tempting to see the 'Solon building' as serving the dining needs of the akropolis sanctuary. It is possible that more dining buildings are located on the eastern saddle of the akropolis or somewhere on the same terrace as the 'Solon building,' but this remains to be explored with further excavation.[62]

Finally, two stoas in public/civic space have been associated with cult dining by scholars, serving as a reminder that the location of dining was opportunistically tied to available space. The rooms in South Stoa I of the fifth century BCE in the Athenian Agora have off-center doorways and a raised platform around the perimeter of the room with space to accommodate seven *klinai* or alternatively, benches, per room (Fig. 8.14).[63] Thompson and Wycherley postulated that South Stoa I, or part of it, might have been referred to as the *Thesmotheteion*, headquarters of the archons, which was a *syssitia*, a place for communal dining in Athens, and that at least one of the dining rooms was possibly used by the *Thesmothetai*, or six junior archons, because they could comfortably fit in a room that

---

60   Ladstätter 2004. Solon is the local toponym of unknown origin. The complex has four baths in one room, an argument against an opulent private house, and a small pool was installed later in place of the baths (Ladstätter 2004, 389); see again Ekroth in this volume on guesthouses.

61   This building awaits further study and publication. The ongoing excavations at Aigeira are under the auspices of the Österreichisches Archäologisches Institut, Athens and are being conducted by Walter Gauss, Director of Excavations.

62   Ladstätter 2004, 390. Geophysical survey revealed no anomalies to suggest that a *temenos* wall existed on this terrace.

63   For South Stoa I at Athens, see Thompson and Wycherley 1972, 74–78.

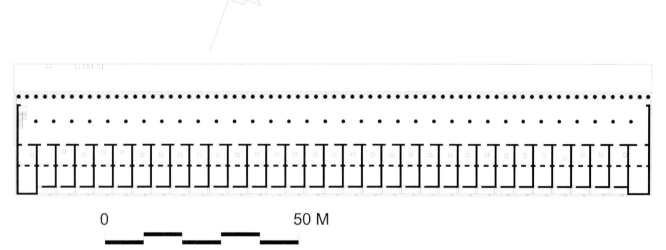

FIGURE 8.15A   Corinth, South Stoa, plan of the late fourth century BCE by author

had seven *klinai*.[64] I think we could also allow the possibility that nine archons would fit, if two of them shared one bed or if there were benches instead of *klinai*.

An example of a stoa that in many ways appears to have been a complete package for drinking, dining, and sleeping, as well as other multifunctional capability, is the South Stoa at Corinth, which is also one of the longest stoas in the Greek world (165 m long), occupying the south side of the later Roman Forum (Fig. 8.15a). It was built sometime at the end of the fourth or beginning of the third century BCE and continued in use with alterations through the Roman period.[65] The original Greek phase of the stoa had 71 exterior Doric columns and 34 interior Ionic columns fronting 33 rooms behind, each with an annex room and latrines on the exterior back of the building.[66] An upper storey above the backrooms may have been for for sleeping quarters for overnight guests.[67] The ground floor rooms have off-center doorways, one of the criteria for dining rooms, but there are two problems.[68] With the exception of the last room to the east, the doorways are offset on the left side, which would be the wrong side for *klinai* to be arranged for right-handed diners.[69] In addition, the interior of each front room is pierced at the back by a door to the back room of the suite, undermining any perimeter arrangement of *klinai*. The reason for the placement of the doorways is unclear.[70] Instead of klinai, dining could have occurred on benches, which is more likely. Unfortunately, any evidence that might appear on the floors, such as plaster along the walls or a border sill is missing, due to Roman renovations that destroyed all the original floors, so this must remain a hypothesis.[71]

As with South Stoa I in the Athenian Agora, the South Stoa at Corinth is not strictly in a sanctuary, but in an area with cult activity alongside public use.[72] Charles Williams suggested that *technitai* related to Dionysos may have held banquets in the stoa.[73] In addition, dining in the stoa may have been associated with visiting magistrates connected to Macedonian aspirations in the Peloponnese and also connected to the games at Isthmia.[74] A flexible aspect of this building, as also with South Stoa I, seems to have

64   Thompson and Wycherley 1972, 77–78.
65   Broneer 1954; Scahill 2012; 2016; 2023.
66   For the latrines as an addition to the building in the third century BCE, see Broneer 1954, 93; Williams 1980, 107, 126. On latrines in sanctuaries, see Trümper in this volume.
67   Scahill 2012, 191–195.
68   Scahill 2012, 290–296.
69   Supra n. 43 for this problem at Labraunda.

70   Broneer (1933, 556) thought the asymmetry was done to avoid door alignment problems with the wells in the rooms. Thompson (1954, 43) suggested that it was to accommodate windows.
71   Broneer (1954, 137) remarks that "nowhere have any traces of the Greek shop floors been discovered."
72   See Williams 1978 for cult activity in the pre-forum area in front of the South Stoa from the Classical through Hellenistic periods. See also Scahill 2016 on other possible connections to cult dining in the South Stoa.
73   Williams 1978, 53.
74   Broneer 1954, 62–64, 98; Scahill 2016, 139–142. I have elsewhere suggested that the South Stoa may have been built and used by the Antigonids for the league first started by Philip and revived

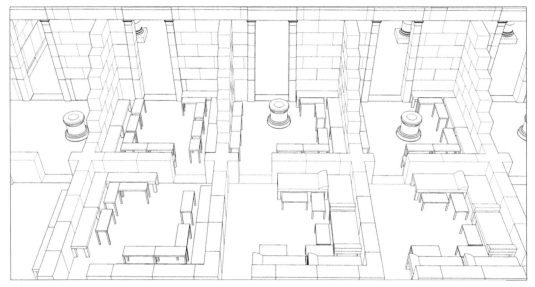

FIGURE 8.15B   Corinth, South Stoa, reconstruction of rooms with benches by author

precluded the use of permanent furniture for dining, unless some of the rooms had stone benches at some point.[75] If *klinai*, benches, and tables were of wood, and therefore portable, then rooms could have been converted for various other uses.[76] Benches and tables can be reconstructed in the rooms; however, the layout of the rooms with an annex doorway eliminates the possibility of using the full perimeter (Fig. 8.15b).

The fact that nearly each room had its own well, its own annex, and its own latrine makes each a self-contained suite. If the rooms were all used at the same time for dining and entertainment, the South Stoa would have been one of the largest banqueting halls known to us. Alternatively, the suites downstairs were probably operated independently as separate apartments or rooms let out for dining and/or commercial purposes. Given the uncertainty of furniture arrangements, speculation on the total number of banqueters who could be accommodated is not possible, but it was clearly a large number.

10   Furniture

The role of furniture in the context of the logistics of dining in sanctuaries is of central importance to the logistics of function, but problematic due to the lack of preserved material evidence, with only a few sites providing definitive proof of *klinai* or bench supports. However, literary, epigraphical, and visual evidence are helpful in reconstructing what was employed.[77] The degree to which special furniture was used in dining contexts is not always clear, unless of stone and preserved since stone furniture would be a fixed, semi-permanent feature of the room. If the furniture was of wood, it would be more portable, implying the possibility of different events and even altogether different uses for a room. In this case, the furniture would have to be stored somewhere.

We have spoken about flexible room use, and the type of material used for *klinai*, benches, and tables may offer evidence of this. At Perachora and in the Asklepieion at Corinth, the *klinai* were made of stone, while the tables are assumed to have been of wood due to the small size of the slots in the floor for inserting table legs.[78] We might ask if the securing of table legs was a measure against boisterous behavior that might overturn a table. The *klinai* could not be moved easily, but wooden tables could have been removed from the room after dinner or drinking, if sympotic activity also occurred here, to make way for entertainment, musical or otherwise.[79]

---

by Demetrios Poliorketes in *c*.302 BCE (see Scahill 2023, 180–183 for discussion and bibliography on the league).

75   Destruction and cleanup debris in the wells of the South Stoa produced pottery and other material that support the idea of a dining function for the rooms. Broneer indicates drinking cups and wine pitchers as evidence for dining and drinking (1954, 62–64, 98–99). See also Edwards 1975, 196–198, deposit summaries 95–118; Scahill 2023, 178–184.

76   For discussion of the function of stoas, see Coulton 1976. The multifunctional aspect is clearly seen in the diverse array of evidence from sanctuaries, as well as from non-sanctuary contexts, especially 16–17 on the visual representation of furniture. On furniture in general, and for additional bibliography on the subject, see also Richter 1965; 1966.

77   See Andrianou 2006, 2009, especially 16–17 on the visual representation of furniture. On furniture in general, and for additional bibliography on the subject, see also Richter 1965; 1966.

78   For Perachora: supra n. 6; for Corinth: supra n. 18.

79   See van den Eijnde in this volume.

The material choice for furniture in the Π-shaped stoa at Brauron, which has stone tables, but sockets for wooden *klinai*, is opposite to that at Perachora and Corinth. *Klinai* of wood could be set aside to allow space for some other activity, but the tables would still be in the way. Wooden *klinai* might be less sturdy, but were a less expensive alternative and replaceable as needed.[80] We may wonder why the tables at Brauron, but not the *klinai*, were of permanent material; perhaps the dining at Brauron differed in some respect from that at Perachora, or this choice was simply a regional preference of materials.

Stone supports to offer stability to wooden *klinai* or benches and wooden tables were used in the three northern rooms in the West Building at the Argive Heraion, the dining rooms at Troizen, and the Banquet Building at Epidauros.[81] If the wooden upper surfaces of the beds or benches and the tables were damaged, they were easily replaceable, and this material choice would also permit some flexibility in room arrangement and use of the room.

Easy portability of wooden *klinai* is debatable, however, due to the considerable weight of even wood ones (and we should factor in size and opulence of additional materials (bronze, ivory inlay, etc.), yet we can infer from the epigraphical record that *klinai* were stored on the Athenian Akropolis and accessible for use. The Parthenon inventories provide one answer, listing "Chian" and "Milesian" *klinai* that were stored in the Parthenon and could have been used elsewhere on the Akropolis, one suggestion being in the Pinakotheke dining room of the Propylaia.[82]

The size of *klinai*, based on both actual measurements of known examples and measurements calculated from room size, shows some degree of variation, slight in many cases, but this variation can become significant when *klinai* are placed along a wall, and lengths are added up.[83] Variation in size would explain the given place names listed in epigraphical testimony such as in the Parthenon inventories to which I just referred. "Chian" and "Milesian" *klinai* might most obviously refer to location of production, style, or origin of the artisans, as Andrianou has pointed out.[84] These names, however, could also signify and reflect differences of size.[85] Although *klinai* variation in dining rooms may be slight, it should be borne in mind that systems of measurement for building varied in ancient Greece, differing between projects, site, and region, so that designating *klinai* by place names could help mitigate problems of size differences as *klinai* were made and procured to fit a particular room.[86]

Furniture in ancient Greek dining contexts had both functional and symbolic aspects. *Klinai* imply reclining guests at a meal or *symposion* and would have aristocratic overtones, while benches and tables would suffice for dining and were used in sacred dining contexts, for instance in the Demeter and Kore Sanctuary at Corinth.[87] The evidence suggests a wide fluctuation in total accommodation for diners dependent on the particular dining requirements of the sanctuary, which would make sense. Typical dining rooms suggest intimacy with a maximum of 11 *klinai*. A hall space would be less intimate, but could hold more *klinai*. Even among this small sample of building types, variation among the buildings in terms of the number of people that could be accommodated is clear and should reflect the differences in dining experienced in each specific case.

11 Other Provisions

Hearths in rooms would have provided illumination and heat and may have been used for cooking or warming food. Permanent hearths do not seem to have been common in dining structures, but two of the buildings discussed here, both in sanctuaries of Asklepios, have them.

---

80   This would also depend on availability of material (i.e., local stone versus imported wood). For Brauron: supra n. 33.
81   For the West Building at the Argive Heraion: supra n. 15; for Troizen: supra n. 18; for Epidauros: supra n. 22.
82   See Andrianou 2009, 32–33 for lists of *klinai* in the Parthenon and Delos inventories, and especially n. 58 for bibliography on couch types and their presence in temple inventory lists. The listing of Milesian *klinai* in the Parthenon inventories starts in 434/3 BCE (*IG* I² 276, l. 14) and continues into the fourth century BCE (*IG* II² 1425, ll. 217, 277). For the full list of the inscriptions from the Parthenon inventories that mention the Chian and Milesian *klinai*, see Harris 1995, 91–92, 136. Harris raises a question regarding the items singled out to be inventoried, suggesting the lists document the items to be distributed for the Panathenaic Procession and other cult needs and were "used only for festivals" (10, 28). The ongoing debate over the specific location of the *klinai* inside the building is beyond the scope of this paper. Sebastian Prignitz is currently working on these inscriptions for new publication in the *IG* series.

83   Miller 1978, 219–224.
84   Andrianou 2009, 32–33. Supra n. 84 for the inscriptions.
85   Hellström (1988, 117–118) discusses the possibility of different sizes of *klinai* in the Pinakotheke on the Athenian Akropolis by calculating the Chian and Milesian *klinai* as two distinct sizes.
86   Regarding *klinai*, Pritchett (1956, 227), notes that "the dimensions must have varied considerably." See Homolle 1886, 467 l. 143; *IG* II² 1638, l. 68. For an overview of ancient Greek measuring systems and regional/local variation, see Wilson Jones 2000; 2001. Standard ancient foot lengths differed around the Mediterranean and even between Greek city-states.
87   See Boardman 1990, 122–131, on *klinai* for *symposia*. For the Sanctuary of Demeter and Kore, see Bookidis 1990 and 1993.

The square building at Troizen has several hearths with evidence of burning in the central hall or courtyard area and in the separate rooms (Fig. 8.4),[88] and built hearths also occur in the dining rooms at Corinth (Fig. 8.5). Whether the hearths in these buildings were for cooking and/or heating the rooms, as well as providing illumination, is unknown.[89] Published reconstructions of the roofing of these structures do not consider how smoke from fire was evacuated. Some means of ventilation, such as opaion rooftiles—that is tiles formed with a hole—would have been necessary to allow smoke to escape.[90] While permanent hearths appear to be rare, portable braziers could have been brought into rooms as needed, provided there was a way to evacuate the smoke produced.

All of the buildings discussed would have had to have access to water, although it is not always visible in the immediate vicinity and could have been brought from a distance when necessary. The huge cistern just to the north of the dining building at Perachora, and the reservoirs off the southern side of the courtyard of the dining complex at Corinth's Asklepieion would seem to provide more than enough water for sanctuary use. One of the most striking features in the rooms of the South Stoa at Corinth is that 31 of the 33 rooms have a well connected to an underground tunnel system that fed water from the Peirene Spring. The water supply in these cases seems excessive for the needs of a particular building or even sanctuary, but this may be deceptive, depending on the number of visitors and even rainfall during the year.[91]

Provision for cooking facilities and water was not always aligned with building size or room space, nor is their presence always obvious from the archaeological remains, which may reflect different dining customs and cult practice. This provision or lack thereof, however, may also have been due to economics and/or site-specific building infrastructure related to a myriad of other internal and external factors.

Availability of water was also a concern for cleaning dining rooms after use. We know that sometimes there were raucous parties at *symposia*,[92] and we can speculate that even the most dignified banquet would cause wear and tear on furniture and floors, mess, and especially if wine drinking were involved, the need for water for cleaning. One is reminded of the 'unswept floor' motif in Roman floor mosaics, the theme of which is traced by Pliny (*HN* 36.60.25) to the artist Sosos at Pergamon in the second century BCE.[93]

Drains in *Andrones* A and B at Labraunda, along with evidence that the floor of *Andron* B may have inclined toward the drain, would have facilitated washing the floors.[94] A similar drain provision occurs in the Aphrodision temple on Delos, where inside the front room of the cella are a mosaic and benches for dining.[95] Sloping floors and drains for ease of cleaning should be looked for in all cases of dining rooms.

12 The Longue Durée

Dining buildings had varying but limited space for visitors. If a building was designed specifically for dining, this leads to questions regarding the type of dining that occurred and the structure's function over time. What about *longue durée* use, for instance from the late sixth century BCE through the Hellenistic period as was the case for the dining building at Perachora? For a dining building in the Archaic period, we would be inclined to see aristocratic overtones in its use, due to the elite nature of the *klinai*. In some sense this aristocratic or elite aspect would continue from the Archaic period through to the Classical and Hellenistic periods.

Were buildings intermittently employed for dining and otherwise vacant, or could the space be used for other purposes? The likelihood that a building would sit empty

---

88 Welter 1941, 32–33.
89 See also van den Eijnde in this volume for discussion of braziers and fireplaces.
90 For an opaion tile in the roof of the South Stoa at Corinth, see Broneer 1954, 87, fig. 61. Opaion tiles from the area of the Tholos in the Athenian Agora may have been for smoke ventilation from the Tholos kitchen; see Thompson 1940, 78, fig. 61.
91 See Klingborg in this volume on the utilitarian needs for water in sanctuaries.
92 See Steiner 2002 on ribald behavior in *symposia* extending to public dining.
93 The most famous example, dated to the second century CE and signed in Greek by Heraklitos, is now in the Vatican museums. It decorated the floor of a domus located in *Vigna Lupi*, south of the Aventine Hill in front of the Aurelian Wall (Parlasca 1963, 277; Donderer 1987, 365–377; Werner 1998, 260; Ribi 2001, 364). On the Pergamon mosaics by Sosos, see Dunbabin 1999, 27; Seaman 2020, 110–131.
94 Hellström and Blid 2019, 38 figs. 54–55 (undressed area at bottom of threshold indicating floor level), figs. 64–72 (continuous boss for the *kline* podium), 41 fig. 73 (*Andron* B: drain at bottom of cella wall just above floor level and through podium foundation), 147–148 fig. 273 (*Andron* A). This drainage system can be compared to similar ones at floor level in traditional timber farmhouses, *Herrstuga*, in Hälsingland, Sweden. These rooms or separate buildings were highly decorated and reserved for special occasions, such as assemblies and other types of festive gatherings, including weddings and meetings with a religious aspect (https://whc.unesco.org/en/list/1282/).
95 Durvye (2024, 41 figs. 3–4, n. 37) points out other buildings on Delos with similar provisions, including the Oikos of the Naxians. See also Durvye 2009, 198–207, esp. 199–202.

for some part of the year seems unlikely from a practical point of view, but must still be considered as a possibility, although evidence is lacking. A building presumably would have to be maintained year-round to be ready for use and avoid dilapidation, and maintenance was probably done at designated times of year. The ebb and flow of traffic in sanctuaries would have a physical impact on a building.[96] Besides wear and tear from use, intervals of non-use would also require attention. An unused building requires airing to avoid humidity problems that would cause the wood in the roof to bend under the weight of the rooftiles.[97] Buildings of both stone and mudbrick with terracotta tiled roofs and wooden beams, windows, and doors would require some degree of maintenance during the year (at minimum once a year?). As Judy Barringer points out in this volume, priests and workers could be on hand for maintenance, and we have evidence in the literary/epigraphical record of specific cases.[98]

13 Concluding Remarks

Greek sanctuaries required some spatial arrangement to accommodate dining. The times of year, festival days, and other special occasions dictated the use of architectural space for dining, and the record indicates a multiplicity of building types used for this function. Special purpose facilities were constructed, and other building types could be modified for dining as needed; nearly all the buildings discussed here could be said to have the potential to be multifunctional spaces. Temples are an exception in not being used for dining; however, the interior spaces in the temple-like buildings at Aigeira and in the Delian Aphrodision were outfitted as *andron* spaces. Whether or not these buildings were still considered temples is a question that lies beyond the scope of this discussion.

Location was an issue. A question remains how close dining buildings in sanctuaries could be positioned with respect to altars and temples, but they were often located at a distance, as we have seen. Building infrastructure depended on the vicissitudes of economic and historical circumstances, as well as topography of the site. Tents were the easiest means to provide shelter for dining, but the tendency toward permanent structures seems to have been desirable, whether these were special purpose buildings or stoa rooms. Making allowance for the different types of buildings that might have served as dining facilities opens up new avenues for assessing the specific logistical requirements and arrangements that were made to accommodate a very practical need in sanctuaries.[99]

Buildings can, and did, remain in use for long periods of time, sometimes centuries, often with modifications. We know that cult activity and ritual use of the building did not remain static for centuries, and we should consider that most or even all the buildings discussed here had the potential to be multifunctional from inception; their use could evolve in different ways depending on the needs of the sanctuary, but evidence is crucial to determine if, how, and why this occurred.

A further step in understanding dining facilities in sanctuaries would be to assess, tabulate, and collate the evidence for the number of possible attendees in dining rooms and buildings, together with evidence regarding the number of participants for specific *symposia*, ritual meals, and other gatherings attested epigraphically and in the literary record at individual sites.

Acknowledgments

I would first like to offer warm thanks to my colleagues and co-editors of this volume, Judy Barringer and Gunnel Ekroth, to whom I am indebted and grateful for the opportunity to join them on this journey to examine logistics in Greek sanctuaries. Part of the research and writing of this article was done within the Aigeira Archaeological Survey Project, funded by the Austrian Science Fund (FWF, Einzelprojekt P 34614), under the auspices of the Austrian Archaeological Institute in Athens. I am grateful to Birgitta Eder, Director of the Institute, and Walter Gauss, Director of the Aigeira Excavations, for their support.

---

96   See Gawlinski in this volume on regulated days of communal worship versus intermittent personal visits to sanctuaries. She notes that evidence suggests healing sanctuaries accepted visitors at almost any time.

97   Roofs and floors are also subject to infestation by birds and other animals, especially when not occupied.

98   See Barringer in this volume on maintenance, and also McInerney for epigraphical testimony regarding building maintenance in sanctuaries at Delos and Athens. *IG* II² 2499 is a lease (of up to ten years) of the property of a cult association in Athens stipulating that the lessee who had fulfilled his caretaking duties could remove the wooden elements from the building(s) there. This may reflect a logistical arrangement for the wooden elements that were susceptible to dilapidation when not in use for some period of time and measures to renovate the buildings with new wood periodically. At the very least, it also indicates the possible recycling value of the used wood.

99   A case in point is the Apollo sanctuary at Delphi, where no *hestiatorion* has been identified within the precinct. Aurigny (2020, 100) has suggested that two buildings, the Lesche of the Knidians and the 'red house,' may have served such a need. This requires further investigation and highlights the importance of keeping an open mind regarding building types used for dining.

Works Cited

Allen, G., and L.D. Caskey. 1911. "The East Stoa in the Asclepieum at Athens." *AJA* 15: 32–43.

Andrianou, D. 2006. "Chairs, Beds, and Tables: Evidence for Furniture in Hellenistic Greece." *Hesperia* 75: 219–266.

Andrianou, D. 2009. *The Furniture and Furnishings of Ancient Greek Houses and Tombs*. Cambridge.

Aurigny, H. 2020. "Gathering in the Panhellenic Sanctuary at Delphi: an Archaeological Approach." In *Pilgrimage and Economy in the Ancient Mediterranean*, edited by A. Collar and T.M. Kristensen, 93–115. Leiden.

Bergquist, B. 1990. "Sympotic Space: A Functional Aspect of Greek Dining-Rooms." In *Sympotica: A Symposium on the Symposion*, edited by O. Murray, 37–65. Oxford.

Boardman, J. 1990. "Symposion Furniture." In *Sympotica: A Symposium on the Symposion*, edited by O. Murray, 122–131. Oxford.

Bookidis, N. 1983. "The Priest's House in the Marmaria at Delphi." *BCH* 107: 149–155.

Bookidis, N. 1990. "Ritual Dining in the Sanctuary of Demeter and Kore at Corinth: Some Questions." In *Sympotica: A Symposium on the Symposion*, edited by O. Murray, 86–94. Oxford.

Bookidis, N. 1993. "Ritual Dining at Corinth." In *Greek Sanctuaries: New Approaches*, edited by N. Marinatos and R. Hägg, 45–62. London.

Broneer, O. 1933. "Excavations in the Agora at Corinth, 1933." *AJA* 37: 554–572.

Broneer, O. 1954. *Corinth 1, The South Stoa and its Roman Successors*. Princeton.

Bouras, C. 1967. *Ἡ Ἀναστήλωσες τῆς στοᾶς τῆς Βραυρῶνος: τα αρχιτεκτονικά της προβλήματα*. Athens.

Coulton, J.J. 1976. *The Architectural Development of the Greek Stoa*. Oxford.

Crouch, D.P. 1993. *Water Management in Ancient Greek Cities*. Oxford.

Dinsmoor, W.B., Jr. 1982. "The Asymmetry of the Pinakotheke for the Last Time?" In *Studies in Athenian Architecture, Sculpture, and Topography Presented to Homer A. Thompson*, 18–33. Princeton.

Donderer, M. 1987. "Die antiken Pavimenttypen und ihre Benennungen. Zu Plinius, Naturalis historia 36, 184–189." *JdI* 102: 365–377.

Dunbabin, K.M.D. 1999. *Mosaics of the Greek and Roman World*. Cambridge.

Durvye, C. 2009. "Recherches récentes à Délos." *RA* 2009: 198–207.

Durvye, C. 2024. "Of things and men in the sanctuary of Aphrodite (Delos): Does the content of a sanctuary define the personality of the god?" In *The stuff of the gods: Material aspects of religion in ancient Greece*, edited by M. Haysom, M. Mili, and J. Wallensten, 35–45. Stockholm.

Edwards, G.R. 1975. *Corinth 8, Corinthian Hellenistic Pottery*. Princeton.

Ekroth, G. 2003. "Inventing Iphigeneia? On Euripides and the Cultic Construction of Brauron." *Kernos* 16: 59–118.

Frickenhaus, A.H. 1917. *Griechische Banketthäuser*. Berlin.

Gauss, W., and R. Smetana. 2022. "Die Forschungen 2011 bis 2018 im Bereich des Theaters, der 'Naiskoi' und des 'Tycheions' von Aigeira." In *Forschungen im Bereich des Theaters von Aigeira, 2011 bis 2018, Aigeira 3*, edited by W. Gauss, 13–96. Vienna.

Goldstein, M.S. 1978. *The Setting of the Ritual Meal in Greek Sanctuaries: 600–300 B.C.* Ph.D. diss., University of California, Berkeley.

Gras, M., H. Tréziny, and H. Broise. 2005. *Mégara Hyblaea 5, La ville archaïque: L'espace urbain d'une cité grecque de Sicile orientale*. Rome.

Harris, D. 1995. *The Treasures of the Parthenon and Erechtheion*. Oxford.

Hellström, P. 1975. "The Asymmetry of the Pinacotheca—Once More." *OpAth* 11: 87–92.

Hellström P. 1988. "The Planned Function of the Mnesiklean Propylaia." *OpAth* 17: 107–121.

Hellström, P., and J. Blid. 2019. *Labraunda 5: The Andrones*. Stockholm.

Hoepfner, W. 1976. *Das Pompeion und seine Nachfolgerbauten, Kerameikos 10*. Berlin.

Hoepfner, W. 2002. *Bildung für Athens Epheben. Das Pompeion-Gymnasium in Athen*. Mainz.

Homolle, T. 1886. "Inventaires des temples Déliens en l'Année 364." *BCH* 10: 461–475.

Jacquemin, A., D. Laroche, S. Huber, and M. Bublot. 2021. "Marmaria, l'*hestiatorion*, le synédrion et le Philippéion." *BCH* 145: 87–113.

Kanellopoulos, C. 2019. *Λισός: η αρχιτεκτονική του Ασκληπιείου*, AURA supp 2. Athens.

Kavvadias, P. 1891. *Fouilles d'Épidaure*. Athens.

Kavvadias, P. 1900. *Τὸ Ἱερὸν τοῦ Ἀσκληπίου ἐν Ἐπιδαύρῳ*. Athens.

Kiriaki, B. 2012. *Τὸ Γυμνάσιο—Τελετουργικὸ Ἑστιατόριο, κτίριο Χ.χ. στὸ Ἀσκληπιεῖο τῆς Ἐπιδαύρου (δ.δ. Παν. Ἀθηνῶν)*. Ph.D. diss., University of Athens. https://www.didaktorika.gr/eadd/handle/10442/33252.

Klebinder-Gauss, G. 2019. "Dining with the Ancestors: The Late Archaic-Classical Westkomplex in Aegina-Kolonna." In *Beyond the Polis, Rituals, Rites and Cults in Early and Archaic Greece (12th–6th Centuries BC)*, edited by I. Lemos and A. Tsingarida, 115–132. Brussels.

Koolhaas, R. 2012. "The Invention and Reinvention of The City." *Journal of International Affairs* 65: 113–119.

Kraynak, L.H. 1984. *Hostelries of Ancient Greece (Hotels, Inns)*. Ph.D. diss., University of California, Berkeley.

Kraynak, L.H. 1991. "The *Katagogion* at Epidauros: A Revised Plan." *ArchNews* 16: 1–8.

Kuhn, G. 1985. "Untersuchungen zur Funktion der Säulenhalle in archaischer und klassischer Zeit." *JdI* 100: 169–317.

Ladstätter, G. 2004. "Grabung Aigeira 2003." *ÖJh* 73: 388–390.

Leypold, C. 2008. *Bankettgebäude in griechischen Heiligtümern*. Wiesbaden.

Linders, T. 1975. *The Treasures of the Other Gods in Athens and Their Functions*. Meisenheim am Glan.

Martin, R., and H. Metzger. 1942–43. "Chronique des fouilles et découvertes archéologiques en Grèce en 1942." *BCH* 66–67: 320–345.

Melfi, M. 2007. *I Santuari di Asclepio in Grecia 1*. Rome.

Miller, S.G. 1973. "The Date of the West Building at the Argive Heraion." *AJA* 77: 9–18.

Miller, S.G. 1978. *The Prytaneion: Its Function and Architectural Form*. Berkeley.

Morris, S. 1995. *Daidalos and the Origins of Greek Art*. Princeton.

Mylonopoulos, J., and F. Bubenheimer. 1996. "Beiträge zur Topographie des Artemision von Brauron." *AA*: 77–23.

Pakkanen, J. 2019. "Reconstructing Building Height: The Early Hellenistic Hestiatorion Propylon at Epidauros." In *Listening to the Stones: Essays on Architecture and Function in Ancient Greek Sanctuaries in Honour of Richard Alan Tomlinson*, edited by E.C. Partida and B. Schmidt-Dounas, 109–120. Oxford.

Papadimitriou, J. 1963. "The Sanctuary of Artemis at Brauron." *Scientific American* 208: 110–120.

Parlasca, K. 1963. "Das Pergamenische Taubenmosaïk und der sogenannte Nestor-Becher." *JdI* 78: 256–293.

Pritchett, K. 1956. "The Attic Stelai, Part II." *Hesperia* 25: 178–328.

Ribi, E.A. 2001. "Asàrotos òikos. Von der Kunst, die sich verbirgt." In *Zona Archeologica. Festschrift für Hans Peter Isler zum 60. Geburtstag*, edited by S. Buzzi, D. Käch, and E. Kistler, 361–369. Bonn.

Richter, G.M.A. 1965. "The Furnishings of Ancient Greek Houses." *Archaeology* 18: 26–33.

Richter, G.M.A. 1966. *The Furniture of the Greeks, Etruscans, and Romans*. New York.

Riethmüller, J.W. 2005. *Asklepios. Heiligtümer und Kulte*. Heidelberg.

Roebuck C. 1951. *Corinth 14, The Asklepieion and Lerna*. Princeton.

Scahill, D. 2012. *The South Stoa at Corinth: Design, Construction and Function of the Greek Phase*. Ph.D. diss., University of Bath.

Scahill, D. 2016. "Dining and the Cult of Aphrodite: The Function of the South Stoa at Corinth." In *Houses of Ill Repute: The Archaeology of Brothels, Houses, and Taverns in the Greek World*, edited by A. Glazebrook and B. Tsakirgis, 129–142. Philadelphia.

Scahill, D. 2017. "Craftsmen and Technologies in the Corinthia: The Development of the Doric Order." In *Material Koinai in the Greek Early Iron Age and Archaic Period*, edited by S. Handberg and A. Gadolou, 221–244. Aarhus.

Scahill, D. 2023. "Ancient Greek Dining Spaces: The Rooms of the South Stoa at Corinth." In *Aspects of Ancient Greek Cult II: Sacred Architecture, Sacred Space, Sacred Objects*, edited by J. Tae Jensen and G. Hinge, 244–261. Leiden.

Schultz, P., B. Wickkiser, G. Hinge, C. Kanellopoulos, and J. Franklin. 2017. *The Thymele at Epidauros: Healing, Space, and Musical Performance in Late Classical Greece*. Fargo, ND.

Seaman, K. 2020. *Rhetoric and Innovation in Hellenistic Art*. Cambridge.

Steiner, A. 2002. "Private and Public: Links Between *Symposion* and *Syssition* in Fifth-Century Athens." *ClAnt* 21: 347–390.

Stewart, D.E. 2009. *οἱ περὶ τὸ ἱερόν. A Study of Sacredotal Housing at Ancient Greek Sanctuaries*. Ph.D. diss., Bryn Mawr College.

Tanner, A. 2020. "Three Hellenistic 'Naiskoi' in the Theatre Area at Aigeira: Small Buildings in the Context of an Urban Sanctuary." In *New Directions and Paradigms for the Study of Greek Architecture, Interdisciplinary Dialogues in the Field*, edited by P. Sapirstein and D. Scahill, 74–87. Leiden.

Tanner, A. 2022. "'Die Naiskoi' D und E im Theaterbereich von Aigeira." In *Forschungen im Bereich des Theaters von Aigeira 2011 bis 2018, Aigeira 3*, 183–202. Vienna.

Tanoulas, T. 1992a. "The Pre-Mnesiklean Cistern on the Athenian Acropolis." *AM* 107: 129–60.

Tanoulas, T. 1992b. "Structural Relations Between the Propylaea and the NW Building of the Athenian Acropolis." *AM* 107: 199–215.

Thompson, H.A. 1940. *The Tholos and its Predecessors*. Princeton.

Thompson, H.A. 1954. "Excavations in the Athenian Agora: 1953." *Hesperia* 23: 39–45.

Thompson, H.A., and R.E. Wycherley. 1972. *The Agora of Athens: The History, Shape and Uses of an Ancient City Center. Agora 14*. Princeton.

Tomlinson, R.A. 1969a. "Perachora: The Remains Outside the Two Sanctuaries." *BSA* 64: 155–258.

Tomlinson, R.A. 1969b. "Two Buildings in Sanctuaries of Asklepios." *JHS* 89: 106–117.

Tomlinson, R.A. 1983. *Epidauros*. Austin.

Tomlinson, R.A. 1990. "The Chronology of the Perachora *Hestiatorion* and its Significance." In *Sympotica: A Symposium on the Symposion*, edited by O. Murray, 95–101. Oxford.

Versakis, F. 1908. "Ἀρχιτεκτονικὰ μνημεῖα τοῦ ἐν Ἀθήναις Ἀσκληπιείου." *ArchEph*: 255–284.

Waldstein, C., H.S. Washington, E.L. Tilton, et al. 1902. *The Argive Heraeum 1*. Boston.

Welter, G. 1941. *Troizen und Kalaureia*. Berlin.

Werner, K.E. 1998. *Die Sammlungen antiker Mosaiken in den Vatikanischen Museen*. Vatican.

Williams, C.K. 1978. *Pre-Roman Cults in the Area of the Forum of Ancient Corinth*. Ph.D. diss., University of Pennsylvania.

Williams, C.K. 1980. "Corinth Excavations 1979." *Hesperia* 49: 107–134.

Wilson-Jones, M. 2000. "Doric Measure and Architectural Design 1: The Evidence of the Relief from Salamis." *AJA* 104: 73–93.

Wilson-Jones, M. 2001. "Doric Measure and Architectural Design 2: A Modular Reading of the Classical Temple." *AJA* 105: 675–713.

CHAPTER 9

The Divine *Symposion*: Logistics and Significance of Drinking Wine in Greek Sanctuaries

Floris van den Eijnde

1 Introduction

The logistics and social significance of drinking wine in Greek sanctuaries is an understudied and undertheorized subject. Reading the major textbooks and compendia of Greek religion might lead one to believe that wine was barely consumed, unless perhaps to wash away the sacrificial meat.[1] This relates to a source problem: if the worshippers drank wine, either with or after their meals, we would not know it because the literary sources by and large fail to mention it. Since wine was an important part of the Greek diet, however, it makes sense that it figured prominently among the necessary foodstuffs provided by a sanctuary.[2] In fact, one might argue that the lack of literary evidence is itself indicative that wine consumption was such an integrated element of the religious feast that it merited little comment by the authors of our texts. And indeed, archaeologists dealing with find assemblages from Greek sanctuaries are constantly reminded that drinking was a very central aspect of the ritual proceedings at cult sites throughout the Greek world: sanctuary deposits are often defined by a large quantity of drinking vessels—the *krater* most prominent among them—and include sets that are commonly associated with sympotic contexts.[3]

Given this abundant material evidence, it is striking that ritualized drinking in Greek sanctuaries is rarely considered as an activity that may perhaps have been worthy of ritualization in its own right, especially in light of the great cultural significance that was attached to wine in the Greek world.[4]

The ubiquity of drinking vessels in Archaic sanctuaries raises the question as to whether something akin to the domestic *symposion* took place in sanctuaries and, if so, whether it shared some of its cultural peculiarities, such as night-time drinking, playful competitiveness, drunkenness, and promiscuity. In *The Rise of the Aristocratic Banquet*, Marek Węcowski sketches the main characteristics of a *symposion*, which we may use as a template for sympotic drinking in sanctuaries.[5] First, the author notes a clear division between the *deipnon*, which takes place in the afternoon and early evening, and the *symposion*, which takes place after sunset. A long nocturnal drinking session could lead to excess, which resulted in the strict exclusion of the wives and daughters of the symposiasts, and in turn opened the door to relationships with courtesans and boys. The *symposion* involved intimate yet provocative and even competitive convivial discourse, with clear winners and losers, while simultaneously fostering group solidarity and a rigorously maintained equality between the symposiasts. The guiding mechanism of the *symposion* is the *epidexia* (*endexia*) ritual, which pertains not only to the *passing of the cup to the right*, but extends to the entire order of events, including the order of speech and gameplay. According to this reading, the circular passing of the drinking cup both emphasized and symbolized the egalitarian nature of the event. This is further developed in the spatial configuration of the *andrones*, with couches placed contiguously in a 'squared-circle' along the sides of the walls and a centrally placed krater from

---

1 The Wiley-Blackwell *Companion to Greek Religion* has in its index one reference to wine, which, upon consultation, does not refer directly to wine consumption in a religious setting (Ogden 2007, 305). Wine typically receives a cursory mention only as a prop within the context of other interests (generally limited to the Anthesteria, Dionysos, and libations): cf. Nilsson 1949; Burkert 1985; Bremmer 1994; Price 1999; Parker 2005; Larson 2007; Bremmer 2008; Mikalson 2009; Parker 2011; Eidinow and Kindt 2015; Larson 2016.
2 A rare exception is a passage in Xenophon's *Anabasis* (5.3.9), which describes how wine is provided for a sacred precinct of Artemis on the author's estate at Skillous near Olympia, where the Spartans had settled him during his exile. The passage offers an interesting view into the logistics of sanctuary provisioning, as the goddess is said to provide "barley meal and loaves of bread, wine and sweetmeats, and a portion of the sacrificial victims from the sacred herd as well as of the victims taken in the chase"—all the ingredients for a religious feast, provided for from the sanctuary's sacred land (trans. Brownson).
3 For analyses of pottery assemblages (including vessels used for votive and/or drinking purposes) in sanctuaries, see Stissi 2002,

231–268; Gimatzidis 2011; Risser 2015. For the social function of kraters, see especially Rotroff 1996. Cf. Węcowski 2012; Węcowski 2014, 39, 69, n. 175, 250, 301; Lynch 2018; van den Eijnde 2018b.
4 E.g., Lissarrague 1990; Papakonstantinou 2009; Pratt 2021.
5 Węcowski 2014, 19–124, esp. 117–124. Cf. Murray 2009.

which to draw wine.⁶ To François Lissarrague, the krater served as the ideological centerpiece of the gathering, "the focal point for the group; (...) the shared cup."⁷ Used in a practical sense to mix wine and water, the krater symbolizes at once the social 'mixing' of the group into a socially cohesive unity. Lavish decoration, of course, reinforced the symbolic meaning of kraters, which could serve as conversation pieces in their own right.⁸

Identifying sympotic activity in Greek sanctuaries is less straightforward than it might seem. Since the literary sources fail us on this account, we largely rely on the archaeological record. But how to differentiate between a cup used for drinking during the *deipnon* and one used in a sympotic context? Or between a dining hall and a room used to stage a drinking party? Two guiding principles derived from the sympotic *praxis* described above can help us navigate this problem: (1) the temporal separation between the *deipnon* (day) and the *symposion* (night); and (2) the functional differentiation between eating at the *deipnon* and drinking at the *symposion*. Finding material or textual expressions of these two distinctions, I believe, is essential if we hope to find evidence of sympotic behavior in Greek sanctuaries.

A short note on terminology is in place.⁹ I use *deipnon* here as a shorthand for the main (domestic or sacrificial) meal of the day, which took place in the afternoon.¹⁰ And while scholars often use *banquet* synonymously with *deipnon*, I use the term *banquet* to refer to the combination of *deipnon* and *symposion*, in coherence with both title and tenor of Węcowski's book. The *deipnon* was thus but one element of the banquet, which also included the *symposion*. The division between eating and drinking is essential to my argument. And since the *deipnon* took place during the day, I avoid the use of 'dinner' and 'dining,' which invoke eating at or after sunset. I similarly speak of banqueting halls—though some scholars prefer *hestiatoria*—rather than dining halls, both because of the daytime setting of the meal, but also because I hope to show that these rooms were also used for drinking rituals at night.

In domestic settings, the social significance of the *symposion* is much greater than that of the *deipnon*, and it is often understood to be one of the key institutions of the Classical Greek polis.¹¹ Conspicuous consumption in domestic settings centered around ritualized drinking at the *symposion* and came at the expense of conspicuous eating.¹² When it comes to the sacrificial banquet, on the other hand, it is invariably the meal that commands attention—both in the ancient sources and in modern scholarship—at the expense of notice given to drinking.¹³ If it is our objective to investigate the nature of ritualized, nocturnal drinking rites in sanctuaries, we must choose a proper terminology that fits the situation. Considering that scholarship has closely associated the *symposion* with (elite) domestic contexts, I propose to speak of *sympotic* aspects when referring to analogous behavior in sanctuaries. It is for this paper to establish—and for the reader to judge—to what degree drinking in sanctuaries conformed to domestic drinking or, to put it differently, whether *symposia* really were conducted in sanctuaries.

It is difficult to overemphasize the cultural significance of separation between conspicuous, ritualized eating and drinking in the context of the Archaic and Classical Greek world. I have previously argued that conspicuous meat consumption was removed from elite domestic contexts at the beginning of the Archaic period and anchored in sanctuaries in a deliberate attempt to defuse the complicated and uneven patron-client dynamics of meat-eating ceremonies in private houses.¹⁴ I also posited that the domestic *symposion* evolved as a replacement for conspicuous food consumption at home, catering to a growing egalitarian ethos among elites. My contribution to this volume investigates an overlooked aspect between the domestic *symposion* and the conspicuous consumption of food during sacrificial meals: the practice of *sympotic*

---

6 Cf. Lynch 2018, 235.
7 Lissarrague 1990, 23.
8 Barringer 2014, 163.
9 Cf. Goldstein 1978, 294–296.
10 The *deipnon* appears to have shifted to increasingly later times of the day. It denotes the midday meal in Homer, whereas Classical sources appear to indicate a moment later in the afternoon. Finally, the *deipnon* was taken in the evening from the late fourth century BCE onward, when it was integrated with the *symposion*; cf. Lynch 2018, who coins the term symposium-feast for it. See also Nielsen 1998, 103.

11 Murray 1983; Schmitt Pantel 1990.
12 Lynch 2018, 237; van den Eijnde 2018a; 2018b.
13 Schmitt Pantel 1990, 14–15. Interestingly, while the title of his book includes the word "banquet," Węcowski 2014 deals mainly with the domestic *symposion*; notably his 'banquets' mostly take place in sanctuaries where the distinction between eating and drinking is lost. Archaic and Classical literary sources, of course, include the lyricists and Plato's *Symposion*.
14 Van den Eijnde 2018b. Commensality is broadly understood to foster social inclusivity while at the same time engendering status differentiation. For the politics of commensality, cf. Dietler 2001. For a recent overview of Greek commensal politics, see van den Eijnde, Blok, and Strootman 2018. The ritualized consumption of wine, however, is articulated differently from eating and carries a distinct social significance; see Lynch 2018; van den Eijnde 2018a. For the egalitarian ethos of the *symposion*, see Murray 1983; 1990; Węcowski 2014.

drinking in Greek sanctuaries. Is there evidence that ritualized drinking, which is generally associated with the domestic *symposion*, also took place in sanctuaries? And if so, what does it tell us about the logistics and social significance of wine consumption in these contexts?

To find an answer to these questions, I will attempt to reconstruct the logistics of wine consumption in Greek sanctuaries from a largely archaeological point of view, drawing on textual sources where they are available. The material evidence discussed in this paper—first the ceramic, then the architectural—not only provides a glimpse into the logistics, but also into the social significance, of wine consumption within or in the vicinity of the Greek sanctuary and opens questions about elite access to sanctuaries beyond specific festival days.

2 Drinking Vessels in Greek Cultic Assemblages

Before we establish whether sympotic drinking can be identified in the pottery assemblages of Greek sanctuaries, we must assess the nature and prevalence of drink-related vessels in sanctuary deposits more generally. These deposits are generally characterized by a high percentage of (often decorated) drinking vessels. Drinking sets are found in cultic contexts from the Early Iron Age onward, clearly peak in the seventh and sixth century, and decline rapidly from the Classical period onward. Illustrating the importance of drinking in early sanctuaries is the fact that drinking wares often constitute the primary (if not only) evidence of cult activity.[15] In what is hitherto the only broad comparative survey of sanctuary deposits, vessels used specifically for drinking (*skyphoi*, *kotylai*, cups) comprise on average about one-third of sanctuary deposits, a figure that rises to about one-half when the larger shapes associated with drinking (*oinochoai*, jugs, amphorae, kraters) are added.[16] These shapes are much more likely to be figurative or simply decorated when compared to domestic deposits.[17] But even the ornate, figurative drinking shapes are difficult to associate directly with sympotic drinking, as they may have been used for other purposes, such as libations, votive offerings, drinking during the sacrificial meal, or even eating.[18]

To help the conceptualization of the various uses of drinking wares, scholars tend to distinguish between 'ritual' and 'votive' vessels.[19] Ritual vessels would have been used repeatedly from one occasion to the next, while votive vessels would have been purchased with the specific intent of leaving it behind as a token of respect for the god. In principle, any or all shapes could end up in either category. High wear and fragmentary preservation could point to ritual (i.e., repeated) use, while the better-preserved objects seem to point to votive use. It is also thought that 'sets' of multiple drinking vessels with matching shapes or decoration, could be suggestive of votive use, as they appear to have been bought for a single occasion to be dedicated after use at the festival. The ritual vessels, on the other hand, would be replaced piecemeal whenever one broke and are therefore considered less prone to appear as sets in the assemblages. On the whole, votive vessels presumably make up the majority of the preserved fragments in sanctuaries.[20]

Miniature vessels are an interesting category as they are too small to eat or drink from but could nevertheless contain small quantities of food or drink to be set up as token offerings to the gods. They could be used for pouring libations or for wine offerings. The chief function of miniatures, however, seems to have been votary, perhaps commemorating a previous moment of libating and drinking.[21] Some of the first attested miniature vessels were themselves probably first used for libations, as in the case of the Late Geometric miniature *hydriai* found at the Aire Sacrificielle at Eretria, where the small size as well as the standardized, home-made appearance of the vessels is indicative of one-time use.[22] Other vessels used for pouring libations, such as the early *louteria* or the *phialai* depicted in offering scenes were probably more

---

15 This is, for instance, the case with deposits found in remote places such as the Early Iron Age peak sanctuaries mentioned below.
16 Stissi 2002, 248. This is consistent with recent findings from the West complex in the sanctuary of Apollo on Aigina, where "the proportion of shapes associated with the consumption of beverages and food is extraordinary (*sic*) high: e.g. various kinds of drinking bowls, craters, and other containers for serving wine," according to Klebinder-Gauss (2019, 120). Stissi interestingly observes that some of the smaller cult sites in his sample have proportions closer to domestic contexts.
17 Stissi (2002, 246–247) compares the percentage of figurative sherds in sanctuaries (15–20 %) to that in domestic contexts (1–5 %) and argues that this is probably a more or less plausible ratio, even allowing for some overcount of figurative pottery.
18 Cf. Morgan 1990, 28–29.
19 Stissi 2002, 240. Cf. Risser 2015.
20 Stissi 2002, 241.
21 Barfoed 2015, 15; Klebinder-Gauss 2019, 122. Cf. Ekroth 2003b for miniatures as votive offerings.
22 Huber 2003, 53–58, 116–120, pls. 79–80.

likely used repeatedly.[23] At the north Greek sanctuary of Sane, on the other hand, medium-sized East Greek jugs in the Wild Goat Style appear to have been favored for libations, their foreign origin perhaps setting them apart for repeated ritual use.[24] In both instances, the unusually high number of these vessels seems to distinguish them from 'ordinary' drinking vessels.

The distinction between 'ritual' and 'votive' use is helpful only to a degree, however, as it fails to capture the manifold uses of drinking vessels in sanctuaries. Exactly how fluid the various ritual uses of these vessels could be is illustrated by the fact that libation or drinking vessels were often set up as votives *post factum*, immediately after their initial use. Common types (i.e., cups, bowls, *kotylai*, *skyphoi*, and *oinochoai*—surprisingly often undecorated) could first be used for drinking, and then dedicated as votive offerings. In some archaeological contexts, vessels appear to have been deliberately broken after they were used for drinking—a kind of consecration in its own right.[25]

Cult regulations record the various ritual uses of wine consumption in sanctuaries. Naturally, wine could be used to pour libations.[26] Wine was certainly consumed, but unfortunately the texts are unclear as to whether this happened during the sacrificial meal, or in a sympotic event following the meal.[27] And wine was frequently part of the perquisites awarded to cult officials after the sacrifice.[28] Wine offerings could also be placed near the altar or on a *trapeza* for a while before consumption.[29] The implication here seems to be that the offerings would be consumed by cult officials and perhaps other participants in the sacrificial banquet. It has been argued that in some instances the wine may have been left to evaporate. The analogy with the holocaust is evident in that neither the meat nor the liquid offering was meant for human consumption.[30] Like the vessels-as-votives, these offerings do not preclude drinking but rather seem to accentuate it. This is borne out by the measures cited in the sacrificial regulations which vary from two *kotylai* (c.0.5 liter) to a *metretes* (c.40 liters) of wine.[31] The larger measures especially seem to suggest that the wine was ultimately meant to be drunk, rather than reserved for libation or evaporation.[32] The smaller measures, in some instances, could represent contributions to a communal krater—the quintessential sympotic vessel—from which the cult community drank.[33] Again, an analogy with meat consumption presents itself. The meat of the sacrificial animal could sometimes be complemented by meat from other animals, either killed in the sanctuary or at home, but not sacrificed in the same sense; the combined meat was subsequently boiled together to eradicate the difference.[34] In either case, a 'sacrificial' portion was diluted with elements of a different extraction, sacralizing the non-sacrificial elements in the process for consumption at the sacred banquet.

Compounding the problem of assigning a clear function to sanctuary pottery is the difficulty of distinguishing between eating and drinking. While vessels connected with cooking or serving food are generally outnumbered by drinking shapes, some assemblages contain a significant amount of cooking ware.[35] The absence of specialized

---

23 Early Attic *louteria*: Callipolitis-Feytmans 1965; *phialai*: van Straten 1995, figs. 136–140, 148.
24 Gimatzidis 2011, 20.
25 Wells, Penttinen, and Billot (2003, 77) state that fragmentarily preserved miniature vessels of fourth-century date found in a banqueting room within the sanctuary of Poseidon in Kalaureia appear to have been deliberately broken and left on the floor. If indeed they were meant for one-time use, this may help to explain why relatively many of the fragments are undecorated.
26 For an overview of literature on libation, see Zerhoch 2020, n. 1.
27 Consumption of wine in sacrificial regulations is clearly indicated by verbs such as ἀναλίσκειν (CGRN 204, ll. 5–8), γεύεσθαι (CGRN 225, B, ll. 47–48), καταχρεῖσθαι (CGRN 202, ll. 57–59), κιρνᾶν (CGRN 187, ll. 26–27; 201, ll. 11–12), χρητηρίζειν (CGRN 98, A, ll. 7–8, 11; B, ll. 13, 19–20, 21; 201, ll. 24–25), πίνειν (CGRN 152, ll. 140–141; 201, ll. 16–17; 225, A, l. 51), or προσαιρεῖσθαι (CGRN 201, ll. 8–9).
28 With verbs as γίγνομαι (+ dat.; CGRN 201, ll. 37–39), διδόναι (CGRN 6, A, ll. 7–8; 156, ll. 13–15), ἐξαιρεῖσθαι (CGRN 157, l. 35), λαμβάνειν (CGRN 157, l. 26), or as ἱερ(ε)ώσυνα (CGRN 56 II, ll. 46–49; 57, ll. 23–26; 74, ll. 4–8).
29 The sacrifice is indicated by the verbs ἀνατίθημι (CGRN 34, ll. 24–28; 139, l. 10), διδόναι (CGRN 6, A, l. 9; 86, B, ll. 11–15; D, l. 25), θύειν (CGRN 34, ll. 6–7, 27–28; 60, ll. 8–13; 86, D, l. 18), παρίστημι (CGRN 34, ll. 6–7, 27–28; 60, ll. 8–13; 86, D, l. 18), (προσ-)φερεῖν (CGRN 35, ll. 8–10; 51, l. 2; 225, A, ll. 24, 32–33, 37; B, 6, 12, 16, 32–33, 38, 47, 55–56, 58, 67, 70–71). In CGRN 6, A, l. 9 wine is set up ἐπὶ βωμὸν (onto the altar).
30 The practice of leaving wine in (usually open) containers is conjectured for some of the votive vessels in excavated sacred deposits. Cf. Stissi (2002, 241–242) helpfully cites the residual evidence left by wine and other organic liquids and foodstuffs, yet objects to the perceived stench resulting from putrefaction, a sentiment that may reflect modern sensibilities. In any case, one wonders how great of a problem this would have been in the case of wine.
31 E.g., CGRN 225, A, l. 24; CGRN 60, l. 13.
32 As would have been the case with the food that is often dedicated on special *trapeza* near the altar. See Ekroth 2011.
33 E.g., CGRN 225, A, l. 37; B, ll. 6, 32–33, 38, 67, 70–71.
34 Ekroth 2007; 2008.
35 Stissi 2002, 249, but here a severe undercount may be at play, as is suggested by the West complex in the sanctuary of Apollo on Aigina, which was clearly a focus of drinking and eating and where about 50% of the pottery consisted of household and cooking wares and included portable hearths; see Klebinder-Gauss 2019, esp. 120–122. Vessels for serving food include bowls, saltcellars, and small containers for oil.

TABLE 9.1 Potential uses of drinking-related vessels (cups, bowls, *kotylai*, *skyphoi* and *oinochoai*, etc.) in sanctuaries

Stage 1	Libation (and/or)	Dedication at the altar, e.g., on a *trapeza*
Stage 2	Drinking during sacrificial meal (and/or)	Drinking after the meal (sympotic)
Stage 3	Storing for further future use (or)	Setting vessel up as votive (including wine?) or deliberate breaking of the vessel

food plates—especially in the early assemblages—further indicates that drinking vessels could double as food containers, blurring the distinction between eating and drinking even further.[36]

We may thus distinguish three stages at which a drinking vessel might in theory have been used: first for libations and/or wine-dedication (stage 1), then for drinking, either during or after the sacrificial meal (stage 2), and finally, they could be left behind, broken or whole, empty or full, as gifts to the gods, signifying the fulfillment of their purpose (stage 3; Table 9.1).

A word of caution is needed here. Even if votive wares seem to dominate the assemblages, that does not necessarily mean that dedicating one's cup or bowl was standard practice. After all, the repeated use of so-called 'ritual' vessels also meant that this category had much less chance of ending up in our record than the occasional votive pot. And in theory at least, a 'ritual' vessel might at some point be dedicated.

The ornate drinking wares that define so many Early Iron Age and Archaic sanctuaries rapidly decrease from the late Archaic period onwards.[37] As we will see, there is no reason to assume that drinking in sanctuaries became any less common during this period. The underlying causes behind the decreasing numbers of drinking vessels are presumably manifold but must at a minimum involve changing trends in votive practices. In other words, rather than the practice of drinking in sanctuaries coming to an end, the habit of dedicating drink-related terracotta vessels as votive gifts seems largely to have gone out of fashion in the Classical and Hellenistic periods. To the extent that terracotta vessels were replaced by metal ones, the dedicating of the latter may well have increased.[38] It seems inconceivable however that the much more expensive metal vessels completely replaced ceramic ones as votives. Underscoring the fact that votive dedications are subject to trends is the simultaneous increase of smaller gifts, such as terracotta figurines, lamps, and coins, which would have cost roughly the same amount as a drinking vessel.[39] Most of the drinking vessels in Early Iron Age and Archaic sanctuaries should therefore be understood as dedications, representing single-use specimens that were either deliberately broken or dedicated somewhere inside the *temenos*. This dedicatory aspect of the pottery in no way denies the use of drinking-related pots for libating and drinking, and it seems likely that many vessels served a multiplicity of purposes (Table 9.1) before ending up in the assemblages.

The dedicatory aspect of many vessels inadvertently brings us closer to answering the question of whether sympotic drinking took place in Greek sanctuaries. I submit that the very fact that drinking vessels were often set up as votives should be understood as a way of commemorating the act of sympotic drinking itself—the moment when drinking was the main focus—rather than the drinking that took place during the sacrificial meal, which revolved around the consumption of sacrificial meat.[40] The latter could be commemorated through the dedication of spits, bones, ashes, or through iconographic references, including animal figurines.[41] The dedication of a drinking cup, on the other hand, celebrates the drinking of wine *per se* and clearly hints at a sympotic gathering quite apart from the sacrificial banquet. This may be supported by the fact that decorated pottery, which was more likely to be used in sympotic settings, is overrepresented in sanctuaries when compared with domestic contexts.[42] A closer look at the sympotic shape *par excellence*, the krater, will further illuminate this point.

---

36 Morgan 1999, 322–323. The krater-*skyphoi* discussed below may in particular have served such a dual purpose.
37 See Stissi 2002, 231–268, esp. 247–248.
38 Cf. Stissi 2002, 256.
39 Stissi (2002, 252–268) discusses changes in dedicatory fashion, noting the surge in votive coins, lamps and figurines during the Classical and Hellenistic period and evaluating the evidence for metal vessels. Referencing Aleshire 1992, he comments: "the unique, detailed epigraphic records of the many, mainly small silver gifts to the Athenian Asklepieion in the 3rd century indicate that most of them would fall in the same price range as a good large pot" (256, n. 1196).
40 Lynch 2018; van den Eijnde 2018b.
41 For the special treatment of bones and ashes, cf. Ekroth 2017.
42 Stissi 2002, 246.

3 Kraters as Votives in Early Greek Sanctuaries

Large, krater-like vessels used for mixing wine with water were part of the ceramic repertoire from the Late Helladic period onward.[43] Susan Sherratt has attributed the 'invention' of the shape to the Mycenaean palaces where many fragments were found.[44] They remained connected with lavish, ruler-centered feasting through much of the Early Iron Age, most famously exemplified by the monumental Late Protogeometric krater found above the burials inside the Toumba building at Lefkandi.[45] These large vessels often measure around 0.50 m in diameter, and it seems natural to assume that they were predominantly used in the context of patron-client feasting.

The kraters that are reported among the drinking shapes in the earliest sanctuary deposits are significantly smaller in size than the regular-sized kraters found in domestic contexts. The smaller shape found in sanctuary deposits dating to the LH-EIA transition has a rim diameter of little more than 15 cm yet is often called 'krater.' Apart from its slightly larger size, the shape itself cannot easily be distinguished from the *skyphos* and is therefore probably better called krater-*skyphos*.[46] At Kalapodi, such vessels date from the final stages of the Bronze Age onward and are accompanied by large numbers of cups and (actual) *skyphoi*, as well as jugs, amphorae, and cooking ware.[47] At Isthmia, krater types of 15–20 cm in diameter are reported from the Late Helladic period to the end of the eighth century BCE.[48] From the Early Iron Age 'Schwarze Schicht' at Olympia, the black layer found between the Pelopion and the Heraion, hail 12 similar krater-*skyphos* fragments in conjunction with the remaining drinking shapes—jugs, cups and *skyphoi*.[49] In addition, two giant, Submycenaean *kylikes* were found, which have been assigned a 'ritual' function on account of their impractical dimensions (0.22–0.24 m).[50] It is not entirely clear if the krater-*skyphos* was used for drinking or for mixing wine, but it seems plausible that these functions had not yet been fully separated at this time. Neither has it been fully established whether the krater-*skyphos* served one individual for an entire session or a group of people for a single round as it was passed around. The Homeric evidence is ambiguous and may itself reflect changing habits.[51] Antonis Kotsonas, however, has argued that an analogous—but slightly later—case of kraters being replaced by medium-sized cups on Crete, must be attributed to individuals tending to their own cups and mixing the wine according to their own tastes.[52] Whatever the case, it is clear that a large, immobile, and centrally placed mixing bowl from which the cup could be filled before circulating was not part of the drinking ritual at Greek sanctuaries before the eighth century, when the first large *symposion*-style kraters made their entry at religious feasts.

The transition from krater-*skyphos* to krater can be witnessed in a few relatively well-preserved sanctuary assemblages from Attika, that of Zeus on Mt. Hymettos and on Mt. Parnes, as well as the sanctuary of Artemis at

---

43 Rotroff (1996, 9) traces the shape back to the Middle Bronze Age at least or "the early years of the 2nd millennium BC." Sherratt (2004, 326) dates the introduction of the krater to LH IIIA1 or LH IIB at the earliest. Late Bronze Age kraters were often lavishly decorated and include the well-known Warrior Krater (National Museum Π 1426) of the early 12th century BCE. Fragments dating to the LH IIIC period have been found in the citadels of Mycenae, Tiryns, and Athens, as well as at Lefkandi; see Lemos 2002, 48, n. 82.
44 Sherratt 2004, 326.
45 Catling and Lemos 1990, 25–26, no. 327, cf. Lemos 2002, 48–53, esp. 52. Many more Protogeometric kraters were found in the fill on top of the building, making it the most significant deposit for this shape in this period; see Lemos 2002, 48.
46 Lemos (2002, 46–48) prefers the term krater-bowl; Langdon (1976, nos. 192–194), giant *skyphoid* krater; Palaiokrassa (2017), *krateriskos*. The krater-*skyphos* is not confined to sacred contexts and is often found in settlement deposits; see Lemos 2002, 47.
47 Jacob-Felsch 1996, esp. 30–40 (LH IIIC); Nitsche 1987 (Protogeometric and Subprotogeometric).
48 Morgan 1999, nos. 136–137 (LH IIIB), with examples cited down to Early Protocorinthian (nos. 456–459).
49 Kyrieleis, Eder, and Benecke 2006, nos. 292–303. The drinking vessels at Olympia were not secondarily burned, which would seem to speak against ritual destruction during the sacrificial ritual and in favor of them having been used as part of the sacrificial meal; see Kyrieleis, Eder, and Benecke 2006, 204. Presumably they were subsequently dedicated to the god.
50 Eder 2001; Kyrieleis, Eder, and Benecke 2006, nos. 5–6.
51 There are a few Homeric passages pointing to drinking *epidexia* (or *endexia*), a single cup passed around among the participants: *Il.* 1.595–604; *Od.* 21.141–142; in *Od.* 17.365–368, Odysseus approaches the suitors in beggars' guise from left to right; in *Od.* 3.51–53 a cup is shared in order to pray, one after another, but this may be a specific case. For a discussion of these passages see Węcowski 2002, 354–355; Sherratt 2004, 306, 310, 322; Kotsonas 2011, 948; Węcowski 2014, 221–225. The standard, recurring passage, however, has youths serving wine directly into the cups (plural) of participants in the feast, *Il.* 1.470–471; 9.176; *Od.* 3.338–342; 21.271–3. If anything, the formulaic verses seem to indicate a deeper, 'historic' stratum in the poems and perhaps the *epidexia* passages are more reflective of 'current' practice at the time of composition, cf. also the "backstage symposium" in Węcowski 2014, 221–224.
52 Kotsonas (2011, 948) argues that the diminishing size of the krater in Crete in favor of an increase in size of the coated cup c.800 BCE should be regarded as a move toward greater flexibility in terms of one's own mixing taste. For a similar consideration of very large *kantharoi* and *kotylai*, see Ekroth 2023, 52.

FIGURE 9.1 Athens, Agora H 487, krater-*skyphos* from the sanctuary of Zeus on Mt. Hymettos, Attika
PHOTO: CRAIG MAUZY, AMERICAN SCHOOL OF CLASSICAL STUDIES AT ATHENS, AGORA EXCAVATIONS
© HELLENIC MINISTRY OF CULTURE / ORGANIZATION OF CULTURAL RESOURCES DEVELOPMENT (H.O.C.RE.D.)

Mounychia, marking the southeastern, northern, and western (coastal) borders of the Athenian plain. Ritual activity at these three sites flourished in the Late Protogeometric period, and the pottery consists of a repertoire of *skyphoi*, cups, *oinochoai*, *kantharoi*, and krater-*skyphoi*.[53] Like the intermediate-sized kraters from Kalapodi, Isthmia, and Olympia, these krater-*skyphoi* (Fig. 9.1) have a diameter of c.15–30 cm: too small for a decent *symposion*-style krater, but too large to comfortably be called a *skyphos*.[54] Significantly, the krater-bowls disappear after the Protogeometric Period in favor of the smaller, 'regular' *skyphoi* (max. diam. 15 cm) from the Early Geometric, and the larger, pedestalled kraters (diam. 30–50 cm) from the Middle Geometric II period, suggesting a gradually deepening, functional divide between krater and *skyphos*.[55] The potential introduction of more fully developed sympotic drinking rituals in Greek sanctuaries thus has a *terminus post quem* of c.800.

Large, *symposion*-size kraters (with an average diameter of roughly 50 cm) had become a standard feature in Greek sanctuary deposits by the Late Geometric period and persisted in cultic assemblages at sanctuaries throughout the Archaic period. Monumental kraters were dedicated, for instance, from the late eighth century on at the Agamemnoneion near Mycenae.[56] We find kraters in Athens among the Akropolis vases throughout the Geometric and Archaic periods.[57] At Perachora, numerous examples date from the Late Geometric to Late Corinthian periods.[58] From the Late Geometric period also hail some fragments of monumental mixing bowls, found at the sanctuary of Apollo Daphnephoros at Eretria and belonging to a type not commonly encountered in domestic deposits.[59] A monumental Late Geometric krater from Eretria, placed on a raised platform in the

---

53 Langdon 1976 (Hymettos); Palaiokrassa and Vivliodetis 2015 (Parnes and Mounychia). A Submycenaean krater-*skyphos* at Hymettos is called a "deep bowl" by Langdon (1976, no. 189), but its upturned handles and conical foot clearly anticipate the LPG examples. Drinking shapes dating as early as LHI include a krater fragment, several bowls, and drinking vessels (Langdon 1976, nos. 177–188).

54 Lemos (2002, 46) characterizes the krater-*skyphos* as "midway between a skyphos and a crater with a lip diameter of 20–30 cm".

55 Mounychia: Palaiokrassa and Vivliodetis 2015, 156–157, nos. 11–13. Cf. Węcowski 2014, 291–292, n. 126; 2017 on MG vases in Samos.

56 Cook 1953, 34–40.

57 Graef and Langlotz 1925, 23 (Dipylon), nos. 611–624 (black-figure).

58 Payne and Dunbabin 1962, nos. 1275–1292 (Protocorinthian), 2240–2266 (Corinthian).

59 Gisler, 1983; 1995; Verdan, Kenzelmann Pfyffer, and Léderrey 2008, 91–95; 2013.

apse of a building (Ed 50) oriented towards the altar of the temple of Apollo, presents us with a tantalizing glimpse of the spatial entanglement of wine and food consumption within the wider sacred precinct.[60] Fifty-six Archaic and Classical kraters were retrieved from the sanctuary of Demeter and Kore at Corinth.[61] Drinking in these places figures not just prominently, but on a seemingly equal footing with eating.

I propose that the transformation of the krater-bowl to the divergent forms of krater and *skyphos*—as well as the fact that many full-size kraters appear to have been dedicated—signals the establishment of a sympotic mode of drinking in Greek sanctuaries. The replacement of the smaller krater-bowl by the larger krater (and *skyphos*) marks a new stage in the development of feasting practices in sanctuaries, where drinking from one's own cup was replaced by drinking from a communal cup filled from the krater, emphasizing the communality of wine consumption.[62] This represents a first step towards the development of a material 'language' that belongs to the broader sympotic discourse defined by Marek Węcowski and others. Based on drinking sets found in Middle Geometric graves, Węcowski traces the emergence of the *symposion* back to the MG II period, or to the beginning of the eighth century, which accords with the appearance of the large, pedestalled krater in Greek sanctuaries.[63] The Early Geometric disappearance of the krater-bowls, however, suggests that attitudes to drinking had been changing in Greek sanctuaries for several generations before then.

The number of large kraters diminishes in sanctuary deposits from the Late Archaic period onwards, following the downward trend of dedicating drinking vessels discussed above. And as was the case with the drinking vessels, the ubiquity of kraters in Archaic Greek sanctuary deposits must be the result of having been dedicated to the gods after use, a practice that gradually lost traction during the Classical and Hellenistic periods. It is unclear if these kraters were routinely left behind as votives after use during a single festival, or whether it was a much more infrequent, even *ad hoc* phenomenon for a krater to be dedicated after use. In any case, the krater dedications must be understood as celebrations of sympotic behavior referencing the drinking, not the eating part of the religious feast.

4 Lamps and Nocturnal Drinking

Greek banqueting etiquette prescribed that the *symposion* began around sunset, and in some cases, could continue as late as daybreak. This meant that artificial light was an absolute necessity. There would have been several possibilities to illuminate sympotic nighttime gatherings. Braziers and fireplaces are commonplace, both in deposits and in epigraphical sources.[64] They provided a suitable source of light (and warmth) but also could be used as cooking devices. Lamps, however, have no function other than illumination and were omnipresent during sympotic gatherings. Alkaios' narrator impatiently encourages his friends to begin drinking early: "Let's drink! Why are we waiting for the lamps? Only an inch of daylight's left."[65] This passage neatly illustrates how nightfall provides the impetus for the *symposion*—as well as the limit for the late afternoon meal, the *deipnon*. "Waiting for the lamps" is here used to announce the *symposion*, showing how crucial these objects were for an event strictly taking place after sunset.

Lamps are also mentioned in sacrificial regulations. A dossier of the familial cult of Diomedon mentions the consecration to Herakles of two lamps (λυχνίας), two bronze lamps with seven flames, a square brazier (ἐσχάραν), as well as a krater, a table, and other items.[66] These offerings were presumably intended for a *theoxenia* ceremony that included night-time drinking, as is indicated by the lamps, brazier, and krater. The sacrificial regulation for the Goddess at Marmarini near Larissa, moreover, specifies that oil is to be supplied for lamps in combination with offerings of wine at the altar, both of which suggest that nocturnal drinking rites were part of the larger sacrificial banqueting ceremony.[67]

---

60 Verdan 2001, 86, pl. 28.2; see also Verdan, Kenzelmann Pfyffer, and Léderrey 2008, pl. 241; Verdan 2013, no. 355, pl. 96.
61 Pemberton, Slane, and Williams 1989, esp. 12–14; Bookides and Stroud 1997, esp. 402. Cf. Bookides et al. 1999, 14
62 Rotroff 1996; Lynch 2018.
63 Węcowski 2014, 271–294; 2017.
64 See Lynch 2011, 41; Klebinder-Gauss 2019, 120, 122. For *escharai* in sacrificial regulations, see *CGRN* 57, l. 33; 96, l. 122. Other illuminating devices, such as torches, are not mentioned in the texts and naturally do not show up in the archaeological record.
65 Alk. frag. 346 (trans. Miller, 48) = Ath. 11.481. Also consider Xen. *Symp.* 5.2 (for a lamp to shine on Sokrates during the *symposion*); Ath. 11.474d ("the lamp, which is suspended from the ceiling, with wide-spreading jets of flame), 15.699d–701b (fragments of other authors who mention lamps [λύχνοι] in the context returning from the *symposion* in the dark); Plut. *Quaest. conv.* 716 d–e (a *symposion* without philosophy is worse than one without a lamp/light); Pollux 6.103 (on lamps in general). See also Węcowski 2014, 31.
66 *IG* XII.4 348, l. 120 = *CGRN* 96, l. 120.
67 *CGRN* 225, B, l. 12 the word for lamp (λύχνον) appearing 6 times, in each case with a measure of oil (either one or one half of a *kotylon*); cf. Bouchon and Decourt 2017.

Lamps have been found in abundance in cultic assemblages, often in conjunction with drinking vessels, throughout the Greek world.[68] It is highly likely that the lamps that ended up in the excavation records were consecrated, like the lamps in the Diomedon inscription. As was the case with the ceramic evidence discussed above, the ritual aspect referenced by the dedication must have been a night-time event, such as the sympotic stage that followed the sacrificial meal. Interestingly, it has been observed that lamps gained in popularity in sanctuary deposits from the late Archaic period onward, notably around the same time that drinking vessels appear to decline, which may suggest that lamps replaced drinking vessels as votives to some degree.[69] This changing trend in votive dedications nevertheless supports the continuing frequency of sympotic drinking rites.

5 Sympotic Drinking in Sanctuary Banqueting Halls

Square, *andron*-type rooms with offset doorways are a familiar feature in Greek sanctuaries from as early as the seventh century. Scholars have generally assumed that these rooms were used for the consumption of the sacrificial meal.[70] However, the function of these rooms was no doubt more multifunctional than has commonly been acknowledged. There can be no doubt that these uses included sympotic drinking. Like the domestic *andrones*, the design of these rooms was eminently suitable for the requirements of sympotic drinking, including an intimate circularity and shelter from the nighttime cold.[71] The square layout, with off-center entrance to accommodate several *klinai* placed along each of the walls, plus one *kline*-width of a bed placed alongside the next wall, adheres to the strict requirements of the *epidexia* principle, which is a key element of sympotic culture. Like the domestic examples, the *klinai* in sanctuaries could be built-in—in which case they were presumably upholstered with blankets and pillows—but mostly they seem to have been portable units.[72] In some cases, stone supports protruded from the *toichobate* to support wooden planks with mattresses, while others were fixed to it or to the floor. The floor itself could be slightly raised along the walls where the couches were to be placed.[73] Sparing one bed for the entrance, the typical layout of the sanctuary *andrones* has either seven (*heptaklinai*) or eleven (*endekaklinai*) couches, the same as in domestic contexts, although more could occur.

This rigidly imposed 'square circle' of *klinai* in the *andrones* of many sanctuaries invoked the sense of equality of the domestic *symposion* as outlined above. While these rooms were suitable for eating as well as drinking, their intimate circularity suggests that the principal motivating idea behind the choice of this particular design was to cater to sympotic gatherings, where the passing of the cup (*epidexia*) was the norm, and circularity was required. As we have seen, the presence of lamps especially serves as a reliable indicator of sympotic drinking in these rooms because of the implication of nocturnal drinking. Of course, once in place, it would be natural to eat inside them as well, and it seems *a priori* likely that the two elements of the banquet, meal and *symposion*, took place in the same (temporary or permanent) architectural environment, and that traces of meat and wine consumption would be mixed together within the same assemblage.[74] More than the *deipnon*, however, which took place during the day, their extension into night-time sympotic gatherings would have required protection from the cold and provided the kind of intimacy that was especially suitable for drinking.

An interesting parallel may be found in the public 'dining' places inside South Stoa I in the Athenian Agora (Fig. 9.2). Ann Steiner has shown conclusively that these rooms were used for eating, as well as sympotic drinking: the drinking rituals conducted by Athenian magistrates in these public spaces give a glimpse of what might be expected at elite *symposia* in private houses: "pederastic flirting" and "sexual games with *hetairai*."[75] While Steiner

---

68   Lamps occur in assemblages from the Archaic period on, but do not become common as votive objects themselves until the fifth century; see Stissi 2002, 249, 256, n. 1204. See also Węcowski 2014, n. 156.
69   Stissi 2002, 256.
70   E.g., Leypold 2008, 12–14 (with references) discusses the variegated nomenclature of these buildings (e.g., ἑστιατόριον, λέσχη, καταγώγειον, οἶκος) but prefers *Bankettgebäude*, for its reference to the sacrificial meal.
71   For the spatial arrangement of sympotic space, see Bergquist 1990; Bookidis and Stroud 1997, 393–402; Lynch 2007, 243; Leypold 2008, 6–10; Murray 2009, 511–512; Węcowski 2014, 30–33. The domestic *andrones* also must have been multifunctional, serving both the eating and drinking element of the banquet, and the meat consumed there could be ritual as well, which further limits the distinction between 'domestic' and 'sacred' *andrones*. Cf. Jameson 1998, 145–146; Ekroth 2007.
72   As in the sanctuaries in Corinth (Demeter and Kore), Isthmia (Poseidon), Kommos, Perachora (Hera), and Thebes (Kabeirion). Cf. Leypold 2008, 143–147.
73   Leypold 2008, 146–152.
74   Węcowski 2014, 171. This seems to be confirmed by many of the assemblages discussed above.
75   Steiner 2002, 373. See also Scahill in this volume.

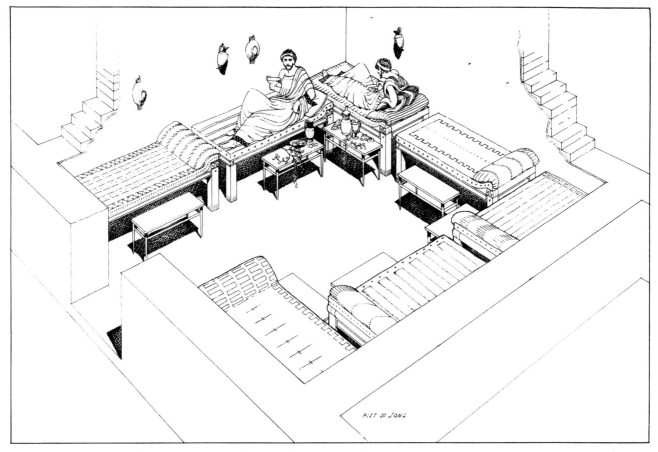

FIGURE 9.2   Athens, Agora, South Stoa I, reconstruction of dining room by Piet de Jong
COURTESY AMERICAN SCHOOL OF CLASSICAL STUDIES AT ATHENS

connects these rooms with the everyday meals of the city's political elites, it is attractive to think that these same elites banqueted there in the context of major state festivals, as well.

Most large sanctuaries possessed *andron*-type rooms, and so did several smaller ones.[76] In many other cases, however, dedicated architectural spaces are lacking, either due to conservation issues or simply because such accommodations never existed. It has, moreover, been pointed out that an architecturally distinct *andron* was not a necessity to host a *symposion*; the participants could just recline on pillows in the house's courtyard, and this could also be the case in Greek sanctuaries.[77] In many sanctuaries, drinking, like eating, was either done in temporary tent-like constructions or out in the open, without formal stone architecture.[78] This was probably the case in small sanctuaries without the financial means for elaborate architecture, but it could also be a function of a huge but infrequent confluence of humanity, such as in Olympia. Of the latter, Pindar notes how Herakles "fenced in the Altis and set it apart in the open and made the surrounding plain a resting place for banqueting."[79] This refers to the so-called *Festwiese* (fairground) where tents and semi-permanent structures housed pilgrims and catered to their needs.[80] Interestingly, a clear separation between the sacred Altis (the *temenos* proper) and the fairground—located to the (north)west, south, and southwest—is conceived of as part of the primordial spatial arrangement of the sanctuary. Excavations have provided evidence for the functional use of this fairground in the form of drinking cups, iron utensils for cooking and butchering, animal bones, and extensive evidence of fire.[81]

---

76   Goldstein 1978; Leypold 2008.
77   Lynch 2007, 243. In some instances, an elongated space was used (e.g., Megara, Thasos, Troizen, Zoster; cf. Leypold 2008). If more irregular spaces (especially without an off-center door) were used, they are potentially more difficult to identify.
78   Węcowski 2014, 174 (with literature). Cf. Goldstein 1978, 8–100; see also Scahill in this volume.
79   Pind. *Ol.* 10.46–48 (translation modified from Race).
80   See also the contributions by Chandezon and Ekroth in this volume.
81   Goldstein 1978, 16–22; Kyrieleis 1990, 180; Sinn 2002, 71–72; Barringer 2021, 52–53.

The very existence of the banqueting halls reflects a conscious choice by a select group of people to eat *and* drink separately from the rest of the cult community. This is an essential element of elite image making. The *klinai* in particular reflect an "ostentatious luxury and sumptuousness laden with almost 'kingly' Oriental overtones."[82] This point deserves emphasis since the sacrificial banquet is often thought to be an egalitarian affair, a notion that is derived from the idea that the sacrificial meat is equally shared between the cult participants.[83] Likewise, the rules of the *symposion* are supposed to create equality between the members of a sympotic group.[84] But the egalitarian ideal of these two civic institutions only goes so far. While the exclusivity of the domestic *symposion* is to a degree concealed within the privacy of the *oikos*, banqueting in sanctuaries strongly defines class and status within a wider societal context. The secret intimacy of these special-purpose buildings would have contrasted markedly with the ostensible inclusivity of the sanctuaries in which they were built, thus emphasizing the exclusivity of these banquets, which is matched by the practice of giving choice portions of meat to certain participants—no doubt often the same individuals—to mark their particular status. The banqueting rooms signify a desire to create an exclusive atmosphere for a select group of peers—priests, cult officials, and other members of the elite—while the common people feasted in the open air.[85] The banqueting halls paradoxically created equality among these elites while establishing a hierarchical ordering of the wider cult community.[86] Thus, to call the sacrificial banquet 'egalitarian' is to refer to the intimate, sympotic atmosphere of the banqueting halls, but it ignores the social stratification implied by their very existence.

6   Banqueting and the Spatial Organization of Sanctuaries

Turning to the broader spatial setting of banqueting, we find that provisions for eating and drinking were nearly always located at the margins of the *temenos*, and this seems to have been the norm from the very beginning. The earliest indication of an architectural provision for banqueting is in the Heraion on Samos, whose seventh-century layout included an almost 70 m long stoa marking the southern perimeter of the *temenos* and oriented northeast toward the rear end of the second *Hekatompedos*.[87] While the stoa does not yet feature distinct, *andron*-like rooms,[88] the pottery assemblage and extensive faunal remains suggest that it provided sheltered accommodation to cult-participants eating and drinking.[89] The placement of the stoa suggests a deliberate relegation of sacred consumption to a second tier behind the temple, spatially subordinating eating and drinking to the ritual focal point located east of the temple, while at the same time demarcating the limits of the *temenos*. But its specific placement may also reveal a desire for social distinction by an inner circle of Samian elites deliberately positioning themselves at the far southwestern end of the *temenos*, behind the inner sanctum and away from the mass of visitors coming in from the island's principal settlement to the east.

Feasting in a secondary location beyond the central area around the temple was the preferred spatial arrangement of several regional and Panhellenic sanctuaries, such as that of Zeus at Dodona and the Archaic sanctuary at Brauron.[90] It is most evident in the Asklepieion at Epidauros: entering through the propylon from the north, visitors to the sanctuary would have had to perambulate through the main temple area in order to reach several subsidiary building complexes to the south, including the feasting halls inside the so-called Gymnasion.[91] It is unclear to what degree these buildings—which include the *palaistra*, the *stadion*, bath building, the *katagogion* (with its own sympotic spaces) and the theater—were understood to belong to the *temenos* proper. All these amenities were placed beyond the main focus of the cult, which was centered on the temple and altar of Asklepios.[92]

To the west of the temple at the sanctuary of Dionysos at Yria on Naxos, two banqueting halls, one apsidal and one rectangular, were erected towards the end of the

---

82 Węcowski 2014, 32.
83 Loraux 1981, 620, cf. Schmitt Pantel 1990, 14–15; 1992, 49–50; Ekroth 2008, 260.
84 E.g., Murray 1990; Węcowski 2014, 33.
85 Cf. Goldstein 1978, 8–60; Węcowski 2014, 174.
86 Cf. Leypold 2008, 193.
87 Coulton 1976, 27; Kyrieleis 1993, 130; Pedley 2005, 158–159. For Samians setting up temporary *skenai*, see Goldstein 1978, 22–23.
88 For curtains or tapestries creating subdivisions, cf. Węcowski 2014, 31. See also Wallensten in this volume.
89 Kreuzer 1998, 36–38; Avramidou 2016, 53.
90 For a similar spatial arrangement at Dodona, see Leypold 2008, 158, pls. 40–41. Ekroth (2003a, 79, n. 101) argues that the main room of the sixth-century 'Sacred House' to the south of the 'Cave of Iphigeneia' (i.e., at the far end of the sanctuary) at Brauron can be reconstructed with a square plan, fitting 11 *klinai* of similar size to those in the feasting halls in the Π-shaped stoa. Pottery shapes retrieved from the area of the cave relate to eating and drinking and include amphorae, kraters, cups, and plates.
91 The identification of the building as a gymnasion is questioned, but the function of the rooms at the back of the building for feasting is not: see Tomlinson 1969, 106–112; Goldstein 1978, 233–246; Tomlinson 1983, 78–84; Leypold 2008, 60–70.
92 See also Scahill in this volume.

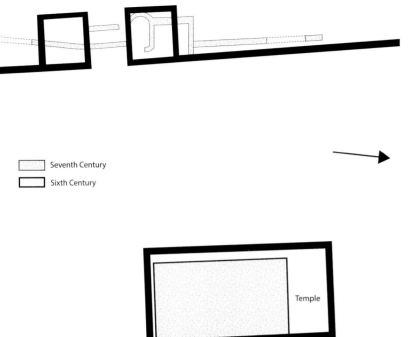

FIGURE 9.3
Naxos, Yria, sanctuary of Dionysos, gateway and banquet buildings
DRAWING BY AUTHOR AFTER SIMANTONI-BOURNIA 2000

seventh century and incorporated into a larger *peribolos* wall demarcating the *temenos* (Figs. 9.3–9.4).[93] It has been suggested that the rectangular banqueting hall owes its design to a desire to accommodate *klinai*. If so, the sanctuary of Dionysos fittingly offers the first evidence of an *andron*-shaped room used for feasting.[94] Given the high proportion of drinking vessels that were set up as votives, these banquets seem to have included sympotic drinking from as early as the Geometric period.[95] It is certain that the two rooms were rebuilt several times from the late sixth century onward. With every rebuilding phase, the banqueting halls remained incorporated within the *peribolos* walls. The late sixth-century arrangement included a gap between the two banqueting halls, effectively creating a rudimentary propylon within the *peribolos* with one square room on each side to demarcate the entrance. Both at Yria and the Heraion on Samos, the banqueting spaces were deliberately placed on the boundary of the *temenos*. This liminal placement of eating and drinking facilities was to become a standard feature in the placement of banqueting halls in the later Archaic and Classical periods.[96]

Contrary to the situation at Samos and Epidauros, however, where consumption was relegated to a secondary tier, the banqueting halls at Yria were prominently placed at the entrance to the precinct. Most subsequent banqueting architecture in sanctuaries follows this second model.[97] The best-known example of this arrangement is the Pinakotheke incorporated into the Propylaia on the Athenian Akropolis. With its not-quite-square design and off-center entrance, this north wing of the main entrance building to the Akropolis could fit 17 benches and afforded a direct view of the Panathenaic processional way leading into the sanctuary proper.[98] The placement of this banqueting hall facing out from the sanctuary seems a bit awkward. It would have been easier to reach had one been able to enter it from the inside of the sanctuary, suggesting that it was deemed appropriate for the banqueting rituals to take place outside of the most sacred area of the sanctuary.

An often-recurring variant of this arrangement is the relegation of banqueting rooms to a forecourt preceding the immediate temple area. Like those at Yria and Athens, banqueting halls can be attached to a propylon, but this is not always the case. The sanctuary of Aphaia on Aigina follows the model of the Pinakotheke in having its consecutive series of sympotic spaces attached to the *temenos* wall, immediately outside (east) of the monumental

---

93 Simantoni Bournia 2000, 215–217; Simantoni Bournia 2002, 277. Cf. Węcowski 2014, 171–172.
94 Węcowski 2014, 172. See also Ohnesorg 2002, 139, fig. 3.; Ohnesorg 2013, pl. 31.
95 Simantoni Bournia 2015.
96 Cf. Klebinder-Gauss 2019, 123.
97 Interestingly, with the construction of the sixth-century 'Rhoikos' temple in the Samian Heraion, the earlier, southern stoa was replaced by an even longer one to the north, ostensibly for the same purpose of accommodating feasting elites while serving as a *peribolos*. A gap within this stoa is reminiscent of the situation at Yria and would have provided direct access to the area in front of the temple.
98 Dinsmoor and Dinsmoor 2004. Cf. Leypold 2008, 33–37. See also Scahill in this volume.

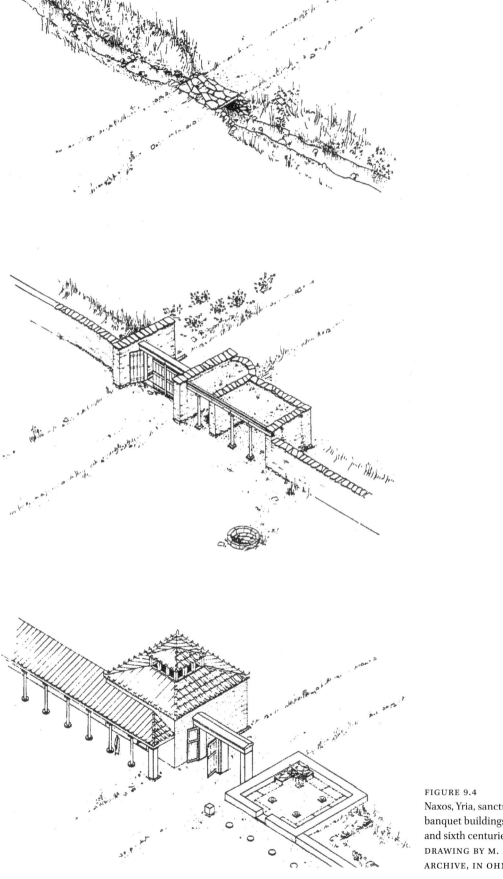

FIGURE 9.4
Naxos, Yria, sanctuary of Dionysos, gateway and banquet buildings during the eighth, seventh and sixth centuries, respectively
DRAWING BY M. LAMBERTZ, PAROS-NAXOS ARCHIVE, IN OHNESORG 2013, PL. 31

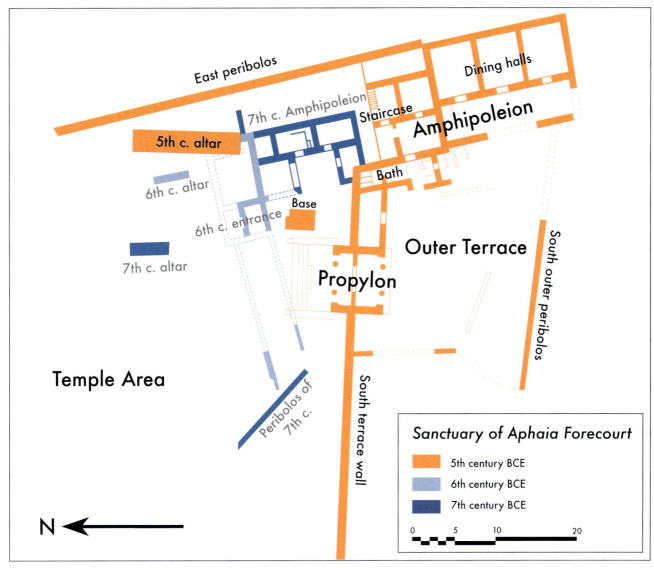

FIGURE 9.5 Aigina, sanctuary of Aphaia
DRAWING BY AUTHOR

entranceway (Fig. 9.5).[99] A second entranceway, no longer preserved, was constructed in the fifth century to create a preliminary court in front of the banqueting halls. This arrangement at once excludes consumptive rituals from the inner sanctum, while including it in the broader configuration of the sanctuary. At the Poseidon sanctuary at Sounion, the banqueting halls similarly were attached to the propylon immediately on the visitor's right and facing in toward the forecourt.[100] This included them within the fortification *peribolos* but placed them outside of the more elevated temple platform. A similar situation exists at the sanctuary of Poseidon on Kalaureia. On a terrace

[99] Goldstein 1978, 143–155; Leypold 2008, 15–25. A curious example of liminal feasting facilities at the entrance of a sanctuary is afforded by the "édifice rectangulaire" or "priest-house" on the Marmaria terrace at Delphi; see Bookidis 1983. Other identifications for this building, e.g., Roux 1965 (temple); Bousquet 1984 (marble workshop), are less convincing because of the off-center doors. While the two suggested banqueting halls are located at the rear of the Pronaia sanctuary itself, the combined cult facilities of Athena Pronaia (Athena-before-the-temple) effectively served as a preliminary stage before arriving at the sanctuary of Apollo from the east. No feasting facilities dating to the Archaic and Classical period have come to light within the premises of the latter, and it is attractive to think that some of the wining and dining connected with the main sanctuary was relegated to the preliminary sanctuary of Athena. Goldstein (1978, 9–14) argues for the setting up of tents within the sanctuary at Delphi from a passage in Euripides' *Ion*, but it is unclear whether this place was *in* or (more likely) *at* the sanctuary.

[100] Staïs 1920, 16; Dinsmoor 1974, 28; Goette 2000, 24–25. Cf. Leypold 2008, 124–125.

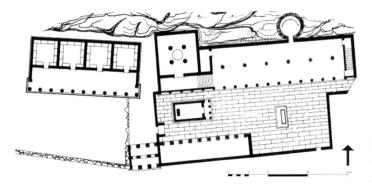

FIGURE 9.6
Athens, Akropolis, South Slope, sanctuary of Asklepios
AFTER TRAVLOS, *ATHENS*, FIG. 171

leading to the second court and the temple platform, a building with two sympotic spaces stood immediately to the right of the entrance.[101] An open space between this building and a stoa with two *oikoi* seems to have directed the processional way towards the plateau from the settlement below. At the Asklepieion in Athens, a monumental propylon afforded entrance to a forecourt, which included banqueting facilities. Immediately to the right within this forecourt, a smaller entranceway provided access to the temple area and incubation space (Fig. 9.6).

The sanctuary of Demeter and Kore at Eleusis had a similar arrangement of feasting halls in front of a propylon leading into the main temple area, but still within a preliminary space.[102] At the sanctuary of Demeter and Kore in Corinth, no less than 52 sympotic spaces of irregular proportion and with built benches were grouped in a lower forecourt before the main temple area (Fig. 9.7).[103]

The fifth-century Π-shaped stoa in Brauron was a multifunctional building containing ten banqueting halls on its ground floor (see pp. 122–123, Fig. 8.8a–b).[104] Two propyla on either side of the elongated open-air entranceway to the north of the stoa provided access to the feasting facilities facing a preliminary sanctuary courtyard and the main temple area beyond and above it. At Labraunda, six sympotic spaces adjoined the propylon immediately to its right upon entering a preliminary courtyard of the sanctuary.[105] At Olympia, banqueting was organized outside the Altis, mostly to the south of the central focus of cult, so in a preliminary position to those who would have visited from the south.[106]

Scholars have claimed that banqueting halls were an integral part of the Greek sanctuary.[107] As we have seen, this holds true to a certain degree, but with an important caveat. While it is clear that banqueting halls were often conspicuously placed upon entering the sanctuary, it is equally evident that they were spatially relegated to a liminal tier of sacrality at the margins of the sanctuary space.[108] Considering that most banqueting halls were placed either in a forecourt of the actual *temenos* or were attached to the propylon on the outside—where competition, inebriation, and promiscuity were hard to avoid—strongly suggests that banqueting was not condoned inside the *temenos* proper or in the vicinity of temple and altar. The sympotic second stage of the banquet in particular, with its tendency toward drunken excess, may have been deemed to be especially problematic. In this light it is understandable that some sacrificial regulations warn against sex inside the sacred precinct.[109] Such regulations are difficult to contextualize without the existence of banqueting halls serving as the backdrop for nocturnal drinking parties nearby.

At the same time, it is striking that most banqueting halls were prominently placed near the sanctuary entrance. This reinforces the notion of cultic elites appropriating the sacred banquet to enhance their social status, thereby undermining the egalitarian ethos of equal

---

101 Wells, Penttinen, and Billot 2003, 75–77. Cf. Leypold 2008, 73–77.
102 Goldstein 1978, 155–161; Leypold 2008, 57–60.
103 Goldstein 1978, 173–192; Bookidis 1990; Bookidis and Stroud 1997; Bookidis et al. 1999. Cf. Leypold 2008, 84–89.
104 Bouras 1967; Coulton 1976, 42–43, 226–227; Goldstein 1978, 114–125; Ekroth 2003a. Cf. Leypold 2008, 124–125.
105 Hellström 1996; 2011; 2019. Cf. Leypold 2008, 98.
106 Banqueting was first organized on the festival grounds outside the Altis (*Festwiese*: Goldstein 1978, 16–22; Kyrieleis 1990, 180; Sinn 2002, 71–72; Barringer 2021, 52–53), and later occurred in built structures, such as the Leonidaion (Leypold 2008, 104–110; Barringer 2021, 56–57) and the Südostbau (Leypold 2008, 110–114; Barringer 2021, 53–56). Cf. also Nemea, Leypold 2008, 159–161.
107 Goldstein 1978, 296–299.
108 It would be interesting to know how this liminal tier relates to the legal concept of *temenos* as used in many ritual regulations.
109 E.g., *CGRN* 5, penalizing a *theoros* at Olympia if he were to have sex inside the precinct. Intercourse appears to be forbidden in sanctuaries from an oft-quoted passage of Herodotos (2.64), who states that "apart from Egyptians and Greeks, almost the whole of the rest of mankind copulate in sacred places and go into shrines without washing after sleeping with a woman." Cf. Parker 1983, 74–103; Pirenne-Delforge 2007, 322; Scahill 2016, 130, n. 5. See also Wallensten in this volume.

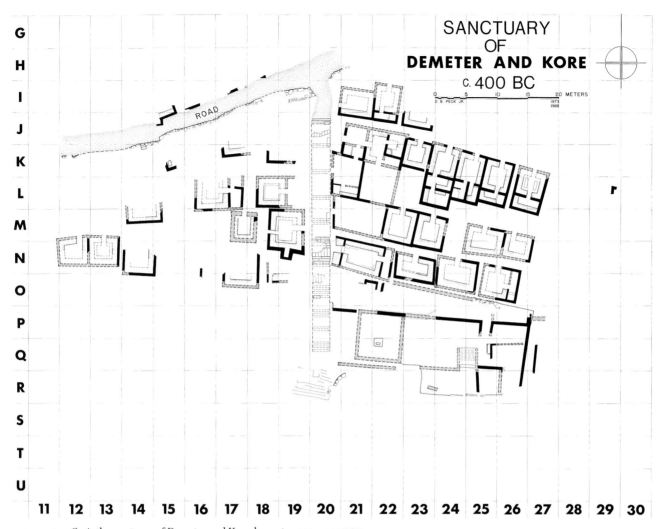

FIGURE 9.7 Corinth, sanctuary of Demeter and Kore, lower terrace, c.400 BCE
PLAN BY D. PECK, AMERICAN SCHOOL OF CLASSICAL STUDIES AT ATHENS, CORINTH EXCAVATIONS

meat-distribution.[110] Receiving one's share may have been important in a civic sense, but *how* and *where* it was consumed, certainly mattered as well.

7 Concluding Remarks

The scholarship of consumptive behavior in Greek sanctuaries has mostly concentrated on the sacrificial meal, a diurnal event that focused on food. I have argued that this aspect covers only part of the 'sacred banquet,' and that a second, sympotic stage formed an integral part of it. The introduction of large, *symposion*-style kraters previously associated with patron-client feasts into Greek sanctuaries c.800, points to the emergence of nocturnal drinking rituals, following the sacrificial feast as described in Homer. Sanctuary assemblages reveal that feasting participants regularly dedicated their drinking vessels as votive gifts in the Archaic period. This widespread votive practice points to a deliberate commemoration of the second part of the festive setting, where drinking, not eating, was the main event. The lamps that partly overtake drinking vessels as votives during the Classical period confirm that both dedications commemorate nighttime drinking sessions, rather than drinking during the sacrificial meal. As the references to lamps in literary and epigraphical sources make clear, lamps were indispensable for nighttime drinking and could function as a suitable replacement of drinking vessels as votives.

It is not difficult to envision that the development of the communal/*isonomic* ethos characteristic of sympotic culture originated in the context of Greek sanctuaries before it was ever adopted in domestic contexts. As the development of the krater-*skyphos* shows, drinking rituals were already changing in sanctuaries during the ninth century,

---

110 The distribution of choice portions, of course, is another deviation from this ethos.

several generations before the commonly accepted 'birth' of the *symposion*. In fact, contrary to common perception, the pre-Classical evidence for the *symposion* is mostly agnostic as to its setting—neither Greek lyric nor black-figure vase painting iconography is particularly informative in this regard.[111] While we may assume that Archaic symposia were also, and perhaps even frequently, conducted in elite houses, conclusive evidence for domestic symposia is paradoxically much harder to find than evidence for sympotic drinking in sanctuaries. In fact, many of our conceptions about the Archaic *symposion* appear to be based on literary sources from the Classical period, Plato most prominently among them. This is a startling observation that has far-reaching implications for the way we understand elite culture in the Archaic period and the root causes for the emergence of the earliest Greek sanctuaries. If we accept the primacy of the sanctuary in the birth and infancy of sympotic culture, it could mean that Archaic elites were tied more closely to the earliest sacred precincts than previously assumed.

We may well ask whether sympotic spaces were used only during festival days or whether the 'ebb and flow' of sanctuary movement allowed for these dining halls to be used on more secular occasions.[112] Did such outstanding special purpose buildings serve, in effect, as aristocratic 'club houses' or 'business clubs,' accessible when the need arose? Could they be leased when necessary, or did access to these halls come with elite cult membership? The analogy of other architecture in Greek sanctuaries, such as theaters or stoas, suggests that specialized cult architecture was often multifunctional and could be used for activities that were not directly related to the cult or used on a cultic occasion. Since cult associations existed year-round, there is no *a priori* reason why they should not have made regular use of the feasting facilities available to them. A good illustration is presented by the West Complex at Kolonna on Aigina, which served as the headquarters of a kinship group based around a hero cult that was not otherwise connected to the main cult of Apollo. According to Gudrun Klebinder-Gauss, the cult participants celebrated important occasions exclusive to their group, such as admitting new members or holding festivities for victorious athletes; shared banqueting, including nocturnal drinking rites, created a common identity between group members and "emphasized ties to the assumed recipients, the ancestors or heroes."[113] This ritual focus on specific heroes or perceived ancestors must have been a common theme of many groups that we assume made use of the banqueting halls at major sanctuaries.

Accessibility may also have depended on the specific context in which feasting was practiced. Sanctuaries with a wider regional or even Panhellenic appeal presumably attracted people in a more uneven flow than poliadic cults, which were accessible year-round. They also had to provide sleeping quarters, and we may wonder to what degree some sympotic spaces doubled as lodgings.[114] It is interesting to note that sanctuaries with sympotic spaces adjacent to the propylon mostly seem to belong to cults that were restricted to the polis. Such a prominent location certainly would have provided local elites with the opportunity to advertise their status to the larger community by regularly wining and dining in close proximity to the entrance of the *temenos*, where they could be seen by their fellow *politai*.

I conclude by addressing two seemingly opposed phenomena encountered in this paper: the decline in votive dedications from the Late Archaic period onward and the proliferation of banqueting halls in Greek sanctuaries throughout the Classical and Hellenistic periods. This paradox vanishes when viewed through the lens of changing access to feasting at sanctuaries. Rather than assuming that sympotic drinking declined around 500 as fewer drinking vessels were given as votives, we may speculate that the reverse may have happened: a widening of access to sympotic gatherings (both in domestic and in sacred contexts) throughout the Greek world. Kathleen Lynch has interpreted an increase of sympotic wares in the Agora deposits around the same time as evidence that non-elites were adopting the *symposion*.[115] The decline in sympotic dedications may therefore be evidence of their declining diacritical function as markers of elite culture. As we have seen, banqueting and sympotic drinking remained important aspects of feasting at or near sanctuaries. Lamps, cult regulations, and the *symposion*-friendly design of banqueting halls indicate that nocturnal drinking rites remained a central element of cult practice throughout much of antiquity.

---

111   For the iconographic sources, cf. Schmitt Pantel 1990, 19.
112   I borrow "ebb and flow" from Gawlinski's paper in this volume.
113   Klebinder-Gauss 2019, 124. *CGRN* 96 (= *IG* XII.4 348) seems to corroborate this practice, stipulating that the cult premises of Herakles Diomedonteios could be used for the wedding ceremony of cult members.
114   The sympotic spaces in the *katagogion* in Epidauros (Leypold 2008, 199, n. 989, with references), for instance, as well as in the Leonidaion at Olympia (Leypold 2008, 104–10; Barringer 2021, 56–57), are thought to have been used for sleeping. Cf. Scahill's paper in this volume. For accommodation in sanctuaries, see also Ekroth in this volume.
115   Lynch 2007, 247–248; Lynch 2011, 272–273.

Acknowledgments

I thank the editors of this volume for their penetrating reading of the various drafts of this paper. The final product has benefited immensely from their suggestions. I also thank Mathieu de Bakker, who read an early draft and provided me with many valuable insights, and Kathleen Lynch for her thoughts and some useful references. All dates mentioned are before the common era.

Works Cited

Aleshire, S. 1992. "The Economics of Dedication at the Athenian Asklepieion." In *Economics of Cult in the Ancient Greek World*, edited by T. Linders and B. Alroth, 85–99. Uppsala.

Avramidou, A. 2016. "Reconsidering the Hera-Pottery from the Samian Heraion and Its Distribution." *AA*: 49–65.

Barfoed, S. 2015. "The Significant Few: Miniature Pottery from the Sanctuary of Zeus at Olympia." *WorldArch* 47: 170–188.

Barringer, J.M. 2014. *The Art and Archaeology of Ancient Greece*. Cambridge.

Barringer, J.M. 2021. *Olympia: A Cultural History*. Princeton.

Bergquist, B. 1990. "Sympotic Space: A Functional Aspect of Greek Dining-Rooms." In *Sympotica: A Symposium on the Symposion*, edited by O. Murray, 37–65. Oxford.

Bookidis, N. 1983. "The Priest's House in the Marmaria at Delphi." *BCH* 107: 149–155.

Bookidis, N. 1990. "Ritual Dining in the Sanctuary of Demeter and Kore at Corinth: Some Questions." In *Sympotica: A Symposium on the Symposion*, edited by O. Murray, 86–94. Oxford.

Bookidis, N., J. Hansen, L. Snyder, and P. Goldberg. 1999. "Dining in the Sanctuary of Demeter and Kore at Corinth." *Hesperia* 68: 1–54.

Bookidis, N., and R.S. Stroud. 1997. *Corinth 18.3: The Sanctuary of Demeter and Kore: Topography and Architecture*. Princeton.

Bouchon, R., and J.-C. Decourt. 2017. "Le règlement religieux de Marmarini (Thessalie): nouvelles lectures, nouvelles interprétations." *Kernos* 30: 159–186.

Bouras, C. 1967. *Η αναστήλωσις της στοάς της Βραυρώνος*. Athens.

Bousquet, J. 1984. "L'atelier de la Tholos de Delphes." *BCH* 108: 199–206.

Bremmer, J.N. 1994. *Greek Religion*. Oxford.

Bremmer, J.N. 2008. *Greek Religion and Culture, the Bible and the Ancient Near East*. Leiden.

Burkert, W. 1985. *Greek Religion*, trans. J. Raffan. Cambridge, MA.

Callipolitis-Feytmans, D. 1965. *Les 'loutéria attiques.'* Athens.

Catling, H.W., and I.S. Lemos. 1990. *Lefkandi 2: The Protogeometric Building at Toumba 1: The Pottery*. Athens.

Cook, J.M. 1953. "The Agamemnoneion." *BSA* 48: 30–68.

Coulton, J.J. 1976. *The Architectural Development of the Greek Stoa*. Oxford.

Dietler, M. 2001. "Theorizing the Feast: Rituals of Consumption, Commensal Politics, and Power in African Contexts." In *Feasts: Archaeological and Ethnographic Perspectives on Food, Politics, and Power*, edited by M. Dietler and B. Hayden, 65–114. Washington D.C.

Dinsmoor, W.B. 1974. *Sounion*, 2nd ed. Athens.

Dinsmoor, W.B., and W.B. Dinsmoor Jr. 2004. *The Propylaia to the Athenian Akropolis 2: The Classical Building*. Princeton.

Eder, B. 2001. "Continuity of Bronze Age Cult at Olympia? The Evidence of the Late Bronze Age and Early Iron Age Pottery." In *Potnia: Deities and Religion in the Aegean Bronze Age*, edited by R. Laffineur and R. Hägg, 201–209. Liège.

Eidinow, E., and J. Kindt. 2015. *The Oxford Handbook of Ancient Greek Religion*. Oxford.

Ekroth, G. 2003a. "Inventing Iphigeneia? On Euripides and the Cultic Construction of Brauron." *Kernos* 16: 59–118.

Ekroth, G. 2003b. "Small Pots, Poor People?" In *Griechische Keramik im kulturellen Kontext*, edited by B. Schmaltz and M. Söldner, 35–37. Münster.

Ekroth, G. 2007. "Meat in Ancient Greece: Sacrificial, Sacred or Secular." *Food and History* 5: 249–272.

Ekroth, G. 2008. "Meat, Man and God. On the Division of the Animal Victim at Greek Sacrifices." In *Mikros Hieromnemon: Studies in Memory of Michael H. Jameson*, edited by A. Matthaiou and I. Polinskaya, 259–290. Athens.

Ekroth, G. 2011. "Meat for the Gods." In *"Nourrir les dieux?" Sacrifice et représentation du divin*, edited by V. Pirenne-Delforge and F. Prescendi, 15–41. Liège.

Ekroth, G. 2017. "'Don't Throw Any Bones in the Sanctuary!' on the Handling of Sacred Waste at Ancient Greek Cult Places." In *Ritual Matters: Material Remains and Ancient Religion*, edited by C. Moser and J. Knust, 33–55. Ann Arbor.

Ekroth, G. 2023. "Citizens as Drinkers? A Glimpse from the Countryside of the Archaic Argolid." In *Politeia and Koinōnia. Studies in Ancient Greek History in Honour of Josine Blok*, edited by V. Pirenne-Delforge and M. Węcowski, 46–64. Leiden.

Gimatzidis, S. 2011. "Feasting and Offering to the Gods in Early Greek Sanctuaries: Monumentalisation and Miniaturisation in Pottery." *Pallas* 86: 75–96.

Gisler, J.-R. 1983. *Céramique géométrique d'Érétrie: les grands vases ouverts du Temple d'Apollon Daphnéphoros*. Ph.D. diss., Université de Fribourg.

Goette, H.R. 2000. *Ὁ ἀξιόλογος δῆμος Σούνιον: Landeskundliche Studien in Sudost-Attika*. Rahden.

Goldstein, M.S. 1978. *The Setting of the Ritual Meal in Greek Sanctuaries: 600–300 B.C.* Ph.D. diss., University of California, Berkeley.

Graef, B., and E. Langlotz. 1925. *Die antiken Vasen von der Akropolis zu Athen 1*. Berlin.

Hellström, P. 1996. "The Andrones at Labraunda. Dining Halls for Protohellenistic Kings." In *Basileia, die Paläste der hellenistischen Könige*, edited by W. Hoepfner and G. Brands, 164–169. Mainz am Rhein.

Hellström, P. 2011. "Feasting at Labraunda and the chronology of the Andrones." In *Labraunda and Karia*, edited by L. Karlsson and S. Carlsson, 149–157. Uppsala.

Hellström, P., and J. Blid. 2019. *Labraunda 5: The Andrones*. Istanbul.

Huber, S. 2003. *Eretria 14: L'aire sacrificielle au nord du sanctuaire d'Apollon Daphnéphoros*. Gollion.

Jacob-Felsch, M. 1996. "Die spätmykenische bis protogeometrische Keramik." In *Kalapodi. Ergebnisse der Ausgrabungen im Heiligtum der Artemis und des Apollon von Hyampolis in der antiken Phokis 1*, edited by R.C.S. Felsch, 1–213. Mainz am Rhein.

Jameson, M.H. 1998. "Religion in the Athenian Democracy." In *Democracy 2500? Questions and Challenges*, edited by I. Morris and K.A. Raaflaub, 197–216. Dubuque, IA.

Klebinder-Gauss, G. 2019. "Dining with the Ancestors: The Late Archaic-Classical *Westcomplex* in Aegina-Kolonna." In *Beyond the Polis. Collective Rituals and the Construction of Social Identity in Early Greece (12th–6th century B.C.)*, edited by I. Lemos and A. Tsingarida, 115–132. Paris.

Kotsonas, A. 2011. "Ceramic Variability and Drinking Habits in Iron Age Crete." In *The "Dark Ages" Revisited 2*, edited by A. Mazarakis Ainian, 943–955. Volos.

Kreuzer, B. 1998. *Die attisch schwarzfigurige Keramik aus dem Heraion von Samos, Samos 22*. Bonn.

Kyrieleis, H. 1990. "Neue Ausgrabungen in Olympia." *AntW* 21: 177–188.

Kyrieleis, H. 1993. "The Heraion at Samos." In *Greek Sanctuaries. New Approaches*, edited by N. Marinatos and R. Hägg, 125–153. London.

Kyrieleis, H., B. Eder, and N. Benecke. 2006. *Anfänge und Frühzeit des Heiligtums von Olympia. Die Ausgrabungen am Pelopion 1987–1996, OF 31*. Berlin.

Langdon, M.K. 1976. *A Sanctuary of Zeus on Mount Hymettos*. Princeton.

Larson, J. 2007. *Ancient Greek Cults: A Guide*. New York.

Larson, J. 2016. *Understanding Greek Religion*. London.

Lemos, I.S. 2002. *The Protogeometric Aegean: The Archaeology of the Late Eleventh and Tenth Centuries BC*. Oxford.

Leypold, C. 2008. *Bankettgebäude in griechischen Heiligtümern*. Wiesbaden.

Lissarrague, F. 1990. *The Aesthetics of the Greek Banquet: Images of Wine and Ritual*. Princeton.

Loraux, N. 1981. "La cité comme cuisine et comme partage." *AnnÉconSocCiv* 36: 614–622.

Lynch, K. 2007. "More Thoughts on the Space of the Symposium." In *Building Communities: House, Settlement and Society in the Aegean and Beyond*, edited by R. Westgate, N. Fisher, and J. Whitley, 243–249. London.

Lynch, K. 2011. *Symposium in Context: Pottery from a Late Archaic House near the Athenian Agora*. Princeton.

Lynch, K. 2018. "The Hellenistic Symposium as Feast." In *Feasting and Polis Institutions*, edited by F. van den Eijnde, J. Blok, and R. Strootman, 233–256. Leiden.

Mikalson, J. 2009. *Ancient Greek Religion*. Oxford.

Morgan, C. 1990. *Athletes and Oracles: The Transformation of Olympia and Delphi in the Eighth Century BC*. Cambridge.

Morgan, C. 1999. *Isthmia 8: The Late Bronze Age Settlement and Early Iron Age Sanctuary*. Princeton.

Murray, O. 1983. "The Symposion as Social Organisation." In *The Greek Renaissance of the Eighth Century B.C.: Tradition and Innovation*, edited by R. Hägg, 195–199. Stockholm.

Murray, O. 1990. "Sympotic History." In *Sympotica: A Symposium on the Symposion*, edited by O. Murray, 3–13. Oxford.

Murray, O. 2009. "The Culture of the Symposium." In *A Companion to Archaic Greece*, edited by K.A. Raaflaub and H. van Wees, 509–523. Chichester.

Nielsen, I. 1998. "Royal Banquets. The Development of Royal Banquets and the Banqueting Halls from Alexander to the Tetrarchs." In *Meals in a Social Context: Aspects of the Communal Meal in the Hellenistic and Roman World*, edited by I. Nielsen and H. Nielsen, 102–133. Aarhus.

Nilsson, M.P. 1949. *A History of Greek Religion*. Oxford.

Nitsche, A. 1987. "Protogeometrische und subprotogeometrische Keramik aus dem Heiligtum von Kalapodi." *AA*: 35–49.

Ogden, D., ed. 2007. *A Companion to Greek Religion*. Malden, MA.

Ohnesorg, A. 2002. "Naxian and Parian Architecture: General Features and New Discoveries." In *Architecture and Archaeology in the Cyclades: Papers in Honour of J.J. Coulton*, edited by M. Stamatopoulou and M. Yeroulanou, 135–152. Oxford.

Ohnesorg, A. 2013. "Die Westanlagen des Heiligtums von Yria auf Naxos." In *Petasos. Festschrift für Hans Lohmann*, edited by G. Kalaitzoglou and G. Lüdorf, 227–240. Paderborn.

Palaiokrassa-Kopitsa, L. 2017. "Ὑψηλόποδες κάνθαροι. Ἕνα τελετουργικό σκεῦος." In *ΤΕΡΨΙΣ—Studies in Mediterranean Archaeology in Honour of Nota Kourou*, edited by V. Vlachou and A. Gadolou, 209–220. Brussels.

Palaiokrassa-Kopitsa, L., and E. Vivliodetis. 2015. "The Sanctuaries of Artemis Mounichia and Zeus Parnesios. Their Relation to the Religious Life in the Athenian City-State until the End of the 7th Century B.C." In *Pots, Workshops and Early Iron Age Society. Function and Role of Ceramics in Early Greece*, edited by V. Vlachou, 155–180. Brussels.

Papakonstantinou, Z. 2009. "Wine and Wine Drinking in the Homeric World." *AntCl* 78: 1–24.

Parker, R.C.T. 1983. *Miasma: Pollution and Purification in Early Greek Religion*. Oxford.

Parker, R.C.T. 2005. *Polytheism and Society at Athens*. Oxford.

Parker, R.C.T. 2011. *On Greek Religion*. Ithaca.

Payne, H., and T.J. Dunbabin. 1962. *Perachora: The Sanctuaries of Hera Akraia and Limenia; Excavations of the British School of Archaeology at Athens, 1930–1933, vol. 2: Pottery, Ivories, Scarabs and other Objects from the Votive Deposit of Hera Limenia*. Oxford.

Pedley, J.G. 2005. *Sanctuaries and the Sacred in the Ancient Greek World*. New York.

Pemberton, E.G., K. Warner Slane, and C.K. Williams II. 1989. *Corinth 18.1: The Sanctuary of Demeter and Kore: The Greek Pottery*. Princeton.

Pirenne-Delforge, V. 2007. "'Something to do with Aphrodite:' Ta Aphrodisia and the Sacred." In *A Companion to Greek Religion*, edited by D. Ogden, 311–323. Malden, MA.

Pratt, C.E. 2021. *Oil, Wine, and the Cultural Economy of Ancient Greece*. Cambridge.

Price, S.R.F. 1999. *Religions of the Ancient Greeks*. Cambridge.

Risser, M.K. 2015. "The City, the Sanctuary, and the Feast: Dining Vessels from the Archaic Reservoir in the Sanctuary of Poseidon." In *Bridge of the Untiring Sea: The Corinthian Isthmus from Prehistory to Late Antiquity*, edited by E.R. Gebhard and T.E. Gregory, 83–96. Princeton.

Rotroff, S.I. 1996. *The Missing Krater and the Hellenistic Symposium: Drinking in the Age of Alexander the Great*. Christchurch.

Roux, G. 1965. "Pausanias, le 'Contre Aristogiton' et les 'Énigmes de Marmaria' à Delphes." *RÉA* 67: 37–53.

Scahill, D. 2016. "Dining and the Cult of Aphrodite: The Function of the South Stoa at Corinth." In *Houses of Ill Repute: The Archaeology of Brothels, Houses, and Taverns in the Greek World*, edited by A. Glazebrook and B. Tsakirgis, 129–142. Philadelphia.

Schmitt Pantel, P. 1990. "Sacrificial Meal and Symposion: Two Models of Civic Institutions in the Archaic City?" In *Sympotica: A Symposium on the Symposion*, edited by O. Murray, 14–33. Oxford.

Schmitt Pantel, P. 1992. *La cité au banquet. Histoire des repas publics dans les cités grecques*. Rome.

Sherratt, S. 2004. "Feasting in Homeric Epic." *Hesperia* 73: 301–337.

Simantoni-Bournia, E. 2000. "Les premières phases du sanctuaire d'Hyria d'après les objets retrouvés." *RA*: 209–219.

Simantoni-Bournia, E. 2002. "The early phases of the Hyria Sanctuary on Naxos: An overview of the pottery." In *Excavating Classical Culture: Recent Archaeological Discoveries in Greece*, edited by M. Stamatopoulou and M. Yeroulanou, 269–280. Oxford.

Simantoni-Bournia, E. 2015. "More Cups for 'Dionysos.' A Selection of Geometric Drinking Vases from the Sanctuary of Hyria on Naxos." In *Pots, Workshops and Early Iron Age Society: Function and Role of Ceramics in Early Greece*, edited by V. Vlachou, 181–197. Brussels.

Sinn, U. 2002. *Olympia. Kult, Sport und Feste in der Antike*. Munich.

Staïs, V. 1920. Τὸ Σούνιον καὶ οἱ ναοὶ Ποσειδῶνος καὶ Ἀθηνᾶς. Athens.

Steiner, A. 2002. "Private and Public: Links between Symposion and Syssition in Fifth-Century Athens." *ClAnt* 21: 347–379.

Stissi, V.V. 2002. *Pottery to the People. The Production, Distribution and Consumption of Decorated Pottery in the Greek World in the Archaic Period (650–480 BC)*. Ph.D. diss., University of Amsterdam.

Tomlinson, R.A. 1969. "Two Buildings in Sanctuaries of Asklepios." *JHS* 89: 106–117.

Tomlinson, R.A. 1983. *Epidauros*. Austin.

van den Eijnde, F. 2018a. "Feasting and Polis Institutions: An Introduction." In *Feasting and Polis Institutions*, edited by F. van den Eijnde, J. Blok, and R. Strootman, 1–27. Leiden.

van den Eijnde, F. 2018b. "Power Play at the Dinner Table. Feasting and Patronage between Palace and Polis in Attika." In *Feasting and Polis Institutions*, edited by F. van den Eijnde, J. Blok, and R. Strootman, 60–92. Leiden.

van den Eijnde, F., J. Blok, and R. Strootman, eds. 2018. *Feasting and Polis Institutions*. Leiden.

van Straten, F.T. 1995. *Hierà kalá: Images of Animal Sacrifice in Archaic and Classical Greece*. Leiden.

Verdan, S. 2001. "Fouilles dans le sanctuaire d'Apollon Daphnéphoros." *AntK* 44: 84–87.

Verdan, S. 2013. *Eretria 22: Le sanctuaire d'Apollon Daphnéphoros à l'époque géométrique*. Gollion.

Verdan, S., A. Kenzelmann Pfyffer, and C. Léderrey. 2008. *Eretria 20: Céramique géométrique d'Érétrie*. Gollion.

Węcowski, M. 2002. "Towards a Definition of the Symposion." In ΕΥΕΡΓΕΣΙΑΣ ΧΑΡΙΝ: Studies Presented to Benedetto Bravo and Ewa Wipszycka by their Disciples, edited by Tomasz Derda, Jakub Urbanik, and Marek Węcowski, 337–361. Warsaw.

Węcowski, M. 2012. "When did the Symposion Rise? Some Archaeological Considerations Regarding the Emergence of the Greek Aristocratic Banquet." Ἀρχαιογνωσία 16.1–3: 19–48.

Węcowski, M. 2014. *The Rise of the Greek Aristocratic Banquet*. Oxford.

Węcowski, M. 2017. "The Middle-Geometric Attic Koine and the Rise of the Aristocratic Symposion." In *Material Koinai in the Greek Early Iron Age and Archaic Period*, edited by S. Handberg and A. Gadolou, 315–322. Aarhus.

Wells, B., A. Penttinen, and M.-F. Billot. 2003. "Investigations in the Sanctuary of Poseidon on Kalauria, 1997–2001." *OpAth* 28: 29–87.

Zerhoch, S. 2020. "The Politics of Religion: Libation and Truce in Euripides' Bacchae." *CQ* 70: 51–67.

CHAPTER 10

What's for Dinner? The 'Menu' in Greek Sanctuaries

Michael MacKinnon

Food is a topic that may present a rather basic, uncomplicated exterior: we all have to eat, and undertake this activity daily, often without much thought. However, when dissected further, it is apparent that the subject of food yields a rich, diversified, multifaceted, and often complicated interior. That 'interior' itself contains practical, logistical aspects, prompting questions such as "from where do we get this food, and how do we prepare it for ingestion?" Then there are the myriad natural and cultural aspects that affect the production, consumption, and general role and interpretation of those foodstuffs. Given that complexity, it is clear that any exploration of the issue of food, especially in past cultures, may pique popular appeal or appetite, but simultaneously suffer from investigatory hunger and famine as we grapple with incomplete datasets and fragmented answers in our reconstructions.

This chapter delves into the topic of food consumption and dietary provisioning at ancient Greek sanctuaries, focusing particularly upon the role and contribution of animals and meat within the activities at these complexes. In pursuing this issue, attention centers upon the zooarchaeological evidence. Obviously, that choice exposes a personal bias: zooarchaeology is my specialty. This is not to say that other foodstuffs did not contribute to sanctuary events; botanical materials, including cakes, breads, fruits, etc., were all consumed, and could comprise substantial commodities. However, at present, palaeobotanical records from Greek sanctuary sites are disparate and problematic, hampered in large part, from an archaeological perspective, by preservation and recovery concerns.[1] Nonetheless, I profess no priority in the selection of one dataset over another in our quest to reconstruct the past. Rather, think of this current chapter as a way to add an ingredient (i.e., zooarchaeological evidence) into a collective stewpot of scholarship on the topic of foodstuffs and foodways in Greek sanctuaries, and see how it flavors the resultant meal.

First, some background to set our investigatory table. Traditional divisions of zooarchaeological remains recovered from ancient Greek ritual contexts are of three general types: (1) altar offerings (i.e., often the materials burnt for the gods or heroes venerated); (2) butchery refuse (i.e., materials associated with the initial preparation of the animal carcasses for offering and consumption); and (3) consumption/dining debris (i.e., materials correlated with ritual dining and feasting at such events). Among these, scholarly attention historically has focused upon the first category: altar offerings. Evidence for the presentation of animal parts, such as the thigh and tail (*thysia* sacrifice), or the offering of, more-or-less, full carcasses (holocaust sacrifice) to such divine or heroic honorees registers fairly distinctly among several ancient Greek ritual sites and contexts, including examples at Eretria, Isthmia, Olympia, Kourion, and Nemea, among others.[2] Correlations these parts share with recovered zooarchaeological remains such as the femur, pelvis, sacrum, caudal vertebrae, or entire animals have been similarly explored,[3] as has the relationship between left and right sides in the choice of such elements.[4]

Butchery refuse marks the second category of investigation. These are the materials associated with the initial preparation of the animal carcasses for offering and consumption. Generally, these comprise elements from the head and lower leg/foot of the animal, parts which may otherwise yield limited meat,[5] or may be contained within the animal's hide after its skinning. Given that these pieces often result as byproducts from the initial division of the animal when it was skinned and prior to the extraction of parts later designated as altar debris or sacrificial cooking/consumption debris from the ritual event, it seems natural that these heads and feet, as butchering debris, might be treated separately and eventually removed from the area, perhaps even to non-ritual

---

1 Bookidis et al. (1999) overviews, in more detail, the challenges and benefits that archaeobotanical evidence brings to our understanding of Greek sacrificial practices.

2 For general syntheses of aspects and examples from various sites (alongside further references), see Ekroth 2008a; 2008b; 2009; 2011; 2013a; 2013b; 2014a; 2016; 2017a; 2017b; 2017c.
3 For further analysis, case studies, and references, supra n. 2, as well as Hägg 1998; Scullion 2013; Trantalidou 2013; Hitch 2015, among others.
4 MacKinnon 2010; 2013, with an example of this from the site of Nemea.
5 Infra n. 8 for discussion of tongues and brains as potential offerings or perquisites.

contexts.[6] To label them 'waste' is not entirely accurate, since they can be integrated into other components, ritual or otherwise, and either remain within, or be exported from, sanctuary compounds. Heads and horns, for example, may be curated in the construction of altars, as at Delos.[7] Feet may be left attached to an entire leg (be this the front or back leg of the animal), which itself may have been among the elements sacrificed, consumed, or provided as perquisites. Similarly, heads (and the meats they housed, such as the tongue and brain) could also have been among the materials offered, consumed or given as perquisites.[8] Nonetheless, outside of these special cases, the impression is that heads and feet of the animals in question were retained presumably within the hides, or otherwise represent the unimportant butchery refuse left over in the quest to extract the select parts either to burn on the altar or to consume as part of the ritual feast.[9] Their potential inclusion within the initial cutting of the hide, and subsequent extraction from that hide at some point in its packaging and preparation, is critical to the location of these skeletal elements. Should they remain within the hide, one might expect them to be removed from sanctuary sites en route to the tannery or other such processing location.[10] Hides are often listed among the perquisites provided to officiating priests, who presumably were permitted to take at least some of these objects outside of the sanctuary.[11] There are references to the sale of hides from sacrificial victims,[12] and thus, there was potential for these parts to move between ritual and non-ritual settings.[13]

Dining debris comprises the final category of interest as regards zooarchaeological evidence from Greek ritual sites. Generally, these materials are more plentiful than altar debris, further differing from them in appearance (e.g., far fewer traces of burning), composition (e.g., more diversified in both taxa and skeletal elements, but in some cases 'lacking' parts that comprise altar debris or butchery debris), and placement (e.g., separate spatial contexts from 'altar debris,' although not always). In whatever form they might be distinguished, however, classification of such materials as 'dining debris' prompts bigger questions about the nature of meat eating in Greek antiquity. Was all meat consumed in Greek antiquity 'sacred' to a certain degree? Was there 'secular' consumption of meat, even if conducted within the context of a sanctuary compound? While opinions vary, responses such as 'perhaps' and 'it depends' may ultimately best answer those questions, as the complexities of the ritual/non-ritual continuum in Greek antiquity materialize. As Gunnel Ekroth, and others, note,[14] the reality within such sacrifices does not always fit neatly into generalized patterns as might be anticipated or expected, and caution is warranted.

Notwithstanding theoretical debates about sacrifice overall in Greek antiquity, an argument might be made that altar offerings, specifically those materials burned on the altar in whatever form they might take, are ultimately presented for the gods or heroes. By contrast, consumption/dining debris might link more directly to the types of animal foodstuffs the sanctuaries' human celebrants and participants ate.[15] This 'dining' component forms

---

6   It is worth mentioning here that bones from cattle feet and lower legs are extremely under-represented among faunal materials collected at the fourth-century BCE altar of Zeus/Jovis at Poseidonia, Italy, where they accounted for less than one percent of bones retrieved. The impression here is that these materials were removed from this 'ritual' region and presumably deposited outside the area. See Leguilloux 2000 for further details. Unfortunately, full NISP (Number of Identified Specimens) statistics for all categories of skeletal parts for this site were unavailable to include in the current study.

7   See Forstenpointner, Galik, and Weissengruber 2013, 238–240 for the Delian 'horn altar.'

8   Carbon (2017, 167–173) explores in greater detail the topic of post-sacrificial division of meat by anatomical element. In addition to bits of muscle tissue (the largest muscle here being the jowl), an animal's head technically also contains the tongue, brain, and eyes, all of which may be consumed. Given that tongues are often listed among materials placed on offering tables or provided to priests/officials as perquisites at Greek sanctuaries, it is likely that they were generally removed, and did not necessarily remain with the head. A tongue can be easily cut from an animal's mouth, without significantly butchering or breaking apart the skull or jaw. The brain may similarly have been offered, gifted, or sold within sanctuary operations but its extraction would typically require the skull to be split to facilitate removal. Half-heads of animals factor within some lists of sacrificial perquisites. Nevertheless—although perhaps impractical—if the brain was to be incorporated into sacrificial operations, it is not impossible to split an animal's skull, obtain the brain, and still leave the remaining cranium in the hide.

9   Ekroth 2009; 2016; 2017a; 2017b proposes this same point.

10 For the preparation of hides from Greek sanctuaries, see Pakkanen's contribution to this volume.

11 E.g., *LSAM* no. 37, ll. 6–15, *LSCG* no. 28, ll. 5–9; see also Naiden 2013, 202; Scullion 2009, 154–156; Carbon 2017.

12 *IG* II² 1496.

13 MacKinnon (2024) investigates the frequency of head and foot bones among Greek sites (sanctuary or otherwise). Patterns are not consistent, but, generally in the case with cattle, non-sanctuary sites register a higher relative frequency of head and foot elements than do sanctuary sites, suggesting some measure of exporting cattle hides (with heads and feet attached) from sanctuaries. The data for sheep and goat hides, however, is less marked in this respect.

14 Ekroth 2009, 35.

15 *Theoxenia* presents a somewhat blurred division between human and divine as regards actual consumption. Within this

the focus of investigation here. Nonetheless, interconnections link all three categories above, so nothing is neatly compartmentalized.

What trends surface in zooarchaeological materials classified as 'dining debris' from Greek sanctuary sites? What animals are noted? What breeds or varieties surface? Whence were animals acquired? Locally or further removed? Are seasonal trends noted? What demographic patterns arise? What skeletal elements are represented? How were parts obtained, processed, butchered, cooked, and prepared? And how might aspects vary in relation to sacrificial altar offerings? In other words, what practicalities go into supplying animals and animal products to Greek ritual sites, and how might these components affect diets? In exploring these aspects, zooarchaeological data for animal taxon, age, skeletal part, sex, butchery, and size from a range of Greek sanctuary and non-sanctuary sites, will be employed. The application of zooarchaeology to our understanding of the world of antiquity has been clearly demonstrated. Nonetheless, as with any category of evidence, it is important to address potential pitfalls and concerns, especially those that might have direct consequences on the interpretation of results in this current investigation of animals in Greek antiquity. Recovery and preservation biases are always an issue when considering zooarchaeological data. Sieving invariably enhances the recovery of faunal materials; taphonomic conditions inevitably shape preservation; teeth survive better than bones; mature bones (from adult animals) survive better than immature ones (from younger animals); denser bones (or sections within) endure better than more porous pieces. Zooarchaeologists are well aware of these biases, and often try to address the impact each may have had on results presented. Even so, difficulties can arise when general comparisons across sites are sought (as attempted in this current study), but which must be formed in the absence of comprehensive assessments of recovery and preservation biases at any individual site. Variations in how zooarchaeological data themselves are determined and reported can add further complications when attempting comparative work,[16] while requisite and detailed contextual information about specific deposits providing the faunal samples of interest is not always made clear.[17] As regards animals, sacral activity in Greek antiquity largely involved the killing of ordinary livestock, an activity that also played a key role in provisioning meat to other contexts, be these within the sanctuary itself (as part of a sacrifice or within the framework of sanctuary dining), or outside of the sanctuary compound (if meat was removed from those areas, not to mention the issue of consumption of meat outside sanctuaries altogether and thus totally removed from ritual events). Components are not always distinct, and linkages of faunal materials within and outside sanctuaries (let alone across sites) are not always explicit. Nevertheless, on the one hand, crafting general faunal patterns across sites, even though problematic, can create a foundation from which to chart broader trends, and in turn recognize outliers. On the other hand, focused attention on faunal patterns within individual sites helps situate their activity at a more refined level. This balance between general and specific foci forms the basis of this current investigation.

1 **General Patterns**

This list is exclusive to sites where zooarchaeological reports are currently published (to 2019) and supplemented with data from additional contexts at Corinth and Athens, locations where I have personally conducted investigations of available faunal materials. To concentrate perspectives, both geographically and temporally, exploration here centers upon contexts from sites on the Greek mainland (with the addition of Euboia) that date to Archaic, Classical, and Hellenistic timeframes—arguably a core temporal bracket for Greek sanctuaries. Although other Greek sanctuaries with excavated faunal samples are known in the wider Aegean and Mediterranean region (e.g., in Turkey, on Crete, in the Cyclades, on Rhodes, in Southern Italy), the choice to restrict investigation here to the Greek mainland may facilitate exploration of movement of livestock within peninsular Greece, as opposed to any maritime trade or movement in stock across islands, for instance. In other words, if any site in peninsular Greece was provided with livestock, it is more likely that such animals originated somewhere on the Greek

---

ritual, the god is invited to partake in dining and presented with a share of foodstuffs and meats on a sacred table. Following display, these materials (all or in part) sometimes may have been burned as further offerings to the god; in other cases, they may have (ultimately) contributed to the foodstuffs consumed by human participants within the sanctuary. See Jameson 1994; Ekroth 2008b; 2017a for more on *theoxenia*.

16 For example, not all reports tabulate counts by skeletal part, by age category, etc.

17 In some cases, samples are pooled across a range of contexts (not always made known, and a number categorized rather generically as 'fills') and reported as broader temporal or site-wide brackets.

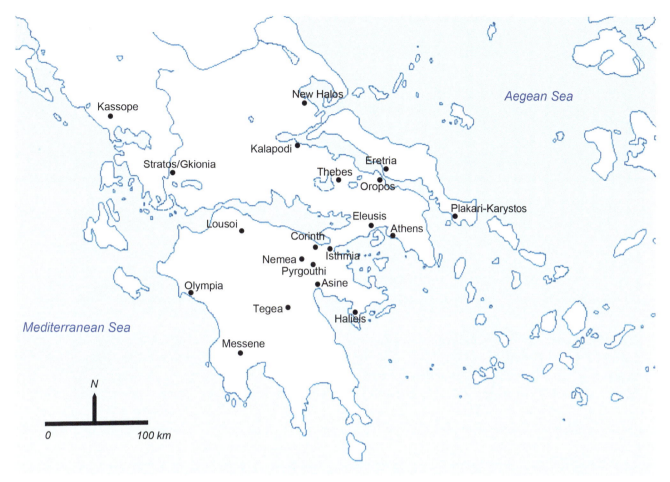

FIGURE 10.1 Location of sites with zooarchaeological remains
Note: References, in alphabetical order, by site: Asine (Moberg 1992; Moberg Nilsson 1996); Athens (MacKinnon 2014); Corinth (MacKinnon, forthcoming); Eleusis (Cosmopoulos, Greenfield, and Ruscillo 2003); Eretria (Chenal-Velarde 2001; Chenal-Velarde and Studer 2003; Studer and Chenal-Velarde 2003; Huber and Méniel 2013); Halieis (Hägg 1988; Reese, unpublished); Isthmia (Reese 1993; Gebhard and Reese 2005); Kalapodi (Stanzel 1991); Kassope (Friedl 1984; Boessneck 1986); Lousoi (Forstenpointner and Hofer 2001); Messene (Nobis 1997); Nemea (MacKinnon 2013; MacKinnon 2018); New Halos (Prummel 2003); Oropos (Trantalidou 2007); Plakari-Karystos (Groot 2014); Olympia (Benecke 2006); Pyrgouthi (Mylona 2005); Stratos/Gkionia (Prust 2013); Tegea (Vila 2000; Vila 2014); Thebes (Boessneck 1973).

mainland as opposed to being imported via the sea from further abroad.[18]

1.1 Taxa

A first investigatory step is to compare what types of animals occur among the pool of sites selected. Figure 10.2 assesses the frequency of the three most commonly exploited mammalian taxa—cattle, sheep/goat, pig—at such locations.

Here, a distinction between sanctuary deposits/sites, 'proper' (on the right side of the graph), and non-sanctuary deposits/sites (on the left) is made, a separation that in turn allows us to explore if faunal resources and underlying supply networks and dietary components varied by site type.[19] Burned ritual deposits (i.e., chiefly, in this case, the altar debris assemblages) are excluded in Fig. 10.2, as these are linked to offerings to gods or heroes. Rather, in keeping with the focus of this chapter, only those deposits characterized as 'dining' waste—that is

---

18 This is not to say that animals were never shipped in such a manner (e.g., horses to sites of equestrian games), but that such a path would likely be costly.

19 Understandably, the labels 'sanctuary site' and 'non-sanctuary site' carry some subjectivity, as 'sacrificial' or 'sacred' activities need not be a component chiefly linked to the former type of site, or, for that matter, absent from the latter. The assumption is that 'sanctuary sites,' as here defined, may better yield evidence for more communal, formal, ritual ceremonies at a more restricted, and presumably fundamentally sacral, location. Whatever the case, division by site type, even if on a generalized and imperfect level, assists in understanding potential variability across archaeological contexts.

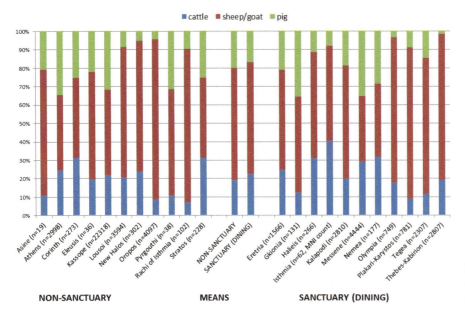

FIGURE 10.2
NISP (= Number of Identified Specimens) frequency values for cattle, sheep/goat and pig among sites

presumably what was cooked and eaten for humans, and not burned on the altar—are presented.

Sanctuary sites can be complex entities with a range of associated activities. This can extend to animal use, as well, and it is important here to note that not all animals eaten within sanctuary sites need be sacrificed; some may have been brought to the site, whole or in part, simply to serve as food or for labor. Whatever the case, various decisions may have an impact upon which animals (or parts of such animals) are brought to (and potentially deposited at) a sanctuary compound for whatever purpose(s)—ritual, sacrifice, burned offering, consumption, acquisition, etc. Among the factors that may well shape the input of animals (or their parts) to sanctuary compounds might be the number of guests/participants, the availability of stock (and seasonal and cultural implications therein), as well as various ecological, cultural, religious, and economic preferences or dictates for certain animals based on their age, sex, or other characteristics.[20] Females are typically more valuable as breeding stock, while males are needed in fewer numbers. Moreover, the age at which an animal is killed can reveal different productive goals.

A first trend to emerge among the 'dining assemblages' for sites explored here is that, in many cases, all three taxa—cattle, sheep/goat, pig—are represented. Second, a balance between sexes within each taxon often registers, although some assemblages, such as dining waste among cults demanding particular taxa and sexes (e.g., Demeter cult at Corinth, which receives female pigs) counter this trend (an issue addressed in more detail later in this chapter). Finally, mortality profiles among most examples typically register what is classified as a 'meat mortality pattern,' as opposed to a 'milk mortality profile' (where surplus young animals are killed), or a 'wool/labor profile' (where adult individuals are emphasized). A 'meat mortality pattern' harmonizes these extremes (some young are killed, some older ones kept), inherently offering flexibility, while focusing on breeding needs. Collectively, the presence of all three taxa—cattle, sheep/goat and pig—across sites, a balance between sexes, and dominance of a 'meat mortality pattern' among them, implies a general rural productive strategy in how these animals were raised and herded. Thus, zooarchaeological patterns best tip towards mixed-farming ventures ultimately claiming dominance in provisioning animals, regardless of site type or region. Within this, small flocks and herds of animals with grazing and manuring strategies are tightly integrated with plant agriculture on small landholdings. That tactic provides security and adaptability, and contrasts with a distinct pastoral productive economy, where large groups of animals are herded seasonally, sometimes through massive transhumant efforts.[21] Perhaps more importantly, the level of homogeneity displayed in these mixed farming zooarchaeological patterns across site type

---

20 Georgoudi (2010, 99–100) acknowledges this diversity and lists some factors with potential input. These include economic and budgetary reasons, importance of the particular cult in question, supply networks, social prestige and benefit, ecosystem, and the 'personality' of the divine or heroic honoree.

21 Where transhumance was practiced in Greek antiquity, its scale was presumably not grand, be that in sizes of flocks and distances covered. There is considerable debate on the issue, cf. Georgoudi 1974; Halstead 1987; Hodkinson 1988; Skydsgaard 1988; Reinders and Prummel 1998; Howe 2008, among others.

Non-Sanctuary		Sanctuary (Dining)	
Site	Sheep:Goat Ratio	Site	Sheep:Goat Ratio
Asine (Helladic contexts)	c. 3:1	Corinth	c. 1.5:1
Corinth	c. 1:2	Eretria	c. 1.2:1
Eleusis	c. 1.5:1	Gkionia	c. 3:1
Kassope	c. 2:1	Kalapodi	c. 1:1
Lousoi	c. 1:1	Messene	c. 1:3
New Halos	c. 5:1	Nemea	c. 4:1
Oropos	c. 1:1	Olympia	c. 9:1
Rachi of Isthmia	c. 0:2	Plakari-Karystos	c. 3:1
Pyrgouthi (Classical & Hellenistic)	c. 1:4	Tegea	c. 3:1
		Thebes-Kabirion	c. 2.5:1

FIGURE 10.3 Ratios of sheep:goat for sites

(large or small, settlement or sanctuary) and geographic region denotes similarity in the goals or methods linked to general animal husbandry schemes across the larger Greek world. This has implications for supply networks. Available zooarchaeological evidence indicates that the bulk of these animals were, for the most part, herded relatively nearby each site, year-round, and thus likely integrated within local agricultural systems. Consequently, one conclusion to reach here is that rural productive farming strategies, and not necessarily sacred or commercial preferences, generally dictate supplies of animals to sites. This is not to say that ritual sacrificial demands (e.g., sheep for this hero, bull for that god, young lamb for that honoree, etc.) were unimportant, but rather that rural productive strategies maintained a level of resource flexibility to cater to different local ritual and commercial demands, as required. Thus, whatever species, sex, age category, etc. requested could typically be supplied from local resources, within reason.

Differences, nevertheless, may register between larger versus smaller settlements in Archaic through Hellenistic Greece. Among smaller sites, such as New Halos and Rachi at Isthmia, for example, sheep/goat often dominate. Conversely, larger settlements (Athenian Agora, Kassope, Corinth) display more balanced distributions among taxa. Given the increasing evidence for settlement hierarchy in this period of Greek antiquity, perhaps smaller settlements focused on specific types of animal husbandry, potentially concentrating upon one species for both export and local consumption, while larger settlements attracted a more diverse range of livestock, potentially supplied from smaller settlements. Nonetheless, it is important not to overemphasize the nature, scale, and impact of any such 'specialization' or 'focused husbandry' that some sites might appear to register and extrapolate this uncritically upon the wider world of Greek antiquity. These are not massive, focused, extensive operations akin to factory farming or herding. Moreover, even those sites that register some 'focus' on specific taxa or husbandry components never do so to the exclusion of raising or incorporating other animals, as well.

1.2   *Sheep/Goat Ratios*

Because of their skeletal morphological similarities, sheep and goats are often lumped together as one taxon (sheep/goat) in zooarchaeological reporting. Nonetheless, certain elements can be distinguished, and by separating out the two taxa, details about cultural and ecological factors influencing husbandry practices for each species can be drawn. Fig. 10.3 presents the ratios of sheep to goat for the sites assessed in this chapter.

Tremendous variation exists across sites and contexts. Overall, however, sheep tend to outnumber goats in more cases, and in greater measure, among ritual, as opposed to non-ritual, dining contexts. Does this imply that sheep were relatively more important for sacrificial dining? And how might that correlate to selection of sheep in burned sacrifice versus their incorporation in dining? Answering these questions is complicated. Sheep are referenced and requested more often than goats among sacrificial calendars,[22] and they tend to outnumber goats across the wider array of sites in Greek antiquity. Presumably, this is a factor of their enhanced cultural and economic value overall at this time. Consequently, there is perhaps some expectation that they predominate. Goats are more limited in ritual operations, as both burned offerings and in feasting. Elevated ratios of goats to sheep in ritual contexts may occur for a variety of reasons, which themselves can mix multiple components. Veneration of Artemis, who received goats among her sacrificial offerings, might explain the high proportion of goats at

---

22   Attic calendars record sheep:goat ratios of 3:1 to 5:1 (Jameson 1988, 89).

Kalapodi. A preponderance of goats at the site of Messene could be a factor of their selection in dining operations here, but given the dominance of goat horn cores (which survive well) in constructing that particular ratio, caution should be exercised to reflect this taphonomic and recovery bias. Moreover, it is always important to assess the ratio of sheep to goat in light of ecological and cultural conditions at each site. This is well demonstrated in the case of Athens, where cultural issues, such as demands for wool and milk (for cheese), alongside ecological factors, such as availability and quality of pasture, drying climate conditions, and so forth, had an impact upon sheep/goat ratios.[23]

Notwithstanding that interpreting sheep/goat ratios requires deeper contextualization of all variables attached to each specific site and situation, results are mixed in the case of sites where a stronger correlation among burned sacrifice, ritual dining, and 'non-ritual' components might be inferred. At the site of Nemea, for example, goats were not identified among burned sacrificial offerings, but do appear (ratio of 4 sheep:1 goat) among ritual dining assemblages.[24] Does this imply that goats were 'acceptable/tolerated' as dining foodstuffs among some sanctuaries, but not (normally) offered in burned sacrifice? The dichotomy here is intriguing, as goats are one of the species frequently forbidden to be sacrificed among various deities, according to the ritual norms. More data for sheep/goat ratios among burned portions of faunal samples for ancient Greece are needed to test this hypothesis. Nonetheless, the inclusion of goat across ritual dining deposits does at least acknowledge a dietary contribution in that respect.

At the other end of the spectrum, sheep/goat ratios for the neighboring sites of Gkionia and Stratos allow comparisons of, respectively, ritual and non-ritual dining operations within a localized area. The fact that both of these sites (Stratos and Gkionia) register a ratio of 3 sheep:1 goat, however, raises the question of recognized 'ritual' feasting presenting no distinct differences than what might be interpreted as 'non-ritual' dining. Does this imply that whatever animals were locally available or accessible were dined upon regardless of situation? If so, such a measure may reinforce arguments already presented about mixed-farming ventures driving general husbandry operations. If the 3:1 sheep/goat ratio at these two sites was principally an instrument of best adaptation to local/regional ecological, environmental, and cultural settings, then those aspects are the key stimuli of the system.

Thus, what was consumed in sanctuaries, in ritual dining, conformed to what options were presented by local practices of husbandry. Again, such a principle reinforces the importance of local supply networks in provisioning animals for many ritual and sacrificial operations in Greek antiquity.[25]

1.3   Age

While inherent local flexibility underscores livestock supply networks to Greek sanctuaries, age variation among these animals may indicate different purposes. What patterns surface in this respect? Exceptions exist, and there is certainly a need for more detailed zooarchaeological data on the ages of animals across sites in question here, but generally, there is a slightly higher incidence of younger animals, notably cattle and sheep, among altar as opposed to dining contexts at Greek sanctuaries. The impression is that younger animals (and parts thereof) may have been offered more regularly among burned sacrifice, leaving older animals to comprise a relatively larger share of feasting debris. Whether or not preferential selection of younger animals links with aspects of fertility, 'first-fruits,' or other symbolic measures is unknown.[26] Conversely, links between mature animals and dining, including practical reasons (e.g., adults yield more meat) require deeper study. It should be pointed out, however, that the pattern noted here does not apply to pigs: younger pigs dominate both dining and altar debris (although pigs are rare among burnt remains as a whole). Most likely, this relates to shrewd husbandry tactics; there is little economic benefit in keeping many pigs to adulthood, given that once they attain their maximum size (around two years of age), they essentially become a drain on food resources without proffering any additional weight gain.

Although available zooarchaeological data (notably for sheep/goat and cattle) might support some selective preference for younger animals in altar sacrifices, and older animals among feasting debris for Greek sanctuary sites, it is important to be cautious before drawing

---

23   MacKinnon 2014.
24   MacKinnon 2018.
25   More routine investigations of isotopic data from faunal assemblages across Greek sites from a wider temporal and geographical perspective will help enhance our understanding of these issues. Vaiglova et al. 2018 use a multi-isotope approach to explore mobilization and acquisition of livestock for Neolithic feasting events at the site of Makriyalos, northern Greece. Similar studies for historic contexts in Greece, however, are currently underdeveloped.
26   Ritual dictates often stress selection of 'perfect' animals (i.e., healthy, strong, attractive) for sacrificial purposes, aspects that are more likely attainable with the selection of younger animals, it may be argued.

widespread conclusions. Two aspects are critical. First, younger age brackets among animals might be underrepresented across sites due to taphonomic, preservation, recovery, and identification biases. It is well demonstrated how zooarchaeological assemblages typically favor adult remains, which in turn then may amplify their relevance, especially among deposits that yield less fragmented (and potentially more ageable) faunal pieces. Burned sacrificial assemblages, thus, might suffer in this respect.

Second, although proportions may vary among the examples assessed here, no altar or dining assemblage (and for the latter this can be expanded to both ritual and non-ritual contexts) yields solely either young or old animals. This applies across all taxa, although it is less marked in the case of pigs, as noted above. Consequently, there seems to be no exclusivity in what age groups could, and were, dined upon, both within Greek sanctuaries and outside them. This flexibility, in turn, fits with the predominance of 'meat mortality profiles' as outlined earlier. Overall, factors such as local availability of resources, seasonality, and general herding schemes, as opposed to stricter cultural or ritual preferences, might be more influential in shaping what was consumed and when. Thus, an elevated proportion of adult sheep/goat and cattle within dining assemblages may reflect wider economic measures to maintain a greater proportion of these animals to exploit their secondary resources (wool, milk, labor, etc.). These groups then might be more readily available, year-round, among local stock that supplied ritual sites. Peaks in supplies of younger animals might be added to that mix depending on the timing of ritual events around schedules of birthing, resource exploitation (e.g., shearing, milking, need for traction animals), herd movements, or other measures that might bring animals to areas on a more seasonal or interval basis.[27]

1.4 Parts

Are there marked differences in the representation of different skeletal parts across contexts at Greek sanctuary sites? Certainly, this is evident among a number of *thysia*-style altar assemblages, where biases in favor of thigh bones and tail vertebrae register. The situation with dining assemblages at these sites, however, is less straightforward. Occasionally, there is evidence for an imbalance within various parts (e.g., a dearth of femur bones or tail vertebrae; a lack, or excess, of head or foot elements; an abundance of a particular element or section, such as ribs or forelegs, among other possibilities) that might indicate dining assemblages received what was 'leftover' from altar offerings.[28] In other cases, it seems that 'supplemental' cuts of meat might have been brought in to bolster dining assemblages.[29] Outside of these special cases, however, no clear pattern emerges as regards what skeletal parts comprise dining assemblages across Greek sanctuaries. Most consist of elements from the entire skeleton, suggesting that at least some whole animals were cooked and consumed. While this generalized representation of skeletal parts among sanctuary dining deposits makes it difficult to draw clear zooarchaeological distinctions as to which types of anatomical elements and/or cuts of meat may have been provided as priestly perquisites in sanctuary activities—for which abundant epigraphic evidence exists[30]—one potential conclusion to draw is that such portions, when awarded, do not appear to have been exclusive or exhaustive. In other words, while *some* parts of *some* sacrificial victims may have been provided to priests,[31] no dining assemblage from any sanctuary site registers a (potential) removal of those elements on any scale to significantly skew results. Nevertheless, examples register where bones from the head and/or foot might be underrepresented, suggesting perhaps some removal of hides, with head/feet attached, or a connection of these

---

27 In this regard, zooarchaeological data bolster many of these same findings presented earlier by Jameson 1988.

28 This is clearly shown at the sites of Isthmia, Nemea, Olympia, and Eretria, among other examples. Ekroth (2017c, 43–45) provides further comment. It should be noted, however, that even in cases where a connection may be inferred, that is with 'missing' or 'leftover' skeletal elements from one deposit (e.g., an altar context) potentially surfacing within another deposit (e.g., a dining assemblage), a true linkage might only be verified through DNA analysis of the bones themselves, to determine concretely if skeletal elements originated from the same animal. Infra n. 35.

29 Such 'supplemental' meats could include a host of taxa (domestic or wild, sacrificed or not), and a range of skeletal elements. See, below, the case studies for: (i) Nemea, for discussion of dogs, equids, and wild animals in sanctuary dining; and (ii) Corinth, for introduction of supplemental pork forelimb sections in ritual dining. Ekroth (2014b) draws attention to the contribution that sausages and minced meat may have fulfilled in ritual operations, be these as consumables in ritual dining or among the perquisites delivered to priests or officials. Notwithstanding questions as to the location of manufacture of such sausages (i.e., inside or outside the sanctuary?) and consequent potential for some of these foodstuffs to be brought into the sanctuary, their mere presence implies the existence of some type of 'supplemental' meat.

30 Carbon 2017 covers this field extensively and provides further references. For a review of the issue from an iconographic vantage, see Tsoukala 2009.

31 Whether these priests removed these or not from the compound cannot be assessed from zooarchaeological data alone.

parts with initial carcass butchery operations.[32] Alternatively, such a pattern might be interpreted as a preferential selection or retention of meatier, central parts of the skeleton (i.e., ribs, long bones, vertebrae) in ritual dining. Whatever the reason, it is important to note that, on the whole, great variability exists among zooarchaeological assemblages that have been interpreted as dining waste (be this ritual dining or otherwise) to posit any fixed conclusion as regards overall skeletal parts. As with aspects of taxa and age, discussed above, a measure of flexibility in what is selected seems to surface.

2 Case Studies

Sanctuary faunal assemblages arguably provide snapshots into specific ritual practices conducted at specific places within a site. Perhaps the best way to contextualize those activities is to compare contexts across a site, ideally sites hosting a range of deposit types: ritual, dining, sacred, secular, etc. Only in this manner can on-site variability be determined. To investigate this issue, three case studies will be outlined: Nemea, Corinth, and Athens. Choice here is partly personal (I have worked at all three sites) and partly calculated to explore variety. Nemea represents a site principally centered around cult. Corinth housed a key sanctuary to Demeter and Kore, but was also a functioning urban settlement. Athens marks a pinnacle among Greek cities, in all their complexity.

2.1 *Nemea*

As the locus of the Nemean games, ancient Nemea was an important Greek cult and festival center, especially during the Archaic period (sixth–fifth centuries BCE). Faunal remains from the site were collected from various regions and contexts.[33] These locations are indicated in Fig. 10.4. As regards 'sacrificial' assemblages, most of which consisted of bone remains of burned offerings collected from the Heroon and Altar of Zeus contexts, the data indicate a preference for sheep as the standard sacrificial animal, but show a definite preference for the hind limb sections of the left side in the case of sacrifice to the hero Opheltes, as opposed to the god Zeus.

Presumed dining debris from Nemea, that is materials associated with the Bath, *Xenon*, and Dining Room assemblages in particular, differs from altar deposits along three principal lines. First, burning is irregularly noted, and where present conforms to charring of articular ends of bones (as opposed to whole elements). Such a pattern denotes cooking fires, as opposed to ritual burning of the entire bone/section of the animal offered in sacrifice. More often, however, this dining debris registers a higher incidence of spirally fractured and broken bone, often in more regular-sized chunks, indicative perhaps of butchering these animals into uniform pieces for stewing or boiling. As widely argued, the most efficient means to cook such materials is through boiling, where mixtures of different foodstuffs—meats, grains, vegetables, etc.—could be produced, which would in turn be easily portioned and distributed among celebrants and diners.[34] Nemea is no exception here.

Secondly, at Nemea, dining debris yields far more taxonomic variability. The *Xenon* assemblage is the only one across the site to record hare and domestic fowl, taxa not normally sacrificed in burnt offerings, but potentially consumed as part of 'regular/secular' diets. The Dining Room assemblage (N17:73) is also special taxonomically in registering a relatively high proportion of juvenile pig remains, and the presence of fish bones. As both commodities were somewhat expensive food types in antiquity, their presence here suggests an elite diet. Perhaps these were meal remains from games officials or dignitaries.

A third aspect in which altar and dining faunal deposits at Nemea diverge is that no side or element preference exists among dining debris assemblages; rather a general mix of left and right parts from entire skeletons occurs. Presumably more whole animals were butchered and consumed in these contexts, which in this case comprised significant quantities of rib, cranial, and vertebral fragments. This pattern registered for both medium-sized (cf. sheep/goat and pig), as well as large-sized (cf. cattle) remains, and contrasts with values for 'sacrificial' contexts. It is possible that those 'missing' ribs and vertebrae from altar assemblages are contained within these dining deposits. Then again, it might be the case that these dining debris assemblages bear no link to ritual events proper, and may simply have been basic dining occasions, outside of feasting dictates.[35]

---

32 Whether these are designated for priests or otherwise cannot be determined on the basis of available zooarchaeological evidence. This issue of heads and feet is discussed in MacKinnon (2024).

33 See MacKinnon 2018 for earlier zooarchaeological studies from Nemea.

34 Ekroth 2007; 2008a; 2008b; 2011; 2014a; 2017a; 2017b; 2017c; among others, provides strong supportive evidence to this effect.

35 Separating out which of the above scenarios may apply (and if so, to what degree) within individual 'dining' deposits among sanctuary sites presents many challenges. As highlighted already,

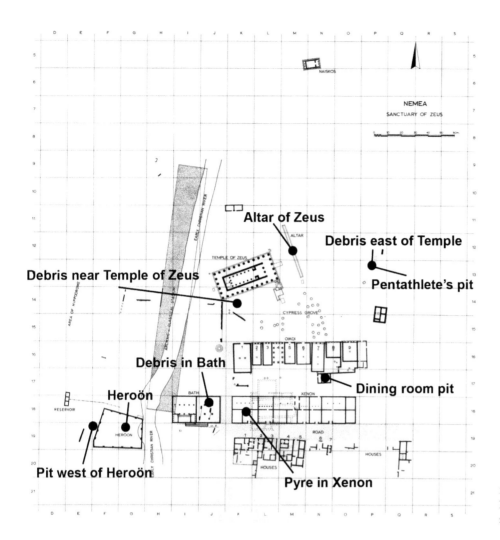

FIGURE 10.4
Nemea, plan with locations of zooarchaeological deposits examined

Remains of wild animals, dogs, equids, and the like, are noted among what have otherwise been categorized as ritual dining deposits (including Nemea) and interpreted, in some cases, as supplemental meats incorporated into communal stewpots for feasting.[36] While such an argument seems sensible, caution is warranted in extrapolating too much dietary significance here. The addition of these components may be more symbolic in nature, such as connections with purification, specialized selection, or some other angle.[37] Typically, these 'supplemental' taxa are scarce additions within assemblages, rarely attaining values above 1% of total NISP counts (Fig. 10.5).

Their apparent abundance at Kalapodi and Thebes rests on questionable contextual evidence for a ritual nature (i.e., levels are predominantly 'fills' and may contain mixed material of secondary deposition). Furthermore, a general overview of skeletal parts within dining contexts favors dentition, in the case of dogs and equids,

---

a discrepancy among skeletal parts among assemblages could have a variety of causes, and the line between ritual and non-ritual is not always distinct. While an argument may be made that 'missing' materials from altar assemblages were incorporated into dining assemblages at sanctuary sites (which may display such elements in higher frequencies), any definitive link to connect contexts may rest on DNA assessments of these bones themselves to verify from which individual animal each element arises (i.e., obtaining a 'fingerprint' for each bone, and then matching up common patterns). Future work may employ these tactics more routinely, but they have, as yet, not been utilized for Greek sanctuary sites to test for movement and/or connection of individual animal parts among different contexts within a site.

36 Ekroth 2008a; 2008b; 2009; 2011; 2013a; 2013b; 2014a; 2016; 2017a; 2017b; 2017c.

37 Although there is little evidence for consumption of animals used in purification practices (most of these otherwise being burnt or discarded to get rid of pollution), it would be difficult to determine their original purpose if the ultimate disposal of these animals was not separated distinctly from dining debris (i.e., contexts mixed).

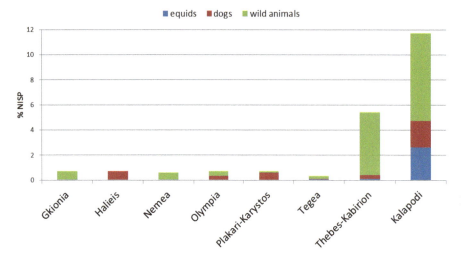

FIGURE 10.5
NISP (= Number of Identified Specimens) frequency values for 'supplemental' taxa (equids, dogs, and wild animals) among sanctuary assemblages

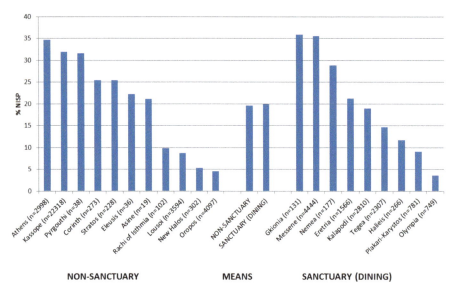

FIGURE 10.6
NISP (= Number of Identified Specimens) frequency values for pigs among sites

and antlers and phalanges, in the case of deer, elements with little meat, but with high archaeological survival rates. Moreover, these taxa and elements surface across otherwise non-ritual sites in Greek antiquity (and elsewhere) in similar frequencies to ritual sites as well, making it difficult to argue distinct ritual roles for them or at least uses that would otherwise not also be applied to non-ritual sites.

Pigs frequently register among dining assemblages at sanctuaries, including Nemea, but rarely account for more than 20% (by NISP frequency) of animals represented (excepting Demeter cults); oftentimes amounts are less than 10% (Fig. 10.6). This contrasts with non-sanctuary sites, where more cases with NISP frequency values over 20% exist. Presumably pigs could have been acquired fairly readily and cheaply from local sources (including households), year-round as well, making them not only a favorite for urban/settlement diners, but also a dependable supplemental menu item among many Greek sanctuaries.

Economics, thus, might have factored in selecting this dietary item even if pigs only served in a limited way for public sacrifice proper (being perhaps more popular among private sacrifice). This is supported by the iconographical evidence—pigs/piglets are the most common animal in votive reliefs that depict private sacrifices.[38]

Returning to Nemea, the choice there, principally of sheep across contexts, aligns with many sites in ancient Greece; as noted earlier, sheep adapt well to Greek landscapes, could be easily acquired, and are commonly mandated in sacrifices. What else can be noted about these sheep? To assist with one aspect of interest, specifically the variability in the size of these sheep, logarithm size-scaling values for sheep bone measurements were tabulated and plotted for comparison. Logarithm values are employed in zooarchaeological work as a means to enable pooling of measurements from different elements.

---

38 Van Straten 1995.

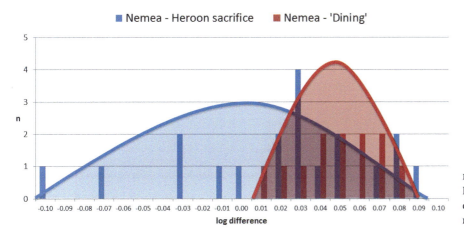

FIGURE 10.7
Logarithm difference values (and distribution curves) for sheep measurements among contexts at Nemea

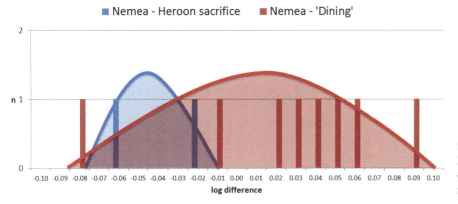

FIGURE 10.8
Logarithm difference values (and distribution curves) for cattle measurements among contexts at Nemea

This helps increase sample sizes for comparison and promotes wider assessments of overall patterns or trends in the data. The values for individual measurements are converted into logarithms and compared against a standard value (in this case sheep values for a Shetland ewe, UK)[39] to gauge the degree of difference. It does not matter so much whence the standard derives provided the same standard values are used in one's statistic. Nonetheless, as only mature bones are measured, comparisons chart only the adult portion of datasets.

Although samples are small, values for sheep (Fig. 10.7) display a greater range for Heroon contexts than for dining assemblages at Nemea. On average, sheep 'dined upon' by humans were larger and more tightly clustered in size than sheep sacrificed to Opheltes. Practical reasons may apply here: feasting might benefit from drawing upon bigger sheep, i.e., more mouths could be fed. These animals also may have been culled from local herds, which displayed limited genetic and morphometric variability (potentially a more compartmentalized, local population). Wider ranges for the Nemean Heroon examples may suggest broader supply networks for sacrificial victims, possibly drawn from a greater area, perhaps reflecting regional migration in celebratory participants. Thus, it may be the case that some worshippers potentially brought their own local sheep to sacrifice.

Logarithm values for cattle at Nemea (Fig. 10.8) add further particulars. Cattle were not the principal victim for Opheltes, and indeed it seems that only smaller representatives are noted among Heroon samples. By contrast, relatively larger cattle occur in dining assemblages at Nemea. A similar bias surfaces with sheep. Perhaps larger individuals were preferred to maximize dining capacity. Textual sources often stress selecting quality stock in sacrifice, sometimes denoting large size, as well. Zooarchaeological data nuance these prescriptive aspects, cautioning that sometimes human diners (and not gods) received larger stock.

2.2   Corinth

The Sanctuary of Demeter and Kore on the slopes of Acrocorinth provides a good circumstance to compare its assemblages with those retrieved elsewhere at Corinth. The bulk of the finds from the Sanctuary derive from 'fill' and 'floor' levels largely associated with Dining Room complexes. Although the Sanctuary operated throughout

---

39   Davis 1996.

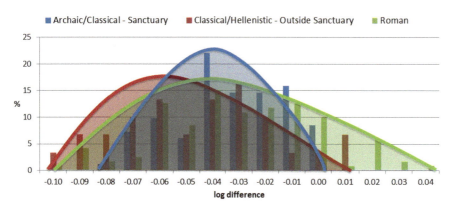

FIGURE 10.9
Logarithm difference values (and distribution curves) for pig measurements among contexts at Corinth

antiquity, its principal phases, and the focus here, center upon the Archaic and Classical periods.[40]

As expected in Demeter cults, pigs predominate, comprising over 90% of sanctuary materials in the Corinth example.[41] Deeper assessments provide more details. First, age and sex data indicate preferential selection of two important classes of pigs, notably (i) young piglets, and (ii) adult females, specifically pregnant sows; indeed, no adult male pigs register among Archaic/Classical contexts at the sanctuary site. While pigs can potentially farrow year-round, birthing schedules are generally timed to occur in spring and autumn. Setting these intervals against sanctuary data favors autumn as the key season of sacrifice (perhaps tied into Thesmophoria festivals). Nevertheless, variability among pig age data underscores a level of flexibility, as well. Thus, the possibility exists that ritual sacrifice and dining episodes were not limited to one season or occasion, and pig supply systems in Corinth, as a whole, adapted well to this.

A second feature of the material from the Demeter Sanctuary centers upon metric data, again using logarithms. Figure 10.9 plots values for pigs across contexts at Corinth. While the average size of sanctuary pigs is slightly bigger than other contexts and timeframes at Corinth, perhaps more telling is that samples for both the Classical/Hellenistic and Roman contexts outside the sanctuary display a much wider range than do Archaic/Classical samples inside the sanctuary. This suggests that pigs incorporated into sanctuary activities (and again it should be reiterated that metric comparisons here refer specifically to the adult pig portion of the sample) were marked by a tighter size (and presumably weight) bracket than those from other timeframes and contexts at Corinth. Might this relate to stricter parameters in selection of pigs for sanctuary functions? As noted, ancient sources often assert the importance of choosing quality, well-formed animals for sacrifice. Naturally, greater visual inspection of available animals would help produce this effect, but the narrower range of sizes exhibited in the profile for the Demeter/Kore Sanctuary pigs might also be linked to a more limited number of (perhaps, specially-bred?) herds from which to collect sacrificial specimens. If greater attention was invested, possibly less variation among sizes and conditions was tolerated, and hence the more limited range of sizes displayed. Unfortunately, dissecting these hypotheses further requires DNA assessments to affirm genetic relationships and connections among stock. Nevertheless, the fact that both larger and smaller pigs than those represented in Demeter Sanctuary contexts existed more generally at Corinth denotes some measure of selection imposed within the sanctuary to exclude those extreme size categories. Moreover, it prohibits the option that only the largest pigs were selected, something one might have expected if size were a chief factor in denoting a quality sacrificial animal. Overall, it may simply be that good stock, as defined along broader parameters, is what ultimately contributed to choice of pigs in this case. Perhaps there were central, favored stocks of pigs reserved for actual altar sacrifice—individuals, who, in turn were selected under stricter protocol—but, a broader range (a greater variety?) of supplemental pigs of varying sizes and weights brought in for dining purposes. Such a scenario would help explain the patterns exhibited.

Finally, data from Dining Room contexts at the Sanctuary of Demeter and Kore at Corinth suggest meat was cooked through boiling/stewing or within casseroles, as opposed to roasting, grilling, or baking. Given the confines of the Dining Rooms, and their limited cooking space, this seems sensible. The bone remains are quite fragmentary and display a range of butchery marks indicative of meat removal and smashing of bones to extract marrow. While

---

40   See Bookidis 1990; 1993; Bookidis et al. 1999 for general overviews of dining and sacrifice at the Sanctuary of Demeter and Kore at Corinth.

41   For further discussion of the topic of pigs in Demeter cults, including case studies involving zooarchaeological remains from sites beyond Corinth, see Clinton 2005; Ruscillo 2013; Miccichè 2020 among others.

whole piglets are noted, additional cuts of pork, most notably supplemental sections from the forelimb (e.g., humerus) also contributed, while other sections, such as vertebrae, ribs, and some hind limbs did not always factor, and may have been removed elsewhere. The inclusion of 'supplemental' forelimb sections denotes introduction of extra cuts of pork in cult operations, and in turn, brings in another potential supply network, possibly preserved salted or smoked pieces (but still on the bone) perhaps acquired through market or household operations. Inclusion of such 'additional' salted/smoked and/or fatty sections of meat, moreover, might also serve to enhance the flavor of the stew, as well.

The notion of market connections in sacrifice is not new. Sacrificial meat was sold, and the recording, commoditization, and pricing of sacrificial animals and cuts of meat implies some commercial linkages. Nonetheless, this issue is complicated and surpasses zooarchaeological data alone. It seems logical that some type of abattoir or butcher shop, even if temporary or make-shift, might operate in tandem with sanctuary animal sacrifices; however, concrete archaeological, or at least architectural, evidence for such among specific sanctuary compounds is lacking.[42] Meat markets do exist in Greek urban settlements (see below for a discussion of this for ancient Athens), but interpretation of these as strictly linked with sacrifice is problematic. Ideally, what is desired is a good example of a butcher shop (with tables, knives, bones, and detailed instruction manuals!) at a site such as Nemea, where cult operations were the principal focus of its existence. For now, such evidence is elusive.

2.3 Athens

Although abundant zooarchaeological evidence for ancient Athens exists, much derives from commercial settings, food shops, bars, and markets. In this manner, Athens presents a more complicated case study for investigating zooarchaeological connections among ritual and non-ritual contexts. Nevertheless, Athens could always draw mouths to feed; indeed, the regular provision of foodstuffs to the city supported the creation of new, specialized craftsmen who were able to leverage their expertise to acquire foodstuffs.[43] Like other large settlements such as Corinth, Kassope, and Messene, Athens registers a fairly even distribution of cattle, sheep/goat, and pig. Larger sites could draw upon animal supply networks as required. Athens presents a special case, however. Judging by its size alone, its pull could have been noticeably strong, and potentially extended far and wide. A study using cattle helps answer two questions of merit. Firstly, is there variation within the range of sizes of cattle consumed in Athens during the Classical period, and if so, what does this tell us about supply networks of cattle for the city? Figure 10.10 displays the logarithm size-scaling data for cattle from excavations at the site of the Athenian Agora by temporal period.

The range of values is extensive; in fact, Classical Athens exhibits the widest variability in cattle measurements across any ancient Greek site. The impression here is that the city was supplied with cattle of diversified stock, presumably from various regions. Comparable statistics for cattle in other areas of Greece displayed in Figure 10.10 show smaller, more tightly clustered ranges. Athenian cattle from the Classical period are not the largest, on average; interestingly, cattle from the Kabeirion at Thebes register bigger values, although that sample is from Hellenistic times (Fig. 10.10). Nonetheless, that finding sets up some interesting questions about the impact of environment upon animal size—for example, was the area around Thebes better suited for cattle herding? Moreover, the average size of cattle everywhere in Greece increased in Roman times, presumably a factor of overall breed improvements. Whatever the case, the point to emphasize here is that Athens was provisioned with the broadest range, and concomitant broadest variety, of cattle during the Classical period. Moreover, available age data indicate that these cattle were slaughtered, on average, at a much older age in the Athenian example, than among other sites.[44] It is unclear if this is due to emphasis on cattle used for labor, or if larger draft oxen were selectively imported to the urban environment.[45] Draft oxen could have been a supply source for civic Athenian sacrifices and beef commerce in the city; thus, larger numbers of older cattle specimens in the Archaic and Classical periods may reveal that draft oxen were disproportionately provided to the urban environment for consumption in feasts or distribution in the marketplace.[46]

A second question involves the treatment of cattle at Athens. In this regard, rather interesting butchery patterns exist for cattle from Classical contexts at Athens. With all

---

42　Although, there is epigraphical evidence for the sale of meat at sanctuaries, including how the meat is to be butchered and prepared, as well as its pricing (e.g., from Didyma: *LSAM* no. 54 = *IDidyma* 482). For further information about the sale of sacrificial meat in Greek antiquity, see Rosivach 1994 and MacKinnon (2024). Parker (2010) examines the issue of the sale and consumption of 'un-sacrificial' meat.

43　Dibble 2017, 305.

44　Dibble 2017, 266.

45　Dibble 2017, 266.

46　McInerney 2010, 180–82; Dibble 2017, 302.

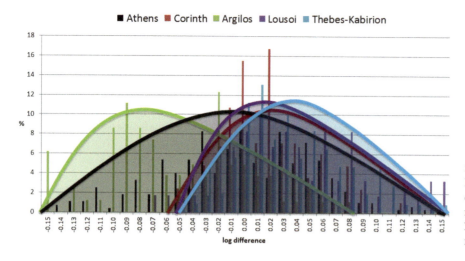

FIGURE 10.10
Logarithm difference values (and distribution curves) for cattle measurements among sites
Note: With addition of site of Argilos, northern Greece, Classical timeframe.

the animals funneling into the city, butchery equipment and techniques professionalized. The cleaver became the tool of choice and distinguished a professional butchery style associated with group feasting in contrast to domestic butchery.[47] Operations were more efficient, but not without some curiosities. For example, investigation of the Athenian zooarchaeological samples noted a lack of butchery marks on cattle femurs (as opposed to those on femora of smaller taxa), which likely indicates that most cattle were initially sacrificed in the context of large-scale feasts, or that butchers expected most cattle thigh bones would be ritually burned and so took extra care in the preparation of this particular element.[48] Whatever the case, the simple fact that these specially prepared femur bones occur alongside other butchered cattle elements blurs some of the parameters between sacred and commercial contexts as regards meat in ancient Athens.

3   Conclusions

To conclude, this investigation of some practical angles to diet at Greek sanctuaries inevitably does not answer all questions we might pose, but nonetheless yields some potential points of interest:

1) It seems probable that many local cult operations could be sustained using local resources. This is argued on the basis of the following criteria: the general variety in animal taxa, the dominance of 'meat mortality profiles' in husbandry schemes, and the fact that stock were principally herded relatively nearby each site, year-round, and thus likely integrated within local agricultural systems. Such tactics helped assure a fairly stable and flexible resource base of animals, even if the size and composition of that base fluctuated seasonally as a consequence of best practices in husbandry operations. Exceptions to this primacy of local resources exist, however, as the case in provisioning cattle (sacred or otherwise) to Athens shows. Here a much wider geographic reach in supplying animals to the city is discernable.

2) Beyond general taxon, age, and sex selection as regards animals in different cults (e.g., adult bull; young female lamb, etc.), sanctuaries may have set their own parameters around what specific sizes, breeds, or varieties of these animals were selected, and how in turn these might be portioned as altar or dining components. These additional parameters for taxon selection among various sanctuary sites might not always be made explicit in our sources.

3) Available zooarchaeological data suggest that younger animals (and parts thereof) may have been offered more regularly among burned sacrifice, leaving adult representatives as a larger relative share of feasting and dining debris. However, any potential significance this may have as regards practical or symbolic aspect needs further study.

4) Menus at Greek sanctuaries display some commonalities, such as incorporation of a range of taxa (not all of which formed part of any altar sacrifice, specifically, or for that matter, might not even have comprised any type of sacred/sacrificial victim *per se*; the purpose of some might be solely as sources of meat for sanctuary dining), a penchant for boiling and stewing, and regularity in butchering patterns to suit that cooking method. Nevertheless, they also yield aspects of uniqueness, regional flair, or other measures of individuality, such as a potential supplement of pig forelimbs for ritual diners in the Sanctuary of

---

47   Dibble 2017, 243.
48   Dibble 2017, 303.

Demeter/Kore at Corinth (a concept further supporting the fact that not all meat provided in sanctuaries derived from sacrificial victims), or the tendency for ritual human diners at Nemea to benefit from incorporation of relatively larger animals on their menu, as opposed to those destined for their honored god and hero.

Zooarchaeological work helps nuance these aspects; my hope is that it will continue to assist.

Works Cited

Benecke, N. 2006. "Animal Sacrifice at the Late Archaic Artemision of Olympia: The Archaeozoological Evidence." In *Archaeozoological Studies in Honour of Alfredo Riedel*, edited by U. Tecchiati and B. Sala, 153–160. Bolzano.

Boessneck, J. 1973. *Die Tierknochenfunde aus dem Kabirenheiligtum bei Theben (Böotien)*. Munich.

Boessneck, J. 1986. "Zooarchäologische Ergebnisse an den Tierknochen- und Molluskefunden." In *Haus und Stadt in klassischen Griechenland*, edited by W. Hoepfner and E.-L. Schwander, 136–140. Munich.

Bookidis, N. 1990. "Ritual Dining in the Sanctuary of Demeter and Kore at Corinth: Some Questions." In *Sympotica: A Symposium on the Symposion*, edited by O. Murray, 86–94. Oxford.

Bookidis, N. 1993. "Ritual Dining at Corinth." In *Greek Sanctuaries: New Approaches*, edited by N. Marinatos and R. Hägg, 45–61. London.

Bookidis, N., J. Hansen, L. Snyder, and P. Goldberg. 1999. "Dining in the Sanctuary of Demeter and Kore at Corinth." *Hesperia* 68: 1–54.

Carbon, J-M. 2017. "Meaty Perks: Epichoric and Topological Trends." In *Animal Sacrifice in the Ancient Greek World*, edited by S. Hitch and I. Rutherford, 151–178. Cambridge.

Chenal-Velarde, I. 2001. "Des festins à l'entrée du temple? Sacrifices et consommation des animaux à l'époque géométrique dans le sanctuaire d'Apollon à Erétrie, Grèce." *Archaeofauna* 10: 25–35.

Chenal-Velarde, I., and J. Studer. 2003. "Archaeozoology in a Ritual Context: The Case of a Sacrificial Altar in Geometric Eretria." In *Zooarchaeology in Greece: Recent Advances*, edited by E. Kotjabopoulou et al., 215–220. London.

Clinton, K. 2005. "Pigs in Greek Rituals." In *Greek Sacrificial Ritual, Olympian and Chthonian*, edited by R. Hägg and B. Alroth, 167–179. Stockholm.

Cosmopoulos, M.B., H.J. Greenfield, and D. Ruscillo. 2003. "Animal and Marine Remains from the New Excavations at Eleusis: An Interim Report." In *Zooarchaeology in Greece: Recent Advances*, edited by E. Kotjabopoulou et al., 145–152. London.

Davis, S. 1996. "Measurements of a Group of Adult Female Shetland Sheep Skeletons from a Single Flock: A Baseline for Zooarchaeologists." *JAS* 23: 593–612.

Dibble, F. 2017. *Politika Zoa*: Animals and Social Change in Ancient Greece (1600–300 B.C.). Ph.D. diss., University of Cincinnati.

Ekroth, G. 2007. "Meat in Ancient Greece: Sacrificial or Secular?" *Food and History* 5: 249–272.

Ekroth, G. 2008a. "Meat, Man and God. On the Division of the Animal Victim at Greek Sacrifices." In *Mikros Hieromnemon. Meletes eis Mneme Michael H. Jameson*, edited by A.P. Matthaiou and I. Polinskaya, 259–290. Athens.

Ekroth, G. 2008b. "Burnt, Cooked or Raw? Divine and Human Culinary Desires at Greek Animal Sacrifice." In *Transformations in Sacrificial Practices from Antiquity to Modern Times*, edited by E. Staviranopoulou, A. Michaels, and C. Ambos, 87–111. Berlin.

Ekroth, G. 2009. "Thighs or Tails? The Osteological Evidence as a Source for Greek Ritual Norms." In *La norme en matière religieuse en Grèce ancienne*, edited by P. Brulé, 125–151. Liège.

Ekroth, G. 2011. "Meat for the Gods." In *Nourrir les dieux? Sacrifice et représentation du divin*, edited by V. Pirenne-Delforge and F. Prescendi, 15–41. Liège.

Ekroth, G. 2013a. "What We Would Like the Bones to Tell Us: A Sacrificial Wish List." In *Bones, Behaviour and Belief. The Zooarchaeological Evidence as a Source for Ritual Practice in Ancient Greece and Beyond*, edited by G. Ekroth and J. Wallensten, 15–30. Stockholm.

Ekroth, G. 2013b. "Forelegs in Greek Cult." In *Perspectives on Ancient Greece*, edited by A.-L. Schallin, 113–134. Stockholm.

Ekroth, G. 2014a. "Animal Sacrifice in Antiquity." In *The Oxford Handbook of Animals in Classical Thought and Life*, edited by G.L. Campbell, 324–354. Oxford.

Ekroth, G. 2014b. "A Note on Minced Meat in Ancient Greece." In *LABRYS: Studies Presented to Pontus Hellström*, edited by L. Karlsson, S. Carlsson, and J. Blid Kullberg, 223–235. Uppsala.

Ekroth, G. 2016. "A View from the Greek Side: Interpretations of Animal Bones as Evidence for Sacrifice and Ritual Consumption." *Journal of Ancient Judaism* 7: 35–50.

Ekroth, G. 2017a. "Bare Bones: Osteology and Greek Sacrificial Ritual." In *Animal Sacrifice in the Ancient Greek World*, edited by S. Hitch and I. Rutherford, 15–47. Cambridge.

Ekroth, G. 2017b. "'Don't Throw Any Bones in the Sanctuary!' On the Handling of Sacred Waste at Ancient Greek Cult Places." In *Ritual Matters: Material Remains and Ancient Religion*, edited by C. Moser and J. Knust, 33–55. Ann Arbor.

Ekroth, G. 2017c. "Sacred Meals in Ancient Greece? Dining in Domestic Setting as Compared to Sanctuaries." In *The Eucharist—Its Origins and Contexts*, edited by D. Hellholm and D. Sänger, 1389–1411. Tübingen.

Forstenpointner, G., and M. Hofer. 2001. "Geschöpfe des Pan—archäozoologische Befunde zu Faunistik und Haustierhaltung im hellenistischen Arkadien." In *Forschungen in der Peloponnes*, edited by V. Mitsopoulos-Leon, 169–179. Athens.

Forstenpointner, G., A. Galik, and G.E. Weissengruber. 2013. "The Zooarchaeology of Cult. Perspectives and Pitfalls of an Experimental Approach." In *Bones, Behaviour and Belief. The Zooarchaeological Evidence as a Source for Ritual Practice in Ancient Greece and Beyond*, edited by G. Ekroth and J. Wallensten, 233–242. Stockholm.

Friedl, H. 1984. *Tierknochenfunde aus Kassope/Griechenland (4.–1. Jh. v. Chr.)*. Ph.D. diss., University of Munich.

Gebhard, E.R., and D.S. Reese. 2005. "Sacrifices for Poseidon and Melikertes-Palaimon at Isthmia." In *Greek Sacrificial Ritual, Olympian and Chthonian*, edited by R. Hägg and B. Alroth, 125–154. Stockholm.

Georgoudi, S. 1974. "Quelque problèmes de la transhumance dans la Grèce ancienne." *RÉG* 87: 155–185.

Georgoudi, S. 2010. "Sacrificing to the Gods: Ancient Evidence and Modern Interpretations." In *The Gods of Ancient Greece: Identities and Transformations*, edited by J.N. Bremmer and A. Erskine, 92–105. Edinburgh.

Groot, M. 2014. "Burned Offerings and Sacrificial Meals in Geometric and Archaic Karystos: Faunal Remains from Plakari (2011–2012)." *Pharos* 20: 25–52.

Hägg, R. 1988. "Osteology and Greek Sacrificial Practice." In *Ancient Greek Cult Practice from the Archaeological Evidence*, edited by R. Hägg, 49–56. Stockholm.

Halstead, P. 1987. "Traditional and Ancient Rural Economy in Mediterranean Europe: Plus ça Change?" *JHS* 107: 77–87.

Hitch, S. 2015. "Sacrifice." In *A Companion to Food in the Ancient World*, edited by J. Wilkins and R. Nadeau, 337–347. London.

Hodkinson, S. 1988. "Animal Husbandry in the Greek Polis." In *Pastoral Economies in Classical Antiquity*, edited by C.R. Whittaker, 35–74. Cambridge.

Howe, T. 2008. *Pastoral Politics: Animals, Agriculture and Society in Ancient Greece*. Claremont.

Huber, S., and P. Méniel. 2013. "Annexe 1: Analyses archéozoologique. La faune terrestre du sanctuaire d'Apollon." In *Eretria 22: Le sanctuaire d'Apollon Daphnéphoros à l'époque géométrique*, edited by S. Verdan, 243–254. Gollion.

Jameson, M.H. 1988. "Sacrifice and Animal Husbandry in Classical Greece." In *Pastoral Economies in Classical Antiquity*, edited by C.R. Whittaker, 87–119. Cambridge.

Jameson, M.H. 1994. "Theoxenia." In *Ancient Greek Cult Practice from the Epigraphical Evidence*, edited by R. Hägg, 35–57. Stockholm.

Leguilloux, M. 2000. "L'hécatombe de l'ekklesiasterion de Poseidonia: le témoignage de la faune." In *Rites et espaces en pays celtes et méditerranéen: étude comparée à partir du sanctuaire d'Acy-Romance (Ardenne, France)*, edited by S. Verger, 341–351. Rome.

MacKinnon, M. 2010. "'Left' is 'Right': The Symbolism Behind Side Choice Among Ancient Animal Sacrifices." In *Anthropological Approaches to Zooarchaeology: Complexity, Colonialism and Animal Transformations*, edited by D. Campana et al., 250–258. Oxford.

MacKinnon, M. 2013. "'Side' Matters: Animal Offerings at Ancient Nemea, Greece." In *Bones, Behaviour and Belief. The Zooarchaeological Evidence as a Source for Ritual Practice in Ancient Greece and Beyond*, edited by G. Ekroth and J. Wallensten, 125–143. Stockholm.

MacKinnon, M. 2014. "Animals, Economics, and Culture in the Athenian Agora." *Hesperia* 83: 189–255.

MacKinnon, M. 2018. "The Faunal Remains from the Hero Shrine." In *Excavations at Nemea 4: The Shrine of Opheltes*, edited by J.J. Bravo, 79–100. Berkeley.

MacKinnon, M. 2024. "Animal Heads and Feet in Ancient Greek Ritual Contexts: Their Relationship between Sacred and Profane." In *From Snout to Tail: Exploring the Sacrificial Animal from the Literary, Epigraphical, Iconographical, Archaeological and Zooarchaeological Evidence*, edited by G. Ekroth and J.-M. Carbon. Stockholm.

MacKinnon, M. forthcoming. *Zooarchaeology at Corinth*. Princeton.

McInerney, J. 2010. *The Cattle of the Sun: Cows and Culture in the World of the Ancient Greeks*. Princeton.

Miccichè, R. 2020. "Sometimes Pigs Fly." In *The Akragas Dialogue: New Investigations on Sanctuaries in Sicily*, edited by M. De Cesare, E. Chiara Portale, and N. Sojc, 253–268. Berlin.

Moberg, K. 1992. "The Animal Bones." In Hägg, R., and G.C. Nordquist, "Excavations in the Levandis Sector at Asine, 1989." *OpAth* 19: 66–68.

Moberg Nilsson, K. 1996. "Animal Bones from Terrace II in the Lower Town of Asine." In *Asine 3. Supplementary Studies on the Swedish Excavations 1922–1930* 1, edited by R. Hägg, G.C. Nordquist, and B. Wells, 111–115. Stockholm.

Mylona, D. 2005. "The Animal Bones from Pyrgouthi in the Berbati Valley." In *Pyrgouthi: A Rural Site in the Berbati Valley from the Early Iron Age to Late Antiquity*, edited by J. Hjohlman, A. Penttinen, and B. Wells, 301–308. *SkrAth 4°*, 52. Stockholm.

Naiden, F.S. 2013. *Smoke Signals for the Gods: Ancient Greek Sacrifice from the Archaic through Roman Periods*. Oxford.

Nobis, G. 1997. "Tieropfer aus einem Heroen- und Demeter-Heiligtum des antiken Messene (SW-Peloponnes, Griechenland) Grabungen 1992 bis 1996." *Tier und Museum* 5: 97–111.

Parker, R.C.T. 2010. "Eating Unsacrificed Meat." In *Paysage et religion en Grèce antique. Mélanges offerts à Madeleine Jost*, edited by P. Carlier and C. Lerouge-Cohen, 137–145. Paris.

Prummel, W. 2003. "Animal Husbandry and Mollusk Gathering in Hellenistic New Halos (Thessaly)." In *Housing in New Halos, a Hellenistic town in Thessaly, Greece*, edited by H.R. Reinders and W. Prummel, 175–223. Lisse.

Prust, A. 2013. "Faunal Remains from Stratos, Acarnania." In *Interdisziplinäre Forschungen in Arkarnanien*, edited by F. Lang et al., 205–217. Bonn.

Reese, D.S. 1993. "Appendix: Faunal Remains from the Well." In "A Well in the Rachi Settlement of Isthmia," edited by V.R. Anderson-Stojanovíc, *Hesperia* 62: 301–302.

Reese, D.S. unpublished report. "Faunal Remains from the Sanctuary of Apollo at Halieis."

Reinders, H.R., and W. Prummel. 1998. "Transhumance in Hellenistic Thessaly." *Environmental Archaeology* 3: 81–95.

Rosivach, V. 1994. *The System of Public Sacrifice in Fourth-Century Athens*. Atlanta.

Ruscillo, D. 2013. "*Thesmophoriazousai*: Mytilene Women and Their Secret Rites." In *Bones, Behaviour and Belief. The Zooarchaeological Evidence as a Source for Ritual Practice in Ancient Greece and Beyond*, edited by G. Ekroth and J. Wallensten, 181–195. Stockholm.

Scullion, S. 2009. "Sacrificial Norms, Greek and Semitic: Holocausts and Hides in a Sacred Law of Aixone." In *La norme en matière religieuse en Grèce ancienne*, edited by P. Brulé, 153–169. Liège.

Scullion, S. 2013. "Bones in Greek Sanctuaries: Answers and Questions." In *Bones, Behaviour and Belief. The Zooarchaeological Evidence as a Source for Ritual Practice in Ancient Greece and Beyond*, edited by G. Ekroth and J. Wallensten, 243–255. Stockholm.

Skydsgaard, J.E. 1988. "Transhumance in Ancient Greece." In *Pastoral Economies in Classical Antiquity*, edited by C.R. Whittaker, 75–86. Cambridge.

Stanzel, M. 1991. *Die Tierreste aus dem Artemis/Apollon Heiligtum bei Kalapodi in Böotien/ Griechenland*. Ph.D. diss., University of Munich.

Studer, J., and I. Chenal-Velarde. 2003. "La part des dieux et celle des hommes: offrandes d'animaux et restes culinaires dans l'aire sacrificelle nord." In *Eretria 14: L'Aire sacrificielle au nord du Sanctuaire d'Apollon Daphnéphoros*, edited by S. Huber, 175–185. Gollion.

Trantalidou, K. 2007. "The Contribution of the Study of Animal Bones in the Social Understanding of Early Iron Age Oropos." In *Oropos and Euboea in the Early Iron Age*, edited by A. Mazarakis Ainian, 379–425. Volos.

Trantalidou, K. 2013. "Dans l'ombre du rite: vestiges d'animaux et pratiques sacrificielles en Grèce antique." In *Bones, Behaviour and Belief. The Zooarchaeological Evidence as a Source for Ritual Practice in Ancient Greece and Beyond*, edited by G. Ekroth and J. Wallensten, 61–86. Stockholm.

Tsoukala, V. 2009. "Honorary Shares of Sacrificial Meat in Attic Vase Painting: Visual Signs of Distinction and Civic Identity." *Hesperia* 78: 1–40.

Vaiglova, P., et al. 2018. "Of Cattle and Feasts: Multi-isotope Investigation of Animal Husbandry and Communal Feasting in Neolithic Makriyalos, Northern Greece." *PLoS ONE* 13(6): e0194474.

van Straten, F.T. 1995. *Hierà Kalá. Images of Animal Sacrifice in Archaic and Classical Greece*. Leiden.

Vila, E. 2000. "Bone Remains from Sacrificial Places: The Temples of Athena Alea at Tegea and of Asea on Agios Elias (the Peloponnese, Greece)." In *Archaeozoology of the Near East* 4-B, edited by M. Mashkour et al., 197–203. Groningen.

Vila, E. 2014. "Étude archéozoologique des vestiges osseux de la fouille dans le temple." In *Tegea 1. Investigation in the Temple of Athena Alea 1991–1994*, edited by M.E. Voyatzis and E. Østby, 547–562. Athens.

CHAPTER 11

Food in Sanctuaries: Markets and Consumption

Annalisa Lo Monaco

Periodic local, regional, or panhellenic festivals involved large—sometimes staggeringly large—crowds of people traveling to big and small sanctuaries, and in some cases, they remained there for several consecutive days.[1] Lucian said that there was "the largest gathering of the Greeks" at Olympia,[2] and the situation must have been similar in the other famous international sites.[3] Spectators could come from far and wide. For example, Kaikilis, a baker from the Macedonian city of Veria, did not miss a single occurrence of the Olympic games in the space of 60 years. Despite the 700 km journey and the difficulties it entailed, he went to the games 12 times and was so proud of it that he had this information engraved in his funeral epitaph![4]

Special areas were set aside for the needs of such large public gatherings, where visitors themselves could erect tents and shelters or simple improvised beds.[5] This information, recalled in reference to Ion's tent at Delphi[6] and Alkibiades' tent at Olympia,[7] is archaeologically confirmed by the discovery of numerous holes for iron supports that held stakes to which tents were attached.[8] Areas of the sanctuaries thus became veritable open-air tent camps and, in the most advantageous cases, were set up near natural water sources.[9]

As well as accommodation, pilgrims also needed water and food: water could be obtained (with some difficulty) from wells or springs.[10] Food could be purchased in special markets intended for the sale of all kinds of necessities,[11] although we should note that some visitors brought their own personal pottery, usually open drinking vessels, *skyphoi* and *kotylai*,[12] more rarely kraters and *aryballoi*,[13] on which the name of the owner was scratched.[14]

The following discussion addresses the nature, supply, and demand in these markets, specifically concerning food consumption within sanctuaries: what kind of food was offered for sale, how these transactions were regulated, what prices were set, the origin of the food sold, and how the goods were handled. Given the nature of the literary evidence, it is not surprising that the remarks are general, simply indicating the occurrence of markets, but lacking useful details about their location, the products sold, or the consumers. At most, we have the indication of *agorai* during festivals or *mercatus*,[15] and the idea that all sorts

---

1 Since at least 472 BCE, the Olympics lasted five consecutive days (Pind. *Ol.* 5.6: πεμπαμέροις ἁμίλλαις; Paus. 5.9.3), with a total of some 45,000–50,000 visitors (Barringer 2021, 10, 44, with references). Cf. Iambl. *VP* 12.58: the *panegyris* attracts men of all kinds, in a huge crowd. On this topic, cf. Dillon 1997.
2 Lucian, *De mort. Peregr.* 1.
3 According to Philostratos (*VA* 4.17), the Eleusinian Mysteries in Imperial times were πολυανθρωπότατα, i.e., "the most crowded of Greek festivals." Menander Rhetor says that the Pythian games were attended by people "from the ends of the world" (*Peri Epid.* 1.366–367), and the crowd in Isthmia was probably even larger, with people traveling from Ionia, Sicily, Italy, North Africa, Marseilles, and Borysthenes (Dio Chrys. 9.5).
4 Tataki 1988, 184–185, no. 647 (third century CE); Pleket 1996, 524.
5 On the more structured accommodation of athletes, cf. Sinn 2004, 130–133, and for accommodation in general, see Ekroth in this volume.
6 Eur. *Ion* 1128–1180 (side of about 100 feet).
7 Ps. And. *Alk.* 30.2.
8 Angeli Bernardini 1997, 184, n. 18. And we have the stakes themselves from Olympia: see Wacker 1996, 91, n. 67. See also Taita 2014, 123–126.
9 The area designated for this purpose at Olympia is to the west of the Altis near the Kladeos River (cf. Lo Monaco 2013, 125–131).
10 For Olympia, see Kyrieleis 2011, 114–115; Barringer 2021, 45–47. For the logistics of water in sanctuaries, see the contributions of Klingborg and Trümper in this volume.
11 On this topic, cf. Dillon 1997, 214–215; Brugnone 2018; Lo Monaco 2020; Chankowski in this volume.
12 Kalapodi: cups, *kotylai*, and *skyphoi* of the Archaic and Classical periods; see Palme-Koufa 1996, 275. Olympia: *skyphoi*, one-handled cups, and cups with feet, and rarely, plates produced in Elis during the fifth and fourth centuries BCE; see Schiering 1965, 149–157, 211; Schilbach 1995, 45. Perachora: *kotyle* from the second half of the seventh century BCE; see Dunbabin 1962, 394, n. A 1, pl. 163. Aigina, sanctuary of Aphaia: chalices and kraters with dedicatory dipinti underneath the rim; see Williams 1983, 169–178. Akrocorinth, sanctuary of Demeter and Kore: black-painted cup of the late seventh century BCE with the graffito: "I am Choirasos' kotyle," and a dedication to Kore; see Stroud 1968, 328, fig. 98g; Guarducci 1974, 335, n. 2.
13 Krater: Dunbabin 1962, 394, no. A4a, pl. 127 (3403), seventh century BCE. *Aryballoi*: Dunbabin 1962, 394, no. A 2 (1555), A3 (1598), pls. 61, 63.
14 According to a custom that was also widespread in Etruscan territory (Guarducci 1974, 330–335).
15 Latin texts indicate *mercatum* regarding the Olympian feast: Heraklid. Pont. apud Cic. *Tusc.* 5.3.9: *mercatum … alii emendi aut vendendi quaestu et lucro ducerentur*; Vell. Pat. 1.8.1: *ludos mercatumque*.

of merchandise, even slaves,[16] were sold.[17] Epigraphic sources are usually sacred decrees and laws, and therefore by their very nature richer in useful details, such as the type of food, its cost, and even portion size. The contribution of archaeology and zooarchaeology differs and enables us to understand the nature of the food consumed, how it was cooked, and occasionally how certain products were sold. The refinement of analysis of faunal remains and organic residues in containers (gas-chromatography and spectrometry) in recent decades allows us to better address issues relating to the subsistence of the visitors inside the sanctuaries on feast days: what did they eat, and in what quantities? Was it dried food they brought with them (e.g., figs, cheese, dried fish), or could they buy fresh and perhaps specially cooked food on site?

1 Markets

The walking distance to a sanctuary from inhabited centers and their respective *agorai* may have prompted visitors traveling to neighboring sanctuaries (e.g., Epidauros;[18] Akraiphia, ca. 2.5 km from the sanctuary of Apollo Ptoios) to avail themselves of the urban *agorai*. It may also have been less costly to shop in a city before entering a sanctuary: although there was certainly a market in Eleusis that could supply visitors with all kinds of goods, a letter from Gallienus, archon in Athens in 264/265 CE, gives the *mystai* easy access to the market in Athens, where they could perhaps benefit from lower prices for the best products and a wider variety of them.[19]

Once at the sanctuary, the sale of goods and food took place in special delimited areas:[20] only within these spaces was it legal to carry out economic transactions.[21] There is no unequivocal data regarding their location, which could fall either inside sanctuaries[22] or near the main access roads, as must have been the case at Olympia (probably in the area between the South Hall and the Alpheios River)[23] and at Delphi (perhaps near the main entrance to the sanctuary).[24]

The location of such markets might not be fixed but indicated by the *hieroi* in spaces specifically delimited for the occasion.[25] Movable structures, stands, and sales counters were mostly constructed of ephemeral material and dismantled in the days following the festivities. The most recurrent term in literary sources and inscriptions is that of counters made of reeds, branches or papyrus, or tents (σκηναί or more rarely γέρρα[26]) covered with textiles or skins.[27] Much more rarely, they could be more fixed structures, such as the stalls used by the merchants (κάπηλοι) at the Heraion of Samos[28] or the οἰκίαι used as storage places

---

16 Slaves were sold in the *panegyris* of Apollo at Actium (*LSS* no. 45; De Ligt 1993, 65, n. 21).

17 Dio Chrys. 8.9 ("and peddlers not a few peddling whatever they happened to have" [around Poseidon's temple at Isthmia]), 27.5 ("Many too bring in merchandise of all sorts, the tradespeople, that is; and some display their own arts and crafts," trans. Cohoon). Cf. the large amount of goods sold at Tithorea (Paus. 10.32.14–16).

18 A stele with the inscription *horos agoras* (350–300 BCE) was found near the slope of the akropolis and is probably related to the location near the coastline of the city agora (Kritzas 1972, 197–199, fig. 10; *SEG* 29.379).

19 Clinton 2005, 419–422, no. 655.

20 This information is derived primarily from the law of Andania (*IG* V.1 1390, ll. 37–38). On these aspects, cf. Soverini 1990–1991, 87; Bresson 2015, 240; Brugnone 2018, 65.

21 E.g., during the *panegyris* of the sanctuary of Artemis Amarysia in Eretria, the merchants have the right to sell their goods inside the sanctuary: *LSCG* no. 92, l. 32 (fourth century BCE); Chandezon 2000, 87, nn. 73–74; Bresson 2015, 237.

22 Eretria, Artemis Amarysia: *IG* XII.9 189, ll. 32–35 (post-340 BCE). The rule contained in the decree goes beyond custom, establishing that during the annual festival, traders could sell their wares inside the sanctuary in any place they liked without paying any tax or rent to the *hieropes* (Brugnone 2018, 60). Also Tegea, Athena Alea: *IG* V.2 3, ll. 26–30 (cf. Dubois 1986, 31–32; Chandezon in this volume); the Heraion of Samos (Soverini 1990–1991); and perhaps Eleusis (Clinton 2005, 278, no. 237).

23 The proximity to the river must have been valuable in facilitating the arrival and unloading of goods. Two excavation campaigns close to the propylon of the South Hall in 2016 and 2017 brought to light stratigraphic levels of only sand (Senff 2018, 43, figs. 1–2), and no trace of the infrastructure used for agora purposes, probably because it was made of perishable material. In the area were also two altars, one consecrated to Zeus Agoraios and the other to Artemis Agoraia (Paus 5.15.5). See now Barringer 2021, 47–48.

24 The function and the chronology of the huge complex near the main entrance of the *peribolos* (500 m²) are still much disputed. The rectangular square, colonnaded on three sides, contained several irregularly shaped rooms on its northern side in which retail shops may have been located. Cf. Amandry 1981, 724, figs. 45, 47, 48; Maass 1993, 67, Taf. IV; Weir 2004, 96; Scott 2014, 281, 300, 453, n. 6; Bommelaer 2015, 111–114, no. 99, figs. 24–26. *Contra*: Lawrence 2012, 162–163, fig. 5.8.

25 *IG* V.1 1390, ll. 37–38.

26 On the two terms, see the recent discussion in Brugnone 2018, 58–59.

27 Andania: the size and positioning of the tents (and even their interior decoration!) are dealt with in two paragraphs in the cultic regulation of 92–91 BCE (*IG* V.1 1390, ll. 35–39). On sacred law, I refer to Zunino 1997, 304–315 (T 7); and Deshours 2006. Abydos: *IGRom.* IV 190 = *IMT NördlTroas* (Roman period), where οἱ σκηνεῖτα⟨ι⟩ and ἐργασ[ταί] are associated. Tithorea: Paus. 10.32.15. Σκαναί are also mentioned in Theoc. *Syracuse* (15.16) in relation to the purchase of sodium carbonate.

28 On the regulation of the *kapeloi* at Samos, much discussed and dated between 246 and 221 BCE, see Soverini 1990–1991; Chankowski in this volume.

for measures and perhaps for valuables.[29] Some vendors may have remained (only) until their wares were sold out, a time period that might not coincide exactly with the duration of the festival. Their stands could also be rented out by the sanctuary.[30]

It was possible to sell food, cooked or raw, as well as all kinds of merchandise, including refined products (golden or silver objects[31]) or items necessary for entering the sanctuary itself (e.g., boots or especially shoes[32]). Coins also were sometimes minted to facilitate sales transactions related to these festivals, as was the case for the Eleusinian Mysteries.[33]

Fraud was also a possibility. An inscription mentions punishments for selling non-genuine or adulterated goods, and the *agoranomos* was responsible for these controls, too (e.g., Andania[34]). Selling stolen goods, as happened in the Kerkopes' market in the Athenian Agora not far from the Helieia,[35] may not have been uncommon even within sanctuaries.[36]

The very nature of markets for sanctuary visitors, which were episodic (yearly or even every five years) and generally lacking in fixed structures, has led to their almost total disappearance. It is therefore very rare to have any archaeological trace of their positions. Recent discoveries in Attika offer additional details on the structure and function of permanent complexes near sacred areas. In the deme of Oe, a vast quadrangular complex has come to light, measuring approximately 1,000 m² and divided into three wings opening onto a central courtyard.[37] It is a structure with a clear commercial use (including an oven in the south wing) as testified by the discovery of lead weights in four different units in direct connection with a sacred area, which may be the agora mentioned in the sacred calendar of the deme of Erchia and the sanctuary of Hermes ἐν ἀγορᾶι Ἐρχιᾶσιν.[38]

Even if buildings are mostly lacking, another valuable indicator of the sale of products can be coins. Exemplary is the recent publication of data concerning the Heroon of Opheltes in Nemea: Jorge Bravo distinguished coins found inside the Heroon and therefore probably used as votives (2–6%) from coins found outside concentrated near the southwestern corner in much larger quantities (94%). He thinks that the latter may indicate commercial transactions related to goods connected to ritual activity inside the shrine, e.g., the purchase of generic, votive items, such as miniature vessels, but also, of course, food.[39] Coins from this heroon also inform us about the origin of the worshippers: most come from nearby poleis (e.g., Corinth, Argos, Sikyon, Phlious), but a residual number derive from more distant cities (e.g., Elea, Syracuse, Ambrakia, Kos).[40]

2 Sale and Consumption of Vegetables

Vegetables—cheap and easily obtained—must have been the main source of food for worshippers and visitors at sanctuaries. Vegetable consumption leaves few archaeological traces. At most, one can make use of analyses of organic remains in ceramic containers (e.g., Kalaureia[41]), archaeobotanical or flotation technology (Kalaureia, Samos, cf. Tas Silġ on Malta[42]), or examination of remains in primary or secondary stratigraphic deposits (Kalaureia, Olympia[43]).

Barley (hulled or not), einkorn, emmer, spelt wheat, broomcorn millet, legumes (lentils, bitter vetch, peas, broad beans), vegetables (mangold, lettuce) and fruit (figs, grapes, quinces, sugar- and watermelons, peaches,

---

29 Eleusis: οἶκος ἐν ᾧ καὶ τὰ μέτρα καὶ τὰ σταθμὰ κεῖται (Clinton 2005, 278, no. 237, l. 62). On the function of the οἰκίαι within sanctuaries, cf. Soverini 1990–1991, 89–91; Ekroth in this volume.

30 De Ligt 1993, 68 with reference to rental of booths near Koronea (*misthosis ton skenon*).

31 In Ephesos, a silversmith named Demetrius made and sold miniature silver temples of Artemis for great profit: *Acta Apostol.* 19.24 ff.

32 It was mandatory to enter the Trophonion sanctuary in Lebadeia wearing heavy boots to consult the oracle (Paus. 9.39.8).

33 Kroll, J.H. 1993, 27–48.

34 *IG* V.1 1390, l. 100.

35 Eust. *Od.* 2.7; Greco 2014, 1135, F 82 (G. Marginesu).

36 Cf. Heraion of Samos: Sokolowski 1978, 144.

37 Kakavogianni and Anetakis 2012, 191–194.

38 *CGRN* 52, col. E, ll. 50–51.

39 Bravo 2018, 46–49.

40 Bravo 2018, 45.

41 Mylona 2008, 93 concerning residues from the dining deposit, west of the Building D: fat residues on *chytrai* indicate the cooking of leafy vegetables, together with consumption of non-ruminant animals (pigs?).

42 Kalaureia: frequent cereals, olives, grapes, figs, and more rarely, nuts, hazelnuts (Sarpaki 2019); in this regard, we await the publication of J. Hansen, *Plant remains from Isthmia*, announced in Sarpaki 2019, 285. Samos: Kučan 1995. Tas Silġ on Malta: Fiorentino, D'Oronzo, and Colaianni 2012.

43 Kalaureia, dining deposit: consumption of olives, grapes, figs, almonds, a few cereals, and seeds (Mylona 2008, 96). Olympia: peach seeds, olives, grapes, walnut shells, and pine nuts were found in wells dug on the slopes of the Kronion in the seventh century and read as remains of meals consumed (along with meat, as evidenced by the discovery of spits and animal bones). Cf. Taita 2007, 50 (concerning the δειπνητήριον mentioned in the scholion of Pind. *Ol.* 10), 55b, e, 57 a–b.

mulberries, olives) are well attested at Kalapodi, Delphi, Samos, and in the sanctuary of Demeter and Kore at Corinth.[44]

The discovery of cooking pottery, e.g., *chytrai* and casseroles, and baking pans for cooking food by boiling or stewing in sanctuaries,[45] e.g., Samothrace, Olympia, Lemnos, may pertain to these foods.[46] Once cooked, vegetables were eaten in cups (*kotylai*), bowls, or plates: their discovery in large quantities in sanctuaries could therefore be related to daily consumption (e.g., Samothrace, Olympia, the Kabeirion on Lemnos[47]).

At Olympia, hundreds of *kotylai, hemykotylai*, and *choinikes* from the late fifth to the late fourth century BCE were found in the south and southeast sectors of the Altis.[48] These shapes comply with local units of measurement with an internal capacity of approximately 200, 400, and 800 cl and were inscribed with Zeus' name;[49] some bear seal impressions of the supervising magistrate (Fig. 11.1). Thus, they were produced specifically for the sanctuary to guarantee the correctness of the sale in containers with a controlled internal capacity. They were used to sell barley and cereal grains, flour or semolina, dried fruit, ground or grated ingredients, and wine in containers of three different sizes, which we know from letters painted on the exterior that indicated the contents within: ἄλφιτον (barley meal/flour), καρπός (fruit), and possibly ψωκτός (minced).[50]

An enormous number of bronze weights were found scattered outside the Altis at Olympia:[51] more than 480 specimens, in various weight formats of four, two, one mina, and fractions of one mina; again, the name of Zeus is inscribed on them (in the genitive), and his symbols (eagle, thunderbolt) in relief on their top surfaces ensured the legitimacy of transactions (Fig. 11.2). It is probable that retailers were obliged, year after year, to purchase weights produced and guaranteed by the sanctuary: since it was impossible to remove them from the sanctuary and use them on other occasions, it is likely that they were consecrated to Zeus at the end of each festival occasion. The relatively small capacities of the clay measures, ranging from 100 gr to 500 gr at most, depending on the density of the food inside, would seem to indicate immediate consumption of the food, within one or at most two consecutive days. A similar indication is given by the unit of bronze weights, ranging from 60 gr to 2 kg: the largest weight units are very rare, while most weights are one mina, half a mina, and their submultiples (from 60 gr to 500 gr), thereby confirming immediate, individual consumption.[52]

The case of Olympia has no equal in the ancient world regarding weights and measures, at least as far as the quantity of evidence is concerned. Official cups and weights have also been found at the Argive Heraion,[53] Corinth,[54] Nemea,[55] Delphi,[56] Oropos,[57] the Artemision

---

44 Kroll, H. 1993; Kučan 1995; Megaloudi 2006, 77–80.
45 I do not propose a rigid formal differentiation between containers used for cooking different kinds of food. In fact, the data is always subject to precise verification by chemical analysis, as demonstrated by the difference between the kitchen ceramics from the sanctuary of Apollo at Hierapolis (used indifferently for cooking animal and vegetable foods) and those from the sanctuary of Tas-Silġ on Malta (with pots for cooking fish or meat stews, and pans for steaming fish). See Notarstefano 2012a, 92–93, 111–112.
46 Samothrace: Lehmann 1969, 209, n. 116 (*chytra*, Augustan/Tiberian), 153, n. 18 (large dish, fourth century BCE). Olympia: Schiering 1965, 231–236; Schauer 2003, 166, nos. A 34–A 35 (*c*.450–425 BCE), 183, nos. D4 (mid-fourth century BCE), D5 (375–350 BCE), D6–D8, 194 (pottery for food preparation and consumption found in wells in the Prytaneion), nos. G13 (late Classical), G15 (late Classical). Lemnos: Monaco in Beschi 2004, 260–261, 262.
47 Samothrace: Mostly locally produced plates and cups of the late fifth-fourth century BCE (Lehmann 1969, 145). Olympia: Schauer 2003, 165, nos. A27 (sixth–fifth century BCE)–A28 (late Archaic/Classical), 178, no. C5 (430–400 BCE), 193, nos. G1–G2 (late Classical). Lemnos, Kabeirion: Monaco in Beschi 2004, 258–260.
48 Such containers could be kept in the Bouleuterion and be used as needed, according to Schilbach 1999, 336.
49 Schilbach 1999, 325. The calculation of the internal capacities of the various types of ceramic vessels has been given considerable impetus in recent years. See Bentz 2002; Engels, Bavay, and Tsingarida 2009.
50 Hamdorf 1981; Schilbach 1999: the inscription δαμόσια is painted on the body of the vessels, corresponding to a *kotyle*, and the word δαμόσιον appears on the shapes *dikotylon, hemikotylion*, and *tetartonkotylion*. On the function of these containers, see Wachter 2001, 282; Kyrieleis 2011, 112; Barringer 2021, 48–50.
51 Kyrieleis 2011, 113–114.
52 Hitzl 1996, 235–244, nn. 404–446.
53 Waldstein 1905, 297, n. 2240, a single specimen from the southern slope (near access to the sacred area?).
54 Apart from a group of only three bronze weights, each weighing one mina of 412 gr from the Greek period, numerous weights of bronze, lead, and even marble from the Roman period have been recovered from the sanctuary (Davidson 1952, 204–206).
55 One example with an inscription ΔΑΜΟΙΟΝ ΑΡΓΕΙΩΝ (Miller 2004, 65, 66, fig. 41).
56 Twenty-four specimens, of which six are in marble, 14 in lead (Roman period), and only four in bronze. See Perdrizet 1908, nos. 709–724; Hitzl 1996, 121–122, where two of the bronze weights, marked ΙΕΡΑ, weigh 1116 gr and 1082 gr, respectively, and are Hellenistic in date.
57 Quadrangular bronze weights, inscribed on the upper side with the name of the sanctuary to which it belongs in the genitive: Ἀμφιαράου. See Pernice 1894, 194, no. 781 (146.27 gr) Petrakos 1968, 125–126, nos. 35 (212 gr), 36 (851 gr).

FIGURE 11.1　Olympia, Archaeological Museum, vessel for the sale of fruit, *karpometron*, terracotta
PHOTO: D-DAI-ATH-1977-0230

FIGURE 11.2 Berlin, Antikensammlung, Ol. 12177, bronze weight from Olympia with Zeus' name and eagle
PHOTO: STAATLICHE MUSEEN ZU BERLIN, ANTIKENSAMMLUNG/JOHANNES KRAMER, CC BY-SA 4.0

of the *chora* of Eretria,[58] Samos,[59] Dodona,[60] Thermon,[61] the sanctuary of Demeter in Dion,[62] and Kalapodi,[63] but their small numbers do not allow us to draw similar conclusions concerning the sale of perishable goods within these sanctuaries.

Epigraphical documents complement this picture. The Andania law states that sellers must use weights and measures that conform to public standards and that they were liable to flogging or a fine if they failed to do so.[64] During the Eleusinian Mysteries, which lasted several days, a public slave at Eleusis supervised the correct use of official weights and measures,[65] and two marble tables with graduated measures for dry goods, such as grain, were found in the sanctuary.[66]

It is possible to think of the purchase and sale of raw products in some cases, while in others, such as flour and legumes, food was prepared and consumed on site (e.g., Kalaureia[67]), perhaps eaten on some kind of tavern tables. The preparation of bread and its derivatives on site is also attested by the frequent discovery of mortars and millstones.[68]

The sale of such goods was regulated by law. For example, the decree of the *kapeloi* of Samos, mentioned above, contains a prohibition on the free purchase of agricultural products from 'unauthorized' dealers and on the sale to persons unauthorized to purchase. This ban, which should be read as an attempt to control and ration cereals because of poor harvests,[69] also indicates the consumption of local agricultural products on Samos.

Vegetables and fruit had to be sold at a short distance from their place of production. Small producers or wholesalers of products would provide larger quantities of their produce than usual during major festive gatherings for intra-regional trade.

3 Sale and Consumption of Fish

Fish bones and seashells from the Geometric to the Hellenistic period attest to common consumption of fish and shellfish in sanctuaries.[70] The percentages are numerically significant from the middle of the eighth century BCE onwards but appear to decrease somewhat in the Roman Imperial period.[71] The overall data are currently incomplete and strongly conditioned by the excavation techniques adopted: in cases where sieving and water flotation strategies are employed (e.g., Kommos, Kalaureia), the quantities are numerically significant.

The multiplication of zooarchaeological investigations has made it possible to appreciate the variety and quantity of fish consumed, which were mostly small- and medium-sized fish (gilthead bream, snapper, and red bream at

---

58 Bronze weight inscribed 'of Artemis,' Imperial age. See *IG* XII.9 893; Knoepfler 1972, 299, n. 45; De Ligt 1993, 258.
59 Two bronze examples, weighing 140 gr (early fifth century BCE) and 751 gr (with indication of ownership on one of the faces HPHΣ), respectively. See Hitzl 1996, 126–127, pls. 42a–c.
60 Three specimens: one bronze of 344 gr (Brommer 1975, 186–187, pl. 59:2; Hitzl 1996, 125, pl. 42d, who dates it as early Hellenistic); one half-ounce of 253 gr (Athens, Karapanos collection: Pernice 1894, 67, no. 703); one silver of 8.52 gr (Roman, half ounce: Pernice 1894, 68).
61 A bronze weight of a mina with a dedication to Apollo Thermios, end of third century BCE. See *IG* IX.1 83.
62 Pingiatoglou 2015, 128, fig. 232 (29.6 gr). Δ is engraved on the upper face.
63 Archaic cup inscribed with the word *hemikotylon* on the exterior and an internal capacity calculated at around 160 cl. See Palme-Koufa 1996, 279–280, 305, no. 46, Taf. 61, 71, 79.
64 *IG* V.1 1390, ll. 99–105. Cf. Zunino 1997, 312–313.
65 *IG* II² 1013, ll. 49–50 of 100 BCE. See Clinton 2005, 278, no. 237.

66 Clinton 2005, 178–180, no. 179, 389, no. 553.
67 The bread was surely cooked and eaten in Kalaureia. See Sarpaki 2019, 285.
68 Megaloudi 2006, 78.
69 Sokolowski 1978, 145–147.
70 Mylona 2008; Mylona 2019.
71 Around 30% of the fish bones found in the sanctuary at Kommos date from 750–650 BCE; see Rose 2000, 495. Fish consumption at the beginning of the Geometric period is attested in Kalaureia. See Mylona 2015, 409.

Kalaureia;[72] cod, sole, gilthead bream, squid, and cuttlefish at Eretria;[73] gilthead bream at the sanctuary of Demeter and Kore at Corinth;[74] grouper, gilthead, bream, scallops and tuna at Tas-Silġ on Malta[75]), and also fish, such as serranids, mackerel, tuna, swordfish (Kalaureia), amberjacks and tuna (Messene[76]), and even angel sharks (Kommos[77]). It is possible that the very low percentage of small fish is due to their integral consumption, which leaves no residue.[78]

The evidence also includes mollusks. A wide variety of edible bivalve shells (mostly rough cockles, also gastropods, such as dog whelks/mud snails, limpets, and mussels) were found inside the *adyton* of the temple of Kythnos in the Cyclades, where they were stored secondarily together with votives, probably on shelves.[79] The secondary location does not make it easy to understand whether the shells were deposited intact as votives or whether they are the remains of a meal, which were collected after consumption. The case of Kythnos is not unique: numerous mollusks (mainly castanets and murici, as well as limpets) were also found at Eretria;[80] gastropods of various families at Kalaureia;[81] oysters and cockles (cerastoderma glaucum) at Samos[82] and Ephesos;[83] and oyster shells, cockle valves, and sea urchins at Tas-Silġ[84] and at the sanctuary of Demeter and Kore at Corinth.[85]

The context in the Poseidon sanctuary at Kalaureia is instructive for our purposes. Most of the bones come from the 'dining deposit' just at the entrance of the area, a triangular space containing an accumulation of much table debris, mainly consisting of drinking, cooking, and serving vessels; animal bones; seashells; seeds; and small objects. It was a one-time deposit in a space specially constructed for the purpose.[86]

More generally, the consumption of fish and shellfish in sanctuaries prompts some reflection on the relationship between dietary practice and the offering of food to the deity. Fish sacrifices are quite rare in the Greek world,[87] apart from tuna and eel,[88] and no proper sacrifice is known to have been related to invertebrates.[89] It would therefore seem to be a food practice aimed at the subsistence of the pilgrims, but without any precise relation to the sacrifice or to a specific deity.[90]

Epigraphic documents provide specific rules on the sale/purchase of fresh fish and the weight-to-cost ratio. We know that saltwater fish (sea bass, mullet, cuttlefish, tuna) and freshwater fish (eel and barbel, perch) could be sold whole or in slices,[91] and that prices varied depending on the slice, the size (Delphi[92]) or whether the females had roe (Akraiphia[93]).

The Roman Imperial government also was concerned about fish markets and food supplies: a letter attributed to Hadrian exempted the fishermen selling wares in the agora at Eleusis, probably during the Eleusinian Mysteries, from paying the 2 obol-tax so as to have "a good supply of food and that the aid through imports may amount to a lot."[94]

---

72 Kalaureia: over 3,500 fish bones of 19 different fish families and many species. See Mylona 2015, 390.
73 Theodoropoulou 2013a, 256, 263.
74 49 bone remains of small/medium-sized fish (11–15 cm). See Bookidis et al. 1999, 38–39.
75 De Grossi Mazzorin and Battafarano 2012, 360; Notarstefano 2012b, 120.
76 Nobis 1994, 303.
77 475 fish fragments from Temple C (375–350 BCE), Kommos. See Rose 2000, 496, 498 (angel shark).
78 Mylona 2019, 200.
79 Archaic to Hellenistic period. See Theodoropoulou 2013b, 199–200.
80 Theodoropoulou 2013a, 256, 263.
81 Mylona 2015, 390.
82 Boessneck and von den Driesch 1988, 42.
83 Bammer, Brein, and Wolf 1978, 109.
84 Notarstefano 2012b, 120, 124.
85 Bookidis et al. 1999, 39.
86 Mylona 2015, 392–393.
87 A list of deities to whom fish are sacred in Rose 2000, 520–528; Lefèvre-Novaro 2010, 39–41.
88 Eel sacrifice by the Boiotians to the Unknown Deities; tuna sacrifice at Halai Aixonides in Attika and Halies in the Argolid. Cf. Ath. 7.297d, 7.303d; Mylona 2008, 91; Mylona 2015, 407.
89 Theodoropoulou 2013b, 204.
90 Cf. Theodoropoulou 2013b, 212–215; Mylona 2015, 410.
91 Some bell-shaped kraters of Apulian production show the rare scene of splitting of fish, e.g., Cefalù, Museo Mandrisca 2, from Lipari, private collection. Usually interpreted as scenes of sacrifice, they have more recently been viewed as depicting the portioning of fish when they were sold at market. See Sparkes 1995, 156–160, figs. 11.7–11.8.
92 Vatin 1966 (third century BCE); SEG 23.326; BÉ 1967, 309 (L. Robert).
93 List of about 70 saltwater fish, grouped alphabetically, with retail prices according to weight, with a lacuna in the text concerning freshwater fish. Few names are discernable due to gaps in the text or hapax. The sale offer perhaps is connected with the occasion of the *Ptoia*, which was reorganized around 220 BCE under the leadership of Akraiphia. See SEG 32.450; SEG 38.377 from the end of the third to the beginning of the second century BCE; Salviat-Vatin 1971, 95–109; Roesch 1974; De Ligt 1993, 64–65, 246; and Lytle 2010.
94 Oliver 1989, 193–195, n. 77; Boatwright 2000, 90–91. Other examples of tax exemptions in connection with *panegyreis* cited in De Ligt 1993, 65–66.

FIGURE 11.3 New York, The Metropolitan Museum of Art 06.1021.241, South Italian red-figure fishplate, perhaps from Cumae, attributed to the Helgoland Painter, c.360–325 BCE, terracotta
PHOTO: NEW YORK, THE METROPOLITAN MUSEUM OF ART, ROGERS FUND, 1906

The frequent finds of fishing tools such as nets, weights, and lead fishing hooks in sanctuaries raise the possibility that fresh fish, whole or in pieces, were brought there.[95] If they were sold to visitors at the sanctuaries during the great feasts, we assume that these fish were eaten after cooking, presumably by boiling, steaming, or stewing. Chemical analyses of the organic residues in containers found in sanctuaries confirm that fish were cooked in ceramic cooking pots or pans.[96] The fish may have been served on 'fishplates,'[97] large dishes c.20–25 cm in diameter, the central cavity of which could accommodate accompanying sauces (Fig. 11.3), which are often recovered from large sanctuaries,[98] and of course, fish could be eaten in smaller dishes.[99] We have no more precise indications of establishments where fish could be eaten and served. The only exception is perhaps Building I at Kalaureia, just outside the sanctuary precinct and not far from the 'dining

---

95 Mylona 2015, 391, 399. Kommos: needles for repairing nets, hooks, bronze fishing hooks, tweezers; see Schwab 2000, pls. 5.48–5.49. Isthmia: bronze fishhooks, lead fishnet weights; see Raubitschek 1998, 127–128, nos. 453–454, 129, nos. 455–456, pls. 72–72. Olympia: bronze hooks and net needles found outside the Altis, and more than a third between the *stadion* and the southeastern sector; see Baitinger and Völling 2007, 57–66, nos. 172–210, 213–232, Taf. 16–17. Perachora; see Payne 1940, 182, no. 80:6, pl. 80:6.

96 Mylona 2015, 396 (a large number of *chytrai* from Kalaureia); Mylona 2008, 94 (Kommos, Temple B); Notarstefano 2012b, 123 (pots and pans, plates and bowls from Tas-Silġ, Malta).

97 It is likely that this form is the πινακίσκος ἰχθυηρός mentioned by Aristophanes (*Plut.* 812–814). Cf. Campanella and Niveau de Villedary y Mariñas 2005, 58–63; Mylona 2008, 113–123 with earlier bibliography.

98 Sanctuary of Demeter at Dion: Pingiatoglou 2015, 101–109, s.v. ψαροπινάκιο. Thesmophorion at Eretria: Metzger 1985.

99 Notarstefano 2012b, 126.

deposit' discussed above. The building, dated to the late Hellenistic and early Roman periods, was a two-storey structure with rooms on three side of an open courtyard. Within was a large quantity of fishing-related objects, such as lead sheets, lead ring weights, and a variety of fish-hooks; this evidence led the excavators to conclude that food preparation and serving took place here, but it seems equally plausible that such material was simply votive. Some rooms were used as kitchens or for food service in both Hellenistic and in Roman times, and handicraft production and commercial activities took place here in the Roman period.[100]

Fresh fish and mollusks certainly came from local districts as suggested by the location of sanctuaries where fish consumption is attested. Many of these are adjacent or close to the sea,[101] rivers,[102] or major ports.[103] These fish are local species,[104] with prevalent exploitation of the coastal strip and fishing by means of nets and pots;[105] fishing on the high seas with fishing rods or dragging submerged baskets was probably less common.

Two documents offer testimony of the transfer of fish from the coast to the interior. A stele at Epidauros records that a fishmonger named Amphimnastos, trading in fish at Tegea and inland Arkadia, attempted fraud against Asklepios by failing to dedicate a promised tithe, and that this was later remedied following a revolt by the fish themselves![106] At about the same time, Aristotle records an epigram in honor of an Olympic winner, who used to transport fish from Argos to Tegea.[107] Additionally, we have ample evidence of the consumption of dried fish, which could be carried by the individual user, sold locally,[108] or even exported over long distances, as was the case with the best quality slices of salted tuna and mackerel exported to the Mediterranean in Punic and Gaditan amphorae as early as the fifth century BCE.[109]

In short, the evidence for consumption of fish in sanctuaries in Greece is similar to that from the Iberian and Phoenician-Punic worlds, where fresh fish (preferably coastal species), salted fish and their derivatives—dried or pickled fish—and mollusks were an integral part of the daily diet.[110]

4   Sale and Consumption of Meat

Meat consumption in sanctuaries, both as the product of animal sacrifice and distribution, and from animals killed solely to procure meat, is central to the topic of food in sanctuaries. Increasingly detailed studies over the last few decades have made it possible to recognize the presence of meat in sanctuaries from the earliest stages of their appearance in the Protogeometric period to the Archaic and late Classical periods,[111] and again in the Hellenistic period.[112] Given the discovery of animal bones and layers of ash, studies have focused on the stature of the animals,

---

100   Mylona 2015, 391.
101   Brauron, sanctuaries of Demeter and Kore in Kyrene and Corinth, Eleusis, Ephesos, Halieis, Kition, Samos, Samothrace, sanctuary of Hermes and Aphrodite at Symi (Crete), Perachora, and Kamiros and Lindos on Rhodes.
102   Artemis Orthia near the Eurotas River.
103   Dion, located 1.5 km from the sea in the Hellenistic period; Demeter sanctuary at Knossos; Delphi, 11 km from Kyrrha; Kalapodi, 17 km from the Gulf of Euboia; Messene, some 20 km from the coastline, see Nobis 1994. Olympia, over 20 km from the ancient port, assumed to be Pheia mentioned by Strabo (8.3.13), who calculates it at a distance of 120 stadia (c.21.6 km); although the distance is actually about 30 km, it can be covered in a day's walk on foot, according to Taita (2013, 346–350, n. 35), who posits the Alpheios River as an alternative for travel and the passage of goods (350–377).
104   Euboian Gulf varieties at Eretria: Theodoropoulou 2013a, 257; coastal fish at Kommos: Mylona 2015, 409.
105   De Grossi Mazzorin and Battafarano 2012, 360; Mylona 2015, 394 (Kalaureia).
106   Herzog 1931, 26–29; *IG* IV².1 123, ll. 21–29 (350–300 BCE); Mylona 2008, 76, 136, n. 23.
107   Arist. *Rh.* 1365a, ll. 25–26: πρόσθε μὲν ἀμφ'ὤμοισιν ἔχων τραχεῖαν ἄσιλλαν / ἰχθῦς ἐξ Ἄργους εἰς Τεγέαν ἔφερον ("with the rough yoke on my shoulders I used to carry fish from Argos to Tegea"); cf. Lytle 2010, 290, n. 151.
108   In Delos, there is evidence of rented premises for the sale of salted fish (ταριχοπώλιον, *ID* 104). For the consumption and sale of salted and/or dried fish, see Linders 1994, 78; Lytle 2010, 291–292; Bresson 2015, 184–186.
109   For the Corinth forum and Olympia, see Campanella and Niveau de Villedary 2005, 37, 52–56; Mylona 2008, 86–88; Lytle 2010, 292.
110   Campanella and Niveau de Villedary 2005, 41, 50.
111   Protogeometric period: Isthmia (sheep, goats, and cattle), see Gebhard 1993, 156; Eretria (goats, cattle, pigs, sheep), see Huber and Méniel 2013. Archaic and Classical periods: Samos (sheep, goats, cattle, sows, and more rarely, fallow deer), see Boessneck and von den Driesch 1988 and Kyrieleis 2020, 31; Ephesos (goats, sheep, cattle, pigs, and more rarely, horses, dogs, and deer), see Bammer, Brein, and Wolf 1978, 107–108.
112   Tenos, sanctuary of Poseidon and Amphitrite: 63.5% cattle, 23.9% pigs, 12.5% rams or sheep/goats; see Leguilloux 1999, 428. Lousoi, sanctuary of Artemis Hemera; see Forstenpointner and Hofer 1997. Thebes, Kabeirion: mainly goats/sheep, a few rams and pigs; see Boessneck 1973.

their size and weight, and their classification into age categories.[113]

In addition to the zooarchaeological data, other material evidence, such as knives, testifies to the slaughter of animals.[114] Small meat hooks,[115] iron spits or forks,[116] and cooking pottery, such as *chytrai*,[117] and trays,[118] sometimes with rims blackened from use,[119] indicate preparation and cooking of meat on site. Some meat was designated for the deity, but later given to the priest, and the rest was distributed to, and consumed by, the worshippers after the sacrifice had been concluded.[120]

Unlike the victuals already discussed, neither literary sources nor the archaeological record allow us to identify specific sales of meat in the *agorai* near or at sanctuaries. We possess no lists of prices or prohibitions concerning false weight from a Greek sanctuary[121] as is the case for fish or the 'Marseilles Sacrificial Fee' from the Phoenician-Punic world.[122]

That is why scholars until now usually discuss the consumption of meat in sanctuaries in the context of sacrifices. After offering a portion of the sacrificed animal to the deity consisting of select bones, usually thighbones and tails, the *mageiros* (butcher) would butcher and prepare the remaining portions, allowing those present to consume the cooked sacrificial meat. Numerous sacred laws regulate the division of portions between deities and worshippers. Studies have focused on the detailed ways in which meat was apportioned;[123] the handling of animals in sanctuaries while awaiting slaughter, including where animals were kept;[124] and how animals were tethered near altars[125] or even to the stylobates of temples.[126]

The question as to what extent sacrificial meat was sold or distributed is central. Epigraphic documents and, to a lesser extent, literary sources indicate the practice of sharing meat, and, more rarely, selling it.[127] In some cases, portions—perhaps reserved for religious personnel—may have been removed from the sanctuary itself,[128] as suggested by the absence of forequarters, and such meat was evidently consumed elsewhere,[129] as was the case with the spinal columns of animals at Eretria.[130]

Some documents even illustrate the minimum weight for the meat portions assigned to each category of

---

113 E.g., see Nemea, Ophelteion of the sixth to fourth century BCE: 85% sheep/goats, 8% cattle, 6% pigs (burnt, preference for left hind limbs). See Mackinnon 2018, tables 11–12 with useful comparative zooarchaeological data for animal sacrifices to Olympian deities in the Greek world; and see Mackinnon in this volume.

114 General overview: Sossau 2019, 33–36. Cf., e.g., Petalidion, sanctuary of Apollo Korythos: Lo Monaco 2009, 726–728 (Mess. Koryth 1), esp. 728. Mt. Lykaon, sanctuary of Zeus Lykaios: Lo Monaco 2009, 406–414 (Arc. MLyk 2), esp. 412. Attika, sanctuary of Zeus Parnessios: Palaiokrassa-Kopitsa and Vivliodetis 2015, 160. Olympia: Baitinger and Völling 2007, 100–110, nos. 402–471, Taf. 37–38 (Archaic and Classical). Perachora: Payne 1940, 189–190, table 86: 16–19. Kalapodi: Felsch 2001; Schmitt 2007, 509–522.

115 Eleusis: *IG* II² 1541; Clinton 2005, 128, no. 140, ll. 13–14 (356–355 BCE).

116 E.g., Stymphalos, sanctuary on the akropolis: Lo Monaco 2009, 454 (Arc. Stymph 1). Tegea, sanctuary of Athena Alea: Lo Monaco 2009, 459–466 (Arc. Teg 1), esp. 465. Mt. Lykaon, sanctuary of Zeus Lykaios: Lo Monaco 2009, 406–414 (Arc. MLyk 2), esp. 412. Attika, sanctuary of Zeus Parnessios: Palaiokrassa-Kopitsa and Vivliodetis 2015, 160. Olympia: Baitinger and Völling 2007, 96, nos. 390–401, Taf. 32 (Archaic and Classical); Kyrieleis 2011, 78, fig. 77. Philia: Kilian-Dirlmeier 2002, 9, nos. 15–31, 253–254, Taf. 4.15–20, 5.21–24, 6.25–31.

117 E.g., Messene, temple of Isis and Serapis: Lo Monaco 2009, 774 (Mess. Mess 60). Dion, sanctuary of Demeter: Pingiatoglou 2015, 93.

118 Eleusis: *IG* II² 1541; Clinton 2005, 128, no. 140, ll. 11–13 (356–355 BCE). The same document also mentions other metal tools useful for cooking meat, such as a στυράκιον and λόγχιον (l. 17).

119 Stymphalos: Lo Monaco 2009, 454 (Arc. Stymph 1).

120 Detienne and Vernant 1982, 13; Naiden 2012, 240–241. For the butchering and allocation of portions to certain categories, e.g., priests, see Le Guen-Pollet 1991, 12–23; Leguilloux 1999, 453–454; to sacred officials, see Paus. 5.13.2. For distribution of meat, see Ekroth 2008; Carbon 2017; Bravo 2018, 94–95.

121 No regulation concerning the origin of meat and its sales (by which means) exists. See Naiden 2012, 241.

122 *CIS* I 165 (Donner and Röllig 2002, no. 69) of the third century BCE offers a detailed list of the sacrifices and quotas, listed in descending order of importance from cattle to birds and concluding with bloodless offerings, which were due in payment to the priests.

123 Detienne and Vernant 1982; Ekroth 2008; Carbon 2017.

124 Cf. McInerney 2014 on the enclosure of Zeus Polieus on the Athenian Akropolis and the management of the animals before and during their slaughter.

125 Dion: Pandermalis 2000, 291–292, figs. 4–5. Klaros: de La Genière and Jolivet 2003, 189–190, pls. v–vii, xxviii, xxxix, plan A. Mt. Lykaios, Sanctuary of Zeus Lykaios: Lo Monaco 2009, 406–414 (Arc. MLyk 2), esp. 412.

126 Olympia: on the first step on the south and east sides of the Heraion. See Herrmann and Moustaka 2013, 110–114, fig. 6. Reused blocks with the usual large iron rings from the late Imperial age also are attested in Olympia; see Herrmann and Moustaka 2013, 112–113, figs. 7–8; Taita 2015, 133.

127 Scullion 1994, 99–101, 103–112; *NGSL*² 276; Naiden 2012, 236, n. 20.

128 Van Straten 1995, 153, figs. 159–162; Ekroth 2009, 141–142. On the other hand, some sacred laws explicitly forbid the removal of consecrated meat from the sanctuary (οὐκ ἀποφορά): see *CGRN* 59 (sanctuary of the Nymphs in Thera, 400–300 BCE); *CGRN* 85, ll. 5, 7 (Kos, 350 BCE); *CGRN* 128, l. 4 (Lissos, Asklepieion, 325–200 BCE).

129 Isthmia, Athens, Corinth, Kyrene (Demeter sanctuary), Ephesos, Kommos, Kourion, Miletos, Mytilene, and Tinos. See Naiden 2012, 260.

130 Huber and Méniel 2013, 251.

participants; this was usually never less than one mina, and in rare cases much higher (two or ten minas).[131] As Carbon pointed out a few years ago, some sacred laws prescribe the portion that priests or staff receive as a reward, usually thighs with specific indication of the cut (the anatomical part) of the portion, and sometimes even the indication of the whole piece down to the surrounding bones.[132]

Rarer is the evidence for the sale of sacrificial meat or portions of it, skins, or even carcasses and remains of dead animals;[133] the Greek term for this practice is πρατόν, signifying something to be sold or referring to the end state of the animal after sacrifice.[134] These sales took place in actual markets, with cuts of meat depending on the animal, their quality, and the type of portion obtained. It remains unclear whether these sales took place within the confines of the sanctuary, or whether the meat portions were sold at city markets. Epigraphic documents and a few literary sources attest to both situations.[135]

A third-century BCE sacred law from Didyma prescribes the sale of the remaining sacrificial parts by weight (l. 3: πωλεῖσθαι δὲ πάντα σταθμῷ), probably after the occurrence of the common meal in the tent (l. 2: ἐν τῇ σκηνῇ). Not everything could be sold, as is shown by the clarification in the next line: a third of the snouts and extremities is set aside, evidently reserved for religious personnel.[136] The heads of the sheep could be sold by the *mageiros* after cleaning (ll. 6–8). The law of Didyma, which is careful as to prescriptions and regulations, is not explicit about the physical space where such transactions could occur; it seems plausible that these could take place inside the sanctuary or immediately next to it, as attested by the occurrence of the sale immediately after meals in the *skene* (ll. 1, 3), the presence of those who still want to stay in the area (ll. 1–2), and the role of the *mageiros* in the sale and cleaning of the sheep heads (ll. 7–9).

The sacred regulations of the Attic demes sometimes offer information concerning locations pertinent to meat sales in the deme and polis. An example comes from the deme of the Skambonidai, which was located within the city of Athens, north of the Athenian Agora (475–450 BCE).[137] The text, engraved on three faces of the pillar, expressly mentions the agora of the deme as the place where sales were held according to the city's liturgical calendar (the Synoikia on the Akropolis, the Epizephyria at the Pythion, and the Dipolieia, and Panathenaia are mentioned) and deme festivals (Leos). The older inscription on face C starts with information relevant to this discussion. After the sacrifice of an adult animal in the sanctuary of Leos (the Leokoreion), the action moves to the agora of Skambonidai, where the meat of the animal is distributed by lot. Not only citizens, but also *metoikoi*, were entitled to receive portions. The text on face A expressly mentions the timing of the practice, which can take place until sunset (face A, ll. 4–5). This distribution was also organized according to regulated portions. In the case of the sacrifice in honor of Leos, each demesman received meat portions from the spits (λέχ[σιν τὸν] [ὀ]βολόν: face C, ll. 5–6).

At some festivals in Athens, such as the Synoikia on the Akropolis or the Epizephyria at the Pythion, raw meat was available for sale (ἀποδόσθαι ὀμά: face C, ll. 18–19; 21–22). The relevant inscription does not mention the precise location of the purchase. However, given the fact that these sales are regulated in the decree of the deme, it is plausible to assume that they took place in the agora of the Skambonidai. If so, we would have to imagine a movement of the participants after having attended the sacrifice, from the Akropolis or the Pythion to the agora of the deme, where meat could be purchased. The sale must also have involved people who had not been present at the sacrifice itself, probably to increase revenues for the deme. This text particularly emphasizes sales methods, quantities, categories of participants, and even degrees to which meat was cooked. The pillar was probably originally displayed in a deme sanctuary, but the activities specified thereon regarding the handling of the meat occurred in the space of the deme agora.

Other deme regulations mention the sale of sacrificial meat, as in the case of the calendar of Thorikos decree (440/430 or 380–375 BCE), which lists the offerings in the name of various deities and consequent sales of sacrificial meat (ll. 9, 11–12, 23, 26, 35; right face, l. 6). The recurring term is, as before, πρατόν. Again, we have here the location of some sacrifices (e.g., the sacrifice for Zeus Kataibates within his sanctuary (ἐν τῷ σηκῷ) near the Delphinion,

---

131 Robert 1945, 48, with reference to Priene (Hiller von Gaertringen 1906, 127, Imperial Age). Amorgos (Aigiale): *IG* XII.7 515, l. 64, second century BCE (one mina to each ephebe). Ioulis: *IG* XII.5 647, l. 12, beginning of the third century BCE (no less than two minas). Kasossos (*CGRN* 184). Hellenistic Age: *LSAM* no. 71 (a leg of not less than 10 minas to those who have acquired the priesthood).
132 Carbon 2017, 153–156, 159–167.
133 *NGSL*[2] 71–72, 129–130; Isenberg 1975; Ekroth 2007, 271.
134 *NGSL*[2] 72, n. 362; *CGRN* 32, ll. 10–12: sacrificial calendar 440–430 or 380–375 BCE from Thorikos, which mentions sacrifice to Zeus Kataibates. See the discussion of the term πρατόν, in the commentary to *CGRN* 32, ll. 10–12.
135 Cf. *Vita Aesopi* specifying the purchase of tongues cut from piglets from the *makellon* (*V. Aes.* §§51, 54; Isenberg 1975).
136 *LSAM* no. 54; *I.Didyma* 482.
137 Lambert 2019, n. 3; *CGRN* 19.

ll. 10–11), and no proper indication concerning the location of the sale, possibly in the deme agora.¹³⁸

One of the most interesting issues in this discussion is whether the meat eaten at shrines always derived from a sacrifice. To address this, we must distinguish sacrificial meat from the meat consumed by worshippers in the sanctuary as sustenance. Unfortunately, the evidence from archaeology does not offer such a clear distinction. Here again, the contributions of recent analyses seem to reveal a varied picture indicating that the consumption of meat in sanctuaries was not strictly linked to sacrificial meat. Gunnel Ekroth discussed this topic more than 15 years ago in a paper that combined literary and iconographical documentation with zooarchaeological analyses.¹³⁹ She argues convincingly that the bone evidence indicates a difference in species between altar debris and leftovers from meals.¹⁴⁰ According to the osteological evidence, in many sanctuaries the presence of sheep and goat is much greater than those of cattle;¹⁴¹ moreover, bones of animal species are more varied than those locally prescribed for sacrifice.¹⁴² Wild animals of different species (e.g., deer, boars), horses, and even dogs were eaten on site as evidenced by cut and chop marks on their bones. Thus, it appears that not all meat deriving from a sanctuary resulted from sacrifice but instead, a fair amount was brought there intended for direct consumption by visitors. Given the state of our sources, it is more difficult to explain how this feasting was organized and managed. The precise stages in the preparation and cooking of the butchered meat, which could take up to a whole day in order for the meat to tenderize after having been sectioned and hung, are unknown.¹⁴³

One last question is fundamental to the logistics of animal sacrifice and consumption of meat in sanctuaries: how were the purchase, the sale, and the movement of animals organized? These could be sacred livestock reared in the sanctuary's pastures or animals of other origins, which arrived en masse near the sanctuary just before feast days. A separate issue, of course, is the case of the hecatombs, which involve the use of large numbers of animals (although not necessarily 100), which likely derived from herds not too far away or even from the pastures and land owned by the sanctuaries.¹⁴⁴ In the Hellenistic period, it was possible to buy some animals (cattle, rams, goats, pigs, and even birds) directly in the sanctuaries: laws record the price, differentiated according to whether the animal was young (unweaned) or more or less adult age, which was to be paid into the lithic *thesauros*.¹⁴⁵ In general, although the origin of the meat for sale in the agora of sanctuaries is not specified, it is likely that it came from regional or sub-regional farms, as is the case with meat for sacrifice (Delos,¹⁴⁶ Magnesia¹⁴⁷).

5   Sale and Consumption of Liquids

Numerous finds of beakers and jugs,¹⁴⁸ amphorae and *kantharoi*,¹⁴⁹ chalices and *oinochoai*,¹⁵⁰ *kylikes*,¹⁵¹ and

---

138 *CGRN* 32; *SEG* 33.147; *AIO* 847; *NGSL*² 115, n. 1.
139 Ekroth 2007.
140 Ekroth 2007, 260–262.
141 E.g., Olympia, Nemea, Tegea, Theban Kabeirion; see MacKinnon in this volume.
142 General overview: Leguilloux 1999, with useful subdivision by type of deity and heroes. Psophis/Tripotama: goats, pigs, oxen, horses, dogs, and boars; see Lo Monaco 2009, 447 (Arc. Psoph 2). Stymphalos, sanctuary on the akropolis: cattle, pig, sheep, and goats, with signs of slaughter, along with snakes, tortoises, hares, deer, donkeys, and foxes; Lo Monaco 2009, 454 (Arc. Stymph 1). Messene, Artemis Orthia sanctuary: 27% steers, 33% sheep/goats, 38% pigs and Altar of the Asklepieion: 41% steers, 15% sheep/goats, 43% pigs; see Nobis 1994, 299, table 4. Olympia: 55% sheep and goats, 34% oxen, 9% pigs; see Benecke 2006, 247; Taita 2015, 131.
143 Verdan 2013, 184; MacKinnon 2018, 94–95.
144 Cf. Taita 2015, 119–120, 126–127 with the cases of Skillous, Delos, and possibly Olympia.
145 Halikarnassos, Artemis Pergaia, third century BCE (*LSAM* no. 73; *CGRN* 118); Olbia Pontica, 230 BCE (*CGRN* 125); Kos, sanctuary of Aphrodite Pontia, end of the second century BCE (*CGRN* 220); Thasos, cult of Theogenes in the agora: first century BCE. See *ThesCRA* 1, 103, nn. 349–352.
146 Wealthy Aitolian pilgrims landed in Rheneia in search of animals to buy for the sacrifice on Delos: Hyp. *Apospasmatia* 13 (*Deliakos*), frag. 70 Jensen; Bresson 2015, 334.
147 The bull to be offered as a sacrifice to Zeus Sosipolis at Magnesia on the Maeander was purchased at the time of the *panegyris* of the *Heraia* during the first weeks of autumn and was bred during winter and spring with a view to its sacrifice in late summer. See *LSAM* no. 32, ll. 12–13, a decree of 197/196 BCE establishing the festival.
148 Olympia from the Geometric period on: Kyrieleis 2003, 72–79; Schauer 2003, 165, nos. A29–31 (Archaic).
149 Samothrace: Lehmann 1969, 145; the *kantharoi* come from the fill layer of the Arsinoeion, so are dated pre-290/280 BCE (35). Olympia: Schauer 2003, 165, nos. A32–A33 (fifth–fourth century BCE). Dion, sanctuary of Demeter: Pingiatoglou 2015, *passim*. Gyroulas on Naxos: a large number of kraters, *skyphoi*, and *kantharoi* of local production with a clear prevalence of open forms; see Labrinoudakis and Ohnesorg 2020, 103–107.
150 Chalices: Psophis/Tripotama, cf. Lo Monaco 2009, 446–449 (Arc. Psoph 2), esp. 447. *Oinochoai*: Messene, temple of Isis and Serapis: Lo Monaco 2009, 774 (Mess. Mess 60), and the heroon at the gymnasion, Lo Monaco 2009, 767–768 (Mess. Mess 54); Phoiniki, sanctuary of Apollo Hyperteleatas (along with numerous *kylikes*): Lo Monaco 2009, 619–620 (Lac. Hyp 1); Tegea, sanctuary of Athena Alea: Lo Monaco 2009, 459–466 (Arc. Teg 1), esp. 465.
151 Petalidion, sanctuary of Apollo Korythos: Lo Monaco 2009, 726–728 (Mess. Koryth 1), esp. 728; Amyklai, sanctuary of

FIGURE 11.4 Olympia, Archaeological Museum, inscribed pointed amphora, terracotta
PHOTO: D-DAI-ATH-OLYMPIA-7392 (GÖSTA HELLNER)

skyphoi and *kotylai* in large quantities in sanctuaries provide clear evidence of the consumption of liquids,[152] and entire wine sets (wine-strainer, cauldrons, *oinochoai*) dedicated at Olympia testify to the use of mixing and buying wine in the sanctuary.[153] As was the case with meat (supra section 4), it is not easy to distinguish between individual food consumption and ritual use. Although individual consumption of wine in sanctuaries is known from as early as the Protogeometric period (e.g., Isthmia), wine also was used for ritual purposes as offerings or libations to deities or heroes (e.g., Olympia).[154] In terms of quantities, open forms usually predominate over closed forms,[155] i.e., more containers for drinking or individual consumption (*kotylai* and other open forms) and less intended for holding or pouring liquids (amphorae, *oinochoai*, *olpai*). Of course, the numerical data must be examined together with the data on the internal capacity of the containers. Cult regulations abound with references to *spondai*, usually with specific indications concerning the nature of the liquid (wine, honey, oil), sometimes combined.[156]

Like other classes of food, wine could be produced and consumed locally,[157] but more often came from long distances as shown by the cases of Eleusis, where sweet Italic wine is documented,[158] and Olympia, where labelled vessels indicate that wine produced in Chios and Kos was used (Fig. 11.4).[159] Visitors were accustomed to drinking wine in sanctuaries, as suggested by the ban on sleeping in the sanctuary of Dionysos at Knidos because of damage previously caused by (probably intoxicated) Bacchants,[160] and by the prohibition engraved on the walls of the *stadion* at Delphi concerning (new) wine during competitions.[161] This inscription at Delphi, engraved in Archaic letters, has been the subject of much debate with regard to its dating and the possibility that its location is secondary. It seems to me that the inscription's use of the preposition ἐς, understood both in the sense of 'outside' or 'inside' the *stadion*, is also problematic: if the prohibition concerns the movement of wine outside the *stadion*, it must therefore be wine intended for celebrations and meals after victories, thus for festive consumption inside the *stadion*

Alexandria: Lo Monaco 2009, 589–590 (Lac. Amyk 2,), esp. 590; Phigalia, temple of Apollo: Lo Monaco 2009, 441–444 (Arc. Phig 1), esp. 443; Haghios Floros, temple of Pamisos: Lo Monaco 2009, 797–799 (cat. Mess. Pam 1), esp. 798; Eretria, sanctuary of Apollo Daphnephoros: Schmid 2006, 19–21, nos. A1–A14, 71.

152 Skyphoi: Gyroulas on Naxos: Lambrinoudakis and Ohnesorg 2020, 104–107 cat. F2:18a–F2:29 (E. Simantoni-Bournia); Samos: Kreuzer 2017, 51; Iria on Naxos: Simantoni-Bournia 2015; Samothrace: Lehmann 1969, 211–213; Nemea, Ophelteion, where drinking/libation vessels form 56% of inventoried vessels with a predominance of *kotylai*, *skyphoi*, and cups of various shapes. Serving vessels from the Ophelteion are rarer and are mainly kraters, *oinochoai*, and jugs, thus suggesting wine consumption/performances: see Bravo (2018, 41), who does not distinguish between wine consumption and ritual acts involving wine. For wine consumption in Greek sanctuaries, see also van den Eijnde in this volume.

153 Siewert 1991.

154 Libation of wine is the most common type. Cf. Burkert 2003, 170–172 (*spondai* of wine); *NGSL*[2] 73, *passim*). Paus. 5.15.10 mentions monthly wine libations, along with other offerings, on the altars in the Altis at Olympia.

155 Gyroulas on Naxos: Lambrinoudakis and Ohnesorg 2020. Iria on Naxos, where open forms constitute almost 78% of the total: Simantoni-Bournia 2015, 192.

156 E.g., *CGRN* 6, A, ll. 2, 4–5, 9, 11; sacrificial calendar of Miletos (525–500 BCE); *CGRN* 7, A, ll. 35, 51; B, ll. 1, 3–4, sacrificial regulation from Athens, probably from the city Eleusinion (510–470 BCE).

157 E.g., Gyroulas on Naxos, where all the amphorae are local: Labrinoudakis and Ohnesorg 2020, 108.

158 Alkiphr. *Epist. Etair.* 4.13.9; De Ligt 1993, 253.

159 Barringer 2021, 49.

160 *LSAM* no. 55 (*c*.350 BCE); Dillon 1997, 206.

161 *CID* I 3; *CGRN* 12; Davies 2007, 52, n. 16.

area.¹⁶² If, however, the text indicates that wine should not be brought into the *stadion*, it is probably intended to prevent any damage to the structures as a result of excessive alcohol consumption by spectators.

6   Concluding Remarks

Over time, *panegyreis* became special occasions: travelling from afar, attending games, consuming food, buying local objects and products, listening to rhetoricians, and acquiring the latest political news. Such occasions involved both necessities, such as food and water, as well as a variety of other things and activities, such as votives, shelter from the sun and the heat, music, and/or dance.¹⁶³ This general picture was clearly outlined 30 years ago by De Ligt and De Neeve, who concluded that "it is against this background that the economic function must be situated … When fairs were held in the country it was especially itinerant traders who profited, while at urban festivals also the local shopkeepers got a substantial share."¹⁶⁴

I agree and conclude by emphasizing the double track on which life and economic activity in the sanctuaries moved. The sanctuaries at more or less short intervals were flooded by huge crowds and filled with merchants from all over the world bringing the rarest of goods. Once the games were over, it was back to the daily rhythm in which sanctuaries were frequented at a local level. Markets also were held but in smaller form and with products restricted to local or intra-regional levels. While the distribution and consumption of food seem to use local or at most regional circuits, wine could be imported from great distances. In this process, great importance must be given to the periodicity of the festivals, which invariably brought huge crowds of people back to the area at expected intervals, ensuring that at least every four years everything could be bought, and everything could be sold.

Acknowledgments

I wish to thank the editors warmly for inviting me to write this paper in the proceedings of the conference held in 2018 and having improved my text thanks to their very useful observations, as well as Judy Barringer and David Scahill for revising my English. I am also grateful to E. Tzimi at the Deutsches Archäologisches Institut Athen, Martin Maischberger and Monique Schröder at the Antikensammlung Berlin, and Judy Barringer for help in obtaining photos and permissions.

Works Cited

Amandry, P. 1981. "Chronique delphique, 1970–1981." *BCH* 105: 673–769.

Angeli Bernardini, P. 1997. "Olimpia e i giochi olimpici: le fonti letterarie tra lode e critica." *Nikephoros* 10: 179–190.

Baitinger, H., and T. Völling. 2007. *Werkzeug und Gerät aus Olympia*, OF 32. Berlin.

Bammer, A., F. Brein, and P. Wolf. 1978. "Das Tieropfer am Artemisaltar von Ephesos." *Studien zur Religion und Kultur Kleinasiens. Festschrift für Friedrich Karl Dörner zum 65. Geburtstag am 28. Februar 1976*, 107–157. Leiden.

Barringer, J.M. 2021. *Olympia: A Cultural History*. Princeton.

Benecke, N. 2006. "Die Tierreste." In *Anfänge und Frühzeit des Heiligtums von Olympia. Die Ausgrabungen am Pelopion 1987–1996*, OF 31, edited by H. Kyrieleis, 247–248. Berlin.

Bentz, M. 2002. "Zu den Maßen attischer Feinkeramik." In *Vasenforschung und Corpus Vasorum Antiquorum. Standortbestimmung und Perspektiven*, edited by M. Bentz, 73–81. Munich.

Beschi, L. 2004. "Il Telesterio ellenistico del Cabirio di Lemno." *ASAtene* 82: 225–341.

Boatwright, M.T. 2000. *Hadrian and the Cities of the Roman Empire*. Princeton.

Boessneck, J. 1973. *Die Tierknochenfunde aus dem Kabirenheiligtum bei Theben (Böotien)*. Munich.

Boessneck, J., and A. von den Driesch. 1988. *Knochenabfall von Opfermahlen und Weihgaben aus dem Heraion von Samos (7. Jh. v. Chr.)*. Munich.

Bommelaer, J.-F., and Laroche, D. 2015. *Guide de Delphes: le site*. Athens.

Bookidis, N., J. Hansen, L. Snyder, and P. Goldberg. 1999. "Dining in the Sanctuary of Demeter and Kore at Corinth." *Hesperia* 68: 1–54.

Bravo, J.J. 2018. *Excavation at Nemea 4: The Shrine of Opheltes*. Berkeley.

Bresson, A. 2015. *The Making of the Ancient Greek Economy: Institutions, Markets, and Growth in the City-States*. Princeton.

Brommer, F. 1975. "Antiken des Athener Instituts." *AM* 90: 163–188.

Brugnone, A. 2018. "Luoghi di vendita e santuari: a proposito di un incensiere iscritto da Selinunte." In *Munus Letitiae. Studi Miscellanei offerti a Maria Letizia Lazzarini 1*, edited by F. Camia, L. Del Monaco, and M. Nocita, 55–75. Rome.

Burkert, W. 2003. *La religione greca di epoca arcaica e classica*, 2nd ed., trans. P. Pavanini. Milan.

Campanella, L., and A.M. Niveau de Villedary y Mariñas. 2005. "Il consumo del pescato nel Mediterraneo fenicio e punico: Fonti letterarie, contesti archeologici, vasellame ceramico." In

---

162   See commentary to *CGRN* 12. See also the contribution by Harris and Carbon in this volume.
163   Davies 2007, 65.
164   De Ligt and De Neeve 1988, 399.

Greci, Fenici e Romani: interazioni culturali nel Mediterraneo antico, edited by S.F. Bondì and M. Vallozza, 27–69. Viterbo.

Carbon, J.-M. 2017. "Meaty Perks: Epichoric and Topological Trends." In *Animal Sacrifice in the Ancient Greek World*, edited by S. Hitch and I. Rutherford, 151–177. Cambridge.

Chandezon, C. 2000. "Foires et panégyries dans le monde grec classique et hellénistique." *RÉG* 113: 70–100.

Clinton, K. 2005–2008. *Eleusis: The Inscriptions on Stone: Documents of the Sanctuary of the Two Goddesses and Public Documents of the Deme*. Athens.

Davidson, G.R. 1952. *Corinth 12: The Minor Objects*. Princeton.

Davies, J. 2007. "The Origins of the Festivals, Especially Delphi and the Pythia." In *Pindar's Poetry, Patrons, and Festivals: From Archaic Greece to the Roman Empire*, edited by S. Hornblower and C. Morgan, 47–69. Oxford.

De Grossi Mazzorin, J., and M. Battafarano. 2012. "I resti faunistici provenienti dagli scavi di Tas-Silġ a Malta: testimonianze di pratiche rituali." In *Atti del 6º Convegno Nazionale di Archeozoologia*, edited by J. De Grossi Mazzorin, D. Saccà, and C. Tozzi, 357–363. Lucca.

De Ligt, L. 1993. *Fairs and Markets in the Roman Empire: Economic and Social Aspects of Periodic Trade in a Pre-Industrial Society*. Amsterdam.

De Ligt, L., and P.W. De Neeve. 1988. "Ancient Periodic Markets: Festivals and Fairs." *Athenaeum* 66: 391–416.

Deshours, N. 2006. *Les mystères d'Andania: étude d'épigraphie et d'histoire religieuse*. Paris.

Detienne, M., and J.-P. Vernant. 1982. *La cuisine du sacrifice en pays grec*. Paris.

Dillon, M. 1997. *Pilgrims and Pilgrimage in Ancient Greece*. London.

Donner, H., and W. Röllig. 2002. *Kanaanäische und Aramäische Inschriften*, 5th ed. Wiesbaden.

Dubois, L. 1986. *Recherches sur le dialecte arcadien, II. Corpus Dialectal*. Louvain-La-Neuve.

Dunbabin, T.J. 1962. *Perachora: The sanctuaries of Hera Akraia and Limenia. Excavations of the British School of Archaeology at Athens 1930–1933, 2. Pottery, ivories, scarabs, and other objects from the votive deposit of Hera Limenia*. Oxford.

Ekroth, G. 2007. "Meat in ancient Greece: sacrificial, sacred or secular?" *Food & History* 5: 249–272.

Ekroth, G. 2008. "Meat, man and god: On the division of the animal victim at Greek sacrifices." In *Mikros hieromnemon: Meletes eis mnemen Michael H. Jameson*, edited by A.P. Matthaiou and I. Polinskaya, 259–290. Athens.

Ekroth, G. 2009. "Thighs or tails? The osteological evidence as a source for Greek ritual norms." In *La norme en matière religieuse en Grèce ancienne*, edited by P. Brulé, 121–151. Liège.

Engels, L., L. Bavay, and A. Tsingarida. 2009. "Calculating Vessel Capacities: A New Web-Based Solution." In *Shapes and Uses of Greek vases (7th–4th centuries B.C.)*, edited by A. Tsingarida, 129–133. Brussels.

Felsch, R. 2001. "Opferhandlungen des Alltagslebens im Heiligtum der Artemis Elaphebolos von Hyampolis in den Phasen SH IIIC-Spätgeometrisch." In *Potnia. Deities and Religion in the Aegean Bronze Age*, edited by R. Laffineur and R. Hägg, 193–200. Liége.

Fiorentino, G., C. D'Oronzo, and G. Colaianni. 2012. "Human-Environmental Interaction in Malta from the Neolithic to the Roman Period: Archaeobotanical Analyses at Tas-Silġ." *ScAnt* 18: 169–180.

Forstenpointner, G., and M. Hofer. 1997. "Kulturhistorische und Landschaftsmorphologische Ergebnisse aus der Untersuchung der Tierknochenfunde von Lousoi in Arkadien." *Anthropozoologica* 25–26: 683–690.

Gebhard, E. 1993. "The Evolution of a Pan-Hellenic Sanctuary: From Archaeology Towards History at Isthmia." In *Greek Sanctuaries: New Approaches*, edited by N. Marinatos and R. Hägg, 154–177. London.

Greco, E., ed. 2014. *Topografia di Atene. Sviluppo urbano e monumenti dalle origini al III secolo d.C. 3: Quartieri a nord e a nord-est dell'Acropoli e Agora del Ceramico*. Athens.

Guarducci, M. 1974. *Epigrafia Greca III: Epigrafi di carattere privato*. Rome.

Hamdorf, F.W. 1981. "Karpometra." *OlBer* 10: 192–208.

Herrmann, K. and A. Moustaka. 2013. "Untersuchungen am Heraion-Altar." *OlBer* 13: 100–128.

Herzog, R. 1931. *Die Wunderheilungen von Epidauros. Ein Beitrag zur Geschichte der Medizin und der Religion*. Leipzig.

Hiller von Gaertringen, F. 1906. *Inschriften von Priene*. Berlin.

Hitzl, K. 1996. *Die Gewichte griechischer Zeit aus Olympia, OF 25*. Berlin.

Huber, S., and P. Méniel. 2013. "Annexe 1: Analyse Archéozoologique. La faune terrestre du sanctuaire d'Apollon." In *Le Sanctuaire d'Apollon Daphnéphoros à l'époque géométrique, Eretria 22*, edited by S. Verdan, 243–254. Athens.

Isenberg, M. 1975. "The Sale of Sacrificial Meat." *CP* 70: 271–273.

Kakavogianni, O., and M. Anetakis. 2012. "Les agoras commerciales des dèmes antiques de la Mésogée et de la region du Laurion." In *Tout vendre, tout acheter. Structures et équipements des marchés antique*, edited by V. Chankowski and P. Karvonis, 185–199. Paris.

Kilian-Dirlmeier, I. 2002. *Kleinfunde aus dem Athena Itonia-Heiligtum bei Philia (Thessalien)*. Mainz.

Knoepfler, D. 1972. "Carystos et les Artémisia d'Amarynthos." *BCH* 96: 283–301.

Kreuzer, B. 2017. *Panathenäische Preisamphoren und rotfigurige Keramik aus dem Heraion von Samos, Samos 23*. Wiesbaden.

Kritzas, C. 1972. "Νέα εκ της πόλεως Επιδαύρου." *AAA* 5: 186–199.

Kroll, H. 1993. "Kulturpflanzen von Kalapodi." *AA*: 161–182.

Kroll, J.H. 1993. *The Greek Coins. Agora 26*. Princeton.

Kučan, D. 1995. "Zur Ernährung und dem Gebrauch von Pflanzen im Heraion von Samos im 7. Jahrhundert v. Chr." *JdI* 110: 1–64.

Kyrieleis, H. 2003. "Die Untersuchungen zur Frühzeit Olympias im Bereich des Prytaneion, 1986/87 und 1990/91." *OlBer* 12: 66–154.

Kyrieleis, H. 2011. *Olympia. Archäologie eines Heiligtums*. Darmstadt.

Kyrieleis, H. 2020. *Ausgrabungen im Südostgebiet des Heraion von Samos, Samos* 28. Wiesbaden.

de La Genière, J., and V. Jolivet. 2003. *Cahiers de Claros I: L'aire des sacrifices*. Paris.

Lambert, S. 2019. "Cult Provisions." *Attic Inscriptions in UK Collections, British Museum* 4.1. https://www.atticinscriptions.com/papers/aiuk-41/.

Lambrinoudakis, V.K., and A. Ohnesorg, eds. 2020. *Das Heiligtum von Gyroulas bei Sangri auf Naxos*. Athens.

Lawrence, K.A. 2012. *Roman Infrastructural Changes to Greek Sanctuaries and Games: Panhellenism in the Roman Empire, Formations of New Identities*. Ph.D. diss., University of Michigan.

Le Guen-Pollet, B. 1991. *Espace sacrificiel et corps des bêtes immolées. Remarques sur le vocabulaire désignant la part du prêtre dans la Grèce antique, de l'époque classique à l'époque impériale*. Paris.

Lefèvre-Novaro, D. 2010. "Les sacrifices de poissons dans les sanctuaires grecs de l'Âge du Fer." *Kernos* 23: 37–52.

Leguilloux, M. 1999. "Sacrifice et repas publics dans le sanctuaire de Poséidon à Ténos: les analyses archéozoologiques." *BCH* 123: 423–455.

Lehmann, P.W. 1969. *Samothrace 3: The Hieron*. Princeton.

Linders, T. 1994. "Sacred Menus on Delos." In *Ancient Greek Cult Practice from the Epigraphical Evidence*, edited by R. Hägg, 71–79. Stockholm.

Lo Monaco, A. 2009. *Il crepuscolo degli dei d'Achaia. Religione e culti in Arcadia, Elide, Laconia e Messenia dalla conquista romana ad età flavia*. Rome.

Lo Monaco, A. 2013. "Fuori dall'Altis. Tende, bagni e propilei a Olimpia in età ellenistica." In *Roman Power and Greek Sanctuaries: Forms of Interaction and Communication*, edited by M. Galli, 125–142. Athens.

Lo Monaco, A. 2020. "I mercati degli dei." In *Spending on the Gods: Economy, Financial Resources and Management in the Sanctuaries in Greece*, edited by A. Lo Monaco, 22–36. Athens.

Lytle, E. 2010. "Fish List in the Wilderness: The Social and Economic History of a Boiotian Price Decree." *Hesperia* 79: 253–303.

Maass, M. 1993. *Das antike Delphi. Orakel, Schätze und Monumente*. Darmstadt.

MacKinnon, M. 2018. "The Faunal Remains from the Hero Shrine." In *Excavation at Nemea 4: The Shrine of Opheltes* by J.J. Bravo, 79–100. Berkeley.

McInerney, J. 2014. "Bouphonia: Killing Cattle on the Acropolis." *Équidés et Bovidés de la Méditerranée antique: Rites et combats. Jeux et savoirs*, edited by A. Gardeisen and C. Chandezon, 113–124. Lattes.

Megaloudi, F. 2006. *Plants and diet in Greece from Neolithic to Classic Periods: the archaeobotanical remains*. Oxford.

Metzger, I.R. 1985. *Das Thesmophorion von Eretria. Funde und Befunde eines Heiligtums, Eretria* 7. Bern.

Miller, S.G. 2004. *Nemea: A Guide to the Site and Museum*. Athens.

Mylona, D. 2008. *Fish-Eating in Greece from the Fifth Century B.C. to the Seventh Century A.D. A story of impoverished fishermen or luxurious banquets?* Oxford.

Mylona, D. 2015. "From Fish Bones to Fishermen: Views from the Sanctuary of Poseidon at Kalaureia." *Classical Archaeology in Context: Theory and Practice in Excavation in the Greek World*, edited by D.C. Haggis and C.M. Antonaccio, 385–417. Berlin.

Mylona, D. 2019. "Animals in the sanctuary. Mammal and fish bones from areas D and C at the Sanctuary of Poseidon at Kalaureia." *Opuscula* 12: 173–221.

Naiden, F.S. 2012. *Smoke signals for the Gods: Ancient Greek Sacrifice from the Archaic through Roman Periods*. New York.

Nobis, G. 1994. "Die Tierreste aus dem antiken Messene. Grabung 1990/1991." *Beiträge zur Archäozoologie und prähistorischen Anthropologie: 8. Arbeitstreffen der Osteologen*, edited by M. Kokabi and J. Wahl, 297–313. Stuttgart.

Notarstefano, F. 2012a. *Ceramica e alimentazione. L'analisi chimica dei residui organici nelle ceramiche applicata ai contesti archeologici*. Bari.

Notarstefano, F. 2012b. "Ricerche sui residui organici nella ceramica di età storica dal santuario di Tas-Silġ." *ScAnt* 18: 119–129.

Oliver, J.H. 1989. *Greek Constitutions of Early Roman Emperors from Inscriptions and Papyri*. Philadelphia.

Palaiokrassa-Kopitsa, L., and E. Vivliodetis. 2015. "The Sanctuaries of Artemis Mounichia and Zeus Parnessios: Their Relation to the Religious and Social Life in the Athenian City-State until the End of the 7th Century B.C." In *Pots, Workshops and Early Iron Age Society: Function and Role of Ceramics in Early Greece*, edited by V. Vlachou, 155–180. Brussels.

Palme-Koufa, A. 1996. "Die Graffiti auf der Keramik." In *Kalapodi. Ergebnisse der Ausgrabungen im Heiligtum der Artemis und des Apollon von Hyampolis in der antiken Phokis 1*, edited by R. Felsch, 271–331. Mainz.

Pandermalis, D. 2000. "Ἀνασκαφή νοτιοδυτικοῦ τμήματος τειχῶν Διοκλητιανοῦ πόλεως στο Ἄργος Ὀρεστικό Καστοριάς." In *Το αρχαιολογικό έργο στη Μακεδονία και Θράκη* 14: 581–590.

Payne, H. 1940. *Perachora: The sanctuaries of Hera Akraia and Limenia. Excavation of the British School of Archaeology at Athens 1930–1933. 1. Architecture, bronzes, terracottas*. Oxford.

Perdrizet, P. 1908. *Monuments figurés, petits bronzes, terre-cuites, antiquités diverses, FdD 5*. Paris.

Pernice, E. 1894. *Griechische Gewichte*. Berlin.

Petrakos, B. 1968. *Ο Ωρωπός και το ιερόν του Αμφιαράου*. Athens.

Pingiatoglou, S. 2015. *Δίον: το ιερό της Δήμητρος*. Thessaloniki.

Pleket, H.W. 1996. "L'agonismo sportivo." In *I Greci: Storia, Cultura, Arte, Società 1. Noi e i Greci*, edited by S. Settis, 507–533. Turin.

Raubitschek, I.K. 1998. *Isthmia 7: The Metal Objects (1952–1989)*. Princeton.

Robert, L. 1945. *Le sanctuaire de Sinuri près de Mylasa*. Paris.

Roesch, P. 1974. "Sur le tarif des poissons d'Akraiphia." *ZPE* 14: 5–9.

Rose, M.J. 2000. "The Fish Remains." In *Kommos 4: The Greek Sanctuary 1*, edited by J.W. Shaw and M.C. Shaw, 495–560. Princeton.

Salviat, F., and C. Vatin. 1971. *Inscriptions de Grèce centrale*. Paris.

Sarpaki, A. 2019. "Plants in the Sanctuary: Charred Seeds from Areas C and D at the Sanctuary of Poseidon at Kalaureia, Poros." *Opuscula* 12: 271–286.

Schauer, C. 2003. "Fundgruppe archaischer und klassischer Zeit aus dem Bereich des Prytaneion." *OlBer* 12: 155–205.

Schiering, W. 1965. "Archäologischer Befund." *OlBer* 5: 137–277.

Schilbach, J. 1995. *Elische Keramik des 5. und 4. Jahrhunderts*, OF 23. Berlin.

Schilbach, J. 1999. "Massbecher aus Olympia." *OlBer* 11: 323–356.

Schmid, S.G. 2006. *Boire pour Apollon: céramique hellénistique et banquets dans le sanctuaire d'Apollon Daphnéphoros, Eretria 16*. Athens.

Schmitt, H.-O. 2007. "Die Angriffswaffen." In *Kalapodi. Ergebnisse der Ausgrabungen im Heiligtum der Artemis und des Apollon von Hyampolis in der antiken Phokis 2. Zur Stratigraphie des Heiligtums*, edited by R. Felsch, 423–550. Mainz.

Schwab, K.A. 2000. "Bronze, Lead, and Bone Implements." In *Kommos 4: The Greek Sanctuary 1*, edited by J.W. Shaw and M.C. Shaw, 391–395. Princeton.

Scott, M. 2014. *Delphi*. Princeton.

Scullion, S. 1994. "Olympian and Chthonian." *ClAnt* 13: 75–119.

Senff, R. 2018. "Olympia, Griechenland: die Arbeiten der Jahre 2016 und 2017." *E-Forschungsberichte des DAI* 1: 42–47.

Siewert, P. 1991. "Staatliche Weihungen von Kesseln und anderen Bronzegeräten in Olympia." *JdI* 106: 81–84.

Simantoni-Bournia, E. 2015. "More Cups for 'Dionysos:' A Selection of Geometric Drinking Vases from the Sanctuary of Hyria on Naxos." *Pots, Workshops and Early Iron Age Society: Function and Role of Ceramics in Early Greece*, edited by V. Vlachou, 181–197. Brussels.

Sinn, U. 2004. *Das antike Olympia. Götter, Spiel und Kunst*. Munich.

Sokolowski, F. 1978. "The κάπηλοι in the Heraion of Samos." *ZPE* 29: 143–147.

Sossau, V. 2019. *Angemessene Anteile. Konsum und Distribution von Fleisch im geometrischen und archaischen Griechenland*. Tübingen.

Soverini, L. 1990–1991. "Il 'commercio nel tempio:' osservazioni sul regolamento dei κάπηλοι a Samo (*SEG* 28, 545)." *Opus* 9–10: 59–121.

Sparkes, B. 1995. "A pretty kettle of fish." In *Food in Antiquity*, edited by J. Wilkins, D. Harvey, and M. Dobson, 150–161. Exeter.

Stroud, R.S. 1968. "The Sanctuary of Demeter and Kore on Acrocorinth, Preliminary Report II: 1964–1965." *Hesperia* 37: 299–330.

Taita, J. 2007. *Olimpia e il suo vicinato in epoca arcaica*. Milan.

Taita, J. 2013. "Olympias Verkehrsverbindungen zum Meer: Landungsplätze bei Pheia und am Alpheios." *OlBer* 13: 342–396.

Taita, J. 2014. "Quando Zeus deve far quadrare il bilancio: osservazioni sul tesoro del santuario di Olimpia." In *Sport und Recht in der Antike*, edited by K. Harter-Uibopuu and T. Kruse, 107–145. Vienna.

Taita, J. 2015. "The Great Hecatomb to Zeus Olympios: Some Observations on IvO no. 14." In *New Approaches to the Temple of Zeus at Olympia*, edited by A. Patay-Horváth, 112–139. Oxford.

Tataki, A.B. 1988. *Ancient Beroea: Prosopography and Society*. Athens.

Theodoropoulou, T. 2013a. "Annexe 2: Analyse Archéozoologique. La faune marine du sanctuaire d'Apollon." In *Le Sanctuaire d'Apollon Daphnéphoros à l'époque géométrique, Eretria 22*, edited by S. Verdan, 255–266. Athens.

Theodoropoulou, T. 2013b. "The sea in the temple? Shells, fish and corals from the sanctuary of the ancient town of Kythnos and other marine stories of cult." In *Bones, behaviour and belief: The zooarchaeological evidence as a source for ritual practice in ancient Greece and beyond*, edited by G. Ekroth and J. Wallensten, 198–222. Stockholm.

van Straten, F.T. 1995. *Hierà kalá: Images of Animal Sacrifice in Archaic and Classical Greece*, Leiden.

Vatin, C. 1966. "Un tarif des poissons à Delphes." *BCH* 90: 274–280.

Verdan, S. 2013. *Eretria 22: Le Sanctuaire d'Apollon Daphnéphoros à l'époque géométrique*. Athens.

Wachter, R. 2001. *Non-Attic Greek Vase Inscriptions*. Oxford.

Wacker, C. 1996. *Das Gymnasion in Olympia: Geschichte und Funktion*. Würzburg.

Waldstein, C. 1905. *The Argive Heraeum 2: Terra-cotta Figurines, Terra-cotta Reliefs, Vases and Vase Fragments, Bronzes, Engraved Stones, Gems and Ivories, Coins, Egyptian or Graeco-Egyptian Objects*. Boston.

Weir, R.G.A. 2004. *Roman Delphi and its Pythian Games*. Oxford.

Williams, D. 1983. "Aegina, Aphaia-Tempel, 5. The Pottery from Chios" *AA*: 155–186.

Zunino, M.L. 1997. *Hiera Messeniaka. La storia religiosa della Messenia dall'età micenea all'età ellenistica*. Udine.

CHAPTER 12

The Question of Temple Merchants: Buying and Selling in Greek Sanctuaries

Véronique Chankowski

The concept of temple merchants refers to a well-known biblical episode concerning the Temple of Jerusalem. After Herod the Great started to transform the architecture of the Temple complex around 19 BCE,[1] economic activities, such as the market for sacrificial animals and the places for money changers and bankers, were moved into the sacred space of the Temple courtyard. They brought benefits to the religious authorities, probably through the collection of market fees. This situation created an economic connection between the cult (with its sacrifices and taxes), priests, and animal suppliers and their customers; both the sale of animals for sacrifice and the payment of the temple tax were activities required by Jewish law and central to the functioning of the Temple.[2] The architectural expansions ordered by Herod made the Temple a hub of economic activity in the city, in which non-Jews also participated. Strongly committed to the values of Hellenism and Greek culture, Herod introduced Greek practices (sports competitions, theater) into Jerusalem. It is possible that he also contributed to the evolution of the Temple's economic activities, according to an economic model coming from the Greek world, but at the same time, this situation was favorable to the Temple clergy who also benefited from it. However, some conservative members of the Jewish community did not consider these changes to be compatible with the rules and the purity requirements of the holy place. In several passages of the New Testament, Jesus appears as the paradoxical figure of an *agoranomos*, armed with the whip that was the attribute of the Greek market magistrates, and fights against this economic dimension of the sacred space in the name of a norm that here is not the justice of trade but divine justice that requires the purity of the place.[3]

However emblematic this scene of conflict between the ritual requirements of religion and the concrete needs of the market-economy has become, it would nevertheless be difficult to apply it in a Greek or a Roman context. In Greek cities, there was no religious power other than that of the city. The use of the funds of a sanctuary and their organization were the sole responsibility of the city, and especially of the *ekklesia*. In this respect, there was no autonomous economic power of the sanctuaries, but rather a system of civic economy in which the citizens were responsible for the finances of the gods. Certainly, the relationship between temples and cities may have been more complex in regions where Hellenization was added to pre-Hellenistic traditions, as was the case in Asia Minor and Anatolia. In some instances, the existence of a clergy, organized along family lines around ethnic religious associations, created local powers that conflicted with the territorial claims of cities and led the parties involved to request the mediation of the royal power. However, these claims did not challenge the economic activity that took place in sanctuaries. Conflicts arose precisely over the economic and financial interests derived from control of the shrines.[4] Unlike the purists of the Jewish religion, the followers of Greek and Eastern cults do not seem to have fought against the development of economic and market activities around sanctuaries.

Thus, the notion of the 'economy of the sacred,' which is often used by scholars to talk about the Greek and Roman worlds, is largely misleading. It is true that economy and sanctuaries work together because a god is always seen as a legal entity, who accumulates property. But this property is usually managed by the city in charge of the sanctuary within its territory. This capital allows the city to organize construction sites for new buildings, interest-bearing loans, celebrations, and sacrifices: the city is the decision-maker and the economic actor.

Even when a conflict arose over the management of a sacred property, such as the dispute between the city of Mylasa and a line of priests concerning the administration of the Labraunda sanctuary, the issue was one of entrusting the caretaking of sacred property to an institutional authority. In case of conflict, the mediator in the person of the king usually chose the city as administrator of the sanctuary.[5] The 'economy of the sacred,' then,

---

1 See Burrell 2014 for the chronology of Herodian works.
2 Busink 1980, 1017–1251; Stevens 2006; Hartman et al. 2013.
3 Matthew 21, 12–17; Mark 11, 15–19; Luke 19, 45–48; John 2, 13–16.
4 Debord 1982; Boffo 1985; Dignas 2002.
5 By insisting on the notion of the economy of the sacred, Beate Dignas confuses two roles (for instance, Dignas 2002, 271–278): the owner and the manager. The fact that the god in his sanctuary is formally the owner of his heritage, which is kept separate from other public goods, does not preclude the sanctuary from being entirely

is part of the economic system of the city in the Greek world. It is even more evident in mainland Greece and the islands, where the civic territory model including one or more sanctuaries prevails.

In the case of large sanctuaries visited by a cosmopolitan population that extended beyond the city or the region, the management of the sacred area and the god's property was the responsibility of the city, which was intended as a civic community and collective owner of the territory, e.g., Delos for the sanctuary of Apollo in the Cyclades, Elis for the sanctuary of Zeus in Olympia, Delphi for the sanctuary of Apollo. This privileged position could give rise to rivalries and conflicts, because a large sanctuary is a source of enormous profits. Thus, between the fifth and fourth centuries BCE, the role of Elis in Olympia was contested by Sparta, which opposed any regional domination (Xen. *Hell.* 3.2.31).[6] The role of the small city of Delos and its ability to administer the sanctuary of Apollo was contested by Athens, which used the sanctuary as an instrument of its imperialism during the Classical period and again in the second century BCE.[7] The city of Delphi held the oracle and provided the clergy of the sanctuary, but the administration of the sanctuary's finances was the responsibility of a confederation of states, the Amphictyony, to which the city of Delphi also belonged.[8]

Religious activity itself (including temple visits, the organization of sporting and musical competitions during major festivals, or sometimes the operation of an oracle that attracted cosmopolitan crowds) required market-based facilities: pilgrims needed to buy sacrificial animals and offerings, but also drink, food and accommodation.[9] Large numbers of visitors to a sanctuary generated significant economic activity for the city and its region. The influx of people during major festivals was beneficial to the economy: pilgrims were also customers. Because sanctuaries were attractive places, they also created captive customers for the local market.

Some population movements occurred in sanctuaries as a consequence of building programs. The financial reserves of large sanctuaries made it possible to undertake major building projects that recruited craftsmen from an often large regional—or even wider—labor pool.[10] These craftsmen contributed to the consumption of essential foodstuffs in the city and to intensifying trade. Other population influxes were due to the major periodic religious festivals in the sanctuaries.[11] Large religious festivals (*panegyreis*) were combined with local or regional fairs. The religious celebration itself had a commercial dimension: Strabo (10.5.4) reports of Delos that "the festival is a kind of commercial affair" (ἥ τε πανήγυρις ἐμπορικόν τι πρᾶγμά ἐστι). Menander compares life to a *panegyris* in which there is "crowd, market, thieves, gambling houses, work activities" (ὄχλος, ἀγορά, κλέπται, κυβεῖαι, διατριβαί, Men. frag. 416, ll. 8–10, ed. Körte).

A Greek sanctuary was therefore a place of daily life as any other public place: in the midst of a crowd that varied in size according to the time, people ate and drank, bought and sold, worked, built, and repaired. Most of this economic activity could take place in the towns themselves: pilgrims and craftsmen generally found all the facilities they needed there. But in the case of more distant, extra-urban sanctuaries, other solutions had to be found to get the necessary equipment at the right place. At such remote locations, the population fluctuations from day-to-day operations to major holidays required management to reconcile the needs of the visitors and the requirements of the sacred space.[12]

1   Places

Most of our information about this coexistence of religion and trade comes from the regulations adopted for festivals, which were special moments in the year: many people came to the sanctuary, and commercial activity occurred parallel to religious rituals.[13] This commercial activity could occur in the *temenos* itself if there was enough space, or in the vicinity because the gods might own land anywhere in the city's territory that would provide a suitable place for the business. It required equipment for sales, and the equipment required space.

For the festival of Artemis Amarysia in Eretria, a regulation from the *boule* and the *demos* of the city c.340 BCE provides that "anyone who wants can sell whatever he wants in the sanctuary, without paying any tax or duty,

---

under the authority of the city for its management. On this subject, see Rousset 2013, which is based on the study of the administration of sacred lands.

6   Cartledge 1987, 248–253.
7   Chankowski 2008, esp. 16–50 concerning the absence of any kind of amphictyony around the sanctuary.
8   Lefevre 1998, 42–51.
9   For these aspects, see also the contributions by Lo Monaco and Ekroth in this volume.
10 Feyel 2006. On the presence of craftsmen in Greek sanctuaries, see Barringer in this volume.
11 Dillon 1997, 206–211.
12 On this aspect, see Gawlinski in this volume.
13 See the comprehensive analysis of the testimonies by Chandezon 2000. See also De Ligt 1993 (including Roman times); Camia 2011 (Imperial period).

and the *hieropoioi* are not allowed to collect any tax from the sellers" (*IG* XII.9 189, ll. 32–35):

> ... · πωλεῖν δὲ ἐν τοῖ ἱεροῖ τὸμ βολόμενον ὅτι [ἄ]μ βόληται ἀτελέα μὴ τιθέντα τέλος μηδὲν μηδὲ πρ-[ή]ττεσθαι τοὺς ἱεροποιοὺς μηδὲν τοὺς πωλέοντ-ας· ...

The regulation on the Mysteries of Andania (Peloponnese, first century BCE or beginning of the first century CE, according to a new chronological assessment[14]) provides that "the *hieroi* must designate a place where everything will be sold" (οἱ ἱεροὶ τόπον ἀποδειξάντω, ἐν ᾧ πραθήσεται πάντα, *IG* V.1 1390, l. 99). These *hieroi* were not exactly priests but members of a religious college, citizens of Messene, and in charge of the organization of the *panegyris*.[15]

Pausanias gives the most complete description of the situation regarding the *panegyris* for Isis at Tithorea (10.32.8–15), northeast of Delphi, on the other side of Mount Parnassos:

> In the country of the Tithoreans a festival in honor of Isis is held twice each year, one in spring and the other in autumn. On the third day before each of the feasts, those who have permission to enter cleanse the shrine in a certain secret way, and also take and bury, always in the same spot, whatever remnants they may find of the victims thrown in at the previous festival. We estimated that the distance from the shrine to this place was two stades. So on this day they perform these acts around the sanctuary, and on the next day the small traders make themselves booths of reeds or other improvised material. On the last of the three days they hold a fair, selling slaves, cattle of all kinds, clothes, silver and gold. After mid-day they turn to sacrificing. The more wealthy sacrifice oxen and deer, the poorer people, geese and guinea fowl. But it is not the custom to use for the sacrifice sheep, pigs or goats.[16]

Such sanctuaries were located several kilometers from the main city, a distance that required special organization of the trade with pilgrims: the sanctuary of Artemis Amarysia is 11 km from the city of Eretria;[17] the festival of Isis took place about 16 km from the town of Tithorea, which had an agora, but that is not where the festival's economic activity took place; and the festival of Andania was 10 km from the town of Messene. By contrast, urban sanctuaries provided more facilities for commercial logistics, but probably less for the accommodation of the pilgrims.[18]

For this reason, regulations generally specify the exact order in which various groups taking part in the procession must march. In Eretria, the festival rules state that, "the demarchs are to organize the procession in the market place where the sacrificial animals are sold (τὴν δὲ πομπὴν καθιστᾶν τοὺς δημάρχους ἐν τεῖ ἀγορεῖ, ὅποι τὰ ἱερεῖα πωλεῖται), first the public sacrifices and the beauty prize, then the selected animals, then the sacrifices provided by private individuals, if any wish to join the procession" (*IG* XII.9 189, ll. 35–38). The starting point is therefore the agora of the city, where pilgrims could buy sacrificial animals, which were then brought in procession through the territory to the sanctuary outside the town, thereby indicating the continuity of territory between the town and sanctuary.[19] After the sacrifices, further sales would take place, this time within the sanctuary: if the meat shared between several authorities was not all consumed, it could be resold, probably immediately, or cured for later resale. The rest of the sacrificed animal was usually also sold for craft (hides, nerves, bristles, bones, hooves, etc.). But other, non-sacrificial, products were also needed. Pilgrims needed to eat and drink, and they might find the opportunity to buy several things at attractive prices and take them home. Therefore, commercial activities were necessary in the sacred space itself (πωλεῖν δὲ ἐν τοῖ ἱεροῖ τὸμ βολόμενον, l. 32), as close as possible to the consumers.

Similarly, the fair, which took place on the third day at Tithorea, was a kind of camp with temporary shelters. The main purpose of the fair was to supply animals for the sacrifices that would take place during the ceremonies, but it certainly supported other businesses, as well. Livestock markets seem to have accompanied the celebration of the festival: according to Pausanias (10.32.14–16), all kinds of goods were sold, but especially slaves, cattle, and precious metals. This clearly shows the economic importance that

---

14 Themelis 2004, 75–79; Themelis 2007.
15 Deshours 2006; Gawlinski 2012.
16 Paus. 10.32.14–16 (trans. Jones and Ormerod).
17 Reber et al. 2018, 52–58.
18 Accommodation in tents is often mentioned in texts relating to festivals. See Ekroth in this volume.
19 In the inscriptions relating to the organization of the *panegyreis*, the word *agora* frequently refers to the market organized during the celebration and not the central place of the city (De Ligt and De Neeve 1988, 392–396; De Ligt 1993, 35–41; Chandezon 2000, 75–76). In the case of the Amarysia, where the city and sanctuary were linked by a procession, the word *agora* more probably refers to the urban market.

these fairs had for the rural population, as they brought the institutions of the market closer to the farmers.[20]

Many epigraphic sources mention commercial activities in sanctuaries, but the archaeological remains, as always with this type of temporary activity, are difficult to identify and very fragile.[21] Much of this trade, as Pausanias shows in the case of Tithorea, involved the sale of slaves and animals at periodic markets, activities whose archaeological traces are often missing from economic studies.[22] In his account of the conflict between the Arkadians and the Eleans for the sanctuary of Olympia (364 BCE), Xenophon (*Hell.* 8.4.32) reports that the combatants destroyed barracks (σκηνώματα) in order to turn them into barricades. They were precarious constructions, like those in Tithorea, erected by the merchants who came to Olympia for the *panegyries*, probably in the southeastern section where recent excavations have revealed the character of the area as a manufacturing place.[23] Several fourth-century BCE weights with the inscription ΔΙΟΣ have also been found in the excavations but outside the sanctuary itself.[24] In Corinth, it has been suggested that an open area just outside the propylon of the sanctuary of Demeter and Kore, where postholes have been excavated, might have been used for a temporary market during the third century BCE.[25] On Samos, in spite of the precise description offered by the regulation on the shopkeepers (*IG* XII.6, 169), which will be discussed below, few archaeological remains can be linked to the shops of the Heraion.[26]

2   Rules

Such masses of people and animals created logistical problems, especially the question of water and food supply, but also the problem of wandering livestock. In addition, if a market was to be held during a festival, it was the responsibility of the organizer to ensure that the transactions went smoothly. As was true of any public place in Greece, the regulation of sanctuaries depended on a civic authority, possibly a royal authority in the Hellenistic period if the community was subject to a king, or if no city was in charge of the sanctuary.[27]

The city was usually the competent authority for economic control. For the commercial part of the festival, the market magistrates (*agoranomoi*) of the city were delegated, sometimes from far away (from Messene to Andania, probably a distance of 10 km).[28] Just as in the market place of the city, their role was both to ensure that people would have enough food to buy and to monitor the behavior of sellers and buyers in order to enforce the city laws.[29] The rules for fairs associated with festivals are well known from several inscriptions and show the same concerns as the rules governing the usual city market.[30] The regulation for the Mysteries of Andania gives a precise description of the duties of the magistrates during the *panegyris* (*IG* V.1 1390, ll. 99–103):

ἀγορᾶς. οἱ ἱεροὶ τόπον ἀποδειξάντω, ἐν ᾧ πραθήσεται πάντα· ὁ δὲ ἀγορανόμος ὁ ἐπὶ πόλεος
ἐπιμέλειαν ἐχέτω, ὅπως οἱ πωλοῦντες ἄδολα καὶ καθαρὰ πωλοῦντι καὶ χρῶνται σταθμοῖς καὶ μέτροις συμφώνοις ποτὶ τὰ δαμόσια, καὶ
μὴ τασσέτω μή[τ]ε πόσου δεῖ πωλεῖν, μηδὲ καιρὸν τασσέτω μηδὲ πρασσέτω μηθεὶς τοὺς πωλοῦντας τοῦ τόπου μηθέν· τοὺς δὲ μὴ πωλοῦντας καθὼς γέγραπται, τοὺς μὲν δούλους μαστιγούντω, τοὺς δὲ ἐλευθέρους ζαμιούτω εἴκοσι δραχμαῖς· καὶ τὸ κρίμα ἔστω ἐπὶ τῶν ἱε-
[ρῶν].

The *hieroi* will designate a place where all transactions will take place. The *agoranomos* of the city will ensure that the merchants sell products that are not counterfeit but authentic, and that they use weights and measures that correspond to those of the city. But the *agoranomos* should not dictate how much or for how long to sell, and no one should demand a right of place. Those who do not sell according to what is written, if they are slaves, should be whipped, if they are free, should pay a fine of 20 drachmas and let the judgment be made by the *hieroi*.

---

20   For the sales of livestock and slaves during festivals, see Chandezon 2000, 92–94.
21   *ThesCRA* 4, 50–51.
22   Grassl 1985.
23   Barringer 2021, 47–57. See also https://www.dainst.org/projekt/-/project-display/13329 and Barringer in this volume.
24   Hitzl 1996, 101–104, pl. 43.
25   Bookidis and Stroud 1997, 201.
26   *ThesCRA* 4, 50–51.
27   Dignas 2002, 59–104.
28   In some instances, a special *agoranomos* for the *panegyris* was designated. In cases of *panegyries* belonging to confederations, such as that of Athena Ilias in Ilion (*I.Ilion* 3), each city member had to appoint an *agoranomos* (Chandezon 2000, 79, n. 38).
29   During the Roman Imperial period, inscriptions indicate that the *panegyriarchoi*, magistrates specially appointed for fairs, inherited the functions of the *agoranomoi* of the *panegyris* (Wörrle 1988, 209–215).
30   Capdetrey and Hasenohr 2012; Chandezon 2000, 79–85.

In this respect, there was no difference between the temporary market and the regular market of the agora: merchants had to sell products of good quality and use legal weights and measures, just as they were required to do in the regular market of the city.

However, since it was a festival and not a normal day, some exceptions are made to the normal rules of the civic markets: very often an exemption from taxes (*ateleia*) was proclaimed for the duration of the festival, whereas normally the levying of market fees enriched the public treasury. In Andania, there was no charge for the *topos* (the place occupied by each seller) contrary to the custom of regular markets. In Amarynthos, everyone had the right to sell anything in contrast to normal market regulations, which usually laid down legal conditions for sellers' access to the market. There was normally no price regulation, either by controlling quantities or timing, during the fairs, and this was also contrary to the customary rules of civic markets.[31]

The trade fair took on the appearance of an economic carnival that lasted only for the duration of the celebration. In the meantime, the city was prepared to yield on some of the usual rules, but still controlled the basic rules of the exchange. The fact that the city was the organizing authority of these markets, whether held in the agora or in sanctuaries during festivals, was manifested by the presence of the *agoranomos*.

The regulations for the festival markets show little concern for the sanctity of the place; they deal only with the economic aspects of the traders' behavior and emphasize that the same rules must be enforced as those in the city's official market to have valid sales. Other regulations concerning behaviors in sacred spaces, known in modern scholarship as 'sacred laws,' dealt specifically with these aspects and were applied during busy periods.[32] Specific regulations often addressed the problem of animals in sacred space, both for ritual reasons and to avoid damage caused by animals wandering in areas not intended for grazing.[33]

All types of regulation contributed to the necessary *eukosmia* (good order and discipline) in the sanctuary,[34] and in this respect, there was no difference between the requirements of the city market and those of the *panegyris* market: the sacred location had no influence on the definition of commercial rules, since the regular market laws seemed to be sufficient to ensure discipline in the sanctuary. In fact, both 'sacred' and commercial laws were created in a civic context: they emanated from civic institutions and reflected fundamental principles of life in a civic community. Their intrinsic coherence did not require any particular adaptation during the period of the *panegyreis*.

The coexistence between gods and men became more complicated, however, with the addition of a market to daily religious life and the arrival of commercial populations whose behavior is often criticized in ancient sources. To enforce the market regulations, the magistrate had the attribute of the whip, which he used against offenders if they were slaves, but other sources from Old and New Comedy highlight that it was also used in the agora against malicious traders or to interrupt disputes.[35] There is no doubt that the ancient market was a place of violence—the violence and deception of some merchants, but also the legitimate violence of the State.

Comedy is full of passages criticizing the behavior of fishmongers, their abuse of the customers, and their unfair and brutal nature.[36] According to literary sources, the order imposed by the legitimate violence of the magistrates, the "cruel hand of the *agoranomos*" invoked by the fisherman of Alkiphron (1.9.3), responded to the aggressiveness of these relationships. It is therefore this whole market society with its conflicting social relations that was transplanted into the sacred space when economic activities took place there. How could this reality concretely coexist with the requirements of behavior in a sanctuary, the *eukosmia* necessary for visiting the gods?

3   People

Festivals required strong economic activity: a well-supplied and well-organized fair enhanced the reputation of the city and the sanctuary, attracted more pilgrims and more offerings, and had a positive economic impact on the city and on the region if the sanctuary were attractive enough. At the end of the third century BCE, the city of Magnesia on the Maeander did not hesitate to invest huge sums of money in the redesign of their central place with the reconstruction of a new temple of Artemis by the famous

---

31 In regular markets, the regulation of prices does not mean fixed prices: see recent developments on this question in Capdetrey and Hasenohr 2012; Chankowski 2019.

32 On the term 'Sacred Laws' and the question of Greek ritual norms, see the analysis of Carbon and Pirenne-Delforge 2012, and Gawlinski and Carbon and Harris in this volume.

33 Chandezon 2003, 293–307; and see Chandezon in this volume.

34 For an example of a regulation dealing with the *eukosmia* during a festival, see Robert 1948, 16–28 concerning the oracle of Apollo Koropaios near Demetrias (*c*.116 BCE).

35 Roubineau 2012.

36 Chankowski 2019, 60–63.

architect Hermogenes (Vitr. *De arch.* 3.2.6) and in the promotion of its new competition, the Leukophryena, throughout the Mediterranean world (*I.Magn.* 16, 61).[37]

For these reasons, cities sometimes provided the sanctuary with permanent shops, sometimes for the sale of offerings, but usually to provide food and drink for pilgrims on a regular basis, especially when the sanctuary was far away from the city center. These shops were conveniently located, for example, in a stoa in the *temenos*. The rent from these shops was also a significant source of income for the sacred treasury.

An inscription of *c.*369/368 BCE from Oropos mentions the shops (*kapeleia*) belonging to the sanctuary. Their income, τὸ [ἀργύριον] ἐκ τῶν καπηλείων, provided additional funds for the repair of a fountain in the sanctuary.[38] The leasing of sacred property was a common practice in Greece.[39] Sanctuaries often received rent from several buildings and land, not necessarily located in or near the sanctuary but anywhere in the city. These properties might have been donated by people to the god to become part of the deity's estate, or they might have been the result of confiscations from insolvent debtors who had borrowed money from the sanctuary.[40] Renting sacred property was simply a matter of income for the treasury: not all economic activity in a sanctuary was necessarily related to religious activity, and the rental of facilities and land in a sacred place was primarily intended to bring money into the sanctuary, not exclusively to meet the needs of worship. Thus, if a deity owned some *oikoi*, they could be rented out without necessarily having any connection with the deity in question.

Renting also led to a frequent change of tenants since the activity that took place in the rented property was not necessarily defined by the landlord. Identical rental activity took place in the agora and in the streets of the city center, according to the same civic rules. Aischines (*In Tim.* 1.124.1) gives a good idea of the turnover that could take place in the shops of the agora in Athens, but which could also affect the places rented out by the sanctuaries:

> If a doctor moves into one of these workshops on the streets, it is called a surgery; if he moves out, and a bronze-smith moves in to the same workshop, it is called a smithy; if a fuller, a laundry; if a carpenter, a carpenter's shop; and if some female prostitutes and their pimp move in, from their activity it is immediately called a brothel.[41]

It was not easy to mix the religious sphere in a sanctuary with commercial activity as trade brought people of bad reputation, especially *kapeloi*, who were retail merchants with shops or taverns, into the sanctuary. The instability associated with the leasehold status made it even more difficult to control these populations over time. This is exactly the situation described in an inscription from Samos, the regulation for the *kapeloi* in the Heraion (*IG* XII.6 169). This unique regulation offers a different picture from the situation of the *panegyreis*: it is not only the context of a festival, but also the regular and permanent supply for the pilgrims in everyday life that is at stake. It was clearly easier for a city to organize the control of the temporary 'economic carnival' of the market alongside the religious festival than to create the conditions for a sustainable coexistence between the needs of trade and the requirements of civic order in sacred space.

The text of the decree is difficult to establish and has been much debated with several reconstruction proposals for the erased parts of the text on the stone. It has been dated to around 245 BCE because it shows some connection with the Ptolemaic control of Samos, a political issue that will not be discussed here.[42] Basically, the regulation deals with the functioning of four shops at the Heraion. These shops were the property of the goddess and were leased to shopkeepers. An earlier regulation (διαγραφή, l. 4) set out the rules for renting, and this inscription documents the Assembly's amendment of these rules made at the suggestion of the magistrates in charge of the sanctuary, the *naopoioi*, perhaps as a result of some abuse.

The first objective of the regulation was clearly to develop the service offered at the sanctuary, which was 6 km from the city: these shops would serve food and drink to pilgrims. However, the city wanted to maintain control over small businesses and insisted on several principles: no monopoly, no interim profit, and stability throughout the year (ll. 5–23):

---

37 Slater and Summa 2006.
38 Petrakos 1997, no. 290, l. 18.
39 See, e.g., Chankowski 2011; Papazarkadas 2011; Rousset 2013.
40 See, e.g., the situation of the sanctuary of Apollo on Delos (Chankowski 2008, 279–294).
41 Trans. Fisher.
42 Tracy 1990, 75, fig. 27; Soverini 1990–91; Hallof and Mileta 1997, 264–268.

```
 5                              ... ἀπομισθ-]
    [οῦν καπηλεῖα ἐν τῶι ἱε]⟨ρ⟩ῶι τῆς Ἥρας τέσσαρα, ἐφ᾽ ὧι οὐκ ἐξου[σία ἔσται]
    [μηδενὶ πλείονα ἔχειν κ]απηλείου ἑνός, ἐφ᾽ οὗ καὶ ἐπ᾽ οἰκήσει οἱ μ[ισθωσά-]
    [μενοι μενῶσιν πάντ]α τὸν ἐνιαυτόν. παρακαπηλ[ε]ύσει δὲ α[ὐτοῖς]
    [οὔτε δοῦλος οὔτε σ]τρατιώτης οὔτε ἄπεργος οὔτε ἱκέτης [οὔτε ἄλ-]
10  [λος κάπηλος οὐδεὶ]ς τρόπωι οὐδὲ παρευρέσει οὐδεμιᾶι πλὴ[ν τῶν μι-]
    [σθωσαμένων· ὁ δὲ] παρακαπηλεύων ἀποτείσει τοῖς μισθω[σαμέ-]
    [νοις ⸻ ζη]μίαν. οἱ δὲ μισθωσάμενοι οὐ παραδώσου[σιν τὰ κα-]
    [πηλεῖα οὔτε ἀπέ]ργωι οὔτε ἱκέτηι τρόπωι οὐδὲ παρευρέσε[ι οὐδεμι-]
    [ᾶι· ὁ δὲ παραδιδοὺς] τούτων τινὶ ἀποτείσει τῆι θεῶι δραχμὰ[ς ⸻ · ἡ]
15  [δὲ ζημία εἰσπραχθή]σεται ὑπὸ τῶν νεωποιῶν καὶ τοῦ ταμίου [τῶν ἱε-]
    [ρῶν. οἱ μισθωσάμε]νοι οὐχ ὑποδέξονται παρὰ δούλου οὐθὲν [οὐδὲ παρ᾽]
    [ἱκέτου οὐδὲ παρὰ σ]τρατιώτου οὐδὲ παρὰ ἀπέργου οὐδὲ ἀγορῶσι[ν οὐθὲν]
    [τῶν σίτων τῶν ἐκ] τῆς χώρας γινομένων οὔτε ἄλλο οὐθὲν τρόπ[ωι οὐ-]
    [δὲ παρευρέσει] οὐδεμιᾶι, πλὴν ἐάν τινες τῶν γεούχων ἢ τῶ[ν ἀπο-]
20  [δειχθέντων σιτ]ωνῶν πωλῶσίν τινα τῶν ἐγκαρπίων. οὐχ ὑπ[οδέξον-]
    [ται δὲ ἐν τοῖς κα]πηλείοις τοὺς καθίζοντας οἰκέτας εἰς τὸ ἱερὸν ο[ὐδὲ παρ-]
    [έξουσιν ἔργα ο]ὔτε σῖτα οὐδ᾽ ὑποδέξωνται παρ᾽ αὐτῶν οὐδὲν [τρόπωι]
    [οὐδὲ παρευρέσ]ει οὐδεμιᾶι· ...
```

Four shops shall be leased out in the sanctuary of Hera, under the condition that no one will be allowed to have more than one shop, at which the lessees will remain in residence for the entire year.

No one will engage in retail trade in addition ... whether a slave, a soldier, an unemployed person, a suppliant or ... in any way or under any pretext, except the lessees. Whoever engages in retail trade in addition (to the authorized shopkeepers) will pay the lessees *x* drachmas as a fine.

The lessees will not hand a shop over whether to a ..., to an unemployed person, or to a suppliant in any way or under any pretext. If anyone hands over the shop to any of these, he will pay *x* drachmas sacred to the goddess. The fine will be exacted by the *neopoiai* and the treasurer of the sacred funds.

The lessees will neither accept anything from a slave, from a suppliant, from a soldier or from an unemployed person, nor will they buy ... those from the land or anything in any way or under any pretext, except if any of the *geouchoi* or ... put some produce for sale.

The shopkeepers will not host in their shops slaves who take refuge in the sanctuary, will offer them neither employment nor food, and will not receive anything from them in any way or under any pretext.[43]

The main problem for the city of Samos is indeed the social identity of the tenants. According to Pollux (7.193), the *kapeloi* are both retail shopkeepers and innkeepers who sell wine. As a retail trade, *kapeleia* has a social and ethical aspect, as shown in Old Comedy as well as in several passages from Athenaios quoting New Comedy, which documents a thriving trading community of all kinds in fifth-century Athens: sellers of sausage, bread, flour, wheat, vegetables, wine, wool, fish, honey, pigs, birds, cheese, cakes, drugs, and other products.[44] These people, especially fishmongers, cheat on measurements and use all kinds of tricks, to sell their rotten goods. Their behavior described in the plays is the exact opposite of what is required by the regulation from Andania: "The *agoranomos* of the city will ensure that the merchants sell products that are not counterfeit but authentic, and that they use weights and measures that correspond to those of the city" (*IG* V.1 1390, ll. 99–100).

The general negative opinion on *kapeleia* is based on the idea that *kapeloi* are people motivated only by their own interest and have no concern for the common good that should characterize a good citizen, a *kaloskagathos*, as are the wholesale traders of the ports (*emporia*), who are praised and honored in decrees for having granted import and export prices beneficial to the civic community.[45]

Moreover, from a religious point of view, *kapeloi* were also known to use curses (*katadesmoi*), a religious practice

---

43 *NGSL*² 289–290. The translation of Arnaoutoglou 1998, 52–53 does not correspond exactly with the text restored in *IG* XII.6.

44 Ehrenberg 1951, esp. 144; Moreno 2007, 225–242.

45 Chankowski 2019, 60–63.

associated with gods other than those honored in major collective festivals of the civic religion.[46] *Katadesmoi*, designated to combat rivals, might have been inappropriate in mainstream cult practice, but appear to have been common in the *kapeloi* sphere. A recently published curse tablet found in a Classical cemetery northeast of the Piraeus shows the involvement of both a *kapelos* and his female counterpart, a *kapelis*, in invoking chthonic deities associated with the underworld (Hekate, Artemis, and Hermes) to curse enemies or commercial rivals:[47]

> [Ἑκ]άτη χθονία, Ἄρτεμι χθονία, Ἑρμῆ χθόνιε,
> ἐπιφθόνησον Φαναγόραι καὶ Δημητρίωι
> καὶ τῶι καπηλείωι καὶ χρήμασι καὶ κτήμασι.
> δήσω τόγ γ᾽ ἐμὸν ἐχθρὸν Δημήτριον καὶ Φανα-
> γόραν ἐν αἵματι καὶ κονίαισιν
> σὺμ πᾶσιμ φθιμένοις. Ο⟨ὐ⟩δέ σε λύσε(ι) πρώτη πεν-
> [τ]ετηρίς. Τοιο⟨ύ⟩τωι σ᾽ ἐγὼ δήσω δεσμῶι,
> [Δ]ημήτριε, ὥσπερ κρατερώτατόν
> [ἐστ]ιν, γλώττγ⟨η⟩ι δὲ κυνωτὸν ἐπεγκρόσω.

> Hekate Chthonia, Artemis Chthonia, Hermes Chthonios:
> cast your hate upon Phanagora and Demetrios,
> and their tavern and their property and their possessions.
> I will bind my enemy Demetrios, and Phana-
> -gora, in blood and in ashes,
> with all the dead. Nor will the next *penteteris* release you.
> I will bind you in such a bind,
> Demetrios, as strong as it is possible,
> And I will smite down a *kynotos* on your tongue.[48]

Such practices help to explain the negative perception of the *kapeloi* in the sources. In this respect, the Samians were no exception. They needed the *kapeloi* in the sanctuary and for other reasons did not allow the god's slaves to perform this function (l. 38: μὴ ἐξουσία δὲ ἔστω τῶν ἱερῶν παίδων καπηλεύειν, "sacred slaves have no right to run a shop"), perhaps because they would not have had time to perform their regular duties for the sanctuary, or because their earnings would have led them to claims for freedom. However, while introducing the *kapeloi* into the sanctuary, the regulation also aimed to prevent undesirable elements from engaging in retail trade and to discourage them from staying in the Heraion. Suppliants, for instance, could become a real burden for sanctuaries.[49] In the peculiar situation of Samos in the middle of the third century BCE after the power struggles between the Diadochs and the establishment of the Ptolemaic power in this part of Asia Minor, the establishment of *kapeloi* threatened to bring into the sanctuary all kinds of unattractive people according to the social norm of *eukosmia*: demobilized soldiers, unemployed workers, slaves, or refugees. They would be attracted by the consumption of wine and perhaps even prostitution in these inns, and above all by the possibility of surviving through all forms of petty trade thanks to the clientele made up of pilgrims.

This regulation is thus chiefly linked to the problem of *asylia* in sanctuaries, which the city of Samos sought to regulate.[50] While many literary sources affirm the sanctity of the general protection to be enjoyed by refugees in sanctuaries in the name of unwritten divine laws, there is evidence that civic institutions tended to limit this right through rules of discipline and order, which, in fact, prevented abuses but violated the general principle of religious asylum.[51] However, since the same civic institutions were responsible for both sanctuary management and public order in the city, there was no conflict of authority in these decisions.

The Heraion of Samos was renowned for its wealth—not only a collection of precious offerings but also deposits of money, including from private individuals (Cic. *Leg.* 2.6). It was therefore necessary to ensure the security that was part of the sanctuary's good reputation. In other words, it was necessary to protect against any form of illicit trafficking that the shopkeepers might bring with them.

It is therefore a whole social network that the Samian regulation sought to control in order to reconcile the needs of supply with public order in the sanctuary. However, good practices were rewarded according to the social order of the city. If the *kapeloi* paid their rent properly and complied with the regulations, they would benefit from a tax exemption, an *ateleia*, of course not for activities outside of their rented shop, but for the specific products that they intended to sell in the sanctuary (ll. 34–38):

> ... τὸν]
> [φόρον] καταβαλοῦσιν οἱ μισθωσάμενοι τῶι ταμίαι τῶν ἱερῶν κατ᾽ [ἔτος ἂν]-
> [τιδ]ικοῦντες οὔθεν οὐδ᾽ ὑπόλογον φέροντες. οἱ μισθωσά-μενοι ἐ[φ᾽ ὧι κα]-
> [ταθ]ήσουσιν τῶι ταμίαι τῶν ἱερῶν, ἀτελεῖς ἔσονται ὧν ἂν ὠνῶν [πωλῶ]-
> [σιν *or* φέρουσιν] ἐν τῶι ἱερῶι ...

---

46 D'Ercole 2013.
47 Lamont 2015, with references to other curse tablets also connected with the *kapeleia* and bibliography about ancient Greek magic and curses.
48 Trans. Lamont 2015, 162–163.
49 See Gawlinski in this volume.
50 Rigsby 1996, 394–395.
51 Chaniotis 1996.

The lessees will pay the rent to the treasurer of the sacred funds each year without dispute or default. On condition that they pay their rent to the treasurer of the sacred fund, the lessees will have tax exemption from whatever they sell (*or* bring) in the sanctuary.[52]

The statement in lines 17–20 concerning the supply of the shops is not clear, but it probably means that the leaseholders had to maintain their status as retailers, i.e., they had to trade on the official market. They were forbidden to engage in illicit trade with farmers in the area, unless authorized persons sold products outside the market, in the case of specific public sales, for example.[53] The *kapeloi* were forced to submit to the city's regular market and its rules, from which they could benefit from an *ateleia* specifically for their work in the sanctuary.[54] It is significant, for example, that the text makes no provision for the sale of sacrificial meat, implying that it was to be sold in the city market rather than in the sanctuary. The Samians organized some shops in the Heraion, but not an entire market.

This regulation is probably stricter than the procedure for renting shops in the city. One of the aims of the Samian law was to increase the income of the Heraion by renting the four shops, but the city carefully endeavored to ensure the correct behavior of the shopkeepers for the *eukosmia* of the sanctuary.

4 Final Remarks

As part of the public space under control of civic institutions, a sanctuary offered a good place for commercial activities because of its attractiveness. In the Greek world, however, a sanctuary never became a second agora. It was a market that was invited into the sanctuary, according to the specific needs of a festival. Under the authority of the city, some of the sales were simply transferred from the institutional site of the city market to the sanctuary.

There is no evidence of interference or contradiction between the needs of the economy and those of rituals. The products to be offered to the gods according to the sacrificial calendars (cheese, honey, wine, flour, animals, etc.) were, in any case, part of the consumer goods in the sellers' stalls or warehouses during festivals. Ritual norms and market regulations thus complemented each other in practice. Moreover, in both cases the same legislator, embodied by the People's Assembly, was at work to enforce *eukosmia* and order for the common good of the community and the pilgrims. Identical social and moral behavior were required, whether in a sanctuary or in any other public place.

It is therefore difficult to see any moral influence or normalization of behavior that would come from the sacred context of such markets, which is unlike the situation in other periods. In the Western Middle Ages, for example, the theory of fair price (*justum pretium*) developed by the Scholastics was inspired by Aristotle but drew on Christian morality and the legacy of Roman law to provide a framework for sales in order to better control market participants.

However, the context of the Greek sanctuary clearly raised heightened regulatory concerns about two major social issues. The first is obviously the security of the property of the gods: since sanctuaries accumulated great wealth, the cities had to protect them and to support the social control of individuals, possibly in contradiction with the general principle of the right of asylum in sanctuaries. The second concern is tax exemption, as *ateleia* is a recurring phenomenon in this context. Tax exemption made a place of sale attractive, but for the city in charge of organizing a sacred festival, it may also have been a question of not taking unfair advantage of the religious need of the pilgrims to visit the gods: such a regulation had a diplomatic, as well as economic, impact. In fact, economic rent based on location, which allows one to make others pay a fee for the use of a collective medium, or the notion of 'free riding,' whereby one benefits from services paid for by others, was rather poorly perceived by the Greeks. Thus, the Delians were pejoratively called "parasites of the god" by their contemporaries (Ath. 4.173b–c). To gain tax revenues from the attractiveness of its tutelary deity would have been an undue advantage for a Greek city with potentially damaging diplomatic repercussions, while *ateleia* could be more profitable in the long run.

This combination of pragmatism, freedom, and strong social constraints seems to be one of the recurring characteristics of the economic functioning of the Greek city-state, even in the logistics of cults.

Works Cited

Arnaoutoglou, I. 1998. *Ancient Greek Laws: A Sourcebook*. London.

Barringer, J.M. 2021. *Olympia: A Cultural History*. Princeton.

Boffo, L. 1985. *Il re ellenistici e i centri religiosi dell'Asia Minore*. Florence.

Bookidis, N., and R. Stroud 1997. *Corinth 18:3: The Sanctuary of Demeter and Kore*. Princeton.

Burrell, B. 2014. "The Legacies of Herod the Great." *NEA* 77: 68–74.

---

52 Author's translation.
53 Chankowski 2019, 58–60 on these practices.
54 The restitution ὧν ἂν ὠνῶν [πωλῶσιν] ἐν τῶι ἱερῶι (ll. 37–38) is problematic since the goods were most likely taxed in the agora or in the harbor market. A better interpretation of the passage would be ὧν ἂν ὠνῶν [φερούσιν] ἐν τῶι ἱερῶι, "of whatever they bring into the sanctuary."

Busink, T.A. 1980. *Der Tempel von Jerusalem von Salomo bis Herodes. Eine archäologisch-historische Studie unter Berücksichtigung des westsemitischen Tempelbaus* 2. Leiden.

Camia, F. 2011. "Spending on the *agones*. The Financing of Festivals in the Cities of Roman Greece." *Tyche* 26: 41–76.

Capdetrey, L., and C. Hasenohr 2012. "Surveiller, organiser, financer: fonctionnement de l'*agoranomia* et statut des agoranomes dans le monde égéen." In *Agoranomes et édiles. Institutions des marchés antiques*, edited by L. Capdetrey and C. Hasenohr, 13–34. Bordeaux.

Carbon, J.-M., and V. Pirenne-Delforge. 2012. "Beyond Greek 'Sacred Laws.'" *Kernos* 25: 163–182.

Cartledge, P. 1987. *Agesilaos and the Crisis of Sparta*. London.

Chandezon, C. 2000. "Foires et panégyries dans le monde grec classique et hellénistique." *RÉG* 113: 70–100.

Chandezon, C. 2003. *L'élevage en Grèce (fin V^e–fin Ier s. a.C.). L'apport des sources épigraphiques*. Bordeaux.

Chaniotis, A. 1996. "Conflicting Authorities. Asylia between Secular and Divine Law in the Classical and Hellenistic Poleis." *Kernos* 9: 65–86.

Chankowski, V. 2008. *Athènes et Délos à l'époque classique. Recherches sur l'administration du sanctuaire d'Apollon délien*. Athens.

Chankowski, V. 2011. "Divine Financiers: Cults as Consumers and Generators of Value." In *The Economies of Hellenistic Societies, Third to First Centuries BCE*, edited by Z. Archibald, J.K. Davies, and V. Gabrielsen. 142–165. Oxford.

Chankowski, V. 2019. "Juste prix, prix libres et prix fixes dans les cités du monde grec antique. Histoire d'un malentendu." In *Les infortunes du juste prix. Justice sociale, bien commun et marchés de l'Antiquité à nos jours*, edited by V. Chankowski, C. Lenoble, and J. Maucourant, 25–68. Lormont.

D'Ercole, M.-C. 2013. "Marchands et marchandes dans la société grecque classique." In *Des femmes en action*, edited by S. Boehringer and V. Sebillotte, 53–71. Paris.

De Ligt, L. 1993. *Fairs and Markets in the Roman Empire: Economic and Social Aspects of Periodic Trade in Preindustrial Societies*. Amsterdam.

De Ligt, L., and P.W. De Neeve. 1988. "Ancient Periodics Markets: Festivals and Fairs." *Athenaeum* 66: 391–416.

Debord, P. 1982. *Aspects sociaux et économiques de la vie religieuse dans l'Anatolie gréco-romaine*. Leiden.

Deshours, N. 2006. *Les mystères d'Andania: étude d'épigraphie et d'histoire religieuse*. Bordeaux.

Dignas, B. 2002. *Economy of the Sacred in Hellenistic and Roman Asia Minor*. Oxford.

Dillon, M. 1997. *Pilgrims and Pilgrimage in Ancient Greece*. London.

Ehrenberg, V. 1951. *The People of Aristophanes: A Sociology of Old Attic Comedy*, 2nd ed. Oxford.

Feyel, C. 2006. *Les artisans dans les sanctuaires grecs aux époques classique et hellénistique à travers la documentation financière*. Athens.

Gawlinski, L. 2012. *The Sacred Law of Andania: A New Text with Commentary*. Berlin.

Grassl, H. 1985. "Zur Geschichte des Viehhandels im klassischen Griechenlands." *Münstersche Beiträge zur antiken Handelsgeschichte* 4: 77–88.

Hallof, K., and C. Mileta 1997. "Samos und Ptolemaios III. Ein neues Fragment zu dem samischen Volksbeschluss AM 72, 1957, 226 Nr. 59." *Chiron* 27: 255–285.

Hartman, G., G. Bar-Oz, R. Bouchnick, and R. Reich 2013. "The Pilgrimage Economy of Early Roman Jerusalem (1st Century BCE–70 CE) Reconstructed from the d15N and d13C Values of Goat and Sheep Remains." *JAS* 40: 4369–4376.

Hitzl, K. 1996. *Die Gewichte griechischer Zeit aus Olympia, OF 25*. Berlin.

Lamont, J.L. 2015. "A New Commercial Curse Tablet from Classical Athens." *ZPE* 196: 159–174.

Lefevre, F. 1998. *L'Amphictionie pyléo-delphique: histoire et institutions*. Athens.

Moreno, A. 2007. *Feeding the Democracy: The Athenian Grain Supply in the Fifth and Fourth Centuries BC*. Oxford.

Papazarkadas, N. 2011. *Sacred and Public Land in Ancient Athens*. Oxford.

Petrakos, B. 1997. *Οἱ ἐπιγραφές τοῦ Ὠπωποῦ*. Athens.

Reber, K., D. Knoepfler, T. Krapf, and T. Theurillat. 2018. "Auf der Suche nach Artemis. Die Entdeckung des Heiligtums der Artemis Amarysia." *AntW* 4: 52–58.

Rigsby, K. 1996. *Asylia: Territorial Inviolability in the Hellenistic World*. Berkeley.

Robert, L. 1948. *Hellenica* 5: 16–28.

Roubineau, J.-M. 2012. "La main cruelle de l'agoranome." In *Agoranomes et édiles. Institutions des marchés antiques*, edited by L. Capdetrey and C. Hasenohr, 47–60. Bordeaux.

Rousset, D. 2013. "Sacred Property and Public Property in the Greek City." *JHS* 133: 113–133.

Sinn, U. 2005. "Kapeleion." *ThesCRA* 4, 50–51.

Slater, W., and D. Summa. 2006. "Crowns at Magnesia." *GRBS* 46: 275–299.

Soverini, L. 1990–91. "Il commercio nel tempio: osservazioni sul regolamento dei κάπηλοι a Samo (*SEG* XXVII, 545)." *Opus: Rivista internazionale per la storia economica e sociale dell'antichità* 9: 59–121.

Stevens, M.E. 2006. *Temples, Tithes, and Taxes: The Temple and the Economic Life of Ancient Israel*. Peabody, MA.

Themelis, P. 2004. "Ἀνασκαφή Μεσσήνης." *Prakt* (2001) 63–96.

Themelis, P. 2007. "Τὰ Κάρνεια καὶ ἡ Ἀνδανία." In *Ἀμύμονα ἔργα. Τιμητικός τόμος γιὰ τὸν καθηγητὴ Βασίλη Κ. Λαμπρινουδάκη*, edited by E. Simantoni-Bournia, A.A. Laimou, L.G. Mendoni, and N. Kourou, 509–528. Athens.

Tracy, S. 1990. "Hands in Samian Inscriptions of the Hellenistic Period." *Chiron* 20: 59–96.

Wörrle, M. 1988. *Stadt und Fest im kaiserzeitlichen Kleinasien. Studien zu einer agonistischen Stiftung aus Oinoanda*. Munich.

CHAPTER 13

'… A Piglet to Clean the Sanctuary': Recurring Costs and the Logistics of Greek Sanctuaries

Jeremy McInerney

1   Preliminaries

The epigraph in the title of this paper is a formula that occurs over 120 times in nearly 30 very long and detailed inscriptions from Delos. In every full attestation and probably in all the partial references too, the line records the cost of a piglet (χοῖρος), which was purchased in order to cleanse the sanctuary.[1] In fact, the sanctuary at Delos was probably purified every month with pig's blood, graphically illustrating the degree to which purification was a matter not only of cleanliness, but also repetition.[2] Although epigraphic evidence like this does not capture all the operational details of Greek sanctuaries, the accounts of the *hieropoioi* (Sacred Officials) on Delos do offer an unusual degree of specificity in recounting the outlays of temple officials and the costs incurred to ensure the daily running of the sanctuary. Some of these operational details overlap with the sanctuary's function as a bank, but the focus of this paper is not on that aspect of sanctuary economics, nor its role as a money lender, whether of small or large loans. This is a topic that has been well studied in the past.[3] Nor do I intend to examine the sanctuary's contracts, leases, and payments recorded in detail in the inscriptions dating to the middle of the third century BCE and the subject of particular legal controls. These have been studied with great perspicacity by a number of scholars.[4] Instead, I wish to see whether the inscriptions can shed light on the practical and mundane business of the sanctuary, the logistics of cult. For example, we might expect expenses relating to charcoal, myrrh, and frankincense, but the inscriptions also refer to 'wood for the altar,' 'faggots,' 'pine,' and 'logs' suggesting a fine set of distinctions and reflecting the practical business of burning sacrificial offerings, issues far removed from the sanctuary's banking functions.

In the accounts of the *hieropoioi* from Delos for 279 BCE, there is one particularly memorable entry: 5 ½ dr paid into the sanctuary's coffers for a dead goose (*IG* XI.2 161 A). The same section lists 1 dr 2 obols (hereafter 'ob') for an Egyptian goose and the eggs of a goose, as well as 1 ob for a partridge.[5] At the end of the section we learn that the coffers were also swelled by the addition of 6 dr paid for pigeons' dung.[6] These are examples of the astonishing degree of detail recorded by the sacred officials' accounts. Despite the fact that these records often deal with amounts of up to 6,000, 7,000 or 9,000 dr, when it comes to miniscule amounts, they forgo the use of categories such as 'miscellaneous.' The accounts of the *hieropoioi* seem not to have employed the equivalent of petty-cash to handle small transactions. These entries are exact to the last obol. This detail is in itself revealing, as if one important function of temple accounts is to create the impression of exactitude, even if, as is frequently the case, net totals often betrayed discrepancies of tens or hundreds of drachmas.[7] Although many of these accounts date to the

---

1 Schaps 1991, 208.
2 Dyer 1969, 43.
3 Bogaert 1968, 126–191; Migeotte 1984, 141–165. The fundamental recent study is Chankowski 2008a.
4 Kent 1948, 243–338; Reger 1994, 127–189; Bresson 2006, 311–339; Chankowski 2008a; Chankowski 2008b; McGlin 2019.

5 Estimating the value of these amounts in modern terms is difficult. A convenient rule of thumb is to take one drachma as the equivalent of a day's wages for a skilled worker. The obol is one sixth of a drachma. Measured this way, the price for the dead goose seems extraordinarily high, perhaps suggesting that the 5 ½ dr were a fine. In the accounts listed below tl refers to a talent, equal to 6,000 dr.
6 Aside from illustrating the high degree of detail in the Delian accounts, this entry also sheds light on the intersection of the sanctuary and the economy of the wider community of Delos. The island is not fertile, and the sanctuary may have played a role in the collection and sale of fertilizer. One is reminded of the famous episode in which Christ clears the money changers from the Temple (see also Chankowski in this volume). According to Matthew 21:12–13 and Mark 11:15–17, he also expelled those selling pigeons, presumably as inexpensive offerings. I thank Mike McGlin for these references.
7 On mistakes in the records of the *hieropoioi*, see Vial 1984, 220–221, as well as Chankowski 2008a, 327, n. 48. Chankowski (2008b) offers a detailed study of Delian record-keeping and reveals the gradual steps especially between 192 and 168 by which the *hieropoioi* improved the exactitude of their record-keeping, beginning with reconciling accounts recorded on the Attic standard with actual deposits made on a variety of different standards. My focus here is not on how such discrepancies arose or were eventually recognized and reconciled, but on the nature of the income and expenditures specifically associated with upkeep and the daily expenses of the

period of Delian independence, this penchant for meticulous record keeping attests to the long-lasting influence of Athenian control. This made sense in a community such as Athens, where elected officials were held accountable at the end of their tenure for the finances under their control, but may have been less important for strictly economic reasons on Delos. Even so, the impression of accuracy created by the accounts confirmed the probity of the Delian officials.

2   Sanctuaries and (Dis)economies of Scale

Accordingly, the Delian *hieropoioi* in the early third century were in the habit of recording the financial transactions relating to the sanctuary, and these are a rich source of information. The major records of this period are the so-called *hierai syngraphai* or sacred contracts, which spell out the terms and conditions under which much of the sacred land of Delos and Rheneia was leased out. These detailed studies have allowed us to situate Delos at the center of a Cycladic economic network but have by no means exhausted what can be learned from the rich epigraphic corpus of Delos.[8] A close reading of some of the economic records from Delos brings us nearer to the experience of interacting with a major sanctuary. The epigraphic record gives us an impression of how the logistical needs of a sanctuary shaped specific patterns of expenditure. Furthermore, lurking behind what might seem simple questions concerned with accounting practices is a larger issue of how the administration of sanctuaries changed as they grew.

Viewed as a locus of social and economic activity, Delos illustrates the diseconomies of scale that characterize Greek ritual economics. This concept may be viewed as an inversion of the better-known expression, 'economies of scale,' which refers to a characteristic of industrialized economies. If one makes a bar of artisanal soap by mixing ingredients and milling the soap by hand the unit cost will be 'X.' If one introduces mechanization one can increase production, and the per unit cost will come down. 60 bars of artisanal soap cost 60 × 'X.' But 60 bars of mass-produced soap have a lower per unit cost, say 20 × 'X.' Hence, the generic soap bar in the supermarket is cheaper than the olive oil soap at the local farmers' market. The opposite, however, can also apply. In contemporary management theory, the notion of 'diseconomies of scale' refers to the disadvantages that afflict firms and governments as a result of increases in firm size or output, which in turn result in increased per-unit costs production for goods and services. For example, if I produce 20 liters of home brew and sell it to my family and friends, let us imagine the cost is $2 per liter. But if I commercialize production and increase output to 2,000 liters of beer, I need more equipment for brewing, facilities for bottling, and a distribution network. This increase in employees, machinery, and bureaucracy leads to a corresponding increase in costs, so that we may be looking at production costs of $3 or $4 per liter.[9] Behind this (oversimplified) picture of economic development lie other features of a disembedded economy: credit and complex mechanisms of investment, insurance, regulation, and debt collection to name but a few. By contrast, the existence of direct accounting practices, such as were employed by small sanctuaries, reflects relatively modest economic transactions. Measured in terms of revenues, expenses, and associated costs, a modest sanctuary can be viewed as a small-scale economic operation with correspondingly small costs.[10] The growth of the sanctuary involves an obvious increase in costs: more wood, more buildings, more animals, more implements, and a need for more services from water supply to waste removal. But does it result in a lowering of costs averaged out across all sacrifices and operations? In other words, does it become more profitable? Or does scaling up production simply lead to an increase in costs and a corresponding lowering of profit? And if so, how does sanctuary organization reflect and mitigate increasing cost? Does the sanctuary generate or inhibit economic activity? Or are there other factors in play altogether that should cause us to modify our view of the sanctuary as an economic operation?

3   Small Sanctuaries and Polyvalence

Complicating the interpretation of the sanctuary as an economic engine is the fact that the boundary between a small or modest sanctuary and a revenue generating

---

sanctuary. For a succinct discussion of Delian accounting, also see McGlin 2019, 94–98. On Athenian accounts celebrating the achievements of the Athenian building program, see Carusi 2020, 86–88.

8   Constantakopoulou 2017, 57–110.

9   This bald summary scarcely does credit to classic studies of diseconomies of scale. Since Knight 1921, 286–287, economists have identified four major conditions leading to diseconomies of scale: specialization, bureaucratic insularity, incentive limits, and communication distortions attributable to bounded rationality. For a recent treatment, see Canbäck, Samouel, and Price 2006, 33–34.

10 For a schema showing direct accounting in the setting of a Greek sanctuary operating as a bank, see Costouros 1977, 42.

establishment, such as a farm, was often highly permeable. Take, for example, the two properties in Attika owned by the *orgeones* (members of a sacrificial brotherhood) of Echelos, one belonging to Kalliphanes and the other to their eponymous hero.[11] At first glance, references to an altar located 'in the sanctuary' (ἐν τῶι ἱερῶι) would suggest that this was a location where religious activities took place, especially sacrifices conducted on behalf of the hero. This sacrifice was arranged by their host, who paid for the event using the *orgeones*' subscription fees. The sacrifice, however, and the feast laid out for members of the association occupied only two days of the year, the 17th and 18th of Hekatombeion (mid/late July). How did the sanctuary of Echelos function for the rest of the year? Presumably as a working property that generated income for the *orgeones*, as is illustrated by a lease of sacred land by the cult of Egretes (*IG* II² 2499).[12] The lease shows that small sacrificial groups would regularly rent out their property to a farmer for up to ten years at a time, during which the lessee had to maintain the buildings on the property and tend to the trees, replacing any that died during his lease. He had to make the house available in which the shrine was located, so the *orgeones* could sacrifice during Boedromion, but otherwise the property and the trees were his to cultivate for the duration of the lease. In addition, at the end of his lease, if he had fulfilled all the stipulations he was permitted to remove all the wood, roof tiles, doors, windows and frames from the building, as if he had taken possession of the entire estate.[13] In effect, this was a working farm for nine-tenths of the year and a part time sanctuary for a month at most. Thanks to it being a multiuse property, a small piece of land owned by a sacrificial corporation was both a locus of religious activity and a traditional, mixed-use farmstead.[14] The arrangement was beneficial to both parties: the *orgeones* received a regular income from their property, and the lessee calculated that he could generate income greater than the cost of the lease. The same conditions applied in other leases. *IG* I³ 84, for example, records the leasing of the *temenos* of Kodros, Neleus, and Basile.[15] The terms of the lease reveal that the lessee was required to turn the land of the *temenos* into an olive grove (ll. 32–35):

τὸ δὲ τ[έ]μενο[ς] τὸ Νελέος καὶ τὲς Βασίλες κατὰ τάδε ἐργάζεσθαι·
φυτεῦσαι φυτευτέρια ἐλαῶν μὲ ὄλεζον ἒ διακόσια, πλέονα δὲ ἐὰν
βόλεται, καὶ τὲς τάφρο καὶ τὸ ὕδατος κρατὲν τὸ ἐγ Διὸς τὸν
μισθοσάμενον.

Let him work the sacred precinct of Neleus and Basile on the following terms: he is to plant no fewer than 200 olive saplings, and more if he wishes; the lessee is to have control of the irrigation ditch and the rainwater.

TRANS. MCINERNEY

Since the lease was given for 20 years, the stipulations concerning planting olives were not unrealistic. After five years the lessee could expect the trees to begin bearing fruit, but the lease nevertheless reflects an investment of time and energy. It also illustrates the overlap between the categories of sacred and productive land.[16]

In some cases, even if a *temenos* was not leased, it was still economically exploitable. This is reflected in the terms of a settlement between two branches of the *genos* of the Salaminioi (*Agora* 19, L4b). The agreement is largely concerned with an equitable division of productive land. After a portion of the sanctuary of Herakles is set aside to be left untilled, the remaining section is specified as common to both parties with the proviso that one group, the Salaminioi from Sounion, must construct a threshing floor the same size as their own and transfer it to the second group, the Salaminioi of the Seven Tribes.[17]

---

11   Woodhead 1997, 161. For full discussion, see *CGRN* 102.
12   The language of *IG* II² 2499 is ambiguous. According to l. 2, it is the *hieron* that is subject to leasing. In l. 27, the terms of the lease state that the lessee must make the house (*oikia*) in which the (*hieron*) is located available for the *orgeones* so they can conduct a sacrifice to the hero. This suggests that the *hieron* was a modest shrine within a larger building. However, at l. 16, the lessee is required to take care of the trees growing in the *hieron*, (ἐπι[μ]ελήσεται δὲ καὶ τῶν δένδρων τῶν ἐν τῶι ἱερῶι πεφυκότων), which means that *hieron* is being used to mean both the property in general, as well as the shrine in particular. The trees are not referred to as an ἄλσος but as δένδρα, further suggesting that they were under productive cultivation.
13   Miller (1994, 87) cites *IG* II² 2499 as evidence for the removal of wood to help explain its absence in the excavation of the *apodyterion* at Nemea.
14   On sacred land, see Walbank 1991, 149–152; Behrend 1970; Osborne 1988, Horster 2004; Horster 2010; Papazarkadas 2011; Rousset 2013; and Pernin 2014.
15   Lawton 1995, no. 4.
16   [Aristot.] *Ath. Pol.* 47.4 reports that *temene* were usually leased for ten years. For a list of 19 leases in Athens and surrounding demes, including both public and sacred land, see the *AIO* edition of *IG* I³ 84.
17   Lalonde, Langdon, and Walbank 1991, L4b, ll. 18–24: ἄλω δὲ κατασκευάσαι Σαλαμινίους τοὺς ἀπὸ Σουνίου τοῖς αὑτῶν ἀναλώμασιν ἐν τῶι τεμένει τῶι κοινῶι τὸ αὐτὸ μέγεθος τεῖ ἑαυτῶν, καὶ εἶναι ταύτην τὴν ἄλω Σαλαμινίων τῶν ἐξ Ἑπταφυλῶν. For full discussion, see RO no. 37; Parker 1996, 308–316; and *CGRN* 84.

The presence of threshing floors allows us to infer that the *gennetai* grew grain on the land. The agreement also splits the gardens and well between the two groups, provides for common ownership of the saltpans (another renewable and exploitable natural resource), and makes reference to the sacred arable land (τὴν ἱερὰν ἄρουραν). Small sanctuaries were nodes of production and integral to the economic health of the community.

The regulations for the *orgeones* of Echelos also reflect other, non-religious activities associated with sacrificial groups. Next to the altar were *stelai* on which were recorded the names of debtors and the amounts they owed. The sanctuary was thus an archive where loan records, as well as 'the old decrees,' were publicly displayed.[18] The lists of debtors and their loans point to an important subsidiary function of the sacrificial group: many functioned as brokers of *eranos* loans, the small-scale loans made between friends and acquaintances that were based on well-established notions of reciprocity, forming the simplest and earliest credit system known in Athens.[19] The web of such loans could extend over a very broad swathe of society, and Polybios (38.11.10–11) reports that in the first stages of the Achaian War in 147 BCE, the *strategos* Kritolaos caused a furor by suggesting the suspension of the repayment of *eranos* loans:

> παρήγγειλε τοῖς ἄρχουσι μὴ πράττειν τοὺς ὀφειλέτας
>   μηδὲ παραδέχεσθαι
> τοὺς ἀπαγομένους εἰς φυλακὴν πρὸς τὰ χρέα, τοὺς ⟨δ'⟩
>   ἐράνους ἐπιμόνους
> ποιεῖν, ἕως ἂν λάβῃ τὰ τοῦ πολέμου κρίσιν.

He suggested to the magistrates that they not exact payment from debtors nor imprison those arrested for debt, and also to suspend the repayment of *eranos* loans until the war was decided.

trans. MCINERNEY

Accordingly, a sanctuary could be viewed as the physical setting in which a religious *koinon* (federation) operated, primarily as a sacrificial group, but it was also the administrative center for a brotherhood whose commercial activities were local, modest, and resembled the recent phenomenon of micro-credit.[20] As such, the property of sacrificial groups like the *orgeones* was an economic resource. These resources and the revenues they created supplied the group's immediate sacrificial needs: animals, firewood, and a place to hold the feast. But just as important as supporting sacrificial needs, the sanctuary complemented its religious functions by operating as an economic zone full of extractable or renewable resources. Through leasing or direct exploitation by the members of the religious corporation that controlled the sanctuary, the *temenos* added another dimension to the economic landscape.

4 Public vs Private?

Further complicating our understanding of small sanctuaries and their place in the economy is that their operations often straddled the line between public and private operations. This is illustrated by the activities of the *orgeones* of Bendis in Piraeus. In addition to being familiar from the opening of Plato's *Republic* (1.327a, 354a), the cult of the Thracian goddess is also known from at least two inscriptions, which preserve details of the regulations of the cult, *IG* II² 1361 and *IG* I³ 136. These regulations make it immediately clear that despite the careful registration of cult members (ll. 1–2), who enjoyed the privilege of sacrificing for free, non-members could also avail themselves of the sanctuary, for a fee (ll. 2–6).[21]

> ἐὰν δέ τις θύηι / τῆι θεῶι τῶν ὀργεώνων οἷς μέτεστιν τοῦ
> ἱεροῦ ἀτελεῖς αὐτοὺς θύειν· / [ἐ]ὰν δὲ ἰδιώτης τις θύηι
> τῆι θεῶι διδόναι τῆι ἱερέαι γαλαθηνοῦ μὲν : IC : [κ]αὶ τὸ
> δέρμα καὶ κωλῆν διανε[κ]ῆ δεξιάν, τοῦ δὲ τελέου ·III·
> καὶ δέρμα καὶ [κ]ωλῆν κατὰ ταὐτά.

If any of the *orgeones* who share in the sanctuary sacrifices to the goddess, they shall sacrifice without charge; but if a non-member sacrifices to the goddess, they shall give to the priestess for a young animal 1½ obols and the skin and the whole right

---

18 *CGRN* 102, ll. 5–9: ἀναγράψαντας τοὺς ὀφείλοντά[ς τι εἰς τὴν κοι]νωνίαν ἐν στήλει λιθίνει στῆσαι παρὰ τ[ὸν βωμὸν] ἐν τῶι ἱερῶι τά τε κεφάλαια καὶ τὸν τόκο[ν ὁπόσου] ἂν ἔχει ἕκαστος· ἀναγράψαι δὲ καὶ τὰ ψη[φίσματα] τὰ ἀρχαῖα εἰς τὴν στήλην·

19 On *eranos* loans, see Millet 1991, 153–159; Cohen 1992, 207–215; Harris 1992, 311–312; and Thomsen 2015, 154–175.

20 Lalonde, Langdon, and Walbank 1991, H84 records the mortgage of a house to a group of *eranistai*; *IG* II² 2721 also records a loan of 3,000 dr to a group of *eranistai*. Other lending groups included demes, phratries, gene, and tribes. Each of the corporate groups of Athenian life had an economic face that complemented its religious and political functions.

21 *IG* II² 1361. For discussion of the inscriptions attesting to the Thracian cult of Bendis at Athens, see Jones 1999, 256–262; and Wijma 2014, 149–152.

thigh, for a full-grown animal 3 obols and the skin and thigh in the same way.

trans. LAMBERT AND PARKER

The sanctuary of Bendis included a house, land, and property, which were leased to generate income for the upkeep of the facilities (ll. 8–11):

ὅπως δ' ἂν ἡ οἰκία καὶ / τὸ ἱερὸν ἐπισκε[υ]άζηται, τὸ ἐν[οίκιον τῆ]ς οἰ[κίας] καὶ τὸ ὕδωρ ὅσου ἂμ πραθῆι, ε-/[ἰς τὴν ἐ]πισκευὴν τοῦ ἱεροῦ [καὶ τῆς] οἰκίας, εἰς ἄλλο δὲ μηδὲν ἀναλίσκειν, ἕ-/ [ως] ἂν [τὸ ἱερὸ]ν ἐπισκευ[ασ]θῆι κ[αὶ ἡ οἰκία], ἐὰν μή τι ἄλλο ψηφίσωνται οἱ ὀργεῶνε[ς].

In order that the house and the sanctuary may be repaired, the rent for the house and the water, whatever they are leased out for, shall be spent on the repair of the sanctuary and the house, and on nothing else, until the sanctuary and house are repaired, unless the *orgeones* make a different decision.

trans. LAMBERT AND PARKER

Subsequent regulations stipulate the timing of meetings, penalties for infractions, a calendar of sacrifice, and terms of membership. It is abundantly clear that most Athenian men were members of some such sacrificial organization, and that every Athenian corporate entity, whether based on blood or putative blood relations, such as the *gene* (clans), or based on locality, such as the demes (municipalities), or based on divisions of the political body, such as *phylai* (tribes), were in practice also sacrificial and feasting groups. That observation is hardly original. It is worth noting, however, that the entanglement of economic, religious, and commensal performances resulted in a distinctive set of practices and features particular to sanctuaries.[22] These can be characterized as follows:

– Like other corporate organizations, the sacrificial and cultic organizations of Athenian life fostered κοινωνία (communality). And as with demes, *gene* and *phylai*, religious groups made decisions regarding the common property of the group.
– These cults and sacrificial groups handled small sums of money constantly in the forms of loans, dues, dedications, and leases.
– Their accounting procedures were direct and subject to oversight and recording.
– Credit did not figure in their economic activities beyond the simple operation of *eranos* loans.
– Their economic activities intersected directly with the agricultural economy in the form of revenues generated by the exploitation of the land.

5   Upscaling: Posideia and Eileithyia

As sanctuaries, local, regional, or panhellenic, developed in the Archaic and Classical periods, this template was employed on an ever-larger scale.[23] This is illustrated by an examination of expenses associated with some of the more humble festivals that took place at Delos. Not every festival was on the scale of the Delia, the greatest festival on the Delian calendar. *CGRN* 199 from Delos dates to 178 BCE and reports the expenses associated with the Posideia festival and the smaller Eileithyia festival.[24] It reads as follows:

Account of the things (i.e., expenses) for the Posideia: an ox [...] 80 dr; 2 rams for Poseidon Asphaleios [and Orthosios ...]; a boar, 18 dr; 3 piglets, 24 dr; nurture for these (animals), 13 dr; 3 *medimnoi* of grape-syrup, price 40 dr; 10 Knidian measures of wine, price 60 dr; barley-groats, (5) 15 dr; for a talent and a half of wood, price 15 dr; vinegar, 4 dr; condiments [...]; olive-oil, 8 dr; dried grapes (raisins), 20 dr; for pottery wares (dishes), 3 dr; coals, 12 dr; anise, 1 dr; for the workers, 16 dr; for the butcher, 5 dr; the thing for roasting the

---

22   To be very clear, I am not attempting here to describe the Athenian economy in its entirety. Neither am I addressing the question of whether economic activity was embedded, nor whether the Athenian economy was primitive. Other important economic institutions, such as state finances and banking, are entirely different questions. On these matters, see Bogaert 1968; Migeotte 1984; Cohen 1992; Migeotte 2014; and Bresson 2015. My inquiry is here concerned with the interplay of economic activity, micro-credit, and small-scale religious groups and the model this provides for larger sanctuaries as they upscale their activities.

23   To observe that large sanctuaries employed a simple form of accounting inherited from smaller corporate bodies is not to deny the complexity of the underlying thinking that envisaged a god or goddess as an active participant in economic activities, such as lending and leasing. For a preliminary study of gods as extraordinary agents, comparable to modern corporations, see Rundin 2007, 323–331.

24   For discussion of these festivals with particular attention to the food stuffs listed, see Linders 1994. For discussion of meat distributions (ll. 8–9), see Carbon (2018), who believes honorands not present on Delos, such as Sosistratos of Knidos, were sent their portions by "regular maritime transport." The stipulation in the Posideia accounts (l. 9) suggests cash payments could be substituted. For payments by the Sacred Treasury at Delos, see Migeotte 2014, 635–643.

entrails (?), 5 dr; chickpeas, 16 dr; nuts, 36 dr; figs, 6 dr; faggots of kindling wood, logs, 2 dr; for those who do not attend the distribution (of meat), (a fund of) 60 dr; (10) 35 Koan measures of wine, price 100 dr; victory-prize for the contest, 20 dr; second prize, 10 dr; we have received the appointed sum, 600 dr; 50 half-obols; (sale?) of the ox-hide, 10 dr; other skins [...]; for the pottery vessel, 6 dr. Account for the festival of Eileithyia, from the 40 (assigned) dr: a sheep, 14 dr; wheat, 10 dr; a cheese, 2 dr; chickpeas, beans 4 dr; sesame-seeds, 2 dr; honey, 2 dr; (15) 4 crowns; for the baker, 2 dr; vegetables, 3 dr; dried fish, 3 dr; relish (sauce?), 6 dr; nuts, 2 dr; wine, 8 dr.

trans. CARBON AND PEELS

This is a very good example of the recurring costs faced by a sanctuary. They fall into various categories. The first involves animals for sacrifice: an ox, two rams, a boar, three piglets, and in the case of the second festival, a sheep. Then there are the accoutrements: spices, supplies, and equipment. These consist of: animal fodder, grape syrup, wine, barley, wood, vinegar, oil, raisins, dishes, charcoal, anise, chickpeas, nuts, figs, kindling, logs, and, again for the second festival, wheat, cheese, chickpeas, beans, sesame seeds, honey, crowns, vegetables, fish, sauce, nuts, and wine. The third category (although the inscription does not group costs by these categories) involves service costs associated with personnel: pay for workers, butcher, and baker. Finally, there are ancillary costs and possible revenue offsets: money set aside for prizes in the games associated with the festival, a separate monetary fund for distribution to devotees who did not make it to the actual festival, and money raised by the sale of skins sold as leather. The totals give us a glimpse of the scale of the festivals: over 600 dr for the Posideia, but only 40 dr for the Eileithyia.

The terms and regulations of the Posideia and Eileithyia are consistent with what we might expect from the Athenian template.[25] Even the smallest costs are recorded, down to a drachma for anise. The animals involved range from a bovine, such as one might have at the Dipoleia festival in Athens, to boars, piglets, rams, and sheep, just as one would have on the calendar of sacrifice from an Athenian deme, such as Marathon or Thorikos. There was payment for the staff, such as the butcher who supplied professional services, and there were provisions for distributing meat to those who were eligible for a share but were not present, corresponding to the *kreanomia* attested in Athenians inscriptions, such as at the Panathenaia, when enormous quantities of meat were distributed at the Dipylon Gate.[26]

One might suppose, then, that sacrificial business was conducted on Delos as it was at Athens. Yet conditions in the two places were quite different. Athens was a hegemonic city with a large democratic population, while Delos, like Delphi, was a politically inconsequential spot. Its status derived entirely from its religious authority and from its central location in an economic network that extended beyond the Aegean. Furthermore, on Delos, in addition to festivals such as the Posideia and the Eileithyia, there were processions and sacrifices by non-state actors. Early in the second century BCE, the Poseidoniasts of Beirut, a corporation of ship captains and merchants from the Levant, built a clubhouse on Delos, the House of the Poseidoniasts. They honored a Roman banker named M. Minatius, who had paid for the completion of the clubhouse and then donated 7,000 dr for the cost of the procession, sacrifice, and banquet that the Poseidoniasts held every year thereafter.[27] He was voted a statue, a portrait, a declaration of thanks at every monthly meeting, and the bovine that was chosen for sacrifice on his behalf was to be paraded with a plaque on it reading, "The association of Berytian Poseidon-devotees on behalf of Marcus Minatius son of Sextus" (ll. 52–53). Given that the bull was to cost 150 dr and the feast another 150 dr, Minatius' gift was enough to endow more than 20 years' worth of feasts, more if the Poseidoniasts invested the endowment.

6 Expenses and Revenues

Now, in terms of authority, one can distinguish between the Poseidoniasts and the sanctuary of Apollo and categorize one as private and the other as public, but in terms of supplying Delos, a relatively small and unwooded spot, with the necessities of large-scale sacrifice, the proliferation of cults, temples, processions, sacrifices, and feasts clearly had a flow-on effect. If wood has to be imported

---

25 On the *hieropoioi* following Athenian practice, see Migeotte 2008, 66.

26 *IG* II³ 447. For other examples, full bibliography, and discussion, see *CGRN* 92.

27 *ID* 1520. For translation and photos, see *AGRW* 224 (Harland). For the excavation history of the Poseidoniasts' meeting place, see Picard 1921. The role of this and other similar fraternal organizations in maintaining solidarity while facilitating professional and social integration in a foreign setting is explored by Baslez 2007.

and every stick paid for, then the presence of small cults does have an effect on the cost of operating big cults since it increases the demand for supplies and probably contributes to rising prices. So, logistically, the epigraphic record should allow us to see how the Delians dealt with their prosperity and the demands it placed on them. This is what makes the accounts of the *hieropoioi* so important. Two inscriptions may serve as test cases: *IG* XI.2 154, a long inscription from 296 BCE that offers a record of the expenses of the *hieropoioi*, and *ID* 98, from 377–73 BCE, which provides an account of the revenues of the *hieropoioi*. Inscribed on two faces of a stele, *IG* XI.2 154 contains over 120 lines of detailed description of expenses recorded in minute detail. The following items (some of which, such as torches and the formula 'wood and log,' are mentioned multiple times) and supplies are listed: pitch, beams, tiles, a sacrificial lamb, wine, wood, a mattock, pinewood torches, blocks, spits, linen, decorations, and wax. The same tendency towards the exhaustive recording of miniscule amounts of monies paid out as is prevalent in the records of small sanctuaries is also evident here: 3 dr, 4 ob for the lamb to Apollo (l. 11); 6 dr for the torches for the choral performances in the month of Hieron; 1 dr 2 ob for pitch; 1 dr for wax.

So far, everything we find suggests, as we might expect, that a big sanctuary had the same demands and was organized in the same way as a small sanctuary. It is, as it were, just a bigger matrushka doll. But on closer examination one can detect signs of difference. Note for, example, that while small sanctuaries can fold capital costs into the terms of a lease or can simply stipulate that income first be spent on the sanctuary upkeep, the maintenance of a larger sanctuary places more demands on the staff. In this inscription, we hear of the following capital works which generated payment for supplies or services (see also Barringer in this volume):

– Plastering or sealing doors and windows of the *hestiatoria* (dining halls)
– Setting the lower beam in the *palaistra* (wrestling ground), and refurbishment of another beam for the foyer of the *palaistra*
– Payment to contractors for the purchase of the new beam
– Purchase of a swing beam for the *palaistra*
– Repairs to the temple wall
– Retiling of the temple of Hera
– Repairing walls in the Thesmophorion
– Leveling the altar
– Repairing the Leukotheion
– Fixing the doors of the Propylon
– Purchasing and installing the doors of a building connected to Artemis
– Clearing the rubble from the shrine of Poulydamas
– Cleaning around the altar of Artemis
– Whitewashing the altars in the Thesmophorion, the wall, and the steps
– Plastering the wall of the *palaistra*
– Plastering the roof of the house at Ortygia and the house at the spring
– Rebuilding the collapsed portion of the Poulydamion
– Repairing the cauldrons
– Whitewashing the well in the *palaistra*
– Repairing a krater and the 'ears' (handles) of a cup
– Rebuilding the collapsed sections of the Archegetes' shrine
– Roofing and fixing the Panionion
– Repair of *oinochoai* (wine vessels)
– Cleaning or purification of the Dioskourion
– Fixing the roof of the Tax-Collectors' quarters
– Cleaning or purifying the Date-Palm in the Letoon
– The removal of a wall that had collapsed by the altar
– Repairing the pigsty
– Transferring the tent to the sanctuary
– Getting the wood and arranging for the carving and painting of a phallos given by Antigonos
– Repairing the cauldron from the temple of Zeus Kynthios
– Obtaining notice board and wax tablet for the accounts, as well as whitening the notice board
– Making a lintel over the door of the house at Ortygia

It is striking that this account does not refer to any major expense, such as the building of a temple or the construction of an entire propylon, but instead lists dozens of smaller jobs. Nor are these aggregated into the hands of a small number of contractors the way that modern corporations favor contractors to provide a whole slew of associated services. Clearly there were running repairs going on all the time. In fact, there are so many references to rebuilding, restoring, or repairing, and so many references either to fallen down walls or piles of collapsed material that one could be forgiven for thinking that the sanctuary had been sacked or hit by an earthquake. Neither is the case. Instead, the refurbishments can be explained by the visits of powerful dynasts: Antigonos Monopthalmos, for example, used Delos as a base, briefly, but both the lead-up to the occupation and the aftermath were peaceful so that there is no need speculate that his men sacked the island. *IG* XI.2 154 refers to a visit in 296 BCE by an Antigonid official, Balagros, and lists the costs associated with torches for a choral performance, wood, and logs (for a sacrifice), suggesting a celebration held during Balagros' visit, an impression strengthened by the fact that the items listed essentially repeat the entries for the Antigoneia, a festival celebrated in Antigonos' honor. Gary Reger has made the attractive suggestion that, while it is possible that Balagros was on a religious visit to Delos, it is also possible that Balagros was on his way to Demetrios to deliver intelligence regarding the political situation in Athens. What is certain is that in the winter or early spring of 295 BCE Demetrios sailed from Asia to Athens.[28]

The movements of these powerful dynasts left their mark in the construction activity of Delos, reflected in the epigraphy.[29] The rather enigmatic reference to the transfer of the tent to the temple occurs in the same segment of the inscription dealing with repairs and costs, as does the reference to the phallos that was prepared on Antigonos' behalf. These appear to be line items that represent the costs the *hieropoioi* had to cover for the honor of a royal visit. Excluding the wood for the phallos, which may have been supplied by Antigonos at 30 dr, the total costs associated with the official's visit were only between 42 and 45 dr, including, unusually, a heading of 'other costs.' Hardly crippling, although perhaps an excuse for sprucing up the sanctuary. Aside from visits by the Antigonids there are no reports either in the historiography, the archaeology, or the seismic literature to suggest the costs had been occasioned by repairs following an earthquake. This just seems to be business as usual: dozens of small-scale transactions on a wide variety of buildings and structures that had to be reroofed, whitewashed, cleaned, replastered, and generally kept in good order.

7 Upkeep

If *IG* XI.2 154 allows us to see the range of activities associated with upkeep of the sanctuary in a single year, 296 BCE, as a continuous work in progress, we can add some granularity to this picture by examining a relatively minor shrine, the *hieron* of Poulydamas, diachronically. This allows us to see how often the structure appears in our records and to follow the types of expenditures associated with its upkeep.[30] Between the mid-fourth and mid-second century BCE, the shrine of Poulydamas is mentioned in 19 inscriptions. On at least six occasions, the expense involves repairs to what is simply called πτῶμα, ruins or collapsed walls. The cost of these repairs can vary from the negligible, 1 dr 4 ob paid to Philokrates (*IG* XI.2 154, 296 BCE) to the much more considerable 50 dr paid to a contractor, name not preserved, in 246 BCE (*ID* 290) and 45 dr paid in 200 BCE (*ID* 384). Aside from these generic references to damaged segments, there are more specific references to repairs to foundations (50 dr, *IG* XI.2 199, 273 BCE), a cross wall (20 dr, *IG* XI.2 139, *c.*300 BCE), and the north wall (2 dr, *ID* 290, 246 BCE). The *peribolos* seems to have been contracted in 273 BCE by a certain Rhodo for 45 dr (*IG* XI.2 199, 273 BCE), and repairs for 'the walls that had fallen down' (τοὺς τοίχους τοὺς πεπτωκότας) were contracted out to two men, Dionysios and Phelys, 66 years later (*ID* 366, 207 BCE). The repairs were contracted at a rate of 18 dr per six feet, and the *hieropoioi* reported 'a first payment for 10 fathoms, or 60 feet, of 180 dr, and a second payment of 120 dr (1/6th subtracted); the remainder was paid to those who completed the work and measured it out at the bidding of the architect: 60 dr.' Smaller jobs are also recorded: 1 dr worth of repairs to a door (*IG* XI.2 144, before 301 BCE); wood (scaffolding?) removed from the shrine to the agora for 3 obols (*IG* XI.2 159, 280 BCE), as well as woodwork completed later (*ID* 324, 250–166 BCE). Metal work is represented by the cost of making keys for the shrine (4 dr, *SEG* 36.731, 272 or 271 BCE) and by plumbing of some sort for the grand sum of 1 dr (*IG* XI.2 219, 265 BCE; *ID* 354, 218 BCE), while a more significant expense came in the form of money spent on gold leaf applied to various statues, apparently including one in the Poulydamas, for a total cost of 87 dr (*IG* XI.2 163, 276 BCE). Aside from these expenditures the shrine figures in a handful of inscriptions as a landmark: a factory near the Poulydamas was leased for five years by a certain Eunous, son of Menestheus (*ID* 1416), and a loan for the purchase or lease of a property near the Poulydamas is recorded (*ID* 354, 218 BCE).

These references to the shrine known as the Poulydamas provide some insight into the economic thinking operative in a major Panhellenic sanctuary in the early Hellenistic period. From earlier and more modest

---

28 Reger 1991.
29 Constantakopoulou 2017, 58–110.
30 The shrine of Poulydamas is relatively obscure. The shrine may have been dedicated to: 1) Hektor's friend and advisor; 2) a famously upright Thessalian citizen entrusted by the Thessalians with public finances; or 3) the famous athlete from Skotoussa. See Bruneau (1970, 453–454), who favors the Thessalian hero-athlete, but admits this is no more than a reasonable guess. He was honored with a posthumous victor's statue at Olympia, where he was victorious in the 93rd Olympiad (408 BCE). See Keesling 2012, 473. Pausanias attributes the portrait of Poulydamas to Lysippos, further suggesting that if the Delian heroon was dedicated to him in the mid-fourth century, he was given heroic honors soon after his death. (I thank Judy Barringer for alerting me to the Olympia statue base.)

shrines, Greek priestly groups inherited certain distinctive accounting habits: the first was to record income and expenses in minute detail. But inherited practices aside, other features of this distinctive system are notable. Contracts were rarely given for particularly large amounts, and in any given year the number of people who received small payments for relatively minor tasks is striking. When considered alongside the specialized craftspeople or contractors who essentially made their money living off the sanctuary by providing expertise, rotating from one job to another, the Delian system appears also to have encouraged a very wide variety of people to perform relatively straightforward tasks that demanded little in the way of specialization.[31] A very high proportion of the tasks consisted of what we might classify as menial or non-specialized tasks: removing rubbish, moving wood, rebuilding walls, whitewashing a building. If the accounting system is direct and uncomplicated, so is the functioning of the sanctuary as an economic hub: many ordinary folks benefited directly from the simple, regular expenses of upkeep, quite distinct from the metalworking or specialized stone working that we associated with temple sculpture or specialized architectural elements, such as guttae, geisons, and the like. In a very simple way, the sanctuary's upkeep benefited the community directly, without middlemen or professional contractors.

8 Status and Shame

In fact, approaching the sanctuary as if economically structured to benefit the maximum number of local people may help us to make sense not only of the many small entries but also of the accounts that record large expenses. Consider the test case: *ID* 98. In this inscription, we have details of payments with interest that came due after four years, 377–373 BCE, carefully spelled out using both the Athenian and Delian calendars to make sure there was no mistake about due dates. The sums were from various Aegean states totaling at least 4 tl 3993 dr 2 obols, accompanied by payments from individuals, often by guarantors on behalf of lessees, of 5,325 dr (all either Delian or Tenian).[32] These payments are referred to as κεφάλαιον τόκου, or sum of the interest, which at a rate of 16% interest yields loans of 33 tl, higher if these were only partial payments.

Thanks to the habit of simple, direct accounting, expenditures were calibrated, as far as possible, to match income. This we can see in the heading ἀπὸ τότο τάδε ἀνηλώθη ("from this income the following expenses were paid ..."), followed by expenditures. For the same period as the recorded income, the payouts are as follows:

1. A crown as an *aristeion* (gift) to the god and payment to the craftsman: 1,500 dr (ll. 32–33)
2. Victory tripods for the choruses and craftsmen: 1,000 dr (ll. 33–34)
3. To the *archetheoroi* (chief sacred ambassadors): 1 tl (l. 34)
4. To the *trierarch* (ship captain) who conveyed the *theoroi* (sacred ambassadors) and choruses: 1 tl 1,000 dr (ll. 34–35)
5. 109 head of cattle purchased for the festival: 8,419 dr (av. cost 77 dr) (ll. 35–36)
6. Gold leaf and payment to the gilder 126 dr (ll. 36–37)
7. *Prothumata* (preliminary sacrifices) (l. 37)
8. Care of the tripods and the cattle and the 2% tax and food for the cattle and cost of wood (ll. 38–40)

The expenditures are much larger than the running repairs we encountered earlier. It is particularly noticeable that compared to the small amounts spent on menial tasks and paid to unskilled laborers, we are now dealing with sums of 6,000 dr to the *archetheoroi* and 7,000 dr to the *trierarch* who conveyed them, as well over 8,000 dr for the purchase of cattle. When set against the revenues totaling 9,052 dr from Rheneia and Delos during the same period, costs associated with high status service emerge as a major drain on the sanctuary's finances. The same picture emerges when one considers how the revenues from rental property were dispersed:

1. For monthly sacrifices, music and athletic contests, and Hyperborean sacrifices and for the trumpeter and herald and attendant: 1,672 dr, 5 ob. (ll. 67–70)
2. Wall rebuilding; preparation of the *epistates*' (chairman's) office and the meeting place of the Andrians (?) and dedication of the crown, and to the allied cities for the men sent by the council for trials ... + 150 dr + ... 550 (ll. 70–74)
3. To the Amphiktyons of the Athenians (Administrators) for the necessaries and to the secretary and undersecretary: 2,658 dr. To the Amphiktyons of the Andrians for the necessaries: 2,100 dr. Total: 7,129 dr 5 obols. (7,130 dr 5 obols in actuality) Surplus: 1,882 dr (ll. 74–76)

---

31 On specialized craftspeople, see Feyel 2006; Mac Sweeney 2017; and McDonald and Clackson 2020.

32 *ID* 98 (the 'Sandwich marble'), Aegean states ll. 11–15, Individuals ll. 15–24. For translation, commentary and bibliography, see Lambert, *AIO*.

This surplus represents a positive balance, and, clearly, the costs of the festivals and capital costs associated with the upkeep of buildings have been taken into account. However, almost two-thirds of the expenditures are payments to the two Amphiktyonic groups involved in the administration of the sanctuary: nearly 5,000 dr of a total revenue of just over 7,000 dr has been spent "on the necessaries." Increasingly Delos' expenditures consist of what today would be called 'administrative costs.'

Even so, in this year there was a surplus, which was added to the previous surplus: "Total of the remainder with the carry-over from the previous accounting 11,861 dr 1 obol. From this to whom of the Delians we lent on the same terms as the others who have been lent holy monies of Delian Apollo: 3,000 dr. Of this sum, the following borrowers owe …" (ll. 77–80) So with a surplus of just under two talents generated over four years, the *hieropoioi* lent half a talent, or 25% of the surplus. Their caution was understandable since there were defaulters and those who were slow to pay back their loans. Defaulters were listed doubtless in the hope that this would act as an incentive to fiscal responsibility. In the four-year period covered by the record, the following were named and shamed for missing their interest payments (B ll. 14–23):

> Agatharchos, son of Ariston, Delian 400 dr
> Agakles, son of Hypsokles, Tenian > 200 dr
> Euphrainetos, son of Euphantos, Delian 110 dr
> Alkmaeonides, son of Thrasydaios, Athenian 510 dr
> Glaukippos, son of Kleitarchos, Delian 400 dr
> D[…]on, Karystian 200 dr
> Skyllias, Andrian 200 dr
> Hypsokles, son of Theognetos, Delian 400 dr
> Praineus, Syrian, Galessios 46+ dr
> … kleides, son of Thrasynnados, Delian 52 dr
> Habron, son of Thrason, Sphettios 280 dr
> Laches, son of Laches, Steirieus 700 dr
> Maisiades, son of Nymphadoros, Delian 140 dr
> Thrason, son of Habron, Sphettios xxx dr
> Aristeides, son of Deinomenes, Tenian on behalf Oinados, son of Kleo[…], Tenian 220 dr

In addition to recording the names of borrowers and defaulters, the accounts also named those who had been fined for an act of *asebeia* during the archonship at Athens of Charisandros, and of Galaios on Delos. They had driven the Amphiktyons from the temple of Apollo and struck them (!) (B ll. 24–27), for which they were fined and condemned to permanent exile. In addition to the individuals who were named, Face B of the same inscription records the monies still owed by cities:

The following cities were short of the interest they were supposed to pay during our magistracy and did not make payment during the four-year period:

> Keians 4,127 dr
> Mykonioi 420
> Syrioi 4,900
> Siphnioi 2,089
> Tenioi 2,400
> Thermaioi 400 (ex Ikaros)
> Parians 4 tl 1,830 (25,830)
> Oinaians 1 tl 80 (6,080) (ex Ikaros) (ll. 1–5)
> Total: 46,246 (7 tl 4,246 dr)

9 Structural Weakness

And here the numbers point to a real problem in the finances of Delos. The sanctuary reports a surplus of 11,861 dr over a four-year period, but also reports over the same period a shortfall in repayments of 42,246 dr, or 11,561 dr per annum. If any bank lost four times what it recouped every year, its long-term viability would be in serious doubt. There is a danger of pressing the numbers too hard, for a variety of reasons. There will have been seasonal fluctuations; there are oddly anomalous figures, such as the Parians' massive debt of 4 tl, and we do not know over what lengths of time these debts were repayable, so the numbers may be the equivalent of a worst case scenario, but without bankruptcy law and without international tribunals or banking regulators except the god's authority, the system of lending emerging from the surpluses and rents depending on the sanctuary economy, looks, frankly, perilously unstable.

So, in answer to the theoretical issues with which we began, namely, were Greek sanctuaries as economic agents subject to diseconomies of scale, the answer is a qualified yes, in this sense: the very basic model of simple accounting that was the inherited template for sanctuary economics was poorly suited to the more complex economic conditions of the Hellenistic period, when international networks of trade fostered a very uneven development of credit.

And finally, this: the expenditures for the successful functioning of the sanctuary were dispersed in such a way that a large number of people profited from small capital outlays. The recording of this and the business of supplying these services meant that the sanctuary was in a constant state of renovation. The psychological effect of this should not be underestimated. Rather than being the pristine spot of our Beaux Arts images, the sanctuary was constantly advertising its piety by being upgraded, and just as people benefited from the business of sacrifice, which put meat on the table, so too the constant drip feed of expenditure on capital works of the sanctuary served as a palliative, advertising to the community that everyone benefited from their piety and status. However, the amount of money to be made for service in the interests of the sanctuary at Delos ballooned massively at the upper end of the scale. Service as an *architheoros*, herald or ambassador, was generously rewarded, so that the elite of Delos benefited disproportionately from the sanctuary's status. Yet the regularity of service, the predictability and repetition of orthopraxy and rituality as it were masked the unequal distribution of the profits that came from the sanctuary. In the Hellenistic period there would be many calls for land distribution and many a wealthy landowner will have cast a nervous eye over not only the slaves who worked his property but also the poorer citizens pushed to the margins of the state's productive land. Sanctuaries, except when sacked by outside forces, were generally immune from such internal stasis, and we have to consider the real possibility that the somewhat brain numbing detail of the accounts of sanctuary finances served to create an impression of accountability, probity, and piety that allowed elites to flourish precisely at a time when secular institutions of property and land ownership were subject to increasing pressure. In that sense, the many laundry lists of revenues and expenses that impress us with the simplicity of their accounting may, in fact, be among the most ideologically charged documents we have from the Hellenistic period.

Works Cited

Baslez, M.-F. 2007. "La question des étrangers dans les cités grecques (ve–ier siècles)." *Pallas* 74: 213–236.

Behrend, D. 1970. *Attische Pachturkunden, Eine Beitr. z. Beschreibung der μισθώσις nach d. griech. Inschriften*. Munich.

Bogaert, R. 1968. *Banques et banquiers dans les cités grecques*. Leiden.

Bresson, A. 2006. "Marché et prix à Délos: charbon, bois, porcs, huiles et grains." In *Approches de l'économie hellénistique*, edited by R. Descat, 311–339. Saint-Bertrand-de-Comminges.

Bresson, A. 2015. *The Making of the Ancient Greek Economy: Institutions, Markets, and Growth in the City-States*, trans. S. Rendall. Princeton.

Bruneau, P. 1970. *Recherches sur les cultes de Délos à l'époque hellénistique et à l'époque impériale*. Paris.

Canbäck, S., P. Samouel, and D. Price. 2006. "Do diseconomies of scale impact firm size and performance? A theoretical and empirical overview." *Journal of Managerial Economics* 4: 27–70.

Carbon, J.-M. 2018. "A Network of Hearths: Honors, Sacrificial Shares, and 'Traveling Meat.'" In *Feasting and Polis Institutions*, edited by F. van den Eijnde, J. Blok, and R. Strootman, 340–375, Leiden.

Carusi, C. 2020. "The Evolving Format of Building Accounts in Classical Athens." In *Legal Documents in Ancient Societies: Accounts and Bookkeeping in the Ancient World*, edited by A. Jördens and U. Yiftach, 74–91. Wiesbaden.

Chankowski, V. 2008a. *Athènes et Délos à l'époque classique. Recherches sur l'administration du sanctuaire d'Apollon délien*. Athens.

Chankowski, V. 2008b. "Banquiers, caissiers, comptables. À propos des methods financières dans les comptes de Délos." In *Pistoi dia tèn technèn. Bankers, Loans and Archives in the Ancient World*, edited by K. Verboven, K. Vandorpe, and V. Chankowksi, 77–92. Leuven.

Cohen, E.E. 1992. *Athenian Economy and Society: A Banking Perspective*. Princeton.

Constantakopoulou, C. 2017. *Aegean Interactions: Delos and its Networks in the Third Century*. Oxford.

Costouros, G.T. 1977. "Development of an Accounting System in Ancient Athens in Response to Socio-Economic Changes." *The Accounting Historians Journal* 4: 37–54.

Dyer, R.R. 1969. "The Evidence for Apolline Purification Rituals at Delphi and Athens." *JHS* 89: 38–56.

Feyel, C. 2006. *Les artisans dans les sanctuaires grecs aux époques classique et hellénistique à travers la documentation financière en Grèce*. Paris.

Harris, E.M. 1992. "Women and Lending in Athenian Society: A 'Horos' Re-Examined." *Phoenix* 46: 309–321.

Horster, M. 2004. *Landbesitz griechischer Heiligtümer im spätarchaischer und klassischer Zeit*. Berlin.

Horster, M. 2010. "Religious Landscape and Sacred Ground: Relationships between Space and Cult in the Greek World." *RHR* 4: 435–458.

Jones, N.F. 1999. *The Associations of Classical Athens: The Response to Democracy*. Oxford.

Keesling, C.M. 2012. "Syeris, Diakonos of the Priestess Lysimache on the Athenian Acropolis (*IG* II^2 3464)." *Hesperia* 81: 467–505.

Kent, J.H. 1948. "The Temple Estates of Delos, Rheneia, and Mykonos." *Hesperia* 17: 243–338.

Knight, F.H. 1921. *Risk, Uncertainty and Profit*. Boston.

Lalonde, G., M. Langdon, and M. Walbank. 1991. *Horoi, Poletai Records, and Leases of Public Lands. Agora 19*. Princeton.

Lawton, C.L. 1995. *Attic Document Reliefs: Art and Politics in Ancient Athens*. Oxford.

Linders, T. 1994. "Sacred menus on Delos." In *Ancient Greek Cult Practice from the Epigraphical Evidence*, edited by R. Hägg, 71–79. Stockholm.

Mac Sweeney, N. 2017. "Separating Fact from Fiction in the Ionian Migration." *Hesperia* 86: 379–421

McDonald, K., and J. Clackson. 2020. "The Language of Mobile Craftsmen in the Western Mediterranean." In *Migration, Mobility and Language Contact in and Around the Ancient Mediterranean*, edited by J. Clackson et al., 75–97. Cambridge.

McGlin, M.J. 2019. *Sacred Loans, Sacred Interest(s): An Economic Analysis of Temple Loans from Independent Delos (314–167 BCE)*. Ph.D. diss., SUNY Buffalo.

Migeotte, L. 1984. *L'emprunt public dans les cités grecques. Recueil des documents et analyse critique*. Quebec.

Migeotte, L. 2008. "La comptabilité publique dans les cités grecques: l'exemple de Délos." In *Pistoi dia tèn technèn. Bankers, Loans and Archives in the Ancient World*, edited by K. Verboven, K. Vandorpe, and V. Chankowksi, 59–76. Leuven.

Migeotte, L. 2014. *Les finances des cités grecques: aux périodes classique et hellénistique*. Paris.

Miller, S.G. 1994. "Sosikles and the Fourth-Century Building Program in the Sanctuary of Zeus at Nemea." In *Proceedings of the International Conference on Greek Architectural Terracottas of the Classical and Hellenistic Periods, December 12–15, 1991*, edited by N. Winter, 85–98, 365–369. Princeton.

Millet, P. 1991. *Lending and Borrowing in Ancient Athens*. Cambridge.

Osborne, R. 1988. "Social and Economic Implications of the Leasing of Land and Property in Classical and Hellenistic Greece." *Chiron* 18: 279–323.

Papazarkadas, N. 2011. *Sacred and Public Land in Ancient Athens*. Oxford.

Parker, R.C.T. 1996. *Athenian Religion: A History*. Oxford.

Pernin, I. 2014. *Les baux ruraux en Grèce ancienne. Corpus épigraphique et étude*. Lyon.

Picard, C. 1921. *L'établissment des Poseidoniastes de Bérytus, Délos* 6. Paris.

Reger, G. 1991. "The Family of Balakros Son of Nikanor, the Makedonian, on Delos." *ZPE* 89: 151–154.

Reger, G. 1994. *Regionalism and Change in the Economy of Independent Delos*. Berkeley.

Rousset, D. 2013. "Sacred Property and Public Property in the Greek City." *JHS* 133: 113–133.

Rundin, J.S. 2007. "Gods and Corporations: Fifth-Century B.C.E. Athena and the Economic Utility of Extraordinary Agents." *Method and Theory in the Study of Religion* 19: 323–331.

Schaps, D. 1991. "When is a piglet not a piglet?" *JHS* 111: 208–209.

Thomsen, C.A. 2015. "The *Eranistai* of Classical Athens." *GRBS* 55: 15–175.

Vial, C. 1984. *Délos Indépendante (314–167 avant J.-C.): Étude d'une communauté et de ses institutions*. Athens.

Walbank, M.B. 1991. "Leases of Public Lands." In *Inscriptions. Agora 19*. Princeton.

Wijma, S. 2014. *Embracing the Immigrant: The Participation of Metics in Athenian Polis Religion*. Stuttgart.

Woodhead, A.G. 1997. *Inscriptions: The Decrees. Agora 16*. Princeton.

CHAPTER 14

Handworkers and Repair in Greek Sanctuaries

Judith M. Barringer

The study of workers in Greek sanctuaries is not new. Scholars, especially those interested in economic and labor matters, have mined ancient building accounts for information concerning individual artisans, their status (*metic*, slave, citizen) and origins, labor and material costs, division of labor, and the acquisition and transport of materials.[1] 'Itinerant craftsmen' are well known in the study of Greek sanctuaries, something Jeremy McInerney alludes to in his essay in this volume;[2] epigraphical evidence attests to workers who wandered far from their homes for major projects, such as the rebuilding of the temple of Apollo at Delphi in the fourth century BCE, and, of course, workers also could be local, such as the many who labored on the Erechtheion on the Athenian Akropolis.[3] While studies of laborers in Greek sanctuaries have focused on big building projects, particularly those with extant inscribed building contracts, this essay takes up a different theme: the day-to-day workers in sanctuaries who tended to all types of maintenance and repairs to objects and buildings. This essay considers evidence for such sanctuary employees, including what types of laborers were needed, then takes up the more problematic question of where such workers were housed.

1 Workers and Workshops in Sanctuaries: a Brief Overview

Fifth- and fourth-century BCE building accounts from sanctuaries attest to the influx of specialized workers—masons, stone cutters, artisans, contractors, and architects—from all over the Greek world. The best evidence is, unsurprisingly, from Delphi and Delos. At Delphi, the organization of building projects was a task that fell to the *naopoioi* (temple-builders), who are first attested in the 360s BCE and were appointed from among the members of the Delphic Amphictyony;[4] among their duties were fundraising and procurement of materials for the rebuilding of the temple of Apollo at Delphi after its destruction in 373/2 BCE. They traveled to the Peloponnese to raise funds and signed contracts for the purchase of stone and wood with Sikyon and Arkadia.[5] The accounts indicate not just the funding, materials, transport, and labor for the new temple, but also funds set aside for maintenance, infrastructure, and new installations.[6] The accounts also indicate a permanent staff, including an architect, who served as an overseer,[7] and while one contractor seemed to be based in Corinth, another was a resident alien at Delphi.[8] In other words, building projects could last a long time, which meant that some workmen remained on the site for years, as was the case at Epidauros, for example, where one marble-worker carved moldings for the Tholos for years, then took up carving inscriptions.[9] On Delos, we have evidence of commissions for sculptors to repair, e.g., re-gild, and maintain cult statues,[10] and financial accounts offer a detailed picture of repairs and maintenance to the sanctuary's many structures, a topic I return to below.

There is no shortage of evidence for workshops in sanctuaries. Testimony is both epigraphical as is the case for the *ergasterion* at the Poulydamas shrine, which was located in a sanctuary on Delos,[11] and a forge (τὰ χάλκια) near the temple of Apollo at Halaesa,[12] as well as physical: the remains of workshops—ceramic, stone, glass, and metal—have left their traces in the form of kilns, wasters,

---

1 See Randall 1953; Burford 1969; Clinton 1972; Davies 2001; Salmon 2001; Feyel 2006 for the Erechtheion building accounts, as well as Mathé 2023.
2 E.g., Risberg 1998, 674 with bibliography in n. 21; Dimartino 2010; Mathé 2023, 61.
3 *IG* I³ 474; *IG* I³ 476. For the building projects at Epidauros in the first half of the fourth century BCE, workers were mostly from Argos and Corinth, but one worker was from as far away as Crete. See Prignitz 2014, 172.
4 E.g., Davies 1998, 4, 12.
5 *CID* II 60; Partida 2009, 311.
6 Davies 2001, 215–216; Partida 2009, 311–312.
7 Davies 2001, 218.
8 *CID* II 84b, ll. 2–4; Davies 2001, 223. Perhaps the contractor in Corinth was the architect Spintharos of Corinth, mentioned only by Pausanias (10.5.13). I thank David Scahill for this reference.
9 Burford 1966, 255 concerning *IG* IV².1 103, ll. 55–56, 136.
10 E.g., Chankowski 2014. See also infra n. 14.
11 *ID* 1416, B, II, l. 36. Cf. *IGRom.* I, 1101 [Kom-el-Gizeh].
12 *IG* XIV, 352, col. II, l. 54 (Hellenistic period); Prestianni Giallombardo 2003, 1075–1077; 2012, 255. I thank Petra Pakkanen for bringing this to my attention; see her essay in this volume.

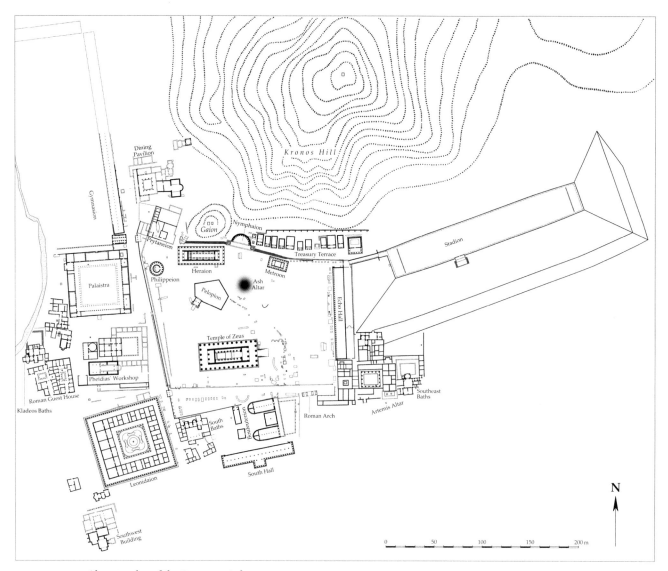

FIGURE 14.1　Olympia, plan of the Roman period
DIGITAL DRAWING BY HANS R. GOETTE FROM HERRMANN 1972, 186, ABB. 129 AND KYRIELEIS 2002, KARTE (H. BIRK)

stone chips, tools, molds, unfinished sculpture, foundries, and scrap material in many Greek sanctuaries.[13] We can point to the following examples (and there are many more). At Olympia, Pheidias' workshop was built atop a fifth-century bronze foundry, and the area in and around it was inhabited by installations and materials for the manufacture and repair of bronze and chryselephantine sculpture from the fifth century BCE onward (Fig. 14.1).[14] A stone workshop operating in the first half of the fifth century BCE was located in the Southeast area,[15] four ceramic kilns were discovered beneath and near the South Hall of c.360–350 BCE,[16] a bronzeworking area at the foot of Kronos hill about 40 m northeast of the Geloan treasury belongs to the fifth and fourth century BCE,[17] and the

---

13　See Lo Monaco (2020, 30–31) with bibliography; Luberto 2023; Maché 2023, 65–66 with regard to the Asklepieion at Epidauros. See also Roux 1961, 86–89, fig. 15; *IG* IV². 1, 102, B, ll. 92–93.

14　*ThesCRA* 4, 23; Heilmeyer 1981, 445–446; Heilmeyer 1987; Zimmer 1990, 39–50; Sinn 2004, 225–227; Sanidas 2013, 178–180. We might think of the repairs made to the Pheidian Zeus by Damophon of Messene in the second century BCE (Paus. 4.31.6).

15　https://www.dainst.org/projekt/-/project-display/13329?p_r _p_1690909578_redirectURL=%2Fsuchen%3Fp_p_id%3 D3%26p_p_lifecycle%3D0%26p_p_state%3Dmaximized %26p_p_mode%3Dview%26_3_struts_action%3D%252F search%252Fsearch%26_3_redirect%3Dhttps%253A%252 F%252Fwww.dainst.org%252Fdai%252Fmeldungen%26 _3_keywords%3Dolympia%26_3_assetCategoryTitles%3D%26 _3_entryClassName%3D. Accessed 26 September 2023; Moustaka 1999; Sanidas 2013, 180–181.

16　Kunze and Schleif 1938/39, 33–36; Sanidas, 2013, 181.

17　*ThesCRA* 4, 23; Heilmeyer 1969, 8–9; Zimmer 1990, 99–100; Sanidas 2013, 177–178.

Southeast building at Olympia had workshops for sculpture and ceramics in the Hellenistic period.[18]

Installations for bronzeworking on the south slope of the Athenian Akropolis were active from the mid-fifth century BCE into the Hellenistic period,[19] and a marble workshop operating from before the Persian War stood on the top surface of the Akropolis in the area of the Pandion shrine.[20] Unsurprisingly, another marble workshop was located south of the Parthenon, which may also have been used for the construction of the chryselephantine Athena Parthenos, although no remnants of the latter material have been found.[21] Another workshop in an Athenian sanctuary is the bronze foundry about 10 m southeast of the Hephaisteion on Kolonos Hill in the Athenian Agora (cf. Andok. *On the Mysteries* 1.40), which Mattusch describes as within the *temenos* of the Hephaisteion.[22]

In the 1990s, Christina Risberg collected the evidence of metalworking in Greek sanctuaries from c.1050–500 BCE.[23] She carefully distinguished between different types of evidence, e.g., tools, molds, or slag versus facilities, such as casting pits and hearths. Installations and sites that show clear signs of production, e.g., spills, drips, are located at the Argive Heraion, Bassai, Kato Symi, Kommos, Philia, Olympia, the Samian Heraion, Oropos, and Tegea,[24] and this list of sites is considerably longer now. For example, the Geometric sanctuary to Apollo at Eretria had a bronze workshop immediately north of the temple,[25] the Amyklaion had a metalworking workshop operating from at least the Geometric through Classical period,[26] and a fifth-century BC bronze foundry operated at the sanctuary of Apollo at Kalapodi.[27] Nemea had a bronze foundry from the third quarter of the fifth century in Oikos 8 extending into the western section of Oikos 9 as indicated by casting pits, tools, ash, carbon, molds and bronze drippings (see p. 167, Fig. 10.4).[28] Evidence of bronzeworking of the fifth-fourth century BCE, but not the foundry itself, has also come to light in the sanctuary of Poseidon at Isthmia.[29]

In addition to the workshops themselves, tools also are common finds in sanctuaries, such as iron tools from Kalapodi,[30] and the hundreds of examples including axes, a drill, saws, wedges, hammers, pliers, files, scissors, chisels, punches, crowbars, a trowel, measures, plumb bobs, awls, needles, and remains of two wooden wheels, from Olympia.[31] To sum up thus far, we know about workshops, tools, and those who used them, both local and non-local, at work in Greek sanctuaries.

Religious personnel were also essential to the daily functioning of major sanctuaries. Seers and cult personnel had to be present on a regular basis between major festivals at large sanctuaries, such as Delphi, Ephesos, and Olympia, where they carried out religious and other duties. For example, we know that priests could handle money: Xenophon (*An.* 5.3.6–7) reports that he left a tithe with one priest at Ephesos, who later returned the money to him when he was at Olympia, perhaps as a representative of his town at the games. Some priests personally contributed to funding for temples (and perhaps this is how they became priests), as was the case for a priest at Priene in 334/3 BCE.[32] Someone had to keep the accounts if the priests did not, and masons had to inscribe them on stone in many locations. I will have occasion to mention religious 'workers' again, but these people are not the focus of this essay.

---

18 https://www.dainst.org/projekt/-/project-display/13329 accessed 26 September 2023.
19 *ThesCRA* 4, 23–24; Zimmer 1990, 62–71, 76–78; Zimmer 1993, 94–95; Monaco 2010, 189–190; Sanidas 2013, 46–47, 52–53; Zimmer and Leopold 2021/2022.
20 Stevens 1946, 22–25; Bundgaard 1976, 77; Zimmer 1993, 95–96; Sanidas 2013, 63–65.
21 Kavvadias and Kawerau 1906, 122–124; Zimmer 1993, 96; Lapatin 2001, 69; Sanidas 2013, 65. Zimmer (1993, 97–98) follows Bundgaard's proposal (1976, 77–78) that the Chalkotheke was used as a workshop for the Athena Parthenos statue before its conversion into a more public space with a colonnaded hall, and notes that epigraphic evidence attests to workshops on the Akropolis for the Erechtheion. In a re-examination of the Chalkotheke's construction and inscriptions, La Follette (1986) rejects Bundgaard's proposal and dates the structure to the fourth century BCE.
22 Mattusch 1977, 348–350. See also Thompson and Wycherley 1972, 142, 145; Zimmer 1990 60–62; Sanidas 2013, 49–50; Miles and Lynch 2024, 197.
23 Risberg 1997. On the frequent occurrence of metal-working installations close to and in sanctuaries, see Sanidas 2023, 5–22, who concentrates chiefly on archaeological material from sites in the north Aegean, especially those on Thasos.
24 Risberg 1997; 1998, 672.
25 Huber 1991.
26 Vlizos 2020.
27 Kiderlen et al. 2016; Hein, Christodoulou, and Fuchs 2017; Sporn 2018/2019, 82; Fuchs 2019.
28 *ThesCRA* 4, 24; Miller 1978, 72; Miller 1990, 162–164; Zimmer 1990, 50–57; Sanidas 2013, 139–140.
29 Rostoker and Gebhard 1980; Zimmer 1990, 74–75; Sanidas 2013, 141.
30 Sporn et al. 2017, 251–252.
31 Baitinger and Völling 2007.
32 Bremmer 2008.

2   'Permanent' Workers at Sanctuaries

In major sanctuaries, particularly extra-urban sanctuaries, where there was a steady stream of visitors, a permanent staff of workers—even a skeleton staff—surely had to be on hand for daily needs and odd jobs; these would not necessarily be people engaged in a major building project, but workers available for smaller tasks.[33] Someone had to tend the altars and temples, to make sure that water lines were intact and maintained, cleaned and functioning properly; plasterers had to repair walls and bath installations; and painters were required to touch up paint on buildings and sculpture.[34] Stonemasons, bronzeworkers, and ceramicists were needed to produce votives and objects (as well as to write inscriptions on a variety of media). Workmen were required to provide wood for fires, wagons, ladders, scaffolding, and written accounts,[35] and woodworkers had to be present to construct such things. Someone had to monitor fires (both to keep them burning and not to allow them to burn out of control); to care for animals, sacrificial or not; oversee and manage votives; and take care of any lands and structures owned by the sanctuary and preserve them from inappropriate use, e.g., squatters,[36] or unauthorized grazing.[37] Tools and those caring for them (e.g., knife sharpeners), measuring devices, rope, baskets, possibly furniture, and provisions for these workers—food, clothing, and shoes—were regularly required, as well.[38] And, of course, upkeep of existing monuments and buildings, e.g., roofs, was an essential component of day-to-day lives in sanctuaries, especially those subject to natural disasters, such as Delphi from landslides, and Olympia from earthquakes and floods. Who were these workers (and by 'workers,' I mean laborers, craftsmen, those who worked with their hands, performing routine repairs and smaller tasks)? What services did they perform, how were they recruited and organized,[39] and where did they live?

Evidence for such tendance in sanctuaries comes from ancient writers (e.g., Xen. *An.* 5.3.13) and inscriptions.[40] For example, a law of the *nomothetai* at Brauron of 354/3–343 BCE describes the bureaucratic procedure for the assessment and contracting of repairs in the sanctuary of Artemis at Brauron: the Athenian *boule* appointed officials to inspect the sanctuary for the condition of the buildings and accoutrements, then an "architect elected for the sanctuaries" (l. 15, trans. Lambert and Pitt, *AIO*) would go to Brauron, take care of the statue, and compile a list of repairs to be made to the sanctuary that would be handed over to contractors, who, in turn, would take care of obtaining funding from the *boule* and allocate the work.[41] Jeremy McInerney explains that the sanctuary of Bendis in Piraeus leased out a house and property for farming to generate funds for repair of the sanctuary (*IG* II² 1361 of *c*.330–324/3 BCE, *IG* I³ 136).[42] In preparation for

---

33   Cf. Linders 1988, 269; Lo Monaco 2020, 33.
34   Burford 1969, 199.
35   Written tablets were used for accounts, contracts, inventories, and notices on Delos. See Kent 1948, 243–244, n. 3.
36   E.g., Clinton 1972, 108.
37   See Chandezon this volume.
38   E.g., Clinton 1972, 98–100, 110–112.
39   Burford (1969, 205–206) points out that *IG* II² 212, ll. 59–63 documents that Athenians could not simply hire workers from another city to do a job but had to obtain permission from the city first. Burford (1969, 198–199) remarks briefly on the odd-job laborers at Epidauros.

40   In addition to the examples adduced here, see also OR no. 144 of *c*.434/3 BCE about repairs on the Athenian Akropolis; *SEG* 42.112 of *c*.360–350 BCE, an honorific decree for the priest of the Apollo sanctuary at Halai, where the priest repaired (or fitted out) the sanctuary (see Gill 1991, 48–50, no. 20); *CGRN* 96, ll. 47–51, 69–77 of the early third century BCE concerning repairs to the precinct of Herakles Diomedonteios on Kos; *IG* XI.2 159, A, l. 45, *c*.281 BCE regarding construction or repair of the *oikema* of the *neokoros* of the Asklepieion on Delos; *SEG* 46.133 of the mid-third century BCE detailing buildings to be inspected, and repaired if necessary, in the Artemis sanctuary at Brauron; *IG* IX.1 2:583, ll. 26–30, 52–56, 58–61 of 216 BCE, a resolution of the Acharnanian League that changes administration of the sanctuary of Apollo at Actium and stipulates that that Acharanians must pay for repairs to the sanctuary; *IG* II² 1324, l. 4 of *c*.190 BCE regarding repairs to the sanctuary of Bendis in Piraeus; *SEG* 42.116 of *c*.180 BCE, an honorific decree for a priestess of the Thesmophoroi, which mentions repairs in the sanctuary of Plouton; *CGRN* 220, ll. 21–22, a late second-century BCE contract for the sale of a priesthood of Aphrodite Pandamos and Pontia on Kos, which indicates the use of funds for the repair of the sanctuary; the well-known regulations of *c*.23 CE concerning the Mysteries at Andania, which mention funding for repairs to the Karneiasion (*CGRN* 222, ll. 55–56); *SEG* 56.1018, a decree of *c*.50 BCE to 50 CE from Thasos about repairs and construction in the sanctuary of a goddess (Artemis?) paid for by one Stilbon, and interestingly, the labor force consists of public slaves, perhaps those assigned to serve the deity in this sanctuary; *SEG* 1.367, an early second-century BCE inscription about repairs to the Heraion temple on Samos (Preuner 1921, 14–19, no. 29; Preuner 1924, 36–38, no. 3); and a decree from the end of the second/beginning of the third century CE from Ithaka concerning funds for repairs in the sanctuary of Artemis (*IG* IX.1 654). See Fournier and Prêtre 2006, 495–496.
41   *SEG* 52.104. See also Pitt 2016, 347.
42   See McInerney in this volume.

the festival to Aphrodite Pandemos in Athens, a decree of c.287–286 BCE details activities to be performed, including covering the doors with pitch and plastering or whitewashing the altars.[43] A contract of c.250–200 BCE for a priesthood at Pergamon, which was contained in a letter, possibly from a Pergamene king, indicates that the sender, i.e., the king, dedicated workshops, which the priest was responsible for leasing and repairing at the priest's expense at the end of his term.[44] In this case, we should note not only the repairs and who is responsible for them, but also the patron of the workshops themselves. The priest of the Asklepieion in Athens was authorized by the boule and demos in 52/51 BCE to repair the propylon, the roof, and the temple at his expense, and the decree also dictates the dedicatory formulas to be inscribed on the works.[45] These day-to-day workers were not famed artisans, but something more akin to handymen doing maintenance (see McInerney in this volume), and presumably this would not be a massive army of workmen, but probably a handful of people: a stonemason, a woodworker, someone skilled in metalworking, a ceramicist, and so on; where workshops existed in the sanctuaries, there may have been one worker present at a given workshop all the time. It is sometimes difficult to draw a line between these workers and sculptors given special commissions in the written record; an inscribed account (IG XI.4 514, ll. 13–16) of the early third century BCE from Delos, for example, records payment and honors for one Telesinos of Athens, who produced statues of Apollo (bronze) and Stratonike (marble), but he also made repairs to other statues in the sanctuary of Apollo. Thus, I do not wish to be too dogmatic about drawing a sharp line between categories of workers, but I have in mind those who were there on a regular basis and 'on call.'

Likewise, other mundane tasks needed to be performed for festival times, as we know from epigraphical evidence, e.g., CGRN 199 of 178 BCE, the accounts for the Poseideia and Eileithyia festivals on Delos.[46] Among the expenses were those for animals, food, and other items, such as wood and coals. Workers and a butcher also received payments; the former surely had any number of tasks, including tending the animals and organizing and managing the distribution of food.

Therefore, we know that these tasks had to be done, but where is the evidence for these day-to-day permanent staff and their labors? One expects them to appear in financial accounts—not necessarily the building accounts, but the routine expense accounts of sanctuaries, such as IG XI.2 154 of 296 BCE from Delos, which details expenses of the hieropoioi.[47] Side A of this inscription includes a remarkably detailed list of small manual tasks, including whitewashing doors and windows of the hestiatoria (ll. 3–4); repairing beams in the palaistra (ll. 5–8); rebuilding a wall for a shrine (l. 9); repairing tiles in the Heraion (l. 10); rebuilding the temple wall of the Thesmophorion (ll. 16–17); leveling an altar (ll. 19–20); repairing the Leukothion (l. 24); repairing the doors of the Propylon (ll. 24–25); building doors for a structure connected to Artemis (ll. 25–26); twice rebuilding the ruins of the shrine of Poulydamas (ll. 26–27, 31–32); cleaning the area around the Artemis altar (ll. 27–28); whitewashing the altars, wall, and krepis of the Thesmophorion (ll. 28–29); whitewashing the palaistra wall (ll. 29–30); plastering the roof of the house at Ortygia and that of the fountain (or spring) (ll. 30–31); repairing bronze cauldrons (ll. 32–33); plastering the cistern in the palaistra (l. 33); repairing a krater and the 'ears' (presumably handles) of a kothon (l. 34); repairing damage to the sanctuary of the Archegetes (l. 35); waxing (waterproofing) the vessel or πανίωνες (ll. 35–36);[48] repairing oinochoai (l. 37); cleaning the Dioskourion (l. 37); providing a roof for the building of the pentekostologoi (ll. 38–39); clearing around (or purifying) the palm tree in the Letoon (ll. 39–40); clearing away the ruined wall near the altar (l. 40); repairing the pigsty (l. 41); bringing down the tent to the sanctuary (l. 43); repairing the cauldron from the sanctuary of Zeus Kynthios (ll. 45–46); obtaining and whitening the notice board and writing tablet (ll. 46–47); and creating a gable for the door of the building at Ortygia (ll. 47–49). The workers who received payments for performing these tasks are named, and it is noteworthy that five names recur—Timokritos who repairs or builds in two instances; Aristokritos, appears thrice, and in all three cases, he is plastering or whitewashing;[49] Philokrates does both; and Sostratos both writes and prepares writing surfaces. Herakleides also receives payment for a variety of tasks (ll. 18–19, 21, 34–37), including repairing the krater, kothon, and oinochoai, and waxing the πανίωνες. Might these workers doing relatively small tasks be resident workers?

---

43 LSCG no. 39; NGSL² 39; CGRN 136.
44 CGRN 124.
45 IG II² 1046; LSCG no. 44; NGSL² 38; AIO.
46 See McInerney in this volume.
47 See McInerney in this volume, as well as IG XI.2 203 of 269 BCE and IG XI.2 287 of 250 BCE, both from Delos, which also mention repairs and cleaning expenses.
48 The meaning of πανίωνες is not entirely clear here. LSJ, s.v. πανίωνες 3b offers ἀμφορίσκος.
49 See also Vial 1984, 351.

We can observe the same phenomenon in another inscription, *CID* II 139 of 247/246 BCE from Delphi, which describes maintenance to the sanctuary in preparation for the Pythia festival.⁵⁰ Several names are repeated, and I think it logical to surmise that these represent the same persons receiving payment for various activities to spruce up the place and ready it for the festival: Agazalos for loosening and leveling the *xystos* and its peristyle area (ll. 5–6), providing white earth (l. 7), and 'making' and cleaning other areas (ll. 33, 43); Kritolaos for fencing something (l. 9) and repairing a water pipe near the Damatrion (ll. 9–10); Kleon twice for repairing walls (ll. 14–15, ll. 18–19); Smyrnaios for cleaning and repairing the *stadion* track and its slopes (ll. 22–25); Nikon for building the odeion (l. 25),⁵¹ the installation of the *proskenion* (ll. 28–29), and building stands in the *stadion* (l. 29); Euthydamos for fencing the *stadion* (l. 28), for making the arched passage to the *stadion* (l. 30), and doing something for the hippodrome (l. 37); and Melissen for repairing that (same?) vaulted passage (ll. 34–35) and for making the stands in the theater (l. 27). The skills required for most of these jobs are not demanding (the constructed structures required light carpentry) and might be well-suited to a skeleton staff on site or living nearby.

Minor expenses sometimes appear alongside the record of major building projects. At fourth-century BCE Epidauros, for example, Aristaios is paid for a variety of minor jobs concerning the Temple of Asklepios, as we know from *IG* IV².1 102: applying pitch to doors (ll. 255–256, 277–278), mending doors (ll. 275–276, 297), removing or providing wood (ll. 275–276, 303–304) for work on the temple roof (ll. 287–288, 289), cleaning the roof (ll. 293–294), providing wood and a ladder (ll. 295–297), for making a ladder (l. 298), for making a money box (l. 300), and for carrying a pair of doors (l. 305).⁵² Aristonikos worked on some wooden beams for the Aphrodite temple and for the peristyle of the accommodation houses, but also installed drains in the horse shelter, and broke limestone blocks for the drainage ditches on the road leading into the city (and these tasks are from accounts covering a few decades' time);⁵³ while Pheidokrates was paid a modest sum for cleaning (l. 2). Burford speculates that it is precisely this kind of small task that was performed by local workers.⁵⁴

It is sometimes difficult to determine when we are looking at long-term, repeat payments since accounts on stone are incomplete, and accounts kept on other materials usually do not survive.⁵⁵ But we have some information attesting to tasks performed regularly, as we might suppose for the Pythia at Delphi discussed above. The Phallophoria for the annual Dionysia festival on Delos required preparations as we know from inscriptions ranging from *c*.304–169 BCE. The image of a phallos-bird, which was paraded on a cart, was constructed anew for this yearly event, and inscriptions describe the materials—wood and metal—and the payments for them and the labor, as well as costs paid to a laborer to level the road.⁵⁶

As further testimony for ongoing repair, we can turn again to Olympia, where natural disasters required repairs and rebuilding of the Temple of Zeus several times, according to Hennemeyer; an earthquake in *c*.464 BCE happened while the building was still under construction (Fig. 14.1).⁵⁷ Another earthquake of *c*.402/1 BCE necessitated rebuilding, which lasted well over half a century and provided a great deal of damaged building material that was reused in other constructions at Olympia.⁵⁸ Two further temple rebuildings occurred; although the impetus for them is unknown, the corner figures of the west pediment were replaced in the second half of the first century CE, presumably because of damage.⁵⁹ The net result was that the two facades were completely rebuilt twice, and their pedimental sculptures were installed twice. I will leave aside the question of the date of the surviving pedimental sculptures, a thorny topic and one that is not directly relevant to this essay.⁶⁰ In many large sanctuaries, there was near constant building and rebuilding, and scholars suggest that this ever-evolving state was intentional, providing labor for workers and their supervisors.⁶¹

---

50 Pouilloux 1977.
51 Made of wood, as was the *proskenion*. See Pouilloux 1977, 118; Bommelaer 2015, 257, 262.
52 Burford 1969, 235, 237.
53 Prignitz 2022, 483, nos. 14 l. 281, 37 ll. 288, 388, 47 ll. 32–33, 49–50.
54 Burford 1969, 199; Burford 1971, 72. Note that Burford (1969) sometimes refers to Aristaios as a contractor (232) and elsewhere as an odd job man (235); he could, of course, be both. See also Prignitz 2014, 289–290.
55 Cf. Burford 1971, 71–72.
56 Bruneau 1970, 312–319. See also Linders 1988, 267.
57 Hennemeyer 2006, 108; Hennemeyer 2010, 188; Hennemeyer 2013a, 19–20.
58 Hennemeyer 2013b, 129; Hennemeyer 2013a, 20–21.
59 Hennemeyer 2013a, 21–23.
60 See Barringer 2021, 136–137.
61 See McInerney in this volume.

3   Accommodations for Sanctuary Workers

If we assume a permanent presence of craftsmen and cult personnel at major sanctuaries, we must then ask where and how these people lived. For a sanctuary like Delphi, one might answer "in the surrounding town." In fact, a third-century BCE inscription from Delphi indicates that the city of Delphi granted tax exemption and the right to possess land and a house to Teisimachos, who had to set up a *proskenion* for the Herakleia in lieu of paying a tax on artisans (χειροτέχνιον), a tax known from another Delphic inscription of the same date.[62] This second inscription grants Akidon exemption from paying the χειροτέχνιον, and awards him and his descendants *proxenia*, *promanteia*, as well as a host of other honors. In exchange for these, Akidon must roof the *hoplotheke* in the Pronaia (sanctuary, presumably), the lower gymnasion, the large portico, the temple, and workshops, and for these tasks, the city will provide the rooftiles. Moreover, the inscription also promises shares of sacrificial victims accorded to those who repair sacred buildings. Thus, we learn that such manual laborers could be recompensed in a variety of ways for their efforts.[63] A similar situation existed on mid-fourth century BCE Kos, where smiths and potters (χαλκέων καὶ κερα[μεω]ν) were singled out for perquisites of the sacrificial ox for Zeus Polieus; they received part of the head.[64]

For sanctuaries at some distance from settlements, what accommodations and provisions were available for the daily staff at sanctuaries? Unfortunately, not much evidence exists to answer this question. Surely this is due in part to the fact that archaeologists have not been 'looking' for residences at major sanctuaries—and this is certainly the case for many of the biggest excavations, where emphasis has always been on major buildings and sculpture—but the lack of data may also be due to the construction materials or methods of such housing, and/or an inability to identify these structures. If there were installations, how would we recognize them?

Accommodations for workers and workers' quarters have been identified outside of sanctuaries, usually close to manufacturing centers, and perhaps these can help us devise some idea of what we should be looking for in the area immediately in and around sanctuaries; in the following, I mostly leave aside production areas of olive oil, textiles, and the like, since these are unlikely tasks for the sanctuary workers under investigation here.[65]

One example of workers' housing is the Street of the Marbleworkers and the fifth-century BCE House of Simon the Cobbler in the southwest area of the Athenian Agora (Figs. 14.2–3). The House of Simon was identified by nails and eyelets for laces, together with an incised cup bearing Simon's name.[66] The marbleworkers' area was identified by modest structures of the fifth and fourth centuries BCE possessing rubble and mudbrick walls, few columns, clay floors, small size, and no decoration, which probably is a description of most average non-elite housing in antiquity. But *these* houses were located near casting pits for bronze statues, and contained a large quantity of marble chips and terracotta molds, strongly suggestive of 'industrial' use from the fifth through second centuries BCE.[67] The House of Mikion and Menon seemed to have served a dual purpose—accommodation and marble workshop—from the fifth through third centuries BCE: marble dust, chips, and unfinished sculptures, as well as an inscribed stylus were found here (Fig. 14.4).[68]

Elsewhere, Olynthos offers examples of houses producing textiles on a scale far too large for household use (Fig. 14.5). For example, House A viii 7/9 held 247 loomweights in the *pastas*, which Cahill claims were sufficient for half a dozen to a dozen looms, as well as another 50 in room B. Because House A viii 9 had no loomweights, Cahill asks if the house served as accommodation for those working the looms in the adjacent western house.[69] Elsewhere in Olynthos, houses, such as House B i 5, contained numerous terracotta figurine molds, and a room in House B i 5 had a large cistern and nearby pit.[70] Likewise,

---

62   Daux 1934, 363–366; Jacquemin 2010.
63   *FD* III 4, 136⁴, ll. 11–14; Jacquemin 2010, who, like Daux (1934), discusses the social status (citizen, metic, etc.) of the two workmen, concludes that Akidon does not usually work at Delphi so is exempt from the χειροτέχνιον tax, whereas Teisimachos does, hence the grant of land and the right to own a house and the need to offset the tax.
64   *Syll.*³ 1025–1027; *CGRN* 86, A, ll. 54–55; RO no. 62, A, ll. 53–54.
65   See also Harrington 2015, 65–68.
66   http://agora.ascsa.net/id/agora/monument/house%20of%20simon%20the%20cobbler?q=house%20of%20simon&t=&v=list&sort=&s=1.
67   Thompson and Wycherley 1972, 173–177; Camp and Mauzy 2010, 181.
68   Tsakirgis 2015. On 'maison-ateliers' on Delos, see Karvonis 2008, 196–197.
69   Cahill 2002, 251.
70   Cahill 2002, 253; Hellmann 2006, 120. See also the Potter's Quarter at Corinth, where the north (end of seventh century BCE) and south buildings (sixth century BCE) were initially interpreted as workshops but may, in fact, be houses (Arafat and Morgan 1989, 324); and the eighth-century BCE ironworking area at Pithekoussai (Klein 1972; Barra Bagnasco 1996, 354). Rooms near a cistern adjacent to the washeries at Agrileza have led some scholars to suggest that they may have provided housing for the slaves who toiled there. See Photos-Jones and Jones 1994, 315;

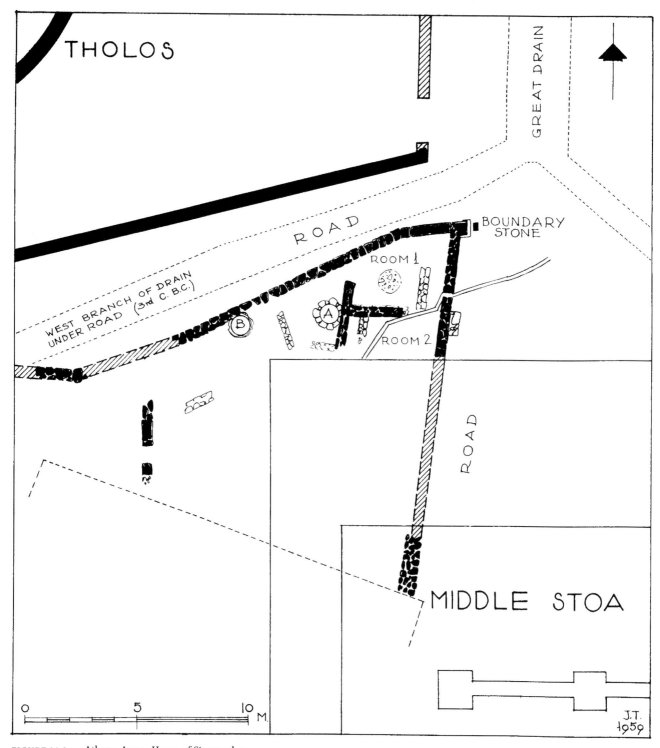

FIGURE 14.2   Athens, Agora, House of Simon, plan
COURTESY AMERICAN SCHOOL OF CLASSICAL STUDIES AT ATHENS: AGORA EXCAVATIONS

late fourth- and third-century *pastas* houses at Heraklea in Lucania clearly were used as both domestic spaces and terracotta production centers as indicated by numerous kilns and hundreds of matrices.[71]

Do we have any such structures adjacent to working areas near sanctuaries or even in sanctuaries? South of

Kalaitzoglou 2004, 90; Hellmann 2006, 115. For the possibility that tower 1 in insula 3 at Thorikos, located within a metal working area, may have served as a house, see Kalaitzoglou 2004, 86–87.

71   Giardino 2014, 1023–1024.

FIGURE 14.3 Athens, Agora, House of Simon, view to west
COURTESY OF THE EPHORATE OF ANTIQUITIES OF ATHENS CITY, ANCIENT AGORA, ASCSA: AGORA EXCAVATIONS
© HELLENIC MINISTRY OF CULTURE AND SPORTS/HELLENIC ORGANIZATION OF CULTURAL RESOURCES DEVELOPMENT (H.O.C.RE.D.)

the *Xenon* at Nemea, houses identified by their domestic contents, specifically cooking implements, a grinding stone, burnt earth, ash, and hearths were constructed in the last decades of the fourth century BCE and in use until the mid-third century BCE at the latest (see p. 167, Fig. 10.4). They are more spacious than typical contemporary dwellings and built of larger blocks than those normally used for houses, so Miller suggests that they are officials' quarters or those of priests, judges, or "caretakers" of the sanctuary during games. Miller also states that the houses are *not* domestic spaces for a permanent population at Nemea because of their larger size, the larger blocks used in their construction, the presence in some of official objects belonging to the sanctuary, and the lack of stratigraphic accumulation that one would expect with continual habitation.[72] But it is worth considering whether such spaces were multi-functional, accommodating a population that fluctuated in number and function as needed. One might ask if they were, at least in part (time or space) dwellings for workers, particularly when the games were not occurring.[73] How could we confirm this? Epigraphical evidence would help; for example, an inscription of the late fourth century BCE from Epidauros refers to the construction of a dwelling in which one room or one portion of the building had something to do with an anvil.[74] But at Nemea we have no such evidence. However, below the north wall of rooms 10 and 12 in Nemea's *Xenon* was a complex of kilns dating to the last third of the fourth century BCE, which seem to have been used exclusively for roof tiles, and a stone workshop lay to the west. Finds from the latter include a bronze sheet with attachment holes on which was inscribed IEPO[Y] ("of the sanctuary"); Miller posits that it was affixed to the end of a wooden beam or the like.[75]

---

72 Miller 1990, 76–77.

73 Miller 1979, 92–93; Miller 1982, 24–28; Miller 1988, 10–19; Miller 1990, 75–78. N.B. that House 3 was already out of use before the second half of the third century BCE; see Miller 1988, 14.

74 Burford 1966, 303–304.

75 Nemea inv. IL 279. Miller 1990, 64–66, 118, 168; Kraynak 1992, 102, 107–108, 157.

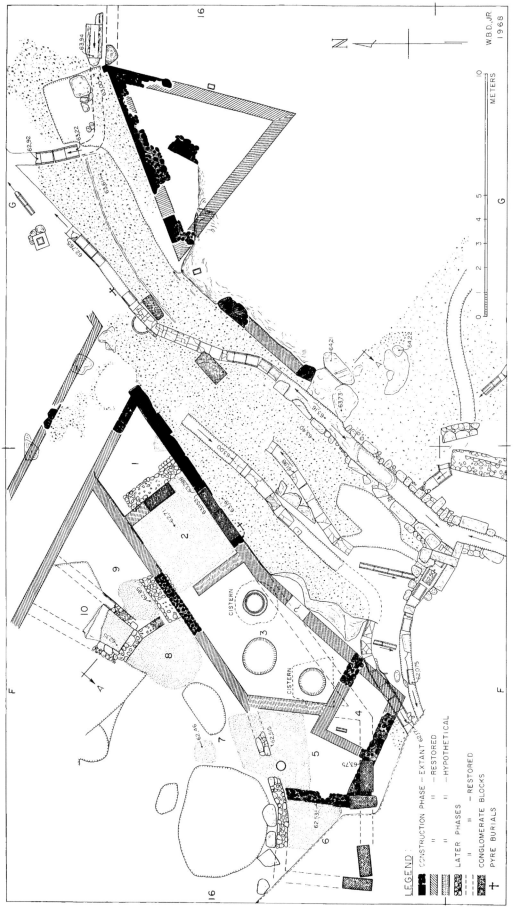

FIGURE 14.4 Athens, Agora, combined state plan and restored plan of the houses (at left) of Mikion and Menon House (5th–3rd c. BC) and (at right) the Triangular Shrine (5th c. BC)
COURTESY AMERICAN SCHOOL OF CLASSICAL STUDIES AT ATHENS: AGORA EXCAVATIONS

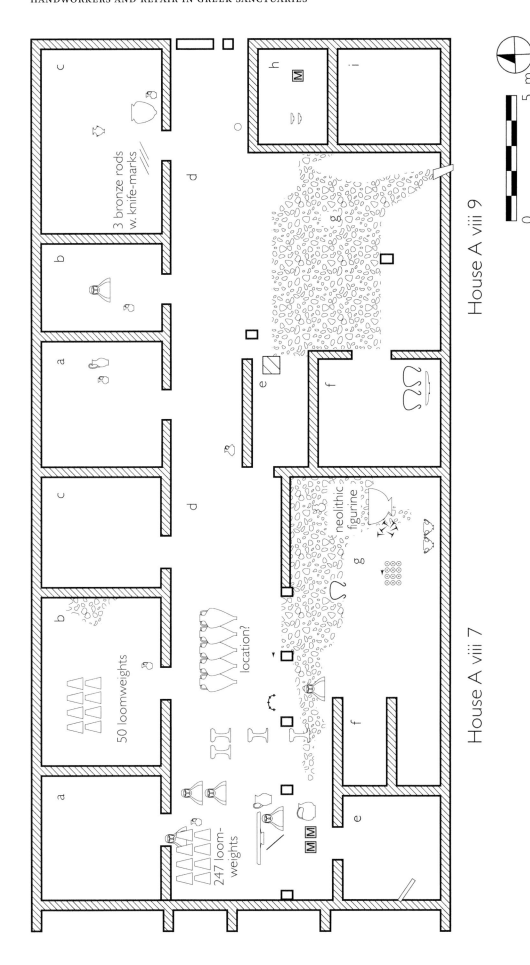

FIGURE 14.5   Olynthos, plan of House A viii 7 and House A viii 9
COURTESY OF NICHOLAS CAHILL

FIGURE 14.6A   Troy, phase plan of the sanctuary prepared by Elizabeth Riorden, Hellenistic period
AFTER ROSE 1998, 78, FIG. 6

Another housing possibility may be a large, multi-room building of c.300 BCE in the west sanctuary of Troy in which were found figurines, as well as industrial remains: murex shell, slag, burnt areas (Fig. 14.6a–14.6b). Bronze casting pits were located just outside. The excavator suggested that this two-storey structure included a workshop with a sheltered area for bronze cold work, although the murex might suggest dyeworks. One might imagine a workshop with space for housing workers,[76] although certain types of labor, including dyeing textiles, usually

76   Rose 1998, 76–85.

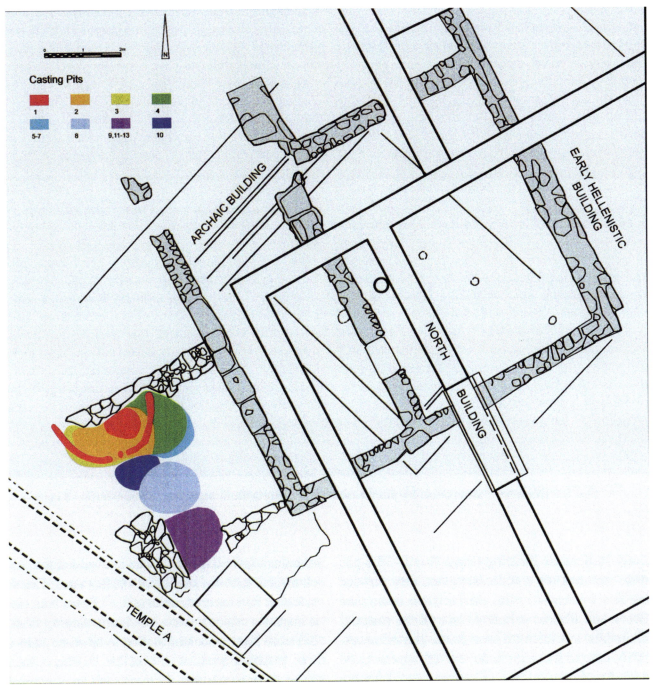

FIGURE 14.6B   Troy, drawing of bronzeworking pits in front of the North Building by Maureen Basedow
AFTER ROSE 1998, 79, FIG. 7

demands distinct living quarters because of the malodorous nature of the industry.[77]

We might also consider the situation at eighth-seventh century BCE Oropos, where there is abundant evidence of metalworking in Building A, and to a lesser degree, the production of ceramics in the areas of Buildings A and B-Γ,[78] as well as of subsistence fishing.[79] Mazarakis Ainian hypothesizes that some buildings may have been used for workshops, as well as dwelling places,[80] and Buildings A and B seem to have operated together as

77 I am grateful to Adeline Grand-Clément for suggesting this to me and steering me toward useful bibliography concerning murex dyeing on Delos, e.g., Bruneau 1969, esp. 790. Cf. Strabo 16.2.23; Bresson 2008, 196. See also Pakkanen in this volume.

78 Mazarakis Ainian 2002, 154, 164–165. For more on metalworking in this central area of Oropos, including Buildings A and B, see Doonan and Mazarakis Ainian 2007.

79 Mazarakis Ainian 2002, 166.

80 Mazarakis Ainian 2002, 166–168.

working and domestic space.⁸¹ Intriguingly, buildings Θ and IA, enclosed together with other buildings in a *peribolos* wall, combine a variety of activities: Θ was domestic space but also accommodated religious gatherings and dining while the adjacent building IA was used for weaving, spinning, perhaps even dyeing of textiles ("an unusual number of murex shells" were recovered here).⁸² In addition, a cult assemblage of the early seventh century, interpreted as evidence of hero cult, was found atop the ruins of building IA.⁸³ In sum, we have close proximity of industry, domestic activities, and religious activities in Early Iron Age Oropos.

So-called priests' houses in sanctuaries may also offer possibilities.⁸⁴ Such buildings are known from literary or epigraphic sources, but rarely from archaeology.⁸⁵ The term is usually applied to buildings whose function remains unknown: 'priest' was not a full-time occupation, and we can presume that most priests lived in their own homes much of the time.⁸⁶ The structures labeled as priest's houses are too small to be major public buildings, their constructions are not elaborate, and they are structures with more than one room. Some scholars now regard such 'priests' houses' as *hestiatoria* or *katagogia* for pilgrims.⁸⁷ Hellmann rightly points out that Pausanias (10.34.7) makes it clear that priests and other religious personnel at sanctuaries need not stay in a dedicated house but could stay in porticos, as was the case at the sanctuary of Athena Kranaia at Elateia,⁸⁸ although this is not plausible as a permanent arrangement everywhere, particularly in the winter.

Pausanias (5.15.8) mentions the Theokoleon, the house of the priest, at Olympia, but Mallwitz interprets the structure to the west of the Altis cited by Pausanias as a lodging space for Pheidias and his workmen (Sinn would place Pausanias' Theokoleon in the southeast of the sanctuary).⁸⁹ The website of the Hellenic Ministry of Culture says of the building in the west (Fig. 14.7), "This was the seat of the *theokoloi*, the priests of Olympia, but also the residence of the sanctuary staff, which included soothsayers, interpreters, bearers of sacrificial animals, musicians and a woodmonger who provided the wood used in sacrifices."⁹⁰ Originally constructed in the fifth century BCE, it was widened to the east in the first century BCE, including the addition of a portico leading to a courtyard.⁹¹ Perhaps this structure also housed the φαιδρυνταί mentioned by Pausanias (5.14.5), who took constant care of the chryselephantine Pheidian Zeus.⁹² The size and proximity to a workshop make this a possibility for worker's accommodation, but without finds to confirm such a proposal, we are in the realm of speculation.

While he conceded that such houses might also be used by pilgrims, Travlos identified several priests' houses in Attika: one of *c*.325–275 BCE at Vari,⁹³ one at the Aphrodite sanctuary at Daphni,⁹⁴ and another (12.40 × 15.20m) of the late sixth or early fifth century BCE excavated by Stavropoullos at Cape Zoster near the Apollo sanctuary (Fig. 14.8).⁹⁵ The Cape Zoster house is intriguing—and promising: originally built *c*.500 BCE or so, it was later remodeled and enlarged in the fourth century BCE. It has been interpreted as a priest's house, later enlarged to be a *katagogia* for pilgrims, but I wonder if, finally, we are not looking at housing and workspace for workers.⁹⁶ The columns might lead one to dismiss this as too elaborate a house for such use, but the finds here include bronze nails, needles, hooks, lead weights, terracotta loom weights, a terracotta rooftile with a ship incised on it, a couple of engraved sherds, a stone inscription from the end of the fifth century BCE concerning funds, as well as a great deal of black-glaze drinking ware, an *askos* painted with the word "*hieros*," a *kernos*, as well as a late fifth-century BCE Attic red-figure pyxis lid, and terracotta figurines. Some of this material could be explained by designating the building a priest's house or *katagogia*, but all of it could be explained by recognizing this as worker's quarters—for work, dining, housing. What would be needed is an area or areas sufficient for sleeping, eating, and safely storing one's tools and personal belongings.

---

81 Doonan and Mazarakis Ainian 2007, 369–370.
82 Mazarakis Ainian 2002, 168.
83 Mazarakis Ainian 2002, 161–164.
84 See Ekroth in this volume.
85 Hellmann 2006, 227. For examples, see Muller 1983, 175, n. 58.
86 Cf. Sinn 2004, 111.
87 Hellmann 2006, 229–231.
88 Hellmann 2006, 227–229.
89 *ThesCRA* 4, 23; Mallwitz 1972, 268; Sinn 2004, 115.
90 http://odysseus.culture.gr/h/2/eh251.jsp?obj_id=5841, accessed 26 September 2023.
91 Mallwitz 1972, 266–268.
92 Mallwitz (1972, 268) suggests space for workers without further specification.
93 Travlos, *Attika*, 448.
94 Travlos 1937, although Hellmann 2006, 211 thinks it is for lodging, generally speaking.
95 Stavropoullos 1938; Travlos, *Attika*, 468.
96 Goette 2001, 197 describes it as a "country house," whose large foundations suggest a tower.

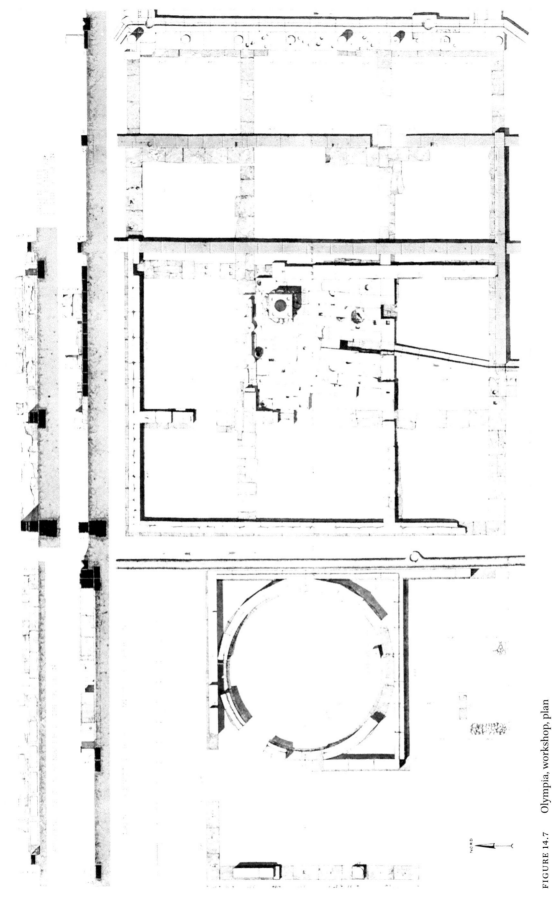

FIGURE 14.7 Olympia, workshop, plan
AFTER MALLWITZ 1972, 267, ABB. 221

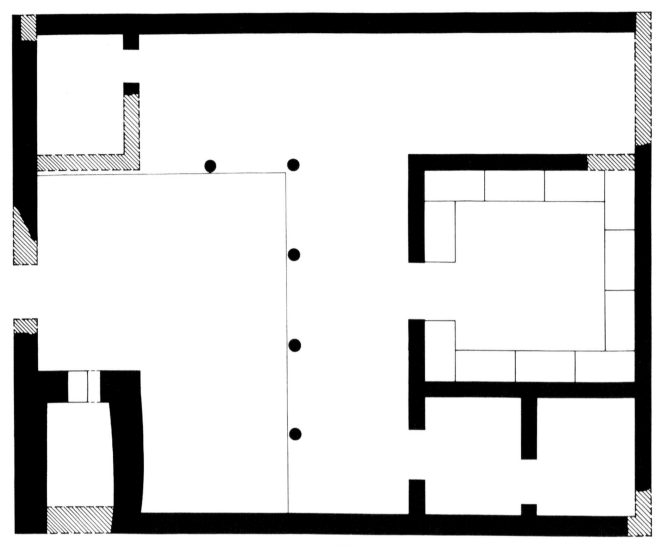

FIGURE 14.8A   Athens, Cape Zoster, plan by D. Giraud, late sixth or early fifth century BCE
AFTER TRAVLOS, *ATTIKA*, 478

Another possibility for this 'priest's house' at Zoster is that it constitutes a multi-purpose building, used at times by the priest or by pilgrims, at other times by workers; or we might speculate if one kind of activity happened on one floor or in one portion of the house, while used for workers in another. This might also be the case for *hestiatoria* with additional courtyards or halls that served as living or sleeping accommodations, as was the case for the Leonidaion at Olympia,[97] the *katagogion* at the late Classical/early Hellenistic sanctuary of Hera Lakina at Kroton (K on the plan),[98] or the South Stoa at Corinth, according to Broneer (Fig. 14.9).[99] I am not thinking of anything quite so elaborate for workers but rustic dining spaces or pavilions might serve this function.

---

97   Barringer 2021, 58, 233–234 with bibliography.

98   Seiler 1996, 253–256; Hellmann 2006, 230.

99   Broneer (1954, 98–99) speculates that the shops on the ground floor also served as dining spaces (he refers to them as "taverns"), while the upper storey may have been used for sleeping. See Scahill in this volume.

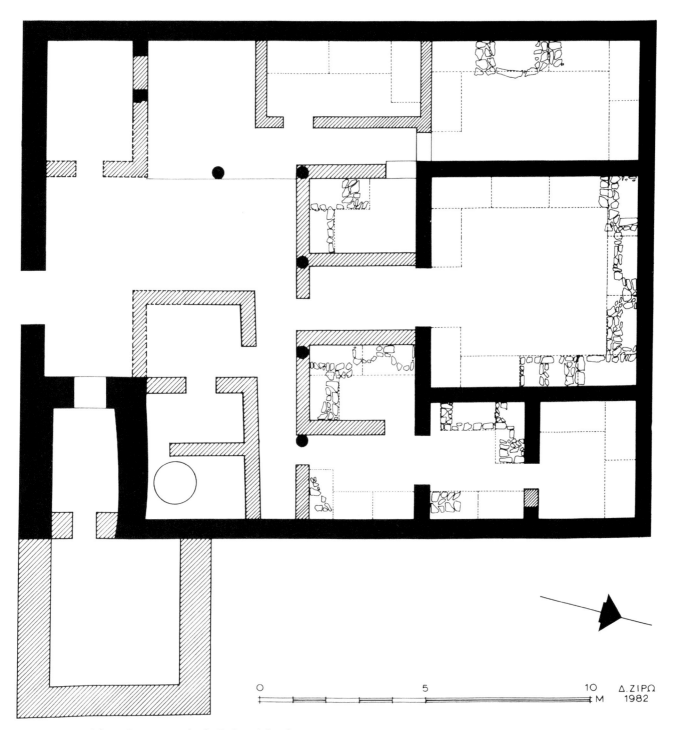

FIGURE 14.8B Athens, Cape Zoster, plan by D. Giraud, fourth century BCE
AFTER TRAVLOS, *ATTIKA*, 479

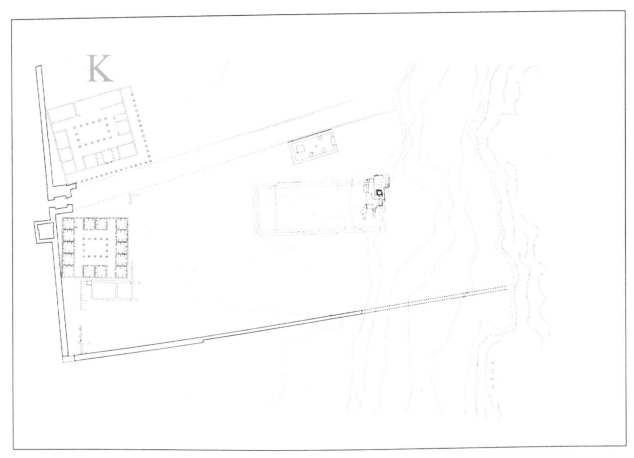

FIGURE 14.9 Kroton, sanctuary of Hera Lakina, plan, late Classical/early Hellenistic
AFTER SEILER 1996, 257 (TOP IMAGE)

4 Conclusions

Day-to-day workers in sanctuaries, particularly large ones, were essential for maintenance, repairs, and doing any number of small tasks that the sanctuary required to function for pilgrims, sanctuary administrators, and the gods. Much work remains to be done on this topic, including excavations with this issue in mind. Rather than looking for houses with workshops, I think we might be more successful if we look for workshops with possible domestic spaces. In particular, expanding our notions of what constitutes a sanctuary by focusing not so much on sacred buildings or sculptures, but considering everything that went on in and around a sanctuary. This involves investigation of peripheral areas; at Olympia, for example, areas to the east of the Altis and west of the Kladeos River. The *temenos* boundary may mark off the sacred area, but human activities essential to the use and functioning of that sanctuary extend far beyond this boundary, and these are also critical to our understanding of how sanctuaries functioned.

Acknowledgments

I am grateful to Gunnel Ekroth, who offered helpful comments and saved me from several errors; David Scahill for his suggestions, Jeremy McInerney for sharing his material with me, Benedikt Eckhardt for his epigraphical help, and Annalisa Lo Monaco who provided a PDF of her new book when I could not access it. I also thank Helga Di Giuseppe, who supplied me with an offprint of her essay, and Nicola Nenci and Hans Goette, who provided bibliographic materials during a COVID-19 lockdown. Finally, I offer my thanks to Nick Cahill, Aspa Efstathiou, Craig Mauzy, Árpád Nagy, and David Scahill for help with the images.

Works Cited

Arafat, K., and C. Morgan. 1989. "Pots and Potters in Athens and Corinth: A Review." *OJA* 8: 311–346.

Baitinger, H., and T. Völling. 2007. *Werkzeug und Gerät aus Olympia, OF 32*. Berlin.

Barra Bagnasco, M. 1996. "Housing and Workshop Construction in the City." In *The Western Greeks*, edited by G. Pugliese Carratelli, 353–360. Venice.

Barringer, J.M. 2021. *Olympia: A Cultural History*. Princeton.

Bommelaer, J.-F., and Laroche, D. 2015. *Guide de Delphes: le site*. Athens.

Bremmer, J. 2008. "Priestly Personnel of the Ephesian Artemision: Anatolian, Persian, Greek, and Roman Aspects." In *Practitioners of the Divine: Greek Priests and Religious Figures from Homer to Heliodorus*, edited by B. Dignas and K. Trampedach https://chs.harvard.edu/chapter/part-ii-variations-of-priesthood2-priestly-personnel-of-the-ephesian-artemision-anatolian-persian-greek-and-roman-aspects-jan-bremmer, accessed 26 September 2023.

Bresson, A. 2008. *L'économie de la Grèce des cités I: Les structures et la production*. Paris.

Broneer, O. 1954. *Corinth 1:4: The South Stoa and its Roman Successors*. Princeton.

Bruneau, P. 1969. "Documents sur l'industrie délienne de la pourpre." *BCH* 93: 759–791.

Bruneau, P. 1970. *Recherches sur les cultes de Délos à l'époque hellénistique et à l'époque impériale*. Paris.

Bundgaard, J. 1976. *Parthenon and the Mycenaean City on the Heights*. Copenhagen.

Burford, A. 1966. "Notes on the Epidaurian Building Inscriptions." *ABSA* 61: 254–339.

Burford, A. 1969. *The Greek Temple Builders at Epidauros*. Liverpool.

Burford, A. 1971. "The Purpose of Inscribed Building Accounts." In *Acta of the Fifth International Congress of Greek and Latin Epigraphy, Cambridge 1967*, 71–76. Cambridge.

Cahill, N. 2002. *Household and City Organization at Olynthus*. New Haven.

Camp, J. 1990. *The Athenian Agora*, 4th ed. Athens.

Camp, J., and C. Mauzy. 2010. *The Athenian Agora: Site Guide*, 5th ed. Princeton.

Chankowski, V. 2014. "Réparer les idoles, entretenir les lieux de culte. L'économie de la restauration dans les sanctuaires du monde grec." *Techne* 40: 42–45.

Clinton, K. 1972. "Inscriptions from Eleusis." *ArchEph* 1971: 81–136.

Daux. G. 1934. "XEIPOTEXNION." *RPhil* 8: 361–366.

Davies, J.K. 1998. "Finance, Administration, and 'Realpolitik': The Case of Fourth-Century Delphi." *Modus Operandi: Essays in Honour of Geoffrey Rickman*, edited by M. Austin, J. Harries, and C. Smith, 1–14. Oxford.

Davies, J.K. 2001. "Rebuilding a Temple: The Economic Effects of Piety." In *Economies Beyond Agriculture in the Classical World*, edited by D. Mattingly and J. Salmon, 209–229. London.

Dimartino, A. 2010. "Artisti itineranti: l'evidenza epigrafica." In *Scolpire il marmo*, edited by G. Adornato, 9–40. Pisa.

Doonan, C.P., and A. Mazarakis Ainian. 2007. "Forging identity in Early Iron Age Greece: implications for the metalworking evidence from Oropos." In *Oropos and Euboea in the Early Iron Age*, edited by A. Mazarakis Ainian, 361–378. Volos.

Feyel, C. 2006. *Les artisans dans les sanctuaires grecs aux époques classique et hellénistique*. Athens.

Fournier, J., and C. Prêtre. 2006. "Un mécène au service d'une déesse thasienne: décret pour Stilbôn (Thanar 1)." *BCH* 130: 487–497.

Fuchs, J. 2019. "A bronze foundry of Classical times in the sanctuary of Kalapodi (Central Greece)." In *Proceedings of the xxth International Congress on Ancient Bronzes: Resource, reconstruction, representation, role*, edited by P. Baas, 319–329. Oxford.

Giardino, L. 2014. "Architettura domestica a Eraclea di Lucania tra III e I sec. a.C.: aspetti architettonici, sociali ed economici." In *XVIII CIAC: Centro y periferia en el mundo clásico: Centre and periphery in the ancient world*, edited by J. Álvarez, T. Nogales, and I. Rodà, 1023–1027. Mérida.

Gill, D. 1991. *Greek Cult Tables*. New York.

Goette, H.R. 2001. *Athens, Attica, and the Megarid*. London.

Harrington, K. 2015. "Privacy and Production: Sensory Aspects of Household Industry in Classical and Hellenistic Greece." *Archaeological Review from Cambridge* 30: 63–69.

Heilmeyer, W.-D. 1969. "Giessereibetriebe in Olympia." *JdI* 84: 1–28.

Heilmeyer, W.-D. 1981. "Antike Werkstättenfunde in Griechenland." *AA*: 440–453.

Heilmeyer, W.-D. 1987. "Die Bronzegiesserei unter der Werkstatt des Phidias in Olympia." *AA*: 239–299.

Hein, A., K. Christodoulou, and J. Fuchs. 2017. "A Classical Bronze Workshop at the Apollon Sanctuary of Kalapodi." *EMAC* https://www.academia.edu/34507288/A_classic_bronze_workshop_at_the_Apollon_sanctuary_of_Kalapodi_Investigation_of_the_pyrotechnical_ceramics.

Hellmann, M.-C. 2006. *L'architecture grecque 2*. Paris.

Hennemeyer, A. 2006. "Neue Forschungsergebnisse zur Cella des Zeustempels in Olympia." In *Bericht über die 43. Tagung für Ausgrabungswissenschaft und Bauforschung*, edited by D. Sack, 103–111. Bonn.

Hennemeyer, A. 2010. "Der Zeustempel von Olympia, Griechenland." In *Geschichte der Rekonstruktion*, 188–189.

Hennemeyer, A. 2013a. "Kontinuität und Wandel: Beobachtungen am Zeus-Tempel von Olympia." In *Sanktuar und Ritual*, edited by I. Gerlach and D. Raue, 19–26.

Hennemeyer, A. 2013b. "Die Wiederherstellung des Zeustempels von Olympia in klassischer Zeit." In *Zurück zur Klassik: ein neuer Blick auf das alte Griechenland*, edited by V. Brinkmann, 127–129. Frankfurt am Main.

Herrmann, H.-V. 1972. *Olympia: Heiligtum und Wettkampfstätte*. Munich.

Huber, S. 1991. "Un atelier de bronzier dans le sanctuaire d'Apollon à Érétrie?" *AntK* 34: 137–154.

Jacquemin, A. 2010. "Qui payait le xeirotexnion?" *RPhil* 84: 243–249.

Kalaitzoglou, G. 2004. "Zur Baugeschichte des Turmkomplexes 1 des Insula 3 von Thorikos." *Boreas* 27: 67–94.

Karvonis, P. 2008. "Les installations commerciales dans la ville de Délos à l'époque hellénistique." *BCH* 132: 153–219.

Kavvadias, P., and G. Kawerau 1906. *Die Ausgrabung der Akropolis*. Athens.

Kent, J.H. 1948. "The Temple Estates of Delos, Rheneia, and Mykonos." *Hesperia* 17: 243–338.

Kiderlen, M., A. Hein, H. Mommsen, and N.S. Müller. 2016. "Production Sites of Early Iron Age Greek Bronze Tripod Cauldrons: First Evidence from Neutron Activation Analysis of Casting Ceramics." *Geoarchaeology* 2016: 1–22.

Klein, J. 1972. "A Greek Metalworking Quarter: Eighth Century Excavations on Ischia." *Expedition* 14: 34–39.

Kraynak, L.H. 1992. "The Xenon." In *Nemea 1: Excavations at Nemea. Topographical and architectural studies: The Sacred Square, the Xenon, and the Bath*, by D. Birge, L.H. Kraynak, and S.G. Miller, 99–187. Berkeley.

Kunze, E., and H. Schleif. 1938/39. "Die 'Sudhalle.'" *OlBer* 3: 30–37.

Kyrieleis, H. 2002. "Zu den Anfängen des Heiligtums von Olympia." In *Olympia, 1875–2000*, edited by H. Kyrieleis, 213–220. Mainz.

La Follette, L. 1986. "The Chalkotheke on the Athenian Akropolis." *Hesperia* 55: 75–87.

Lapatin, K. 2001. *Chryselephantine Statuary in the Ancient Mediterranean World*. Oxford.

Linders, T. 1988. "Continuity in Change: The Evidence of the Temple Accounts of Delos (Prolegomena to a study of the economic and social life of Greek sanctuaries)." In *Early Greek Cult Practice*, edited by G. Nordquist, C. Güllog, and R. Hägg, 267–269. Göteborg.

Lo Monaco, A. 2020. "I mercati degli dei." In *Spending on the Gods*, edited by A. Lo Monaco, 22–36. Athens.

Luberto, M. 2023. "Aree sacre e quartieri artigianali in Magna Grecia: les colonie achee." In *Travailler à l'ombre du temple*, edited by O. de Cazanove, A. Esposito, N. Monteix et al., 173–195. Paris.

Mallwitz, A. 1972. *Olympia und seine Bauten*. Munich.

Mathé, V. 2023. "Construire dans un espace cultuel en Grèce Classique et hellénistique: aspects socio-économiques et pratiques." In *Travailler à l'ombre du temple*, edited by O. de Cazanove, A. Esposito, N. Monteix, and A. Pollini, 49–64. Paris.

Mattusch, C. 1977. "Bronze- and Ironworking in the Area of the Athenian Agora." *Hesperia* 46: 340–379.

Mazarakis Ainian, A. 2002. "Recent Excavations at Oropos (northern Attica)." In *Excavating Classical Culture: Recent Archaeological Discoveries in Greece*, edited by M. Stamatapoulou and M. Yeroulanou, 149–178. Oxford.

Miles, M., and K. Lynch. 2024. "The Hephaisteion in Athens: Its Date and Design." *Hesperia* 93: 191–250.

Miller, S. 1978. "Excavations at Nemea, 1977." *Hesperia* 47: 58–88.

Miller, S. 1979. "Excavations at Nemea, 1978." *Hesperia* 48: 73–103.

Miller, S. 1982. "Excavations at Nemea, 1981." *Hesperia* 51: 19–40.

Miller, S. 1988. "Excavations at Nemea, 1984–1986." *Hesperia* 57: 1–20.

Miller, S. 1990. *Nemea: A Guide to the Site and Museum*. Berkeley.

Monaco, M.C. 2010. "1.35 Il chalkourgeion." In *Topografia di Atene 1*, edited by E. Greco, 189–190. Athens.

Moustaka, A. 1999. "Unfertige Marmorplastik und andere Reste von Steinmetzwerkstätten." *OlBer* 11: 357–366.

Muller, A. 1983. "Megarika." *BCH* 107: 157–179.

Partida, E. 2009. "From Hypaethral Depots to Hypaethral Exhibitions: Casting light on architecture and society in 4th–3rd B.C. Delphi." *AM* 124: 273–324.

Photos-Jones, E., and J. Jones. 1994. "The Building and Industrial Remains at Agrileza (Fourth Century BC) and Their Contribution to the Workings at the Site." *ABSA* 89: 307–358.

Pitt, R. 2016. "Inscribing Construction: The Financing and Administration of Public Building in Greek Sanctuaries." In *A Companion to Greek Architecture*, edited by M. Miles, 344–360.

Pouilloux, J. 1977. "Travaux à Delphes à l'occasion des Pythia." *BCH* supp. 4, 103–123.

Prestianni Giallombardo, A.M. 2003. "Divinità e culti in Halaesa Archonidea. Tra identità etnica e interazione culturale." In *Quatre Giornate internazionali di studi sull' area Elima 1*, edited by A. Corretti, 1059–1103. Pisa.

Prestianni Giallombardo, A.M. 2012. "Tusa: Fonto letterarie, epigrafiche e numismatiche." In *Bibliografia Topografica della Colonizzazione Greca in Italia e nelle Isole Tirreniche 21*, edited by G. Nanci and G. Vallet, 251–262. Pisa.

Preuner, E. 1921. "Aus alten Papieren." *AM* 46: 1–26.

Preuner, E. 1924. "ΣΑΜΙΑΚΑ." *AM* 49: 26–49.

Prignitz, S. 2014. *Bauurkunden und Bauprogramm von Epidauros I (400–350)*. Munich.

Prignitz, S. 2022. *Bauurkunden und Bauprogramm von Epidauros II (350–300)*. Munich.

Randall, R. 1953. "The Erechtheum Workmen." *AJA* 57: 199–210.

Risberg, C. 1997. "Evidence of Metal Working in Early Greek Sanctuaries." In *Trade and Production in Premonetary Greece*, edited by C. Gillis, C. Risberg, and B. Sjöberg, 185–196. Jonsered.

Risberg, C. 1998. "Production in a Sacred Place." *Topoi* 8: 671–679.

Rose, C. 1998. "The 1997 Post-Bronze Age Excavations at Troia." *StTroica* 8: 71–113.

Rostoker, W., and E. Gebhard. 1980. "The Sanctuary of Poseidon at Isthmia: Techniques of Metal Manufacture." *Hesperia* 49: 347–363.

Roux, G. 1961. *L'architecture de l'Argolide aux IVe et IIIe siècles avant J.-C.* Paris.

Salmon, J. 2001. "Temples the Measures of Men." In *Economies Beyond Agriculture in the Classical World*, edited by D. Mattingly and J. Salmon, 195–208. London.

Sanidas, G. 2013. *La production artisanale en Grèce: une approache spatiale et topographique à partir des exemples de l'Attique et du Péloponnèse du VIIe au Ier siècles avant J.-C.* Paris.

Sanidas, G. 2023. "Activités artisanales et espaces religieux dans les fondations grecques en Égée: exemples et image globale." In *Travailler à l'ombre du temple*, edited by O. de Cazanove, A. Esposito, N. Monteix, and A. Pollini, 2–38. Paris.

Seiler, F. 1996. "L'archittetura sacra." In *I Greci in Occidente: Santuari della Magna Grecia in Calabria*, 250–256. Naples.

Sinn, U. 2004. *Das antike Olympia*. Munich.

Sporn, K., et al. 2017. "Forschungen zur Anlage, Ausdehnung und Infrastruktur des Heiligtums von Kalapodi: Die Kampagnen 2014–2016." *AM* 131/132: 193–278.

Sporn, K. 2018/2019. "Kalapodi—Die Kampagne 2018." *DAIatheNEA*: 78–83.

Stavropoullos, F. 1938. "Ἱερατικὴ οἰκία ἐν Ζωστῆρι τῆς Ἀττικῆς." *ArchEph*: 1–31.

Stevens, G. 1946. "The Northeast Corner of the Parthenon." *Hesperia* 15: 1–26.

Thompson, H., and R. Wycherley. 1972. *The History, Shape and Uses of an Ancient City Center. Agora 14*. Princeton.

Travlos, J. 1937. "Ἀνασκαφαὶ Ἱερᾶς Ὁδοῦ." *Praktika* 25–41.

Tsakirgis, B. 2015. "Tools from the House of Mikion and Menon." In *Autopsy in Athens*, edited by M. Miles, 9–17. Oxford.

Vial, C. 1984. *Délos indépendente*. Paris.

Vlizos, S. 2020. "Metallwerkstätten, Produktion und Infrastruktur des Heiligtums: Der Fall des spartanischen Amyklaions." In *Spending on the Gods*, edited by A. Lo Monaco, 37–46. Athens.

Zimmer, G. 1990. *Griechische Bronzegusswerkstätten*. Mainz am Rhein.

Zimmer, G. 1993. "Werkstattbauten des fünften Jahrhunderts." In *Die griechische Polis: Architektur und Politik*, edited by W. Hoepfner and G. Zimmer, 94–101. Tübingen.

Zimmer, G., and M. Leopold. 2021/2022. "Die große bronzene Statue der Athena. Eine Werkstatt des Phidias am Südabhang der Akropolis." *AM* 136/137: 241–362.

CHAPTER 15

Handling of Hides in Greek Sanctuaries: Practical, Spatial, and Conceptual Considerations

Petra Pakkanen

This essay addresses three questions relating to logistical procedures in ancient Greek sanctuaries regarding production of leather: 1) practical: what type of raw material for leather processing was provided by sanctuaries, and how and by whom the hides from sacrifices were handled; 2) spatial: if there was a connection between tanning establishments and sanctuaries; and 3) conceptual: if hides, and consequently leather produced from sacrificial animals, were perceived in a specific way. In order to localize these questions within the framework of tanning, it is necessary to clarify briefly what actually was done when skins were tanned into leather.

1   What Kinds of Skins Were Produced by Sanctuaries?

Leather has been called antiquity's plastic,[1] and for good reason: hardly any individual could avoid encountering leather in his or her daily life. Regardless of its importance, the production patterns of ancient Greek leather have received surprisingly little attention, and this includes the connection between tanning and sanctuaries. As with meat and meat consumption, there is no reason to believe that all leather for tanning originated in sanctuaries,[2] but sacrificial contexts nevertheless seem to have been a significant provider of hides and skins for leather production alongside less regulated methods, such as hunting and domestic farmhouse processing of hides for one's own consumption. By Classical times, commercial tanning had become quite a substantial and profitable trade.[3] It was not a centralized and organized industry in ancient Greece as it later became in the Roman Empire when the massive scale of operations and the high degree of organization are attested in the size and variety of leatherwork complexes.[4] However, leather production was an important component in the Greek *polis* economy: the creation of skin in sacrificial ritual ensured the economic viability of animal sacrifice and thereby supported the temple economy.

Particularly in the major sanctuaries in ancient Greece that regularly employed large-scale animal sacrifices, the sheer number of hides and animal skins must have been significant, at least occasionally during the major 'supplementary sacrifices' (*epithetoi heortai*). In the fourth century BCE, thousands of oxen and far more sheep and goats were required yearly for both the deme and *polis* sacrifices in Athens and Attika alone.[5] The fact that the value of the hides of the animals sacrificed at festivals was recorded on the so-called *dermatikon* accounts signals that they were valuable and significant parts of the profit from sacrifices.[6] The money from the sales of the hides also could be used for political ends: with the intention of gaining revenues for the state, Lykourgos

---

1   Van Driel-Murray 2008, 482.
2   Echoing the old argument that most meat was consumed by the ancients during special occasions, i.e., religious festivals, and was connected with sacrifice, it also has been claimed that hides most often originated in cultic activity in sanctuaries. For the argument, see esp. Jameson (1988), later criticized by, e.g., Ekroth 2007, with references to earlier discussion, esp. 251–252; McInerney 2010, 183.
3   Howe 2011, 11–12; 2014; Acton 2014, 163. The view on profitability is based on the knowledge of certain rich tannery owners or their heirs, in particular Kleon, who was wealthy due to an inheritance of his father's tannery in Kydathenaion (this tradition is based on Ar. *Eq.* 44 and schol. *ad loc*) and on numerous passages in Aristophanes' plays.
4   Literature on the theme is vast. For just a few recent studies, see Leguilloux 2002; Van Driel-Murray 2008, 487–490; 2011; Bond 2016, 114. For the most recently excavated monumental tannery built by Septimius Severus in Trastevere, Rome, see De Christofaro, Di Mento, and Rossi 2017, 10–25.
5   Ferguson (1948, 134) calculates that on one occasion 240 victims were sacrificed at Athens in 334/3 BCE; Wilson (2008, 97) thinks that *c.*200 oxen for the City Dionysia would be a realistic figure; Howe (2011, 12) reckons that 6,528 oxen and 15,186 sheep/goats were the minimum numbers of animals required yearly for both deme sacrifices and the *epithetoi heortai*; Naiden (2012, 64–65) estimates that up to 15,000 kg of meat would be distributed at the festival of Artemis Agrotera at Agrai, and 10,000 kg at the Panathenaia in Athens. See Rosivach 1994, 52–56, 78, n. 27. See also Lohmann 1992; and Blok 2010 for funding the *epithetoi heortai* with *demosion*-money of the *polis*.
6   Rosivach 1994, 48–64, 155–157; van Straten 1995, 178; Mikalson 1998, 36–37, 39; Gebauer 2002, 291. Jameson (1988, 107–112) and von Reden (2010, 166–716) discuss the value of ox-hides.

systematized arrangements for the sale of skins of animals from major public sacrifices in Athens (334/3 BCE),[7] and this 'dermatic fund' was one of the treasuries used to pay for the equipment and costs of cult in Athens and elsewhere in Attika.

In private sacrifices, individuals offering a sacrifice were often expected to retain the valuable skin for themselves along with other portions allocated to them.[8] Whether skins and hides from private sacrifices were further treated to be tanned into leather most probably depended on unregulated private initiatives, and the number of skins and hides from these sacrifices was rather small. It is therefore probable that cults that had any facilities for the first stage of skin and hide processing, i.e., preparing them either for further sale or transportation to tanneries, were only those at major sanctuaries where public, large-scale sacrifices took place. Assigning the skin from a sacrificial animal to the priest or priestess was a standard practice in these official sacrifices, and priests and other important personnel profited a fair deal by selling the skins granted to them.[9] Perquisite of skins and legs was the most important of the priestly prerogatives and usually listed first or at the beginning of the list specifying honorific portions (*hierosyna* or *gera*) to priests, priestesses, or to other important officials. The assignment of a skin was stipulated following the standard formula in ritual norms, namely δέρμα ἔστο τô ἱερέος / ἱερέας τὸ δέρμα / ἱερέαι δέρμα, and in addition, they often received certain other parts of sacrificed animals, such as the tongue, thighs, head, kidneys, etc.[10] In our epigraphical evidence, the difference between flayed and non-flayed animal, δαρτὸν and μὲ δαρτόν, is quite often specified. If a priest or priestess was to receive a share from a singed animal, a hind leg was often designated for this purpose as a compensation for the loss of the valuable separate skin or hide.[11] When porcine animals are concerned, the nature of the animal, or rather its skin, is characterized as εὑστόν or εὑστόν (singed), and the priests or priestesses do not receive skin separately but as part of meat portions.[12] In other words, these animals were not flayed but singed instead. Singeing was a carcass-handling process, and a singed portion denoted a carcass or part of a carcass from which the skin was not separated. Hence the inscription from Miletos (300–275 BCE) states that "if the city sacrifices an animal whose skin has been singed, he [the priest] will receive the tongue, singed sacrum, the foreleg (or tail):

---

7   IG II² 1496, ll. 68–92 shows that in 334/3 BCE, the revenue was nearly 6,000 dr from seven months' worth of hides from at least nine festivals in Athens. See, e.g., Wilson (2008, 96–97), who notes that the public sacrifices at the Panathenaia and the City Dionysia were most probably unparalleled in Greek society; and Naiden (2012, 74–76).

8   E.g., CGRN 81 (= LSAM no. 39), which regulates pastoral sacrifices in Thebes on Mt. Mykale c.350 BCE: perquisites of skin and a leg, together with a kidney and the small intestine, are attributed to the shepherds who have "brought the κουρεῖον," ll. 20–23; see Carbon 2017, 157. A regulation of a priesthood of Herakles on Chios, CGRN 50 (= von Prott and Ziehen 1896–1906, II, no. 113; LSCG no. 119, 400–350 BCE), informs us that in the sacrifices of a *genos*, the tongues, entrails, a double portion of meat, and skins go to the priest; see Carbon and Peels in the commentary to CGRN 50. For the recipients of choice portions, see esp. Ekroth 2008, 267–269.

9   Le Gruen-Pollet 1991a, 23; Tsoukala 2009, 10–11; Gawlinski (2012, 129) states that priests often also controlled the sale of the skins; Carbon 2017, 152–153.

10 For the priestly prerogatives and the share of sacrificial victims, see esp. Le Guen-Pollet 1991a, 17–19; Carbon 2017, 157–159. Tsoukala (2009, 6, n. 33) presents a list based on LSCG and LSS. See also NGSL² 309–310; Patera 2012, 114–114, 117–119. For the inscriptions mentioning skins as prerogatives, see Prestigianni Giallombardo 1988, 1467, n. 60; Carbon 2017, 165–166, 171–175.

11 We have numerous cases of the practice in epigraphical evidence. These are to be found in CGRN with discussions and commentaries. Here, I offer two representative examples: CGRN 26, col. B from 430 BCE regulates cults probably belonging to an Attic *trittys*. Face B concerns the prerogatives of a variety of priests and priestesses from sacrifices offered either by private individuals or by the city. It specifies (ll. B 5–7, 10–19) that a priestess was allotted the hides of animals that were flayed (*dartoi*) in addition to 1 dr per animal. If an ox was sacrificed at a public sacrifice, she received multiple shares of the meat, whereas at a private sacrifice, she obtained a hide and legs from the skinned animals, but only the legs from animals whose skin was singed. The other example is the Decree of the Salaminioi in Attika CGRN 84 (= LSS no. 19; RO no. 37) from 363/2 BCE, ll. 31–33: of the sacrificial animals that he [the priest of Herakles] sacrifices for the whole group, he shall take the skin and the leg of an animal that has been flayed, the leg of an animal that has been singed; of an ox he shall take nine pieces of flesh and the skin (τῶν δὲ ἱερείων ὧν ἂν κατάρξηται τῶν κοινῶν λαμβάνειν δαρτô δέρμα καὶ τὸ σκέλος, εὑστô τὸ σκέλος· βοὸς δὲ ἐννέα σάρκας καὶ τὸ δέρμα).

12 The accounts for priestly perquisites and other sacrificial expenses from the deme of Aixone in Attika from 400–375 BCE (CGRN 57 = IG II² 1356) state (ll. 5–6): [Ἡρώ]ινης ἱε[ρείαι ἱερε]ώσυνα ⊢·, τὰ δέρματα ἐκ τῶν ἱ[Ἡρ]ωινίων, ἄπαν[τος εὑστô] τελέο ⊢⊢⊢·. Here the priestess of Heroine is to get 5 dr as priestly emolument, the skins of the animals sacrificed during the *Heroinia*, and in the case of an adult animal whose skin has been singed (a porcine), 3 dr as compensation for the absence of the skin; the priestess of Hera receives the same emolument, and for an adult singed animal 3 dr as compensation for the skin and an (equal) share of the meat ("Ηρας ἱερείαι ἱερεώσυνα ⊢· [τὸ δέρμα τῆς οἰ]ός, εὑστô τελέο ⊢⊢⊢· δεισίας κρεῶν, ll. 12–13). See commentary on CGRN by Carbon and Peels, also Le Guen-Pollet 1991a, 17. Rosivach (1994, 62) reads εὑστô τελέο as meaning the value of 3 dr of the swine's skin, but in light of skinning-treatments, it could be interpreted as signifying the value of a fully grown pig that is not skinned but singed, in addition to the compensation of 3 dr for the loss of skin.

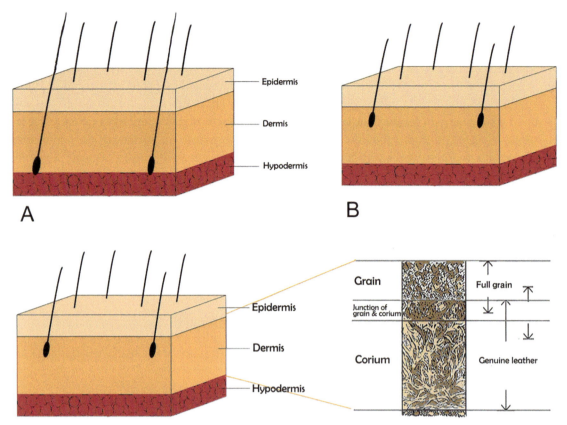

FIGURE 15.1 Simplified structure of animal skin and leather layers. Above, A: skin structure of porcine animals; B: skin structure of most animals. Below: layers of leather processed from dermis of most animals
DRAWING: AUTHOR

ἢν δὲ εὐστὸν θύηι ἡ πόλις, λάψεται γλῶσσαν, ὀσφὺν δασέαν, ὤρην" (ll. 5–6).[13] The meaning of the word δασύς—rough, hairy, or shaggy surface—could denote a part of animal with its hairy skin still attached, i.e., singed porcine.[14] In the *Odyssey* (14.74–76), the swineherd executes the singeing procedure: he chooses two piglets (χοῖροι), brings them in, slays (sacrifices) them, then singes them, cuts them up, spits them, and finally roasts them.[15] Flaming or blazing with a torch was probably used for singeing (as is still the case today): a scholiast on Aristophanes explains in *Knights* 1233 (where the term εὔστρα, a place for singeing pigs, appears) that the term φλογίστρα also means a place where slaughtered swine are singed, pointing to the use of fire in the process.[16]

When a slaughtered animal is singed, its hair is initially removed or partially removed by torching, scalding, and scraping, and hence the skinning method differs for those animals that are singed and those that are not.[17] Pigs are not flayed and hence their skin stays attached to the carcass. Pigskin differs from the skin of any other animal: it has long, thick hair with indistinguishable grain and corium layers, and the hair shafts pass all the way through them rather than stopping in the grain layer as in the skin of other animals (Fig. 15.1).[18] This is why pigskin cannot easily be removed from the flesh. Ovines (sheep and lamb) are partially flayed, usually with a knife, whereas bovines and equines are 'peeled' completely.[19] The bulk of flaying

---

13   *CGRN* 100 (= *LSAM* no. 46), trans. Carbon, Peels, and Pirenne-Delforge in *CGRN*.
14   Carbon (2017, 158) explains that ὀσφῦς with the attribute δασύς indicates a solid segment of meat and bones cut out of an animal as an honorific share. Already Ziehen (1899, 270–272) discussed the meaning of the two words here, and Puttkammer (1912, 11) suggested that they refer to sacrum bone extending to a meatier part of the animal. For further discussion, see Pakkanen 2021, 138–139.
15   See a similar process for a hog: Hom. *Od.* 14.426–430.
16   This is explicit also in Homer's description of Patroklos' funeral pyre (*Il.* 23.33–34) where "many white-tusked swine, rich with fat, were stretched to singe (εὐόμενοι) over the flame of Hephaistos."
17   For the idiosyncrises of pigskin and its treatment, see Pakkanen 2021, esp. 133–137 (on flaying) and 137–141 (on singeing).
18   Haines 2006, 15–17.
19   Vialles 1994, 96–100. In this anthropological study, the butchers tell of their work in anonymous citations.

is carried out bare-handed.[20] Modern butchers note that sheep and lamb are slower to work on and may require a long time, whereas calves and larger animals are worked faster. Pigs are least valued among these species for the reason that they are not flayed.[21]

The difference between 'singed' (εὑστόν or εὐστόν) portions and those from δαρτός (flayed) animals in our ancient sources therefore has implications for what kind of hides sanctuaries produced. No skins or hides were obtained from non-flayed, singed animals in sanctuaries, and thus processing hides after sacrifices within sanctuary space or in the vicinity concerned ovicaprids, particularly bovines, which could maximize the economic profit. Regardless, pigskin was used in leather production, but pigskin leather was presumably regarded as being of lower quality, at least in comparison to that of bovines, since pigskin does not produce full-grain leather, which is more durable; leather from larger porcines is particularly 'rough' and densely pierced through with holes of hair tracts (Fig. 15.1). This also could partly explain the attitudes and perceptions toward pigskin in our evidence.[22]

In sum, the reasons for the distinction between skins from porcine and other animals were both pragmatic and subsequently ideological, probably emanating from the practical physical difference of skins of these animals, which resulted in pigskin leather being held in lower esteem. A purity regulation, *IG* XII.1 677 (*CGRN* 90), issued by the *polis* at the sanctuary of Alektrona at Ialysos on Rhodes (350–300 BCE) may reflect this attitude. It states that it was not "righteous" (*hosion*) to wear shoes or anything made of pigskin (ὕειον, ll. 25–27) at the sanctuary (ll. 25–27).[23] This points to the special nature of pigskin leather, and as it concerns a sanctuary norm, symbolic associations concerning pigs also may be read into it.[24]

2 What to Do with Hides in Sanctuaries?

When the ritual meal in a sanctuary ends, the rest is entirely given over to the human domain, the 'after-care' and clearing up the facilities.[25] Keeping the sanctuary clean and free from any defilement included disposing of hides and forwarding them for further treatment. Destroying the skins altogether by burning them to the gods was rare, but we have evidence of partial destructions, although also exceptional.[26] Without further treatment, a skin from a flayed animal quickly becomes hard, and even if it is dried slowly it will putrefy, a process that is under way within hours of death. Hides and skins to be tanned into leather therefore had to be removed from a sanctuary or promptly treated for storage in order to avoid the dangers and nuisances of putrefaction. Epigraphical evidence seems to indicate that the time lapse between the slaughter of the animals in sacrificial rituals and the distribution of meat to the public in connection with official sacrifices could have been as much as two days.[27]

---

20 See, e.g., Hippocratic text *De haemorrhoidibus* 4.1.14–16: "There is no more difficulty in this than in skinning a sheep, to pass the finger between the hide and the flesh" (trans. Adams).

21 Vialles 1994, 97–99.

22 Leathers from various animals naturally occur in different thicknesses and this, together with the quality of the leather, dictates how and for which kinds of products it will be used and how the leather is valued as material. Leather made of ox-hide or from a large bovine is resistant, thick and strong, whereas pigskin leather, although thick, is porous due to the holes of the removed hair tracts; hence pigskin leather is not as durable as leather from bovines. Pigskin was available corresponding to the availability of porcines, but the process of turning pigskin into leather is far more labor intensive and time consuming than that for other animal skins, starting from treatments in the initial stage of tanning when skin is separated from the carcass.

23 Prohibitions of shoes are known from other similar regulations, but pigskin is not specified in these cases. See the decree at Andania (*CGRN* 222) discussed infra; the purity regulation at the sanctuary of Despoina at Lykosura (*CGRN* 126 = *LSCG* no. 68, ll. 6–7); a purity regulation from an unknown sanctuary at Eresos (late second-beginning of the first century BCE), *CGRN* 181 (= *LSCG* no. 124), l. 17: μηδὲ ὑπόδεσιν μηδὲ ἄλλο δέρμα, so all leather products were prohibited; cultic regulation of various gods at Kyrene, 150–100 BCE; and *CGRN* 190 (= *LSS* no. 116), col. A, ll. 7–8, which forbids entering the sanctuary while wearing any footwear. In *CGRN* 17 = *IG* XII.8 358, l. 2, pigs, together with sheep, are not permitted in the sanctuary of Apollo, Nymphs, and the Charites at Thasos in the fifth century BCE: ὄϊν οὐ θέμις οὐδὲ χοῖρον; and *ID* 1720 = *CGRN* 216, of c.100 BCE from Delos prohibits sacrificing any swine (products) or any goat (products): ὑϊκὰ μὴ θύειν μηδ[ὲ] αἴ[γ]ει[α], ll. 7–8. See Harris 2015, 61; Brøns 2017, 336–340.

24 For further discussion of this theme, see Pakkanen 2021, 141–145.

25 The purity regulation from Kos, *IG* XII.4 72 (= *CGRN* 148; *LSCG* no. 154) of c.240 BCE, is a good example of meticulous rules concerning cleanliness of the sanctuary space.

26 Ekroth (2002, 216–217, 228) regards the cutting or burning of the skin of the animal sacrificed as a partial destruction and gives testimonia of this from Erchia *CGRN* 52 (*LSCG* 18, 375–350 BCE) and Kos *CGRN* 86 (*LSCG* no. 151A–D, RO no. 62 A–D of 350 BCE). *CGRN* 128 from the Asklepieion at Lissos (c.325–200 BCE) rules that the skin is for the god: τὸ δέρμα τῶι θεῶι (l. 5). The editors of *CGRN* (Carbon and Peels) are hesitant to believe that the skin would have been dedicated (i.e., burnt) to the god, but instead suggest that it may have been placed on a cult table and most probably ended up as a priestly perquisite.

27 *IG* II² 1183, ll. 32–35 = RO no. 63, third quarter of the fourth century BCE, an Athenian deme decree from Hagnous stipulates that on the fifth of the month, the *demarch* is to hold the sacrifice of the Plerosia in honor of Zeus and to distribute the meat on the seventh of the month to those present, those who

Therefore, logistics, including possible temporary storing of hides, must have been regulated somehow and arranged in major Greek sanctuaries during the festival days when these operations were rather massive in terms of the amount of raw material.

So, what was done with the skins and by whom? Alongside the priests in the sanctuaries mastering the sacrificial ritual were their helpers—*parasitoi*,[28] *hieropoioi*,[29] as well as *mageiroi*, who were, as attested by numerous epigraphical and textual sources, sacrificants, meat-cutters, meat-sellers, and cooks, multitasking meat-specialists, and businessmen in both public and private domains, who also could profit from trading the meat of the sacrificed animals.[30] Their task as meat-cutters at sanctuaries was complemented and assisted by such functionaries as *artamoi*,[31] *kreokopoi*,[32] and *kreodaitai*[33] (butchers and meat-cutters), who may have been at work separating hides of sacrificed victims. Slaves could also have been employed to assist in the tasks.[34] From Athens and Delos, we know of officials called *boonai* (βοῶναι), who were appointed to buy cattle for sacrifice from private sellers and to take care of the sale of hides and payments to priests.[35] They appear also in the *dermatikon* accounts, and thus it is reasonable to assume that *boonai* were officials who took as much care of the provision of cattle for sacrifices as dealing with the sales of the hides of sacrificed animals. Their role could be characterized as purchasers and dealers of commodities. According to *IG* II² 334 (ll. 17–18), they, together with the *hieropoioi*, are to buy cattle for the Little[36] and Demosthenes likewise talks about them in conjunction with the *hieropoioi*,[37] thus placing them rather high in the hierarchy of cult officials. Pollux (8.114, 6.34, 7.25) later includes *boonai* in the (ancient) *polis*-functionaries (in Athens), grouping them together with *teichopoioi* (officers charged with repairing the city walls in Athens) and *hieropoioi*. Officials collecting various taxes, *hellenotamiai*, first and foremost, precede *boonai* in Pollux. Thus, the role of a *boones* could have been rather important indeed.

The most obvious method for storing hides temporarily is dry salting to stop putrefaction. Salt was generally an easily accessible commodity.[38] Skins have to be salted within a few hours after they have been removed from carcasses since once decomposition begins, tanning is no longer possible. Dry salted rawhide resists putrefaction for several months,[39] allowing even long-distance transportation, usually by sea.[40] Modern data shows that dry salted hides weighed up to 45% less than those freshly flayed.[41] Who the functionaries responsible for carrying out the

---

join in the meeting, and to those who join in offering. Rhodes and Osborne comment (RO 317) that such a delay between sacrifice and distribution seems to be unparalleled. Ekroth (2008, 277–279) suggests that the meat was tenderized by hanging before it was distributed, probably in cooked form. See also Tsoukala 2009, 12.

28   For the role of *parasitoi*, see Naiden 2012, 75–79.
29   *Hieropoioi* were chiefly cult administrators functioning in a variety of organized bodies in cities and sanctuaries alike. See, e.g., *NGSL*² 265–266.
30   *Mageiroi* have received much scholarly attention after Berthiaume's (1982) work. Bundrick (2014, 565–566), following Gordon (1989, 568), is probably correct in noting that this stress on their role may overestimate their status and that they were more like hired hands, not even particularly well-paid, whose standing is reflected in the rarity of depictions of them in Classical vase paintings.
31   Berthiaume (1982, 10–12) refers to this functionary as a butcher who slaughtered a sacrificial victim but worked also as a cook in further food processing.
32   Dion. Hal. *Ant. Rom.* 12.2.8, in which Maelius tries to take refuge, ending up in a butcher's shop (μαγειρικόν) where he seizes a cleaver (κοπίδα) used by the meat-cutters (κρεοκόποι). This is the only mention of such tradesmen, hence Berthiaume (1982, 57) thinks that Dionysios chose this name for a *mageiros* for the sake of literary style in order to avoid repetition of the same term.
33   Κρεοδαίτης is a distributor and carver of meat at public feasts (*LSJ* s.v.). In Plut. *Lys.* 23.7 and *Ages.* 8.1, Agesilaos appoints Lysander to be his carver of meats. Pollux 7.25.12 presents *kreodaites* together with *mageiros* under "On meatselling (*kreopolia*) and meatsellers (*kreopolai*), their work and tools" (7.25).
34   Tsoukala 2009, 8–9, also Bundrick 2014, esp. 664–667.
35   McInerney 2010, 17; Howe 2014, 145. On the Delian *boonai*, see Vial 1984, 243–244; Liddel and Low 2015, 247; and *ID* 399, A, ll. 7, 14, 17, 18 (192 BCE). For *boonai* in Athens, see, e.g., *IG* II² 334, ll. 17–18 (Little Panathenaia 335/4 BCE); 1496, ll. 70–71, 80–81, 88–89, 118–119, 133 (*dermatikon*-account, 331/0 BCE). See Reger 1994, 148, n. 41. As cattle is imbedded in their title, it is reasonable to believe that it was mostly bovine hides that were factored into the economic transactions of hides from sanctuaries.
36   = *IG* II³ 447, ll. 43–44, c.335/4 BCE.
37   Dem. 21 (*Against Midias*).171 *boones* in parallel with *hieropoios* (sacrificer on one occasion and buyer of the animals). Also Harp. s.v. *boones*, who regards their office as rather honorable.
38   Carusi 2016, 344–346.
39   Beyries 2008, 12.
40   E.g., two Eleusinian inventories from 408/407 and 407/406 BCE, *IG* I³ 386 and 387 (Clinton 2005, no. 52; 2008, 72–82), list various items owned by the gods, i.e., stored at the sanctuary. Hides are mentioned four times, including 18 Sicilian hides (βύρσαι Σικελικαὶ) listed twice under the rubric σκεύε (equipment). Thus, hides destined for use as building material or for other purposes at Eleusis were transported to Attika, even from Sicily, already at this relatively early date. See the full commentary in Cavanaugh (1996, 119–209) and Clinton (2005, 64–70); see also Habermann (1987). Hide transport, usually large-scale by sea, is attested also in various textual sources, e.g., Dem., *Androkles against Lakritos* (*Or.* 35.34) and *Against Phormio* (*Or.* 34.10).
41   Douglas 2015, 35.

practical operation of salting were can only be guessed, but possibilities range from *mageiroi* to *parasitoi, artamoi, kreokopoi* and from *kreourgoi* to *boonai*. Handling of the hides from (major) sanctuaries falls therefore to the two groups of people, those who took care of the handling of the sacrificed carcasses when meat was separated from the hides and personnel specialized in dealing with the commercial transactions connected with the hides and skins of the sacrificial animals.

3 Were Tanneries Near Sanctuaries?

Where was the first phase of the skin and hide processing carried out, and do we have evidence of the connection between sanctuaries and tanneries? This takes us first to the *mageireion*, a butcher's premises or shop, not a 'kitchen' for cooking. Such installations connected with sanctuaries do not necessarily have to be permanent, as any structure erected for temporary use would serve this purpose. Major sanctuaries needed more substantial facilities for handling the first phase of hide-processing than, for example, a religious association. The latter's *mageireion* was a 'kitchen,' like that of a *thiasos* for a goddess in Piraeus in 219/218 BCE, where the *epimeletai* (supervisors) of this *thiasos* "had voted to repair the kitchen ... from their own resources and accomplished the things that had been voted upon with due haste" (ll. 5–6).[42] This *mageireion* did not necessarily have any connection with tanning procedures. However, a possible *mageireion* would have been directly connected with a tanning establishment in the vicinity of the *naos* of Adranos in Halaesa (Alesa), Sicily, whence an inscription records and details the rules of property and land boundaries, subdivision lines, buildings, and related details within the sanctuary sites of Apollo, Zeus Meilichios, and Adranos.[43] It locates an already existing *mageirikon*[44] and specifies the borders of a double-allotment (*diklaron*, no. 13), an extension of the olive-yard, a large coppice near the river Opikanos, and the *naos* of Adranos, the borders of which are detailed. The text regulates (col. I, ll. 70–71) that "those who have leased the olive-yard (ἐλαιοκόμιον) shall not make a tannery or a *mageireion* (βυρσοδέψιον οὐδὲ μαγειρικὸν)." Prohibiting tannery and *mageireion* together suggests that both establishments would have served a shared purpose relating to handling of the meat and hides respectively. The river and existing drainage,[45] and hence a water resource, together with the large road, would have made a good site for a tannery, and logistics were in place: raw material from a sanctuary and the surrounding fields, water, road, and possibly the oak bark for tanning from the large oak forest nearby.[46] These factors indicate that the connection between a sanctuary, slaughterhouse, and tannery existed as a concept. Furthermore, the existing *mageirikon* at the *temenos* of Apollo was situated next to a forge (τὰ χάλκια), indicating manufacturing activities connected with the sanctuary.[47] We can only speculate on the reasons for the ban of a new tannery and *mageireion* at Halaesa, nasty smells being a possibility, but here it is also the vicinity of the temple that is of concern. The prohibition is preceded by a statement (l. 69) 'in the respected area of the olive-yard, olive trees are sacred' (περίστασις τῷ ἐλαιοκομίῳ εἴ τίς ἐστι ἱερά). In this circumscribed area of the olive-yard very close to the *naos* of Adranos,[48] the olive-trees had to be kept 'sacred,' i.e., left undisturbed and protected/guarded/sheltered/overseen by the god whose property they were, thus, untainted by pollution.[49] This stipulation also protected the trees from being felled for use as fuel and their branches as animal fodder.[50]

In another example, a tannery is directly connected with a sanctuary. This is the so-called 'tanner-decree' *IG* I³ 257 from 440–430 BCE, found in 1923 in the vicinity of

---

42 *IG* II² 1301. The word before *mageireion* is missing and is therefore heavily reconstructed (by Kloppenborg and Ascough 2011). The facility referred to is nevertheless most probably a 'kitchen,' not a slaughterhouse or butcher's shop.

43 *IG* XIV 352 = *SEG* 45.1363 (*Tabulae Halaesinae*) dated variously from the third to first century BCE. For the discussion of the text with full bibliography, see Facella 2006, 317–341. For the details concerning ll. 69–71, which are of interest here, see Prestianni Giallombardo 1988. See also Prestianni Giallombardo 2003, 1059–1063 for the discussion of the interrelation of the Halaesan sacred areas in terms of the concepts of *temenos, hieron, naos, chora,* intra/extramural or extra-urban, central, and peripheric; 2012, 254–256.

44 This *mageirikon* is in allotment 4, section 6, which follows the culvert below the temple of Apollo: there is a forge (τὰ χάλκια) next to it (col. II, ll. 54, 63–64). See Prestianni Giallombardo 2003, 1076–1077.

45 Water resources include the drainage (ὀχετὸν, l. 8), probably connected with the fountain of Ipyrra; see Prestianni Giallombardo 1988, 1457.

46 The large oak forest surrounded the *temenos* in Halaesa. Prestigianni Giallombardo (1988, 1449–1451, 1462, 1466) and Burgio (2014, 488–489) heed the importance of the olive cultivation, existence of large woodlands, and cattle herding in the area and emphasize the agricultural character of the site where manufacturing activities also took place.

47 Prestianni Giallombardo 2003, 1075–1077; 2012, 255.

48 Ll. I 63–64 stipulate that the lessee will provide a six-foot approach road to the Adranieion and will keep a distance of 20 feet away from the temple (*naos*) on all sides.

49 For discussion, see Prestianni Giallombardo 1988, 1458–1460, 1465–1466.

50 I am grateful for this comment to the reviewer of this article.

the monument of Lysikrates in Athens. The text forbids anyone to tan hides or to soak them in the river Ilissos upstream from the sanctuary of Herakles (ll. 4–8) or to throw rubbish into the river (ll. 4–10).[51] The obvious aim was to prevent the river from being polluted by *katharmata*. The texts attest to the connection of the raw material for tanning operations by the Ilissos with the sanctuary of Herakles, but which of two Herakles shrines in the area is meant is unclear. The exact locations of the shrines along the river Ilissos have been debated in scholarship since the early 19th century. The question of the location concerns two separate Herakles shrines north of the Olympieion by the right bank of the river, one at the gymnasion of Kynosarges and another for Herakles Pankrates along the river further north and closer to Kallirois near the *stadion*.[52] The banks of the Ilissos are described in ancient texts as an idyllic place where flowers bloomed, and the river glittered tranquilly in near bucolic beauty.[53] The exact location of the shrine of Herakles mentioned by the 'tanner-degree' notwithstanding, our first associations of the ban on polluting the water with tannery waste are therefore environmental reasons: we connect this with the wish to save the beauty of nature by the Ilissos valley from the disturbing waste of a tannery.

Scholars have argued that the decree was connected with the activities of washers working nearby so as to protect the purity of the water for their work.[54] This argumentation is partly based on a mid-fourth-century BCE relief, divided into two parts by a narrow horizontal register, which bears the inscription IG II² 2934: "Washers (οἱ πλυνῆς) dedicate this to Nymphs and all the gods fulfilling a vow" and lists 12 names of its dedicators ('washers'). The relief depicts Pan, Acheloos, the Nymphs, and all the gods (θεοῖς πᾶσιν).[55] The scene is a grotto, and the logical topographical reference would be to the shrine of Pan, Nymphs, and Acheloos by the Ilissos. The trades of tanners, fullers, and even washers were, in fact, loosely related crafts requiring somewhat similar premises and processing facilities, and hence it could have been logical that these traders operated in close proximity to one another.[56] However, none of these branches was in fact 'clean' in terms of modern associations of cleanliness (smelling clean and fresh, sterilizing unhealthy particles, etc.), and hence Plato's perfumes of summer in his bucolics is not necessarily the scenery corresponding to his everyday reality on the banks of Ilissos, at least at the point where the hides from the Herakles sanctuary were tanned, wool fulled, and clothes washed using urine.

What then was the role of the *katharma* mentioned in the 'tanner-decree?' It might be tempting to connect these *katharmata* to the religious purity ideology of the Greeks and speculate on the concept of 'sacred' more generally since *katharmata* were impure offscourings, refuse of a sacrifice that had to be discarded in cleansing.[57] However, I would rather regard them here as an actual harmful, concretely polluting nuisance, as filth. After the sacrificial ritual was over, the hides were literally harmful and could be toxic, including potentially polluting waste, which had to be cleaned away, as the word *katharma* implies: there is a notion of the return to a clean or pure state.[58] However, the *miasma*-ideology in which

---

51 Ll. 4–10: μεδὲ δέρματα σέπεν ἐν τôι ιλισôι καθύπερθεν τô τεμένος τô hερακλέ[ο]ς· μεδὲ βυρσοδεφσêν μ[εδὲ καθά]ρμα[τ]α ⟨ἐ⟩ς τὸν π[οταμὸν βάλλεν ..]. See, e.g., Lind 1990, 155–159; Le Gruen-Pollet 1991b, 60–61, no. 13; Billot 1992, 155–157; Sanidas 2013, 181–182; Dercy 2015, 179–181; Salta 2019, 81. Papazarkadas (2011, 23) assumes that the *temenos* in question is that of Herakles at Kynosarges.

52 See Billot (1992, 130–145) for the detailed examination of the earlier topographic studies with the focus on connecting the shrine(s) of Herakles and Kynosarges from W.M. Leake's 1829 study to J. Travlos' publications in the 1960s and 1970s; see also Chiotis 2016, 7–11.

53 Pl. *Phdr.* 229a–229d delivers a description of an idyllic landscape with plane trees, crystal waters, and grassy slopes filled with the constant sound of cicadas.

54 Billot 1992, 156; see also Dercy 2015, 36, 179–181; Sanidas 2013, 181.

55 Berlin, Staatliche Museen, inv.no. K 87, now SK 709, see https://id.smb.museum/object/699167/weihrelief-attischer-w%C3%A4scher-und-w%C3%A4scherinnen; Blümel 1966, 77–78, no. 90;

figs. 123–124; Travlos *Athens*, 289, no. 196. See also Jones 1999, 309; Taylor 2015, 43–44; Dercy 2015, 180–181.

56 Fullers have been well covered in the scholarship, see esp. Bradley 2001; Wilson 2003; and Flohr 2013.

57 The term is also used for purification of refuse in Aisch. *Cho.* l. 98 (refuse carried away [from a rite]). A Hippocratic writer (*Morb. sacr.* 1.99–102) wrote about *katharmata* (used in healing rituals): "They bury some of them in the ground, they throw some into the sea, and others they carry off to the mountains where nobody can touch or tread on them." *Katharsia* fall in the same semantic field as *katharmata*: Plut. *Mor.* 280b–c (*Quaest. Rom.* 68.111) relates that dogs are brought for Hekate with the other *katharsia* (purification refuse), while puppies were used in cleansing rituals themselves (*periskulakismos*). See Parker 1983, 30; Johnston 1991, 221; Zografou 2005, 197; and Georgoudi 2018, 175–179 for purification ritual (*katharmos*), especially dogs as purificatory animals (*katharsia*) in such rituals.

58 The words *katharma* and *katharsis* are interlinked: the term means also 'a purified place' as in Ar. *Ach.* 44, where *katharma* is sacred space: πάριθ᾽, ὡς ἂν ἐντὸς ἦτε τοῦ καθάρματος (move on, to get within the consecrated area). Cf. the term with *peripsema*, anything that is wiped off, offscourings, something of no value, and of persons, a scapegoat (*LSJ*, s.v.), as in 1 Corinthians 4:13 "We [the Apostles] have become the scum of the earth, the garbage of the world" (ὡς περικαθάρματα τοῦ κόσμου ἐγενήθημεν, πάντων περίψημα, ἕως ἄρτι). See, e.g., Lloyd 2003, 9–10; Compton 2006, chapter 1.

katharma would be regarded as 'sacred waste' seems not to be the foremost indication here, but instead the practical need to eliminate unclean detritus and animal waste from a tannery. Byproducts of tanning are mentioned, for example, by Theophrastos, who advises the application of *kopros* as manure[59] and further explains (*Caus. pl.* 3.9.3, 3.17.5–6), e.g., for cultivating myrtle and pomegranate, "we are told to use even stronger manure, such as tanner's (οἶον τὴν βυρσοδεψικήν), and pour urine round them when the shoots come out." Tanner's manure is a byproduct of tanning,[60] most probably the leftovers of the dehairing liquids that included both animal dung and human urine. This is smelly stuff, and if a tannery by the Ilissos produced these odors, together with the remains of animals, including hair, pieces of flesh, etc. that might be thrown into the Ilissos, some sort of environmental regulation is no surprise. This does not mean that the pure-impure dichotomy would not have pertained to tanning and handling of animal skins in the ancient world view. On the contrary, within the religious-ideological world view, tanning could be seen essentially as a cleansing process, and there are interesting nuances where this sense applied to the attitudes towards tanners (there were frequent requests for them to be sent outside the borders of the cities to deal with animal carcasses) and to the dichotomy between freshly flayed animal skins and processed, 'purified' leather.

The regulation of the tanner-decree can be placed further within its socio-political setting in which it reflects political, social, and economic conflicts of interests. This discussion takes us into the local politics of the fifth-century Kydathenaion, where tanneries are believed to have been situated.[61] Aristophanes' systematic and sustained attack targeted the popular leader Kleon, 'The Tanner,' who had inherited a tannery in Kydathenaion and amassed considerable wealth thanks to it. Aristophanes was legally from Kydathenaion and may have had connections with a cult association of Herakles in the district. It is not possible to delve into these intrigues here,[62] but we should note that this tanning operation might have been involved in a financial dispute on which Aristophanes commented by mocking Kleon as a stupid nouveau riche, stinking tanner, who, together with his tannery, had to be banished to a place outside of the city.[63]

4 The Process of Transforming Hides into Leather

When hides from sacrifices were transferred to be turned into leather, tanning had to be performed. A brief explanation is offered here. Tanning permanently alters the chemical structure of the skin and involves replacing the animal protein in the skin with tannins, resulting in flexible, resistant, strong leather.[64] In principle, all three layers of the skin (Fig. 15.1) require different treatment depending on which end-product is desired: cured leather, fully tanned leather, or fur.

It is important to distinguish between 'true tanning,' i.e., vegetable tanning, and 'pseudo-tanning,' regardless of the somewhat misleading nature of the terms. According to some scholars, 'true' vegetable tanning cannot be traced back much further than the fifth century BCE, at least not in the archaeological record.[65] We begin here with the pseudo-tanning or curing. When tannins extracted from plants rich in them are not used, we refer to this as 'curing,' which employs relatively simple methods for delaying the onset of decay of skins, for example, by smoking or applications of fat, oils, or mineral earth.[66] The first textual reference in ancient literature to leatherworking methods is Homer *Il.* 17.389, a rather representative description of fat-curing of an ox-hide, hence 'pseudo-tanning:' "when one gives men to stretch a great bull hide, swilled with grease, they take it and stand in a ring and stretch it, then in a moment all moisture is gone and the grease sinks in." Dressing hides with oil to produce 'pseudo-tanned leather' continued parallel with vegetable or 'true tanning' throughout antiquity.[67]

'True tanning,' in which plant tannins are used, is a more complex process than 'pseudo-tanning' or curing. Fleshing of the skins is part of the pre-tanning procedures

---

59 E.g., *Caus. pl.* 2.6.3, 3.9.5; *Hist. pl.* 7.3.5, 7.1.8, 7.5.2.
60 Note that in *Caus. pl.* 3.17.6, the term for tanner's manure is ἡ σκυτοδεψική.
61 See supra n. 3. E.g., Faber 1938, 303–304. Acton (2014, 164) claims that "the archaeological evidence suggests that [in] Athens tanneries clustered in one district, Cydathon," but does not reference this archaeological material.
62 For the discussion, see esp. Welsh 1983, 52–55; Lind 1990, 141–148; O'Bryhim 2001, 9–10; Henderson 2013, 282.
63 This is the view especially of Lind 1990, 141–148.
64 Leguilloux 2004, 7–8; Haines 2006, 11; Jablonski 2006, 31; Beyries 2008, 11–12; Dercy 2015, 20.
65 Falcão and Araújo 2018, 1. See also Lau 1967, 56; and van Driel-Murray 2002b, 17; 2008, 483, 487–491, despite her tone of skepticism regarding a centralized, organized tanning industry in the Classical world before the Roman conquest of northwest Europe.
66 Rahme 1991, 68–70; van Driel-Murray 2002a, 252–253; 2002b, 17; 2008, 485; Strid 2010, 8–9; Dercy 2015, 39–40.
67 Van Driel-Murray 2002b, 17–18; 2008, 486. See also Blümner 1912, 267.

in which any loose pieces of membrane, fat, or meat still attached to the underside of the skin were removed before the tanning operations.[68] In the beginning of the tanning process, hair is removed from skins using an alkaline solution that attacks the hair, which then can be wiped off.[69] This is a malodorous stage of tanning, particularly so if one of the most straightforward (and common) means to dehairing hides is employed, namely folding and piling them, then letting putrefaction set in until the hair roots loosen. This process could be hastened by sprinkling the hair with urine or liquid mixed with pigeon dung.

Pigeon excrement, among other animal manure, was collected in ancient Greece and used as fertilizer, but pigeon dung is also an excellent dehairing agent in tanning due to its ammonia content. Keepers of the temple of Apollo on Delos turned revenue into sacred treasure by selling bird dung (κόπρος περιστερῶν) from their dovecote,[70] and there were even grand dovecotes regarded as sacred elsewhere in the Greek world.[71] Thus, not only was pigeon dung used as fertilizer, but also was very likely employed in tannery operations.

Urine contains nitrites, and it was largely utilized as a cleansing agent, as well as fertilizer. In Classical Athens, persons called *koprologoi* collected human sewage and waste from the streets, removed and disposed of it, and probably also sold it to be used as fertilizer of the fields nearby.[72] Citizens were forbidden to foul on streets and were obliged to empty waste and sewage into statutory dumps, which were then periodically cleaned by *koprologoi*.[73] Urine is thought to have been used in tanning in ancient Greece, as deduced particularly from the texts of Pliny and other Latin writers.[74] It would not be surprising if urine would have been separately collected for the demand of the tanneries by individuals or officials appointed to this duty to the profit of the collector and seller.[75]

In addition, mulberry leaves and the fruit of bryony (*bryonia dioeca*) are said to have been used to loosen hair in ancient Greece, although our testimony for this comes from later writers.[76] Hair itself was removed by manually scraping the skin with a (two-handled) dehairing knife/carver over a wooden beam. The entire dehairing process requires one to five days.[77]

In vegetable tanning, the tannins are made to work their way into the structure of the skin. This phase was time-consuming, yet after the first renewal of the tannin-solution in vats and pits, it was not labor intensive; the entire treatment took from six months to a year to achieve quality and durable leather.[78] Hides were set horizontally in layers in pits or vats with vegetable tannin material (such as crushed barks, leaves, or fruits) and water to immerse the skins.[79] Tanning in pits or vats set in the ground is the most suitable for the treatment of large animal skins to produce strong leathers, whereas the tanning of small to medium skins could be carried out in wooden or clay vats, where the skins were combined with coarsely crushed or ground vegetable material, or an aqueous liquor of these

---

68 For details and equipment in this procedure in Medieval tanning, see, e.g., Rahme 1991, 46–54; Strid 2010, 7–8. For the discussion concerning ancient Greece, see Dercy 2015, 36–37.

69 Chahine 2002, 16–17; Leguilloux 2004, 149–152; Dercy 2015, 36–39.

70 IG XI.2 287, ll. A 20, 23–24 records the revenue of the sales of *kopros peristeron*. Chamoux (1992, 638–640) provides details of the secular and religious use of pigeons as revenue. On selling pigeon guano on Delos, see Bruneau (1970, 420), who regards it as a usual source of profit in sacred funds.

71 For monumental dovecotes, especially the one in Apollonia in Kyrenaica, see Chamoux 1992.

72 Alcock, Cherry, and Davis 1994, 147–155; and Auden 1999, 156–158 for *kopros* as manure.

73 Owens 1983, 45–46, 48; Hughes 2014, 120. *Koprologoi* are mentioned only twice in the textual sources: Arist. [*Ath. Pol.*] 50.2 states that it was the duty of the *astynomoi* to ensure that the *koprologoi* deposit the *kopros* at least ten stades outside of the city; Ar. *Pax* 9, where a *koprologos* is called to empty a dung heap. For the role of *koprologoi* as either public employers or private entrepreneurs, see Martin 1974, 62–63, 68.

74 Esp. Pliny, *HN* 17.51, 23.140. Faber 1938; Michell 1940, 170. However, see Dercy (2015, 37–38), who notes the absence of the explicit mention of urine in Greek texts.

75 A special vessel, a handled urinal, ἀμίς for men, σκάφιον for women, would allow collection, transport, and emptying the contents in a certain location. For *amis* of c.440–425 BCE, see Sparkes and Talcott 1970, fig. 14, pl. 96; Owens 1983, 47.

76 Plin. *HN* 23.140 notes that mulberry leaves soaked in urine help remove hair when skins are tanned. Dioskourides, writing in the first century CE, gives information regarding white bryony (or common bryony) in his *De Materia Medica*, where he explains that hides are made bare of hair with this plant, ἄμπελος ἀγρία (*Vitis alba* 4.184).

77 For the process and equipment, see Blümner 1912, 266; Deferrari 1997, 364–365; Borgard et al. 2003, 13–18; Thomson 2006, 68–70; van Driel-Murray 2008, 487; Dercy 2015, 49–50; Bond 2016, 112–113; De Cristofaro, Di Mento, and Rossi 2017, 16, 22. Procter (1903, 144, 179–182) provides instructions for the operations over a period from ten days to three weeks. Leguilloux (2002, 270–274; 2004, 17) and Brun and Leguilloux (2014, 132, 152) depict a tanner's tools recovered from Pompei Insula Vb I tannery: a curving dehairing knife, half-moon knife (*culter craepidarius*), and rectangular blade.

78 Procter 1903, 9, 220: 2–12 months (depending on the desired result and nature of the raw material); Deferrari (1997, 356): 15 months; van Driel Murray (2008, 487): 6–12 months; Volken 2010, 426: from 8 months to one and a half years.

79 Thomson 2006, 69–70; Falcão and Araújo 2018, 2.

materials stewed in layers between the hides.⁸⁰ Tannins, *pharmaka*, were obtained from plants, which can produce high yields (20–50%).⁸¹ In addition to the tissue of such plants, galls were used in ancient Greece as sources of tannin. They are found in the branches, leaves, or domes of plants as a response to the bites of certain insects or other parasites and can contain as much as 60% tannins.⁸² The *Chemical Dictionary of Economic Plants* (2001) lists 20 tanning plants, eight of which are native or grow in the Mediterranean region,⁸³ and Classical authors explicitly mention six of these as tanning plants used in leather tanning,⁸⁴ a valid attestation of rather high-level, even sophisticated, knowledge of tannins already at that time. Theophrastos' writings on plants are an important source on the tannins used in ancient Greece. The sources of tannins used by tanners that he mentions can be grouped into galls, barks, and fruits. He especially discusses oak galls,⁸⁵ barks, and sumac leaves, plants that were the most widely used tannin sources in Europe in leather production until the 20th century.⁸⁶

5 Sacred Hides and Leather from Sacrificial Animals

In a well-known cult regulation of 386–374 BCE from the Amphiareion in Oropos,⁸⁷ the *dermata*, hides of sacrificial animals, are termed 'sacred': the hide of every animal sacrificed in the sanctuary is to be sac[red] (τῶν δὲ θυομένων ἐν τοῖ ἱεροῖ πάντων τὸ δέρμα [[ἱερ[ὸν εἶναι]]], ll. 29–30). The text also describes sacred portions from the sacrificial animals and the perquisite for the priest. The original specification (still partly legible) stipulating the 'sacred' nature of the hides was later erased by chiseling it out.⁸⁸ The hides at the Amphiareion indeed had a special status probably because they had a particular cultic or ritual role in this sanctuary as indicated by sculptural evidence,⁸⁹ and, as often pointed out, Pausanias' (1.34.5) description of the ritual healing processes in the sanctuary. It seems plausible that the hides referred to as 'sacred' in the original inscription were so because everything kept in the sanctuary was the god's property and therefore inherently sacred. Therefore, the location (inside of the sanctuary) and the ownership (gods' property) stipulate the sacred nature of the hides here. However, their sacrality was a flexible concept as they also had a role to play in commerce. In 334/333 BCE, probably after the inclusion of the Greater Amphiaraia into Athenian civic festivals, the Athenians used the money from the *dermatikon* for covering the festival costs and expenses of the cults on the Akropolis and elsewhere in Attika, as shown by *IG* II² 1469 and 333. Hence the erasure and change in the 'sacred' status of the skins would have allowed the selling of skins from the Amphiareion sacrifices. When released from the god's property at the sanctuary and sold, the hides lost their 'sacred' nature.

This change in status has implications for the consideration of how leather originating in sanctuaries and leather from other contexts were perceived in terms of sacredness. We have one epigraphic mention that points to the concept of 'sacrificial leather.' The Andanian rule for regulating the Mysteries in Messenia stipulated that no woman in the sanctuary is to wear shoes unless they are made of felt or of leather or hide from a sacrificial animal (μηδὲ ὑποδήματα εἰ μὴ πίλινα ἢ δερμάτινα ἱερόθυτα, ll. A1 22–23).⁹⁰ Contrary to the hides at the Amphiareion, the leather in this case is not 'sacred leather,' but sacrificial hide, which itself was not 'sacred' when taken out of a sacred precinct. I would be cautious about qualifying a processed commodity as 'sacred' outside the physical confines of sacred space since anything outside sanctuary space was no longer sacred, i.e., the god's property, regardless of its origin in a sacral context. One way to understand the stipulation is to regard the approved type of shoes as of better-quality footwear than rough footwear probably

---

80 Procter 1903, 328; Harborne and Baxter 2001, 123; Falcão and Araújo 2018, 2.
81 For chemical composition of tannings, see Falcão and Araújo 2018, 1–3.
82 Harborne and Baxter 2001, 123; Falcão and Araújo 2018, 13.
83 Harborne and Baxter 2001, 121–128. Tannins from these plants come from bark, galls, acorns, and leaves, and some of them also are used as dyeing agents.
84 For the summary of these plants, see esp. Dercy (2015, 203–206 Annexe 1).
85 Due to the importance of galls as source for tannins, Theophrastos deals with them in detail and describes ten different types produced by oak trees (*Hist. pl.* 3.7.3, 3.7.4–5, 3.16.1). Identifying galls described by Theophrastos is difficult, yet of the ten oak galls that he mentions, nine have been identified by scholars; see Senn 1942; Thanos 2005, 31–32.
86 Thanos 2005, 31; Falcão and Araújo 2018, 9.
87 *IG* VII 235 = *CGRN* 75; *LSCG* no. 69; RO no. 27.
88 Petropoulou 1981, 60–63, followed by RO 132–133; Lupu 2003, 333; Carbon and Peels in their commentary on *CGRN* 75. *NGSL*² no. 24 (= *SEG* 28.750), a short regulation from the Asklepieion in Lissos on Crete (Hellenistic or Roman) states that "Meat shall not be carried away. The skin goes to the god" (κρεῶν οὐκ ἀποφορά. τὸ δέρμα τῶι θεῶι, ll. 4–5), thus becoming divine property.
89 Discussed with illustrations by Lupu (2003, 323–325).
90 *CGRN* 222 (= *IG* V.1 1390; *LSCG* no. 65), 92/91 BCE. See Gawlinski 2012, 113–132.

made of cured or untanned leather. Shoes made of cured leather are not durable, nor waterproof. Aristophanes makes the Sausage-seller in *Knights* (315–318) claim that Kleon (the Tanner) "cuts on the slant the hide of a low-grade ox (δέρμα μοχθηροῦ βοός)[91] to cheat to make it look stout and sell it to the peasants at a dishonest price." He implies that Kleon, a specialist in leather work, knows how to deceive customers and sell worse-quality leather from wretched oxen. Read against the background of what we know of tanning methods presented here, we should regard the leather sold by Kleon to peasants as untanned or cured, not fully tanned, leather.[92] Accordingly, he tried to pass his low-quality leather off as fully tanned leather, which would have come across as thicker or stouter, and hence of better quality (ὥστε φαίνεσθαι παχύ).

It seems that certain leather—that which originated in sacrificial rituals—was regarded as, if not special, at least distinguished from poorer quality leather. This is because sacrificial animals had to be perfect specimens (healthy, without blemish), and as discussed above, lesser quality porcine-skin leather would not have originated in sanctuaries. The situation is the same as with meat: meat from sacrificial animals was a highly regarded commodity sold separately on the market[93] and was designated as meat of *hierothyta*.[94] The hides kept at the Amphiareion sanctuary were sacred (the god's property), whereas the leather of the sandals in the Andanian rule is not *hieron*, but simply made of ἱερόθυτα.

In conclusion, I take full imaginary liberty and follow Sokrates to the Athenian Agora,[95] where he would discuss philosophy with his companions at a shoemaker's shop. Could there have been a sign at the shop advertising "Quality-shoes sold here. The best materials used?" This shoemaker could price his items high as his materials would be the best quality with added value of leather from sacrificial animals to guarantee their worth. Thus, the business of hides and skins was both sacred and profane business. As often with Greek concepts, opposites coincide.

Works Cited

Acton, P. 2014. *Poiesis: Manufacturing in Classical Greece*. Oxford.

Alcock, S., J. Cherry, and J.L. Davis 1994. "Intensive Survey, Agricultural Practice and the Classical Landscape of Greece." In *Ancient Histories and Modern Ideologies*, edited by I. Morris, 137–170. Cambridge.

Ault, B.A. 1999. "Koprones and Oil Presses at Haleis. Interactions of Town and Country and the Integration of Domestic and Regional Economies." *Hesperia* 68: 549–573.

Berthiaume, G. 1982. *Les rôles du Mageiros. Étude sur la boucherie, la cuisine et le sacrifice dans la Grèce ancienne*, préface by M. Detienne. Leiden.

Beyries, S. 2008. "Modélisation du travail de cuir en ethnologie. Proposition d'un système ouvert à l'archéologie." *Anthropozoologia* 43: 9–42.

Billot, F.M. 1992. "Le Cynosarges, Antiochos et les tanneurs. Question de topographie." *BCH* 116: 119–156.

Blok, J.H. 2010. "Deme Accounts and the Meaning of *hosios* Money." *Mnemosyne* 63: 61–93.

Blümel, C. 1966. *Die klassisch griechischen Skulpturen der Staatlichen Museen zu Berlin*. Berlin.

Blümner, H. 1912. *Technologie und Terminologie der Gewerbe und Künste bei Griechen und Römern 1*, 2nd ed. Leipzig.

Bond, S.E. 2016. *Trade and Taboo: Disreputable Professions in Roman Mediterranean*. Ann Arbor.

Borgard, P., J.-P. Brun, M. Leguilloux, and M. Tuffreau-Libre. 2003. "Le produzioni artigianali a Pompei: Ricerche condotte dal Centre Jean Bérard." *RStPomp* 14: 9–29.

Bradley, M. 2001. "It All Comes Out in the Wash: Looking Harder at the Roman *fullonica*." *JRA* 15: 20–44.

Brøns, C. 2017. *Gods & Garments: Textiles in Greek Sanctuaries in the 7th to the 1st centuries BC*. Oxford.

Brun, J.-P., and M. Leguilloux 2014. *Les installations artisanales romaines de Saepinum. Tannerie et moulin hydraulique*. Naples.

---

91 Schol. ad Ar. *Eq.* 316b explains this as deadly, sickly, weak with thin skin: θανασίμου ἢ ἀσθενοῦς, ἰσχνοῦ καὶ λεπτοβύρσου.

92 Dercy (2015, 55) interprets δέρμα μοχθηροῦ βοός in this passage as leather that is cut slantwise, i.e., to thinner parts resulting in thinner leather.

93 Ekroth 2007, 271. She adds that "This meat was not only of guaranteed good quality as coming from recently killed and healthy animals, it was the most sacred of all meat, imbued with the divine." See also Isenberg 1975, 271–273; Berthiaume 1982, 65, 67–69; *NGSL*² 71 for the sale of skins in sacred laws. See Cheung 1999, 32–34, 250–251; and McDonough 2004 for the distinction between *eidolouthyta* ('idol meat') and meat not from 'idol' sacrifices among early Christian communities, esp. in Corinth.

94 Berthiaume 1982, 67–69 with examples in the texts. Regardless of accepting the difference between sacrificial and non-sacrificial meat, Berthiaume is doubtful whether the first was by rule sold in the sanctuary context and the second at the Agora. See also Lo Monaco in this volume.

95 Sokrates is said to have frequented manufacturers' shops in the Athenian Agora: Xen. *Mem.* 4.2.2 and 4.2.8 mention a leatherworker's shop frequented by the handsome and knowledgeable youth, Euthydemos, who: "would be found sitting in a saddler's shop (ἡνιοποιεῖόν) near the market. So, Sokrates went to this shop with some of his companions" wishing to question him about the wisdom to be gained from books. See, e.g., Collins 2013, §3, 15; Sobak 2015, 700. See also Hock 1976, esp. 46–47; Clay 1994, 33; and Cast 2008, 1–2.

Bruneau, P. 1970. *Recherches sur les cultes de Délos à l'époque hellénistique et à l'époque impériale*. Paris.

Bundrick, S.D. 2014. "Selling Sacrifice on Classical Athenian Vases." *Hesperia* 83: 653–708.

Burgio, A. 2014. "Alesa Arconidea: dal 'paesaggio mediterraneo' alle dinamiche storiche e culturali del territorio." In *Paesaggi in trasformazione. Teorie e pratiche della ricerca a cinquant'anni dalla storia del paesaggio agrario italiano di Emilio Sereni*, edited by G. Bonini and C. Visentin, 487–494. Bologna.

Carbon, J.-M. 2017. "Meaty Perks: Epichoric and Topological Trends." In *Animal Sacrifice in the Ancient Greek World*, edited by S. Hitch and I. Rutherford, 151–177. Cambridge.

Carusi, C. 2016. "Vita humanior sine sale non quit degere: Demand for Salt and Salt Trade Patterns in the Ancient Greek World." In The *Ancient Greek Economy: Markets, Households, and City-States*, edited by E.M. Harris, D.M. Lewis, and M. Woolmer, 337–355. New York.

Cast, D. 2008. "Simon the Shoemaker and the Cobbler of Apelles." *Notes on the History of Art* 28: 1–4.

Cavanaugh, M.B. 1996. *Eleusis and Athens: Documents in Finance, Religion, and Politics in the Fifth Century BC*. Atlanta.

Chahine, C. 2002. "Évolution des techniques de fabrication du cuir et problèmes de conservation." In *Le travail du cuir de la Préhistoire à nos jours*, edited by F. Audoin-Rouzeau, and S. Beyries, 13–29. Antibes.

Chamoux, F. 1992. "Un pigeonnier antique près d'Apollonia Cyrénaïque." *CRAI* 136: 623–642.

Cheung, A.T. 1999. *Idol Food in Corinth: Jewish Background and Pauline Legacy*. Sheffield.

Chiotis, E. 2016. "Springs, Sanctuaries and Aqueducts in the Ilissos Valley, Attica, and the Enchanting Scenery in Plato's Dialogue *Phaedrus*." Symposium paper at the international conference *L'eau dans tous ses états. V^e symposium international HYDRΩMED*, Aix-en-Provence, 30 May 2016.

Clay, D. 1994. "The Origins of Socratic Dialogue." In *The Socratic Movement*, edited by P.A. Vander Waerdt, 23–47. Ithaca.

Clinton, K. 2005–2008. *Eleusis: The Inscriptions on Stone. Documents of the Sanctuary of the Two Goddesses and Public Documents of the Deme*. Athens.

Collins, J. 2013. "Socrates in the Marketplace." *Center of Hellenic Studies Research Bulletin* 2. https://research-bulletin.chs.harvard.edu/2014/02/12/socrates-in-the-marketplace/.

Compton, T.M. 2006. *Victim of the Muses: Poet as Scapegoat, Warrior and Hero in Greco-Roman and Indo-European Myth and History*. Washington D.C.

De Cristofaro, A., M. Di Mento, and D. Rossi 2017. "Coraria Septimiana e Campus Iudeorum. Novità dai recenti scavi fuori Porta Portese." *Thiasos* 6: 3–39.

Deferrari, G. 1997. "Per un'archeologia della produzione in conceria: Possibili percorsi di indagine." In *I congresso Nazionale di Archeologia Medievale*, edited by S. Gelichi, 363–368. Florence.

Dercy, B. 2015. *Le travail des peaux et du cuir dans le monde grec antique. Tentative d'une archéologie du disparu appliquée au cuir*. Naples.

Douglas, C.R. 2015. *A Comparative Study of Roman-period Leather from Northern Britain*. MA theses, University of Glasgow.

Ekroth, G. 2002. *The Sacrificial Rituals of Greek Hero-Cults in the Archaic to the Early Hellenistic Period*. Liége.

Ekroth, G. 2007. "Meat in Ancient Greece: Sacrificial, Sacred or Secular." *Food & History* 5: 249–272.

Ekroth, G. 2008. "Meat, Man and God. On the Division of the Animal Victim at Greek Sacrifices." In *Mikros hieromnemon. Meletes eis mnemen Michael H. Jameson*, edited by A.P. Matthaiou and I. Polinskaya, 259–290. Athens.

Faber, G.A. 1938. *Dyeing and Tanning in Classical Antiquity*, Ciba Review 9. Basel.

Facella, A. 2006. *Alesa Arconidea: Ricerche su un'antica città della Sicilia tirrenica*. Pisa.

Falcão, L., and M.E.M. Araújo 2018. "Vegetable Tannings Used in the Manufacture of Historic Leathers." *Molecules* 23: https://doi.org/10.3390/molecules23051081.

Ferguson, W.S. 1948. "Demetrius Poliorcetes and the Hellenic League." *Hesperia* 17: 112–136.

Flohr, M. 2013. *The World of the Fullo: Work, Economy and Society in Roman Italy*. Oxford.

Gawlinski, L. 2012. *The Sacred Law of Andania. A New Text with Commentary*. Berlin.

Gebauer, J. 2002. *Pompe und Thysia. Attische Tieropferdarstellungen auf schwarz- und rotfigurigen Vasen*. Münster.

Georgoudi, S. 2018. "Couper pour purifier? Le chien et autres animaux, entre pratiques rituelles et récits." In *Purity and Purification in the Ancient Greek World*, edited by J.-M. Carbon and S. Peels-Matthey, 173–205. Liège.

Gordon, R.L. 1989. "The Moment of Death: Art and the Ritual of Greek Sacrifice." In *World Art: Themes of Unity and Diversity*, edited by I. Lavin et al., 567–573. University Park, PA.

Habermann, W. 1987. "$IG\ 1^3$ 386/387, sizilische Häute und der athenisch-sizilischen Handelsbeziehungen im 5. Jh v. Chr." *Münstersche Beiträge zur antiken Handelsgeschichte* 6: 89–113.

Haines, B.M. 2006. "The Fibre Structure of Leather." In *Conservation of Leather and Related Materials*, edited by M. Kite and R. Thomson, 11–21. Amsterdam.

Harborne, J.B., and H. Baxter 2001. *Chemical Dictionary of Economic Plants*. Chichester.

Harris, E. 2015. "Toward a Typology of Greek Regulations about Religious Matters. A Legal Approach." *Kernos* 28: 53–83.

Henderson, J. 2013. "The Comic Chorus and the Demagogue." In *Choral Mediations in Greek Tragedy*, edited by R. Gagné and M. Govers Hopman, 278–296. Cambridge.

Hock, R.F. 1976. "Simon the Shoemaker as an Ideal Cynic." *GRBS* 17: 41–53.

Howe, T. 2011. "Good Breeding. Making Sense of Elite Animal Production in Ancient Greece." *Scholia* 20: 4–24.

Howe, T. 2014. "Value Economy. Animals, Wealth and the Market." In *The Oxford Handbook of Animals in Classical Thought and Life*, edited by G.L. Campbell, 136–155. Oxford.

Hughes, J.D. 2014. *Environmental Problems of the Greeks and Romans. Ecology in the Ancient Mediterranean*, 2nd ed. Baltimore.

Isenberg, M. 1975. "The Sale of Sacrificial Meat." *CP* 70: 271–273.

Jablonski, N.G. 2006. *Skin: A Natural History*. Berkeley.

Jameson, M.H. 1988. "Sacrifice and Animal Husbandry in Classical Greece." In *Pastoral Economies in Classical Antiquity*, edited by C.R. Whittaker, 87–119. Cambridge.

Johnston, S.I. 1991. "Crossroads." *ZPE* 88: 217–224.

Jones, N.F. 1999. *The Associations of Classical Athens: The Response to Democracy*. Oxford.

Kloppenborg, J.S., and R.S. Ascough. 2011. *Graeco-Roman Associations: Texts, Translations, and Commentary 1: Attica, Central Greece, Macedonia, Thrace*. Berlin.

Lau, O. 1967. *Schuster und Schusterhandwerk in der griechisch-römischen Literatur und Kunst*. Bonn.

Leguilloux, M. 2002. "Techniques et équipments de la tannerie romaine: L'example de l'officina coriaria de Pompéi." In *Le travail du cuir de la préhistoire à nos jours*, edited by A. Beyries and F. Audoin-Rouzeau, 268–282. Antibes.

Leguilloux, M. 2004. *Le cuir et la pelleterie à l'époque romaine*. Paris.

Le Gruen-Pollet, B. 1991a. "Espace sacrificiel et corps des bêtes immolées. Remarques sur le vocabulaire désignant la part du prêtre dans la Grèce antique, de l'époque classique à l'époque impériale." In *L'espace sacrificiel dans les civilisations méditerranéennes de l'antiquité*, edited by R. Étienne and M.-T. le Dinahet, 12–23. Paris.

Le Gruen-Pollet, B. 1991b. *La vie religieuse dans le monde grec du Vᵉ ai IIIᵉ siècle avant notre ère. Choix de documents épigraphiques traduits et commentés*. Toulouse.

Liddel, P., and P. Low 2015. "An Honorific *gnome* of the *koinon* of the Phrikyladai: A new Inscription from Liverpool." *BSA* 110: 263–284.

Lind, H. 1990. *Der Gerber Kleon in den 'Rittern' des Aristophanes. Studien zur Demagogenkomödie*. Frankfurt am Main.

Lloyd, G.E.R. 2003. *In the Grip of Disease: Studies in the Greek Imagination*. Oxford.

Lohmann, H. 1992. "Agriculture and Country Life in Classical Attica." In *Agriculture in Ancient Greece*, edited by B. Wells, 29–57. Stockholm.

Lupu, E. 2003. "Sacrifice at the Amphiareion and a Fragmentary Sacred Law from Oropos." *Hesperia* 72: 321–340.

Martin, R. 1974. *L'urbanisme dans la Grèce antique*, 2nd ed. Paris.

McDonough, C.M. 2004. "The Pricing of Sacrificial Meat: *Eidolothuton*, the Ara Maxima, and Useful Misinformation from Servius." In *Augusto Augurio. Rerum Humanarum et Divinarum Commentationes in Honorem Jerzy Linderski*, edited by C.F. Konrad, 69–76. Stuttgart.

McInerney, J. 2010. *The Cattle of the Sun: Cows and Culture in the World of the Ancient Greeks*. Princeton.

Mitchell, H. 1940. *The Economics of Ancient Greece*. Cambridge.

Mikalson, J.D. 1998. *Religion in Hellenistic Athens*. Berkeley.

Naiden, F.S. 2012. "Blessed Are the Parasites." In *Greek and Roman Animal Sacrifice. Ancient Victims, Modern Observers*, edited by C. Faraone and F.S. Naiden, 54–83. Cambridge.

O'Bryhim, S. 2001. "Introduction." In *Greek and Roman Comedy: Translations and Interpretations of Four Representative Plays*, edited by S. O'Bryhim, 3–13. Austin.

Owens, E.J. 1983. "The *Koprologoi* at Athens in the Fifth and Fourth Centuries B.C." *CQ* 33: 44–50.

Pakkanen, P. 2021. "Beyond Skin-deep. Considering the Pig in Ancient Greece through the Particularities of Its Skin." *Kernos* 34: 123–158.

Papazarkadas, N. 2011. *Sacred and Public Land in Athens*. Oxford.

Parker, R.C.T. 1983. *Miasma: Pollution and Purification in Early Greek Religion*. Oxford.

Patera, I. 2012. *Offrir en Grèce ancienne. Gestes et contextes*. Stuttgart.

Petropoulou, A.B. 1981. "The *Eparche* Documents and the Early Oracle at Oropus." *GRBS* 22: 39–63.

Prestianni Giallombardo, A.M. 1988. "Ἐλαιοκόμιον δίκλαρον. Una interpretazione di *IG* XIV 352, col. I, ll. 69–71." *AnnPisa* 18: 1447–1467.

Prestianni Giallombardo, A.M. 2003. "Divinità e culti in Halaesa Archonidea. Tra identità etnica e interazione culturale." In *Quatre Giornate internazionali di studi sull' area Elima 1*, edited by A. Corretti, 1059–1103. Pisa.

Prestianni Giallombardo, A.M. 2012. "Tusa: Fonto letterarie, epigrafiche e numismatiche." In *Bibliografia Topografica della Colonizzazione Greca in Italia e nelle Isole Tirreniche* 21, edited by G. Nanci and G. Vallet, 251–262. Pisa.

Procter, H.R. 1903. *The Principles of Leather Manufacture*. London.

Puttkammer, F. 1912. *Quomodo Graeci carnes victimarum distribuerint*. Köningsberg.

Rahme, L. 1991. *Skinn. Garvning och beredning med traditionella metoder*. Stockholm.

Reger, G. 1994. *Regionalism and Change in the Economy of Independent Delos*. Berkeley.

Rosivach, V.J. 1994. *The System of Public Sacrifice in Fourth-Century Athens*. Atlanta.

Salta, M. 2019. "Under the Care of Daemons: From the Athenian Acropolis to Kallirrhoe on the Ilissos." In *Ascending and Descending the Acropolis. Movement in Athenian Religion*, edited by W. Friese, S. Handberg, and T.M. Kristensen, 63–101. Aarhus.

Sanidas, G. 2013. "La question des activités à 'nuisance' dans les villes grecques: intra ou extra muros?" In *Proasteion. Recherches sur le périurbain dans le monde grec*, edited by P. Darcque, R. Étienne, and A.-M. Guimier-Sorbets, 173–191. Paris.

Senn, G. 1942. "Oak Galls in the *Historia Plantarum* of Theophrastos." *Transactions of the Royal Society of Edinburgh* 60: 343–355.

Sobak, R. 2015. "Socrates among the Shoemakers." *Hesperia* 84: 669–712.

Sparkes, B., and L. Talcott. 1970. *Black and Plain Pottery of the 6th, 5th, and 4th Centuries B.C. Agora 12*. Princeton.

Strid, L. 2010. *Identifiering av garverier i en arkeologisk kontext— Metoder och möjligheter*, Uppsats fördjupningskurs i arkeologi, Högskolan på Gotland (Gotland University), unpublished dissertation.

Taylor, C. 2015. "Social Networks and Social Mobility in Fourth-Century Athens." In *Communities and Networks in the Ancient Greek World*, edited by C. Taylor and K. Vlassopoulos, 35–53. Oxford.

Thanos, C.A. 2005. "Theophrastus on Oaks." *Botanika Chronika* 18: 29–36.

Thomson, R. 2006. "The Manufacture of Leather." In *Conservation of Leather and Related Materials*, edited by M. Kite and R. Thomson, 66–81. Amsterdam.

Tsoukala, V. 2009. "Honorary Shares of Sacrificial Meat in Attic Vase Painting: Visual Signs of Distinction and Civic Identity." *Hesperia* 78: 1–40.

van Driel-Murray, C. 2002a. "Ancient Skin Processing and the Impact of Rome on Tanning Technology." In *Le travail du cuir de la Préhistoire à nos jours*, edited by F. Audoin-Rouzeau and S. Beyries, 251–265. Antibes.

van Driel-Murray, C. 2002b. "Practical Evaluation of a Field-Test for the Identification of Ancient Vegetable Tanned Leathers." *JAS* 26: 17–21.

van Driel-Murray, C. 2008. "Tanning and Leather." In *The Oxford Handbook of Engineering and Technology in the Classical World*, edited by J.P. Oleson, 482–495. Oxford.

van Driel-Murray, C. 2011. "Are We Missing Something? The Elusive Tanneries of the Roman Period." In *Leather Tanneries: The Archaeological Evidence*, edited by R. Thomson and Q. Mould, 69–83. London.

van Straten, F.T. 1995. *Hierà kalá: Images of Animal Sacrifice in Archaic and Classical Greece*. Leiden.

Vial, C. 1984. *Délos indépendante (314–167 avant J.-C.). Étude d'une communauté civique et de ses institutions*. Athens.

Vialles, N. 1994. *Animal to Edible*, preface by F. Héritier-Augé, trans. J.A. Underwood (original *Le sang et la chair: Les abattoires des pays de l'Adour*, Paris 1987). Cambridge.

Volken, M. 2010. "Le fer et la peau: Le cuir et ses outils en milieu urbain romain." In *Aspects de l'artisanat en milieu urbain: Gaule et Occident romain*, edited by P. Chardron-Picault, 415–424. Dijon.

von Prott, H.T.A., and L. Ziehen, eds. 1896–1906. *Leges Graecorum sacrae e titulis collectae, ediderunt et explanaverunt*. Leipzig.

von Reden, S. 2010. *Money in Classical Antiquity*. Cambridge.

Welsh, D. 1983. "*IG* II² 2343, Philonides, and Aristophanes' Banqueters." *CQ* 33: 51–55.

Wilson, A. 2003. "The Archaeology of the Roman fullonica." *JRA* 16: 442–446.

Wilson, P. 2008. "Costing the Dionysia." In *Performance, Iconography and Reception. Studies in Honour of Oliver Taplin*, edited by M. Revermann and P. Wilson, 88–127. Oxford.

Ziehen, L. 1899. "Εὐστόν." *AM* 24: 267–274.

Zografou, A. 2005. "Élimination rituelle et sacrifice en Grèce ancienne." In *La cuisine et l'autel. Les sacrifices en questions dans les sociétés de la Méditerranée ancienne*, edited by S. Georgoudi, R. Koch Piettre, and F. Schmidt, 197–212. Turnhout.

Index of Inscriptions

CGRN

4: 22, 37
5: 37, 152
6, A, 2: 188
6, A, 4–5: 188
6, A, 9: 141, 188
6, A, 11: 188
7, A, 35: 188
7, A, 51: 188
7, B, 1: 188
7, B, 3–4: 188
11, 2–3: 11
12: 44, 188, 189
13: 36, 38
13, A, 1–2: 11
17, 2: 239
19: 186
23: 13
25, A, 9–11: 42
26, B, 5–7: 237
26, B, 10–19: 237
27: 22
31: 47
32: 11, 69, 187
32, 10–12: 186
33: 22, 40, 106, 111
34: 42
34, 6–7: 141
34, 24–28: 141
34, 27–28: 141
35, 8–10: 141
36: 45
36, 7–11: 108
36, 8–11: 13
36, 11–13: 13
37, 14–16: 46
38: 41
38, B, 9–11: 46
42: 46
42, 6–7: 41
43: 43
43, 24–28: 29
45, A, frag. 3, 30: 11
50: 13, 45, 237
50, 12–14: 13
51, 2: 141
52: 239
52, E, 50–51: 178
53: 69
56: 69
56, II, 46–49: 141
57, 5–6: 237
57, 23–26: 141
57, 33: 145
59: 185
60, 8–13: 141
62: 22
63: 22
65: 38

65, 7: 61
71: 22
74, 4–8: 141
75: 12, 42, 245
75, 2–6: 12, 30
75, 20–24: 30
75, 25–32: 45
75, 31–32: 30
75, 39–43: 30
76, 25–30: 15
78: 41, 46
81: 236
82, D, 19–29: 43
84: 205
84, 31–33: 237
85: 71
85, 5: 185
85, 7: 185
86: 71, 239
86, A, 54–55: 221
86, B, 11–15: 141
86, C, 8: 64
86, C, 13: 64
86, D, 18: 141
86, D, 25: 141
90: 41
90, 14–18: 22
90, 21–25: 60
90, 30–33: 58
91, 24–26: 43
91, 36–38: 14
92: 43, 70, 208
96: 71, 154
96, 18–21: 72
96, 47–51: 218
96, 69–77: 218
96, 80–85: 104
96, 82–86: 111
96, 25–27: 239
96, 86–113: 12
96, 120: 145
96, 122: 141
97: 41
97, 2–4: 29
98: 71
98, A, 7–8: 141
98, B, 13: 141
98, B, 19–21: 141
99: 71
99, A, 26–32: 45
99, 26–29: 72
100: 238
102: 205
102, 5–9: 206
106: 71
106, 10–14: 71, 76
118: 187
121: 22
124: 219

125: 187
126: 22, 239
128, 4: 185
128, 5: 239
129: 111
136: 71, 72, 219
138, 2–3: 15
139, 10: 141
140: 73
142, 20–23: 45
144: 22
147, 10–11: 44
147, 117–118: 44
147, 124–126: 44
148: 71, 239
148, 75–78: 43
152, 140–141: 141
155: 22
156, 13–15: 141
156, 24–26: 22
157, 26: 141
157, 35: 141
163, 1–2: 12
163, 2–4: 12
163, 3–4: 26
164, 8–9: 44
166: 38
167: 16
175, 2–6: 108
181, 17: 239
181, 21–22: 70
183, 8–10: 47
184: 186
185, 24–28: 36
186, 27–29: 29
187, 26–27: 141
188: 26
188, 8–10: 26
188, 8–13: 12
190, A, 7–8: 239
191, 25–32: 38
199: 69, 71, 207, 219
201, 8–9: 141
201, 11–12: 141
201, 16–17: 141
201, 24–25: 141
201, 37–39: 141
202, 57–59: 141
203: 22
204, 5–8: 141
208, 18–19: 44
208, 20: 45
211: 40
212: 49
212, 22–28: 41
216, 7–8: 239
217: 22
220: 187
220, 5–6: 11

CGRN (*cont.*)
   222: 42, 48, 74, 239, 245
   222, 1–11: 108
   222, 21–22: 218
   222, 25–26: 42
   222, 25–28: 29
   222, 34–37: 64, 106
   222, 36–37: 36, 39, 107
   222, 38: 107
   222, 42–45: 29
   222, 55–56: 218
   222, 70–71: 59
   222, 78–80: 14, 36
   222, 80–84: 16, 110
   222, 98–103: 62
   222, 103–105: 68
   223: 56, 57, 59
   225: 72, 90, 99
   225, A, 6–8: 42
   225, A, 24: 141
   225, A, 32–33: 141
   225, A, 37: 141
   225, A, 51: 141
   225, B, 2–6: 42
   225, B, 6: 141
   225, B, 12: 141, 145
   225, B, 16: 141
   225, B, 32–33: 141
   225, B, 33–34: 42
   225, B, 38: 141
   225, B, 47: 141
   225, B, 47–48: 141
   225, B, 55–56: 141
   225, B, 58: 141
   225, B, 67: 141
   225, B, 70–71: 141
   225, B, 80–81: 91, 108, 110
   233: 72
   234, A, 2–4: 61
   234, B: 39, 48
   249, C, 10–12: 45
CID I
   3: 188
CID II
   60: 215
   84b, 2–4: 215
   139: 220
   139, 5–6: 220
   139, 7: 220
   139, 9–10: 220
   139, 14–15: 220
   139, 18–19: 220
   139, 22–25: 220
   139, 28–29: 220
   139, 30: 220
   139, 33: 220
   139, 34–35: 220
   139, 37: 220
   139, 43: 220
CID IV
   54, 7–11: 106
   85, 9: 106, 108
   108, 25–27: 70

CIRB
   939: 73, 81
CIS I
   165: 185
I.Amyzon
   10: 40
   11: 40
I.Chalcedon
   12, 23–24: 26
I.Didyma
   482: 171, 186
I.Ilion
   3: 7, 196
I.Knidos
   160: 111
IK.Priene
   191: 30
   192: 30
I.Labraunda
   46: 40
I.Lampsakos
   9: 36
I.Lindos
   487: 38
I.Magnesia
   16: 198
   61: 198
I.Smyrna
   728: 40
   753, 27–29: 110
I.Stratonikeia
   203, 17–21: 106, 107
I.Thasos 3
   4: 41
   9: 36
ID
   68 a–b: 39
   97, 36: 109
   98: 5, 209, 211
   104: 184
   290: 210
   324: 210
   353, A, 28: 57
   354: 210
   366: 210
   384: 210
   399, A, 7: 240
   399, A, 14: 240
   399, A, 17: 240
   399, A, 18: 240
   440: 69, 71
   445: 69, 71
   1416: 210
   1416, B, II, 36: 215
   1520: 208
   1720: 239
   1830: 26
   1875: 26
   1876: 26
IG I^2
   276, 14: 133
IG I^3
   3, 6–10: 12

   4: 41
   78a: 11
   82, 24–28: 42
   84: 74, 205
   136: 206, 218
   256bis: 11, 69
   257: 241
   386: 240
   387: 240
   474: 215
   476: 215
   977a: 74
IG II^2
   212, 59–63: 218
   333: 244
   334, 17–18: 240
   995: 15
   1013, 49–50: 181
   1046: 219
   1126: 39
   1183, 32–35: 239
   1237: 39
   1301: 241
   1324, 4: 218
   1356: 237
   1358: 69
   1361: 218
   1361, 2–6: 206
   1362: 49
   1365: 40
   1366: 40, 44
   1366, 11–12: 40
   1425, 217: 133
   1425, 277: 133
   1469: 245
   1496: 159
   1496, 68–92: 237
   1514, III, 22–23: 25
   1534, 102: 25
   1541: 185
   1635, 36: 70
   1638, 68: 133
   1672: 109
   2499: 74, 111, 135, 205
   2721: 206
   2934: 242
   3453: 30
   3464: 30
   3474: 30
   4964: 37
   4971: 69
IG II^3
   352: 70
   447: 43, 70, 208
   447, 43–44: 240
   879: 71, 72
IG IV
   768: 26
   840: 71, 76
IG IV^2.1
   40: 42, 108
   41: 42, 108
   102, B, I, 92–93: 216

102, B, II, 255–256: 220
102, B, II, 277–278: 220
102, B, II, 275–276: 220
102, B, II, 287–288: 220
102, B, III, 289: 220
102, B, III, 293–294: 220
102, B, III, 295–297: 220
102, B, III, 297: 220
102, B, III, 298: 220
102, B, III, 300: 220
102, B, III, 303–304: 220
102, B, III, 305: 220
103, 55–56: 215
103, 136: 215
116: 74
121: 37
122: 37
123: 37, 184
297: 26
393: 42, 108
401: 42, 108
402: 42

IG v.1
  1312: 11
  1390: 14, 16, 68, 74, 245
  1390, 34–37: 64
  1390, 35–39: 177
  1390, 37–38: 177
  1390, 98–103: 62
  1390, 99–100: 199
  1390, 99–103: 196
  1390, 99–105: 181, 195
  1390, 100: 178

IG v.2
  3: 4, 52–62
  3, 26–30: 177
  4: 61
  6, 8: 57
  22, 8–9: 59
  81: 58
  142, 6: 59
  142, 12: 59
  142, 22: 59
  142, 32: 59
  142, 37: 59
  262, 1: 57

IG vii
  235: 245
  4255: 74

IG ix.1
  83: 181
  654: 218

IG ix.1²
  2:583, 26–30: 218
  2:583, 52–56: 218
  2:583, 58–61: 218

IG xi.2
  139: 210
  144: 210
  154: 5, 209, 210, 219
  159: 210
  159, A, 45: 218
  161 A: 203

163: 210
199: 210
203: 219
219: 210
287: 219
287, A, 20: 244
287, A, 23–24: 244

IG xi.4
  514, 13–16: 219

IG xii.1
  677, 25–27: 239

IG xii.2
  499: 40

IG xii.4
  72: 43, 71, 239
  274: 71
  275: 71
  275, 8: 64
  275, 13: 64
  276: 71
  277: 71
  278: 78
  285: 73
  297: 45
  304, 38–39: 45
  304, 39–40: 44
  319: 11
  319, 1–2: 43
  326, 66–67: 45
  328, A, 20–24: 16
  330, 1–2: 12
  330, 2–4: 12
  332: 71
  337, 14: 45
  348: 12, 71, 154
  348, 18–21: 72
  348, 86–113: 12
  348, 120: 145

IG xii.5
  225: 22
  569: 73
  647, 12: 186

IG xii.6
  169: 5, 15, 196, 198
  261: 28

IG xii.7
  515, 64: 186

IG xii.8
  358, 2: 239

IG xii.9
  189, 32–35: 177, 195
  189, 35–38: 195
  189, 36–38: 14
  893: 181

IG xii.Supp.
  126, 21–22: 70

IG xiv
  352: 241
  352, II, 54: 215

IGRom. I
  1101: 215

IGRom. IV
  190: 177

IPArk
  2: 52–53

LSAM
  5, 23–24: 26
  5, 24–26: 110
  6, 1–3: 41
  8, 24–26: 36
  12: 41, 49
  18: 40
  20, 25–32: 38
  28, 7–10: 27
  32, 12–13: 187
  37, 6–15: 159
  39: 237
  46: 238
  54: 171, 186
  55: 111, 188
  61: 41
  71: 186
  73: 187
  74: 15, 46
  79, 8–10: 47
  84: 40
  86: 72

LSCG
  18: 239
  19: 39
  28, 5–9: 159
  36: 41, 46
  37: 49
  39: 219
  41: 46
  43: 15, 46
  44: 219
  53: 91
  55: 40
  55, 12–15: 44
  60: 42
  65: 36, 42, 48, 245
  65, 36–37: 39
  67, 4–5: 47
  68, 6–7: 239
  69: 42, 245
  70, 48–52: 47
  78, 47–48: 39
  80: 46
  83: 42
  83, 28–30: 47
  84, 8–14: 70
  84, 82–87: 58
  91: 74
  91, 2–6: 47
  91, 9–12: 70
  91, 11–12: 58
  92: 43
  92, 32: 177
  93, 29–31: 47
  100, 2–4: 61
  101: 39, 48, 111
  104: 74
  105: 59
  110: 22
  115: 48

LSCG (cont.)
   116: 62, 74
   116, 2–6: 70
   116, 17–20: 14
   116, 27–30: 14
   119: 237
   121: 37
   122, 1–5: 47
   122, 6–8: 47
   124, 17: 239
   127, 7–10: 40
   136: 41
   136, 30–33: 58
   144, A, 5–6: 47
   151A–D: 239
   151B: 27
   154: 239
   168: 65, 106
   173, 110–114: 47
   178: 69

LSS
   3 B: 37
   15, 40–43: 47
   19: 237
   24: 73
   24, 4–7: 48
   43: 46
   45: 177
   49: 39
   50: 73
   53: 73
   69: 36
   75: 38
   75 a: 38
   91: 38
   107: 46
   112: 38
   115: 71
   115, 26–29: 72
   116, A, 7–8: 239
   121, 25–30: 47

   123: 46
   128: 37

Malay and Petzl, *New Religious Texts from Lydia*, 2017
   1, 10–12: 38
   1, 15–20: 40

MAMA
   5, 205: 27

Minon, *Les inscriptions éléennes dialectales*, 2007
   3: 37
   4: 37
   7, 2: 36
   8: 37
   13, 1–5: 35
   19: 37
   20: 47

NGSL²
   14, B, 26–28: 44
   16: 109, 111
   18, 20–23: 15
   20, A: 41
   24: 245
   26: 109, 111
   29: 72

OGIS
   483: 73
   610: 112

OR
   141, 18–21: 47
   144: 218

RO
   1, C, 10–16: 14
   5: 39
   27: 245
   27, 2–6: 13
   37: 205, 237
   59, 36: 14
   59, 50: 14
   62, A, 53–54: 221
   62, A–D: 239

   63: 239
   81: 43

SEG
   1.367: 218
   17.415: 36
   23.326: 182
   23.498: 91
   26.1225: 37
   28.750: 245
   29.379: 177
   32.450: 182
   32.1167: 22
   33.147: 187
   36.371: 210
   37.34: 124
   38.377: 182
   41.182: 12
   42.112: 218
   42.116: 218
   43.568: 73
   45.1363: 241
   46.133: 124, 218
   47.134: 124
   47.1314: 28
   48.1037: 14
   52.104: 124, 218
   53.103: 124
   55.307: 12
   56.950: 73
   56.1017: 41
   56.1018: 218
   68.288: 37

Syll³
   338, 21–25: 60
   729: 7
   914, 7: 57
   914, 33–34: 57
   1025: 221
   1026: 221
   1027: 221
   1157: 42

Index Locorum

Aischines
    1.124.1   198
    1.183   40
    3.18   47
    3.52   43

Aischylos
Cho.
    98   242
Supp.
    508–509   65

Aelianos
VH
    4.9   107

Alkaios
frag.
    346 (Miller)   145

Alkiphron
Epist.
    1.9.3   197
    2.3.11   18
    4.13.9   188

Andokides
On the mysteries
    1.40   217
    1.110–116   15, 49
Against Alkibiades
    4.30   107

Pseudo-Andokides
Alk.
    30.2   176

Antiphanes
frag.
    152.2   73

Antiphon
    5.82   22

Apollodoros
Epit.
    E.66   29, 44

Aristophanes
Ach.
    44   242
    719   16
Eq.
    44   236
    315–318   246
    1233   238
    1311–1312   15
Lys.
    913   73

Pax
    9   244
    879–880   107
    1020   72
Plut.
    812–814   183
    1183–1184   108
Thesm.
    181–182   40
    624   107
    625   40
    655–658   107
    658   107

Aristotle
[*Ath.Pol.*]
    47.4   205
    50.2   244
    56.3   108
Mete.
    349b   75
Pol.
    1322b   47, 108
Rh.
    1365a   184

Athenaios
    4.173b–c   201
    4.170e   73
    4.143a–b   110
    7.297d   182
    7.303b   182
    10.423–427   69
    11.474d   145
    11.481   145
    15.672b–c   25
    15.699d–701b   145

Bacchyl.
    11.110–111   72

Cicero
Leg.
    2.6   200
Tusc.
    5.3.9   176
Verr.
    2.4.94   27

Demosthenes
    19.266   59
    20.158   22
    21.1–2   43
    21.8   43
    21.10   43
    21.11   36, 43
    21.11   36, 43
    21.13–21   43
    21.28   44

    21.43   38
    21.171   240
    21.175–176   43
    21.176   44
    25.23   18
    34.10   240
    35.34   240
    37.59   38
    59.85–86   40
    59.87   40
    59.116   47

Dio Chrysostom
Or.
    8.9–10   1, 177
    9.5   176
    9.22   107
    11.163.15   25

Diodoros Siculus
    5.44.1–5   112
    5.63.3   29
    10.28.1–2   24
    11.25.4   94
    14.109   106, 107
    16.60.1–3   39

Dionysius of Halikarnassos
Ant. Rom.
    12.2.8   240

Dosiades
ap. Ath.
    4.143a–b   110

Epiktetos
Diss.
    1.6.26–28   1, 76, 99

Euripides
Ion
    154–183   72
    226–232   23
    1122–1166   107
    1128–1180   176
IT
    65–66   112

Eustathius
Od.
    2.7   178

Heliodoros
Aeth.
    2.33.7   112

Herodas
    4   23, 30
    4.19–20   25

Herodas (cont.)
4.41–56	27
4.45	23, 30
4.55–56	28

Herodotos
1.9	40
2.64	152
5.71	16
5.72	22, 23, 29, 30, 39
5.119	74
6.81	39
6.133–136	38
6.134–136	29, 31, 44
8.36–37	29

Hesiod
Op.
596	69
757–759	73

Sc.
99	74

Hippokrates
De haemorrhoidibus
4.1.14–16	239

Morb. sacr.
1.99–102	242

Homer
Il.
1.470–471	143
1.595–604	143
2.776	64
6.297–301	26
6.303	25
9.176	143
17.389	243
23.33–34	238

Od.
3.51–53	143
3.338–342	143
6.291	74
9.196–215	112
14.426–430	238
17.365–368	143
21.141–142	143
21.271–273	143

Hyperides
Deliakos
13	187

Iamblichos
VP
12.58	176

Isokrates
4.157	38

Livy
31.14.6–11	14
31.14.7–8	38
42.15–16	36
45.5–6	36

Lykophron
Alex.
1193	72

Lucian
De mort. Peregr.
1	176
19	76

De sacrificiis
13	22

Dial. Mort.
27.2	6

Her.
8	107
62.1	25

Pseudo-Lucian
Erotes
15–16	24

Menander
Dys.
406–418	12
546–549	73

frag.
416, 8–10	194

Menander Rhetor, *Peri Epid.*
1.366–367	176

Pausanias
1.21.7	74
1.22.6	126
1.25.7	24
1.26.5	25
1.27.3	111
1.34.4	73
1.34.5	245
2.1.7	74
2.3.7	111
2.10.4	28
2.13.3	74
2.17.3	30
2.25.6	23
2.27.1	111
2.27.6	88, 111
2.31.2	27
2.35.1	98
2.35.8	27, 30
2.35.11	27
3.22.7	40
3.23.3–5	29, 31, 44
3.25.8	73
3.26.10	24, 27
4.17.4	27
4.31.6	216
5.2.2	35
5.9.3	176
5.12.4	28
5.12.5	25
5.13.2	185
5.13.10	23
5.14.4	27
5.14.5	228
5.15.1–4	104
5.15.2	105
5.15.5	177
5.15.8	228
5.15.10	188
5.17.5	25
5.21.13	36
6.20.3	23, 24, 27
6.23.1	97
7.25.7	30
8.11.4	59
8.23.6	24
8.25.4	52
8.28.1	57
8.37.2	22
8.45.4	52
8.45.5	52
8.47.3	55, 58
8.47.4	55, 59
9.27.6–7	111
9.39.8	178
10.5.13	215
10.23.2–3	29
10.24.4	27
10.32.8–15	195
10.32.12	27, 110, 111
10.32.14–16	177, 195
10.32.15	60, 64, 177
10.34.7	228
10.34.7–8	110, 111
10.35.15	106

Philo
On Sobriety
36	74

Philochoros
frag.
30	17

Philostratos
VA
1.8	112
1.16	112
4.17	176
4.31	112
5.43	97

Pindar
Ol.
5.6	176
10.46–47	106
10.46–48	147

Plato
Leg.
761c	74
945e	112
946d	112

Phdr.
229a–d	242
230b–c	23

Plt.
279e	40

Resp.
327a	206
354a	206

Pliny
HN
17.15	244
23.140	244
36.60.25	134
34.19	30

Plutarch
Ages.
8.1	240

Arist.
7.4	17, 18

De Alex. fort.
340d	74

De stoic. repugn.
22	108
1045a	72, 91

Lys.
23.7	240

Mor.
280b–c	242
657	69
847a	18
1045a	72, 91

Quaest. conv.
716d–e	145

Quaest. Rom.
16	39

Sol.
12	16

Thes.
36.4	15

Pollux
6.34	240
6.103	145
7.25	240
7.193	199
8.20	17, 18
8.114	240
8.123	17, 18
8.124	17, 18
8.141	17, 18

Polyainos
Strat
6.45	106, 107

Polybios
38.11.10–11	206

schol. Ar.
Eq.
44	236
316b	246
1233	238

Pax
879–880	107

schol. Pind.
Ol.
10.46–47	106
10.55b	178
10.55e	178
10.57a–b	178

schol. Plutarch
Thes.
36.4	15

Sophokles
OC
9–20	23

Strabo
8.3.13	184
9.2.33	65
10.5.4	194
12.8.9	112
16.2.23	227

Theokritos
Id.
15.16	177

Theophrastos
Caus. pl
2.6.3	243
3.8.3–4	74
3.9.3	243
3.17.5–6	243

Hist. pl.
3.7.3	245
3.7.4–5	245
3.16.1	245
7.1.8	243
7.3.5	243
7.5.2	243
7.6.2	64

Thucydides
1.126	16
2.13.5	24
3.68.3	105
4.97	39, 69, 111
5.16.3	111
5.49.1–5	35
5.50.1	36
5.50.3–4	36

Velleius Paterculus
1.8.1	176

Vita Aesopi
51	186
54	186

Xenophon
An.
5.3.6–7	217
5.3.7	63
5.3.7–13	63–64
5.3.9	106, 138
5.3.13	218

Ap.
25	24

Hell.
3.2.21	35, 36
3.2.31	194
3.4.3–4	45
6.4.29	70
7.4.32	106
8.4.32	196

Mem.
4.2.2	246
4.2.8	246

Symp
5.2	145

General Index

abaton 37, 105, 110–111, 118, 120–121, 123, 127
accommodation 4, 64, 103–112
   for merchants 64, 65
   for sanctuary personnel 2, 4, 105, 108–109, 110, 111–112
   for visitors 2, 4, 64, 103–112, 118, 154, 176, 194, 195
   for workers 6, 221–230
   guesthouse 85, 87–88, 91, 93, 99, 104, 129–130
   hotel 4, 103–105, 109, 110, 111, 121
   house 4, 105, 110
   huts 65, 106, 107
   katagogion 93, 104, 105, 112, 121, 148, 228, 230
   oikia/oikos 94, 109, 111, 112
   'priests' houses' 108–109, 115, 117–118, 223, 228, 230
   tents 4, 16, 43, 64, 65, 99, 104, 105–108, 115, 135, 147, 176, 177, 186
   See also camping; Olympia; stoas
Acheloos 23
Agesilaos of Sparta 45
agora. *See* market
agoranomos 43, 48, 68, 90, 178, 193, 196, 197, 199
agriculture 12, 58, 62, 109, 162–163, 164, 205–206, 218
Agrigento, Zeus sanctuary 94, 96
Aigeira
   naiskoi 125, 135
   'Solon Building' (guesthouse) 129–130, 135
Aigina
   Aphaia sanctuary 25, 27, 118, 149–151
   Kolonna, West Complex 140, 141, 154
Aliakmon River 75
Alkibiades 107, 176
Alpheios River 54–55, 75, 76, 91
alsos 63, 64, 74, 110
   See also grove
altar 1, 2, 13, 15, 44–45
   accessibility of 23
   animal sacrifice on 5, 11, 13, 24, 44–45, 65, 72, 158–160, 161–162, 164–167, 170, 172, 187
   anointment of 72
   blood on 72
   cleaning around/of 72, 209
   location of 24, 25, 27
   refurbishment of 72, 209, 219
   supplication at 16, 49
   urination on 72–73, 108
   wine offerings at 141, 142, 145
   zooarchaeological remains from 5, 158–159, 163–167, 172, 187
Amarynthos (Euboia) 14, 197
Amphiareion. *See* Oropos
Amyklaion 187, 217

Andania regulations 28, 31, 48, 59, 108, 196, 197
   cutting wood in the sanctuary grove 14
   female attire 42
   shoes worn in the sanctuary 245, 246
   suppliants 16
   temporary boundaries 18, 43, 106, 107
   tents 64, 65, 106, 107
   uninitiated forbidden entry 39
   use of space 16, 43, 106, 195
   water 68, 74, 90–91
   weights and measures 181, 199
andreion 110
andron 115, 124–125, 130, 134, 135, 138–139, 146–147, 148, 149
animals 52, 58, 62, 108, 158–172, 196
   age of 162, 163, 164–165, 171, 172, 185, 187
   bones of 2, 142, 165, 166, 170, 184–185, 187
   care of 218, 219
   cleaning of 73, 77
   confiscation of 57–58, 59, 60
   for labor 6, 60, 69, 70, 165, 171
   hides of 159, 165, 195, 236–246
   husbandry 162–163, 164, 172
   origin of 5, 7, 160–161, 163, 187
   sacred 70, 187
   sacrificial 5, 6, 59, 60, 97, 163, 164, 171, 172, 185, 193, 208, 245
   sale of. *See* markets: livestock
   size of 71, 171, 172, 173, 184–185
   skins of 6, 45, 177, 186, 208, 235–240, 242, 243, 245, 246
   supply of 7, 161, 162–163, 164, 165, 169, 171, 172, 187, 195
   transhumance 60–61, 162
   transport of 160–161, 187
   water for 2, 69–70, 76, 77, 98, 196
   wild 167, 187
   See also boar; bull; cattle; cow; deer; dining: debris, donkey; excrement; goat; grazing; horse; leather; markets: livestock; oxen; sacrifice; pig; sheep; tanning; zooarchaeological remains
Antigonos Monophthalmos 209–210
Antikyra 27
Apollonios of Tyana 112
architect 24, 115, 129, 198, 210, 215, 218
architheoros 211, 213
archons/*archontes* 14, 17, 43, 130–131, 177, 212
Argive Heraion 39, 118, 120, 133, 179, 217
   West Building 118, 120, 133
Argos 30, 36, 178, 184, 215
argyroskopos 48
Arkadia 56, 60–61
artamoi 240, 241
   See also butcher; cook
artisans. *See* craftsmen; sculptors; workers
asebeia 39, 212

ash 72, 91, 142, 184, 217, 200, 223
   ash altar 23
astynomoi 46, 72, 90, 244
asylum 3, 10, 15–16, 17, 65, 110, 111, 200, 201
ateleia 197, 200–201, 221
Athens 12, 43, 164, 194, 203–204, 206
   Agora 17–18, 163, 198
      bronzeworking 216, 221
      court 17
      Eleusinion 15, 38, 47, 49
      Hephaisteion 74, 216
      House of Mikion and Menon 221
      House of Simon 221
      Klepsydra 75
      South Stoa I 130–131, 146
      Stoa Basileios 11, 17
      Street of the Marbleworkers 221
   Akropolis 23, 29, 30, 37, 39, 133
      Erechtheion 25, 27, 215
      'Hekatompedon inscription' (*IG* I³ 4) 41
      Northwest Building 126
      Parthenon 23, 25, 133
      pottery 144
      Propylaia 126–127
         Pinakotheke 115, 126, 133, 149
      workshops 216
   Aphrodite 12, 72, 219
   Asklepieion 26, 88, 122–123, 129, 152, 219
   Delos and 194, 204, 208
   dermatikon funds 6, 158–159, 165–166, 236–246
   Dionysia 43
   Dipoleia 208
   Hephaisteia 29, 31, 43
   Herakles sanctuary (Ilissos River) 6, 242
   Kerameikos, Pompeion 115, 118
   Panathenaia 11, 70, 75, 115, 126, 208, 240
   Pan, Nymphs, and Acheloos shrine 242
   Theseion 15
   zooarchaeological remains from 160, 164, 166, 171–172
attire. *See* dress
Aulis 27, 45, 104

bakers. *See* baking
baking 41, 71, 170, 176, 179, 208
bankers 7, 193
banqueting 4, 5, 54, 60, 65, 120, 124, 138, 139, 143, 145, 152, 154, 159, 171
   groups 154, 207, 208
   location of 148, 152, 154
   sacrificial 139, 141, 142, 145, 148, 152, 153, 187
   See also dining; *orgeones*; wine
banqueting structures and locations 4, 83, 88, 94, 110, 115–135, 139, 146–153, 154, 206
   See also *andreion*; *andron*; *hestiatorion*; Labraunda

GENERAL INDEX

bathing   4, 77, 81, 82, 85, 90, 92–94, 98–99, 130
bath   73–74, 85, 88–89, 90, 92–94, 110
bench   4, 26, 83, 92, 115, 117, 118, 120, 121, 124–125, 128, 130, 131, 132–133, 134, 149
blood   22, 36, 40, 72, 91, 200, 203, 207
boar   207, 208
boonai   240–241
boundaries   16–18, 28, 31, 36, 121, 241
   lustral basin   28, 29, 31, 98, 148–151, 241
      See also *perirrhanterion*
   temenos   23, 36, 37, 59, 122–123, 147, 149, 230
   temporary   3, 16–18, 106, 107, 177
   walls   23, 24–25, 37–38, 66, 149, 151
      See also *horoi*; *perischoinisma*
bovine. See bull; cattle; cow; oxen
Brauron, Artemis sanctuary   110, 123–124, 133, 152
brazier   134, 145
bread   63, 71, 73, 138, 158, 181, 199
bronzeworking   216, 218, 221, 226
building activity/construction   11, 62, 68, 70, 212–213, 215
bull   163, 208, 243
butcher   185, 186, 219, 240, 241
butchering   5, 147, 158, 165–166, 171–172, 185

calendar   11, 15, 56, 62, 69, 163, 186, 201, 207, 208, 211
camping   17, 46, 65, 104, 105–108, 109, 110, 111, 112, 176, 195
      See also accommodation: tents
cart   6, 61–62, 64, 70, 108
cattle   27, 41, 58, 59, 61, 70, 71, 75, 91, 161–162, 164, 165, 169, 171–172, 187, 195, 208, 211, 238, 239, 240
      See also bull; cow; oxen
cephalopod. See fish
ceramicist   7, 218, 219, 221
Christians   3, 104, 105, 201, 246
chryselephantine   24, 25, 28, 216, 228
cistern   75–77, 94, 96, 116, 134
cleaning   4, 7, 48, 62, 71–73, 81, 90, 91, 110, 134, 242–243, 244
      See also altars: cleaning of; purification; washing
clothes. See dress
coin   12, 48, 142, 178
cooking   5, 7, 177, 187
   boiling   71, 75, 141, 166, 170, 172, 179, 183
   facilities   73, 115, 118, 121, 124, 134, 170, 184, 241
   fire   7, 166
   grilling   170
   implements   73, 147, 223, 185, 186
   roasting   170, 207, 238
   steaming   183
   stewing   68, 166, 170, 172, 179, 183
   ware   2, 141, 143, 179, 182, 183, 185
      See also butcher; fireplace food; hearth; *mageiros*; meat; water: cooking with
cook   240

Corinth   160, 163, 166, 169, 179, 215
   Apollo temple   72
   Asklepieion   74, 88, 118–120, 129, 132, 134
   Demeter and Kore sanctuary   11, 17, 73, 76–77, 133, 145, 152–153, 162–163, 169–170, 179, 182, 196
   Peirene fountain   75, 134
   South Stoa   109, 131–133, 134, 230
   zooarchaeological remains   160, 162, 169–171, 172–173, 179, 182
coroplast. See ceramicist
couch. See bench; *kline*
cow   27, 61, 70, 71
craftsmen   5, 7, 90, 171, 194, 218, 221
   itinerant   6, 194, 215
   sculptors   7, 215, 219
      See also workers
Crete   110, 143
Crimea, Nymphaion   81, 90
curtains   28, 107, 148

damiourgoi   47, 57
debtors   43, 198, 206, 212
dedications. See votives
deer   54, 167–168
defecation   4, 73, 81, 82–83, 89–91, 98, 99
deipnon   138–139, 145, 146
Delos   46, 104, 116, 159, 194, 201, 203–204, 215
   Antigoneia   210
   Aphrodision   125, 134, 135
   Apollo sanctuary   111, 194, 198, 244
   Archegetes sanctuary   39, 209, 219
   Asklepieion   218
   Delia   207
   Dionysia, Phallophoria   220
   Dionysos altar   91
   Eileithyia   71, 207–208, 219
   Inopos reservoir   73
   Leto sanctuary   73, 91, 209, 219
   maintenance and repairs   135, 208–211, 215, 219
   Minoe Spring   73
   pandokeion   104
   Poseidoniasts of Berytos   208
   Posideia   69, 71, 75, 207–208, 219
   Poulydamas shrine   210, 215, 219
   sacred accounts and regulations   5–6, 46, 69–70, 73, 133, 184, 203–213, 219, 239
   Thesmophorion   209, 219
   xenon   104
      See also Athens: Delos and
Delphi   36, 39, 65, 77, 85, 110, 112, 194, 208, 215, 218, 221
   Amphictyony of   39, 46, 106–107, 194, 215
   Apollo sanctuary   23, 29, 37, 135
   Apollo temple   23, 27, 215
   Attalid stoa   46, 106, 108
   baths   88, 93
   maintenance and repairs   220, 221
   market   177
   Marmaria sanctuary   118, 151
   oracle   11, 194
   pandokeion   104

Pythia festival   70, 220
Pythian games   6
regulations   14, 43, 62, 70, 106, 108, 188, 220, 221
sacred herds   60, 70
stadion   44, 188–189
town surrounding sanctuary   1, 221
weights   179
zooarchaeological remains from   178–179
Demeter   38, 39, 42, 46, 168
Demosthenes   43, 44
dermatikon funds. See Athens
dining   17, 46, 106, 133, 141, 145, 187
   debris   5, 147, 158, 159–171, 172, 182, 187
   ware and implements   73, 140, 141–142, 179, 182, 183, 185, 188
      See also banqueting; *deipnon*
dining structures and locations   2, 4, 7, 17, 92, 93, 99, 104, 109, 110, 115–135, 139, 146–154, 158, 159, 228, 230
      See also *andron*; Athens: Akropolis: Propylaia: Pinakotheke; banqueting structures and locations; *Festwiesen*; *hestiatorion*; *naiskos*; stoas
Dion, Demeter sanctuary   181, 183, 184, 185, 187
Dionysios I of Syracuse   106, 107
dog   167–168, 187
donkey   41, 69
dress   22, 28, 29, 31, 40, 64, 73, 195, 218, 242
drinking   4–5, 44, 68–70, 77, 131, 132, 138–154
   vessels   73, 132, 138, 140–142, 143, 144, 145, 146, 149, 153, 154, 176, 179, 182, 187–188, 228
      See also fountain; spring; *symposion*; water: drinking; wells; wine
drunkenness   44, 138, 152, 188
dung. See excrement

economies of scale, and diseconomies of scale   204, 212
ekecheiria (truce)   6, 35, 37, 39
Eleusis, Demeter and Kore sanctuary   11, 14, 23, 37, 39, 85, 93, 152, 177, 188
   House of the Kerykes   109
   Mysteries of   15, 17, 37, 38, 43, 178, 181, 182
Elis   1, 35–36, 37, 194
enkoimeterion   110, 118, 120, 122
Ephesos   47, 63, 178, 182, 184, 185, 217
Epidauros, Asklepieion   49, 85, 88, 91, 105, 120, 148, 149, 216, 220
   Asklepios temple   25, 148, 220
   Banquet Building (Gymnasion)   120, 133, 148
   baths   74, 88, 89, 93
   katagogion   93, 105, 118, 121, 148, 154
   latrines   88, 89, 110
   propylon   76, 77
   Stoa of Kotys   88, 90
   Tholos   105, 215
   well   76–77
Epiktetos   99
epimeletes   48, 71, 108, 241

epimenioi   47
epinician poetry   7
equine   60, 167–168
   See also donkey; horse; mule
eranos loans. *See* loans
Eretria   47, 58, 144–145, 184, 185, 194–195, 216
   Aire Sacrificielle   140
   Apollo Daphnephoros sanctuary   144, 188, 217
   Artemis Amarysia sanctuary   177, 195
   Artemisia   43, 194
eukosmia (in sanctuaries)   41, 48, 197, 200, 201
Eumenes II, king of Pergamon   36
Evander of Crete   36, 37
excrement   7, 41, 62, 64, 65, 72, 81, 82, 85, 88, 90, 91, 98, 99
   as fertilizer   7, 72, 83, 90, 91, 203, 244
   for tanning   90, 243, 244

fair. *See* markets
farming. *See* agriculture
feasting. *See* banqueting
feces. *See* excrement
fertilizer. *See* excrement: as fertilizer
festivals   5, 10, 76, 77, 91, 176, 189, 194, 212
   ancient   10–18, 24, 28–30, 31, 35–37, 40–43, 46–47, 48, 49, 52–54, 56–65, 69–71, 75, 77, 81–82, 98–99, 105–108, 126, 140, 154, 176, 178, 186, 189, 194–198, 201, 207–208, 210, 217, 219–220, 236, 245
   modern   82, 91, 92, 99, 106, 107–108
   personnel costs   208
   recurring expenses   194, 207–208, 220
   supplies and equipment   208, 219
Festwiesen   4, 65–66, 91, 106, 107, 147
   See also Olympia: *Festwiese*
fines   13–14, 16, 35–36, 37, 40, 41–42, 43, 44, 45–46, 47–48, 49, 58, 59, 61, 73, 91, 181, 196, 212
fire   7, 22, 38, 41, 46, 52, 61, 70, 107–108, 111, 115, 147, 166, 218
   regulations concerning   38, 41, 46, 51, 52, 54, 107–108, 111
   See also fireplace; hearth
fireplace   145
fish   5, 166, 181–184
   dried   5, 177, 184
   price of   182, 185
   sacrifice of   182
   transport of   184
fishing equipment   183–184
fishmonger. *See* merchant
food   2, 4, 5, 7, 73, 91, 99, 139, 158, 176–177, 178, 194, 196, 218, 219
   cereals and grain   64, 166, 178, 179, 181
   fruits and vegetables   5, 158, 166, 178–179, 181
   legumes   178, 181
   See also bread; cooking; fish; market; meat; sacrifice; votives: food; wine

foreigners   29, 39, 43, 45, 48, 58, 60, 62, 107, 111
fountain   55, 64, 70, 73, 75, 76, 85, 120, 123, 130
fowl, domestic   166
fraud. *See* market: fraud in
fuller   241

games   1, 6, 11, 12, 22, 25, 35, 36, 39, 59, 65, 69, 76, 77, 89–90, 91, 92, 93, 97–99, 103, 104, 131, 161, 166, 176, 189, 208, 217, 223
   See also Delphi: Pythian games; Isthmia: games; Nemea: games; Olympia: Olympic games
garbage   7, 106, 108
garden   4, 62, 68
goat   13, 58, 60, 61, 64, 69, 70, 71, 161–164, 165, 166, 171, 187, 236
grazing   13, 52, 57–61, 62, 70, 74, 162, 197, 218
grove   14, 16, 57, 74
   See also alsos; tree
guard   17, 23, 42, 91, 108
   See also sanctuary: policing
guesthouse. *See* accommodation
guide   6, 7
gymnasion   2, 94, 97
gynaikonomos   28, 31, 40, 42

Halaesa (Alesa, Sicily)   6, 215, 241
hare   54, 166
healing   4, 11, 13, 68, 73–74, 76, 93, 105, 245
   See also incubation
hearth   27, 118, 120, 133–134, 223
heating   7, 92, 145
   See also hearth
hecatomb   69–70, 75, 187
Hekatomnids of Karia   124
Heraklea (Lucania)   222
Herakles   12, 27, 145, 147, 205
   See also Athens: Herakles sanctuary
herd   60, 61, 64, 69, 162, 165, 169, 170, 187
   See also Delphi: sacred herd
herding   163, 165, 171, 172
Hermione   27, 30, 97–98
   Demeter Chthonia sanctuary   27, 30
Herod the Great   193
Herodotos   25
hero   12, 111, 154, 163, 166, 188, 205, 228
   Egretes sanctuary, Athens   74, 111, 205
hestiatorion   2, 4, 73, 77, 110, 115–116, 126, 139, 228, 230
   See also banqueting structures and locations; dining structures and locations
hetaira   7, 40
hide. *See* animals: hides of; tanning
hieroi   28, 43, 177, 195, 196
hieromnemon   47, 48, 54, 57, 58, 61–62
hieron   22, 29, 56, 57, 63, 111, 205, 210, 246
Hieron II of Syracuse   97
hieropoioi   13, 29, 31, 41, 42, 43, 47, 195, 203, 204, 209, 210, 212, 219, 240

hierosylia   29
hierothytes   54, 57, 59
holocaust. *See* sacrifice
horoi   17, 23, 35, 37
horse   41, 60, 61, 69, 187
hosios   11–12, 26, 239
hostel. *See* accommodation
hotel. *See* accommodation
house. *See* accommodation
hygiene   81, 82, 83

Ialysos (Rhodes), Alektrona sanctuary   41, 58, 60, 239
Iasos   46
Ilion. *See* Troy
Ilissos River (Athens)   6, 23, 29, 242, 243
incubation   13, 109, 120, 121, 129, 152
   See also enkoimeterion; healing
India   4, 82, 91, 92, 99
   Allahabad, Kumbh Mela pilgrimage   82, 92
   Pandharpur, Ashadi Ekadasi festival   82, 92
informers   3, 13–14, 29, 43, 44, 45, 48–49, 91
initiation   11, 17
inphorbismos   54, 57–58
Isthmia, Poseidon sanctuary   23, 75, 77, 85, 91, 94, 107, 163
   baths   88, 93, 94
   bronzeworking   216
   cistern   75, 76
   games   6, 131
   Large Circular Pit   75
   pool   94, 97, 98

Jerusalem, temple   193

Kalapodi   26, 143, 144, 163–164, 167, 176, 179, 217
Kalaureia, Poseidon sanctuary   76, 151–152, 182, 183–184
kapeleia   104, 171, 196, 198–200, 201
kapeloi   5, 15, 65, 177, 181, 189, 196, 198, 199–201
Kassope   163, 171
Kastabos, Hemithea sanctuary   29, 68
katadesmoi   199–200
katagogion. *See* accommodation
katharmata   242–243
   See also purification
Keos   73
key, temple   26
kiln   6, 215, 216, 223
Kladeos River   91, 94
Kleomenes of Sparta   23, 29, 39
Kleon of Athens   242, 245
kline   4, 27, 94, 110, 116–117, 118, 120, 124–126, 130–131, 132–133, 134, 146, 148, 149
   See also bench
Knidos, Dionysos sanctuary   111, 188
koimeterion. *See* enkoimeterion

koprologos 90, 244
kopros. *See* excrement
Korope 42, 47, 58
Kos, Asklepieion 12, 23, 26, 44, 45, 72, 73, 85, 93, 221
krater 138–139, 140, 141, 142–145, 153, 176
 See also drinking; *symposion*; water: wine and
kreanomia 208
kreodaites 240
kreokopos 240, 241
kreopolia 240
kreourgos 241

laborers. *See* craftsmen; workers
Labraunda, Zeus sanctuary 17, 106, 109, 124–125, 134, 152, 193
 andrones 124–125, 134
lamp 145–146, 154
land 1, 3–4, 13, 14, 22, 46, 48, 52, 62–63, 64–65, 187, 194, 213, 218, 221, 241
 See also lease: of land; Tegea: Alea (pasture)
Laodikeia-by-the-Sea 46
latrine 2, 4, 82–89, 92, 98, 99, 115, 131, 132
 See also toilet
lease
 guarantors 211
 of buildings 104, 109, 154, 198, 200–201, 210
 of land 5, 198
 of sacred property 60, 74, 198, 204–206, 207, 210, 218
leather 6, 106, 208, 236, 237, 239, 243–246
 See also tanning
libation 140–141, 142, 188
Lissos (Crete), Asklepieion 127–129, 239, 245
livestock. *See* animals; bull; cattle; cow; goat; horse; pig; oxen; sheep
loans 5, 193, 203, 206, 207, 210, 211, 212
lodging. *See* accommodation
Lourdes 103, 105
Lousoi, Artemis sanctuary 70, 163, 184
Lucian 76, 77, 107, 108, 176
lustral basin 23, 106
 See also perirrhanterion

mageireion/mageirikon 241
mageiros 41, 185, 186, 240
 See also butcher
Magnesia-on-the-Maeander, Artemis sanctuary 85, 197–198
manure. *See* excrement
marbleworking 6, 63, 215, 216
 See also Athens: Agora: Street of the Marbleworkers
markets 2, 5, 7, 16, 62, 64, 110, 176–189, 193–201
 city and sanctuary 177, 194–198, 201
 economic impact of 189, 193, 197
 fraud in 178, 197, 198

liquids 187–188
livestock 187, 193, 194, 195–196
 location of 62, 65, 177, 178, 193, 195, 196, 198
 meat 171, 187
 metals 195
 offerings 194
 prices 176, 177, 197
 regulations of 5, 15, 64, 176, 181, 182, 187, 193–195, 196–197, 201
 structures (physical) 17, 177–178, 196, 198
 timing of 62, 176, 178, 189, 196
 weights and measures 5, 43, 178, 179–181, 196
 See also agoranomos; fish; *kapeleia*; meat; slaves: sale of
Marmarini regulation 72, 145
Marseilles Sacrificial Fee 185
Maussollos. *See* Hekatomnids of Karia
meat 158–173
 consumption of 139, 158–159, 160, 173, 184, 187
 cooking 160, 165, 187
 See also cooking; sacrifice: meat
Mecca 103, 105
Menander 194
merchants 1, 31, 64, 65, 178, 189, 193, 196, 197, 208
 See also kapeloi
Messene 42–43, 88–89, 164
metalworking 6, 211, 216, 219, 227
 See also bronzeworking
metoikoi 186
Miletos, Thesmophorion 29, 38, 39, 44
Miltiades 29, 31, 38, 39, 40, 44
Mina, tent city 103
mollusks. *See* fish
money changing 7, 193
Mounychia, Artemis sanctuary 143–144
Mt. Hymettos, Zeus sanctuary 143–144
Mt. Parnes, Zeus sanctuary 143–144
mule 58, 60
murex shell 226, 228
mystai 177

naiskos 115, 125–126
naopoios. *See* neopoies
Nemea, Zeus sanctuary 74, 93, 164
 bath 77, 93, 166
 Dining Room 166
 Heroon of Opheltes 166, 169, 178, 185, 188
 houses 222–223
 Nemean games 6, 69, 93, 166
 Oikoi 76, 105, 217
 stadion 69
 temple 105
 wells 76, 77
 workshops 216, 223
 Xenon 76, 93, 105, 166, 223
 zooarchaeological evidence from 158, 164, 166–169, 171, 172

neokoros 13, 30, 35, 39, 40, 42, 45, 48, 111
neopoies 40, 46, 47, 198, 199, 215
nomophylakes 42, 47
norms, ritual/sacred laws 1, 3, 11, 22, 31, 35, 37, 40, 44, 48, 49, 69, 70, 72, 74, 90, 164, 177, 185–186, 197, 201, 237
nymphs 23, 68, 76, 90, 96, 242

oathtaking 12, 48
odor 40, 83, 99, 108, 226, 241, 242, 243, 244
offering. *See* votives
oikia/oikos. *See* accommodation
oil 145, 188, 221, 242
Olympia, Zeus sanctuary 1, 23, 35, 36, 37, 42, 77, 85, 143, 147, 152, 176, 188, 194, 196, 217, 218
 agora 177
 Altis 23, 147
 baths 85, 88, 92, 93, 98, 99
 Eileithyia temple 27
 Festwiese 65, 99, 106, 107, 147
 Heraion 25
 Kypselos chest 25
 latrines 85, 87–88, 99
 Leonidaion 7, 87–88, 92, 97, 104–105, 230
 maintenance and repairs 220
 Olympic games 1, 6, 11, 25, 36, 39, 65, 69, 76, 77, 89–90, 91, 92, 93, 97–98, 99, 103
 Palaistra 91, 92, 93, 106
 pool 94–96, 97–98
 South Hall 97, 216
 Southeast area/complex 97, 179, 196, 216
 Stadion 69, 76
 stoas 91, 93, 97
 Theokoleon 92, 228
 weights and measures 179
 wells 76, 77, 99
 workshops 216
 Zeus altar 27, 36
 Zeus statue (Pheidian) 228
 Zeus temple 25, 27, 28, 220
Olynthos 104, 221, 225
oracle 42, 47, 104
 See also Delphi: oracle
orchard 64, 74
orgeones 205–207
Oropos (settlement) 161, 163, 227–228
 Amphiareion 12, 13, 27, 30, 42, 44–45, 73, 74, 108, 179, 198, 245
ostracism 17–18
oxen 58, 64, 69–70, 71, 171, 208, 221, 236, 246

Pan 12, 76, 242
Panathenaia. *See* Athens: Panathenaia
pandokeion 104
parasitoi 240, 241
pasture. *See* grazing
Patara, Zeus Labraundos sanctuary 111
Pausanias 7, 25, 27, 41, 73, 104, 228
penalty. *See* fines; punishment
Perachora, Heraion 115–116, 120, 121, 132–133, 134

Pergamon   73, 83, 219
    See also Eumenes II
peribolos. *See* boundaries: walls
perichoros   54, 59
perirrhanterion   24
perischoinisma   17–18
Perseus, king of Macedon   36
Philip, king of Macedon   105
pigeon   72, 203, 243
piglet   168, 203, 208, 238
pigs   58, 60–61, 69, 70, 71, 161, 162, 164, 165, 166, 168, 170, 171, 238, 239
pigskin   60, 238–239
    see also animals: skins of; leather; tanning
plants. *See* garden; tanning
Plataiai, Hera sanctuary, *katagogion*   105
Plato   7, 74, 107, 154, 242
Pleistoanax of Sparta   111
polis, sanctuary controlled by   41, 42, 43, 45, 46, 47–49, 57, 61, 62, 91, 193–194, 196–197, 200, 201
pollution (environmental)   73, 82, 242–243
pollution (*miasma*)   22, 28, 36, 37, 81, 91, 110, 111, 241–243
pools   92, 93, 94–98
postholes   17, 18, 56, 106, 115, 196
potter. *See* ceramicist
praton. *See* sacrifice: meat
prayer   13, 27, 30, 45
Priene   30, 70, 83, 217
    Athena sanctuary   73
    Demeter sanctuary   70
priestesses   23, 26, 27, 44, 58
    perquisites for   45, 237
    punishment of   45–46
    residence of   108–109
    responsibilities of   11–12, 26, 29, 46
    statues of   3, 30–31
priests   4, 11, 12, 13, 15, 24, 26, 35, 46, 49, 52, 57, 58, 61, 107, 109, 135, 148, 193, 217
    absence of   13, 30, 42, 44–45, 47, 108
    accountability of   47, 48
    herd belonging to   58–59
    perquisites for   13, 41, 45, 141, 159, 165, 186, 237–238, 240, 245
    punishment of   41, 45, 46, 47
    responsibilities of   2, 10, 13, 16, 18, 26, 41, 42, 44–45, 46, 47–48, 110, 219, 240
    statues of   30, 31
    See also accommodation: 'priests' houses'
privacy   18, 115, 128, 148
probole   43
processions   3, 22, 24, 27, 72, 115, 208
    management of   14, 29, 43, 195
prostitution   7, 200
punishment   13, 35, 36, 38–39, 40, 41–42, 43, 44, 46, 47, 48, 58, 178, 207
    physical   36, 38–39, 40, 42, 43, 57–58, 181
    See also fines; priestesses: punishment of; priests: punishment of
purification   4, 22, 35, 38, 40, 41, 68, 72–73, 77, 81, 91, 110, 167, 203, 209
    See also cleaning; washing

purity/impurity   29, 39, 43, 242–243
    regulations concerning   40, 41, 90, 91, 111, 106, 193, 239
    See also pollution: *miasma*

reservoir. *See* water: reservoir
rhabdophoros   28, 31, 43, 48
rhabdouchos   35, 36, 37, 42
Rheneia   204, 211
rhetorician   7, 189
Roman/Romans   4, 7, 11, 36, 75, 77, 82, 83, 85, 88, 92, 93, 94, 98–99, 105, 131, 134, 170, 171, 182, 184, 201, 208, 216
Roskilde music festival (Denmark)   106–108

sacrifice, animal   1, 2, 10, 11, 18, 23, 24, 27, 41, 44–45, 57, 70, 72, 158–173, 193, 205, 206, 208
    by-products of   5, 6, 158–159, 195, 236–245
    costs of   41, 203, 207–208, 209, 210, 219, 228
    exclusion from   39, 40, 45
    holocaust   141, 158
    in the absence of an official   13, 44, 45, 47, 108
    invalid   45
    meal   71, 139–140, 141, 142, 146
    meat, sacrificial   77, 138, 142, 148, 159, 171, 184, 186, 187, 201, 244, 245
        consumption of   2, 4, 5, 106, 141, 142, 146, 159, 170–171, 184, 185, 187
        cooking of   2, 70–71, 77, 141, 170, 185, 186, 187
        distribution of   5, 70, 148, 152–153, 184, 185–186, 208, 239, 245
        perquisite   45, 159, 165, 186
        sale of   171, 185–187, 195, 201
        supplemental   70, 141, 165, 167, 171, 235
        weight of portions   71, 185–186
    private   12, 14–15, 18, 23, 41, 48, 60, 71, 77, 108, 168, 206–207, 237
    regulations concerning   5, 10, 11, 12, 13, 14, 15, 22, 35–37, 39, 40, 42, 44–46, 47, 57, 63–64, 72, 81, 90–91, 107, 185–186, 197
    See also norms, ritual/sacred laws
    See also animals: sacrificial; *deipnon*; fish; tanning; wood: for sacrifice
sacrilege. *See asebeia*; *hierosylia*
Salaminioi of Attika   205–206
Samos, Heraion   16, 17, 76, 107, 148, 149, 177, 179, 181
    kapeloi regulation   5, 15, 196, 198–201
Samothrace   4, 11, 35, 36, 37, 38, 85, 91
sanctuary
    access to   3, 22–24, 28, 31, 37–38, 140
    activities forbidden in   111, 152
    as economic operation   5–6, 7, 189, 193–194, 196–198, 201, 203–213, 236
    boundaries of   36, 37–38, 111, 123, 149, 230
    cleaning of   71–73

construction projects in   11, 62–63, 68, 70, 97, 193, 194, 197–198, 215, 220
    exclusion from   3, 35, 36, 37–41, 43, 48, 58, 59, 60
    expenses of   203–213
    extra-urban   4, 41, 82, 85, 89, 91, 92, 97, 194, 195, 218, 221
    finances of   2, 5–6, 193, 194, 203–213
    living/staying in   4, 5, 30, 39, 41, 60–61, 62, 64, 76–77, 81, 82, 103–112, 118, 200, 228, 230
        See also incubation; sleeping in sanctuaries
    maintenance and repairs   2, 5, 6, 11, 18, 72, 82, 98, 112, 124, 135, 194, 207, 209–210, 211, 215, 218–220, 230
    management   1, 2, 3, 4, 7, 10, 13–14, 18, 35, 61, 64, 65, 99, 103, 106, 108, 112, 193, 194, 200, 204, 212
    officials   3, 6, 10, 13–14, 18, 24, 28–29, 31, 35–49, 81, 91, 93, 96, 103, 108, 166, 193, 203–204, 208, 217, 218, 221, 223, 240
    Panhellenic   1, 11, 97, 98, 148, 154, 176, 207, 210
    policing of   2, 3, 7, 13, 18, 28–31, 35–49, 91, 108, 111, 196, 197, 201
    revenues of   2, 5, 6, 7, 64, 104, 193, 194, 198, 201, 204–210, 211–212, 213, 239, 244
    sack of   29
    travel to   3, 6, 7, 11, 13, 22, 103, 176, 177, 189
    warfare in   196
    weddings in   12
    workshops in   6, 215–217, 219
    See also accommodation; festival; markets; sacrifice, animal; *temenos*
sanitation   2, 4, 81–99
sculptors. *See* craftsmen: sculptors
sex (activity)   12, 22, 24, 38, 40, 91, 111, 121, 146, 152
sex   6, 22, 29, 40, 81, 82, 83
sheep   23, 58, 60, 61, 64, 69, 70, 71, 160–164, 165, 166, 168–169, 171, 172, 186, 187, 208, 236
shellfish. *See* fish
shoes   60, 178, 218, 239, 245–246
shops. *See kapeleia*
shopkeepers. *See kapeloi*
signs   3, 35, 38, 43, 91
singing   17, 26–27, 29
Skillous   60
    Artemis Ephesia sanctuary   63–64, 106
skins. *See* animals: hides of; animals: skins of
slaves   2, 15–16, 29, 40, 43, 73, 91, 107, 108, 110, 111, 181, 197, 200, 213, 239
    manumission of   7
    sale of   7, 16, 177, 195, 196
sleeping in sanctuaries   7, 29, 93, 105, 106, 107, 109–111, 124, 129, 154, 188, 228, 230
    in stoas   124, 131
    See also incubation
smith. *See* bronze working
Sokrates   23, 29, 246

Sounion   17, 44, 151
   Athena sanctuary   17, 28
   Men   40, 44
   Nymphs   69
   Poseidon sanctuary   151
Sparta/Spartans   35–37, 39, 76, 194
   Apollo Karneios festival   108
   Menelaion   76
sponde. *See* libation
spondophoroi   6
spring   58, 69, 70, 73, 75, 76, 94, 120, 123, 127, 130, 176
   See also Athens: Akropolis: Klepsydra; Corinth: Peirene Spring; Delos: Minoe Spring
statues   2, 24, 16, 71–72, 208, 210, 219
   cult   3, 24, 25, 26, 27, 28, 31, 64, 68, 72, 77, 215, 218
   See also priestesses: statues of; priests: statues of; votives: sculpture
stele   35, 64, 91, 177, 184, 206, 209
stoas   2, 46, 91, 104, 105, 109–110, 111, 115, 121–123, 124, 131, 135, 148, 152, 154, 198
stone working   211, 216, 218, 219, 223
   See also marbleworking
supplication. *See* asylum
swimming   97–98
Symi (Crete), Hermes and Aphrodite sanctuary   184, 217
symposion   5, 133, 134, 138–154
   See also drinking; *klinai*; krater; wine
Syracuse   25, 94, 97, 98
syssitia   110, 130

table
   dining   115, 116, 117, 120, 123, 132–133, 181
   offering   26, 27, 44, 141–142
tanning   6, 90, 159, 236–246
   See also animals, skins of; leather
tax   46, 182, 193, 194–195, 197, 201, 211, 221, 240
   exemption (*ateleia*)   197, 200, 201, 221
Tegea, Alea Athena sanctuary   4, 52–66
   Alea (pasture area)   57, 58–62, 65–66
   regulations concerning the *panegyris*   52–66
temenos   4, 5, 22, 23–24, 28, 29, 31, 38, 44, 46, 57, 59, 64–65, 70, 74, 75, 82, 93, 94, 103, 105, 110–112, 112, 123, 147, 148–149, 152, 154, 194, 198, 205, 206, 232, 241
   See also boundaries; sanctuary
temple   1, 2, 3, 4, 63–64, 104, 135, 185, 193, 217, 241
   access to   22, 23–28, 29, 38, 40
   protection of   28–31, 38, 40
   repairs to   6, 215, 220
tents. *See* accommodation
textiles   28, 107, 177, 221, 226, 228
Thasos   13, 22, 36, 41, 47–48, 187, 218, 239
theft   28, 31, 43, 49
Theophrastos   243, 245

theoxenia   27, 145, 159
thesauros   2, 3, 12, 37, 42, 109, 187, 220
Thesmophoria   40, 41, 170
Thesmophorion   29, 38, 39, 41, 46
   Delos   209, 219
   Eretria   183
   Paros   29, 38–39, 44
   Piraeus   41, 46
thesmothetai   17, 130–131
Thorikos   11, 69, 186–187
thysia. *See* sacrifice
timber. *See* wood
Tithorea (Phokis), Isis festival   60, 64, 110, 177, 195, 196
toilet   4, 81, 82, 83, 85, 92, 98, 99
   See also latrine
tools   6, 215, 216–217, 221, 218
trade. *See* markets
trapeza. *See* table
trash. *See* garbage
treasurer   41, 46, 47, 48
treasury. *See thesauros*
trees   23, 54, 57, 74, 77, 97, 98, 108, 111, 205
   oak   54, 240, 245
   olive   54, 74, 205, 241
   regulations concerning   43, 62, 108
trials   16, 17
Troizen
   Artemis Soteira temple   27
   Asklepieion   118, 120, 121, 133, 134
Troy   29, 226

urination   4, 81, 82–83, 90–91, 98, 99, 108, 110
   See also altars: urination on
urine   81, 91, 108
   as cleaning agent   242, 244
   as fertilizer   83, 243, 244
   in tanning   244

vendors. *See kapeloi*; merchants
VIPs   7, 106, 109, 116, 148, 154, 209–210
visitors, environmental impact of   7, 41, 57, 82, 108, 111, 112, 188, 189, 197
votives   1, 2, 3, 5, 7, 12, 15, 24, 25, 26, 30, 35, 37, 41, 44, 142, 182, 189, 218
   coins   12, 46, 142, 178
   food   23, 25, 27, 147
   lamps   142, 146, 153
   melting down of   46, 47
   pinakes   46
   placement of   15, 27, 30, 46, 182
   regulations concerning   3
   sculpture   12, 23, 168, 241
   spits   142, 185
   tax on   46
   vessels   140, 141, 142, 143–145, 146, 149, 153, 154, 178
   weights   179
   See also wine: as votive

washing   4, 24, 68, 71–74, 76, 77, 81, 82, 92, 98, 134, 152
   rules concerning   73
   See also bathing; cleaning
water   2, 4, 16, 54–55, 68–78, 81, 83, 90, 92–99
   cooking with   68, 70–71, 77
   drinking   4, 5, 60, 64, 68, 68–70, 77, 81, 91, 99
   regulations concerning   43, 69, 70, 73
   pipes   14, 74, 130, 218
   reservoir   73, 120, 134
   supply   58, 68, 69, 70, 76–77, 81, 83, 85, 87, 88, 90, 91, 115, 116, 120, 123, 130, 134, 176, 196, 204
   wine and   69, 75, 77, 143
   See also cistern; fountain; pollution, environmental; spring; tanning; washing; well
weaving. *See* textiles
weights and measures. *See* markets
well   2, 75, 76, 91, 132, 134, 176
   See also Epidauros: well; Nemea: wells; Olympia: wells
wine   4–5, 68, 134, 138–154, 188, 200
   as perquisite   141
   as votive   141, 142, 145
   origin of   188, 189
   regulations concerning   44, 68, 141, 188–189
   sales of   179, 188, 189, 199
   See also libations; water: wine and
wood   14, 18, 118, 204, 206, 210, 211, 218, 219, 220, 223
   for barriers   18, 25, 28, 29
   for sacrifice   203, 206, 208–210, 228
   for structures   29, 46, 64, 83, 106, 107, 135, 205, 215, 220
   for tanning   244
   regulations concerning   43, 74
   See also alsos; bench; grove; *kline*; orchard; postholes; table; tree
woodworker   218, 219
workers   5, 6, 7, 82, 135, 208, 200, 210, 211, 215–230
   See also accommodation: for workers; craftsmen
workshop. *See* sanctuary: workshops in

Xanthos, Letoon   109, 111
Xenophon   60, 63–64
Yria (Naxos), Dionysos sanctuary   148–150

zooarchaeological remains   5, 54, 55, 58, 61, 66, 142, 147, 158–173, 177, 178, 181–182, 184–185, 187, 238
Zoster, Cape   27, 228–231